640 Acres
and
Dirt Poor

Janet Godwin Meyer

authorHOUSE®

AuthorHouse™
1663 Liberty Drive
Bloomington, IN 47403
www.authorhouse.com
Phone: 1 (800) 839-8640

Published by AuthorHouse 09/11/2017

ISBN: 978-1-5462-0555-5 (sc)
ISBN: 978-1-5462-0554-8 (e)

Print information available on the last page.

Any people depicted in stock imagery provided by Thinkstock are models, and such images are being used for illustrative purposes only. Certain stock imagery © Thinkstock.

This book is printed on acid-free paper.

Contents

Chapter 1

Mary Lizzie, the oldest girl, was holding the lantern while the old man took his mules out of harness. Ice was in his hair and beard and his hands were numb. He made three trips to Muscadine today hauling hand hewn cross ties on the dray. He had twelve dollars and ninety-six cents in his pocket. It had been a good day.

"You better get on home to your family; " the old man tried to sound cheerful, and he wanted to caution his daughter to protect her unborn baby walking home in the dark, but he let it go so as not to cause embarrassment.

"I know Pa, but I'll just go inside first and wash up the supper dishes. Essie needs all the help she can get, and I'll come back tomorrow evening"

"There's no need, you better stay home. It'll be another cold day tomorrow, mark my words."

Twenty-eight year old Mary Lizzie turned from her Pa, walked toward the long front porch and climbed the steps to go inside the house, but before the old man returned to his work, his gaze settled on the wavy images visible through the windows, and he couldn't help but think how the once welcoming, warm and beckoning scene now looked cold and lonely without Mattie. Damn the typhoid, and damn Mattie for dying and leaving me with all this. How can I do it all? Most of the children still at home are up big enough to manage but the baby and little Sugar desperately need their mother, Little Sugar's only four years old, and Baby Nell's just six months old. Baby Nell nearly died too, and she would've died if Mattie hadn't shook the life right back into her. But the typhoid was too much for my beloved Mattie, too young to die, at age forty-seven, healthy all her life except for the pain and suffering of carrying babies thirteen times and birthing fourteen, one set of twins, but she found joy in our family and never once complained. She was kind and gentle to the end, and she loved Baby Nell just as much as she loved her first born, Aaron now Doctor Godwin. I've lived a good life until now, all the good times were made possible through love and sharing with my sweet wife, but now without you, my beloved Mattie I don't have the strength to put one foot in front of the other, God's dealt me a cruel and devastating blow this time, and no way in hell can I face this lonely, hopeless future. Doc's young bride Essie is a God send for the children and she herself not yet seventeen, but she works from sun up to midnight everyday caring for the young'uns, why it's a full time job just cooking for this big crowd, and now for me the glow coming through the window has lost its warmth and there's no peace awaiting me, and drawing me in. I'm sixty-seven years old and too lonely and weary to face life's hardships. How can I go on? Damn the typhoid for taking my wife Mattie and my son, Right Handy named for my ancestor the honorable Right Handy Godwin who lived a distinguished life in North Carolina back in the 1700's. The loss hurts down deep inside of me and sometimes it's more than I can abide, right now I feel like I can't breathe.

"Hold still old Dan, let me pull your harness off, rub you down, and feed you, so I can go inside and rest a while. Essie will have supper waiting. This old man is cold and hungry and tired."

"The biscuits smell good, Essie."

"Get out of that wet coat before you're laid up sick. Doc's still asleep."

I know the reason for my oldest son's stupor, he's as good a doctor as any of the best wealthy specialists in the big city, and he's accomplished remarkable and unbelievable successes a treating the poor folks of this county, but his reward must needs be something besides monetary wealth for the poor folks of this rural county can't pay in cash money, but make no never mind, they have medical emergencies just the same as rich folks, and they desperately need a good doctor and in him they get good care for he is the best doctor for miles around, at least when he's sober, and while he cares for the poor and gets no pay the only return is some high minded concept that it's God's work he's a doing, but it's obvious to me that he feels trapped in poverty and at the same time he can't deny the need, and it is pitiful to watch his inner battle on the one hand he rides high for his sacrifice and on the other hand, he's forfeited prosperity and the base reward of putting food on the table, on the one hand he solves baffling medical problems and yet he failed to save his own sweet Ma's life. All the long destitute, penniless years of studying at the Atlanta School of Physicians and Surgeons with nothing and still nothing, for there's no money to be made practicing medicine in the dirt poor backwoods of Alabama and constant sacrifice can drag down the spirits of any man, and even though he accepts there's a desperate need for his healing hands, he's the first to admit that his patients who need him the most have the least so most times he goes without getting any pay atall, and that is a predicament he's locked into by his honor and dedication. I heard they've changed the name of his medical school in Atlanta to "Emory" but it's the same school as where Doc earned his license to practice medicine and now he's come home to the responsibility of caring for the pore folks of the county who pay with a few eggs, or a slab of home cured ham, maybe a live chicken. Come the spring of the year maybe some will pay with fresh turnip greens, that's all the pay he gets for no one around these parts has any cash money, no one, and Doc's lucky to get what he does from a few of the better off patients for the one's that are starving have nothing to give and the typhoid epidemic was mighty hard to watch as it spread through the county and took so many of these poor ole farmers which he won't be getting over that for some time, but now he's happy to have a new bride, Essie, but he can't recover from the horror of watching helplessly as his mother and brother died of the typhoid so maybe the whiskey will dull his guilt for he's got the idée that he should of prevented the typhoid outbreak, so there's nothing more to do but let him sleep it off, and maybe when he wakes a miracle will change the world.

Essie opened the cast iron oven door and pulled out two long flat pans filled with golden brown biscuits, and the family gathered round the table as she placed on the table the biscuits and two seventeen-inch iron skillets of bubbling hot gravy. it takes a lot to feed this crowd and hot biscuits and gravy is a good meal that sticks to the ribs, and we'll survive the hard times with good food like this.

Whenever any land that adjourns my farm comes up for sale, I buy it and I'm proud to own six hundred and forty acres, but I think that's where I'll stop buying for now we're land rich and money pore and this size farm is more than one man can handle so my boys got no choice but to help out, and they know very well how to do ever job involved on this farm, and there's plenty a jobs to go around, but that being said, I'll remind Joe to winter plow under the long bottoms come morning for we'll plant cotton again this year for it's the best money crop. At ten years old, the twins Thomas and Mose are big enough to help with the planting. I have to chuckle at my boys' shenanigans, I got a house full of roughnecks, and it's a wonder Thomas didn't break a leg falling fifteen feet to the bottom of the old dry well. I know he was pushed but I don't know exactly who did the pushing. My boys are all guilty and can't resist the chance to push one another in, and they all know and accept the responsibility which falls to the one's remaining on top outside the well to figure a way to pull the one's in the bottom of the dry well back up and out again, and that's the hard part but they don't think ahead to the problem for the fun of the actual scuffle and ultimate pushing in is far too hard to resist, but I'm afraid that one of these days, somebody will get hurt, but there's nothing to be done about it.

I'm cold to the bone, but at least Alabama winters are not so harsh, just the dogged cold rain and fog that can make a man ache for a warm blazing fire. Inside the house it's warm on the kitchen side anyway, but as convenient as the long open hall is in the summer, it's a nuisance in the winter, in the summer it's a relief after supper to get out of the hot kitchen and go outside through the open hallway and back inside into the cool half of the house which I planned for cool summer sleeping. The sleeping room is plenty big enough for four beds all lined up in a row, but my plan for cool summer sleeping was short sighted and didn't allow for warm winter sleeping with no fireplace and no way to heat the big room except now after all these years we now have a wood burning stove finally as a result of the typhoid epidemic and thanks to our generous neighbors, we burn a pile of wood and heat up the big room and also thanks to our good neighbors we now have a pretty plenty enough quilts to cover all the children in all the beds, and we'll forever be beholding to the goodness of John Owens in particular for now weeks later, we've recovered from the worst of the typhoid, and it's mighty good of Cynthy McElroy who is still coming every day to help with baby Nell. Cynthy 'chews-and-feeds' the baby just like Mattie did. Oh Matt, you're gone; and Doc thinks he should a done more to save you and I guess in a way that makes his pain worse than mine. He's a good doctor and he is respected in these parts by other doctors and his patients, and sometimes other doctors ask for his advice, like Doc Downey from Tallapoosa and Doc Gilmore too, but in his own mind he's laid the blame on himself for he's fought a battle inside his own mind, and he's lost that battle and wound up convincing himself that he stood by helpless and watched his own mother die of the typhoid, and now the guilt he's a carrying, he can't shed and worse yet, he believes that other's in the county put the blame on him too which isn't so, but nonetheless he's judged himself as guilty. It's a mighty big burden for a man to carry, and none of us can change this madness he's cooked up in his own mind.

I need to go to Tallapoosa tomorrow. Essie's getting near the bottom of the flour bin. She's a good cook, but she can't make biscuits out of thin air. I'll have to wait a while longer to buy kerosene. Burning pine knots will be the only light in this house at least till I can sell some charcoal. I'll buy kerosene with the charcoal money. I hope the rain stops because it's a misery to travel the seven miles in the rain. Things are booming in Tallapoosa, a new business or factory every time I go, but the Tallapoosa boom doesn't reach across to this side of the state line. Here in this northeast part of Alabama all our neighbors are just as bad off as we are, and it's only the strong sense of loyalty and unity that we all have around here which helps us get through the hard times. It's a mile to the nearest house, John & Sally Owens's place, but the narrow wagon road is walked every day, at least once a day because we all look out for each other and help each other and check on each other, and when you think about it, life in rural Alabama can't be any other way, everybody has to pull together to survive.

John Owens is a good man, always some foolishness going on when he's around. It's been hard on both John and Sally to lose two babies. The first one lived four months, the second one only twelve days. The first, a little girl, died in the night after Sally washed her hair, and that was three years ago, an eternity for grieving parents, God bless Sally, I've heard her say she'll never wash a head of hair again. John is the strong one while Sally's quiet and never was much of a talker, but when her sister Ollie moved off to Oklahoma to be a mail order bride, Sally seemed to withdraw into a sadness that's always with her. I know I sure can't help her bear the burden of her grief, I've got my own grieving to do for I'm lost and alone without Mattie.

I stood up from the table and walked into the adjoining room where a fire was blazing in the big fireplace. I twisted and twirled a straight back chair from the kitchen table into the fireplace room and sat down facing the fire. The big room was full of young'uns ages six months to young adult. And sleeping in the small office room in this half of the house was Doc, my oldest now twenty-nine years old. In twenty-eight years, Mattie had fourteen babies. Now Mattie's gone and our little son Handy gone too, both taken by the typhoid. This inconceivable loss runs over and over through my mind, and now all the little'uns in this big house have to look to Essie, Doc's young wife, to be their mother. I guess we all have to look to Essie to do the cooking and cleaning and all the hard labor that goes with living in these penniless times, it's every day's business, every day's sadness, every day's hateful reality which is we work for no more than enough food to keep us alive, we have no luxuries, none more than the luxury of happiness we find in each other's company and simple pleasures.

Mostly through my long sixty-seven years, I've felt a deep sense of well being, which I've always called my talent as to look for the good in every situation and profit from the good and not let the bad take a hold of me for there's more good in life especially when a person works because working is the cure all, for any feeling of helplessness that can sometime creep around and try to knock a hole in a good man's happiness and that is precisely what I'm facing in my lonely life without my good and faithful wife, but I'll look around me tomorrow and figure out a way to contentment again which will be through my children and grandchildren, and by and by, I'll want to find enjoyment again maybe, but right now the sadness weighs heavy, and it's mighty hard to find my way.

The floor boards creaked as the family moved about, Mary Lizzie leaned across her big belly to wipe the crumbs and spills from the table as she and Essie washed up the supper dishes by the pitiful light from a pine knot set to burning in an iron skillet. The boys were pushing and shoving as was their normal pastime, and little Sugar was playing with a button on a string, and the look of concentration on his face made me wonder if he feels the same black, meanness of our loss, and I can guess that he does and with special grief that only an orphan can feel. If Mattie were still alive, she would be laughing and playing with all the children, and little Sugar would be happy and carefree, but I'm not like Mattie, I'm more sober and just as Mattie always said, I'm too gruff. I guess that's right, and now more than ever I don't want to smile let alone laugh and play. I am not a silly person, I like to plan, think things through and plan, all my life I've been planning for the future. I try to show my sons that planning for the future is important and buying land is important. Education has it's place, that's for sure, but I'll never agree with Mattie that education is the only way out of this poverty. She never convinced me of that, but it's obvious she made a lasting impression on her boys because they're all educated even the young ones can figure and read, and of the older boys (now men) one's a doctor and one's a teacher James who for now is in the military. When I think of my oldest son Aaron I don't say 'Aaron' in my mind anymore, instead, I think of him as 'Doc' when did I start calling my own son 'Doc?' I long for James to come home from the war. He's in far away Europe.

"Oh Lord, my God, bring James home safe."

Doc knew early on that he'd work at any job, do what ever need be done to finish high school, and so he lived off in Heflin, boarded with Judge Glasgow and worked at chores around the place to pay for his room and board. He was up before light every morning to do the milking and shoveling the judge's barn clean, feeding the judge's animals and toting the judge's fire wood into the house which was hours of back breaking work every morning before going to Heflin High School, and I got to hand it to him, he stayed with it and went on to medical school in Atlanta with no more money than the little he made doing odd jobs.

As I came out of my reverie, I noticed my youngest son 'Sugar' a standing in front of me, hands locked at his back, a real serious look about him. At four years old, he's handsome, proud, and strong, I wanted to hold him to me like I'd hold to a lifeline but that'd embarrass him.

"Pa, I don't want you to call me 'Sugar' any more."

"Why not?"

"That's what Ma called me, and she's dead and not coming back. If she'd come back, I'd let her call me 'Sugar' or if Handy would come back from the dead, I'd let him call me 'Sugar'. But they're not coming back, and I don't ever want to be called 'Sugar' again."

My silence left the room quiet, until I said, "Well then, what'll we call you?"

"I don't know, Pa."

My youngest boy crawled into my lap and together we quietly watched the crackling of the logs on the fire. One of the older boys was holding and swaying baby Nell, and now all the boys stopped their scuffling and instead of playing some game like rough necks always picking at each other, in unity they softly moved closer so as to coral their strength in numbers and willfully combine their minds and magically without hands, hold up and comfort their little brother 'Sugar.'

"Your brother Thomas calls you 'Eb'. Do you want everybody to call you 'Eb'?"

"No. I call Thomas 'Kit' and that's just between him and me."

I knew the nickname 'Kit' was personal to my boys as it was for me; it brought back memories of my sister Katharine called 'Kitsy.'

"Do you want to be called Elbert or Stewart?"

"No."

Baby Nell started crying and Essie took her into her arms and started a slow dance-walk back and forth first in front of the fire with the baby looking over her shoulder so as to watch the snap and pop before Essie walked and swayed her way to the shelf holding the clock where she stopped again with the baby facing the clock because the baby likes to watch the slow swinging rhythm of the clock's pendulum, and while Essie swayed the baby Nell, Mary Lizzie went to the dry sink to wash some of the baby's soiling rags; she dipped water from the handy hot water reservoir on the cook stove, and scrubbed the stains from the soiling rags with homemade lye soap, and when that was done, Mary Lizzie walked out the door and up the road to her own husband and children, I'm thankful for the help and they're all doing the best they can to care for my little motherless baby.

"Well then we'll have to think up a nickname for you. Your ma thought you were sweet enough to be called 'Sugar,' but I can see as how you might not like it for anybody else to call you a name like 'Sugar.'"

"No, Sir. I don't like it."

"I know a shorter version of the nick name 'Sugar' which sounds strong instead of sweet, and maybe you'd like to be called the short version of the name your ma thought up for you."

"What name is short for 'Sugar'?"

"Shug."

The little boy twisted around again to lean back on me. The fire was quiet for a long time until he said, "Shug's a good name and I like it and that's what I want to be called from now on."

After sweeping the floor with a fresh-bound-straw broom, Essie took the baby out-a-doors like Mattie always did last thing at night and first thing in the morning for the cold outside air causes the baby to wet herself, then back inside wrapped in dry rags and bound up in a quilt she'll sleep dry till morning. Most times as the cold air shocks the baby and if the rag is untied and held aside, she wets and the water falls to the ground at the edge of the porch saving one washing of that rag. Mattie said baby Nell seemed to understand this body function earlier than any of the other babies.

Essie began tying on a clean rag, and some of the boys began to visit the outhouse. When Joe took his little brother by the hand to walk beside him through the dark, Shug looked as brave as any little four-year-old orphan could look, and as the cold night air greeted little Shug, he raised his head high and lifted his shoulders back as if conquering his fear. The whole family, of course, overheard the conversation about his new name and in turn they all called him 'Shug' as everyone finished their evening chores, visited the outhouse and settled down to sleep.

I am an old man who loves to wake up to the aroma of coffee. Even though the roaring fire in the fireplace opposite my bed has warmed this half of the house, I noticed I could still see my breath, and I was careful not to touch the bed stead because I knew from past experience that my skin would likely stick to the freezing cold iron. There are three rooms on this side of the open-air-hallway, the kitchen with a cook stove, and this room with a fireplace and both these rooms are big and spacious, but the third is a much smaller side room that now serves as both a medical office and a bedroom for Doc and his new bride. All totaled there are seven beds in the house, two in this fireplace room, mine and the one where Shug and the baby Nell were still sleeping. I pulled on my shirt and overalls, grabbed my socks and boots and shuffled into the warm kitchen. I guess most of the boys are still asleep in the four beds in the other half of the house across the open-air, covered porch. Already this morning, Essie built a blazing fire in both the kitchen cook stove and in the next-room fireplace so she must have started working an hour or more ago. As I entered the kitchen, she poured me a cup of coffee and said, "The biscuits are just about ready. I'll start the gravy."

I have difficulty getting about first thing in the morning, my joints are stiff and sore, and I tried my level best to straighten my aching back as I hurried out-a-doors and across the open-air hallway to enter the big room where the boys were sleeping.

"Wake up boys! We gotta get cracking."

Now for the first time since I built this house, the sleeping room is heated by John Owens's pot belly stove, and I have John Owens to thank again and again for one 'thank you' is not enough to fully express to the good Mr. John Owens our gratitude which is boundless and this warm room is a mighty fine gift, that is pleasant to receive each time the warmth is experienced, and I relived the weakness of the typhoid which is a physical memory powerful enough to knock the breath out of me. The memory of big John Owens hauling in the pot belly stove and setting it up and keeping a fire burning to warm my sick children, and likely saving their lives. Last night's roaring fire in the potbelly stove was now burned down to embers but the room was warm. I leaned down to pick up several sticks from the wood box and as to prepare the embers for the added wood to spark the embers into flame with the first stick of wood I stirred the ashes so as to sift them through the grate and into the removable metal drawer at the bottom of the stove which had it's own smaller door, and then each stick of wood which I tossed onto the embers caused a small explosion of sparks and flames as the fire caught and blazed into another dazzling hot source of heat. As I closed the stove door, I tried to straighten my weary backbone and started mentally planning the day's work.

Today the charcoal pit is first on the list of chores. It'll take four boys to saw down one big hardwood tree, strip the branches, saw the tree trunk into shorter lengths, and then snake the two to three foot logs into the pit. Of course the mules will balk every step of the way at pulling the short but heavy logs. Next the boys will work at filling the pit with the short hardwood logs, cover them with a layer of dirt, and pile the good-for-nothing hardwood limbs on top of the dirt, this top layer of hardwood debris will then be set ablaze. When they finally roll the last of the short logs into the pit, the boys know the rest of the job in the charcoal producing process is easy and that's when they'll more'n likely fight over who gets to do the firing. Two of the younger boys will stay through the last bit of sunlight and into the night feeding the fire, and when it's good and dark and ever body else has finished supper, replacements will relieve the two so they can eat what's left of supper, and if I know my boys, they'll turn the job into a pleasure game and they'll all go and stay at the pit to watch the show as the fire's sparks lift and curl into the starry night sky. My gang will sit on the ground around the fire and tell stories for hours on end before coming in to bed. They will cover the last embers with more dirt so it's safe to leave the fire unattended. The boys are young and strong and they find great pleasure in each other's company. They know the firing has to be a slow steady burn till bedtime, so they consider themselves unlucky doing the back-breaking labor and lucky doing the easy job of watching and stoking the long burning fire. The dirt layer under the long burning fire allows the buried logs to char or become carbonized. After days of cooling, the charcoal logs can be uncovered and snaked out of the pit and onto the dray for hauling. This batch of charcoal will be delivered to the waiting neighbors. They're always in need of the extra hot fire charcoal produces when they fire up their blacksmith shops and begin the process of sharpening and repairing plows for spring planting, and I appreciate the ready market for my winter charcoal for might near every farm has a blacksmith shop and it turns out winter's the time of the year when all the county farmers become blacksmiths. There's a bigger market for the charcoal in Tallapoosa because the glass works depends on a steady supply, but because of the large and constant demand the factory mostly buys from larger operations than mine. So I'm proud to have the farmers in this county depending on me.

Everyone was at the table ready for breakfast as Essie once again placed two skillets of gravy and two long pans of biscuits on the table. It seems like biscuits and gravy is the standard for every meal, but frequently, someone brings in fresh game as an added dish. There's a good supply of rabbits and squirrels in these parts and birds are plentiful too, but they're harder to kill and don't have as much meat, but whatever the game, Essie batters and fries it and seems to have a magical talent to make it delicious with nothing more than a little salt and pepper. All the children drink coffee for breakfast, right down to little Shug. Coffee helps warm up the body for the hard work ahead.

The boys decide on their own job assignments for the day. Besides the work at the charcoal pit, someone has to chop firewood for the house, draw and carry well water into the house and closer by to the watering trough. Someone has to shovel the barn stalls. As the kitchen bustled with preparation, I announced, "Shug is going with me."

Shug kept up behind me as I set out walking to the southeast, I wanted to show him once again the two lone, tall pine trees that I purposely left standing when the hardwood timber was cut from the rolling hills all around them.

"See these little pine trees, Shug?" I pointed to the new saplings covering the slopes.

"Yea, Pa."

"Someday, these trees will belong to you."

"I won't be getting' much; they're just little old scrubby sticks."

"You're growing every day aren't you?"

"Yea, Pa, I'm getting taller."

"Well then these trees that you call sticks are growing every day too, and when you are a grown man, these little scrubby pine trees will be a whole lot taller than you'll be. I want you to remember what I've told you and that is we cleared and cut the timber on this forty-acre parcel when you were a tiny baby. Now in those four short years, these trees are as tall as you are. And there's new trees coming up every day. Do you know why?"

"No, Pa, but I think it has something to do with the two tall trees over there," Shug said as he pointed.

"You're right, look at the two big strait and true pine trees we left standing," I motioned to the big twenty-foot tall trees he'd pointed to.

"I see 'em Pa."

"The two big pine trees we left standing when all the hardwoods around them were cut to feed the charcoal pit. The two tall pine trees make hundreds of pinecones every year, don't they? And every single pinecone drops seeds to the ground and every year the seeds start new trees a growing, and when you're a grown man, these here little trees will be just like money in your pocket. Remember pine lumber is the best for building and hardwood lumber is the best for making charcoal."

I reached to the ground and picked up a pinecone before I found a sunny place to sit and lean against one big pine.

"Sit down on the ground here beside me."

Shug ran to catch up. He sat down beside me, and watched as I pulled the pinecone apart, he was interested in the seeds which he said could grow more trees like the seeds we keep each year to plant and grow more vegetables in the next year's garden, but he tired of the pinecone lesson, and asked if we could hunt for rabbits on our way home. So as we walked back in the direction of home, I noticed him lift his coat and check for his slingshot still held safely in his little back pocket. We walked in silence and pretty soon I pointed to a rabbit at the edge of a thicket.

Shug motioned for me to hold up and go quiet as he too spotted the rabbit hiding at the edge of the cleared land just where the thicket cast a shadow to serve as rabbit cover, and so as not to scare off the rabbit, Shug slowly slipped his flip out of his back trousers pocket as he silently found and picked up a marble sized rock and carefully placed the rock in the pocket of his flip. His big brother Joe made the flip and gave it to him for Christmas. Joe used the tongue from a worn out pair of shoes to make the rock pocket, and now Shug aimed and pulled back the leather trap which took all of the little boy's strength to sling the rock with force, and he did a pretty good job, but I saw the ammunition fall short, but he was so intent on his target that he paid no attention to my slight retreat behind him, and I was able to sling my own rock just at the same instant Shug let go of his flip pocket, I let go of mine from my flip and sent it hurling toward the rabbit which of course hit the target and it was a true pleasure to watch as little Shug jumped for joy thinking he'd been the successful hunter and killed the rabbit with one strike. I've trained my boys never to leave the house without a flip handy in their back pocket, and I'm proud to say Joe can kill a quail on the rise with a single stone.

Shug ran to retrieve his proud addition to the supper table, and as he skipped over the laying straw in the clearing, his wool coat flapped open so I could see he was wearing his rabbit fur under vest. The boys wear wool long handles their Ma makes from the wool cloth she weaves. First Mattie cards and spins the sheared wool into thread then she weaves the thread into wool cloth and every year after the sheep shearing she goes through the long process a making tight fitting long handles for all the boys to wear under their clothes. She also pieces squirrel and rabbit pelts into vests for the children to wear inside their wool coats, and she's discovered if the fur side of the vest is worn facing the body it holds the body heat. Mattie makes outer pants of wool too because wool cuts the cold that can go right through thinner overhalls. She makes hand coverings, straight like socks only for hands, out of rabbit fur. They're mostly in the way, except when riding any distance. A man can't work while wearing them.

I realize that I talk about Mattie as if she's still alive. My grief is crushing, when I think of Mattie I think that she's still alive, how can I ever think of her in the grave?

"Pa, can I skin the rabbit over by the creek?" Shug ran off.

Shug was gutting the rabbit by the time I caught up to him, and we were working together to skin it when he said, "I'll stretch this skin as soon as we get home, Pa. It's a good-sized pelt from an old rabbit, and that means the meat will be tough, but Ma, I mean Essie will know how to cook it tender."

I'm pleased with my little four-year-old son's skill as a hunter. Another year or so and he'll make the kill himself without my help. He knows how to survive. Shug knelt at the water's edge and washed the meat and pelt in the cold rushing creek water. "Pa, why does this creek run all through the winter, and the little branch over yonder dries up by Christmas?"

"The little branch is run-off water, it doesn't last. This creek water is lasting water, which means it never dries up because it's fed by the Indian Spring not just rain or run-off water. You know where the Indian Spring is don't you?"

"Yea, Pa."

I smiled as my son instantly pointed in the direction of the Indian Spring. You can turn him till he's dizzy, and he never loses his direction, and that's the kind of learning that matters. Mattie always said that reading and writing and figuring are more important. In my mind I've figured out she held that book learning is the most important because she never learned to read nor write, and that was always a belittling for her. She always said she wanted her children to know what she didn't know. Doc couldn't read till he was fifteen, but by the time he was twenty-four, he was a doctor. Mattie always worried that we didn't send the little ones to school early enough, but I prefer that the older ones teach the younger ones, and later when they're old enough to finish their chores and get to school on their own, then they can go part of the time to Bethel school, but the work around here has to come first. James was the teacher at Bethel when he enlisted to fight in Europe, and Mattie was mighty proud of his teaching at Bethel and his fighting in Europe.

Little Shug struggled to carry the rabbit which was actually longer than Shug was tall so he had to hold it up above his head with his little arms stretched high in order to keep the rabbit from dragging the ground, and frequently he switched his heavy load to the other hand, but he didn't complain or ask for help. We were coming to the Section Corner, ahead where lay the Ingram grave, a section of land consists of six hundred and forty acres, and here at this corner where four sections of land come together is buried Liziebeth, wife of M.L. Ingram, this forty acres of the Godwin home place was homesteaded by M.L.'s mother, Mary Ingram, and I have the deed dated December 1, 1851 and signed by the president of the United States, Millard Fillmore. I asked for the original homestead deed when I bought the property. Mary Ingram's son M.L. married Liziebeth who died in childbirth in 1862, at the young age of twenty-two years. On the headstone, her birth year is listed as 1840. Shug stopped at the headstone, and as we sat down beside Liziebeth Ingram's grave, I read aloud the inscription on the marker,

"She was a loyal friend,

A noble daughter,

And a devoted wife and mother."

Shug spoke the last words in unison with me.

"Did you read that, Shug?"

"No Pa, I know it by heart."

"Well you'll be reading before long. You've already made the first step. Now sit still and listen to the story of Liziebeth Ingram."

"Liziebeth was twenty-one years old in 1861 and mother to three little children. Before her husband went off to fight in the Civil War, he promised he'd return home within six months so as to be at her side for the of birth their fourth baby. As he rode out of sight a ribbon of dust drifted across the barren, rolling fields, a lonely and painful mark of his path leaving Liziebeth mesmerized and intent on watching as the last image of security faded into the horizon and Liziebeth let her mind wander to the unthinkable, would she ever see her beloved again? With resolve and inner strength, she found encouragement in knowing his return would include planting crops and the renewal of life with another happy birth in this house. To feed his family during the winter months of his absence, M.L. made arrangements for the nearest neighbor (more than three miles away) to butcher their hog in return for half the meat, and together the milk from the cow and the pork to eat surely would sustain Liziebeth and the children but for the confiscation."

"What's confiscation, Pa?"

"Well, it's what the army has the right to do in order to feed the soldiers."

The Ingrams had a small but nice house down this very lane going south from the grave. You know where the shallow, old dry well is, don't you?"

"Yes Pa, it's right down yonder," answered Shug as he pointed to the south.

"That old dry well is just precisely where the Ingram house stood. Now, back to the story, with her husband off fighting the War, the Confederate government and most southern states including Alabama enacted laws to intercept crops and cash money owed to the United States government up north in Washington, and for that matter, any debt owed to any private individual in the northern states, and that was a stark and overwhelming reality for wives left behind when their husbands rode off to war, and Liziebeth was faced with this unfair (what I'd call criminal) confiscation of her property, and she struggled with the loss of her ability to sustain her life and the lives of her children including one unborn when in fact the two levels of government overlapped and a single debt owed to the North was collected by both the southern state of Alabama and the central Confederate government in Richmond, Virginia. As I heard the story, after the Ingram livestock (the hog and cow) were confiscated by the Confederate government, Liziebeth's troubles became life threatening when the Alabama militia (in the name of the state government) confiscated stored potatoes, dried apples, and any and all supplies not hidden under a loose board in the floor of the house, and which I have a very difficult time a figuring how any actual, lawful Alabama militia men could a performed a low down despicable act of what amounted to stealing from a helpless woman and her children. So in my mind, I lay the blame on bureaucrats and the governing system which when it gets too unwieldy to serve the people on a personal level then what happens when orders go out from a far away government and the orders must be carried out by individuals who have no means with which to understand the orders in real life situations, but however it came about, it did happen and Liziebeth had to scrimp together barely enough food to keep the children alive, which meant on the lowest level of the system, a young woman right here is Cleburne County Alabama was forced to dig through the dirt of the potato mound time and time again to find maybe one or two small potatoes, and sometimes she was able to cut enough young turnip green sprouts to make a weak soup which was mostly pot-liquor (water and lard maybe flavored by a pitiful one or two turnip green leaves), and occasionally perhaps she found a new carrot in the garden. These meager food scrapes were all the Alabama militia men left behind after the confiscating which was a necessary part of fighting a war, but in this case, it was an extreme and impossible hardship for a woman and three children to endure."

All that aside, the point of the story is that Liziebeth prepared every single bit of food and put it on the table for the children, and she made the conscious decision to feed the children and not herself, which was a mistake, because she starved herself to death, and of course the baby she was carrying died too, and on the very day that her husband returned home, he found his wife's dead but still warm body, and her shortsightedness could have been a disaster that also took the lives of her children if her husband had not returned at that precise minute, because the children were too young to dig a grave and bury their ma, and beyond that immediate catastrophe, the children might have died of starvation like their Ma if they'd been left alone for the oldest of the children was only four years old and as the three little children were in a very weakened, starvation state which would bear completely on their ability to make any kind of simple decisions let alone make life and death, difficult, decisions of vast consequence."

"Shug, it's a sad story to be telling a little boy, but you need to hear it just like your older brothers have heard me tell it more than one time; and for this reason which I'm telling you, son, you will be faced with many difficult decisions in you life, and let this story be a lesson to you, son listen careful, it is imperative that you understand you have to take care of yourself first and by that I mean, you look out to make sure you are strong in mind and body, as you grow into a man and for your entire life, weigh every decision with the heaviest emphasis on taking the path that will keep your body strong, and healthy and well fed, for with a mind and body working at it's level best, in turn you'll be able to help others. Now my son, tell me if you understand my reasoning for telling you this sad story?"

My boy answered, "Yes, Pa, I understand."

I added another piece of advice, "When you are older, I think you'll find opportunity for betterment in every difficult situation, and right now your opportunity for betterment lies in your little sister, I'm confident you'll do the right thing, you'll make yourself strong, and in turn you'll take care of Sis."

That day at the Ingram grave, as little Shug sat beside me on the cold ground, he pondered all I'd said, and I watched his face as he tried to reason through the process of acceptance and storing this pitiful disaster in his own mind, and the blank, lost look on his sweet face led me to make another decision which is starting right now, I'll tell Shug more stories of his Ma, both happy and sad. Oh, my beloved Mattie, I miss you so. Maybe Shug can carry some of my memories with him throughout his life. Lord knows my little son has lost his mother far too early for his own memories of her to be planted in his head. While her death is hanging like a black cloud over him, he might find sustaining strength in hearing, and I might find solace in telling.

1885

Shug, this story is from 24 years before you were born. My sister Jenett, called Nen, greeted me at the door of the small house situated at the end of the lane from our house to the main road, Nen lived there with her husband Jasper Hicks, and I'm grateful to Jasper for he's good to Nen and through his kindness to his own widowed sister Harriet Hughes, I met his niece Mattie, Harriet's daughter. Jasper's good heart kept Mattie, her mother and sister from starving when Mattie's pa came up missing in 1883. The day Mattie's pa disappeared, he worked a full day at building McBride's bridge over the Tallapoosa River, and he left work to walk the two miles home, but never showed up. With his good wife Harriet waiting and watching for him 'til far into the night. Most people suspect he was killed for the pay in his pocket., and that's one mystery we'll never know the answer, the how or the what. He was just gone like he dissolved into a puddle in the road.

As I entered the little house, I greeted my two children and my ma Ferraby with a hug for I'm a man who loves his family, and glancing to the corner of the room, I saw Mattie's fleeting look my way as I hung my heavy coat and hat on the peg by the door. This cold snap in October is normal, we'll have Indian summer yet to warm the last days of harvest. Jasper sat at the end of the long table near the fire. Nen and Ma were busy with the cooking, and Mattie in the corner of the room near the spinning wheel was intent on rolling the newly spun wool into a ball. The thread tangled as she pulled against the loop of yarn on the floor so I picked up the loop, inserted my big clumsy hands and stretched the tangled wad, and slowly Mattie was able to begin to work through the mess of yarn and again roll the thread into a ball. She wore a drab but clean work dress, which was actually too small for her slight figure. Each time I looked at the pitiful sight of her wearing this dress or one other, for I've seen her in only the two dresses and both of which are too short (above the ankles) to be stylish and both are thread bare at the elbows. Mattie was slightly taller than five feet, I'd guess about five feet, two inches, but the shoes she wore lifted her another inch to my six-foot frame. She was very shy, but she boldly looked up to my sun browned face and smiled her thanks, but she didn't say a word, she seemed too conscious of my towering height. She was a sweet girl of seventeen, I was a man of thirty-eight years, married once but now left alone and single. I loved to look at her girlish innocence, and it was my common practice to be careful not to speak too loud or boastful around her. I wanted her to learn to be comfortable with my presence; I wanted to earn her trust.

Nen called us to supper and Mattie's ma and sister came from the other room. Jasper and Nen sat at opposite ends of the long table, and Mattie and her sister climbed onto a small bench with little room to maneuver, but after the contortions to seat themselves, they were quite comfortable leaning back against the wall; and I sat on the opposite bench on the other side of the table next to my Ma and my two children, John now seven years old and Martheny six years old.

The mother of my children just up and walked off and left us, but I guess the desertion was understandable for she never loved me anyway, and I'm not exactly sure if she loved the children. Her only feeble explanation was the complaint that she saw no recourse but to leave or else go crazy with the love she felt for Whitley. She was right to go because we knew in our hearts and agreed on that one thing that I never felt the same passion that Whitley always had for her. She abandoned my children, John and Martheny, because she had no choice. I'd rather die than give up my son and daughter.

I broke the silence, "Did John and Martheny complete their chores here today?

I yawned for I was weary of traveling all the way to Tallapoosa in the bitter cold which the trip started before daylight when I set out this morning and pulled the horse to a stop outside this little house so my children and Ma could spend the day with Nen, Jasper, and Mattie. I know Mattie is kind to my children for they seem to adore her and she them.

Nen replied, "Both the children were a big help in the house. It was too cold to work outside, so we peeled and sliced a bushel of apples, and the children climbed the ladder to the loft with each bucket full, and I climbed the ladder to look in on their work, which I can say they were careful to spread the peeled apples out to dry in a single layer like I showed them."

It was obvious that my children were proud of their good work. It never hurt anyone to work, and pride in that work is a sweet reward. My children know because I preach it to them just about every day. A lazy man gets nowhere in life and we won't be shiftless nor will we ever expect the other fellow to do our work. An honest man does and honest days work every day of his life.

I spoke a bit louder than intended when I said; "It's time we started for home. We're grateful for the good hot supper, and we're nourished by it, and I thank y'all for watching after John and Martheny today."

I helped the children and Ma climb into the wagon seats, I clicked the horse into motion and the four of us rode the short distance to our new house where I coaxed the horse into the big barn and Ma and the little ones climbed down from the tall wagon as I instructed John to go in the house with grandma and lay a fire. Martheny stayed to help with the bridle, which she couldn't reach the nail to hang it, so in the dark she felt her way over to the feed bucket, returned with it in hand, and turned it upside down, so as to stand on it to reach the nail. With the gear put away, I sent her on into the house while I fed the animals. When I walked to the well to draw water for the watering trough, I saw the light through the window, for John had a fire blazing inside the house, and I choked with emotion looking through the fine, wavy glass to see my children and Ma standing with their backs to the warmth, happy to be home.

As I walked across the yard toward the door of my home, I proudly surveyed my handiwork in cutting the trees and sawing every plank to build this spacious new home. I had the idea to build the kitchen under the same roof as the sleeping room, but separated by a long open-air hallway or dogtrot. Some other houses in this part of the country have kitchens out back in a separate building behind the house, and in the hot Alabama summers, it's a blessing to have the cooking stove in a room away from the sleeping part of the house, but that separate kitchen design is a nuisance in the winter, for the cook is constantly running back and forth between the outbuilding kitchen and the bigger house which I improved considerable on that inconvenience by designing this open covered dog- trot through which a person can cross over even on a rainy day and stay dry, and I placed two beds in the cavernous fireplace room on the kitchen side of the house for sleeping in the winter where John sleeps with me and Martheny sleeps with Ma in beds placed right before the fireplace which together with the big iron cook stove in the kitchen makes that side of the house the warm and cozy winter sleeping quarters.

"Mattie said she'd be over tomorrow to help with the apples," little Martheny spoke to me with excitement as I entered the house for she liked Mattie and looked forward to seeing her again.

"It's good to have her help."

Mattie's kind and good to help with the household chores and with the children, though she herself is just a girl, but she's a good cook and can do the heavy work that Ma can't do. I can't tend the farm and help with the house chores too, and Ma, at seventy-eight needs the help and Mattie says she's glad to do it, and she likes this big new house. Jasper's house is half this size with five people living there, but just four of us living here in this big rambling place.

"When we take the dried apples to town to sell, we'll pay Mattie cash money for the work she's done to help us."

I planted the apple orchard back in 1874, when we first moved west from Union City near Atlanta. I brought apple tree seedlings to these Alabama woods, and now eleven years later the apple harvest is plentiful, I hauled the last load of fresh apples to Tallapoosa this day, and with Mattie's help, the remainder of the apple crop will be sliced for drying tomorrow. Come Thanksgiving and Christmas we'll sell some of the dried apples to the town folk for their holiday pies, but mostly we'll use them for our own table, and hopefully, I'll see Mattie in this house helping to cook fried apple pies. The sight of her in my house warms my heart.

The next morning Mattie walked the short distance on the wagon road from the Jasper Hicks' place to the Godwin home-place. She wore a heavy shawl and bonnet and yet the cold penetrated beneath her thin cotton dress and underskirt. She was glad for wearing long cotton stockings pulled up and above the knee and tightly stretched and bound around her leg before twisting the stocking around and around her finger to form a knot, and rolling and tucking the knot under the tightness. This held the stockings up to maximum length for greatest warmth. She tucked her hands inside her homespun wool shawl and pulled the ends together and hugged herself inside.

At the top of the hill in the narrow wagon lane, Mattie gasped in wonder at the sight of a cloud lying in the valley ahead of her. She liked the way she could see right over the top of the thick cloud-fog, and the spectacle gave her a feeling of importance that she normally did not feel, and actually most times she felt small and insignificant, but this morning, she was confident and enabled to float on her high mindedness and be lifted above and see ahead a distance, and the ordinary was transformed and the disguised and unclear hollow or low points of her mundane life now seemed that they must have of course led to this very scene which seemed a terrestrial experience for she could see all the way there from here. The exact points of 'there' and 'here' were obscured in the shroud, but this defining clarity seemed unchallenged by all she'd known up to now, and her thought was to walk down into and through the cloud where her view of what lay ahead would be blurred but still ahead lay a new-found sense of purpose made easy. She had a new power, the power to see over the obstacles immediately in front of her, and she could see that her destination was filled with sunlight, and in the distance, lay the new home she loved to visit, and her thoughts and desires were of me, the man inside that house.

I opened the door when she walked onto the porch. I was gruff with my invitation to sit down for coffee. She put her head wrap and shawl on the peg by the door, and spoke a quiet 'Hello' to everyone. My little daughter Martheny took Mattie's hand, and they sat down side by side on a bench at the table while Martheny whispered something, and they both giggled. I didn't see anything to laugh about so I finished my coffee, snorted, pushed back from the table, and said, "I'll be in the barn."

I stayed busy all morning with the chores of caring for the livestock. I like working hard and I enjoy the smell of hay, and sometimes I imagine the animals are talking to each other in their soft bellowing sounds which are a comfort to me, and I appreciate the farmer's life in it's safety and warmth. I've been to the big city of Atlanta a few times when I was younger, and I don't like the crowds of people and I feel it's unnatural to see buildings next to more buildings without open pastures in between. I love this place and my joy and peace lies in mindlessly going through the motions and losing track of time while completing the chores. Sometimes I think to myself, "This is as it should be."

Toward evening I saw Mattie walking along the road away from the house, and she looked so like a child, and I questioned if I should complicate my life by courting her, but she catches my fancy each time I look at her, and she is gentle as a spring rain and soft as a newborn calf, but she's young, maybe too young for me. Before I went inside the house to supper I stood and watched her disappear down the road into the holler. Because I deliberately stayed away from the house and Mattie inside it at noon, I was very hungry, and I appreciated that Ma had supper ready and on the table. She looked at me in understanding like she knew of my feelings for Mattie. She never said anything, but I knew she could read me like a book. The next morning Mattie once again set out for the Godwin home place as she pondered yesterday's rebuff. She wanted to continue her position as helper in the house and let matters come as they may, and her resolve was to admit the strong attraction she felt for me and simply respect and trust me to do the right thing.

Over the coming days, I continued to keep a distance from Mattie, which she accepted and actually the time blew past because it was a busy time on the farm with the work of picking cotton and hauling it to the depot in Muscadine which two trips consumed an entire day. When the railroad came west from Atlanta through Tallapoosa and on to Anniston and Birmingham, Alabama, I started hauling my goods to the depot at Muscadine because it is closer than Tallapoosa by three miles. Each time I haul goods to Muscadine, I buy sugar or coffee or some other staple at the small general store there, which serves the surrounding farmers and the three families living in the Muscadine settlement. It is a picturesque village nestled in the rolling green hills with each house set at its own elevation and the train track winding along the floor of the valley along side the only building besides the depot, the store. In 1885, Tallapoosa was a boomtown of more than five hundred residents, and boasted of a telegraph office, six good-sized mercantiles, a livery stable, a bicycle shop, a drug store, and a shoe store. If we had a need, any need well it was available in Tallapoosa.

All this hullabaloo caused Mattie to wake from a fitful sleep to find herself crowded into the narrow bed with both her sister Julie and her Ma. It was somewhat fortunate that she was not in the middle, although on really cold nights the middle spot definitely is the warmest position, but tonight she turned her back to her mother and sister which afforded her a modicum of privacy in which to think her own thoughts, and naturally, her first thought was of her poor missing Pa and her fervent hope of seeing him again, and of course thinking of her Pa prompted the usual tears cried quietly into the pillow, but then she began to think beyond her grief to the comfort she could bring to her ma if she married well. Deep down inside, she understood that her Ma would be glad to have one of her daughters well loved and cared for by an honorable man. Just then her sister Julie, situated in the middle, turned from side to side which forced Mattie to hold onto the cover quilt in order to prevent yet another upset down onto the cold floor. When the three were finally settled once again, Mattie's tears were dry and her last thought was a bold determination to stand her ground with me on Thanksgiving Day.

The harvest feast at the Hugh Godwin table included an iron skillet of battered and fried squirrel and a big pot of corn made creamy with a little added flour and bacon grease. Another big pot contained the last of the season's squash, and there were two pones of cornbread. My favorite dish set on the table was the fresh, tender, turnip greens gathered that morning and cooked with a little sugar, salt, pepper, and bacon grease. The turnip greens will last well into the first weeks of December and longer if the mild weather holds, and when the greens no longer sprout from the turnip, which if left alone and buried in the ground and pulled up only as needed, we can eat the turnip roots throughout most of the winter. On the pie safe which was purposely positioned in the kitchen on the cooler wall opposite the cook stove, were two dish pies of golden brown crust laid under and a top the dried apple filling, a dessert fit for a king, which for the festive feast seems slightly more formal than the usual method of preparing an apple dessert which is to wrap the dried apples softened with sugar, water, and butter, inside a pillow of dough and fry in sizzling hot lard. This was a Thanksgiving to be proud of, a gracious plenty food for two families, grown by the will of our Almighty God right here on this farm. This farm provides all our necessities leaving only sugar, coffee, and flour that must be store bought, which depends entirely on the chance that we have the money to buy the luxuries, and which sugar is by no means a necessity, for desserts are just as delicious when sweetened with honey harvested from bee hives found right here usually in hollow tree trunks. We don't grow sugar cane in these parts, and I don't grow wheat. I've never even seen sugar cane growing, but syrup cane is a common crop, and some neighbors produce sorghum syrup in the fall of the year. I let them do that job and consider myself lucky to swap some of my charcoal for a few quarts of the tasty syrup.

Mattie was particularly pretty that day. Her golden hair glimmered in the sunshine and formed a golden halo around her head, which made her look as sweet as an angel. She contributed to the conversation, but never out of turn, and she always waited to speak until her words could be easily heard for she was never bold or out-spoken. My children loved her and wanted to be near her. John sat on one side of her and Martheny on the other, and no one in the same room with Mattie could ever resist her contagious laughter she was her prettiest when laughing. She seemed to be the center of the gathering, and that day I understood my deep love for her was like none I'd ever felt for another woman, but she was not yet a woman, she was just seventeen. Lord, help me.

Jasper and Nen stayed on a while after Mattie and her ma and sister walked on down the slope through the hollow and up hill to the little house. Nen was in the kitchen, helping Ma. My sister Nen and Ma came with me to Cleburne County, Alabama from Union City, Georgia, near Atlanta in 1874, after Pa died and we buried him there. We had a good producing apple tree back in Union City, and the last thing I did at the old place was to dig up all of the shoots coming up around the big tree, and carefully pack them in wet rags to hold some dirt and moisture around the roots, and on the journey west, every time we crossed a creek, I poured water over the rags, and once we reached this place, I planted the orchard before doing anything else, and every single shoot I planted grew into a tree, but of course I nursed the seedlings through two long, hot summers with might near a barrel of water a day hauled from the nearby creek.

Pa's lone grave back in Union City is marked with a stone that stands three feet high, and Ma always wanted to go back to visit his grave, but the seventy-five miles each way is a two day journey over and two days back, and we never felt free enough to spare four days from the work of our farm, and as a consequence, we never went back to Pa's grave.

Here in this place, I feel a freedom, with nothing weighing me down, I can do the work that I love, and the bonus is that I can provide for my family on this farm, and as is the usual thing, the harvest is bountiful with corn and cotton in the fields and okra, tomatoes, potatoes, peas and beans in the garden near the house, which the garden needs hours of back breaking tending, but we live and thrive all summer and into the winter on the bounty of this good land. The apple orchard takes care of itself for the most part, but in another a year or two I'll have to prune the trees again. After gathering the apples each fall, I do spread manure from the cured pile around each tree. I call it the curing pile, where I dump the manure shoveled from the barn stalls into a mound, and let it stand in the weather through at least one winter so then it can be used as fertilizer without a worry of scalding the tender new crops. I don't mind the work of shoveling, and the pungent odor is part of the vigor of this life. I'm jealous of my power to control the earth, and I know that I can carve and shape this red Alabama clay just as an artist carves and shapes clay into forms, the only difference being that I use a plow and with my carving, I prepare the clay to produce and bring forth food. I relish all the phases of cultivation, and the reward is that with diligence and hard work I coax and coach the land, which then as a result of my labor, supports my family and me.

I have a lot to offer Mattie, but I worry about the twenty-one years difference in our ages, but on the other hand she'll be well off living her life with me because I will care for her and keep her safe from hunger and cruelty, and if her mother decides to move away from here and go down south to live with other brothers there, I'll have to speak my peace for I can't or won't live my life without Mattie. I need to settle all this so as to rest assured that I'll see Mattie everyday for the rest of my life, and I'll accept nothing less for the sight of her brings untold joy to me, and I am certain she cares for me in return, but on the other hand, it's best to wait.

I was in the barn before sun-up on butchering day, which in Alabama is usually the first cold spell after Thanksgiving, so as to eat the first ham at Christmas. The salt cured and smoked ham and bacon lasts through the winter, and we have ten-gallon crocks for in which to cold pack the smaller cuts of meat. First, we slow cook in the cauldron over an open fire and then dip the meat from the cauldron into the crock, and then pour the liquid fat in to fill the crock. The crocks are stored in the root cellar and when we need meat, we dig into the cold congealed lard and retrieve the preserved chops of pork. That year I butchered two hogs and traded it in town for coffee, sugar, flour and salt. It's good luck when the weather immediately after Thanksgiving is cold enough for butchering which gives a man time to barter in town for Christmas English walnuts, pecans and oranges.

Mattie and Ferraby, as Mattie calls Ma, were in the kitchen washing and placing cucumbers in a five-gallon crock of brine. After soaking the cucumbers in the brine, they cook them in apple vinegar, a small amount of sugar and herbs raised in the yard. That year I hauled two full crocks of pickles to market in Muscadine, The pickle crocks stand upright in the corner of the slide. I built the dray (slide) out of oak which is the hardest wood to work with and the most durable because of the great amount of stress which is naturally put on the slider boards while hauling heavy loads, and the next week I again made the trip to Muscadine this time with a load of railroad ties. There was always a demand for railroad ties back then for construction was still underway to the west of Birmingham. Forming the railroad ties by hand is tedious work, but the hard labor is rewarded with good pay. In designing and building the dray, I fashioned detachable side and end planks for easy loading of the heavy railroad ties, also for easy loading, the bed of the dray is only a foot off the ground. The weight of the crossties makes the initial pull difficult for the mules, but once the runners are set in motion a gliding, the momentum is easy to maintain and many times I can park the dray on a slight, very slight downhill slope, but being mindful of the importance in parking the dray crossways of the slope or perpendicular to the down slope and with the initial pull, lead the mules in a shallow turn which helps the mule a pulling the load downhill, and of course, a man never adds his own weight to the dray, but instead he rides his horse alongside, and another boost to heavy-load hauling is to walk alongside when moving from loading sight to loading sight. But back to the building of the dray, I round cut the front end of each runner from a two by ten oak board, which when rounded and smoothed along the front edges prevents them from digging into the ground, and the dray is used only for the heaviest loads, of course a wagon (wheels a turning) is more efficient in hauling lighter loads, but when hauling maximum loads of railroad ties, a man relieves the mules by riding along side on a horse.

With ingenuity and hard labor, I regularly accumulated money, and each time I reached another goal, I purchased another parcel of land. I was becoming a common visitor at the county recorder's office, and I garnered more respect each time I added acreage to my estate. My tall, slim but muscular physical stature helped to give me visual authority, and I learned to look any man in the eye, hold my head high, and always use kind words and that has been a good part and reason for my success for I learned early in life that strength in a man is emphasized by calm methods and easy-ness in demeanor, and by the time I was thirty six, I enjoyed considerable influence, and to this day I am careful to conduct myself with dignity, and I deserve this position of respect because I've worked hard to earn it.

My trip into Tallapoosa on the twentieth of December gave me the opportunity to buy surprises for my family, including Nen and Jasper, and also for Mattie and her ma and sister. I figured the ladies would appreciate store bought yardage for making new dresses so I bought an entire bolt of brown cotton material, it cost less per yard to buy by the bolt. I was unaware that the ladies might object to wearing dresses made from the same brown colored material, things like that were of no significance to me. My practical side told me to save money, and I was proud to find a logical solution when faced with putting new dresses on all the women. I also purchased a bolt of white cotton so the ladies could make shirts for the men. Ma and Nen were teaching Mattie to sew, and in our houses as in all others in the county, the Singer sewing machine stood in a place of honor. Two or three dresses can be sewn on the Singer in the same amount of time it takes to sew just one dress by hand without the amazing and wonderful sewing machine, and the Singer makes straighter, more durable seams.

While I was in town five days before Christmas, Nen, Ma and Mattie decorated both houses with Christmas trees. They roamed through the woods in search of two cedar trees but they found only one to be what they considered the correct size and so they settled for one cedar and one loblolly pine. The children joined in the search and anticipated finding the perfect tree, and time after time, they ran ahead, over the next rise knowing in their hearts their search would be rewarded. Mattie kept up with them, but Ma trailed behind with Nen at her side. The yelling of the children urged them on, and they found two trees each about five feet tall, cut them with my hand saw and started back to the house with Mattie dragging one tree, and Nen pulling the other.

They found hanging in the barn the old cross-boards nailed together many years ago, and while Mattie held the boards in place, Nen pounded the rusty nails into the bottom of the trunk of one slender tree. Nen decided to go home so's she could hunt for Jasper's cross boards for the bottom of her own tree. While Nen and Ma pulled our tree inside the house, Mattie and the children skipped off to the holly bush. The berries were brilliant red and the leaves shinny green, and they broke off as many limbs as they could carry. The prick of the spikes made them yelp in pain, and each time one screamed, the other two laughed with silly delight. They found the twine in the barn and started the task of tying the holly sprigs to the twine. They worked at this in the sun under the leafless cottonwood tree at the edge of the yard and they added sweet gum balls and cottonwood burrs to the twine garland by first binding the sweet gum balls and cottonwood burrs into clumps which then might be added to the garland. They remembered to use loose knots in all this preparation so as after Christmas the twine could be saved for other uses. With this garland bundled and stretched between Mattie and the children, they went a hollering and laughing into the house. Everyone joined together in placing the long rope of holly boughs, cottonwood burrs, and spiked balls from the sweet gum tree into a beautiful pattern a going around and around the tree. It was very festive.

When I came in from my trip to town, the children were sitting on the floor in front of the hot fire both a facing not the fire but the whimsical tree. They were so intent on admiring the Christmas tree that I managed to slip the packages into the small room before they noticed I'd entered the house. "I met Nen and Mattie on the road. Nen was dragging a Christmas tree and Mattie was hollering that she was bleeding from the pricks of the holly garland she carried. Nen was laughing at her torture and they told me a Christmas secret."

In secret, everyone took turns working on one Christmas gift for each of the children, a corn shuck doll for Martheny and a pine-straw-sled for John, and by Christmas Day with both toys complete, the families came together with a noticeable static excitement in the air. Early in the morning Nen, Jasper, Mattie, her Ma and sister walked the narrow lane down the hill across the creek and up to our house, they were early so as to help with the cooking of dinner, the noon meal, and as usual the children were up at dawn to find their Christmas surprise and by now of course they were outside the house hard at play and the sound of their laughter put a look of contentment on every adult face, and I do believe the adults enjoyed each and every slide down the hill fully as much and the children, and the intervals of comparative quiet meant a child was pulling the amazing new toy back up the hill and sure enough the next trip down brought more squeals of delight and so on went the parade, up and down, up and down. Riding down, toting up, riding down, toting up, as the new and actually crude sled served the purpose of entertaining the entire family and all this from a simple sit down board about three feet long, cut from a one by ten, flat down on the ground and another two foot cross board cut from a two by four and nailed perpendicular to the sit-down board and by which John or Martheny while seated precariously on the contraption stirred and slid down the hill lick-a-de-split over the slippery brown pine straw, and of course, John and Martheny took turns sitting on the wide board, hands waving above their heads, and feet positioned out front on the foot rest cross board which actually did little to stir the contraption, but instead served as a means by which to prompt the child to lean into their anticipated turn, and they learned right off to lean side to side while bracing as best they could on the cross board, a making slight turns as they went faster and faster down the hill with arms a flailing and the only measure of stirring amounted to body weight corrections. John loved the excitement and the danger and continued the down and up routine far longer than Martheny who tired and eventually preferred watching John and holding her corn shuck doll.

Inside the cozy house an enchanting pine tree perfume mingled with the delicious aromas of baking ham and apple pie. The home cured, brown colored ham is delicious like none other for the method of curing which is to separate the hams at the joint at the time of butchering and leave them to soak overnight in twenty gallon oak kegs of brine, and I've learned it's best to place a heavy rock on top of the hams which keeps them submerged in the salty solution, and the next step in the curing process is to tie the pork to nail hooks inside and high up in the peak of the smoke house and a smoldering fire-kept-burning inside the little house slow cooks the meat, and the smoke rises to cure the hanging hams and shoulders. I use my own secret combination of oak and hickory wood chips and the home smoked taste is better than any store bought, and sometimes I feel sorry for the town folk because their store bought food supplies can not compare to the food prepared here on this farm, except of course unless a family is lucky enough to dine on the hams and pickles which I haul into town.

After the noon Christmas dinner, I proudly handed out bags of nuts and oranges, and my added surprise gift (of two bolts of cotton cloth) made everyone giddy with happiness. Ma and Nen were hugging and laughing, and the love in the room created a blessed peace, a Christmas gift from the Lord God Almighty. Out-a- doors the morning chill vanished, and the afternoon sun warmed the earth, and I asked Mattie to go for a walk. We strolled leisurely along the wagon road. The slight breeze curling Mattie's hair around her chin caused her to lift her shawl over her head, which made me disappointed to lose sight of her soft golden hair. My wide brimmed hat pulled down on my forehead cast a shadow and Mattie could not read my thoughts, and she wondered as to the meaning of my silence. I sensed she was mesmerized by the constant wind ruffling my string necktie. My white shirt in the brilliant sun was almost blinding.

I spoke first. "Mattie, I know the difference in our ages is frightening for you. But, I suggest to you that the benefits of age in my case can give you safety and comfort."

Mattie replied, "I'm not frightened."

Her delicate, confident words astonished me, and I stopped to catch her arm, and pull her back toward me. She willingly melted into my arms, and she indicated confidence that our life together was beginning in that minute. She went limp, and I held her close to me, and our kiss was at first soft and timid and for Mattie a new and wondrous thrill full of promise, and for me our first kiss was filled with more love than any ever experienced in my here to fore mundane and void life, and when she sighed with pleasure, the passion exploded for us both.

"Oh, Mattie, I want you like none other. You alone make me feel powerful and you bring meaning to my lonely life. I want your sweet charm to be constantly in my life, I am incomplete without you, please say you will live with me and be mine? Tell me you are old enough to understand the commitment that I'm asking of you?"

"Yes, Hugh, I understand. I want to be with you everyday and every night. I love you and I admire you, and I know that you are a good man."

I knew that I should give her time to examine her heart. "If you still feel this way on New Year's Day, 1886, one week from today, then we will begin our life together. I won't come to you until then, you should have time to search your inner self and make your own decision. On New Year's Day, I will wait for you at the apple tree behind Jasper's house. If you find that you are brave enough to start a new life with me, meet me at five o'clock. If you do not come to the apple tree by five thirty, I will walk away, and we will never speak of this again."

We walked back to the house in silence each feeling the strength of the commitment that lay ahead. Our attraction was all consuming and she seemed to adore my browned skin, hawkish nose, clear blue eyes and dark straight, shiny hair. She loved my big, callused hands and the clean smell of lye soap about my clothes. She was not afraid, but at the same time she did not feel brave. Her contentment was much simpler than that.

This glimpse into her future was for her a calming and reassuring force, and somehow she knew that we would live together forever.

I felt that I had finally been able to put down a heavy load from my weary, aching shoulders and from my conscience. Before this day, I denied my love for Mattie for months leading up to that day because her youth gave me doubts about my honorable intentions, and just then, I felt again that she was mature beyond her years. It's her sensitivity and her intelligence that I first admired. Two people who have strong feelings should act on those feelings. I trusted that she would be my family and be faithful to me forever. By all that's holy, she would be faithful to me because at that minute I realized I simply could not tolerate the notion of ever loosing her.

The week between Christmas and New Year's Day 1886 seemed endless, and I worked from sunup to sundown to force my mind to let it go. Mattie came everyday to help in the house, and in a deliberate attempt to avoid her, I was sure to be out of the house hours before she arrived, and I returned to supper only after watching her walk away. I wanted her to know that in all things I am a man of my word. I said she would have this week to ponder her decision, and I intended to keep my word.

Mattie felt that the week of waiting was unnecessary because she knew no other path for her life to take. She could see no other way to face the years ahead. In 1886, she would be eighteen years old and when she looked into the far distant future, and the year turned to 1896, she pictured herself as she turned twenty-eight and she believed and realized the only possible way she could look to the future was to picture spending her life by my side. She declared that life would not be happy except spent with me. She loved her ma and sister, and she loved her poor lost pa, but that was a different sort of love and not at all like the assured feeling that she belonged to me for as long as she lived and even into eternity. This new sense of belonging to a man held mystery and joy beyond any she had experienced. A man and a woman sleeping together was for her a mysterious unknown but also she understood the boundless joy lying ahead in her future and it was fundamental to her need to care for me, to cook for me, to wash and mend my clothes. Simplicity is the foundation of life.

1886

On January 1, 1886, the year that Mattie would turn eighteen, she first helped Nen clean up the kitchen after the noon dinner of hog jowl, turnip greens, cornbread and buttermilk. Her ma and Nen followed the same superstition of eating hog jowl and turnip greens on the first day of the year so as to insure prosperity throughout the coming year, and when she completed all her chores that day, Mattie went into the bedroom carrying a clean cotton feed sack and quickly folded her clothes and stuffed them into the sack. She made a loop knot in the top of the feed sack and slipped silently out of the house. She found a good hiding place behind a rotting log near the apple tree and she tucked the white sack into the safe place and covered it with leaves. She ran back to the house to bathe and leave behind her sister's borrowed dress.

All that week after Christmas, she and the other ladies worked every day a sewing brown dresses, and on New Year's Day, Mattie's nice new brown dress with the white collar was finished and ready to wear. It was Mattie's Ma who helped her attach a white rounded collar because Mattie wanted this special dress to be elegant for this the most important day of her life. All day on that first day of the new year, Mattie was careful to keep her secret for she was determined to say goodbye to her family and declare our plans just at five o'clock.

The evening sun was in her eyes as she approached the apple tree where I was standing with my back to her. I was standing and leaning into the old, gnarled tree with one hand lifeless at my side, and because I felt a heavy weight of uncertainty that might crush my hopes for happiness, I was face down, head resting in the crook of my arm, eyes closed as I said a silent prayer, "Oh, Lord bring Mattie to me."

I was a tense coil of nerves, and I jerked and sprang toward Mattie when I heard the rustle of the leaves in the path. I smiled brighter than the heavens and folded my arms around her and kissed her with the unashamed enthusiasm of a man in love, and at that precise minute our lives together began, and we knew our love was meant to be and would last forever.

Panic in my voice, I asked, "Didn't you bring your things?"

She sensed my concern and quickly reassured me that earlier in the day she hid her belongings behind the log. I turned away from her warmth and took three long strides to the log, and when I returned a glance to her, she pointed, and I easily found the white sack, and holding her pitiful few possessions in my left hand, I closed my right arm about her as we walked arm in arm up the path, across to the road, and down the narrow lane away from the Jasper Hicks house. If we had been interested, we might have turned to see four smiling faces in the window with the one face of Mattie's ma shedding tears of happiness and good hope. Mattie and I did not look back because we were intent only on the road ahead for we both saw a clearly defined path to our future. When we approached my home place, I kissed her once more before going inside where Ma and the children were expecting us. Ma didn't look at us, instead she kept rocking in her rocking chair and watching the fire, but John and Martheny ran to us and started babbling about how happy we would all be with Mattie here to stay forever, and that was my clue that Ma had a talk with the children, which as I look back should a been my responsibility, but truthfully I was not at all positive what Mattie's choice would be.

I took Mattie's hand and led her into the small room walled off from the fireplace room, I closed and latched the door, and despite the cold, we were happy to have some privacy. The day before in preparation, I moved one of the beds into the little room, and now with the warmth of the fire shut out of our sight, I carefully placed Mattie's under garments from the white sack into a drawer in the bureau, and next, I hung her work dress on a peg in the shiff-robe and when I turned to once again face my beloved, she stretched to put her arms around my neck and kiss me with the first demonstration of her love for me, and we could no longer hide our delight in each other.

Mattie was so sweet; I could hardly contain my boundless joy. We were shivering in the cold, little room, and we stood facing each other for an eternity, holding hands and making our promises.

I asked if she would live her life faithful to me in mind and body.

She answered, "Of course."

She asked me if the children could call her 'Ma.'

I said, "Yes. I love you."

She said, "I love you."

We undressed each other and loved each other with a reverence for the solemn words we spoke. Mattie wasn't one bit shy, and we made each other very happy.

Ma and the children ate alone the celebration supper she prepared earlier in the day, and with the remaining food she placed in the pie safe, and the dishes washed and put away, Ma and the children sat by the fire until all three crawled sleepily into the warm bed. Ma slept in the same bed with the two children, and in the middle of the night, Ma heard us as we tiptoed through the room into the kitchen. She heard us laughing and whispering as we ate the cold food and when we crept back through the fireplace room, she heard me add two logs to the embers in the fireplace. A man always takes care of his family.

Mattie and I were happy. She helped Ma with the house chores just like before and most days, at noon, she brought a basket of food to me where ever I was working in the field or barn or woods which we planned our meeting place each morning before I left the house. At least once each month I hauled goods to market and Mattie wanted to go with me, but I knew the mule could do without the extra one hundred pounds of weight and more important was the consideration that Ma and the children needed her at home with them. Ma was about to turn eighty years old and I felt uneasy about leaving her at home alone with the two children. The three of them were safe with Mattie.

On occasion, Mattie talked about going into town to stand before a magistrate or a preacher and say again our vows, and we agreed to plan an outing in the spring that would include the entire family. We enjoyed dreaming of the time when we could register our marriage in a legal book and make our announcement to the world now and forever more we will live as one.

In the winter, a woman has carding, spinning and weaving to do if she is to have cotton cloth for making clothing and quilts for the family, and besides the normal work of cooking and washing Mattie stayed busy with that year's very good cotton crop which allowed me to keep back a large cotton bonus for our personal needs. Mattie liked to set aside Monday as wash day, and she was up before dawn for an early start so as to be assured of accomplishing the chores before sundown, so most Monday's she was up before sunup out in the yard a filling the cauldron with water, building a fire under it, pushing and agitating the clothes into the boiling water and lye soap, moving the clothes from the wash pot to the rinse pot, pulling clothes up and above the water level so as to drain the excess before slinging each item onto the porch railing or the garden fence. She took great pride in keeping a clean house and a well-fed and clean family. When agitating the clothes in the wash pot, she stood as close as possible to the fire and leaned forward to stir the clothes with the battling stick, and this awkward pose usually gave her a backache, but she never complained. The dirtier clothes she lifted out of the boiling water and spread on the wash rock where she scrubbed the spots clean by rubbing the cloth between her knuckles and the scrub board and sometimes she scrubbed the skin right off. For the sores on Mattie's overworked fingers, Ma boiled the dried leaves from the ground around the sweet gum tree to make a soothing sweet gum soak, and Mattie sat with her hands in the pan of sweet gum water every evening at the end of the day's work.

A favorite pastime for Mattie and Ma was to walk with the children through the woods, and these strolls became foraging excursions as Ma began to teach Mattie to recognize and gather the healing plants. Ma included instructions regarding which healing plants not available in the winter, can be dried for use year round and Mattie learned by examining Ma's collection in the root cellar, but the sweet gum balsam which is best for cleaning sores can be brewed from dry sweet gum leaves but it is more potent when brewed from the stronger sap, and the time for collecting is when the sap is up in the spring and through the summer and is gathered in the spring and summer through a hatchet cut on the rough sweet gum tree bark which lets the sap run, and it can be captured on rags and saved in the root cellar and by ripping off a small portion of the saturated rag and boiling the rag itself it makes a good strong soak which Mattie's tender knuckles responded to and by Tuesday evenings after Monday's wash day, the cracks sealed over and Mattie hands were in good shape for the week of baking, cooking, cleaning, carding, weaving, and sewing. She was never idle.

Our time together was full of love and happiness and contentment. Mattie was good to John and Martheny and she wanted the children near her at all times. I wondered how Mattie could persuade them into helping with the chores; and more importantly, I wondered how she could tolerate their help which many a times resulted in a mess to be reckoned with which in most instances Mattie magically cleaned up with a blinding smile and a splash of stardust, or equally as magical, Mattie somehow managed to transform the cleanup-chores into a game that delighted the children, and I have to admit, it fascinated me and Ma too, to watch my beloved in action as she charmed every one in sight. Once, I saw Martheny drop a clean wet white shirt in the dirt as she tried to spread it out on the fence to dry, and once, when John was chopping stove wood, he cut himself with the ax. Mattie was not flustered by any happenstance, and with the skill of a fine doctor, she sewed two stitches in John's gash. She coaxed the boy to clench his teeth and look the other way, and the stitching was made easier of course because Ma first made him some strong tea from the dried and pounded root of the wild flower called 'Lady's Slipper.' The Lady's Slipper tea helped to calm John, and after the stitching, another cup of tea settled him down and he slept soundly right through the night, and beginning the very next morning, Mattie cleaned the wound with an antiseptic tea made from the inner bark of the white oak tree and applied with a clean-rag-poultice made from the dregs and laid directly on the sore, and by the third day, the redness and swelling was gone.

About the middle of February, I noticed that Mattie was pale and throwing-up-sick every morning, and when I saw her walking away from the house carrying a white feed sack and to make it all the more unusual, she was alone, which might near never happened, and if she was just going-a-calling, as a normal habit she would be walking with the children and Ma by her side. I bided my time, and at noon when I went into the house for dinner, Ma looked like she'd swallowed more than she could chew, and her face was red, and she was fussing about the room without getting much done. Dinner was still in the pot on the stove, and the children were sitting cross-legged in front of the fire when they should have been in the kitchen a helping Ma.

"What's wrong, Ma?" I asked.

Ma replied, "Mattie was sick again this morning, and she packed her clothes in a feed sack and left without saying a word."

I grabbed my coat and hat off the peg and slammed the door so hard the whole house shook. I was half way down the wagon road before I had my arms in the sleeves, and when I reached Jasper's house, I practically pulled the door about off the hinges, and once inside, I controlled my voice, "I'm here for Mattie."

No one spoke when Mattie came out of the bedroom a crying. It was a shock to me for I'd never seen her cry before that minute.

"Let's go home, Mattie."

"I'm sick. I want to stay with Ma."

I growled, "No, you belong with me. I'll take care of you."

She wailed, "No. I want to stay here."

I wasn't about to argue for everyone to hear, so I went to her and put my hands on her shoulders, and when she looked up at me. I bent down in front of her and took one small wrist in my hand, pulled it over my head and easily lifted her off her feet and onto my shoulder; and when she tried to kick, I held her knees against my belly, and I held a good tight grip on her wrist. She was hitting me in the back with the other pitiful little fist, and she wasn't saying nothing, but she was sobbing, she was quietly sobbing which tore me up, and my legs seemed liquid and about to puddle us both on the floor, and she just kept a crying as I carried her like a sack of feed out the door and down the road. Mattie's Ma handed me the white sack of Mattie's belongings and I clutched it with the hand at the back of Mattie's knees, and as I walked down the road the sack kept bumping into and bouncing off of the front of my legs, and it beat a rhythm that was comforting to me, but might still be alarming to Mattie.

Mattie said, "Put me down Hugh. You're hurting me."

I put her down. I would never do anything to hurt her.

I said, "Mattie, you promised to stay faithful to me."

She said, "I'm sick, and I want to be with my Ma."

I said, "Well, I won't let you go back to your Ma because you belong with me now. I know you're too young to know why you're sick, but I know why and it's because you haven't had your monthly and you're carrying my baby. Listen carefully to me Mattie, I love you and you love me and I will never let you leave me, and for damned sure, I won't let you leave me and take my baby. I am your family and you are my family, and you promised to be faithful in all things. In October, we'll have a baby to care for, and you my sweetheart, will never leave me."

Mattie didn't say a word, but she walked beside me up the slope to our home, and once we were inside the house, in her confusion she was very shy in front of Ma and the little children, and none of us understood this development, but we let her stay to herself for several days after, and she did all her chores, but she didn't play games and she didn't laugh, and it was a good while before she really came back to us because she was pitiful embarrassed and throwing-up-sick a lot.

It was along about Easter when Mattie smiled again and with the return of hot weather, the family walked with her down by the creek to escape the heat of the day because it was cooler in the shade of the tall hardwoods that lined portions of the stream. The young'uns loved to wade in the clear, cool water while Ma pointed out healing herbs growing along the banks. Ma said to Mattie, "I might not be able to gather remedies when the baby gets sick, so you have to know what to look for."

That summer on June 26, 1886 Ma turned eighty years old and Mattie cooked a peach pie for desert from the dried last year's crop, it was a might early for the peaches on the tree to be fully ripe. It was difficult for Ma to get about but she was mentally alert and we treasured each day with her. Pa died at the age of seventy-eight, in the grave for twelve years now, and Ma spoke of him often, "You never stop missing your mate. Sometimes I look at the door and wish he would walk through it. There are lots of things I want to talk to him about."

Mattie listened to Ma's teaching and learned the healing art very quickly. She had a natural ability to absorb the smells, feels, colors and shapes of the remedies. In turn, as she learned a remedy's uses, she tried to teach ma to recognize the plants without looking or feeling them just by the aroma, but this was something Ma could not learn. Mattie said that some remedies smelled bitter, some like the wild garlic and onions had what she called 'a jerk away smell, and the sweet smell of honeysuckle was her favorite. She learned to dry and crush the garlic and onion bulbs and use the powder mixed with grease as a salve for insect bites in the summer and a chest rub to get up phlegm in the winter. The powder makes a terrible tasting tea to purge the bowels of parasites that cause stomach cramps.

Ma told Mattie to use the garlic and onion bulbs and green shoots in her cooking for flavor and for happier babies. The bulbs stay fresh in the ground through the winter, and most times the greens last year round. Ma remembered way back when she was a young girl, her mouth was sore, and her legs were weak from the scurvy. Her Grandma made her eat onions and garlic right out of the ground and made her drink tea made from pine needles, and Ma was cured in just a few weeks. Mattie took all Ma's teachings to heart, and thought up her own ways to make the remedies even better.

One warm spring day as I was clearing some of the old hardwoods in a field close to the house I noticed Mattie walking toward me from across the field of standing rabbit tobacco and as she waded through the broom straw and rabbit tobacco, she bent to pick a handful by grabbing the rabbit tobacco stalk down low might near down at the ground and well below the foliage level, and with the stalk held tight in her hand, she pulled up the length of the stalk and separated the dried leaves as she stretched and pulled her clinched hand the length and to the top, and now clutched in her hand the dried leaves formed a clump from which she could bite and chew the leaves which provided some relief from the sickness that still plagued her, and with the rabbit tobacco safely in her apron pocket she focused on gathering a good hand full of broom straw for she always took advantage of every opportunity to replace the house broom with fresh more pliable straw, and with this welcome image of her seared in my mind, I turned away and went back to my work of chopping the downed oak into six foot long logs from which I'd next begin the process of squaring into six by six cross ties, and with my mind of other matters, I was lost to the world when, with a start, I realized that Mattie was no where in sight. I did a wild dance hither and yon in the field until I found that she had strayed from the straight line leading in my direction, and when I came within close proximity, I heard her soft sobbing. She was lying on her back looking up at the sky with her arms spread wide. Her bonnet had fallen back away from her head, and now rested on the ground, the string was still around her neck, and when she heard my approach she clutched her shawl close about her. She was bathed in the warm sun in what she considered to be a secret place out of my sight where the broom straw stood all around her to keep her misery private. I stooped to a crouched position beside her and came to rest on my knees, "What's wrong, Mattie?"

She didn't answer. I could see her tears sparkle in the sunlight as they ran from the outside corner of her eyes down into her hair. I could smell the rancid odor of her food come back up, and I saw the remains in the straw beside her head, and she pleaded, "Don't look at me. I'm ashamed."

I dropped my head to my chest and looked at the ground beneath my knees and with deliberately slow and calculated moves, I picked a straw and put it between my teeth as I allowed my beloved to roll away from the vomit's retched odor now several feet behind me. "Why are you ashamed?"

"I'm sick."

I crawled over her slight body and sat on the clean straw close on the other side. I pulled her up off the ground into my lap and wiped her chin with my hand and then I wiped my hand on the straw. I folded my arms around her and rocked her. At first she was stiff and curled into a ball, her feeble stab at avoiding me, but I held her against my chest and kept on rocking. She stopped crying, "How can you hold me when I am so ugly and sick?"

"Mattie, I love you when you are sick just as I love you when you are well, and it makes no matter to me, I want to take care of you all the time. You took care of little John when he cut himself with the ax didn't you?"

"That's different. He's just a little boy."

"It's not different, Mattie, I love you when you are happy and well of course, but I'd be a weasel of a man if I stopped loving you when you are sick. Everybody gets sick some times, Mat, everybody. You can't be pretty and smiling all the time. When you're sick, my heart aches for you and I want to hold you and help you."

"Let me go, I want to wash my face."

I let go of her and when we both stood up I prevented her escape from me and I surprised her by picking her up and walking toward the house, and once inside the house, I put her in a chair and took her bonnet and shawl. I poured water in a pan and brought a clean rag to the table, and I washed her face and hands. I wouldn't let her help, and I wouldn't let her turn away. I chuckled with the children and Ma as they came close and I kissed Mattie on the forehead and smiled at her. I would not let her turn away, and I looked her straight in the face until she smiled back at us.

Before my eyes Mattie became a woman, and her pitiful shyness faded as she accepted the love we offered to her. In her eyes glowed new life and peace and serenity, as she let her restraint slide away and leave in it's wake nothing more to hide, nothing more to fear, and we all laughed loud and long, and Mattie's first words were to Ma, "Hugh's Pa was named Aaron?"

Ma nodded yes.

Mattie touched her belly and said, "In October, there'll be a baby, and his name will be Aaron after his grandpa."

Mattie worked hard all day every day. She studied the art of healing with Ma and the children, and she learned from her Ma, and Nen took an interest too. Every day the ladies searched out and gathered wild plants, and with her keen senses, Mattie began to connect plants into groups. It all came so easy for her. She was as good at healing as anybody could be and she seemed almost to have an extra power.

Mattie kept after me to trade for some sheep because she wanted to make warm woolen clothes for the family. She wanted wool for winter, cotton for summer. It took three days of traveling the countryside out to the west of Cleburne County to find a farmer willing to split his flock, and I came prepared to trade apple tree shoots (seedlings), one small crock of pork congealed in lard, and another crock of pickles which I deemed a good swap for two sheep, a ram and a ewe. I planted the apple shoots for the farmer and instructed him as to their care before I loaded the two sheep on the slide and headed back east, and I made it back home by sundown the next day. I sheared the adult ram and ewe that first spring and Mattie began her job of cleaning and carding the wool before she dusted off the old spinning wheel and began spinning the wool into yarn. With Ma's help she mastered the art of weaving the yarn into cloth, and with in a few weeks she gathered wild plants from which to make dye for the coloring of the wool in the wash pots in the yard. She made trousers for me and John and shawls for Ma, Martheny and herself, all this and the bonus that the ewe dropped two lambs that summer.

Mattie figured and practiced the importance of drying healing plants as a way to have remedies on hand for winter ailments, and when the goldenrod bloomed in the fall, she dried the flowers for chewing the goldenrod petals and slowly swallowing the juice to cure a sore throat, and she collected small chips of the inner bark of the Dogwood tree knowing that she could collect more at any time for the dogwood bark tea reduces fever, even the high fever of malaria, and is good for cleaning wounds. Mattie wrapped all her remedies in clean rags and stored them in the root cellar.

Mattie's belly was well rounded and the extreme heat of the summer of 1886 especially in August made her misery all but unbearable, and each night after supper eaten cold so as to keep the house from the blazing hot temperature of a cooking fire, we sat on the porch and watched the children catching lightning bugs. We ate and enjoyed our cold supper in hopes of sleeping better in a slightly cooler house. Ma and the children now slept in the opposite side of the house entirely away from the heat of the cook stove, but Mattie and I preferred to have our privacy and so we continued to sleep in our little room off the fireplace room.

When our first baby came on October 17,1886, the days and nights were considerably cooler and Mattie learned from the midwife that tea made from the roots of the cotton plant relieves the pains of labor which of course she remembered for future births, and as a result, Mattie proudly proclaimed her successful birthing of baby Aaron with little or no screaming which gave her an immense reason to boast, and as she said, "Blessedly saved Martheny and John from undue fear."

She kept all these precious cures in her remarkable memory for she never learned to read nor write, and therefore she never labeled her remedies, but more importantly, she never forgot any plant or it's medicinal purpose, and our root cellar became an apothecary shop, but admittedly there were sometimes when she had to unwrap more than one cloth to hunt for a remedy, but most times she remembered what the folds of cloths contained for she was a brilliant woman, always full of surprises.

Mattie was a good ma and now she had three children John, Martheny and Aaron. The baby sometimes cried with the colic, but Mattie knew what to do. She dipped a clean rag in elder tea and let the baby suck the tea from the rag. This soothed the baby and reinforced Mattie's confidence in her own healing skills. Mattie had a gift for watching the body and learning its reaction to foods and healing herbs. She taught herself to figure out how to treat any symptom and since her first time pregnant will always be remember for the constant retching and agony, still after the birth of Aaron, she gained confidence in her own worth and power, and she remembered the taste of vomit and never again ate anything with that taste at least when she was carrying a baby.

She told me many times that her first berthing sickness was caused by fear of the unknown more than anything else. Never again was she afraid while she carried a baby, because she understood the necessary changes and was happy and confident in the wonders of her body. She rejoiced in knowing she was building a new life inside her, and her confidence made everything work for her. The years of her discovery were rich and meaningful, and she made our lives full and content. I loved her more every day.

When she was carrying our second baby Mary Lizzie, of course she took care of herself and the unborn baby, but beyond that she began unraveling the relation between her pregnant-sickness (which many times became violent, lurching heaves) during the carrying of Aaron, and in her analytical mind to the colic he often suffered as an infant and she decided there was a direct correlation between the pregnant sickness and the baby's colic, and I believe she was right in that notion for when she taught herself to avoid her own sickness, she helped prepare for a healthier baby, and as a matter of fact, Aaron, her first, was the only baby out of fourteen to cry and spit up from colic, so she learned from her mistakes which the most important education was to watch carefully what she ate.

Through Aaron's first winter the little baby boy had a red irritation that sometimes looked like it might bleed. Mattie kept a clean rag tied to him all the time, and she changed it every time it was soiled, but the baby still cried from the pain of the rash. In the spring, when he was about six months old, she stopped tying a rag on him and let him crawl free inside the house and outside in the sun, and her hands bled might near every day through the winter from washing so many rags for the baby, and she decided the fresh air and sunshine would dry up the pustules on the baby, and this was the time when she started holding the baby away from her side when she felt the first warm drops of urine and allowing the water to fall past her skirts and onto the ground or even to the floor inside the house and it kept the rash in retreat both on the baby and her pitiful raw knuckles, and to clean the floor puddles, she kept a stick and a rag leaning in the corner by the back wall which she used as a mop as she poured a little water from a dipper onto the rag and then keeping her hands virtually dry by pushing the rag along the floor with the stick, and she took all of this farther by actually learning to sense when the baby was about to urinate, and more times than not she rushed out the door and to the edge of the porch before the flow started. She smiled at the baby and cooed to him that it was a good thing to perform this body function as his mother held him over the edge of the porch. The baby seemed to understand and link all of this together, and Mattie laughed when his skin rash cleared, and her hands stopped bleeding, and Mattie said of her discovery, "It's easier to let nature show us what's best."

The garlic that grew wild in the fields around the house added a delicious flavor to the watercress Mattie gathered from along the creek banks in the spring of the year. Mattie loved to wander alone by the creek in search of watercress and she could quickly collect enough for a meal and carry it to the house in her apron held together to form a sack and her creative mind led to pictures of words when she described to the children the scene of the watercress dancing in the cool rushing water, and when she took the children with her, she delighted them by telling stories of the fairies dancing in the water wearing little green hats, and after the story telling, when it was time to wade in the cold, clear, fast-running water and pick the watercress, she left the baby on the bank with Martheny, but John liked to wade in the water with Mattie, pulling as much of the watercress as Mattie. One day, I was indeed a lucky man to catch a show of this when I saw Mattie talking in a whisper to the two children and baby Aaron, and their spellbound expressions were of disbelief as they inspected the creek rushing past. Then with a smile, Martheny sitting on the creek bank, rocked baby Aaron in her lap as John rolled up his pants legs and Mattie bent over reaching between her legs to catch the back of her shirt, pull it through her legs and up to her waist and tuck it into the apron at the same time twisting her apron to one side so as to free the apron for the purpose of hauling the soon to be collected watercress. The children and Mattie walked barefooted from early spring through late fall, but since this was their first day without shoes, Mattie and John were dancing a jig in the creek bed as sharp little rocks pricked their tender feet, but with all the distractions, they harvested a mess of watercress and our evening meal was fit for a king. After supper that night, when Mattie sat down to nurse baby Aaron, she called out to me in an anxious voice, "Hugh, come here. Look at this! The baby won't suckle. Every time I add garlic to the cressy greens, Aaron won't suckle at my breast."

I found it fascinating that she could piece all this together in her quick mind. She figured that the garlic must taint her milk just as bitter weed taints a cow's milk and everyone knows when a cow eats bitter weed, her milk is too bitter to drink. That's when the milk goes in the hog's slop.

Our Christmas together in 1887 was wondrous for all and especially the children. Aaron was walking and took great delight in the miracle of tree brought inside the house, but he pricked his finger more than once on the holly leaves tied to twine and wrapped around the tree from top to bottom. Mattie could do little more than call out to him when he approached the prickly attraction because she was moving about at a slow pace with the bulk and weight of carrying around another rounded belly and this second time she was bigger for now she understood what foods agreed with her and she ate a lot, probably twice as much as with the first. She relied on Martheny to corral the rambunctious little feller knowing that Ma was ailing with joint pain and a stiff back, and Mattie simply could not bend over to pick up the heavy one year old for her giant belly restricting her movement and her back which was in constant pain. Three days after Christmas, Mattie delivered a baby girl and declared that the baby's name would be Mary Lizziebeth from the Ingram grave inscription, and that we'd call our daughter Mary Lizzie, and this sweet little girl was a peaceful and quiet baby who slept long hours which was a welcome change from the constant colic of Aaron's first months.

1918

Shug was seven years old and Nell was three when my health was deteriorating such as to keep me bed ridden for weeks at a time through that long winter, and my problem in it's entirety, is that I have a lack of strength and resolve to face the future. The mere word 'future' turns my heart to stone for how can there be such a thing if I cannot picture what my lonely future can possibly be. I have proved to myself that the reality of the here and now is that I cannot recover from the death of my beloved Mattie and life without her is sad. However, there is a comfort in this barren despair, and that comfort lies in Baby Nell and little Shug for many are the days when they stay inside the house with me and their presence alone is a huge encouragement for an old man like me. They are as precious to me as each and every one of my sixteen offspring, and I take delight in their eagerness to help around the house with simple chores, and that is exactly what young uns need in order to establish their own independence and self-reliance. That will be a necessity all too soon when I pass from this earth and cross into the great beyond to join my Mattie, and I might ought to feel some sense of failure or anguish at the prospect of leaving my youngest children to find their own way, but it's not despair that I feel, instead, it's with positive anticipation for the blessed day when I'll begin eternity by the side of my sweet Mattie. These are the circles of my thinking that take me back through this old worn out reasoning again and again. It is to little Nell's credit that she wants to help with chores and she is remarkably adept at handling and drying the supper dishes from her perch a standing in a straight back chair, and like Mattie, Nell seems to have an affinity for tidiness and perfection. Why Nell stacks the dishes in strict order just as her Ma did, and she already folds the clean clothes with a precision of detail that brings Mattie's presence right into the room with us. It is inborn in little Nell for the traits of her Ma can have no place in Nell's short memory, no sir, it is inborn in Nell to be a replica of her Ma.

Doc is still practicing medicine out of the little room that I first shared with Mattie when that first night I brought her here to be my wife and which now Doc calls his office, and sometimes I feel as though I've become unnecessary to this life and I'm just an old man in the way. I know too well and wrestle every day the empty feeling in this old house since Mattie died. I want to tell my youngest children Shug and Baby Nell as many stories of their loving Ma as I can remember, and every day Shug and Nell climb on the high bed and listen to their old Pa. I draw comfort in the obvious which is they are completely reliant on each other, and it is a solace to see them feel responsible for each other. I imagine a lifetime of caring between them, and maybe that will make up for the loss of their Ma and the loss of me when my time comes. I'm sure they'll stand together and support each other's need to lean toward the other.

We could hear Essie in the kitchen washing the breakfast pots and pans and my youngest children were respectfully quiet and still as I talked to them in a whisper. My little girl snuggled into the tight space between her brother Shug and me.

Today, I want to tell you about the typhoid epidemic of 1915. Nell, you were just a baby, six months old when you and all of us, the entire family came down with typhoid fever. Since your mother was a healer, she always knew how to cure any sickness, but she didn't know how to heal the typhoid. Your brother, Right Handy was eleven years old that winter, and he was the one who took sick first, and night after night your Ma stayed by his side all through the night, and if she got any sleep atall it was maybe an hour or two in the still of the night when the house was quiet and everyone was asleep. Only then, did she dose off as she lay on the floor beside Handy on a pallet, which at that time consisted of only one quilt folded once and spread on the floor in front of the fireplace. For three or four days, Handy was out of his head moaning and tossing. He was wet with fever and your Ma's energy and devotion seemed never ending. One by one, she watched helpless as all you children came down with the fever. She never complained or rested from nursing the whole family, me included and by the fourth day (or maybe the fifth), every inch of the fireplace room was covered with floor pallets, and on each pallet was a shivering, deathly sick child. One night your ma screamed and started shaking you, Baby Nell, because you were lifeless and quiet, and her grief was devastating when she couldn't revive you, she was crying and hollering, "Wake up my precious baby, oh please wake up."

Again and again she squeezed you close to her breast and then with an agitated and erratic motion she extended you to arms length high in the air above her, and it must have been that jerking motion that caused your limp little body to shudder as air filled your lungs and then a miracle happened and you started to cry, and your Ma said the sound of your crying was the sweetest song she'd ever heard. You were dead, but you started breathing again thanks be to God. The next morning at about sun-up, John Owens came into our house with his big arms loaded down with quilts and cash money collected from our good neighbors all over the county. We knew full well not one of our neighbors had either quilts or money to spare; but out of the goodness of their hearts, they saw fit to share their meager subsistence with us in our time of need, and Big John Owens, was an agent of God and an angel of mercy the day he was helped by Ab Whitley to bring in and set up a brand new pot belly warming stove bought and paid for with the donated cash money. The two men worked all day at cutting a hole in the wall of the sleeping room and splicing and extending and running the brand new stovepipe through the hole to the outside. They chopped and brought into the house enough stove wood to warm both sides of this old drafty place, and they gently carried each sick child into the sleeping room and placed them into beds under piles of quilts and big John Owens stayed here in this house, night and day for two weeks and he spoon fed the sick, steadied the children and adults when they had to eliminate liquid or solid from their weakened and fragile bodies, and he was a vigilant guardian for the entire Godwin family as he cooked the soup we sipped and changed the clothes we soiled.

I shutter to think what would have happened in those dire circumstances if we'd been left to attend to our body functions without his selfless acts of mercy, and it's not in excess to imagine that most of us would have died just the way your brother Right Handy died the very first night when John and Ab completed the installation of the warming stove and as they stood a warming their own frozen hands right there in that God forsaken room of gloom and darkness when John said good bye to Ab Whitley and no sooner than he turned in place to begin his rescue mission did he hear the gasping and wailing of my sweet Right Handy and unbeknownst to me or his Ma, Right Handy died in the big compassionate arms of John Owens. In the lonely solitude of a deafening silence before the sun rose again, your Ma, my darling Mattie, died too, and the only comfort my lost soul could find when I came to was to think that Mattie and our son held each other in rejoicing when they met our Lord, and they are happy and forever pain free except for the fleeting moments when they are tugged back to this life with the hateful interruption of their bliss by our pain and sorrow.

I felt the sobs building inside me for my little children, and it was a strange and welcome relief to witness little Shug finally grieve openly for his lost Ma. The three of us (me and my two youngest children) huddled together for an eternity, and then my remarkable little son and daughter wiped the tears from their eyes, and Shug spoke first.

"Come on Sis, we've got work to do."

The transformation that was obvious to me might have been subtle to others, but I could rest assured that another level of maturity had developed in my youngest two children.

"Off with you both. Tomorrow I'll tell you more about the John Owens family."

Alone in the room, lulled back to sleep by my children's ruckus accomplishing their morning chores, I am a lonesome man who somehow accumulated six hundred and forty acres of land, and when I was working toward that end, I enjoyed life's sacrifices and embraced them with the hope of a better tomorrow, but here I am at the end of my life, I can call mine one square mile of the state of Alabama, and this position is not what I worked for, not what I dreamed about, not what I intended, this land is just dirt that cannot comfort me. I married a beautiful young woman twenty-one years my junior, and the bet was that she'd be the one to grieve for the loss of me, but I lost that bet, it was not to be, and this is the cruel hand of God that has mocked my intentions and left me to mourn the death of my beloved Mattie.

Chapter 2

Back to 1903, Spring

The Roberds sisters, Sally and Ollie, were holding hands sitting on the creek bank. Their bare feet dangled from the moss-covered overhang.

Ollie said, "Lean out over the water Sally and look at that big fish."

Sally was slow to follow her sister's direction just as if she knew ahead of time what was about to happen. The sisters felt a slight movement of the ground where they were sitting, and then they heard a slurp as the wet red Alabama clay started to break apart. They were screaming and laughing as the creek bank overhang collapsed beneath their weight, and the sliding mud pulled them down with a slow easy gurgle and bubbles of air escaped to the muddy surface of the once sparkling clear water. They found themselves standing in two-foot deep mud and watched fascinated as the swirling clumps disappear downstream. They tried to remain in a standing position, but some of the rocks in the creek bed were sharp enough against their bare feet to cause them to begin a wild jumping dance. As their arms flailed in search of balance, the inevitable poking and pushing landed the two sisters in a sitting position in the water. Now they were soaked through every layer of clothing and the weight of their wet step-ins, underskirts, dresses and aprons caused them to round their young strong shoulders. As they tried again to stand, their long sleeves cupped and caught water heavy enough to bend the slender girls into a bowing stance, and the inevitable water fight brought squeals of laughter. Neither girl had the strength to throw sleeves full of water, but they managed to splash a shower deluge on each other. Their hands skimmed just beneath the surface, and with every jab, they coughed and gasped and spit mud and water in every direction. Necessity finally brought them together in a hug and each welcomed the mutual support now the only means of escape.

Struggling hand over hand the girls tried to crawl out of the creek and some advancement came when they grabbed hold of exposed tree roots. Both were virtually blinded by the mud and Sally's apron pulled away from her body as she stumbled over its trailing edge. The slippery slope and the dragging apron forced her to admit she had no choice but to fall back behind her sister and start her climb again. Ollie reached the top of the bank first and turned to pull her younger sister up beside her to a footing on the soft green pasture grass.

"We should take a bath here in the creek and try to wash some of this mud out of our clothes."

"No, I want to go home. This is wash day and Ma will have the wash pots boiling."

They giggled all the way up the hill. Inside the house, as they were trying to remove their sticky dresses, Ollie remembered to check her pockets.

"Sally, I forgot to tell you. Look at this." Ollie was holding a scrap of newspaper.

"I found this in the paper yesterday. It's a name of a farmer in Oklahoma. He's advertising for a wife. Now that I'm twenty-one, I think I'll write to him."

"Let me see that," Sally reached for the paper. "The date on this paper is way back last winter."

Then Sally read aloud, "Christian Oklahoma farmer needs a wife. Please write to Mr. Hooper."

1903 Fall

Sally and Ollie were sitting in the parlor, each working feverishly with needle, thread and thimble. Sally sewed buttons on the bodice of a honey brown suit, and then she carefully hemmed the wrist-edge of the leg-of-mutton sleeves. Next, she tacked around the neck of the stand-up collar. An open trunk sat on the floor between the two girls, and folded inside were two new, work-dresses made of cotton calico. Also, in the trunk stood a neatly folded stack of white cotton underclothes, and above the opened trunk lid, on the table next to the oil lamp lay another stack of newly sewn under garments. The girls and their mother had completed one chemise, and two each of step-ins, underskirts and camisoles all made of crisp white cotton. The girls were proud of their finger work, but their mother was more experienced at using the treadle sewing machine so the young girls sewed the delicate, hand stitches to perfectly finishing each of the undergarments. Just this minute as Sally tied off the last of the buttons on the brown suit waist, she stood, stretched the kinks from her young back, picked up a dishtowel, and gingerly retrieved a hot iron from the stove. Carefully she ironed the honey brown fabric, the lining fit perfectly into the gored bodice. The artfully placed darts and seams created a closely form-fitted jacket that would cling to Ollie's midriff from her shoulders to her waist. Below the waist, the jacket's wider gores caused the soft material to fall into graceful flounces hanging below the shirt's waistband and accentuating Ollie's tiny figure. Sally finished the ironing and stretched the cotton shirtwaist on the long kitchen table, and this time with her hands, she again flattened the warm material.

"Sally, stir the beans while you're in there," called her mother.

Sally stirred the beans and returned to the task at hand. Another month and Ollie would be leaving. The sisters and their Ma were working with urgency to complete Ollie's hope chest. For Sally, this precious time spent with her beloved sister was heaven on earth. Both the girls loved to sew, and they loved thinking wistful thoughts about this joint endeavor as they spent their time making preparations for Ollie's future in Oklahoma with Mr. Hooper. They whispered secrets and dreamed together and swooned at length throughout every day and every night in the dark, still, quiet time in their shared, cozy bed their youthful excitement was often expressed through squeals of hope and promise for Ollie's about to be realized adventure, but now and then, Sally was struck with the sober fact that was more than sad, it was catastrophic. Sally realized that Oklahoma is a long way off from Alabama. Their Papa figures it will take only five days for Ollie to travel from Alabama to Oklahoma, and that seems like lightening speed. The trains move along at a fine pace, sometimes as fast as forty miles an hour, why the countryside will be only a blur going at such high speeds. Nevertheless, the solemn hateful fact froze Sally's exuberance with the force of a sledge hammer, if it takes five days to get there, it will of course take five days to return, and facing the truth, Sally reasoned to herself the obvious conclusion, when in the world will a new bride have time to leave her home and travel such a long distance to visit her family back in Alabama when the travel time alone is ten days? Sally knew the answer, and with a wash of grief she realized that this next month would be her last month with her sister. She was happy for Ollie and sad for herself, and above all she knew and understood that she could not speak of this to Ollie for to verbalize these feelings would hurt Ollie and diminish her happiness, but no matter, Sally grieved for her impending loss and shed secret tears when no one could hear.

Ollie positioned herself to stand in a straight chair so Sally could measure the correct length of the honey brown travel skirt, and with Sally's basting stitches in place, Ollie jumped off the chair, stepped out of the skirt and returned it to Sally who hugged the skirt under her arm and threaded a needle to hem the skirt and tack the waistband. When Sally finished hemming and ironing the skirt, she passed it back again to Ollie and said, "That does it, your travel suit is finished, and I'm just dying to see it on you, please try it on,"

The warm brown color complemented Ollie's dark complexion. "It's almost the same color as you hair." Sally said pensively.

"I know your mail-order husband will be smitten with your beauty the minute you step off the train," said Ma.

Ollie swirled around making the skirt float away from her slender figure. She had been in a dancing mood for a month now, ever since Mr. Hooper's first letter in answer to hers had arrived from Oklahoma. The letters came to her delivered by the peddler, and each morning she woke with starry-eyed anticipation, although the peddler only came through this part of the county once or sometimes maybe twice a week. Her fervent hope each morning was that today would be the magical day for another letter from Mr. Hooper.

Ma chided, "Back to work, girls, it's mid afternoon, the day's a waning, we have to stay focused on the job at hand while the light's still good for sewing."

Sally picked up another bodice, this one a soft blue taffeta with white lace collar and cuffs, which could only be described as a Sunday-go-to-meeting dress. Ollie's plan is to wear the brown suit for travel, and if privacy can be found on the train, she'll change into the blue suit for her arrival and marriage ceremony. Mr. Hooper has written they will see the preacher in town then they'll drive the horse and wagon to Mr. Hooper's land holdings. His last letter included a daguerreotype of himself. He looks strong and determined, not a hint of a smile. His clothes look shabby, but Ollie can fix that. She will be a welcome help for this lonely man now responsible for all the work on his large land holdings. His last letter described his need to work both inside and outside the house, which settled their first whispered concern if Ollie might have to live in a soddy, but Mr. Hooper definitely used the word "house." Along with the daguerreotype, Mr. Hooper included cash money for Ollie's train ticket, and in his generosity, he sent enough cash money to buy all this material and thread. On Pa's trip into town last week, he used the cash money to buy the piece goods and thread before stopping at the depot and directing the train agent to figure the fair and route.

The ladies heard a commotion outside. Sally stood up and ran to the window. "It's John Owens." Sally said in an excited whisper

Sally turned and flew across the room to the little mirror above the washstand. She patted her disheveled hair and quickly splashed some cool water on her face, wiped it dry and glided on thin air to open the front door. John Owens stood on the porch as Sally nervously gasped to fill her lungs. This big man always made her fumble and stammer but she managed a cordial invitation to come inside, and he walked purposefully to bend at the waist, remove his hat and greet her ma. "How do Ma'am?"

"How do, John?" Ma replied

Sally was scurrying around trying to make a place for John to sit. She became flustered as she gathered the ladies' under things and tried to hide them from his notice, but, as he sat down, Sally saw the look of recognition on his face. His handsome face lit up in a smile, and she knew with a flutter that he would start to tease. He couldn't resist teasing her.

After dropping her armload of under garments into the chest and quickly closing the top, Sally sat down next to her Ma. She caught John's eye once more, then modestly looked at the floor, her heart was pounding out of her chest.

"Miz Roberds, Ma'am, I just spoke with your husband. I declared my intent on courting your daughter. If it is to your pleasure, Ma'am, I will walk Sally home from church come this Sunday."

"It is to my pleasure, John. Will you stay to dinner?"

"No Ma'am, I have chores still waiting at home."

"Well then can you come to Sunday dinner?"

"That I will do, and thanks to you for the invite. I'll be going." Again he tipped his hat, "Until Sunday."

"Good bye John," said Ma.

Sally was still staring at a crack between the wide pine floorboards when John let himself out the front door, and without explanation she and Ollie started giggling. Ollie took Sally's hands in her own and pulled Sally up from the straight chair, and together the girls began dancing at arms length, around and around in dizzying circles.

"You girls stop that nonsense before you break my last oil lamp; a woman can't have nothin' in a house full of rambunctious young'uns. Sally go stir the beans, I think I smell 'em burnt."

Sally thought Sunday would never come though it was a distraction each day they sewed and packed more into Ollie's hope chest. On Saturday evening when the sewing machine was folded into it's cabinet and the chickens, hogs, and cows were fed and in their designated quarters, the supper cooked and dishes washed and put away, finally all their work accomplished, the women bathed by the warmth of the kitchen fireplace and dressed in clean nightgowns, Ma settled down in bed with one last buttonhole to finish by the light of the kerosene lamp, and the girls crawled into their shared bed to allow the men some privacy to take their turn, and one by one Pa and the boys filled the wash pan with clean hot water and bathed in preparation for Sunday's attendance at church, and as on every other Sunday morning, the entire family walked to Camp Ground Church. Sally loved the old church building. Her life seemed to revolve around the social gatherings at this church and as always, her eyes found John Owens as soon as her Pa opened the door for them to enter.

After church, John and Sally walked behind the others lost in comfortable silence. The sun seemed to shine only on them on this bright and beautiful day. The dirt road was packed from the recent rain and formed a wide red clay ribbon winding ahead through the pines, the birds were singing and a deer bounded into the woods. Sally thought her legs would fold beneath her when John caught her small hand in his, and with brave daring she looked up at him and smiled. She stood only five feet four inches to John's well over six feet of muscle and brawn, his handlebar mustache and his full head of hair were red as was his face and Sally watched awestruck as his beautiful sky blue eyes picked out birds on tree limbs deep into the shadows, and with precision, he directed her attention to birds unknown to her, and of course she knew most bird calls and most budding trees, but she pretended ignorance when she asked him the name of the now blooming sourwood trees lining their way. Sally washed her hair the night before, and consequently she was confident that John was admiring her black hair glistening as a crow's wing in the sunlight, and when she looked down, she was mesmerized by the sight of her sun darkened small hand wrapped in John's large fair-skinned freckled hand as she thought to herself, "I love this man, I always have."

At home, Ma covered her Sunday-go-to-meeting dress with a long apron flipped over her head and tied behind her back in one seamless motion as she headed out the back door and down the steps behind the house to catch and kill one of her prized chickens. Quickly, she grabbed the nearest chicken by the head and with a practiced to perfection movement held the chicken directly in front of her frame and with the force of a strong and determined woman she swung the young fryer around and around in circles until it dropped to the ground headless and flopping. Ma tossed the chicken's head to the dog, sat on a stump, plucked the feathers, collected them in a flour sack, and was climbing the back steps in minutes with the plucked chicken in one had and the flour sack of feathers in the other. Once inside she handed the plucked chicken to Ollie and dropped the flour sack in the corner behind the door. Ollie cut the chicken into pieces and slid the slippery pieces into a bowl of water on the table where Sally stood waiting to take the chicken pieces from the water and dip each piece into the biscuit pan of flour before placing the battered chicken pieces into the big iron skillet on the stove where the bubbling hot lard popped and spattered. Sally tended the frying chicken while Ollie mixed up the biscuits in the biscuit pan using flour, leavening, buttermilk, and lard. She first pushed her fist into the mound of flour with just a dash of leavening, rotated her fist from the middle of the pan in wider and wider circles forming a nest in the flour to which she added the lard and buttermilk. Still using only her hand, she squeezed the mixture through her fingers again and again until she achieved just the right smooth consistency, as the next step in the process she sprinkled and patted more flour into the dough and with the other hand she continued to turn the pan round and round adding more and more flour to stiffen the dough ball. With the dough ball as big as her two fists, she scooped it up and lifted it with one hand, and with the other hand she settled the flour into the center of the pan where she then plopped the dough ball on top. She was careful to knead the mixture one last time before she pinched a small ball between her thumb and first finger and rolled it between her flour-covered hands. She tossed the dough ball back and forth from one hand to the other knocking off excess flour while at the same time, evenly covering the small ball with flour all around. She followed this ritual with each biscuit and placed them on the long greased biscuit sheet. She filled the sheet with neat rows, and one last punch with her knuckles to each mound of biscuit dough left it flattened with a slight indentation in the center. With her apron scooped up to protect her tender hand from the hot oven door handle, Ollie opened the door of the Dutch oven built into the side of the stone fireplace and quickly inserted the long, flat pan of white dough balls. Again using her apron to touch the hot door latch, she pushed the heavy iron door closed and locked it by lifting the latch securely into the hasp.

Outside in the garden, Ma in a bent at the waist approach, shuffled down the rows of knee high collard leaves, and cutting with a butcher knife, she whacked at the base of each tender newest leaf, and when she reached the end of the row, she laid the stack of leaves on the ground and continued working her way up and down the rows and stacking her load until time to retrace her steps and systematically pick up all piles and place them in the makeshift carrying sack she formed by holding together the bottom corners of her long cotton print apron. She hauled her heavy load inside the house, removed and submerged her apron in a bucket of cool water, and began washing and looking the stack of collards, and when she was satisfied there were no more lady bugs or specks of dirt on the greens, she emptied the collard wash water out the back door, she drew a bucket of water and refilled the dish pan splashing each dipper full over the mountain of collards greens, and back inside the kitchen she worked each hand full of greens into and out of the water with a push under pull up motion before plopping the water coated greens into the bubbling hot lard in the big iron cooker where of course the drops of water erupted in pops and sputters, and as the collard leaves came in contact with the boiling hot lard each leaf instantly wilted and withered to a very small fraction of it's garden size. As the collards cooked down she added a small handful of sugar, a splash of vinegar, a good sized pinch of salt and peppercorns wrapped in a dishcloth and pounded to bits, and last and probably most important she added two dippers full of water for she meant everyone to have their fill of pot liquor sopped up with biscuit. Thus working together as a team, Ma, Ollie, and Sally called the men into the house for dinner within the hour, and no finer, or fresher dinner was ever served to any king.

John kept the conversation lively from his place on the bench across the table and opposite to Sally. He told hilarious stories about his fourteen brothers and sisters which included two sets of twins, Roy and Ramer who were the normal set and the famous prankster set of twins, Elijah and Elisha.

"I know my brothers, the twins Elijah and Elisha are known throughout the county for their mischievous nature, and it's obvious to all just how much they enjoy playing pranks on anyone and everyone, so here's the latest prank which happened just last week. Elijah pretended to be hurt in the barn loft and let out a loud cry for help, but somehow Mr. (Fancy pants) Elijah miscalculated Elisha's whereabouts, and in fact Elisha was actually a good distance away from the barn in the field behind the house where naturally Elisha did not hear Elijah's cry, but Pa was in the barn right down below Elijah and Pa heard his son's call for help, and when Pa started up the ladder to get to his obviously seriously injured son, Elijah. Pa failed to confirm his identity and made a very big mistake in his clamor climbing the loft ladder and as a consequence Elijah poured a bucket of water on Pa's head which drenched Pa through and through, and what happened next I cannot repeat in front of the ladies, but I expect you all can imagine the scene, and I expect that Elijah will be more cautious in the future."

When the table was cleared and the dishes washed and put away, John took Sally by the hand and led her out onto the porch. All afternoon they sat in the swing and talked and laughed.

"Time to head on down the road," John leaned over and kissed Sally on the cheek.

"I'll come courting again next week, Sally," he said over his shoulder as he walked away.

In these last weeks together, Sally and Ollie found boundless joy in each other's company. They worked long hours each day, and at night they lay side-by-side in the same bed sharing stories and giggling. They loved to whisper to each other in the quiet dark house. They dreamed about their future and dreaded the day when their time together would end. They didn't talk about the day when they'd be a thousand miles apart; if they didn't say it maybe it wouldn't happen.

The next week in church, John sat beside Sally and whispered an apology that he could not visit her family today, but he asked if he could walk her and Ollie to the barn dance on Friday night.

"Friday at last!" exclaimed Sally as she milked the cow. Ollie was behind her throwing down fodder for the livestock. Then without saying so, Sally felt the familiar veil of sadness settle over her. Only two weeks more with Ollie. How can I say good-bye to the best friend I've ever had? Without reserve, Sally stood up from the milk stool, rubbed her hands on her apron, and caught Ollie in a death grip. Ollie knew and hugged her back. Their sobs echoed through the big barn.

"What will I do when you're gone?"

"How can I go?"

This day went by too quickly, all week Sally had wished for time to fly because she wanted to dance with John. Now she felt that she had wasted her precious time with Ollie. She berated herself for tending to forget the importance of these last days with her sister when in reality nothing else should matter. The girls took turns bathing in the kitchen, each poured hot water from the kettle into the wash pan and washed her body standing in front of the fire. They wore their best dresses and waited on the porch. John arrived precisely at six o'clock; the girls stopped swinging to look closer as he approached. There was enough light in the sky to see that John was walking up to the house in his dripping wet Sunday suit.

"What happened John?" asked Sally.

"That damned Liege and Liesh sawed the foot log to the point of breaking, and when I started to cross the creek and got to the middle of the foot log, the foot log broke and I fell into the water. Those boys aren't fit for a thing but to fill up old wells. I can't go to the barn dance like this. I wanted to let you know." John turned and walked away.

Without saying so out loud, both girls were just as happy to stay home together, and they couldn't hide their laughter as they watched the wet John Owens disappear down the road.

Letter from Ollie
Dearest Family,

The train ride will be a fond memory for the rest of my life. Mr. Hooper met me as expected, and a man of God in a small white chapel married us. The wagon trip to Mr. Hooper's land holdings took two hours, the last hour in a drenching rain. My trunk suffered from the soaking. Some of the clothes inside were wet but none were stained. Sally, I was wearing the blue suit in the chapel and on the wagon trip in the rain, and as a result, my blue suit is now stained from the resin found on the wagon seat. Nevertheless it remains my favorite garment.

Mr. Hooper is a fine, strong man. He prepared the house for my arrival. The wood floors were scrubbed clean, and the few pieces of furniture were well dusted. He has purchased a bolt of cotton from which I will make shirts for him, and as a surprise he presented to me bolts of calico and gingham for household decoration; and another surprise, a new Singer sewing machine. There is no well but a creek that runs near the house. Until next time, love from yours truly.

Ollie

"Christmas and John will be here soon," thought Sally.

"Ma, I feel so much older this year. Last Christmas Ollie was still here. She had no notion that Christmas next would find her in Oklahoma," sighed Sally

"We all miss her, my child," said Ma.

John opened the door and hurried into the room. He boldly kissed Sally and embraced her Ma. That Christmas Day 1904, John Owens reached across the table for Sally's hand and in front of the family asked Sally to be his wife. Sally had just turned twenty. John would be twenty in May.

John came to court Sally several times a week. He always brought life into the sad lonely house. Sally and Ma hoped each day for word from Ollie. Watching for the peddler became a constant preoccupation, but so far only one letter from Ollie to date.

John started preparing the site to build a home for his bride, one room with a fireplace. The neighbors took turns helping him dig the well. John wanted to locate a good supply of water first and then begin to lay the logs so as to have the well just out side the back door. John cleared the pine trees and built a log tripod centered directly over the best water site as determined by Mac Thompson using a divining rod. With the tripod in place, the digging progressed steadily. Each day another two to three feet of red clay was hauled up out of the well and down the hill behind the site. Beginning at five or six feet a candle was let down into the well each morning before any worker went down, if the candle went out it was unsafe to enter. Now the buckets of dirt were hauled to the surface by means of a block and tackle suspended from the tripod. At a depth of seventeen feet, the dirt turned to mud, and at this point the good bucket was replaced with an old rusted one with holes punched all around and through the bottom to allow the heavy water to drain away from the mud. The work slowed because of the extra weight of each shovel of mud and because the worker down in the well was now standing in the sloppy, oozing mud. When the water depth reached four feet, the last bucket of mud was hauled up and the last worker crawled out of the well and onto solid ground. John built a strong pine log frame, six feet tall, up and over the open well, and to this frame he permanently attached a pulley. Next he built a wooden curb four feet high all around to enclose the open well. On one side of the pulley frame he built a spool support and to the spool he anchored a metal crank or hand pedal at one end, and in the middle of the eighteen inch spool he attached one end of a rope by slipping a noose onto the spool, pulling it to a tight snug fit, and securing it with nails driven through the rope and bent double (as a staple) solidly attached to the spool in three different places. This done he tied the other end of the rope around the water bucket handle, and over the next weeks, as the mud settled out of the well water, John worked on the log cabin. Once the exact location was marked with twine stretching from four corner stobs, he piled and secured stacks of stone on which to lay the log floor joists and next he and neighbors raised the walls into place. The west end of the cabin was three feet off the ground while the east end was only a foot off the ground. The construction moved along quickly when one day each week, the neighbors gathered for a joint effort workday. The men arrived at sun up and worked all day only taking a short break when the neighbor women arrived at midday carrying baskets of fried chicken, biscuits, and dried peach pies. This became a once a week social gathering; the work of building and cooking almost as much fun as a barn dance.

In two short months, the finished Owens home-place included a well, a log cabin, a smoke house, a corncrib and a barn, all made of pine logs cut on site. Now all the cleared land would be fenced in for pasture for John was well off a owing six sheep, one milk-cow, a mule and a horse. Not bad for a young man, and he looked forward to and planned a bright future working in the lumber business, along with the farming of course, but farming would be for him a pastime, with the lumber business as his main interest and focus.

In the fall, John moved into their new home as Sally planned a church wedding in December and worked at a feverish pace with her mother a filling her hope chest with hand made sheets, towels, curtains, rugs, and clothing just as they'd done for Ollie the year before. The latest news from Ollie delighted the family for Ollie and Mr. Hooper were expecting and every day they hoped to receive a letter announcing the happy news of a new baby.

December 16, 1905

John and Sally were married at Camp Ground Church. Sally wore a white shirtwaist with a beautiful home tatted white lace collar and a black skirt gathered into a slight bustle at the back. She was radiant when she promised to love and honor none other. John was handsome beyond description in his Sunday-go-to-meeting black suit. Every member of the Roberds family and every member of the Owens family were witness to the solemn ceremony, and most of the neighbors came to see the handsome couple and wish them well, and Sally thought the day was perfect in every way, if only Ollie could have been there.

"Ma John, is here," Sally called from the back door.

Ma came into the warm log cabin through the front door as John came in from the smoke house with a slab of venison he set to cure last week. With a long face, Ma pulled a letter out of her pocket.

"Sit down, Sally. This letter is from Mr. Hooper."

Ma read the letter, and when she looked up, Sally was crumpled across John's lap, gasping for air through her uncontrollable sobs.

Letter from Mr. Hooper:

Dearest Family,

I have a son. I have named him OK. He is doing fine. It is with a sad heart that I tell you of his mother's death. It was a difficult birth. I could be of little help to her. After three days in labor, I knew no other action but to ride into town for the doctor. She was alone for four hours though I'm confident she was unaware. The doctor was able to save the baby, but he could not revive Ollie. I buried her in the blue suit she was wearing when I first laid eyes on her.

Yours,

Mr. Hooper

In January, Sally received another letter from Mr. Hooper. This one was inside Ollie's hope chest along with all of Ollie's clothing except for the blue suit with the lace collar.

Letter from Mr. Hooper:

Dearest Family,

It is very difficult to part with Ollie's personal belongings, but reason prevails. Mrs. Roberds and Sally will have more use of these things than I. The doc has procured a bottle with a feeding cap. I have a producing milk cow. The baby is thriving. I load him in his basket and keep him near me as I work. I am lonely without Ollie. She was a comfort and help to me in all things.

Yours,

Mr. Hooper

Sally picked up the brown suit, the color of Ollie's hair and held it to her face to absorb the last sweet aroma of her beloved sister. For the pain it caused, Sally could only glance at the remaining contents of Ollie's hope chest. Gently she replaced the brown suit, closed the lid and once again fell into John's arms for comfort.

Happy news, in the spring Sally told John that she was expecting a baby come fall. Pa brought a pig to Sally, and said if she would raise the pig and then sell it in town, she'd have enough money to order that dresser with attached looking glass from the Sears and Roebuck catalog.

Sally's grief lifted slightly as the spring flowers appeared and she was grateful to John for planting the jonquil bulbs and creeping roses all around the house. Sally loved to cross the road and sidestep down the steep hill behind the corncrib to watch the cool bubbles of the spring, this cavernous, sanctuary soothed her soul and she was lured by the seclusion and spender of towering hardwoods and luxurious, velvet green moss which always seemed to thrive with the cold of winter. She sat for hours on the creek bank after first drinking from the dipper hung on John's steel peg hammered into the trunk of the hollowed, big oak tree spanning the creek's beginning. The tree stood just at the point where the spring bubbled out of the ground, and on the spike, John had the fore site to hang a short handled dipper (more of a tin cup) for drinking the cool spring water. This quiet, shaded spot suited Sally's somber mood.

Now and then, she'd follow the little creek down through the towering trees and out into the open pasture where the sheep came to greet her with a nuzzle. The milk cow kept her distance and the horse wanted a treat, knowing Sally kept an ear of dry corn or a shriveled apple in her apron pocket. John had the mule in the east field, plowing to plant the spring crop. He was out of sight on the other side of the hill, but sometimes if the wind was right she could hear him yelling at the top of his lungs for the poor old mule to, "Haw, gee, haw god damn ye, gee!"

This outrageous mule talk always brought a smile to Sally's face. She loved the cursing man more with every passing day for he was kind and ever vigilant in caring for his wife. Sally's morning sickness seemed to last well into the afternoon, and John spoiled her by doing all the livestock chores and the housework. He drew a bucket of water each morning and filled the kettle, and when the water was steaming, he filled a wash pan for Sally to bathe. John scrubbed the pine floors once a week and in the wash pot behind the house he washed their clothing, towels, and sheets made from shorts sacks (the heavy cotton sacks which contained the livestock feed produced as a by product of wheat milling and consisting of bran, germ and course meal). He built the fire under the blackened iron wash pot, filled the pot with water, collected the soiled clothes, soaked the clothes in the hot lye water, beat the clothes on the battling rock, and finally returned the clothes to fresh hot rinse water before hauling the wet clothes in buckets to the garden fence. With only one wash pot, he had to stack the wet soapy laundry on the porch while he dipped the hot water out of the wash pot into a bucket which he toted a few steps downhill of the well and poured the dirty wash water to run down the hill safely avoiding any contamination of the clean, drinking, well water, then he drew more fresh water to refill the wash pot. He rekindled the fire under the pot; and as he waited for the water to boil, he called out to Sally, and when she appeared he stepped aside as she gently dropped into the fresh boiling water all the eggs she'd collected from the hen nests. This tradition John himself initiated in the months before their wedding when he lived here alone, and now he wanted to continue this ritual in an effort to repay the neighbors for their help with digging the well and building the log cabin and surrounding shelters, and this simple idea of sharing hard boiled eggs with the neighbors was a means and excuse for visiting which was pleasing to all and especially to big John Owens who was a mighty sociable feller, and the neighbors anticipated with enjoyment this little break from their normal work week, and come washday at the Owens home place every last neighbor appeared one by one to enjoy a boiled egg cracked and peeled, and devoured right there a standing by the wash pot and this informal weekly meeting served as a means of getting the latest news and gossip before returning home to their own chores.

When the entire garden fence was littered with wet clothes strung out to dry, John carried each heavy bucket of wet clothes on a little farther to scatter them on the pasture fence finally finding a drying space for all the wet things.

Although John continued to carry the bulk of chores around the place, Sally still had responsibility for the cooking at the open fireplace inside the cabin, but in all respects, John gladly became her protector and provider in hopes of returning his shy and delicate wife to her former happiness. His only regret was that he could not do more and his heart was cheerful for their upcoming birth, and he was confident the baby would bring sunshine back to their lives and turn his grieving wife into a busy mother and mercifully stop his wife's tears shed daily for Ollie, and until the happy birth, John was willing and eager to shoulder any burden from Sally's childlike frame. Mr. Hooper was faithful with letters of OK's growth and for that John was grateful, but each letter brought renewed sadness with each of many daily readings, Sally carried the newest letter in her apron pocket, and possibly read it a dozen times a day, and each time Sally looked to John to bring her solace, and each time he tried as best he could.

Spring of 1907

In the spring, Sally's first baby was born and like Ollie, Sally had a difficult time. John watched her struggle for only a few hours before fetching her Ma who assessed the situation and without hesitation directed John to go for the mid wife. Sally was in hard labor for three days with the mid wife by her side day and night, and when Sally's exhaustion was total, her muscles failed into a slight relaxed state which brought on a semi unconsciousness, and then is when the midwife successfully reached her small hands into the womb to surround the baby's head, but the tremendous effort needed to pull the baby proved more than the small woman could accomplish, so she called John in to help, and through his tears he wrapped his bear-like clumsy hands around the small baby's head and pulled, one strong powerful pull until he could slide one fore finger beyond each tiny arm and finally pull the baby free, and when the midwife sent him from the room, he realized he couldn't have stayed any longer because Sally had the look of death from the pain he'd caused.

Sally's recovery was slow, and her Ma stayed from sunup to sundown every day to care for the baby and do the cooking. John and Sally named their baby girl Hazel, the color of her eyes, and her Ma stayed away only when she felt that Sally was strong enough. In the next month, Sally once again began to laugh. John loved to tease, and she loved to respond, and most times she suffered embarrassment, but she learned to put her rambunctious husband in his place with a simple phrase. "Pshaw, John."

When she chided him in this manner, she felt a little modicum of control, and happily John watched her strengthen, and he was encouraged as she became stronger, and her power over him was greater than any power on earth.

Sally took to walking down to the spring again but now she took baby Hazel with her, and the mother and baby spent many hours a sitting beside the peaceful gurgle, and when she scooped the tin cup full of water, she and Hazel found it refreshing, and Sally decided the spring water was improving their health. Sally let the baby drink by capturing a drop on her finger and placing it to the baby's mouth. These days filled with love and wonder, helped Sally's loneliness and grief for Ollie to fade into the distant past, and most times she could remember the good times with her sister and actually forget about her loss, because the baby's demand for constant attention helped to move all other thoughts into a safe recess of her mind. John's crops were coming in and of course he worked many hours at harvesting, and their evening meal together and restful sleep with the baby between them brought peace. This was a very happy time.

After supper on a Saturday night, when Hazel was almost four months old, Sally bathed the baby and washed her hair. In preparation for attending church the next morning, Sally and John both bathed and washed their hair that night, and they all three slept soundly in the same bed. Sally woke with the sunrise, and rolled over to tend to the baby, but when she touched baby Hazel, Sally screamed like a banshee and John sat up like a bolt of lightening. Baby Hazel was blue and cold. Dead.

They buried Hazel in the small Roberd's cemetery near Sally's parent's house, and the first night without the baby, Sally waited to hear John's heavy breathing in sleep; then she put her shawl around her shoulders and walked the two miles to the cemetery where she lay down beside the cold grave. John found her there at first light and carried her from the cemetery across the road and into her Ma's house where Sally stayed through the long weeks while John harvested the crops, and each night he came to Sally, and together, they went to Hazel and slept on the ground beside their baby's grave, and when the first frost came, Sally asked John to take her home.

The winter was long and cold. Sally had nightmares of her baby crying in the grave, and she became convinced they buried the baby too quickly for if they had given her time surely Hazel would have stopped holding her breath, and in her demented state, Sally began to rethink the time when John was bathing Hazel and preparing her for burial, and Sally asked John time and time again for assurance of Hazel's actual state, "Did she cry, John?" "Did she breathe, John?" Did she move, John?" and with each answer Sally asked for reassurance. "Are you sure she didn't cry?" "Oh, John are you absolutely sure you saw no tears on her face?" And on and on and on Sally asked insane questions until John finally shocked his mournful wife with a heartless description of their cold, lifeless baby, and his cruel words stalled off more questions of the likes that John could not tolerate for he knew the ugly truth and it was time to force the reality on Sally, and finally she vowed to accept and learn to deal with it, but John knew that she cried in the night when she thought he did not notice. John tried to return to normalcy with teasing his wife, but she could not smile. She could find no peace. The darkness of grief closed in all around her. Christmas came and went. She could find no solace, and again her morning sickness lasted into the afternoon.

"This birth is bound to come easy," John encouraged her.

Sally feared another long painful labor. The torn tissue damage from Hazel's delivery was slow to heal, and she wondered if she had the strength to survive, but she kept these worries from John, and in her mind favored the simple approach of letting him carry the load while she relied on his courage to see them through.

One morning as John sat on the front pouch, he sharpened his razor against the leather strap, lathered his face and leaned toward the mirror hanging by a string wrapped around a nail. He shaved his neck and cut a clean line around his handlebar mustache, and as he wiped the remaining soap from his face, Ab Whitley came into the yard. "How do, John?"

"Fair to midlin' and you?"

"Fine, I'm doing fine. How's Sally?"

"Aw … She's all right I guess; mean as hell," chuckled John.

Ab laughed outright at John's exaggeration. "Sally Owens wouldn't know how to be mean to the devil himself" he responded.

"I'm riding into town. Good day to you, John."

John watched as Ab rode off to the east. When deciding on the place to build, John positioned his log cabin very close to the road because he so enjoyed every chance to visit with neighbors. The corncrib sat directly across the road from the house and the barn stood a few steps to the west of the corncrib and all the buildings hugged the road for maximum friendly greetings and exchanges as neighbors rode past.

Sally came out of the house, and John swept her into his arms.

"My little wife is getting fat."

"Pshaw, John."

Sally smiled remembering what she'd heard John say to Ab. *My husband always brings delight to my senses. I can be strong through all the sadness of life as long as I have John to shock and embarrass and poke fun.* "Put me down, John. I gotta puke."

As she leaned over the porch railing, John placed his big hand under her forward so as to assume some of the weight of her sickness and Sally welcomed the support as she allowed the powerful convulsions to rid her of her biscuit and gravy breakfast. When she could, she straightened with shame, embarrassed at vomiting, and quickly she wiped her chin with her lace edged handkerchief and stumbled toward the door, but before she could hide inside the cabin, John once again had her in his arms. She was determined to get away; and with her chin resting on her chest, she managed to squirm loose.

"Sally, there's no need for embarrassment."

"Pshaw John," she said as she went through the door.

After supper, Sally mixed the corn bread scraps with water, and John carried the bucket of slop to the pig trough, next he threw down fodder for the livestock while Sally scattered dry corn for the chickens. Her hands were rough and bleeding from removing the hard kernels of corn from the cob, and back inside the cabin, she rubbed lard over her dry cracked knuckles. When she placed the lard bucket back in the cupboard, she closed and latched the door, and stood back to look at John's handiwork. With George Vaughn's help, John finished building the cupboard last week and today he built a bench for the table. They now had two straight chairs, one bench, the table and the cupboard near the fireplace. Along the far north wall next to the window looking out to the road, stood their bed. Their clothes hung from pegs along the wall near the bed. White cotton curtains covered the windows. "Right homey in here," thought Sally. The baby kicked and all seemed right with the world.

John was sitting in his straight chair next to the fire whittling a poplar twig into a whistle. The wood was dry enough and he separated the bark from the wood core, and through the sleeve of bark, John cut a notch. By sliding the wood core into and out of the sleeve, he could change the pitch of sound as he blew into the bark cylinder. To Sally's delight he played a simple tune and she swayed and turned with a laugh. The only light in the room came from the fireplace. They had no oil for the lamp. Sally had some mending to do so she placed a pine knot in her one and only iron skillet and she drew a burning twig from the fire and when the pine knot caught fire, she dropped the burning twig into bright fire now burning in the skillet. Holding the skillet handle with her apron, she placed it on a flat stone on the table and pulled her chair closer to the light. By the light from the burning pine knot, she threaded her needle and mended John's shirt.

"I'm going into town tomorrow." John said.

"I'll walk to Ma's, I can't stand to be alone." Sally replied.

They made ready for bed. John spilled the pine knot ashes into the fireplace, and then leaned the hot empty iron skillet against the blue slate fireplace. He took a few minutes to admire his handy work in building the fireplace and chimney from the blue rocks he found all around the countryside, and then he added a few logs to the fire making a big enough mound of wood to last through the night.

The next morning, John hitched the mule to the wagon knowing Sally was inside by the window watching him, and John was evasive as to his reason for taking the wagon and mule and the horse into town. When he saddled the horse and tied it to the back of the wagon, he drove away up the hill toward town, and Sally walked to her Ma's with an uneasy feeling, and later that day after dinner with her Ma and Pa, when Sally walked back home, she felt very weak and she noticed her vision was blurred, and when she was finally back home and inside the cozy, one room cabin, she washed her clammy face with cool water and fell asleep on top of the bed covers. Her sleep was fitful and when she woke she was shivering in a pool of sweat, but thankfully, she heard John outside talking to Eb and Lula Kilgore. Vaguely she realized that John and Eb were unloading something from the wagon, and when the door opened, she watched as John backed into the room. Sally could see that John and Eb were struggling to move a brand spanking new cast iron cook stove. It was a thing of beauty with a shiny black and white enamel oven door and matching swing doors on the upper warming oven, and she could see a hot water tank to the right of the cook top. With the cook stove positioned against the west wall beside the window, John went back to the wagon to fetch three lengths of stovepipe and two elbows.

"Come here John," Lula cried, "Sally's burning up with fever."

Baby Paul lived only twelve days, and when he stopped breathing, John carried Sally out to the wagon and gently placed her on a spread-out quilt along side the tiny pine box, and he gently stuffed a feather pillow under her head. The old mule pulled the wagon at a slow and careful pace as John loosely grasped the reigns and knelt to support himself on one knee behind the seat and beside his pathetic wife. When they reached the Roberds cemetery, it took every bit of Sally's pitiful strength to pull herself into a sitting position and lean her heavy numb head onto the top rail as she watched John slowly pull the baby's pine box to the back of the wagon. He then carried it around to the side and placed it on the ground. John's ma and pa and Sally's ma and pa stood shoulder to shoulder forming a safety circle around him when he lowered the baby into the ground. Sally still could not walk for she had no feeling in her legs. Since his birth, Sally's ma had cared for the baby, and though she longed to, Sally could not help. She could not even hold the baby for the weakness in her arms, and now John watched as his wife slipped partially away into a cold barren stare. The blue sky looked cruel and heartless to her and her head felt hollow, and the buzzing in her ears blocked the sound of her husband's sobs as he covered the pine box with dirt. John drove the mule and wagon back to the log cabin leaving behind not one but two graves filled with their lost youth and happiness. He carried Sally inside the cabin and carefully laid her in bed while he went back outside to tend to the mule. Once the chores were done, he noticed a stream of snot a foot long hanging from his nose. He'd been unaware that he was crying, he pulled the snot rag from his back over hall's pocket and blew his nose before he went inside and slipped into bed beside Sally, and they held onto each other and cried through the night with shared pain and desolation. This young man and his quiet wife struggled with their loss over the next months. Sally slowly regained strength, but they found no joy in their daily life. Through out each day they completed their meaningless chores, and at night they held each other as they cried.

In the winter, John hauled Sally's hog to town and mailed the money along with her order form to Sears and Roebuck, and four weeks later the peddler pulled into the yard with Sally's oak dresser strapped to the top of his wagon. John helped the peddler unload; and together, the men moved the dresser base and then the mirror inside the cabin. Sally directed them to place it near the window. She rubbed her hand over the smooth golden oak. What a thing of beauty! A store bought dresser!

1912

For longer than three years, Sally and John lived together in grief. Neither wanted the pain of losing another baby, so they slept in a gentle embrace but refrained from the intimate contact between husband and wife. Their love remained strong and sustained them through this valley of the shadow of death, until finally with the anticipation of another birth, joy and laughter returned to them. The new baby was noticeably willful and healthy, and in 1913, another healthy baby was born. The two boys Chester and Jack, easily chased away the cloud of sadness, but the hateful loss forever molded Sally into an inescapably melancholy demeanor.

1914 August, at age forty-six, Mattie Godwin's fourteenth, Baby Nell was born, and in February of 1915, a typhoid epidemic spread through the county, and Mattie Godwin was one of the first cases. That winter was especially cold and when John Owens heard of the typhoid just up the road at the Godwin home place, he left Sally and his own little boys to go about the county collecting quilts and cash money. Afraid to go home and risk spreading the typhoid to his family, he stayed nights at the Godwin place nursing the sick, and days he traveled to other houses involved in the massive epidemic, and he continued collecting quilts and money and when John collected enough money, he rode back home to his cabin and from the yard, he called out to his wife.

"Sally, don't come outside. Stay indoors with the boys. I'm taking the mule and wagon into town to buy a potbelly, heating stove for the sleeping room at the Godwin place. I have a job there and there I'll stay nursing the sick and keeping the fires burning."

"We need you here, when can you come home, John?" Sally cried out.

"When the typhoid has run it's course. They're all sick, all the children, Doc and Essie, and Hugh and Mattie, and they'll all die if I leave them alone with no heat and no one to nurse them. Be strong Sally and don't let nobody come inside the house. You and the boys are safe here as long as you have no contact with the outside world."

1916

In the first month and the seventh day of nineteen and sixteen, Sally had another baby girl, and both she and John silently thanked God for their beautiful brown-eyed daughter. They shared a fervent hope they'd never have to look at hazel eyes again. This baby they named 'Vesta' (Roman goddess of the hearth). Vesta's hair was a mass of red curls and she smiled easily. John already proudly suspected his son's to have his gift of laughter, he so believed in the power of humor, and he hoped to pass on his giant capacity to appreciate wit to all his children. Physically, Chester and Vesta inherited his fair complexion and red hair, and so far only Jack had Sally's dark skin and hair, but all three children inherited Sally's brown eyes, thanks be to God.

Sally bathed her boys and sweet baby girl every Saturday night, but she refused to wash a single head of hair. John's wife and children were healthy in all regards except for Sally's continued fear of another devastating loss! John teased his wife and was rewarded with a smile, but the sound of her outright laughter was seemingly silenced forever.

Sally's spirits lifted slightly as John worked on building more living space for his growing family. He laid out two rooms, one to be a new kitchen and the other a much-needed bedroom. In the kitchen he built another fireplace of the blue slate rocks plentiful in the area, and Sally praised her husband's choice for she loved the almost sky blue veins running through the beautiful rocks, and the new part of the house would be only a step or two from the well which Sally marveled at the convenience, and John's promise to her was to build a porch around the well and thereby making the well even more accessible just outside the back door and imagine the ease of carrying buckets of water only a step or two.

Sally's ma came almost every day after Baby Theda's birth. Now with two boys and two girls, Sally needed help with the chores and once in a while John managed to talk Mrs. Roberds into taking home a chicken as pay for her many hours of work. Little Vesta watched over the baby and called for help if Baby Theda crawled too far from the house. John, his Ma, and Sally's Ma all three worked very hard to allow Sally time to regain her strength, but she continued to be physically weak and perhaps and almost certainly sweet Sally Owens faced a lifelong struggle with her loss.

Pretty little Vesta Owens is just one year younger than my youngest, Baby Nell, and I say a prayer for the Owens family who will stand in stead as family to my children who'll have Doc and Essie and this big Godwin family and they'll also have friends and neighbors all through these parts who'll befit them with the next best thing to family which is the wider family of this Bethel community, and now there's another new baby girl in the Owens house, her name is Theda, the fourth for John and Sally, and a happy crowd it is. "Shug, go to the outhouse with your little Sis, and when you come back in, wash up and climb into bed with me, let's get some rest and sleep in God's arms."

I watched my two youngest children with a sober premonition that my time with them would be very short and possibly only a matter of days, and with great joy and heavy sorrow, I considered the vast happiness they've brought into my otherwise sad existence but no matter, these two have enforced an old man's attention to their good beginning whereas without responsibility of them, I might have been more inclined to give up and slow down and wallow in my lonely misery, but now my concern for their uncertain future leaves me with an unwanted helplessness never before experienced for I cannot prolong my life and I have no choice but to leave them to their own means however young they are and however much I hate to go, for it is quite certain my youngest children will grow up as orphans. I look to the older ones to watch over them, but the best sisters and brothers are no substitute for parents, and therefore my youngest children will be required to mature before their time, and realistically, they will not have a childhood. I've left instructions for a headstone inscribed with, 'Love Is Eternal,' and I'm happy and eager to be reunited with my beloved Mattie, but for the pain of leaving my children.

Chapter 3

I Know You're The Bully, But I've Come Now

1960

My youngest (eight year old) Randall was sitting on the toolbox on the D6 Caterpillar while I worked on rebuilding the starting engine, which I'd been working on now all morning long; and still the dogged new part didn't fit. All I could figure was I'd have to go back to the store and swap it for another.

"Let's quit for dinner, I'm starving!"

I opened the paper dinner sack and pulled out two baloney sandwiches wrapped in wax paper, one for my son and one for me while Randall dug back a pile of leaves away from our gallon jar of tea, cold and sweet, ice cubes still a floating.

"That's a pretty good trick Daddy, you're right the tea stays cold in the shade and buried under the leaves."

My son unscrewed the half-gallon, wide-top, glass jar and turned it up for a drink before passing it to me.

After dinner, I watched my boy as he chased blowing leaves and dropped to his knee in deep dead leaves on the steep hillside before I finally called him back to work, but this time we made headway. I guess we'd wasted three days a trying to fit a part into the starting engine, and now my young son pointed into the engine from his perch on the tool box situated right beside the cab of the caterpillar, and with a stroke of genius or maybe a stroke of luck, Randall said, "Why don't you turn it over, I think it might fit that way."

I scowled, "Is'at so?"

I withdrew the part and securely held it above the starting engine despite my slippery, grease-covered hands, and I slowly rotated the part as a generous smile declared that in fact it will now fit, but still I held our breath and watched as the overturned part slipped easily into place, and we could not hold back our stunned surprise and we yelped like we'd been hit by a two by four, and one more time, my son jumped off the caterpillar and played his child's game of tag through the knee deep leaves, and this time and before my eyes he rolled down the steep hill with lightning speed over and over a holding on to his locked arms, and when he reached the bottom of the dizzying ride he was on his feet in a flash and a running back up the hill to the sound of my laughter, and we worked on at the repair job until the light of day failed us and with the paper dinner sack and the half gallon jar in tow, we climbed to the top of the hill and walked toward the house and along the way we found Janet had walked to meet us and was sitting on what she calls HER moss garden at the bend of the narrow lane near the rock garden (another of Janet's designates), and now the three of us walked along in darkness and right down in the woods (just about close enough to touch) on the north side of the narrow lane we heard an old whip-er-will calling, and it's lonely wail led me to tell another story. My children quieted down to listen to my story as we walked along in the darkness.

Back to 1919

Marvin stood beside me in the red-dusty front yard of the Godwin home place and the awful, mournful sound a coming from inside the house covered our faces with a gray, ashen film for we were about to bury my Pa. My oldest sister Mary Lizzie came out of the unpainted house whose boards had darken to almost black with years of weathering, and she made her way through the dogtrot and onto the front porch a toting Sis, my youngest sister, for my baby sister was just five years old when our Pa died, Sis's birthday was August 4th when she turned five and Pa died that same month, and looking at her little scared face made me recall what that felt like because I was the same age, almost five when our Ma died and now four years later, the sadness of that loss washed over me like a dipper of cold water splashed in my face, it was a painful reality that's never left me to this day.

It don't do no good to cry and I didn't cry but I started feeling like an old man when I learned the truth about death. I never wanted to feel like an old man at the age of eight years and two months, but that's what happened. As Sis ran down the steps and into my arms, Mary Lizzie called out, "Marvin, you help Shug take care a Sis,"

"I will Ma."

The three of us kids, me and Sis and our nephew Marvin stood there in the hot sun. I was eight, Marvin was ten and Sis was five years old, and I can tell you for sure we were old enough to recognize that lonely feeling that comes from understanding we'd never see our Pa again. Sis fell against my legs wanting me to hold her up. She was pitiful crying.

We three kids stood in the blazing hot sun as eight men hauled their burdensome pine box out of the kitchen side of the house, into the long, shaded, open dogtrot dividing the kitchen side of the house from the sleeping side of the house. The men were sober and intent on their job of maneuvering their load. The glaring sunlight at the far end of the dogtrot transformed the eight men toting the long box into a giant, scary, black, creepy-crawly figure with no face, just a body and eight sets of legs, and the monster struggled to come through the door, and as the giant black bug slowly turned toward us, the massive hideous thing shuffled from side to side a walking through the dogtrot and onto the front porch, and still in the shadow and backlit against the brilliant sunlight at the far end of the tunnel, the faceless figures stepped one by one into the open air of blinding sun and then the fantasy ended, but the nightmare was real for we recognized the eight men holding the pine box containing Pa, and they were lined up four on each side. As they neared the porch steps leading down to the dusty front yard, one dark figure moved from the left side to the front end of the box and another man moved from the other side to the back end of the box. We watched as they loaded our Pa onto a wagon bed, and then one man walked around to the front of the wagon, took a hold of the bridle, and led the mule down the road to Bethel cemetery, it was all cleared land back then between the Godwin home place and Bethel cemetery, and we let the procession get a little ahead of us, and we watched mesmerized as the crowd of people spread out almost the entire length from up there at the front of the procession back to us kids at the tail end which was about exactly one mile. It was a big crowd, and we fell in line behind the people following the mule and wagon, and Marvin tried to carry Sis part of the way, but within just a few steps, Marvin had to put her down, and when he did all three of us stopped and waited way back behind the crowd, and we stood there a watching as they moved farther and farther away from us, and then me and Marvin both held onto Sis who was a looking down at the ground and holding on tight to our hands. Everything was muffled and gloomy. My older sisters were crying softly as their skirts swayed side to side in a bereavement dance, and I remember Thomas and Mose too were sniffling along in a dirge walk ahead of us but still toward the back of the crowd, and they were closest to us but still several yards in front of us, and when we reached the hated cemetery, Mose was miserably sobbing aloud which caused Sis to wail and jerk for air. I don't remember much about what the preacher said that day; I couldn't listen for the ringing in my ears.

Marvin and Sis and I stayed in the cemetery after everybody else left, and the three of us young uns sat alone on the fresh turned mound of red clay which was Pa's grave. We talked some. It was real peaceful. After dark, we were still sitting there, still talking. Marvin left us for his ma expected him home for supper, and we listened to his departure as his quick steps pounded the hard clay soil in the roadbed.

We heard the rattle of the wooden bridge as he crossed the creek on his way home up across the road from Bethel church and school, but Sis and I remained in the cemetery and listened to an old whip-er-will, and to this day, that's what I think about ever time I hear an old whip-er-will calling in the night. It was the usual thing to be scared of ghosts, but we weren't one bit scared in the cemetery that night for we felt close to Pa, and we even talked to Pa, and I think he heard us. I looked at Ma's grave beside Pa's and I got goose bumps when I realized I could not remember my Ma's face. I remember her ways, her actions which demonstrated her love for me and all my brothers and sisters and for Pa, but it makes me shiver thinking about her kindness and sweetness and there's one thing I'll never forget even if I can't remember exactly the lines of her face, I'll never forget how she held her head at a tilt, and now forty-five years after she died, if I close my eyes I can see her pretty sun spun hair, and by now, in my mind I've kind a replaced her face with your face Janet because once in a while, I notice you holding your head at a tilt and your hair has always been the exact color I've carried around in my special memories, and I know my ma was pretty because that's the word people use to describe her; but Lord help me, her face has faded from my mind, and no matter how old I get and no matter that I have five children of my own now, and no matter how much I love my kids, there's a hurt deep inside of me that sometimes knocks the wind out of me; I miss Pa and Ma.

That night in the cemetery, I said to Sis, "Sis, there's no need to be scared. You can't walk through life always looking over your shoulder. I don't feel brave. I don't feel grown up, but we have to be brave, and we have to be grown up for each other."

So that's what we did. From then on we acted brave and grown up, and me and Sis always depended on each other, and we walked with out heads up, and we watched out for each other. We both had a lot of doubts and fears, but we knew what we had to do, and we did it.

That day changed me and Sis! We were the youngest of fourteen children, but we grew up in the house with Doc and Essie's five children who were younger than we were. Most of our older brothers and sisters were married and moved out raising their own big families. Our brother James taught at the Bethel school until he left home to go fight in a war. That was World War I, and back then those words didn't mean a thing to me. All I knew was that James was gone.

One night at the dinner table when the whole country was going down struggling to find food or shelter, just a little while after we buried Pa, four-year-old Sis asked for more milk, but the milk pitcher was empty. We were dirt poor, I mean dirt poor. We had one old cow to give milk for that big table full of hungry people, and when Thomas heard little Sis ask for more milk which there was no more, he looked at his ration which was mostly all of his milk still in his cup. He stood up and walked around the table to Sis, and he poured his milk into Sis's cup. Sis started crying and put her little head down on the table, and Thomas stood there patting little Sis's head real gentle. Thomas didn't walk away from Sis until she raised her head and drank the rest of his milk. It was a defining minute in Thomas's life. He was honorable and selfless. He was hungry, but he gave his milk to Sis, and he did it with kindness and love in his heart.

The next day, without saying much to anybody, Thomas rolled up his Sunday shirt and poked it in a clean white feed sack. He dropped his flip in the sack and stuffed his hand-me-down winter coat in the sack. He was thirteen, would be fourteen on October first. He made the rounds hugging everybody, and as he walked out the door, he turned back to us and said, "While I'm gone, I want Sis to have my share of milk. You're all hearing me say this, and I want to walk away from here knowing it will be like I say."

From Martheny's house in Valdosta, Georgia, Thomas wrote a letter telling of his travel south. It was a comfort to hear from him.

We'll never forget that day. It just about ripped my heart out of my chest. In a day or two when he could talk, Mose said, "When my twin brother left, part of me went with him."

In that same year, 1919, the year we lost Pa, and then Thomas up and left. It was mighty lonesome. Letters from Thomas came from Valdosta, Georgia. When he left home, he walked all of the way to Tallapoosa where he went inside the new model-T emporium, he asked for a map, if it was free. The older man dressed in real fancy Sunday-go-to-meeting clothes handed Thomas a Goodrich Road Map of GEORGIA-ALABAMA. Thomas thanked the man, took the map outside, sat down under a tree and began to decipher the information on the map. Thomas could read and write, and do figures in his head. He twisted his body and turned the map so the arrow in the corner of the map was pointing north and was straight with the world, and now he could read the map. (Let me interrupt here, you got to remember this was before the highways were paved and numbered, and that dirt, east-west road today is Highway 78 and remember Thomas was just a boy who'd never been more than ten miles away from the Godwin home place) To his delight, the map showed that Alabama should be to the west of Tallapoosa, Georgia, and he knew this to be true because he walked into town from the west for it was late afternoon and the sun was behind him. The map showed the next town to the east of Tallapoosa was Bremen. Thomas turned back facing south in front of the Model T emporium and crossed the east west road but stopped short of crossing the train tracks also running east and west. He stuck out his thumb to hitch a ride when an automobile passed by heading east. When the car kept on going leaving Thomas choking in the dust, the map donor came out of the new car emporium and asked,

"How far are you a going young feller?"

"I aim to go east to Atlanta and then south all the way to Valdosta where my half sister lives."

"Well you're in luck, I'm driving all the way into Atlanta first thing in the morning. I'll close up shop and you go ahead and climb in my car parked over there. (Thomas looked where the man pointed.) It'll work out fine for you to come home with me and sleep in the barn loft. My wife will have supper waiting, I'll bet you're hungry."

"That's mighty kind mister. But I couldn't impose."

"I'm betting my wife will need your help with chores. Would that ease your conscience?"

"Yes, Sir, I'm much obliged."

This gentleman and his wife treated Thomas with respect and hospitality. Thomas chopped firewood, fed the chickens, and swept the house. He filled the water basin on the wood-burning cook stove, and after supper, he dipped out the hot water and toted the buckets to the bathtub set up in a small room. This beat anything Thomas had ever seen, the bathtub had a corked hole in the bottom, and before pouring the hot water into the tub, Thomas pulled out the cork and looked down the hole, but it was too dark to see anything so he replaced the cork and filled the bathtub with hot water. Thomas went out-a-doors into the barn and climbed the ladder to the loft. Like most model T owners, this man kept a horse to draw his carriage. The model T was a good, reliable car, but a ready supply of gasoline was not reliable. Thomas slept in the small barn loft on a pile of fresh hay, and at sunup, he was eager to look under the house where he saw a pipe to let water from the bathtub into a sluiceway, which continued down a slight incline and emptied into a trough. From the trough, the water could be carried in buckets to the vegetable garden and to the fading rose bushes along the front of the house. It was August; Thomas would be fourteen on October first.

The next morning, the man's generous wife handed Thomas a dinner to carry with him. It was wrapped in a clean rag. Thomas protested but bashfully accepted. In addition to the supper last night and a hearty breakfast this morning, this lady was sending him off with another meal for the road. The clean rag was wrapped around the food and tied secure with a piece of string. Riding in the model T, Thomas untied the string, slid the wrapped dinner into his feed-sack/satchel and placed it carefully on top of his coat, then he used the lady's string to tie the top of his feed-sack/satchel shut, and the string was long enough to form a loop for hanging the feed-sack over his shoulder. This was a very handy way to carry the feed-sack/satchel.

As they rode along, Thomas stopped chewing his hay straw, pulled it out of his mouth and measured the hay straw to the scale of miles on the Goodrich Road Map, next he broke the straw to the exact length to equal sixty miles, and on the map, he held the hay straw with one end at Tallapoosa and the other end reached all the way to Atlanta, so he reasoned it to be just about sixty miles from Tallapoosa to Atlanta. Then he measured the hay straw to his finger and tossed the hay straw out of the car because now he could use his finger to make future calculations of distance. This map represented a world of opportunity for a thirteen-year-old Alabama country boy. He could read all the words on the map, and now he could judge the distance from one place to another place. This map symbolized his accomplishments. Deciphering and making the map work for him was a great big success not a small thing for a boy who'd never before been more than ten miles from the home place.

The man and the boy talked and laughed a lot on the ride to Atlanta. Thomas was amazed at the speed of the car, nearly forty-five miles an hour when the road was good enough for that high a speed. Including one stop in Douglasville to buy gasoline, the trip took about three hours. The man said so when he let Thomas out in the big city at the junction of a major north south road. The man pointed off to the right and said, "This is the main road going south and the next town will be Jonesboro. This corner will be a good place to hitch a ride. Good luck, son"

The man drove off and Thomas was left alone in the middle of town, the biggest town he'd ever seen. Maybe the biggest town in the world, for all he knew. For a minute, Thomas considered crossing to the other side of the road, sticking out his thumb, and hitching a ride back to Alabama, back home. At least he knew what to expect back home. But then, he thought about the crowded home place and the empty milk pitcher so he took a deep breath, pulled his shoulders back, and started walking south toward Jonesboro. He walked slowly, looking up at the tall buildings, one had a giant Coca Cola sign painted on it so as to take up a full and entire side, and pretty soon he saw another building-size painted sign for Levi's jeans, and how do you suppose a painter could reach that high? He passed dozens of stores with glass windows so expansive he wondered how in the world you'd ever be able to transport a piece of glass that size, why just the glass alone was worth more money than the entire Godwin home, and looking through the astonishing glass store fronts, he could see every single store was packed full of merchandise, and as he sauntered along he realized that every single person who walked past him seemed to be in an immensely important hurry, and after a deliberate stroll south down an easy slope, Thomas reached a wide open intersection where he counted five bustling streets coming together at one spot, and in a seemingly frantic stricken crowd, he purposely stopped, and enforced his position (which was not easy) because he thought it interesting to study a multistory building called Rich's Department Store. The sights and sounds of Atlanta were more amazing than anything he could ever have imagined, and he was a very imaginative young feller.

Walking at a good pace, he reached the edge of the big city and left the busy traffic behind, and now in the countryside he noticed fewer and fewer cars until finally no cars passed by, and he resigned himself to walk as far as he could before sundown. He estimated Jonesboro to be another ten miles, he'd already walked maybe five or six miles, and with the afternoon sun beginning to place visibility limits on his traveling much farther today, he found himself on another stretch of road running along beside a train track, and when he heard a train coming, his first reaction was to place himself in a position favorable to the idea of jumping a free ride so he ran to the edge of the tracks and waited, and as the train passed he was able to catch a glimpse into some cars that looked to be empty, completely empty, no seats and no freight, and these cars had no windows only big wide open doors. He'd never considered jumping a train before for the whole idea seemed haphazard at best, but somehow this looked like as good a time as any, here he was on a deserted stretch of road, the daylight hours were diminishing, and he was anxious to make progress south, and if he took this opportunity as it presented itself, he might actually be delivered somewhere in the vicinity of Valdosta, and realistically, the chances were probably better than fifty-fifty that he'd move closer toward his southern goal because let's face it, the train was moving toward the south, and a reversal of that direction would call for drastic, sporadic, and idiotic engineering plans for laying of the train's track. So having reasoned through the positives and avoided the negatives, he pulled his sack up onto his shoulder and reached out for and grabbed a hold of a ladder on one of the slow moving cars, and as he grabbed on tight to the ladder his sack swung free to dangle by the still attached string, and as he was able to manage it, he made every effort to reign the sack in closer to his body where he could control it between himself and the metal for he realized if he dropped his sack, he'd have to plunge himself off the train back to the ground so as to recapture his belongings for his sack contained all his worldly possessions, that being, his clean shirt, his flip, his hand-me-down winter coat and his rolled-up dinner. His feet flew high in the air and the ladder jerked his arm just about out of it's socket. He struggled to bring his feet up to the bottom rung of the ladder and was finally able to pull his weight up to the next higher, and then the next higher rung. He was on the train.

He found the ladder to be close enough to an open door that possibly if he let go of the ladder with one hand, he might reach out and catch hold of the door's edge, then he threw one foot onto the floor of the open car, and remarkably he was inside the car laying on the hard wooden floor. He was completely winded, out of breath mostly (he realized) from the excitement of facing and conquering a very dangerous situation. He rolled over to his back and tried to slow his breathing. He pulled himself to a sitting position on the floor and watched out the door as the trees and a house or two passed by. At first and for several minutes what he saw was mostly trees, but then there were more and more houses, and incredibly he read a sign on a building. "Welcome to Jonesboro."

He looked at his Goodrich Road Map and reckoned the next big city would be Macon. The train rolled through three small towns, but he didn't see any signs to tell him the name of any of the three little towns. He stood in the open door way as the train slowed to enter a fourth town, and when the train came to a stop in the middle of this town, Thomas saw the big black letters "Griffin Dry Goods." Workmen toted supplies off an open flat bed car, and the train pulled out of Griffin, Georgia. Thomas checked his Goodrich Road Map once again as the train picked up speed and now whizzed along through the open countryside, and cotton pickers in the fields at the end of their day's work returned his wave. Three more unnamed small towns zoomed past in a blur, and by his map calculations they would be Orchard Hill, Milner and Barnesville. It was pitch dark, probably close to ten o'clock, when the train stopped again and like before workmen hauled big wooden crates from another flat bed car. The clue to his location this time was a sign that read, "Forsyth City Lumber." Late that night maybe around midnight the train stopped in Macon.

When Thomas watched the work crew leave the train, he decided this must be the last stop, so he jumped down to the ground and made his way into the small train station through a door which was open and in fact had no lock, and Thomas was accustomed to doors without locks for no country folks ever needed a locking door, and by the looks of the number of people inside this small station house, the building must be a travelers refuge. He found a corner inside the building and leaning against the stationary wall as he let his wobbly legs buckle beneath him, he sat down by sliding onto the floor for he was dizzy with the hours of motions unlike any sustained motion he'd ever experienced, and when he felt a bit more steady, he unfolded the clean rag wrapped around his packed dinner and to his great pleasure he discovered two biscuits and a piece of fried chicken, a leg. He ate the chicken and saved the biscuits for another day. He curled up on the floor with his sack under his head to act as a pillow and to keep his possessions safe, and he slept through the night in the big open room of the station house. The other travelers were also asleep on the floor along the wall. No one spoke, and Thomas was mighty proud to be on his own, independent and in Macon, Georgia.

The next morning, Thomas walked south away from the train station past the Macon Post Office, and in front of the Court House, he asked a man hurrying by, "Pardon me Sir, could you direct me to the road out of town heading south to Valdosta?"

The stranger replied, "Go back past the Post Office and turn right. That is 4th Street. Keep on that street. The name will change to Broadway, and farther out as you're leaving town, the name will change again to Houston Road. That road goes south to Perry and Tifton and Valdosta. It's a hundred miles or more to Valdosta."

After studying his map and getting his bearings, Thomas went into a mercantile and asked the proprietor if he could find work. The man was glad to have the help sweeping up and stocking shelves, and Thomas worked a full day. The man paid him cash money and offered to have Thomas sleep in his barn. Thomas was much obliged and before walking out the door of the mercantile, he picked up a cake of soap, and asked, "How much?"

Thomas paid the man for the cake of soap, went to the wagon out back, and climbed up to the wagon seat as the man directed, and first thing Thomas made sure to safely tuck his sack on the floorboard at his feet, and soon the proprietor climbed onto the wagon, picked up the reins and clicked to the horse, and once in motion Thomas and the proprietor enjoyed their first chance at conversation. Thomas told the man he was heading to Valdosta to pay a visit to his half sister.

The man said, "My home is on this very street which is the street that you'll keep to out of town and to the south, all the way to Valdosta, and along the way you'll pass through Perry and Tifton."

Thomas was glad to confirm his travel plan, and when the man drove his horse and wagon into his small barn, Thomas volunteered to bed the horse down and the man went inside the house. Thomas washed up using his new cake of store bought soap and a bucket of water dipped from the horse trough. He sat under a tree in the cool of the evening to eat one biscuit. He had one more biscuit for tomorrow evening, and he had a little cash money to buy a meal or two after that. So far, so good.

As he hitchhiked south, day after day, he caught only a few rides, and many times the ride took him only a mile or two and then left him strung out alone on deserted roads, and mostly Thomas did a lot of walking. On several more occasions he found work along the way, but these jobs earned no cash money instead he was paid a good evening meal, a dry night's sleep in a barn, and a piece of bread for the journey, and generally speaking, the farmers were poor but very kind, and without exception as he came in contact with perfect strangers along the way, they asked him into their home for supper. As luck would have it, some rides took him in to good-sized towns, and all in all, most everyone seemed glad to help because he was still just a boy, and he looked younger than he really was because he was shorter than most boys his age, and I guess maybe his small size helped to inspire strangers to be kind hearted. As was his routine each night of his journey he pulled his precious Goodrich map from his pocket, held it gently along the edge and easy as could be he added a small rip, and then, once again he counted the rips, and by his calculation tomorrow he expected to arrive in Valdosta on the twenty-fifth day of travel, and this last night on the road, after working for his supper and meticulously storing his sack in the barn loft, Thomas bathed in a creek and took off his clothes and washed all over including his hair. He rubbed soap on his shirt and britches and scrubbed them on a big rock. He wrung out as much water as he could and with difficulty he forced his legs into the wet trousers which was a another first in his life, and as he cleaned up his shoes as best he could in the creek water, he noticed a hole just about all the way through the sole of both shoes. He'd have to find a cobbler in Valdosta. That last morning when he woke in another man's barn loft, he quickly dressed in his good shirt which he'd been saving to wear for his meeting with Martheny and despite the wrinkles, it was in good repair and had not a single hole in it. His britches were fresh washed and his hair was clean and finger-combed off his face, and his shoes were presentable. He was a handsome young feller, and he felt on top of the world, invincible, able to meet any challenge, and he thanked his lucky stars for his ability to read, write, do arithmetic, and above all decipher problems and find a solution.

When our Pa died, Mary Lizzie wrote a letter to our half sister Martheny in Valdosta telling her of the sad news, and knowing this Thomas walked over to Mary Lizzie's house the night before he left home, and copied down Martheny's street name on a scrap of paper, and now in Valdosta after twenty-five days a traveling, he pulled that neatly folded paper from his sack and asked the nice stranger he was riding with to direct him, and Thomas jumped to the ground from the running board of the man's car, and walked down a block and although there was no street sign, he turned on the street the man said was Martheny's street, and he counted the houses just like the man said, and when he found the house, he crossed through the white sandy front yard to the front porch steps, and he knocked on the door of a house with faded and peeling paint, but in those days, most houses in town needed a new coat of paint, and for that matter, houses in the country rarely, if ever, got the first coat of paint, and when Martheny came to the door, Thomas recognized her to favor Pa and when he choked up, she did the talking after she hugged the wind right out of him.

"Well land sakes, I don't know which one you are, but I know by looking at you you're a Godwin."

Essie worked hard cooking and cleaning for her own family of four little children all of which were younger than five-year-old Sis, and on top of that she took care of about six or more of us kids (Doc's youngest brothers and Sis), and the only possible result was that poor old Essie stayed busy from sun up till after dark and that first year after Pa died and Thomas left home was difficult for everybody, and to help get through the bad times sometimes the pack of boys in the family played devilish tricks on each other, and I've often wondered if it was a means for us to vent our pain over the loss of Thomas and Pa, and some of the shenanigans that went on might have bordered on criminal to a saner bunch of people, and Essie pretty much threw up her hands in surrender for she was unable to control us. One night during a thunder storm we witnessed a lightning strike which sparked a field fire that spread quickly in the direction of the Ingram Grave, and in the light of day the next morning we boys headed out to inspect the damage, and the continuation of black soot included the dry well south of the Ingram Grave, where we turned around to walk back toward home but naturally someone got the bright idée to look down in the well which went dry many years before the fire, and in fact the dry well was the main reason the place was deserted back in the 1800's. We looked into the well alright, and we saw it was no more than twelve or fifteen feet deep, and that was surely not deep enough ever to have provided lasting water, and looking around the place the old rotten barn was now nothing more than more black soot on the ground, and starting that very day this old dry well many a times called to us boys like the forbidden fruit in the Bible, and more times than not when we passed by, we fell to our stomachs for our ritual look into the deep dry hole. Bert was always the worst one to play tricks and that morning at age ten, he was bursting full of mischief, and we understood we better watch out for Bert's bedevilment, but somehow both me and Mose found ourselves in the bottom of that dry well, and that was just the first time of a recurring temptation that seemed the hardest thing in the world to resist.

Down in the well, Mose let me stand on his shoulders so I could reach a stick that Bert was holding, and the boys standing on top made Bert lie down on the ground with half of his body hanging over the edge. He was screaming like a girl, afraid he'd fall in too for the others were holding Bert's legs and sliding him farther and farther over the edge, and when I barely caught hold of the end of the stick with one hand, I was finally able to pull myself up and hand over hand catch hold of the stick and place one foot a top the other foot walking up the steep walls of the well. I was out, and I did a jig of celebration, but then we all got quiet because Mose was still screaming from down in the creepy well.

Mose was yelling at the top of his lungs, "Y'all better get me out of here."

Being the one that got us into this mess, Bert understood without argument that he'd be the one to hold the stick again, so he went looking for a longer stick, and he found a fine light-weight pine limb; and once more, Bert elbow-crawled up to the edge of the well and stuck his feet in the air, and the first standing-up boy wrapped his hands around Bert's ankles and slid him down the shaft, and it worked again. The pine limb was long enough such that Mose stretched up on his tip toes as high as he could from his feet planted in the bottom of the well, and miraculously, he grabbed a hold of the tip end of the pine limb, but this time the pull was a little bit more tricky because the weight was more and this time all the boys quickly lined up one behind the other with arms locked around the next one in front all the way up to the one at the well's edge holding onto Bert's feet, and Bert's position was precarious to say the least for the weight pulled him farther and farther into the well, and at some transition point every last boy in the caterpillar line broke the human chain and ran to the front of the lineup and belly on the ground grabbed onto Bert's britches and bare feet, and it was a good thing Bert had the foresight to take off his shoes, and finally someone was able to reach Mose's hand and that did it; we pulled Mose the last few feet to safety, but the pile added to Bert's danger because those reaching for Mose had to trample on Bert who whimpered to be in such a predicament, and of course considering Mose's rankle, as soon as Mose scrambled out over the rim of the well, Bert stood up with a smooth, liquid single bounce from belly-on-the-ground to running-for-his-life for Mose tore out chasing Bert, and I wondered just what Mose was gona do to Bert when he caught him, but Bert was just a little faster than Mose that day, and he explained later that he was genuinely convinced he was actually fighting to continue breathing in God's precious air which pumped up his ability to run faster than ever before, and Bert disappeared off to the south, over the rise, and down the slope running barefoot through the black soot and into the trees, and finally Mose gave up chasing Bert and came back to walk home with us, and before supper that night, back at the house, Mose had Bert down on the floor trying to beat and tickle him to death when Essie came out of the kitchen to call us to supper.

She didn't say a word more than, "Come on in, supper's getting cold."

But at the supper table, Doc talked at length to each of us and then he directly chastised Bert, "You bunch of hooligans better slow down on these pranks, somebody's bound to get hurt, and don't come running to me with a broken leg or worse."

From then on, I don't think that pack of ruffians ever walked past the old deserted Ingram place without at least one of us winding up at the bottom of the old dry well. It got real tiresome.

—————◆◈◈◈◆—————◆◆

Doc's children were more like brothers and sisters; I mean we've been mighty close all through the years. Doc still tended to patients from all over the county mostly by walking his rounds, but some came to be treated in his office off the big fireplace room on the kitchen side of the house, and sometimes, he also drove a horse and buggy to make house calls.

I remember one time a neighbor man named Pruitt and his wife brought their little girl Arbelle in to Doc's office. The two-year-old had a big ole pone on the side of her neck, and the poor little thing was squirming and twisting in her mother's arms obviously in a lot of pain, and both the mother and little Arbelle were crying, a soft whimper. The boil or as it's called in the south, the risen (pronounced with a long 'I') was bigger than little Arbelle's fist, and the poor little girl was in misery from the swelling pressure, and her mother answered Doc's questions and explained that she and the baby had slept a precious few hours over the last week. With this information, it was plain to see why both the mother and especially little Arbelle were listless and in a dazed state. Doc examined the risen very carefully and decided the best course of action was to do nothing for a few more days until the boil came to a not yet formed head and to try to lance too soon would cause unnecessary pain and might possibly have a detrimental effect, so he told the Pruitt's to take their baby back home and apply hot compresses to the swollen area, and to continue the hot compresses every hour through the day and night except he warned they should leave the child alone if she happened to fall asleep for she and her mother were to the point of breakdown and needed sleep to restore their strength. Doc told them to watch for a white point to form in the middle of the pone and bring her back when they could see the infection rise to the surface in the middle of the swelling. He explained to the worried parents that a circle of red would appear, flame red about the size of a quarter, and in the center of the red circle, they would see a head or hard white point, a pocket of puss at the skin's surface. They were pitiful with disappointment as they walked out of the office, but within ten days they were back, and poor old Mrs. Pruitt was pale and utterly exhausted from sleep depravation because she'd held and rocked her baby all through the days and nights. At the initial glance of the grotesquely enlarged boil (now the size of Mr. Pruitt's fist) Doc began immediately sterilizing his sharp pocketknife over the flame of a candle. The parents helped Doc hold the baby still as he lanced the risen, and with one small prick of the sharp blade precisely in the white head, the risen burst opened with an unbelievable popping sound as the pressure release on the swelling caused the puss to explode into the room, covering the parents, the baby and Doc. The stinking yellow puss penetrated their cotton clothing, and understandably, Arbelle cried and squirmed as the puss drained, and with Doc's added squeeze the puss finally stopped oozing, and Arbelle collapsed against her mother's shoulder and fell instantly asleep and slept for a solid twenty-four hours from that minute.

Doc was a good doctor. Everybody in the county knew he was a good doctor. Everybody in the county also knew he got drunk from time to time, and most folks knew the reason, and that being Doc still blamed himself for the typhoid that killed our ma. In his mind, a twenty-nine-year-old doctor should have known enough to make the boys in the family go down-hill of the well to empty their bladder which no one realized that the urine produced at the edge of the porch might and probably did filter down through the dirt and quite possibly into the well water. Just a drop into the well water could have made for a dangerous situation. Looking back, Doc was a very busy man practicing medicine. He failed to notice the one most important and consequential thing in his daily life: the boys urinated while standing on the edge of the porch instead of going out into the yard beyond the well or better yet, farther down the hill to the outhouse, after all, the placement of the outhouse down-hill of the well, was common practice, and everyone with any brains atall knew to protect the well water from possible outhouse seepage. When the house was built way back before Doc was born, the outhouse was deliberately place down-hill of the well, and although the well was a good twenty feet from the porch, Doc accepted lethal responsibility for his failure to enlighten his younger brothers as to the hazards of urinating up-hill of the well.

Doc convinced himself that his delinquent instruction resulted in contamination of the well water. When the boys urinated while standing at the edge of the porch, the urine seeped down through the ground and eventually found it's way at least six feet down into the well water.

Again from porch to well, not more than a drop of water could have seeped into the well's large and deep reservoir, but no matter how infinitesimal the amount, even one drop in the drinking water could have caused the outbreak of the dreaded and highly contagious typhoid. This highly unlikely reasoning was settled in Doc's mind, and what he believed was an indisputable conclusion, and through the years no matter how improbable, Doc doggedly contended that any damn doctor worth his salt should have noticed, should have pieced together the facts, and his mistake in vigilance ended in a damned stupid oversight that nothing could undo now.

He'd just have to carry his guilt with him to his grave, and after years of self hatred and belittlement, and no matter how much Pa tried to render Doc blameless, and no matter how many times we all tried to convince Doc, in fact he shouldered the blame and responsibility for Ma's death, and as a result, Doc drank too much moonshine whiskey, which caused me to pity Doc for giving in to an unreasonable equation which actually had no winner, but instead set up a justification for escaping future responsibility, and his family was shortchanged in the process.

He was never mean or abusive, but he was never one hundred percent available either, and this situation with Doc might be an explanation and a means to justify my own over developed sense of responsibility which developed at an early age in response to my obligations to Sis; I've often wondered about that, and it might have some valid arguments for I understood from a very early age that I did not want and would not accept the luxury of a carefree childhood, but instead I've always been committed to watching out for and taking care of others, and from way back before Pa died in my mind I pictured Sis getting into dangerous and life threatening situations if I shucked my role in keeping her safe. I'm not talking about doing things for Sis or anybody else, what I'm talking about is bigger in scope than that, it's difficult to explain, but somehow my role in life is to act as a back up safety and security shield while and at the same time I inspire and teach self reliance and independence. I look back over my life and my way of thinking and I realize that I could never have left home like Thomas did, but at the same time I'm proud of Thomas and his adventurous spirit, and I envy him for his travels to far away places! It's simple in my mind: I could choose no other path except to stay at home and care for and provide for and instill self-determination within my family and friends. I've always wanted nothing out of my time on God's earth, nothing more but to help and protect the ones I love. It's a crowd of people, but I understand that no man can do everything needed to care for another person and as a matter of fact that would be exactly the wrong thing to do, so it's my role to set about instilling self reliance, and I will never know any other course of action, I don't seek any other course of action, and I will be true to this deep seeded role of humanitarian, and I guess maybe Thomas is actually my counter self, and he's the one person who's never needed me to take care of him, and much less, he has never needed me to be anything more than his little brother and he's needed me to read his letters and wait for his return home.

1922

During the cold winter months, when farming work fell into a lull, we attended Bethel School, a one-room schoolhouse built right beside Bethel church. Nobody had time to go to school in the farming season so the school was open only in the winter. The teachers traveled about from one school to another, and the family who lived closest to the school boarded the teacher. We lived close to Bethel school, but we never boarded any teachers except, of course, brother James that year when he came home from the War in Europe. That was the last winter James lived at home for he was about to get married to a real nice young lady named Lillie McElroy. Our house was always crowded, and I liked it that way. That one year when I was about seven years old, James was the teacher and I wanted to go to school because James made learning seem like the exact right thing to occupy a boy's time, and because he was fair to everyone and expected everyone to pay attention make an honest effort to understand the subject and carry our own selves along the road to getting an education, and it was that attitude of putting us in control of our own lives which offered us a window of opportunity in those difficult times and also empowered us and me especially, but the next year when James did not return to Bethel School I lost interest and instead of going to school, I spent my time hunting and thinking, and anyway, I did not return to school until finally when I was eleven years old, I decided to go back for I realized I needed more book-learning, and besides that, seven-year-old Sis had a lot to do with it for she begged, and begged until I finally gave in, and she was the one who wanted to go to school but she was scared to go alone because she didn't know what to expect when she got there, and when I gave in to her pleading, she spent a full week planning what we'd wear, making me sit still so Essie could whack off some of my long hair, and mending (with Essie's help) a dress for herself and a shirt and britches for me, and finally the night before the wondrous first day, she bossed me around and ordered me to wash all over, even my too-short hair, and the next morning when we left the warm fire and walked through the cold morning frost, I admitted we both looked pretty good and when I said so, a tear or two rolled down her cheek. The short walk to Bethel was no quicker through the cemetery or past the Jasper Hicks place and that morning we went down through the holler, over the creek bridge, up the hill past the Jasper Hicks place and down the main road, and when we walked past the church and into the schoolhouse yard, pretty little six-year-old Vesta Owens came rushing over to us and I saw tears glistening in her eyes too, and these girls looked like they'd just seen a ghost, they were so nervous and fidgety, and it made me feel mighty proud to know they both were ready to conquer their fears and bravely begin their first day of school. The old teacher called for everyone to come inside the schoolhouse, and he snapped at us, "Keep your coats on for I'm still trying to build a fire in the stove."

Vesta and Sis sat down together on the same short bench kind of hugged each other to get warm, and for no explicable reason, he yelled at them to sit on separate benches, so Vesta stood up and quiet as a rabbit moved to sit beside me, side by side on the same short bench, and after the teacher allowed as how Sis and Vesta might be disruptive if they sat together, and he even used the word 'giggle' in his long speech which was completely out of line for this mean old teacher rambled on with no understanding of our basic character in Cleburne county, and his consequential mistake was a far fetched notion that Sis and Vesta could be disrespectful which of course would never happen, never in a million years would these timid little girls be even slightly disruptive for they were just like everyone else in the county. They were courteous, simple, well mannered and in every way lived up to our unspoken guiding principle as integral as breathing, and this banner of honor strictly dictated that no one ever caused a ruckus and everyone operated with respect for one another, and never ever did anything that might cause a commotion, we never talk out of turn, and without hesitation we were honest in every action and word, but for some reason that teacher proved himself to be a mean old son-of-a-bitch which sure made me wish James would come back to teaching at Bethel, but he didn't, and we went to school every day wondering just what the teacher would say about us, and one of the worst days was a day close to Christmas when the mean teacher called on Vesta to read aloud, and she started crying because she didn't know how to read, and the teacher practically jumped down her throat as he screeched, "Vesta, you're never gona learn if you don't study."

After school let out that day, Vesta followed right behind me and outside she asked me a question.

She said, "Shug what does 'study' mean?"

I told her it meant looking at a book and teaching yourself, so she went back in the schoolhouse and asked the teacher if she could take a book home to study, and he let her, and the next week the old mean teacher called on Vesta again, and this time she started reading words out loud, but the words didn't make any sense, and right quick I understood her problem, she was pointing with her finger as she read each word out loud, and she was beginning each line of words with her finger on the wrong side of the page, she was reading from right to left. I put my hand on top of her hand and she stopped reciting the non-connected words for a minute while I gently moved her shaking finger to the opposite side of the page, and I slowly guided her trembling finger from one word to the next going from left to right, and beginning the next line back at the left side of the page and as she called out the words this time she was amazed to hear her voice reading sentences as they were meant to be understood, and she didn't stumble but instead she read the words in an order that made sense, and I was amazed that this brilliant little girl took a book home and taught herself to decipher words and that was an incredible act of genius especially since she was learning words with no context, and then from that day on with the hard part behind her, Vesta learned every subject easily as if she had been starved for knowledge, and actually she inspired me to pay attention and work on my own education for it was high time I worked on building up my own independence.

The poverty in the county was a constant and quiet battle, the smothering poverty was all we'd ever known, nobody had enough to eat, and it seemed like every house was full of hungry children, so in the spring of 1924, before my thirteenth birthday in June, I decided to put up my own whiskey still for my contribution to our livelihood now seemed a dire emergency situation. I was old enough to understand the rules of survival, which as I sorted through the positive points of making money, I also had to reconcile the possible consequences of actively working outside the law, and I wrestled with the idea that I could go to jail if a revenuer caught me making whiskey, they'd send a boy to jail just like they'd send a man to jail, so I decided I could be smart about making whiskey and I could manage to keep secrets, that was the main thing, keep secrets, and number one secret to keep was the still location, and number two secret to keep was all details of whiskey making and never put any member of my family in the middle of something that could get them mixed up in breaking the law, so

I decided all my secrets had to be kept from all members of my family for their good and for my good. I was old enough to drive the mule and wagon to town, and desperately, I needed money to buy food, we had to eat, and this seemed a simple direct solution, and in a logical manner, I thought about it long and hard, and finally, me and Marvin talked about it long and hard which was a general discussion with no mention of details, and so my only option (making whiskey) became a reasonable course of action with no turning back, for once I made the initial investment I could not justify abandoning the project and forfeiting the expense, and just as 'b' follows 'a' me and Marvin found ourselves on a one way path with no looking back for we knew the basics of whiskey making, and we were hungry.

First, we each picked a good secret supply of water, and I picked a good secret place deep in the woods along the lasting-water creek that flows down through the long-bottoms, and though we were a young age, we figured it never hurts to be independent, and I managed a line of thinking that let me hide my illegal moonshine work behind the cover of my legal farming work, for early in the mornings I hitched up the mule behind the plow and set out for the long bottoms and it was common knowledge as to my whereabouts, and about mid morning when I was sure no one was in the vicinity, I parked the mule under a shade tree and waded down stream in the branch to my secret still location, and by wading the distance, I left no trail, and if any questions come about my whereabouts, all concerned could answer truthfully that I was in the long bottoms plowing. It seemed as good a cover as any, and it worked for as long as the long bottoms needed plowing. My secret moonshine place was on a sandy built-up shoal at the base of a seven-foot bluff, which in my mind, I named Eagle's bluff. There over time the creek has washed away the clay and tunneled under the overhang of a big rock where the creek makes a lazy turn under the overhang and meanders into another swing at the solid rock base of the bluff which forces the flow to double back in the opposite direction. Both these turns have eroded the soft ground into a deep and narrow ravine. So on the west side of this secret place there was the cover of a steep cliff and also the opposite, east creek bank was pretty high making a good hide-out at the water level. No revenuers would see the still or even the fire until they were right above on the tall Eagle's bluff or on the lesser bluff across on the other side of the creek. Since I worked only a couple of hours each day, it took a month or more to dig the three-foot round holes for the vats because the ground was hard clay under the top three inch layer of sand. It was Marvin who gave me the information about digging in the vats, and setting the vats on big rocks leaving enough space for the fire down in the pit underneath the vats. This made sense for two reasons first the fire down in the pit was not visible from a distance and second the pit contained the fire that is to say, the fire could not spread out of the pit into the dry leaves which I left in place for clearing the ground of undergrowth, pine straw, and leaves would be a dead give away of the still's whereabouts, and I had to be very careful to hide all the operations and of course, the more natural and undisturbed the woods remained, the less likely a revenuer would notice.

The last thing you wanted was to set the woods on fire so the pit for the fire made real sense to me. So during the plowing and planting season, I accomplished hauling in the equipment, digging in the vats, and setting up the pipes and runoff, and after that my whiskey making business went from day time work to night time work because me and Marvin agreed that the cover of night was our best bet for keeping our secrets. It's a good thing I liked to be in the woods alone at night where I could think my own thoughts, and it was a necessity to stay long hours so as to stoke the fire to boil the mash. To me it was quiet and peaceful at night in the woods, I wasn't afraid of nothing and I liked the solitude. I felt well hidden and safe in my secret place, and in the long hours with not much to keep me busy, I had time to think about a lot of things and I planned how I'd escape if I heard a noise and I formed emergency escape plans if: 1) I heard a noise that came from the east, my escape plans were different if: 2) I heard a noise coming from the north and again different plans 3) if a noise came from the south, and 4) pretty much just pick any escape path if the noise came from up on top of the bluff, and when I no longer felt the need to review escapes from this location, I went over in my mind selecting an alternative secret location if and when I was run out of this place, and back upstream about a mile was a place I'd avoid for sure because the water rushed over some pretty big rocks and made a loud roar which for one thing I'd never hear approaching revenuers, but these were the ramblings of my mind which always came back to right here at Eagle's bluff where the water's flow was silent and swayed in slow motion and rippled and sparkled in the moonlight, and I could sit here for hours and watch the soft dancing motion sliding past me.

It's good for a man to appreciate the beauty in the world and to stand tall and be independent and not afraid, and that's really the only choice for a man who wants to take care of the people he loves.

Every chance I got, I drove the wagon into town for more whiskey making supplies, and most times I went into Tallapoosa. Sometimes I went the farther distance to Heflin, Alabama. I had no money, so I had to ask for credit, and I was lucky even way back then for all the store owners in Tallapoosa and Heflin knew my family and for that matter they knew every family in both Haralson and Cleburne counties, so in both towns, I got credit on my name alone and that made me feel good to have a good reputation, and there's probably nothing more important than a good reputation for if your reputation is bad, it spreads like wildfire that you can't be trusted, but with a good reputation, there's no limit to what people will do to help you get started in life, and it follows you all through the years, making your life easier for trust in a person is without exception irreplaceable in a man's future which is made easier in every respect, and there's no measure of the significance.

Those Who Farmed

Way back when I was just a little feller, my pa made legal whiskey and I remembered a good bit about his whiskey making process and me and Marvin shared information, and he taught me some things, and I taught him some things, but Marvin knew just about every thing about setting up a still so he got into the business at the same time but remember my nephew Marvin (his mother is Mary Lizzie) Marvin is two years older than I am) but he never knew just exactly when I worked or where I worked, and we talked about everything but the specifics. Neither of us ever let anybody know exact particulars, no sir, we both knew that was information to keep to ourselves, and another thing, I never thought about the question if it was right or wrong to make whiskey for I had a responsibility to help feed a house full of children, so I did the best I could and besides, I reached the conclusion: if I didn't make whiskey, those that want to drink whiskey will buy it some place else, and in the desperate times back then in our part of the world, you made whiskey or farmed, and those that farmed starved.

I had whiskey customers all over Cleburne County, Alabama and Haralson County, Georgia. When Pa was alive, he had regular customers in Cedartown Georgia. That was back when he had a temporary license to make whiskey After I sold my very first batch of whiskey, I went straight into Tallapoosa and Heflin and paid off my debts for I wanted to keep my good standing because a man never knows when he might need credit. Two years later when I was fourteen, I was turning a sizable profit. Marvin was doing a good business too, and we both had a ready supply of cash money. For safekeeping I buried my extra money in the woods and of course Marvin hid his somewhere, but we kept all that to ourselves. We worked our own stills and kept our own secrets, but we talked over problems and shared recipes. Running a still is a one man job for many reasons and the first is if a man gets caught, he'll never rat on the other no matter what the law threatens to do if there is no other man working the same still so the safest way to do business is to keep to yourself cause if you don't know something, you can't tell it, and it's best all around for only one man to risk the dangers, make the decisions, and own the profit. Back then making and selling whiskey was the only way to climb out of the smothering poverty. I've never been a selfish man, and I help other people any way I can, and if I'd had a choice and could a made money any other way besides making whiskey, well then that's what I would a done. I've never considered making whiskey was evil and in fact, in my case it was the opposite from evil for it was a means to be of use to others in a very bad time, and the law against making whiskey was unreasonable, but it was the law anyway, but being against the law did not make it sinful, and maybe the lawmakers committed a sin by making laws against a feller, and I strongly believe that sometimes there are laws that are themselves the source of evil, and looking to lawmakers to dictate what's evil is a fool's folly, for the lawmakers don't have the blessing of God on everything they do or every law they make, and from my point of view God is just shaking his head sometimes with the gumption of some lawmakers in believing they're doing God's work when in reality they've no right atall to claim God's on their side. I interpret that a good man can come close to God's will by listening to the inner struggles in his own life, and if a law leaves out any poor old soul from making a living and feeding his family, well it's difficult for me to accept that God wants little children to go hungry, but I don't presume to speak for God, no sir, but in my own dealings I hope God looks at my unselfish motives and dwells on my generosity and ongoing desire to help the little feller who's wound up at the bottom of humanity's heap by no fault of his own, so I'll keep on doing the best I can to make money in the illegal whiskey making business, and by this means I have been completely independent since age twelve; I have relied on no one and I don't need anybody to give me anything.

The whiskey money gives me the freedom and power to be strong and kind at once. I like to buy things for all the little young 'uns and especially for Sis for she is, and forever will be, always to the end of time my special little sister who makes me very proud because she's not afraid of work, and she helps Essie all the time with the cooking and cleaning and whatever work presents itself. From a real early age, Sis and Essie's little girls washed all the clothes for that big family, and by way of making it seem more like fun than work, you can hear them laughing and carrying on while they work, it's a heart warming sound. Once or twice a week, Sis builds a fire under the wash pot to boil the clothes clean, that's a hard job and way too dangerous for anyone younger than Sis, and even Sis is really too young, but what has to be done has to be done and Sis always liked things to be clean and neat, so she never stopped working, sweeping and scrubbing the floors or ironing the clean clothes. Sis has a contagious laugh because she is happy and wants others to be happy too. I took her to town now and then and also gave her some money to buy what she wanted. She wouldn't let me go in the store with her, she wanted to take care of herself, and it's a fact that she is good at it too.

Growing up in the woods, I mean roaming the woods and watching creatures in the wild and learning what to fear and what to enjoy was a good education that you can't get from a book, and I learned I'd better watch out for snakes but that's not saying much because everybody in this part of the country knows to watch out for poisonous snakes and spiders, and there's a lot of them too, the woods just crawl with a lot of dangers.

One morning while I was bathing in the deep creek, I came face to face with a water moccasin. I was quick enough to grab it just behind the head with one hand and with the other hand fish in my pants pocket for my knife. I cut that snake's head just about off with one lick of the sharp blade and I stayed calm by thinking to myself that I was whittling at a big old wooden stick instead of a dangerous snake. I rationalized that I'd not let the cotton mouth scare me away from bathing in the creek cause I got in the habit and I didn't want to go around looking dirty like a poor old tramp so most mornings after working the still through the night, I stripped off my soot covered work clothes, scrubbed my skin clean with lye soap, and put on my good clothes which was a nice pair of pants, a white shirt and a knock about jacket which was made out of corduroy, and I've always worn a nice felt hat with a feather in it. I kept a piece of a comb in the feed sack with my shaving mug, lye soap and shaving brush and I shaved by feel which all my life has been easier for me than looking in a mirror, and the last thing was to spread out my wet clothes on a limb in the woods, and walk away from the still all cleaned up and looking like a dandy for to make my whiskey deliveries of last week's batch already loaded in and covered with a dirty strip of sugar sacks sewed into a big rectangle, and I followed a variation of this routine seven days a week.

I never made a path into or out from my still for that would be too easy for the revenuers to track so as a precaution I walked a different way into the woods and a different way out of the woods, never going the same way twice and sometimes I swung out in a big circle (either going or coming) in order to leave no sign atall of my passing. This was a good trick to use for throwing off the revenuers, but it was dangerous for walking into spider webs so I always picked up a stick and swung it out in front of me and this habit I'll never break for swinging a stick up and down with a rhythm just for the purpose of swiping down spider webs and most of the time it works, but sometimes, I still get a face full of dogged old spider webs and I'll be the first to tell you that it is a spooky feeling to walk right into a big ol' spider web and wonder if the spider is down your shirt and that can give a man a creepy crawly feeling and make him do a dance like a sissy a getting' his shirt off to shake it out. I managed to avoid the poisonous brown spiders that can kill you before you know what happened and all my life I've had a healthy out and out fear of them devils because they spin their giant webs between trees in order to catch big insects like dragon flies and bumble bees. Another poisonous spider is the black widow that lives under rocks or logs right on the ground. I always move rocks and logs and other stuff on the ground with a clear respect because I don't want to stick my hand right into a black widow's nest under there. The woods can be peaceful and quiet but you have to be aware of your surroundings to survive. I guess that goes for all places and all times not just walking in the woods.

I worked at the still at night and delivered whiskey or bought supplies in the daylight hours, and the old mule and wagon was slow transportation but it was reliable, but I was impatient because I wanted to get things done in a hurry so after my birthday. When I was fourteen, I bought my own jalopy. I was almost six feet tall and looked older partly because I went around dressed up like a city dude and looking back I never felt like a child after my daddy died, and I really can't remember a single time in my life when I felt like a kid in fact I've never dreamed about being irresponsible and I certainly never wished for it, but I've been glad to watch my brothers horse around and play pranks on each other and it sure gives me pleasure to watch younguns a playing, but I've never wanted to act or feel like a kid, but once in a long while, I sometimes wonder what it would a been like to be a kid, but I guess that's something I'll just never know. Anyway, I bought a Model T so I'd have faster transportation to get it all done, to go into town and buy supplies for my still and pay the usual hush money that I slipped to the sheriff and make my whiskey deliveries to my customers, and about once a week, buy staples like flour, coffee, and sugar for the family. The Model T gives me speed in getting it done. So one day, I put on a clean fresh ironed shirt and a clean fresh brushed suit, and a clean fresh brushed felt hat and I went to town and paid three hundred dollars saved-up cash money for a brand new model T with a four cylinder, twenty horse power, gas engine. It was fast, up to forty-five miles an hour, and I knew I could outrun the law if I had to. It had a hand crank on the front at the radiator, and I had to be careful of that crank 'cause it had a kick to it, enough to break a grown man's arm. I learned to pull back real fast. The spoke wheels were made of wood and it was called an open touring car. I didn't want the roadster model because it was smaller, and I needed room to haul whiskey and supplies. The lights were electric and set in gleaming brass lamps, and both the horn and the radiator were made of brass. I liked all this shiny brass and the shiny black paint.

I learned how to drive in one turn around town with the salesman sitting in the car beside me. The car had to be in neutral to crank it up and you found neutral with the parking brake lever. To shift from low speeds to higher speeds, I worked the floorboard pedals, and I gave it gas with a lever on the steering column. I was proud that I could afford such a fine touring car and I looked the part of a successful young man.

Vesta and her sisters, Sis, and two of Doc's girls, our nieces (six little girls in all) from the Godwin family and the Owens family, planned their Saturday before Easter just like always, they met at the Bethel Cemetery and from there the girls walked together through the newly plowed fields that stretched over the rolling hills of the Godwin farmed land. There were a total of six hundred and forty acres, but not all was in cultivation. Last year these same six girls made their Easter nests on the one hundred acres owned by John Owens because Ruth was just three then and Sally wanted the girls to stay close and build their Easter nests right around the Owens home place, but this year the three Owens girls headed in the direction of the Ingram Grave to meet Sis and her younger nieces Beulah and Pauline who were just toddlers but the excitement of building Easter nests was something they could not bear to miss. It was mid morning and each girl carried a dinner pail because they planned to keep working until they'd made at least six nests and there was little or no chance they'd finish the nests in time to be back home by dinner, and besides a picnic along the creek shoals in the warm sunlight was part of this year's Easter outing. As the girls began their journey into the plowed fields, Vesta pointed to the blackberry bushes surrounding the cemetery. Sis wondered to herself if she would have noticed the delicate, little white flowers on the blackberry stalks, she easily noticed the blackberries when they were ripe for eating, but the flowers that came before the berries probably would have escaped her completely except for Vesta so it was lucky to have Vesta along to point out the beauty. The girls knew of several picnic spots and Vesta hoped they'd wind up at her favorite spot down the hill east from the Ingram grave, this place all the girls knew by name as the Rocky Shoal, and as they walked through the cultivated fields, Vesta pointed to the distant woods adorned with the white blossoming dogwood trees. The dogwood trees were little more that big bushes that dotted the hill side at a level considerably below the new green leaves of the tall oak, black gum, and sweet gum trees.

Vesta pointed to a tall flowering tree, "Look at that beautiful tree with the hanging white blooms high above that little dogwood tree. Do you see it? That is a sourwood tree."

The white dogwood blooms were at the peak on their glory and Vesta used the word "decorated" to describe the rolling hills of the distant woods now full of the dogwoods, and with shear pleasure, the girls stopped and put down their pails and stood looking and admiring the colors and sounds and aromas and because of Vesta awakening their senses, they practically held their breath afraid the flowers would vanish from this beautiful scene.

Vesta directed, "Y'all close your eyes and listen and smell."

They all closed their eyes and spread their arms for balance, and the girls swayed from side to side and rolled their heads up to face the sky, and while all six girls, kept their eyes shut tight, Vesta spoke, "Can you smell the sweet blooming honeysuckle?"

Vesta led the way into the woods straight to the Ingram grave, and as always, they stopped to read the inscription on the lone headstone. This time Sis found a slender pine stick just the right size to fit into the grooves of the words carved in the stone, and letter by letter, she followed the lines with the stick, and when she finished tracing every letter she threw the stick to the ground and read the inscription with surprising ease for the words on the headstone were now outlined in black, and aloud they wondered if the words would always remain blackened.

> She was a loyal friend, a noble daughter,
> And a devoted wife and mother
> 1840-1861

Vesta spoke again, "Liziebeth Ingram was twenty-one years old when she died."

Sis and Vesta could do the arithmetic and read the words because they were smart, but mostly because of the repetition of many visits has emblazoned in their memories a young twenty one year old mother. As the girls skipped down the hill in the woods beyond the Ingram grave, they hushed their giggles and listened to Vesta describe this as a reverent place with tall shade trees stretching to the blue sky like church spires. They walked down to the creek, and Vesta told the girls of a story she read about a white church with a tower pointing to heaven. None of these girls had been into town more than once or twice in their lives to see such a sight for themselves, but Vesta's words painted a good picture in their minds. At the creek bank, they jumped down to the rocky shoal and were glad to see that their secret place was just as they left it last fall when they ate their packed dinner shivering in their winter coats, but in stark contrast, on this warm Saturday before Easter none of the girls wore a coat. Like last fall, they sat on the big log at the rushing water's edge, it was too big around for their feet to reach the ground so they sat with their legs and feet swinging and bumping the giant log. The smooth, bark free log was dry and comfortable through their light-weight cotton dresses and against their tender legs, and the warm sun found it's way through the high canopy of new leaves into their secret, secluded hideout. The creek banks were high enough to conceal even the tallest little girl, and they loved the privacy and were completely unaware that their chatter and laughter could have led any intruder directly to them, but such a foreign thought could never even flash through their minds for their seclusion was total and undeniable.

Vesta said, "Yall listen to the crow's cawing. A whole flock of the big shiny black birds followed us all the way down here, and now they're calling to each other and to the ones back up the hill in the trees above the Ingram Grave, and they're spreading the news that we are safe and now they can stop worrying about us."

The girls loved this idea that the crows were acting as their guardians, and when the girls finished their dinner they packed the clean, food-wrap-rags back in their dinner pails, climbed off the big log and scampered up the creek bank, and once again Vesta took charge.

"We'll build our Easter nests right here in this thicket and everyone has to make at least one nest. There's plenty of moss growing along the creek's edge, and keep an eye out for tree stumps where moss loves to grow on the rotten wood, and the best place to build an Easter nest is where the moss is already growing and thriving for then you don't have to transplant and disturb the green velvet which guarantees your nest will last longer, and next year we can clean out the leftover nests and easily add new flowers which will cut out nest building work in half, " she directed.

Vesta pointed to a huge rotting tree blown down by a powerful wind, which pulled the roots right up out of the ground, and they followed Vesta's example and stored their dinner pails in the cage of upturned roots, and then they saw for themselves that just like Vesta said, the moss was plentiful, and they easily peeled off large portions of the decomposing wood covered with brilliant green velvet moss, and the happy to be busy little girls spread out into the woods each to pick out the perfect place for an Easter nest, and only a few steps away, Vesta found a remarkably, hen-nest-size round indentation in the ground where a small broken tree's roots decayed underground and produced a cave-in, already lined Easter nest, which was actually just as she'd envisioned for it was surrounded by four small blooming dogwood trees which she decided added a halo of white around her soon to be decorated nest, and she began quickly to remove unwanted debris from the larger scene, and this became an all inclusive setting much larger than she'd anticipated, and so as to turn her attention to helping the younger girls, she quickly pushed down the last remains of the soft, rotten small tree, threw it away, and then filled in a few gaps in the shallow nest with moss peeled from only a portion of the giant decaying tree, and once the lining moss was continuous and seamless except for the exact center, she went in search of violets to adorn. She spotted a small mound of slender, delicate almost threadlike stems each ending in a tiny blue-it wildflower with petals opened into the shape of a fragile four point star no bigger than the tip of her little finger, and using a firm stick as a shovel, she scratched the dirt from around the base, grasped the green stems, and gently but firmly pulled the blue-it mound free from it's anchor, and with the blue-its cupped in her hands, she danced back to her moss nest and knelt to her knees to make a place in the moss for the beautiful pale blue flowers which fit just right into the center of the nest and she was stunned by the beauty of the clump of pale blue wildflowers surrounded by the dazzling green moss. Next she transplanted bigger dark purple and light lavender violets, and as a special crowning touch all around the perimeter. She could imagine no finer design, and as a mark of her creativity she added single dogwood blossoms spaced evenly in the ring of emerald circling the inner blue core, and the contrast of white on green was magnificently finished by the outer lavender and purple border. She stood back to admire her Easter nest and quickly changed her focus to the other girls, and happily she traveled skipping through the woods to inspect each completed nest and in keeping with the optimist inside of her, she found all six nests to be far prettier than last year's. As a last minute inspiration of glory, Sis collected a length of vine and added to her nest a handful of small, cream-colored trumpet flowers pulled from the honeysuckle. The girls paraded around and around through the holler admiring each nest and singing 'The Old Rugged Cross,' until they were shocked out of their euphoria by a loud clap of thunder, and they looked up to a find a dark, cloudy sky; when did that happen? Vesta motioned for the girls to gather their dinner pails, scurry off up the hill past the Ingram Grave and finally run as fast as they could into the plowed field. The Godwin girls Sis, Beulah and Pauline cut across the field to their home place while Vesta, Theda and little Ruth headed toward the cemetery and the Owens home place beyond. When they reached the top of the hill above their house, they were drenched and out of breath, but they continued running down the hill through the rain laughing hysterically and they were glad to hear their Papa grumble something about getting sick as they climbed up the steps to join him on the porch where he was sitting in a straight back chair watching the rain, which was a favorite pastime and always a novel thing to do for he carried a life long appreciation of what he called the simple shocks of life, and this he passed on to his children as an inheritance of greater value than gold.

Vesta's Four Dresses and a Store Bought Hat

Later on that very summer word came from the Owens family that nine-year-old Vesta had an accident while sitting on the porch in a straight back chair. It was stifling hot and not a breeze to be found that afternoon as John pushed himself back and forth in the porch swing in an effort to stir the air, he always said this was more pleasant and productive for him than fanning which in his estimation was for the ladies, and in fact he pronounced many times that the exertion necessary to pump a fan in his case at least just worked up more body heat and was overall a deficit in the cooling business. So he continued his slight swinging motions as he recounted to his daughters another of his worn out old stories, and he was the last to realize their minimal attention for the three girls were half listening and half not and each girl was immersed in her own preoccupation. Theda was dancing up and down the steps in a choreographed repetition of hopping up one step and back down two, Little Ruth was playing with a corn shuck doll a rocking her 'baby' to sleep although her position was constant and almost motionless in her own chair, and as kids will sometimes do, Vesta repeatedly rocked her chair forward as far as possible so as to balance the chair's straight-ladder-back between her crouched body and two chair legs, and without realizing her proximity to the porch edge was becoming dangerously precarious as with each cycle her chair slid slightly closer and closer until finally it worked it's way inch by inch to the edge of the porch where one chair leg dropped off, and little Vesta toppled with the chair off the porch and hit the ground in a crash of ominous proportion. The chair hit first, and the bone broke when Vesta's flailing arm slammed against the now unmovable chair seat which if she could have avoided contact with the stationary chair seat now backed up against the solid ground, the accident could have been reduced in magnitude, but this was unavoidable and that's why the word accident is used with dread.

From inside the kitchen, Sally joined John's screeching chorus for their evil images were not erasable and once again these two good parents were forced to relive painful memories of burdensome helplessness that tossed them about like feathers, and now as in the past, their profound inconsequence rendered them unable to protect another of their beloved children. John actually heard the bone crack and said it was a sickening sound, and in a matter of one second, John was out of the swing, down the steps and at Vesta's side kneeling in the dust, positioning Theda and little Ruth and barking instructions to comfort and hold their screaming sister, "Keep her as still as possible! Don't let her move, leave the chair alone."

It was impossible for Vesta to move even marginally for it seemed that any replacement of even her big toe sent shock waves into her hideously crooked arm. Sally flew out of the house carrying feather pillows, and John hitched the mule to the wagon and practically threw little Ruth and Theda onto the wagon seat to sit beside him, and at that point he realized he was unaware as to how it came about, but Sally (with Vesta in her arms) somehow came to occupy the wagon bed behind the seat and now leaned against the upturned very chair that broke his sweet daughter's arm, and with a surrendering acceptance of unreality, John at once steadied and drove the mule as fast as he dared for he knew better than to push or excite the animal if he wanted to be successful in getting Vesta into town to a doctor for this was a time when Doc Godwin was not available, and what a shame because of course the Godwin home place was the closest choice in a dire emergency, but more than the close proximity was the glaring fact that Doc Godwin was a better doctor than any doctor to be found in any town. Sally was crying and holding her sweet daughter's head in her lap, and even with the arm cushioned in the feather pillows, Vesta cried out in agony when they forded the creek and every single bump in the road was pure torture.

Doc Gilmore set the broken bone as best he could, and in private he told John he could feel a wide space between the two pieces of bone meaning that after impact, the bone fragments traveled some distance apart, and as a consequence one sharp point jutted toward the surface and almost punctured the skin which bone movement through soft tissue added to little Vesta's piercing pain. So with limited resources his only approach was to push and twist Vesta's elbow and hand until he thought maybe the bone pieces might be lined up, but there was so much swelling, he couldn't be sure, and he had no stomach to continue this torturous process although she was very brave in her resolve to assist him in returning her arm to it's original straight nature, but no matter how valiant little Vesta was determined to be, she could not physically endure much more of the excruciating pain, so he splinted and bound the arm unwilling to place it in a cast and possibly deny the bone pieces the latitude to 'settle' into a more reasonable location. John carefully picked up his precious wounded angel and carried her out to the wagon and settled her once again in the shield of her Mama's arms, and their two younger girls scampered up to the wagon seat as Sally leaned back against the despised upturned chair situated in the wagon bed, and the doc pulled John aside with, "I'll make arrangements for Vesta to see a surgeon in Atlanta."

Back at home Vesta was in such misery she couldn't eat or sleep, and because he knew no better way to care for his daughter, John drove her back into town to see Doc Gilmore every week for six long weeks, until finally, Doc Gilmore journeyed out to the Owens home place with the news they'd leave the next day on the trip to Atlanta, as the surgeon in Atlanta was expecting them. Doc Gilmore insisted he should ride to Atlanta with John & little Vesta for the matter of introduction, and so the next morning Sally bathed and dressed her little girl as had become the custom since the accident, and when the wagon disappeared out of sight up and over the hill, Sally prayed for a speedy and safe return, for potential bad unwanted results loomed as a distinct foreboding possibility.

In town, John stored the mule in Doc Gilmore's own pasture, and parked the wagon beside his barn to remain there until John and Vesta returned from Atlanta which hopefully would be on the turn around trip of the Jitney Bus, and Vesta and John anticipated this extraordinary journey into Atlanta, all the way to the distant city, an implausible sixty miles which certainly seemed to them as far away as the moon, and to make the trip in a gas, motor driven Jitney Bus was both inconceivable and foreign. They learned from the good doctor the particulars of the Jitney Bus, which passed through Tallapoosa three days a week on the eastbound trip, and in 1925 this was the finest sort of public conveyance. So as Doc Gilmore described the Jitney Bus, he explained they'd buy tickets to board the long, three-seated car (not counting the driver's seat of course) and John imagined this Jitney Bus must be a giant automobile if each public seat could accommodate two adults or three children, and the engine could only be a powerful monstrous piece of machinery to pull such a load in comfort at speeds upwards of forty-five miles an hour (if road conditions permitted), and on this fine and wondrous day as they waited for the Jitney Bus, John took his daughter into O.D. Lipham's Dry Goods Store and picked out a hat for Vesta to wear to the big city. Vesta tried to be brave through all this commotion, but her pain never eased and John knew this to be true when she showed no interest in picking out her new hat. He himself, admired his daughter's shiny red curls, but he understood their bright auburn color was a source of embarrassment for his beautiful little girl, and in fact she considered her hair to be ugly, and that is why she always wanted to hide her red curly hair under a hat which now she owned a brand new store bought one picked out by her Papa.

They were not prepared to stay overnight in Atlanta and were astonished when the surgeon examined little Vesta and told them they'd have to stay at least two weeks. The surgery was very serious, he'd have to break and reset the bone and Vesta's recovery would be slow. He wanted to keep a close eye on Vesta and do everything possible to immobilize the arm, for even in a splint, the bones could shift and worse still, any slight infection could lead to gangrene. This hospital was a fine medical facility with twenty-six beds in all, and in preparation for the surgery, the nurses removed Vesta's dress but did not remove her underslip when they noticed her aching modesty, and her humiliation was somewhat lessened when they covered her with a brilliant-white, ironed-crisp sheet.

John kissed his little girl's forehead and followed the bed-on-wheels procession down the hall, and when she was out of his sight, he cried like a baby, the sobs shaking his giant frame and causing him to find support against a nearby wall. Vesta was anesthetized (put to sleep) with ether, and the surgeon was successful in reconnecting the bone fragments, and her Papa was holding her hand when she came to, and as soon as she was conscious enough to look under the white sheet, she was mortified to discover her underslip had been removed, and with this final crushing blow, little Vesta started wailing and John became acutely aware that her crying convulsions might damage the fragile bone repair and start up the bleeding again.

This was before the time of hospital issued gowns, and Vesta begged her Papa to please find her dress and please cover her nakedness, and when he gently pulled the dress over her head, and she eased her one good arm into it's sleeve at that minute, a massive, uncontrollable, violent storm of vomiting soiled her one and only dress which she was wearing when they arrived in Atlanta, and before she realized what was happening the nurses appeared in the room and began stripping her naked again but thankfully, her extreme distress caused her to cry herself to sleep, and after a short nap a nurse bathed the putrid slime from her chest and removed the rancid soiled sheet while simultaneously replacing it with a clean one, and the soothing warm bath and riddance of the sickening odor helped somewhat to calm her dry heaves, and then much to her pleasure, the nurse slipped a white dress over her head, and explained the dress was her own, it was her spare work dress. The dress was twice Vesta's size but she imagined herself to be a nurse in uniform, and best of all she was glad to hide her nakedness

On the second day in the hospital, another very kind nurse came into Vesta's room and spread out a child's size dress which made Vesta inhale in wonder at the sight of such a beautiful rounded collar, puff sleeves and gathered low-slung waist, and then an exceptionally amazing thing happened, the nurse said, "Here honey, I altered one of my dresses to fit you. I'm tired of wearing it and the color is just right to flatter your beautiful red hair, you can wear it while you're in the hospital, and when you go home, I want you to take it with you."

Next, this kind and selfless person carefully bathed and dressed Vesta in the most elegant, seamed up to fit dress she'd ever seen, and when the nurse combed her red curls and handed her a mirror, Vesta felt pretty; but she did not believe the part about her hair. The ether's nauseating effect lingered well into the second day which left her weak and pale, and each time she soiled her dress (or underslip) the nurses quickly washed it, hung it up to dry, and ironed it, and once she was dressed in a slightly damp underslip, but Vesta insisted that she'd rather be sopping wet than lie naked under the sheet. Her modesty was debilitating.

Doc Gilmore stayed overnight one night at the hospital and returned home on the Jitney Bus the next day and back in Tallapoosa, he decided his first duty would be to visit the Owens home place and convey the news to Sally, but before he hitched his own horse to the buggy, he hitched John's mule to the Owens wagon, and subsequently tied the mule to the back of his buggy so as to deliver to Miss Sally Owens a means of transportation, and as Sally listened to Doc Gilmore's story of her daughter's predicament, Sally began formulating her idée to get busy sewing two dresses for her little girl. Luckily it was peddler day and the peddler must a met the doctor within a mile of the house for within minutes of the doctor's departure, the peddler pulled up to the house, and Lula Kilgore jumped down from the peddler's wagon, and after retelling Vesta's ordeal, Sally traded to the peddler one chicken, one dozen eggs, and a dozen fresh-made teacakes in exchange for enough material. Also, she asked the peddler to pass on to John's ma (at that stop) the message to come help her sew and bring her needle and thimble, and it was a lucky thing that Lula Kilgore got off the peddler's wagon, for she could now help sew dresses for Vesta. So these two ladies, Lula Kilgore and Amanda Owens set in to help Sally make two dresses, one a green dotted Swiss with lace on the sleeves, and the other a real pretty tan material with a tiny wire check. This dress too was trimmed with lace.

I heard Vesta describe these two dresses (in exactly this manner) at least a thousand times over the years and always included in her story, 'Grandma Owens and Lula Kilgore helped Mama sew the dresses and they finished the job in two days.'

By the time the peddler came again, Sally had the package ready with the dresses and a fresh shirt and overalls for John bundled into a clean feed sack and with black thread, Sally hand embroidered on the white cotton feed sack, Vesta's name, the name of the hospital (except it was called a sanatorium back then) and Atlanta Georgia. The peddler took the bundle to the post office and mailed it to Atlanta, and incredibly, Vesta received the two new dresses on the very day which marked the end of her first week in the hospital, and by this time, she was still very weak and in a lot of pain, but she was thankful to be over the vomiting. When the bundle arrived, John was glad to get a change of clothes, and the hospital staff showed him into a room with a shower stall, and it was the first time in his life to bathe all over standing up under running water.

At the end of the second week with her arm in a cast, Vesta was strong enough for the trip home on the Jitney Bus and the whole family was waiting in the wagon when the Jitney Bus pulled into Tallapoosa, and it was a very exciting day.

Vesta was proud to tell her story again and again, and each time, she ended with what she called her 'enormous good fortune' to actually own FOUR dresses and a store bought hat.

I was mighty glad to hear that Vesta was back home, and of course John and Sally watched Vesta's every move. When she was inside the house, one parent or the other stayed in the room with her to cover her if she was cold or to fan her if she was hot for they could not be any other way, and when their little girl went out-a-doors, John stayed by her side every minute because he suspected that Sally was too weak to catch Vesta if she happened to fall, and most definitely Sally was not strong enough to pick her up and carry her any distance, not counting of course Sally's single handed, unbelievable lifting, transport and placement of Vesta in the wagon bed on the day of the accident! John and Sally showed a degree of caring that pitifully reflected their loss of baby Hazel and baby Paul, and they tried in their every action to keep their little girl safe knowing that another loss would be unbearable, totally and completely unbearable!

I Know You're the Bully, but I've Come Now

While sitting beside Vesta on the extra wide porch rocker one day, John leaned down to hear her whisper, "Papa here comes that old mean man again."

"What old mean man?" John asked surprised at Vesta's apprehension.

Vesta whispered to her Papa, "The man who's moved into one of the share cropper cabins."

John twisted around to looked over his shoulder and search the road up to the hilltop and sure enough he saw a man carrying a stick and beating a young boy. The man and boy were barefooted and wore only overalls, neither had on a shirt or a hat. They both had uncombed, oily, straight, stringy, dirty hair long enough to touch the shoulder, and the hot summer sun had reddened their skin. The man was growling like a dog as he hit the child again and again with the stick.

John pointed his finger at Vesta's nose and emphatically said, "You stay here on this porch."

He was down the steps and in the road in a split second, and Vesta saw her giant Papa walk up the road about ten paces, and before the man could react, John ripped the stick from the man's hand.

"My name is John Owens, I know you're the bully, but I've come now. I live right here and God as my witness, you won't hit that boy again or so help me, as easy as I took your stick, I'll take your arm off at the socket."

The angry little man doubled up both fists and stood on his toes to bring his face almost to the level of John's chin and defiantly said, "I know who you are and you're not the kang of me, John Owens."

John placed his strong giant outstretched hands on the feisty little man's upper arms and squeezed his shoulders tight together and pushed him away to arm's length, and he did not let go as the little man squirmed, and the little man sort of whimpered as John applied more pressure and raised him up off the ground and when the little man was finally at John's eye level, "Don't make a damn if I'm the 'kang' or not, you are not gona beat that boy."

John put the little man's feet back down on the dusty road and turned to walk away, but then he changed his mind and confronted the little man again. John pointed toward the spring and said, "There's a spring just down the hill here behind the corn crib, you're gona have a cool drink of water. Now git on down to the spring"

Before the little man could respond, John retraced his steps to the porch and scooped his little girl into his arms. He was very careful not to hurt her as he carried her to the spring with the boy and the man following along behind down the hill and into the dark shade of the tall trees. After successfully negotiating the steep slope, John gently placed Vesta on the moss covered creek bank.

"Papa, I can walk! Don't you remember it's just my arm that's broken, both my legs are working just fine like they always have," said the exasperated Vesta.

John chuckled and roughed up his beautiful little girl's pretty red curls, and then he turned to the little man and the boy. He motioned to the big oak tree at the head of the spring, "I drove that steel pin into the tree, and you are welcome to use the tin cup hanging on it, and anytime you pass by, whether I'm around or not, I want you to come down here for a cool drink of spring water."

Without saying so, the little man was glad for a drink of the cool water, but he cupped his hands instead of using the tin cup. When the little boy knelt at the water's edge, the welts, bumps and red stripes of the beating were obvious on his exposed back.

John carried a cup full of spring water to Vesta and then enjoyed two cups himself. He replaced the cup on the steel pin and sat down beside Vesta on the mossy creek bank. Then the little man jerked his son's arm and motioned for him to climb the hill back to the road. John snarled through his teeth, "Sit down."

The little man and the boy understood the order, and decided to comply. To make his point, John told the story of Vesta's broken arm and the helpless feeling of watching her suffer. Next he told these miserable, dirty strangers the sad story of the deaths of his first two babies, Hazel and Paul. The little man looked at John with a blank stare when he heard John's voice crack with the pain of remembering, and still the little man showed no emotion, and then big burly John Owens cried openly as his little girl with a broken arm climbed into his lap and hugged him and kissed his cheek.

This very well could have been a moment of transformation for the little man, but instead he was not swayed by John Owens, a big man not only in stature but also in principle. Together, the four climbed the hill back to the road, and in the bright sunlight John Owens gently pushed aside the little boy's overall galluses and the mean man had no choice but to look at his son's pitiful wounds, then John toted Vesta back to the porch before catching up to the little man and the boy as they walked away down the hot dusty road.

John said to the little man, "I want you to know that everybody in this county will have an eye on you from now on, and believe me they will tell me if this boy ever has even one more bruise. So you better make the rest of your time with your boy count for something good."

A few days passed and word spread through the settlement and John received a report from at least one person each day, and one afternoon to John's surprise the mean little man walked into the yard and up the steps of the Owens' home place and asked for help writing a letter. John asked him in, and called out to Sally. The mean little man could not read or write a word so Sally wrote as he spoke his words. Before beginning, he directed Mrs. Owens to write down the words exactly as he said them, and then he cleared his throat and recited like he'd memorized each word.

Dear Mr. Sears and you too Mr. Roebuck,

I got this pair o' shoes out of your catalog summer 'fore last. As you can see, there's a hole clean through the bottom on the left shoe and one might near through on the right. I know you'll make this good on account o' I buy a pair of shoes every three years regular. I'm returning this here pair and telling you, I ain't wore this pair o' shoes all day nary day. Please send a new pair just same size and color and I'm much obliged.

Yours Truly,

Sally tore an addressed envelope from the Sears and Roebuck catalog and she wrote the man's name for return, but she added 'in care of John Owens,' and then she used her pencil to write the Sears and Roebuck address on a clean white sugar sack. Next she placed the letter and the shoes inside the sack, and with a needle and thread she whipped the sack opening shut. Then the feller walked up to the main road in hopes of catching the peddler, and in a matter of only three weeks, the peddler left a package for the little man and John hand carried it over to the sharecropper's cabin. The little man was pleased to open a box containing a brand new pair of shoes.

While the little man was examining his new shoes, John Owens looked to the man's wife and two children. John nodded his head to the little boy, but the little boy didn't nod back, he just dropped his head to look at his feet. John looked at the wife and though it was dark in the cabin, he could see she had a black bruise on the side of her face, and even more disturbing, John noticed the young girl probably no more than twelve years old, was too shy to come from behind her mother. Back home John told Sally of the frightened and bruised wife, and together they planned to return to the sharecroppers' cabin the next morning.

When Sally and John walked into the yard, it became obvious that the wife and children were trapped in a cruel existence. The mean little man and his wife and two children were situated on the far side of the house in the shade and no one saw John and Sally enter the yard, but John and Sally heard the little man's voice barking orders to the children as the wife begged him to leave them alone. She was babbling to him that she did not need help, and she'd get the work done. Then as the little man drew back his hand, John tried to shield Sally from witnessing as the mean little man struck his wife so hard that she landed on the ground in the dust. Sally took on her inner strength and would have none of her husband's shielding, and in a flash, she was on her knees beside the woman and through clenched teeth she ordered the little man to, "Get away from here!"

With this the children came out of the shade, and John and Sally dreaded to think, why the little girl's skirt was bloody. At this point, John doubled up his fist and knocked the little man so hard that his feet came off the ground and the little man was blown backwards until he slammed into the watering trough. John stood over the little man and shouted, "If you get up, I'll let you have it again and harder this time."

While John had the man cowered on the ground, Sally went inside with the wife and children and she heard John growl the words, "Mark my words, you filthy buzzard, if you've forced yourself on your own daughter, it'll be hell to pave and no pitch hot, so help me God."

When Sally and the little man's wife and children came out or the cabin, Sally walked to her husband and pulled on his sleeve and John leaned his head down to Sally's level to hear her whispered words, "This excuse of a man has raped his own daughter."

John said nothing as the little man picked himself up and dusted the dirt from his backside, and dumbfounded, watched as Sally herded his wife and children to the edge of the yard, and when John was convinced that the little man would not follow, he turned, took three long strides and caught up with his brave wife and her three frightened wards, and John's heart caught in his throat when he heard Sally's soothing words to the pitiful bunch, "All three of you will be safe from now on. I know it because my husband will make sure of it. You'll stay with us for a few days, and then we'll decide what is to be done."

At home John and Sally made up a corn shuck pallet in the sheltered corner of the back porch and the woman and her two children slept there, safe and well fed for the first time, and at first light, John hitched the mule to the wagon and drove through the county gathering the descent men.

Each one of the vigilantes was remarkably level headed when they dragged the mean little man from the sharecropper's cabin. In the yard under the big oak tree each man asked the little man a question and each man listened to his remarks which added up to a complete denial of any wrong doin' even whippin' his boy as he walked past the Owens place. Then it was John's turn and the little man once again stood in defiance as John spoke.

"These men know me to be a good and law abiding husband and Pa. They know I would never accuse anyone unjustly and you sir, are a liar and a rapist and right here and now, you will be punished for that."

This group of six men beat the little man to within an inch of his life, and it was a beating well deserved but no one took any pleasure in it. The last words spoken were from John Owens, "I'll bring your family back to this cabin in a few days, and when I do this better be a different place. Now you get busy cleaning up yourself and this pigsty you live in, and both had better stay clean in all manner of speaking. Do you understand?"

The little man said nothing until John shook his fist in the little man's face, and finally the little man nodded his head that he understood. John warned, "You can count on some one of us to come calling at least once a day every day from now on and if we ever see any sign that you're back to your old tricks, the lot of us will come here, ask no questions and hang you from this here big oak tree and that is our solemn promise to your family"

Back at home, John watched as Sally rekindled a sense of pride and good hope in the wife and children. Sally tended their wounds to body and spirit, they were strays to be nurtured and petted, and her kindness captured in their faces shouted louder than the mean and destructive hell of their lives thus far, and on Sunday they walked with the Owens family to Campground Church wearing clothes the good neighbors of the county found fit to share which looked mighty nice when Sally finished altering and patching, and they learned to hold their heads high confident they themselves as victims were not judged as inferior and the future would certainly bring better times.

I've never mentioned any names involved in this sad story, and this telling is far removed and completely disconnected to the Bethel settlement today, the sharecropper's cabin is rotten with age and no more than a pile of debris, and the family has moved on, and it is my intent to tell this story this one time and never again because it's best to look ahead and not back, and these sharecroppers would a never been able to look ahead if they were branded by gossip, they'd never of had a chance a getting past these unspeakable things, and the total of six vigilantes have never mentioned the little man's disgusting and vile crimes, never, not once, to any soul in the world.

As it so happened, the little man and his family stayed in the sharecropper's cabin and worked the fields for many, many years, and they are well thought of to this day. But as long as they lived in the sharecropper's cabin and that was onwards to thirty years, well there was never a single day that went by that some one of the six men didn't enter that cabin unannounced just to pass the time of day.

1927 Shooting Accident

When Bert was eighteen he lost his left arm in a shooting accident; I was with him when it happened. I was sixteen. It was a dusty June day and me and Bert went off into the wood to walk along the creek since we knew the lay of the land like the back of our hand, but we set out anyway a carrying a shotgun, for in the summer months, we never walked any where not in the woods, not down the road, not in the fields, and sometimes not even across the yard to the barn without carrying a shot gun, and it certainly was not for hunting because everybody knows better than to shoot any animal when there might be young ones depending on the mama, no sir we didn't hunt in the summer, but we carried a shotgun to shoot snakes and I don't mean just any non-poisonous snakes for we never wasted ammunition in killing them, but there were plenty a poisonous snakes which we recognized copper heads, rattlers and water moccasins, and we thought it wise to use as many bullets as it took to kill one of them mean snakes, and that day when we came out of the woods onto the road after walking the creek for hours, we stopped on the little wooden bridge between us and the Jasper Hicks place, and Bert had the single barrel, twelve gauge shotgun, and we were picking and eating big old juicy blackberries from the briar bushes a leaning way out over the bridge weighted down with dozens of heavy, big, ripe blackberries. I was down stream of the bridge in my own blackberry heaven while Bert stayed on the bridge propped on the shotgun with the discharge end tucked under his left arm like a crutch, and as he leaned beyond the edge of the bridge in order to reach a bunch of blackberries, the stock of the shotgun slipped off the bridge, and the hammer hit the bridge and fired directly into Bert's upper left arm and shoulder.

I must a made a big commotion coming into the yard, and I don't remember it, but I guess I carried Bert from the bridge to the home place with his bloody arm a dangling, and I must a been yelling cause what I saw was everybody a coming a running in a panic, and I heard the chicken feed bucket crash to the ground, and Doc was yelling, "Take him into the kitchen."

Someone went running ahead of me into the house and pushed everything off the table, and I had plenty of help when it come to placing

Bert's lifeless body on the kitchen table and I leaned down to Bert's mouth hoping to feel his breath against my cheek and I stayed standing in place at the end of the table for I knew only one thing to do and that was to hold Bert's head in an effort to comfort him, and Mose grabbed the dish rag and pushed it into Bert's bloody shoulder, and without hesitation, Doc pulled his sharp knife from his pocket, poked it into the red hot coals inside the cook stove and cut the remainder of the arm away from Bert's body, and like a man with blinders on he began skinning the severed arm. When Doc could remove a six-inch by six-inch piece of skin from the dead arm, he raced to the washbasin and poured boric acid over the skin, and thankfully, Bert was still unconscious.

Doc washed the wound with boric acid while Essie retrieved his little black medicine bag from the office, and Doc cauterized the blood vessels in Bert's shoulder to stop the gushing blood. With the grafting skin in place, Doc began sewing ragged edges together. Mose struck a match to light kerosene lamps for it was getting dark, and under adverse conditions, Doc worked into the night. Essie added wood to the fire in the cook stove and everybody was doing something, anything to help. Two or three held lamps for light in the now pitch dark kitchen and a rotation started when the lamps became too heavy. No one spoke.

Doc instructed Mose to wrap the remainder of Bert's dead arm in a clean white sheet, which all sheets back then were made out of sugar or feed sacks. I did not leave Bert's side, and I held his face in my shaking hands and leaned over as I talked to him. He was still out cold, but I thought he might hear my soothing words so I kept on crooning as Essie and Sis cut his bloody clothes from his body. Essie's younger children drew water from the well, and someone went outside to bury the clothes, and Essie bathed Bert's twitching body, and I kept on talking to Bert and to God.

"You're gona be alright."

"Doc knows what to do."

"Dear God, please help Doc know what to do."

"Just rest now."

"God please don't forsake us."

About midnight, Doc instructed Mose to take Bert's arm to the cemetery.

"Bury it by the light of the moon. Dig a deep grave, and when it's covered, hard pack the dirt and scatter the leaves to hide the grave for you alone will know where the arm is buried and if Bert wants to know you will be the one to tell him."

As the night dragged by, a few of the children curled up on the floor and maybe they slept for an hour or two, but Mose, Sis, Essie, and Doc sat at the table surrounding Bert all through the night, and I stood holding Bert's head until sun-up, and at first light, Essie made coffee and biscuits and gravy which no one ate much, but the coffee helped us stay awake. Bert was moaning and still unconscious. The children stood up from the kitchen floor, stretched out the kinks and one by one ate a little and drank some coffee, The work of a farm waits for no one, but as soon as the chores were done, again everyone gathered around Bert's quiet still body, and each time he twitched or cried out, we too were stabbed with his pain.

Bert was on that kitchen table unconscious for two days, Doc considered loading him in my car and driving him to the hospital in Heflin, but each time Doc ended that line a thinking with the decision that Bert was better off right here until he made some progress away from the catastrophic accident and gained a modicum of strength, and when Bert finally came to, he was pitiful sorry to be a one-armed man. We gently pushed a quilt under him and grabbed a hold, three of us on each side, and carried him to bed where he passed out again. Essie and twelve-year-old Sis washed his red puffy shoulder all through the night and day as a means of calming infection and with Doc's suggestion they added a tidbit of salt to each wash pan of clear well water poured from the kettle on the cookstove. Bert's fever caused him to talk out of his head in nonsensical ramblings until on the tenth day when his medical supplies were exhausted, Doc decided we'd take Bert to a hospital and the best facility within reasonable driving range would be Anniston, Alabama. We loaded Bert into Doc's Model T and made him as comfortable as we could with feather pillows and quilts and Mose and Sis crouched in the floor board to hold him steady on the seat and Essie rode up front with Doc, and we filled my Model T with everybody else who would not hear to staying behind, and we set out driving to Anniston, and it was a good thing we got him to a hospital for Doc realized blood poisoning had set in and Bert stayed in the hospital for ten days with Doc overseeing his care, and when we brought him back home, one morning while Essie was cooking breakfast, Bert staggered into the kitchen not yet strong enough to pull his clothes on, but as a matter of expediency he wrapped himself in a quilt and walked the distance to the table bundled up; and he sat there while Essie pinched a biscuit into little pieces and spooned gravy over the pieces, and he fed himself and held a cup of coffee so he could sip (Essie poured only a half cup for his hand was shaky and weak), and he ate everything on his plate and finished his coffee, and he stayed up sitting at the kitchen table for an hour or more, while Mose shaved him, and I helped him pull his pants on, and he said it sure felt good to be alive, and it was mighty hard to find fault with that way a putting it, but he asked for help getting back to his bed, and he slept through the afternoon and all through the night and into the next day, and that was the beginning of his return to good health, and with every passing day he gained more and more vigor, and he profited by so much help and mothering that finally he got a little cross and belted out that he was ready for the molly coddling to end, so we all stepped back so he'd have the space to rebuild his life, and he made us all proud as he learned to shave one handed and button his shirt one handed, and pretty soon, he was doing most things for himself, but he was weak, and one day a neighbor come to visit and brought in a newspaper, The Cleburne News, and he read out loud to us:

Loses Arm In Gun Accident
Bert Godwin, young farmer in Beat 2, was shot in the left arm by the accidental discharge of a shotgun about ten days ago, and was reported on Wednesday to be slowly recovering in an Anniston hospital where he was carried for medical attention, following the accident. The arm was badly mangled above the elbow by the discharge of the shot and as blood poisoning set in, it was amputated at the shoulder joint.

This newspaper depiction was not quite accurate, as to the actual facts, and the article didn't give Doc the credit he deserved, but anyways, it was a fine thing to have the accident written about so all the county would know and after it's appearance, there was a steady stream of Cleburne County neighbors stopping by to visit and to help pass the time as Bert continued on the long road to recovery.

During that time of adjustment Bert and Doc stayed drunk sometimes for a week or more at a time. They'd sober up for a while, and then go on another drunk, and Mose did double time completing their chores and his too and shielding them so none of us could find any reason for getting irritated with them, but I'm not sure that was necessary for we all realized they had every right to handle this uniquely difficult situation in whatever manner they figured was best, but I guess Mose thought they needed the numbness of a drunken stupor free from explanation or justification for sooner or later Bert had to accept the loss of his arm, and Doc had to accept his failure to prevent the typhoid that killed Ma.

1928

Mose hated the whiskey making trade, but he was running two stills (his and Bert's), and Mose did this for his one armed brother, out of the goodness of his heart. This way Bert could go back to running his own still when he was completely recovered, and meanwhile, Mose kept Bert's still operating and producing enough whiskey so Bert's regular customers wouldn't leave him and find another supplier. The sad thing was that Bert was drinking the profits. Mose used the cash money to buy sugar and jars and every batch produced a bonus of several gallons that a smart businessman could turn for a profit, but Bert and Doc drank that bonus and swallowed the profit.

We got a letter from Thomas. He was still working in the Bakery of Valdosta and was sorry to hear of Bert's accident. Mose wrote back to Thomas that Bert was doing fine and getting stronger every day, and all the boys, now 'bout near grown, were still playing pranks, except now, Bert was just a little more selective about who he pushed in the dry well, and when he couldn't resist doing the mischief, at least he was sure to have at least one two-armed brother close by so as to have help a pulling 'em out, and even though Bert continued with the pushing, never again, not even once did Bert himself get pushed in the well .... Any body with eyes could see why.

I saw defeat in Bert's and Doc's attitude, it seemed like they both sort of lost their will to get ahead in life. Bert was running wild and kept company with one girl in town. I was about to turn seventeen and I could see as plane as the nose on my face that at nineteen, my one armed brother needed a good solid education if he was to amount to a hill of beans, so I convinced him to enter Tallapoosa High School, and God bless his soul, he was more than willing for a chance at a future. Those were mighty hard times for any man with two eyes and two arms, so I made arrangements for Bert's room and board in Tallapoosa, and I set up a schedule to pay his room and board and to give him a little spending money all along. I suggested the spending money part for he needed to concentrate on his studies instead of working, and I was happy to pay for my brother's paper and pencils, and thankfully the school and books were free.

Tallapoosa High School had a football team, but just barely for the school was small, but they had eleven boys and that was exactly the correct number needed to make up a football team. Bert got to going to Friday afternoon football games which pushed his time to come home into Saturday morning, he'd hitch hike or walk home even though it was fourteen miles each way but he wanted to get home so as to share with us the excitement of the football game, and he was real good at comparing Tallapoosa's football team to the opponent's team, and he pretty much described every minute of the game to us, and before long, we looked forward to the report and felt like we knew the players, but Bert's description of the rules of the game were sketchy at best, but no matter we got involved in his post game analysis, and it became an amusing pastime which the whole family anticipated all through the week, and we were mighty proud that Tallapoosa High School's football team was doing pretty good that year.

Bert had lessons on week ends so at home I helped him with his arithmetic because arithmetic was easy for me and had made sense to me since real early in my life when my Pa started me doing figures in my head, but when it come time for Bert's science and reading lessons well then the situation reversed and he was my teacher, but he said he learned more a working with me than he learned all week in the classroom, and I liked learning all subjects right along with Bert. After his first year at Tallapoosa High School, Bert made use of his summer out of school to work his still, and he was proud to tell me he'd saved some money and wouldn't need spending money from me at least not for a while. So in the fall, I drove Bert back to his boarding home in Tallapoosa for he was entering his second year of high school, and he was dressed in his new store bought clothes, a white shirt like mine for I bought both his and mine at O. D. Lipham's in Tallapoosa. I bought a lot of my clothes in that store, but some clothes I ordered from the Sears and Roebuck catalog and the peddler was always real nice to go about returning an order in case of a bad fit, but still it was a lot easier to buy clothes at O. D. Lipham's because of that private little room at the back of the store under the wide staircase where I could try on the clothes before I paid for them. The small up-stairs at O. D. Lipham's was used mostly as a bookkeeper's office although some dry goods like snuff and chewing tobacco and cigarettes were kept up there in a long glass display case. This up-stairs was built to protrude from the back wall out over the main floor by no more than about twelve feet, and the ceiling under the up-stairs was still pretty high at ten or eleven feet, so you can imagine that the main part of the store which was real big and roomy from the front door all the way back to the up-stairs part had a very high ceiling of way on up to twenty foot. When I was looking at the men's clothes in this fine and roomy store, if I found anything I liked, Mrs. Lipham took the articles from me and placed them on the nails pounded into the walls on the inside of the little trying-on room, and once inside the little under-the-stairs changing room, which was no bigger than an outhouse, you had to hold the curtain open with one hand in order to have enough light to see how to switch on the electric light bulb hanging at the end of an electric wire swinging from the ceiling which I hit it with my head the first time I entered the little room, and so I knew to feel around and find the dangling pull string and turn on the electric light, and then close the cloth curtain for privacy, and I understood why Mrs. Lipham did not turn on the electric light and that was because it would be an unnecessary expense added to the already too high light bill. Inside that little room, there was a long mirror propped up in a straight back chair so I could see what I looked like and how the new britches and shirts fit me before I put down a penny of cash money payment. The fit of my clothes was important to me 'cause I like nothing better than going around dressed up like a big time operator, and I don't like to wear clothes that look like they were bought for a taller man, I want my clothes to look like they were made for me.

Football Game

Anyway, on our way into town me and Bert rode right past the football field where the team was practicing for the upcoming game against Bowdon on Friday night, so after we watched the practice for a while, Bert commented that he could count only ten boys out on the practice field, this didn't mean anything to me, until Bert explained again that a football team needs eleven boys to play a game. Another feller was watching the practice and his name was Bant Bailey, and I noticed that he too was dressed real nice, and when Bant heard us talking, he told us that one team member was out with a broken toe and then Bant said, "He'll more 'an likely be out for this Friday night's game, and if Tallapoosa doesn't have eleven players for the game with Bowdon, we'll be forced to forfeit the game."

So we watched the football practice for a little while longer, and then I left for I had whiskey deliveries to make and Bant Bailey was to give Bert a ride on to the boarding home so Bert transferred his shaving mug and razor, and his one change of clothes from my car over to Bant's car.

That next Friday afternoon I drove into town to pick up Bert because I had to buy ten sacks of sugar at Mini Jackson's store for at that time, I was running a ten sack pot, which means I was running a good sized still producing enough whiskey to make me a lot of money in a time when men in other lines of work were making just enough money to keep from starving to death. When I pulled up to the boarding home, Bert came a running out to the car all excited. He was babbling about the football game in Bowdon, and he directed me to drive south out of Tallapoosa, so I was heading south which was not the way back to the Godwin home place, when Bert mentioned that I was to play in the football game tonight.

"What do you mean when you say, 'You've got to play in the game?' Are you crazy? I watched practice for ten minutes, and I've never seen an actual football game."

"Come on, Shug, you know I'd play if I had two arms." This one got me every time and Bert knew it.

"I'm not a student at Tallapoosa High School."

"Well your one-armed brother is."

With that one, I knew just exactly what he was doing because it was just another jab in Bert's now familiar tactic. This banter continued until we pulled up to the football field at Bowdon High School which is about fifteen miles down south of Tallapoosa, and we saw that the game must a been delayed because nobody was playing football, instead everybody in uniform or not in uniform was just wandering around the field, and it was getting on toward sun down, and I found out later that they actually delayed the game until I got there. When I got out of the car, somebody grabbed me by the arm and pulled me along while he unbuttoned and took off my shirt, and on the other side of me was another son of a bitch undoing my belt buckle to drop my pants, and before I got my bearings, I was wearing a pull-over-the-head shirt with a big number sewed to the front, and I was skipping along and about to fall for I was tangled up in some knee length pants which were jerked up onto me and rope tied at my waist. Somebody else placed a leather hat (they called it a helmet) on my head and pulled the chinstrap in place, which was too tight, and some good for nothing idiot slapped me on the butt and pushed me out on the grassy field. It was getting dark and a great big hubbub somehow produced enough cars parked door to door all the way up and down on both sidelines, and with the headlights turned on and aimed to the center of the playing field it lit up the place real good, and now everybody wearing a numbered shirt lined up on the field in two lines facing each other, eleven boys on the other team, and now eleven counting me on the Tallapoosa team. Somebody pushed me into position, and I watched as everybody got down in a crouching position, so I did too.

Somebody yelled, "Hut" and all hell broke loose.

I was busy trying to save a life, my own, when a great big old boy grabbed me and slung me to the ground, I guess because I happened to be standing beside the man with the football tucked into the crook of his arm, and while I was on the ground, two or three boys ran over me, I mean they stepped right on me and it hurt too. The Tallapoosa team pushed me into the line-up again where I found myself facing the same Bowden player, and this time I knew enough that nobody had to tell me to get into a crouching position, and I crouched down just before that dreaded word.

"Hut"

The same big ugly boy threw me to the ground again, and I got up and walked off the field before they had time to push me into the line-up one more time, and you can believe that I was as mad as a hornet. I walked to the sideline of the field right to Bant Bailey again, "Bant, give me my knife out of my pants pocket, I'm gona cut the next son of a bitch who punches me in the ribs or steps on me while I'm down."

Bant said, "Listen Shug, a lot's depending on you. This year is the big chance for Tallapoosa's team. They did real good last year, and they're gona be even better this year, and they could wind up being the state champions, so you've just gotta get 'em through this game. They'll have eleven players for every game the rest of the season, just not tonight, and if they forfeit this game, they're out of the running for the championship. Now go out there and try to figure out what you're supposed to do, and then do it."

So I did it, I played the entire game, and I might have been pretty good, but I didn't like being pushed and shoved and stepped on and thrown to the ground over and over again. I was sore for a week, and another thing, I for damn sure, never went into town on a Friday night again, or at least not near the football field.

Vesta was thirteen years old on January 7, 1929, and back then all the girls in the county worked in the fields and most of the boys made whiskey, which wadn't by choice, but by necessity. Making whiskey wasn't considered a bad or evil thing, but simply a way to keep from starving. It was hard work, but it paid well if you knew how to manage your business. We'd go to school in the dead of winter, and the rest of the year Bethel and Crossroads schools were shut down.

I found out that one of my brothers fathered a baby and didn't marry the baby's mother or give her any money to help feed the baby. Most everybody in town knows which one of my brothers it is that's the baby's pa, everybody has always known, but I don't talk about it, and that little boy and his mother became another responsibility of mine, but I'm not complaining, I wanted to give the poor girl a little money, and I did because I thought of that baby as a part of the Godwin family, and I still do to this day. That baby is a grown man now and so is his brother. There were two babies born out of wedlock, and I've never been ashamed to claim them because they are fine upstanding men.

"Vesta, walk the rows and lay down the fodder."

"Aw Papa, let Theda, I want to sew my dress."

"Vesta, you know your sister'll need a recipe to walk the rows and lay down the fodder."

Vesta knew her Papa was right. Theda might be awkward and slow moving, but she was not stupid. She just needs a recipe to do anything, and in contrast, Vesta could stomp down the fodder and then finish sewing her dress before sundown. She wanted a new dress to wear to school the next day, her first day in sixth grade.

The teacher, Mr. Mullino decided where the pupils sat in class. Since we were in the same grade in our studies, Mr. Mullino assigned Vesta to sit beside me on the same bench in the back row. We were in the sixth grade at the same time, sitting side by side on the same bench, and me five years older. The work on a place comes first and school has to come second so most of the boys in Bethel school were several years older than the girls in their same grade.

Sitting next to Vesta made the school day go by faster because I liked her a lot, and she was for sure the prettiest girl in the Bethel Community and when I could, I walked her home from school. She was so sweet and I liked talking to her for she seemed to be interested in learning and improving her mind.

As we ambled along I asked, "Why are you toting the science book home?"

Vesta replied, "I want to read more about today's lesson."

It was hard for me to keep my mind on Science when all I really wanted was to admire Vesta's red curls and creamy white skin, but by nodding now and then, I managed to convince her of my sincere interest which wasn't atall the truth, and actually, I was mesmerized by the sunlight's emphasis on the dancing ringlets that covered her head and bounced off her shoulders, and their glossy shimmer left me befuddled and oddly adrift, and I purposely let her get just a step or two ahead of me so as the distance gave me a full vision of her beautiful curls, and when I paid her a compliment, her embarrassment was obvious, and she revealed to me that her hair was a source of shame, and certainly not pride which melted my heart with compassion.

I guess that was the first time of many times that I tried to convince Vesta that her hair is not ugly, but instead and to the contrary it is easily the prettiest hair in the county if not the world, and when the sun hit it just right, the lighter streaks mixed in with the darker red curls in a pattern that could stop a healthy man's heart from beating, and that day as we lagged along behind the others by a greater and greater distance which offered a degree of privacy or else I never would have had the nerve to squeeze her hand in mine.

I stayed at the Owens home place till after nightfall helping with the chores and sitting down to supper, and when I set out for home, I inhaled the pine perfume, watched the path of a falling star, and listened to a chorus of four or more whip-er-wills which as was the usual thing filled my heart with longing at first for my Pa, but now the sadness I carried inside me included a hope for another chance to hold Vesta's hand.

As I walked along, I came to from my dreaming to the eerie cry of a screech owl, screaming like a woman getting killed off down in the woods so I took my felt hat off and held it in my hand and started running as fast as I could, and when I finally reached the clearing at the Bethel Cemetery, I heard a rustling sound in the leaves on the far side which drained the blood right smack out of my head, and I thought I was about to pass out, and when I tried to introduce some sanity into my panic, I could reason with myself all I cared to, but the truth found a back recess in my mind when I argued the two new tall monuments I knew very well were in place because me and Sis walked past them just this morning and again after school let out, and we all walked right past them on our way to the Owens home place, and even though I knew just exactly where the tall new monuments stood and what they looked like, my mind played a trick on me, and in the shadows and moonlight, the tall monuments looked like two short men, and it was a simple matter to encourage my self-induced hallucination as the two short men moved and nodded agreement in their scheme to kidnap me, and it was plain to see they both wore covers like hoods over their heads, and I was pretty sure they were plotting some evil deed that would count as my demise, so my feet (now unattached from my body and carrying out their own accord) decided to make a run for it, past the short, devious strangers wearing the eerie drapes hiding their faces and as I ran full speed into the open space of the cemetery, I heard the crunching sound of feet breaking through the knee deep forest floor of dead leaves and sticks and as a third devil came closer and closer in pursuit and right when I reached the spot close enough to where the two monuments could reach out and grab a hold of me, in my mind I calculated there had to be at least three and maybe more of these evil doers hemming me in, but at once, I deciphered the unusual idée that the two hooded demons waiting in ambush couldn't possibly stand so still, stone still, which I'd a figured out right about that minute the incongruous phenomena and maybe my lungs could a been allowed to fill with oxygen, except for the scariest possibility which unfolded when my tracker came running across right through the middle of the cemetery and stopped me dead in my tracks and somehow the wicked thing slipped right between the two tall monuments and jumped up on me, I mean two cold wet slimy fists slammed against my chest and expunged the last little oxygen remaining in my lungs and a mighty wave of relief washed over me when Ole Boss started licking my face, and I can tell you that old dog and me ran the rest of the way home, one full mile, and we didn't slow down for nothing.

Vesta said more than once that she thought I was the smartest boy in school which always made me feel like a million dollars, and a course she more-n-likely just believed me to be brilliant because none of the other boys could do figures in their head, but to me that was a simple thing that might near anybody could do, for I was only eight when my pa died, and by that time he'd been making me learn arithmetic in my head for years and that's something that's always come easy for me.

Vesta kept chickens, and sold eggs and sometimes a fryer to the peddler and sometimes when the peddler didn't have any money to pay her, she'd trade her eggs for a piece of material. She wore pretty dresses all the time for she was like me and wanted to look nice, but she also wore a hat all the time, and one day I asked her why, and she told me again just how much she was ashamed of her red hair, she thought it looked unnatural and hideous, and again like many times before, I tried to get her to understand that her hair was beautiful to look at for it was shiny, curly and a knock out gorgeous deep red color, but she thought the color was ugly and nothing I could say was going to change her mind.

She finished the last stitches of her new dress just as Sally called out that supper was ready so Vesta folded the treadle Singer sewing machine into its cabinet and stood back to admire the Singer sewing machine's beauty, and thought to herself "It's as beautiful as any fancy piece of art work."

She loved the graceful scrolling black wrought iron base and the beautiful, quarter-sawn, oak wood cabinet for she's an artist who sees beauty in places that ordinary people don't see, and as she carefully placed her new dress on a peg in the back bedroom and headed for the kitchen, she heard her Papa ask Theda. "Where's Vesta? I need some milk."

"Here Papa, I'll get the pitcher." Theda said.

"All right Theda, slosh me some buttermilk."

Vesta smiled and understood her Papa's choice of words for Theda remained in an awkward stage and usually poured as much on the table as in the glass.

Sally came in the back door with garlic and onion stalks in her hand, the first greens on the table in the spring and the last in the fall. John especially liked the fresh garlic stalks with his cornbread and buttermilk. He crumbled the cornbread into his glass and waited as Theda poured buttermilk over it, this time spilling only a drop or two on the oilcloth table cover, and as was the custom, with a spoon he ate and drank the mixture right out of the glass. Sally poured a little hot bacon grease from an iron skillet directly over the cornbread crumbs and green onion bits on her plate. She preferred the taste of the hot-grease-wilted spring onion and garlic greens and she ate this off her plate with a fork and drank her glass of well-cooled buttermilk (which means the jar of buttermilk was capped tightly and rope lowered to the bottom of the well to cool.)

Theda sat down on the bench along the back side of the table and slid to the middle winding up in the middle next to Chester who was already seated at the other end of the bench next to the tall home built cabinet which had never been painted or finished in any way but the aged and gray wood grain was obvious and beautiful to both John and his oldest daughter. Vesta sat down on the bench to sit next to Theda, Jack brought the pump organ stool to the table and Little Ruth stood beside Jack for at age seven, she was just the right height to stand up to eat at the table. Sally's chair was closest to the wood burning cook stove and the back door and John sat at the opposite end at the head of the table with the tall cabinet to his left. He remembered and appreciated George Vaughn's help in building the simple cupboard years before when he and Sally lived here alone.

In the comfortable silence, Vesta dreamily admired the shape of the old milk pitcher, and in her mind, she imagined the pattern of greenish blue spots on the ceramic pitcher to represent fluid drops that increased in size as they dripped from the small diameter of the rim and became larger spots increasing in size down the sides from top to bottom. "Do you like the curtains I made?"

Theda and Ruth both said they did.

John asked, "Where did you get the money for that foolishness?"

"I traded the peddler two dozen eggs for the cloth, Papa. Don't you think the curtains are pretty?"

"Yeah, the curtains are pretty," her Papa said with a snort.

Vesta looked around the room and admired the cast iron cook stove and the clean, wavy-glass windowpanes on each side of the fireplace sparkling in the evening sunlight. The beauty she appreciated all around the room and for that matter all around her everywhere she looked outside the house and inside the house was of no importance to most of her family except for her Papa's great admiration for the out-a-doors. It was John Owens who studied wildlife and taught himself the names of trees and birds and wildflowers and all manner of nature in the wild, but Sally and the other Owens children looked past all this and found no need to take notice. They all looked right past every day what Vesta prized and for an example, Vesta even admired the curves of the boric acid bottle her papa kept on the sill above the door for the door frame was exposed as were all the two-by-fours used to frame out this newest part of the house. It made for cold winters and hot summers inside the house and a family joke was that sometimes you could go to sleep in one bed and wake up in another if the wind picked up in the middle of the night.

None but Vesta in the family and not even John himself could see the beauty of that old boric acid bottle, and when flowers bloomed, Vesta brought them into the house and put them in water in an old rusty tin can and combined with the sparkling clean window panes, the freshly washed and ironed floral print curtains, and the cherished furnishings of the house, Vesta could see what was as obvious as the nose on a face, that the world was a beautiful and charming place and such furniture pieces as her mama's Sears and Roebuck dresser with the quarter sawn oak patterns provided peace and serenity through delicate loveliness, all be it though the wavy glass mirror kept Theda convinced she was deformed since her reflection looked not at all like the other members of her family.

Pump Organ

Along then John ordered a pump organ from the Sears and Roebuck catalog because he wanted to hear music in the house, and he figured that Vesta could learn how to play since she could do just about anything she set her mind to, and when the peddler brought the six foot tall pump organ to the Owens house, it was strapped to the peddler wagon rooftop because it was too big to fit inside, and at his last stop before turning off the main road and heading for the Owens place, the peddler asked Eb Kilgore to follow him so as to help haul the tall heavy oak pump organ into the Owens house, and Sally and the girls were dancing and giggling to see such a grand piece of furniture, and when the peddler and Eb rode off, John answered his family's excited questions with, "I've already paid for twenty lessons, Vesta starts learning to play this here pump organ tomorrow."

Vesta walked to the music teacher's house which was over close to Crossroads School, and for an hour once a week she began to learn how to play the pump organ, and the teacher said she learned quicker than anybody she'd ever taught, and that fall after just about ten lessons, Vesta played the piano at Camp Ground Church one Sunday, and she played one Sunday every month for many years. This whole business was because John wanted to hear music in his home and Vesta entertained the family and visitors just about every night, and it was plain to see that John was very proud of his little girl.

One Sunday in church, while Vesta was playing "Come Thou Fount of Every Blessing," Sally's brother Alec's girl Geneva and Theda started giggling out of control until John finally pinched Theda, but the pinch did nothing to calm the girls and when the song ended and every one sat down their continued laughter actually caused the pew to shake and make a squeaking racket and of course this made the situation even more laughable for the young girls.

On the walk home, Theda told her angry Papa that when everybody sung out the words, "Here I raise mine Ebenezer." Geneva whispered into Theda's ear, "I'm not raising mine til I find out what it is."

The next night after supper, Vesta cleared the table and washed the dishes and went to the well on the back porch to draw water to refill the hot water basin on the side of the cook stove, and as Theda dried the dishes and put them away, she declared she'd tell another funny story about the spelling bee at Bethel school today.

"Maskal's word to spell was "shirt." He wasn't sure of the spelling and slowly said, "S......H......" The waiting was agony for Mr. Mullino who finally prompted Maskal to continue. Standing next to Maskal in the line of spellers was Shug. Shug bent his head down to his chest so the teacher couldn't see his lips move and whispered just loud enough for Maskal and no one else to hear "I ...T." Without considering the consequences, Maskal blurted out the last two letters just as Shug had whispered them. Even the teacher had to laugh. All the children were shouting to Maskal that he had spelled a bad word. Maskal started laughing too, and he watched as Shug threw back his head and lifted and slapped his leg as laughter shook his shoulders in a familiar jerking motion. Shug's the best one to have a good time."

Vesta went to the edge of the back porch and threw out the dishwater and returned to the kitchen and started dipping more hot water into the wash pan.

"Vesta, what are you doing?"

"I need to wash my hair, mama."

"You washed your hair last week after we made soap. Surely you aren't going to wash it again so soon."

"A week's long enough to wait, mama, I want my hair clean and shiny."

"Well, I'm just afraid it'll make you sick."

No one in the room spoke of the pity they all shared for their gentle Mama. They understood her endless pain grieving, and they understood that nineteen years is not long enough to recover from loosing a baby and since baby Hazel died on the very night that Sally washed her hair somehow along the way the act of washing her baby's hair had become entangled in her mind and now the cause of death was certainly Sally's mistake of washing the baby's hair, and now all these many years later, John and all five of Sally's children understand that their Mama will never get past the pain.

The family drifted out of the kitchen and gathered by the fireplace in the old log cabin part of the house, which everyone in the family calls the 'big house'. The weather had been unseasonably warm so they didn't build a fire to knock off the slight chill in the room and besides that they all knew not to waste, so as not to want, and it simply wadn't cold enough to waste a single stick of firewood. John asked Vesta to play the organ, Jack retrieved the organ stool from the kitchen and Ruth and Theda sat on the bed while Vesta played "Amazing Grace."

The half log, half plank house was double the size of the original log cabin, and now the Owen's home place was big and spacious with four rooms. John and Sally started out married life in the one room log cabin, but after their five children were born, John built a new kitchen and a new bedroom out of rough sawn planks, and not until the girls got up old enough to require more privacy a bathing and dressing did the one last inside wall come into being, so while the men worked outside of the house tending the farm, the girls and Sally worked inside the house building a partition to separate off a small bedroom from the biggest part of the original roomy oversized log cabin, and the plank wall they built was very nice on the fireplace side but was never finished (or planked in) on the back side, but this resulted in a handy storage wall on the small bedroom side as the framing two-by-four's became convenient shelves on the bedroom side while the plank side of the wall facing the big fireplace room was a very nice solid wall with an open door way right in the middle, and for more privacy, Vesta made and hung a white feed-sack curtain to cover the door opening, and the feed-sack curtain could be pushed aside to open or easily pulled shut to close, and directly in the middle of this long, to-the-floor, door-way curtain, along the seam that joined the top large feed-sack section to the bottom large feed sack section, Vesta embroidered a fancy angular block design using very nice thick, shiny red embroidery thread, and the top half of this long feed-sack curtain was an exact copy of the shorter feed-sack curtains hanging at the two windows, one window in the little back bedroom squarely across the room from the doorway, and the other short curtain hanging at the window to the left of the fireplace in the larger log cabin room. The only difference in the three curtains being length for the window curtains were short and hung just to the bottom of the windowpanes. On the short window curtains Vesta embroidered the red block design along the bottom, and as it turned out the red designs embroidered on all three curtains were precisely at the same level up from the floor, which was very artistic.

The little long, narrow bedroom was just wide enough for a bed at one end and the girls and Sally placed a small table and wash pan at the other end of the room, and they drove ten penny nails into the exposed two-by-fours and these nails together with the wooden pegs already drilled into the logs created a place to hang all the family's spare clean clothes, and this made a fine room where Sally and little Ruth slept. Vesta and Theda shared the bed by the fireplace, and also in that room stood the pump organ, the Sears Roebuck oak dresser (with the wavy mirror), and the Singer sewing machine which was placed in front of the window beside the fireplace for to sew by the best daylight, and even with a portion of the room partitioned off, this was still the largest room in the house, and because of its comfortable size, it now served as the parlor and bedroom combined.

After church when the preacher came to Sunday dinner, Chester and Jack took down the bed and leaned it against the wall, and Sally covered the leaning bed with one of her prized hand made quilts made from leftover sewing scrapes, and there were a gracious plenty of leftover sewing scraps since Vesta now sewed for the whole entire county it seemed like. It was and still is a general way of life to make your own clothing and curtains and whenever store bought material is used it is imperative that each and every scrap no matter how small be added to the scrap bag, which is anything BUT a bag stuffed with trash as it's name implies, no indeed just the opposite is true, the scrap bag is treasured beyond imagining because from these little scrap pieces of fabric ladies everywhere exercise their finest artistic skills and create works of art, and just by looking over a quilt remembering the garments worn on special occasions, the garments worn in infancy, the garments worn everyday working in the fields picking cotton or laying down the fodder, or burning the fields in the fall when an enchanting embers light show is carefully contained and managed late into the night.

Sally took exceptional steps and sewed into every quilt one small sentimental scrap of her sister Ollie's brown traveling suit or scrap from Ollie's blue marrying suit, which made Sally sad and happy at the same time. She liked to show off her quilts, and after dinner, the men moved the chairs and the bench from the kitchen table into the makeshift parlor, and Vesta played the organ. It was very nice.

One cold January, after completing their morning chores, the five Owens children Chester, Jack, Vesta, Theda and little Ruth left the house to walk the wagon road through the thick woods to Bethel school. It was quiet and peaceful, the air felt crisp and clean. The boys were wearing over-hauls, long sleeve shirts, and denim jackets they called jumpers. The girls were wearing cotton dresses and each had a wool coat but not one coat fit properly, the sleeves of Vesta's coat hit her arm well above the wrist, although Vesta was the oldest, Theda was now a little bit taller and so Theda was wearing the biggest coat and even the biggest coat was actually too little for her, and Little Ruth's smallest coat was so long on her that to be safe she held it up when she ran because a time or two she had tripped on the hem which almost dragged the ground. The ill-fitting coats and clothes didn't matter to the children as they chattered and laughed and skipped along happy as could be. Vesta was intent on the wild life, and in fact she urged them to listen, "If yall'll be quiet, I'll identify the bird calls we hear along the way."

John taught Vesta to recognize birds and trees by name just as he would have taught all his children, but the others weren't interested, but there was one tree in the forest that all of the Owens children recognized, and I mean they recognized it in any season and that was a black gum tree because in the fall of the year every one in the family knew to watch for the breath-taking colors as the black gum trees leaves turned spectacular colors including purple and gold and deep brownish red all on the same black gum tree, and with the memory of the black gum trees' brilliant colors seared into their minds, all of the Owens children could easily locate them in any season where they grew along the road and bordering the plowed fields, and even in the dead of winter when the only leaves were the brown dry ones on the ground they all followed their Papa's requirement for he insisted with zeal that they brush their teeth at least once a day with a stem off a black gum tree. John Owens believed in taking care of his own teeth, and he was absolutely passionate that his children do the same, so he taught each one at an early age how to make a black gum toothbrush and to scrub their teeth and massage their gums. John instructed his children to chew on the end of a live black gum twig, "Break it from the tree, not from the dead limbs on the ground around the tree."

He insisted without exception that all his children follow this ritual of hygiene every day. In some ways, he was very strict.

There is one other tree easily recognized by all of the Owens children and that is a sweet gum tree because just at the top of the hill above the house across the main road from where the small wagon road cuts through the woods to Bethel school, there's a giant old sweet gum tree standing a proud watch over the Owens place and each year when the sap starts to rise and that's more-n-likely in February unless it's been out of the ordinary cold, John hacks a gash in the sweet gum tree so the rising sap can be collected because chewing the sweet gum sap is a pleasure like none other. The balsam makes a good antiseptic for sores too.

Mr. Fincher

Back to the story, as the children walked to school on this cold January morning, they passed by the Fincher cabin, which was the only house on the road and it stood about half way between the Owens home place and the cemetery. The children heard the back door slam at the Fincher place, and they all stared in stunned silence when Mr. Fincher, without a stitch of clothes on his skinny body, ran full speed from his house to the outhouse. Feeling more than a little uneasy, the children walked faster so as to be out of sight beyond the house when the naked man returned from the outhouse, and when they reached the darkness of the dense woods on the other side of the Fincher place, Theda was the first to start laughing, and from that day on until this very day the word 'naked' is never used in the Owens part of the family, no sir, that whole bunch uses 'Mr. Fincher' instead of the word 'naked' and I guess it is thought of as a more civil way to express the idée, and I'm well aware I don't have to tell you any of this because just this morning I heard you call your brother 'Mr. Fincher' when he ran from the bathroom to the bedroom with nothing but a towel wrapped around his nakedness.

The same morning when the Owens kids saw Mr. Fincher, Sis and me walked around by the Jasper Hicks place on our way to school. Most mornings we walked through the cemetery, it was just about a mile either way from the Godwin home place to Bethel. I walked just about every place I had to go in the Bethel Community because any fool could see it was not practical to waste gasoline and walking gets you limbered up and gets your mind a working so my Model T sat in the yard at home just about all the time.

For as far back as I can remember, I've wanted to walk up to any stranger any where a knowing that I looked as good as anybody, and so I buy nice clothes and I wear my dress up clothes just about every where I go because I want to have a reputation in the county of being a successful business man. I didn't need any more education, but I went to Bethel School just about every day because I knew that Vesta would be there because her attitude toward education is completely different than mine, she wants to learn every thing about every thing and some days I sat beside her in school and felt like she might change me into another book worm just like her, because she's always had a mighty powerful effect on me, but when you get right down to it, I knew I'd do just fine for the rest of my life with the book learning I already had. Anyway, that morning me and Sis walked by the Jasper Hicks' place which meant we passed over the bridge in the holler and as we walked down the porch steps and away from the house, I led the way down the road to the creek because I happened to notice a ring of dirt around Sis's neck, but I didn't want to embarrass Sis and I knew her to be easily embarrassed so I didn't say anything until we got to the creek and that's when I told Sis to put her dinner bucket down on the bridge.

"Why?"

"Cause we're gona wash your dirty neck in the creek."

Just like I thought she'd be, Sis was pitiful embarrassed, but she put her dinner pail down on the boards of the bridge and pulled off her coat and dropped it down by the dinner pail, and she wouldn't let me help her down to the creek bank because she didn't want me to get wet too, so she slid down the bank to the creek and washed her neck with the cold water, and as she climbed back up the creek bank, she lifted her cotton skirt to dry the water from her neck and then she adjusted her white cotton slip and tugged and slapped her wet cotton dress in place over her slip and next she jerked her coat up from the bridge boards and poked her arms into the sleeves before she just about ripped it in two forcing it up on her shoulders and then she bent down and grabbed her lunch pail and huffed off up the road ahead of me leaving me to slither along behind her, but by the time we climbed up the hill by the Jasper Hick's place, she slowed down for me to catch up, and when she turned to look me in the face, she saw that I was grinning wide watching her display of childish anger and she smiled at me to let me know she understood it was my job to take care of her just like I've always done and today is no different than the past and she can just face it, yes-sir-re-bob I'm gona take care of my little sister no matter what.

That cold morning when Vesta and the others walked into the Bethel School yard, me and Sis were already there waiting for them and Sis went running over to Vesta and I saw Vesta look down at Sis's wet dress and I'm sure Vesta noticed because Sis was shivering in the cold, but she didn't say anything which would have made Sis more self conscious. I saw Sis take a picture out of her pocket and hand it over to Vesta. "Vesta, look at this pretty dress in the Sears and Roebuck catalog. Can you make it for me? I bought the cloth from the peddler." Sis offered a torn page from the catalog, and now I understood why Sis asked me for a dollar yesterday.

Vesta said, "Let me look at it. ...... Yeah, I can make it for you Sis. It's really a simple dress but for the collar has a briar stitch around the edge and that will be a new embroidery stitch for me to learn, but I can figure it out. So let me keep the picture." Vesta tucked the Sears & Roebuck dress picture into her pocket.

"Thank you. I'll bring the cloth tonight, and Shug said he'd come with me to your house after supper. You're the same size as me, so just make the dress to fit you. I'll have to help Essie cook supper and wash up the dishes, so it'll be after dark when we get there," Sis finished telling all this to Vesta as they entered the Bethel school house. Now I don't want you to get the idée that Sis could not sew for she most certainly can sew and she sews real good, but Vesta was maybe just a little bit better at sewing back in the days when nobody could afford to buy a pattern, and in fact the peddler did not carry patterns, he just carried material, thread and needles, and

Sis asked Vesta to sew that dress for her because it was a complicated dress to make with the rounded collar and inset sleeves.

Anyway that morning the teacher was swinging the school bell to bring everyone in out of the cold and once inside, I was happy to sit down on the same bench with Vesta. The teacher had all the students recite in unison the two's, three's and four's multiplication tables which was easy because me and Vesta knew all the multiplication tables by heart.

The teacher spent about the whole morning explaining how to weave wool or cotton thread into cloth. It was a useless lesson because just about every house in the county had a spinning wheel and a loom, but I guess the teacher thought it was important, because he sure went into every detail of the process. I couldn't keep my mind on what he was saying, and even Vesta started to yawn. Maskal was sitting on a bench at the far back of the room with his feet up kinda stretched out, and when I looked back at him one time, he was asleep. I guess the teacher saw his eyes closed, because he said real loud, "Maskal."

And when he heard his name yelled out like that, Maskal sat up straight and listened for a while, and then he raised his hand, and the teacher called on him and Maskal said, "Well, that's sort a like weavin' ain't it?"

Everybody started whoopin' and laughin' and pore ol' Maskal laughed too, even though he didn't really know what was so funny.

The teacher called on different ones to read aloud from the primer, and me and Vesta followed along leaning our heads close together so we could read from the same book. I touched Vesta's hand under the table, and my heart did a somersault. We held hands for a long time in school that day.

That evening as Vesta washed the supper dishes, John handed the cross cut saw to Theda. "You and Ruth better go out and saw some firewood for your Mama."

Theda took the long, limber saw blade from her Papa and carefully refolded it into a loop, and with her hands stretched wide to make the grasp, she held both handles side by side and walked across the kitchen floor toward the door with Little Ruth close behind her, and John held the door open as the girls went through. Once Theda was outside, she stumbled, did a dance across the porch, and tumbled down the steps to the ground with the six-foot saw still tightly clutched in her hands. John raced out the door, down the steps and knelt on one knee at her side, "Theda are you all right?"

"I'm not hurt Papa, I know how to fall."

When Vesta finished washing the dishes, she went out to help saw the firewood, and it was Little Ruth and Vesta who pushed and pulled the cross cut saw back and forth through the log while Theda stared dreamily up at the full moon and brilliant stars, and on his way to tend to the animals in the barn when John shuffled past his three daughters, two of which were actually working, he remarked, "Theda, you'll better things a hell of a lot by gazing up at the stars. You're never gona learn how to saw firewood by dreaming at the sky."

"I know Papa, but I want to gaze at the sky, and I don't want to learn how to saw firewood."

Sis and me toted the firewood into the kitchen, which we were happy to help, and I always jumped at the chance to do anything that served as a means of bringing me close to Vesta, and back inside the house, she set inst to spread Sis's material on the long kitchen table and cut out the pieces for Sis's new dress. She used the one and only pair of scissors in the house, which were twice the size of John Owens's hand and the scissors dwarfed Vesta's hand and made it seem very small and frail. John always made sure the scissors were sharp for he used these giant scissors every spring to shear the sheep.

Vesta looked at the picture torn from the pages of the Sears and Roebuck catalog and without the use of a sewing pattern; she cut out the bodice, skirt, sleeves, and collar. In my mind this was the work of a genius, cutting the material into pieces that would fit around Sis's arm and come into the bodice at the shoulder without using a pattern to go by, and of course the question of money was a constant problem and who could afford to buy a sewing pattern? Anyway, I stood in wonder as twelve year old Vesta cut out the dress and sat down at the treadle sewing machine to sew these flat pieces of material into a three dimensional dress. To me that was nothing short of brilliant.

It was getting cold inside the house as the kitchen cook stove fire burned down, so I built a fire in the big house fireplace which was easy for John always had plenty of rich, pine knot kindling stored in a bucket by the hearth, and then Sis and me said our 'good nights' and we left the warmth of the roaring fire that burned at a lesser degree than the love and joy binding the Owens family together with each other and with all who visited their haven of peace in a depressed country, and me and my little sister walked back home through the cemetery at pitch black night without the slightest twinge of fear because our Ma and Pa sort a watched out for us, and we talked about this idée as we walked along, and we expressed our luck to be a part of two families, the Owens's and of course the Godwin's, and it wadn't the first time we talked about this. We knew then and we know now how remarkable it is to be loved and cared for and to love and care for others in return, and we are glad for the rewards are great and by thinking out loud to one another the idée that our Ma and Pa might a left us through death, but not through spirit, and we are part of a long standin' tradition of honesty, and decency, and pride and trust. And one common, southern greetin' applies to what we talked about that night, for me and Sis are as close as any brother and sister can be, and we look out for each other and we understand what is expected of us, and that is to live by the rules and "just try to hold it in the road."

And the meaning of that expression is simple and easy to understand when you think about the way we came up in a time when ever body was pore but nobody stepped on another person or turned a blind eye to suffering. In those days, the roads ever where were dirt and when it rained the dirt turned to slick mud, and if you were driving through the road of life in a wagon and mule or a Model T automobile, you had to keep your eye on the road and watch out so as not to slide off into a ditch, and in life as in driving you just "tried to hold it in the road."

Countywide Tests

The next week on Wednesday, all the Bethel six grade students went to Heflin, Alabama for countywide tests. I drove a load in my car, and I took the tests too, but I didn't do too good on some parts of the test, but I'm sure I got the right answer on every problem on the arithmetic part. I was proud to drive a car load of neighbors who all seemed like family because our lives were so entwined, and on this exciting day, everyone came to school in their Sunday-go-to-meetin' clothes which were old and patched, but clean and ironed. The girls in cotton print dresses looked like a fine bunch of rich folks if you didn't notice the repairs, and the boys in high water pants up to their ankles and shirt sleeves that didn't reach their wrists might look like a motley crew to some big shots from Atlanta, but when we entered the high school building in Heflin everybody looked right in place, and I just about cried to watch them act like they were just as good as anybody. I had a little uneasy feeling that some rich Heflin folks might make fun of us country pore folks, and I was prepared to knock'em cold, but it didn't happen, and in fact a knowing full well that Vesta would beat me to it anyway and do as her Papa always taught about dealing with bullies, "Just squint your eyes, raise you chin up to the sky and stare them down, and if that don't work, say, 'I know you're the bully, but I've come now' and that'll work ever single time. They'll soften up and before long they'll be squintin' down the next bully that comes along."

But it didn't happen and in fact there was not a single mean spirited person in the whole building, and Vesta looked like a million dollars a wearing the new dress she made out of feed sacks, but you'd never know the material came from feed sacks because it was white like feed sacks only in leaf shaped spots. She told me later she put the leaf design on the feed sacks by spreading them out on the ground and carefully placing leaves all over the feed sacks and then she dusted soot gathered from inside the chimney and covered the leaves and the feed sack material so as the soot formed a black background and when she lifted the corners of each feed sack and snapped the soot and the leaves off, a design of white leaves each one surrounded by the black background was revealed, and next she washed the feed sacks so as not to get the soot all over her hands, the giant sheep sheering scissors and the Singer sewing machine. And boy howdy she could make the Singer sing, but 'hum' would have been a better word to use, but the sewing machine was a 'sing er' not a 'hummer' anyway it was a real pretty dress and Vesta wore it proudly and looked like somebody and the other girls looked real nice too, and I wondered how many girls were wearing dresses made by Vesta, and I knew for a fact that she made most of the coats the girls had on and some of the boys' jackets too, and the warm coats were made out of wool sheared from the sheep that just about every farm in the county raised and sheared in the spring. Most folks swapped eggs or garden produce to the peddler in exchange for a cutting of material off the bolts he carried in his wagon. The peddler's wagon was a little house structure with walls, a roof, and wood panels on each side hinged at the top and when propped opened with a stick displayed the dry goods for sale inside the little structure, and when the panels were closed shut they protected the contents of the little store on wheels from the dust kicked up by the horse's huffs and the wagon wheels rolling along, and another factor was the contents stayed dry even if it was pouring down rain which naturally turned the roads into red mud splashing up and all over the outside walls but not on the for sale cargo inside.

It was about the last week of February when we learned that one of our Bethel School students scored very high on all parts of the county-wide tests and that all of the Bethel students did real good enough on the tests a proving we were poor but not dumb, but we knew that already for all the young folks in the Bethel Community worked hard every day to make a living and also come to school and do their best, and beyond that all of them were honest and loyal and true friends through good times and bad times and everybody was mighty proud that right in our little one room school house was the smartest student in the whole of Cleburne County and that student was Vesta Owens and that is a matter of fact for Vesta made the highest grade of all the sixth grade students taking the county wide tests and it was printed in the Heflin newspaper and Mr. Mullino brought the newspaper to school and read the article out loud to us. I was the proudest strutting' rooster for I always knew Vesta was smart, and now everybody in the county knew it and not just our backwoods Bethel neighbors. It's always been obvious to everybody that Vesta is very pretty and very talented, and now there's proof she is very smart.

We did very little book learning that day for everybody was fidgety and sort a anxious and busting to get out a there and tell the good news. So as to pass the time, Mr. Mullino started reading aloud to us a book about horses, and in the second chapter, a horse with a broken leg had to be shot. At the end of each short chapter everybody had a chance to talk and ask questions, and I glanced over to Maskel and it was pretty sure he was asleep, but when Sis said sadly, "Rob Roy was a good horse but they had to shoot him in the end."

Well that's when Maskel finally rubbed his eyes, stretched his long arms over his head and blurted out to Sis, "Did you say they shot him in the end?"

With his emphasis on "the end " it was certain to everyone including Mr. Mullino that Maskel confused the "end" to be the horse's rear end and not the "end" of Rob Roy's life, and in spite of the sad story about the death of a good horse, the entire room got a good wha-wha-ing big laugh out a Maskel's disinterested and mistaken query.

Most Sundays in the cold winter months, the John Owens family walked the shorter distance to Bethel Church, and that next Sunday morning the Bethel preacher announced from the pulpit, "In case some of you didn't read about it in the Cleburne News, I want to say we are mighty proud to have in our fellowship the smartest student in all of Cleburne County, and that being 'Vesta Owens' and she's a sitting right here with us in our cold little church, and our warmest congratulations to you, Vesta! Well folks, we're hovered together as close to the pot belly warming stove as we can get and on these freezing Sundays, I'm reminded of the scripture from Matthew 22:14, 'Many are called, but few are chosen.' and in my mind on mornings like this one when we are forced to wear our warmest coats inside our church, and we can see our breath forming little clouds in front of each face, well at times like these I sometimes make a reverent twist of that scripture, 'Many are cold but few are frozen.'"

That winter was my last year of schooling, I quit because I had to work and make a little money, and I simply couldn't work all night making whiskey and stay awake in school. I couldn't learn under those circumstances but I already knew how to read, write, and do figures in my head so I decided I had all the education I needed, but I didn't stop learning, no sir re, I always found things to learn and I understand it's a mark of a strong man to admit he needs help with some kind of subject about which he knows nothing, but at that time me and Vesta both had a good sixth grade education so I quit school, I'm not proud of it, but I'm not ashamed of it either for I had it to do, but Vesta did not quit school, no sir, she went on with her schooling and started in the fall in the seventh grade at Crossroads School. She walked the two miles each way and sometimes she walked together with other girls from the Bethel area, but she went more days than anybody else so most times she walked the distance alone which she wadn't afraid of nothing and nothing would a happened to her for every house she passed along the way sort a gave her a shield of protection that was just the natural way of conducting business in those days. Sometimes it worked out for me to go along the road in my jalopy and pick her up and give her a ride, and I guess about once a week, I was lucky enough to catch her in the morning and more afternoons than not when Vesta's school day ended, I was sitting in front of the big old white two story school house, and every single time Vesta came out of that Crossroads School house door and walked toward me sitting in my car I had to catch my breath for she had a smile on her face showing me the most beautiful set of white teeth I've ever seen. She was so pretty and sweet and talented and smart and I loved her and I can't ever remember a time when I didn't love her.

Some of the times on the rides between Crossroads School and the Owens home place, I switched places with Vesta so as she could learn how to drive my Model T and she caught on real quick. You have to understand that all the roads were dirt back then and not even the bigger roads were paved so Vesta learned how to handle a car on uneven dirt roads and sometimes the ruts were so deep that if the bottom of the car got positioned on the high center ridge, the wheels might be suspended and not even touch the ground, so I cautioned her to keep the wheels out of the ruts and up on the high road and she did. The roads were too narrow to meet another car or a horse and wagon so one or the other had to pull off into the ditch and let the other pass and getting back up out of the ditch and on the road required a skill in handling that came as second nature to Vesta.

From an early age, Jack and Chester spent very little time in school because John needed the boys to help in running the steam powered sawmill for it was a big operation which one man could not handle alone. I've heard Jack joke of getting all the education he needed at Bethel College. Jack was fifteen years old and quick enough physically and mentally to set the blocks; and Chester, with one more year of growth, was stout enough to fire the boiler for that job could only be done by a man with a strong back. John and his boys started their grueling work day every morning at sun up and worked til after dark, but they kept at it for every load of lumber they hauled into town helped to put food on the table and they knew somehow that no matter how much they worked, they were not a gona get rich for no man can get ahead in a market that offers no or close to no actual reward for a man's honest labor, and in fact the cycle of depression beats down a man's effort for when a product like lumber is offered for sale, most times the product don't bring a dime for there's no buyer who can pay the dime You have to remember it was the great depression and people all across the country in big cities and little towns were so poor they could not afford to buy food, and they were lining up once a day for a bowl of free soup. We saw these pictures in the week old newspapers the peddler brought by when he got the chance. John Owens worried that his family might have to cut back even more for the price of milled lumber was in a steady decline, and already his family ate only breakfast and supper, but they were proud to have two meals a day which were earned and paid for by honest work, but it is humiliating for a man to work for little or nothing and watch his wife struggle to make ends meet. During the years when John and the boys worked at the sawmill, Sally and the girls continued the chores inside the house such as cooking the meals, cleaning the house, patching, mending, and washing the clothes, and in addition, the women took on the responsibility of caring for the livestock, working in the fields and chopping enough firewood for the cook stove and two fireplaces.

It was an unnecessary waste of money to buy new material to make clothes when we all had a plenty sugar sacks and feed sacks, so when the family out grew their clothes, the women let out seams and hems and when that wasn't enough, they added strips of feed sack cloth down the sides of the garments and the strips came to be worn as a flag of pride and proof of independence from soup lines like the poor old city folks were standing in, but it seemed like a never ending sewing task of adding wider and wider strips of sugar sack material, and it just seemed like the young folks' clothes were perpetually too little. In the worst year the girls handed down their one dress to the next youngest and Sally and her girls worked on a total remake of the smallest dress to pass as a new dress for the oldest. First, they pulled out all of the stitches and laid the old material out on the table and cut the new bodice and collar pieces from the old skirt, and then they cut the new dress sleeves and skirt from feed sack material which Vesta was ashamed to wear this half feed sack dress as long as the blue feed advertisement lettering was readable, but the blue letters faded from the feed sack material quickly for Sally and the girls washed clothes in the wash pot out behind the house every Saturday morning, and the homemade lye soap and hot boiling water stripped the blue lettering from the feed sacks. There was a quandary of how to wash dirty clothes when the dirty clothes amounted to the only clothes with which to cover their nakedness, but this dilemma was solved by every member of the family dressing up in any rags they could find for the women also washed all the tattered work clothes worn throughout the week. So for the entire Bethel Community wash-day-rags became the uniform worn on Saturdays. The girls were always afraid somebody would come calling while they looked like hobos, so they worked especially fast washing and ironing their good clothes because Saturday nights were a favorite night for company to come calling, but neighbors dropped by to visit many weeknights also because the Owens house was so much fun with all the laughter and nonsense going on all the time. The Owens girls might have imagined that others in the county were not faced with the 'what to wear on washday' predicament, but they should have known they were as well off as the neighbors, and wash-day-uniforms were a common occurrence.

Through the summer, the girls and Sally worked all day every day in ragged, tattered scrap clothing that gave them the appearance of ragamuffins, but each day at sunset, each member of the family filled a small wash pan with hot water from the reservoir on the right side of the wood burning cook stove and with a clean rag for a washcloth and another clean rag for drying off, the girls and Sally escaped one by one to the privacy of the little back bedroom. Most times the men one by one bathed on the back porch and often on summer nights they went across the road, past the corncrib and down the steep hill to bathe in the cool spring water. Weary, tired muscles loosened up and relaxed with a nightly bath, and every evening each member of the family dressed in their one presentable change of clothing, and the girls and Sally cooked a good supper, and more nights than not, while the girls washed the supper dishes company came a knocking at the door, but the knock was just a short signal that the visitor was walking on in for no one felt the need to wait on an invitation to enter anybody's house and most especially the Owens house for it was common in the Bethel Community to walk in and set a spell and every house was the same but more nights than not, the Owens house filled up with visitors because everybody loved to join in the good times. At these get-togethers, the girls giggled and poked fun at each other happy to have the gift of laughter and just about every night Vesta played the organ and usually about nine o'clock, the boys and men went outside to dip snuff or smoke a cigarette which me and most of the boys in the county started smoking at about twelve years old, but John Owens forbid his boys to smoke, and one night Chester told me about the only whippin' he ever got was when his Papa caught him smoking. John and Sally Owens both dipped snuff, but John didn't believe in smoking.

Usually, as we all walked off into the night, John Owens called out after us, 'Good night and yall come back tomorrow night,' but if he didn't say, 'Yall come back tomorrow night,' we knew enough not to come back the next night but it was uncommon not to gather at the Owens's.

At bed time back then people put on the next day's patched but clean work clothes for to sleep in, and by wearing tattered and threadbare clothes to work in that way their good Sunday-go-to-meeting clothes were kept from going to rags too quick. Nobody wanted to parade around at these nighttime get-togethers dressed like poor old hillbillies, and me especially me. From the time when I first started making whiskey, I bought good clothes, good pants and shirts and I like to wear a knock-about jacket and a tie a lot of the time, and from an early age, to put the finish touch, I liked to wear a felt hat with a little feather in the band, but back then I had only one good hat at a time, but I kept the old out of shape hats to wear while working at the still, and it was a kind of a symbol of a bootlegger to wear a felt hat, and the logic was that walking through the woods a toting heavy sacks of sugar or other supplies leaves no free hand to swing a stick to knock down spider webs, and the brim of a hat sweeps the spider webs down just before the dogged old spiders could drop down into your shirt and that is what gives me the spooks so I always make sure to wear a wide brimmed hat to work in the woods like any smart bootlegger. A felt hat also keeps ticks from dropping off trees onto your neck and you can always brush them off you shirt or britches, but if they drop onto your head or neck, then they bite down and that's the reason why you always have to be careful to feel your scalp and neck and all over your body ever time you wash so as to find and pull off the dogged ole ticks, and it's a mystery to me why one tree in the whole area is always the only tree where the ticks will drop on you as you walk by, well not the only tree for ticks will drop from just about any bush or tree, but as a usual thing, it is mainly from one tree or bush, and after a while, if you pay attention, you get to know the trees and bushes to stay away from. My good dress hat is usually a kind of dark brown color which looks good with both brown and gray pants and jackets, and I like to wear the brown jacket with the gray pants and the gray jacket with the brown pants, and another thing, I always want my shoes shined so on the weekend when I go into town, I get a shoeshine in the pool hall after I give a nickel to every boy waiting for me at the moving picture show.

For two or three years while John and the boys worked twelve hours every day at the sawmill, Sally and the girls put in the crops in the spring, tended the crops through the summer and brought in the crops in the fall, the main crop being corn for it is good feed for the livestock and for the family but Sally, Vesta and Theda did most of the work letting Little Ruth do just a little bit of light work and none of the heavy work, and although Theda is two years younger than Vesta, the girls are just about the same size, and they both are already as tall as their mama because Sally Owens is a little bitty woman who looked slight and dainty but could fool you with all the work she can do, and she can hold out to work for as many hours as it takes to get the job done, and I guess that's where Vesta got the idée that if there's something to be done, just get it done and don't shy away from work, and so Vesta and Theda did just as much of the work as their Mama did, but Theda complained and whined and cajoled until sometimes even her sweet Mama might get a little short with her, but everybody sort a just overlooks this about Theda because she means well and doesn't shirk any work a tall once her complaints are registered and her so called laziness was well established. In fact, I think John and Sally both took a lot of pleasure in watching Theda's delay tactics that changed with every situation and everybody enjoys Theda's light hearted easy laughter even if the joke is on her, and without fail, when it comes down to 'do' or 'don't', she always does what she has to do. And when these seemingly frail women realized they'd inherited the job of farming and the farming was waiting', well they went about getting it done even though the whole business seemed impossible starting with the job of putting the bridle on the mule, but they devised a method that worked out just fine. First, they coaxed the mule from the pasture into the barn's open hall between the stalls and then Vesta climbed up three stall boards, lifted the horse collar from the nail on the support beam, and reached out from the stall boards and holding' on good and tight with one hand so as to place the horse collar over the mule's head with her other hand, and then she lifted the bridle from it's nail and leaned out again from the stall boards again holding' on tight so as to find the maneuvering room to throw the bridle over the mule's head which Theda caught the loose end and slipped the bit into the mule's mouth, then passed the leather strap under the mule's head back to Vesta where she now stood on the next lower stall board and with the leather in her left hand she leaned against the mule in a way to free up both hands, and she buckled the bridle in place. Next the girls walked the giant mule up the road, over the hill and down to the field by the creek bridge where they left the plow yesterday, and the first few days of this just walking along behind the strong muscular mule intimidated the women for they felt insignificant in comparison, but pretty soon they shrugged off the perspective of wonder, swallowed their fear, and shouldered the attitude of confidence and pride in their ability to do anything and that meant even commanding this big old mule.

In the field, the women hooked up the harness traces to the hames on the horse collar. They learned the horse collar allows the horse to use its full strength and changes the dynamic from pulling to essentially allowing the horse to push forward with its hindquarters into the collar. Sally went first, she threw the reins over her shoulder, around her body and off she went plowing' the day's first row with Vesta walking beside her to the other end of the field where Sally stopped the mule, pulled the reins from over her shoulder and stepped back so Vesta could step in, throw the reins over and around her own body, turn the mule and plow the next row about two feet from the preceding' row. Each learned the trick of lifting the plow handles behind the mule in order to force the plowshare into the soil which was a job that required every single bit of strength these women could muster, but they could sustain this extrude for no more than one length of the field, so the three strongest Sally, Vesta and Theda set up a sort of relay system whereby at the end of each row, a replacement stepped in, took over, turned the mule and plowed the next row back to the other end of the field to find the waiting' replacement. The hardest part of plowing' a row was the delicate location of placement by eyeballing the previous row and plowing and holding the plow straight so as to put the next row the correct distance over so as to maximize corn planting and production, and meanwhile the relief female was resting' in the shade at the far end of the field.

The ladies understood the crucial and fine points of plowing a field and so before the first row was plowed in the morning, they carefully checked the plowshare's condition, which had to be sharp, and if it was beginning to dull that meant they'd come in from the field just a little early at the end of the day bringing the plowshare with them so John could fire up the blacksmith equipment and sharpen the edge.

Their team relay system of plowing was a sight to behold when these slight females stepped behind the plow, leaned far enough forward to drag their skirts in the dirt lifting' and pushing' the plow handles above their head so as to get enough leverage to keep the plow in the ground turning the soil away, and they got real handy at making the rows straight, and mostly Little Ruth followed behind dropping corn into the furrows and kicking soil over the kernels which were dropped about three fourths a foot apart, but sometimes Little Ruth might set down in the shade of a tree and let Theda drop corn in the rows for a while, and when that happened, it meant that Sally and Vesta each had to plow the length of the field down and back before getting' relieved.

This work was done on hot days with the sun beating down on the smothering 'protective clothing' they wore to keep their fair skin white and freckle free. They learned real quick to pull their oversized shirt sleeves down over their hands to serve as gloves in an effort to avoid the painful blisters the plow handles could rub on their palms, and in fact, they wanted to cry in pain when the blisters broke. But taking all these hardships into account, these women actually seemed to enjoy themselves with singing and laughing and carrying on even though they had nothing to eat from morning to night except sometimes they had the early dew berries and later on the blackberries and huckleberries growing wild along the field's edge, and when the roasting-ears grew to six inches long it was a feast reward for their work planting and weeding and thinning and harvesting when they helped themselves to the delicious and tasty corn-on-the-cob uncooked right there in the field all the while working as though the clock was a running down, and all farmers find the unique pleasure of eaten' roasting-ears in the field right off the stalk and cobb and anybody who's ever grown a single field of corn can tell you the roast-n-ears taste better fresh off the stalk, shucked in the row and eaten off the cob while standing in the noon day sun. I guess that's one of God's rewards for doing the dirty work of a farmer.

These women farmers dressed up in big long sleeved, ragged shirts and hand-me-down britches they tied with a rope around through the belt loops or else they'd fall off, and sometimes when they were lucky they wore old socks to protect their tender palms, and of course, they wouldn't leave the house without their homemade feed sack sun bonnets with wide brims reaching out over their face and little gathered 'skirts' to protect the back of the neck, and all these layers of clothes they wore to protect their fair skin from the burning sun because they wanted to fool people into thinking they didn't work in the fields, when everybody knew they did work in the fields, and at night they even soaked a rag in buttermilk to lay on their freckles while they slept thinking the buttermilk would fade the freckles which they deemed to be ugly, but to my way of thinking, Vesta's freckles were beautiful.

Sally Owens and her girls acted like they loved this hard work of farming and you could hear them cackling a mile away, but from my point of view, I never did like the work of a farmer, I guess I didn't like any part of the process, but I did plenty of it in my day, and then when I found out the money was better for selling whiskey I guess from then on I tried to get out of doing the work of farming.

One day it was time to run cut lumber into town and John drove the load on the second wagon while Jack drove the first wagon in the lead. John's Model T truck was also loaded with lumber and ready to go, but they had no gasoline so Chester stayed at home. Both Jack and Chester usually went along with their Papa into town each driving either a team and wagon or the truck, and it took the three of them at least a week to cut and mill enough lumber to fill the two wagons and the truck, and they pushed themselves to the limit for a pitiful little bit of money. Chester and Jack both wanted to get into the whiskey making business, but John argued against it, so they kept on with the back breaking' work of sawmilling. John felt guilty about working the boys such long hours, but he figured it was better than going to jail for bootlegging which more and more of the bootleggers had to do.

On this particular trip into town, John in the second wagon coming along behind watched as his son's head began to bob in sleep. The team of horses knew the way, and this wasn't the first time Jack had fallen asleep while driving, but always before when he fell asleep, his chin rested and bobbed on his chest while the wagon wheels continued their rhythm, but this time John watched in horror as Jack's head rolled over to his right shoulder and nodded and bobbed a pulling his body farther and farther over to the right, and in a split second, the weight of Jack's head started a downward free fall that brought him off balance on the wagon seat and caused him to plunge head first from the wagon seat five feet to the ground. His head hit the ground first and his body followed with a sickening thud, and next his legs flew and waved up in the air over his crumpled shoulders and thankfully he landed just a might clear of the back wagon wheel as it rolled right on along for at least the length of the wagon leaving behind Jack's slumped body. John's spontaneous protective reaction was to rein in his team but this sudden jerk caused the hemmed-in horses to rare up dangerously close to Jack's still body and the spooked horses continued to rare up as John pushed himself off the wagon seat, his own feet flying through the air and landing him on the ground helplessly watching as his son's lifeless body was trampled, and of course John blamed himself for following too close, if he'd been just a few feet back the horses wouldn't have been penned in when Jack's wagon came to a stop. Anyway, in a sorry daze, big John Owens gathered his unconscious fifteen-year-old son up into his arms and close to his chest, and as he took his first steps he locked Jack's head under his chin and contained Jack's limp arms from swinging by squeezing him tighter and closer. John's quick mind deciphered first that Doc Godwin was a good six or seven miles closer than Tallapoosa, and second that it would not be feasible to lift Jack back up onto one of the wagons and besides, on this narrow country road, it would be impossible to turn the team and wagon. The next wide place in the road might work but if he loaded Jack on the front wagon, proceeded toward town, turned the wagon at the wide spot and retraced the wagon tracks back to the second wagon, but then what? He certainly could not meet and maneuver around the second wagon, and towing the second wagon along behind the first would just waste precious time so to John's way of thinking, the only rapid course of action was to tote Jack to Doc Godwin. So big John Owens walked his precious cargo back along the road toward the Bethel Church and on to the Godwin home place and every step of the way he forced his mind to remain clear and focused and he saw no choice but to continue with calm concentration, and he actually lifted himself above the invasion of fear by counting the rhythm of his steps like he was counting' the rhythm of Sacred Harp singing:

Sacred Harp singing is a non-denominational community musical event emphasizing participation, not performance. Singers are invited to take a turn "leading" and beaten' time with their hand. Sacred Harp singing means there's no accompaniment by harps or any other instrument. The notes are read from The Sacred Harp, which is an oblong songbook first published in 1844. The music is printed in "patent notes," wherein the shape of the note head indicates the syllables FA, SOL, LA, and MI. The repertory includes psalm tunes and revival hymns. In the rural South, some call Sacred Harp 'fa so la singing.' Usually there is a singing at St Michael's church about once a month through the spring, summer and fall, and the singings last all day and at noon everybody opens up a picnic basket and spreads a quilt in the shade of the tall oak trees. It is a mighty fine pleasure.

As he trudged along, John let his mind wonder to shield himself from the painful reality, and without feeling, he methodically put one foot in front of the other while his heart raced hard enough to break open his chest, and when he finally climbed the steps of the Godwin home place, he glanced down for the first time at his son's face and when this giant among men saw blood draining from Jack's mouth he felt an actual hole poked right through his own heart, and he tried to call out, no he tried to cry out, but his own mouth was too dry to form words and so with mechanical movements only, somehow he managed to kick open the door, bust inside the house and stagger across the fireplace room into Doc's office where Doc was sitting at his desk with his head in his hands unaware of John's presence until John pushed the side of his chair.

Then like a rock from a flip, Doc was on his feet motioning John to place Jack's body on the kitchen table. For the grieving John, the last steps of the two-mile walk carrying his son were no more difficult than the first steps, and in a trance like state, he turned, re-entered the kitchen and gently set down his precious load. Doc opened his black medical bag and first listened to Jack's heart and lungs, then he tried to make John leave the room, but he realized this was not possible and so together he and John removed Jack's shirt and revealed two hoof-print-shaped bruises on Jack's chest and both men knew that Jack's ribs could not have held under the impact. So while the boy was mercifully unconscious, the two men bound his chest with rag strips as fast as Essie could rip the sugar sacks.

Back out on the road where the accident happened, I came up on the two wagons loaded with lumber, and I knew something was bad wrong. Before I could pass, I backed my car to the wide spot in the road, ran back to the two wagons, hitched the team reins of the second wagon to the back of the first wagon, climbed to the driver's seat of the first wagon, and drove the two teams to the wide spot in the road. When I had the two wagons positioned off the road in the weeds, I jumped back in my car, and now I had a decision to make … where to go? Before I really realized what I was doing, I was on my way home and I'm glad that's where I went cause I found John sitting by the kitchen table staring at Jack's bound, still body. John was not talking, so me and Doc decided that me and Chester had a job now of driving the two wagon loads of lumber into town, so I turned the car around in the yard and when I drove up to the Owens home place which was unusual for me to show up there in the middle of the day, I pulled into the yard and Sally was out of the house and down the porch steps before I got out of my car. I didn't have to tell her what had happened, and without a word being said, she climbed into the passenger side of my car and waited, her hands clasped together and fidgeting in her lap while Chester and all three of her daughters came out of the house and climbed into the back seat. I drove like a steak of lightening up to the main road and on to the site of the accident. I could see Miss Sally reach into her apron pocket for her handkerchief to wipe her eyes as I explained about Jack's accident, "Chester and I will drive the two wagons into town and Vesta will drive all y'all to the Godwin home place to pick up Jack and John."

When Vesta drove into the yard at the Godwin home place, Sally opened the car door and actually jumped to the ground before the car stopped rolling. At age forty-six, Sally was spry and agile but her once straight back was beginning to bow into a hump. She never complained, and she certainly didn't slow down because of it, and she still looked young in every other way, her hair was black as a crow and her very prominent black eyebrows unexpectedly softened her sun-bronzed kind face. By her appearance you'd think her to be weak and helpless, and maybe even frail as is often the case after a lifetime of carrying more weight than seems fair as a mother carries and delivers and cares for her children, but actually Sally Owens was strong and definitely in control as if the years of grief and despair which should have laid her flat, had indeed toughened her into a monolith of strength. Rarely did she sit down, and when she did it was her normal demeanor to bow her head and watch her hands as she fidgeted her thumbs in a little game of chase. She worked every day of the week except Sunday tending the fields, cleaning the house, sweeping the yards, weeding the garden, gathering the produce for meals and for canning, and she helped John with the sheep shearing in the spring. She was as strong as any man in a lot of ways.

When Sally entered the Godwin kitchen, she stopped in her tracks to watch as Mose and Doc placed a wide pine board on the table next to Jack's body and positioned themselves one at Jack's head and one at his feet, and just as they were about to lift Jack's body onto the wide pine board, John stepped in and with purpose and urgency gathered his fifteen year old son into his arms again, hugged him close to his chest and carried him to the car obviously afraid Jack might slide off of the pine board when they started down the porch steps. Jack was not aware of his groans, but John and Sally winced at the sound of their son's misery, and they were grateful to have him remain unconscious at least for now until they could get him home. Doc called out instructions and promised to come calling tomorrow as Sally scrambled into the car and settled in the back seat and John stooped to maneuver his son's head under the car top and through the tiny door and with the single encompassing purpose of preserving all that mattered in the world, big John Owens stepped one foot onto the floorboard inside the car and carefully placed Jack's head in Sally's lap, this giant of a man handled his full grown son as if he were putting an infant to bed. Sally's lap, more bones than flesh, would do little to cushion Jack's head, but these two parents both knew in their hearts that her gentle touch would convey to Jack their presence and their fathomless love, and now the tiny and meek Sally actually barked orders to her husband because she could see what we all saw, John was disconnected from reality and Sally's stern commands might be the only way to penetrate his blank stare; and so with Jack in place on the small back seat, Sally's murmurs guided John to sit in the front seat, and without acknowledgement all present witnessed the exposed chasm of John's shock as he mechanically responded to Sally's voice and none other.

Jack's quiet sprawl left no room inside the car for Theda and Little Ruth so each girl closed the door on her side of the car and climbed onto the running board to ride standing up, Little Ruth on the driver's side and Theda on the passenger's side. The girls grabbed a hold of the windshield support frame and the fragile top of the Model T and held on for dear life as Vesta expertly backed out of the yard and turned the car to head toward the Bethel cemetery. It was a bumpy ride and Jack's moans tortured them all, and when Vesta finally pulled the car as close as possible to the porch at the Owens home place, it was no more effort than picking up a feather for John to pick up his son's lifeless body and carry him up the steps, across the porch and into the house.

John laid Jack down on the bed in the front bedroom and Sally covered her son with a quilt and assigned eight-year-old Little Ruth to watch over him while she and Theda and Vesta finished the job of scrubbing the walls and dousing them with buckets of boiling rinse water in an attempt to kill the dogged old bedbugs and chinch bugs for this job had to be completed or else they'd all be sleeping on the floor tonight.

The blasted old bed bugs and chinch bugs were a torment all through spring, summer and into the fall, and the ritual of removing all furniture and thoroughly scrubbing down the walls and scouring the floors cut back on their population for a few days or maybe a couple of weeks, but then it was all to be done again. The first step in this elaborate cleansing / purging ritual was to open up the end seams of all the bottom mattresses and dump the old brittle corn shucks out on the ground behind the house, down the hill on the far side of the field, and once set a blaze, Theda stayed with the corn shuck fire while Vesta trudged back up the hill to the wash pot toting the last empty mattress ticking; and with the battlin' stick she lifted and removed another ticking from the wash pot, plopped it over into the rinse pot and then thankfully pushed the last mattress ticking into the boiling wash water. She poked and stirred it in the wash pot then turned her attention to the rinse pot. She stoked the fire under each pot convinced the boiling water would kill any chinch and bedbug eggs remaining in the mattress ticking fabric.

When the corn shuck fire finally burned safely down in the field, Theda came along back up the hill to help wring out the washed and rinsed mattress ticking, and when the girls spread them out on the porch railing to dry, they went back inside to help Sally with sweeping and spreading to dry the last of the standing water on the back bedroom floor. All this time, Little Ruth stayed by Jack's side in the front bedroom where she continued to sooth him by singing to him or whispering his name or smoothing the worry lines from his brow, and John sat in a straight back chair beside the bed and watched through dazed eyes.

That was a very sad and sobering time for John Owens always the anchor for his family and friends, but now this strong and honorable man felt for the first time in his life that he might loose control, and he imagined himself as a liar and anything but the rock of strength he'd been 'til now, his shoulders began to slump as he came face to face with the years of personal disaster heaped on the years of a gripping country-wide hunger and depression and he began to feel the heavy relentless weight that might actually crush him.

Doc and me walked down to check on Jack early the next morning. My Model T was still at the Owens home place, and that was just as good a parking space as any and there was no need of wasting gasoline just for the sake of moving it up the road a piece, and for that matter, we would have walked the short distance anyway or maybe hitched up the horse and wagon because in them days you never burnt precious gasoline unless it was a work trip (which involved hauling whiskey to customers or hauling in whiskey making supplies from town) because gasoline was too hard to come by. Just a few weeks after I bought my Model T, I made the wise purchase of two five gallon galvanized tin gas cans and strapped them both full of gas to the back of the car because it was so damned inconvenient to run out of gas way out on the country roads for the only remedy was to walk the long distance to the gas pump back in Tallapoosa. Anyway that happened to me twice and that was one time too many so I made sure from then on that the two spare gas cans strapped to the back of the car were always full of gasoline and that took care of that.

When we walked in at the Owens home place, we found Jack awake and talking, he was in real good spirits but we soon realized his memory of the past week or more was wiped clean. Sally fixed Jack a breakfast of eggs and biscuits and gravy and brought the plate to him in the front bedroom, and we watched as he devoured the food. Obviously he had a very good appetite. The sun was just beginning to lighten the sky, and John and Chester were out of the house already working at the sawmill. Doc listened to Jack's heart and lungs and he felt along Jack's arms and legs, no broken bones, except his ribs of course, and Jack complained that the rag strip bindings around his rib cage were too tight, but Doc said they needed to be tight to remind him to restrict his movements because, "You can't be moving around and expect your ribs to heal."

Doc told Jack to stay in bed for at least a week and be quiet and still, and he stressed to Sally the crucial importance of Jack's remaining immobile, "Tote all Jack's meals to the bed for at least five or six days and make him stay in bed."

Jack tried to argue that he was needed at the saw mill, but Doc wouldn't hear to it, so Doc and me walked out of doors past my car and on up to the top of the hill and when Doc turned left to walk up the narrow lane and go home through the cemetery, I turned right and walked toward the screaming noise of John's steam powered sawmill because I knew Jack was right when he said John would be short handed.

Prettiest Girl in the World and Me a Saw Miller

The sawmill was situated just a little ways past the big sweet gum tree and into the clearing beyond cleared expressly to allow the loading of timber boards onto the truck or wagons. I guess I looked at it for the first time that very morning, I mean I'd been to the sawmill site lots of times, but I never paid attention to any of the particulars. This time as I came closer to the singing of the steam engine, I looked with respect at the long shed-roof built over the boiler and the long belts and pulleys running to the equipment. I breathed in the acid of the pine sawdust and appreciated the amount of work put into building the shed, digging away and moving the dirt, and setting up this amazing, complicated machinery.

I watched Chester guide a team of horses away from the log dump area, park them in the shade still harnessed to the empty dray before turning back to the work site. He noticed me and waved his arms motioning me to come on over. At the log dump area, I saw John moving one log from the pile of logs using a four or five foot pole. When I got close enough I recognized the tool he was holding as a cant hook and when he saw me, John nodded his head and sure enough he handed me the cant hook and put me to work right that minute a doing Jack's job which was setting blocks. It was might near impossible to hear with the steam engine chugging so when John handed me the cant hook, he made hand motions a telling me to stay at the log dump area, and then he turned and circled around the logs piled on the elevated dump area. John side stepped down the four-foot drop off to the lower level and made his way to the sawyer's station. Nobody had to tell me what my next move had to be and that was to maneuver the logs from the dump deck one at a time down the skid poles and onto the carriage

With the dray, John and Chester had off loaded logs to the deck. I noticed the hillside was dug away and a wall drop off formed a four foot cliff just about exactly the height of the moving carriage leading to the big circular saw turning and whining off to my right. Skid poles installed side-by-side running lengthwise from the deck to the carriage formed a slide so as to roll the logs directly down onto the carriage which was waist high level for John.

With the cant hook, I maneuvered and rolled a log down the skid poles and onto the carriage and I let it roll up against the blocks which I wondered why they were called blocks because they were not in the shape of blocks but were shaped like tall handles with levers a holding' weighted locks which I slammed down onto the log so that the sharp end of a spike went nearly an inch into the log. This is called setting the blocks, which sounds easy, but before I could push down the lever, which dropped the weights, I had to set the distance of each block from the saw cut line and judge the diameter of the log at the base end. I compared that to the diameter of the log at the tree top end and then set the blocks as quick as I could to get a good cut on the straight from the tree top end down through the base end. Sometimes this meant adjusting the position of the blocks so the cut-off slab would be thicker by as much as several inches at the base end. I could see as how operating the sawyer's levers might scare a man 'cause just standing close to the giant turning saw blade made my insides feel jittery. John didn't back away from any challenge and I took his lead and decided the best way to go was to face the danger.

I admit I was completely spellbound as I watched John's expert work, all done with his left hand at the levers. I stood waiting with the cant hook. The other lever made slight adjustments to the position of the log on the carriage, and he was working foot levers too.

After cutting the first slab off the first side of the log, John sent the carriage all the way back and motioned for me to turn the log so the flat cut side faced into the blocks, and then is when I saw my mistake, my first block set caused way too much to be sawed off of the top end of the log. As quick as I could I repositioned the blocks and then with the cant hook which had a handle of about four feet long I pulled the log back up tight against the blocks and again I pushed down the lever on the blocks which dropped the weights and locked the log in place on the carriage. It was all new to me, and my guess is that John Owens let me make mistakes that first day knowing I'd learn faster by doing than by trying to hear and follow orders.

I learned how to handle the cant hook and I figured out that it was called a cant hook because the metal was canted or curved with respect to the metal sleeve part. The point of the hook was sharp enough to dig into the wood and the pivot point of the cant acted as a fulcrum for the four-foot long wooden handle or lever and this design made it easy to move heavy logs

I learned to imagine the saw line and with that line in my head, I positioned the blocks so the saw took off less bark from the front end or tree top end. Each log had its own characteristics that John calculated as fast as I could roll the log onto the carriage.

As fast as I could I turned the log like he called for and dropped the weights in place and then signaled to him that I was free from the carriage by slinging both arms into the air, and he pushed the lever and started the carriage moving toward the saw blade. If he sawed opposite sides of the log and sent the carriage back to me, I learned to leave the log unturned and move the blocks over two inches if John showed me two fingers, this meant he needed some two-bys to fill a order.

Another way to cut the logs is after the first cut, the carriage is brought all the way back past the saw and the front end of the log is brought all the way back to the sawyer and the log is turned so it is riding with the flat surface on the bottom, now the whole thing (if it is symmetrical) is cut again exactly as before so that the second cut on the second side is just like the first cut. The sawyer has to decide what is needed to fill the order or what is needed to produce the most efficient cut if the lumber is cut into two-bys or four-bys or maybe even for rafters or support beams which are six-bys or eight-bys.

We quit work at sun down and at the end of that first day working at a saw mill, when John shut off the steam engine, I did what I'd wanted to do all day but couldn't spare the time, I kindly squatted down and let my weight fall into my right hand down on the edge of the log deck and I pushed off throwing my legs out in front of me, and jumped down to the level of the sawyer's station, where before all the light left the sky, I squatted down to examine the series of pulleys and friction wheels that moved the carriage back and forth on rails. I stretched back a standing up and realized just how dog-tired I was, but still I could not understand how a whole day could have slipped away in what seemed like just a few minutes. I had a ringing in my ears from the loud noise of the steam engine, but I missed the scream of the saw tearing through the wood like I'd been listening to some music makers.

I didn't want to quit because this saw milling work is more interesting by a long shot than the work of making whiskey, so as I stood up and placed my hands on my tired aching back, for a quiet minute I turned my face up to the sky and looked at the beautiful tall standing pine trees swaying in the clear moonlight and I felt the captivation I've always felt only now I noticed every little detail of the long pine needles fanned out in a design that could only been made in heaven, and I wished that minute would never end, and as I beat and brushed the layers of saw dust off my shirt and pants, I sucked in the crisp fresh aroma of the loblolly pine dust that for me is far more pleasant than smelling a sweet shrub held in hot cupped hands. I felt sorry for the pore ole city dudes who've lived their lives with never getting to enjoy the acidic and sweet fragrance of fresh cut pine lumber.

Anyhow, I knew that first day and possibly the first hour that I'd found the work I want to do for the rest of my life, and as me and Chester and John walked along talking and laughing about our good day's work, it made my chest swell with accomplishment and brotherhood to understand what they were saying and why they were saying it.

When John and Chester turned down the hill to the Owens home place, I continued straight across the road into the darkness beneath the big hardwood trees lining the narrow road leading to the cemetery and there I saw Vesta just as she stood up from sitting at the base of a giant oak tree, and she came out in the road to me and all I could see in the dark was her pearl white teeth, and she walked beside me through the darkness. We walked a few feet not saying a word, and in our silence everything between us was absolutely, totally and completely known and understood. I'll never forget the mighty power of the few steps I made with the prettiest girl in the world and me a saw miller.

Every morning Doc walked down to check on Jack and I walked with him as far as the top of the hill above the Owens home place, and there we'd split up for I walked straight on to the sawmill and every day while Jack's ribs were healing, I did his job of setting blocks and I got pretty good at it too, but Chester couldn't do all the other jobs by himself, so I helped at all the stations of the sawmill just like Jack always did, and after a week and a half when Jack showed up back at work there was a good sized pile of logs waiting for him on the deck and me and Chester told him to take it as easy as possible and stay at the deck and set the blocks while we went into the woods with the mules where we cut the logs into lengths to fill the orders that we all kept in our heads, and using the straight twelve foot pole that was notched at the ten foot point, and the eight foot point, we measured for exact cuts of eight foot, ten foot, twelve foot and fourteen foot logs. Chester couldn't no way lift a log more than fourteen foot long. So with the logs cut in exact lengths, we snaked them to the dray using the team of mules, me and John and Chester all agreed that if I wanted to keep on working at the saw mill then naturally Jack would again take over the job of block setter and me and Chester would work as a team, sawing down trees with the cross cut saw, snaking them to the dray, loading them on the dray, hauling them to the log deck, unloading them and when that work got caught up, then me and Chester worked at firing the boiler, running the boards through the edger, shoveling the piles of sawdust from the ground around the circular saw into a wagon that we by hand pulled out and around and backed into position close to the boiler door. We shoveled the sawdust from the wagon into the boiler.

The pile of slabs built up mighty quick where the conveyer belt dumped them and that alone was a full time job just keeping all the slabs cut into pieces and hauled to the boiler where naturally they too were used as fuel.

John tried to pay me some when we hauled into town two wagons and the truck loaded with lumber, but I had my mind made up that I'd not take it and though John tried his best to make me take the money, I wouldn't have it for it was not fair to Jack to take the money that was rightfully his and besides I was working at my still through the night which was an easy enough job that I could just about do it in my sleep, and that's what I did, I slept on the ground at the still, the only problem being, I'd been slippery so far when it came to revenuers, but I could've been caught during that time when I was working two jobs but sleeping most of the night on the ground right at the still, but I figured it was worth the risk, cause I didn't see how I could give up the chance to learn every detail about saw milling.

I walked around feeling real smug about running enough whiskey to fill my orders and holding out to work from sun up to sun down at the sawmill with just a few hours of sleep at night. I did change my whiskey delivery times from my routine of doing that in the early morning hours, but when you think about it I should've been switching the delivery hours around a long time before then just as another precaution to fool revenuers who might be watching me or my customers. I notified every single customer when I caught 'em at the pool hall or on the road, or in some cases at their house, but this was not very smart for I sure didn't want any good customer to be in no way put into the uncomfortable position of being a link between me and my shady business. Deep inside I felt that working at the sawmill probably served as a real good way a throwing off the nosey revenuers who saw me delivering lumber or what not, and I'm for sure the revenuers figured no man could do both jobs and since it was plain out there for everybody to see that I was working at the saw mill, then naturally, they all believed I must a quit making whiskey.

Right here, I want to make sure you understand the code of honor that was followed between boot-legers and revenuers whereby it was possible for us to be friendly to one another and talk to one another and even shoot pool with one another, in fact there wasn't a single one of the revenuers that I didn't like, and they all liked me, but they had a job to do and would do it and I knew that if they caught me making whiskey, they'd think nothing of putting me in jail. I had a lot of people depending on me to put food in their mouth, so I had to be smart and watch the revenuer's every move just like they were watching me, but I never was afraid of being mistreated, no sir, for I knew that if a revenuer caught me red handed, nothing bad would happen to me like getting shot or pistol whipped or beat up, no sir, for that was not in the code of conduct because the revenuers respected me, and even though they carried a gun and they were sworn to uphold the law which meant they'd arrest me if they caught me for making whiskey was illegal even though in my case there was not a victim to this supposed illegal act, and actually the exact opposite was the case. There were a lot of people who benefited from my making whiskey, and that being said, at the same time I was sure as shooting positive, there wasn't a single revenuer that would ever under any imaginable circumstances draw a gun on me. It just wasn't done that way, but I had to face facts, they all knew where I lived, and they all knew I was feeding a whole lot of people and most likely I was coming by my money by making whiskey, but the point is that none of them ever treated me like I was a criminal, for I damned sure wasn't.

Every week when the weeks work was sold in town, the honorable John Owens tried over and over again to make me take a little pay for working at the sawmill, and every week, I refused to take it, knowing the three of them, John, Chester and Jack all added together were probably making about the same amount of money or maybe a little less than I was making selling whiskey to my regular customers so they better just keep their money, and it was clearly theirs and not mine because in my way a thinking, all fair money dealings have to consider 'need' as the biggest consideration and besides to even out the equation, at sun down every day, in my way of thinking, I got paid more than all the gold in the world when Vesta met me at the top of the hill and walked a ways by my side.

Me and the other bootleggers (them that carried a half pint of outlaw whiskey in the leg of their boot) liked to get together and tell about our close cuts with the revenuers. Sometimes at a barn dance or in town standing on the street corner or maybe in the pool hall, we'd tell lies and sometimes we'd tell the truth about our wild escapes running from the law. I always added a little to make my stories sound bigger. Everybody did that.

I was working at my still one night, when the sounds of somebody coming up woke me from a deep sleep, and the approaching sounds were coming from the west back in behind me and as I turned my head toward the ruckus, I caught the faint glow of a lantern which was just a quick glimpse through the thick trees. I was sitting on a log on the west side of the branch where I'd dug the vats into the ground, which I always dug the vats into the ground as part of my system to hide my fire. This was a lot of work, but well worth it for by having the fire below the ground level the flame was not visible except right at the spot, and it was easy to douse a flame with a double handful of creek water and then take off a running which I did after I further concealed the vats by spreading out the vat cover which I made out a sugar sacks and sewed them together to make a big sheet, and I changed the white material to make it blend in with the woods by spreading it out on the ground and scattering shovels of dirt all around on it and stomping the dirt in by the twisting of my boots. And before dawn each morning, when I finished running a batch of whiskey into fruit jars, my first job was to put out the fire, my last job was to spread the cover, place a few rocks along the edge, and pick up and scatter leaves on top of the cover, and a few times even I had to hunt for my still because it was well hidden from me, the very one who was supposed to know the where abouts.

Back to the story, I had a pretty good hunch the noise I heard was revenuers approaching from the west, so I doused the fire, spread out the cover and as fast as I could, I rolled the fruit jars full of whiskey under the edge of the cover and dropped a last bunch of leaves on top. Then I waded through the branch a heading away from the revenuers and started my escape up the far creek bank scrambling through the dense woods to the east. There was still no light in the sky, but I knew the lay of the land like the back of my hand and when I rounded up over the ridge out of breath, I slowed down thinking I had out tricked them, and then's when I discovered two or three more revenuers a waiting for me with their lanterns held high. I didn't take time to count the rascals and I guess their lanterns worked against them in a way and gave me the edge because they could see only as far as the lantern light spread, but I on the other hand, didn't need a lantern, never had for I can see in the dark, and for that matter, I can't understand people who say they can not see in the dark, anyway, I diverted my path and avoided running right smack dab into the revenuers who could hear me but couldn't see me, and I was running lick-a-de split through the trees toward the long bottoms, and I didn't slow down for nothing and I was mighty glad they had no bloodhounds to track me down.

I could always out run the revenuers in a race for my freedom, but the revenuers had another trick up their sleeve. They started hiring football players from the University of Alabama, and I for sure could not out run the football players, and word was that they hired enough football players to have relay teams ready and in place to take up the chase when one team got too tired to run any more.

For sure John never worked at the sawmill on Sunday for that was a day of rest, and most everybody, everywhere observed the no work on Sunday rule, but Saturday he and Chester and Jack went about the heavy farming work that comes up regular and has to be done, and on Saturdays every member of the family worked about the place, and the men specifically completed what was too heavy for the women to do, but the women folks stayed busy with many menial, daily tasks requiring attention which were said to 'wait for no one' both inside and outside the house and when the depression reached deep down into the pockets of desperately poor country folks, the women everywhere went to planting crops and raising cattle and sheep, and in addition to saw-milling, the men picked up the slack of jobs unsuited to the women, but on the other hand, Saturday for me became sobering for I was denied the exhilarating work of saw-milling so I put Saturday mornings as my time to catch up on loose ends in my whiskey making job, and by mid Saturday afternoon, I put it all down, covered it all up, and washed up to go to town. In town, I started by getting a haircut and shave and after that most times I found myself in the pool hall, and in the pool hall one Saturday, Morris Hare told the story of a young man learning the whiskey making trade. Morris called him a bootlegger's apprentice and described the young apprentice running like the wind through the woods with the revenuers running right along behind him chasing him, and when they got close enough to grab the collar of the young man's coat, the apprentice didn't slow down one bit and actually ran out of his coat, leaving the revenuers behind out of breath and holding nothing but his coat. He was mighty sorry to loose that coat.

Working at a whiskey still was grimy, dirty work, and I didn't want to go around town looking as filthy as an old buzzard so most nights I brought to the still a change of clothes and when the night's work was done, I walked downstream along the creek to a favorite bathing place where the water was up to my chest. I knew of many of these deep swimming holes, and that morning, I stripped off my clothes and waded into the water holding a bar of lye soap which was about the only thing that would cut the oily black soot from my face, hands and hair. After my bath in the swimming hole, I dried off and put on clean clothes for this was a delivery day and once I completed deliveries and before I showed up at the Owens sawmill, I wanted to drive the road to Cross Roads School in the hopes of giving Vesta a ride. It was not out of the ordinary for me to slide over and let Vesta drive, and she could maneuver the car through even the muddiest and slipperiest spots, and she didn't shy away from any difficulty.

Just about every Saturday, knowing the Owens saw-mill would be silent, I managed to spend a little time in the pool hall, I like it there because it's a dark, men-only hideout right on Head Avenue in Tallapoosa, and a man can always find a willing opponent for a friendly game of eight ball.

Two buildings south of the pool hall was the new Grand Theater, and on Saturday afternoon, the boys in town waited in line at the ticket window, and every week, as soon as I got into town, I headed for the Grand Theater and the line up of boys waiting on me to go down the line giving a nickel to each boy. For a nickel, a boy could see a cowboy movie, a weekly serial, a comedy and previews of coming attractions, and these boys come to rely on me to pay their way into the show, and I like to help out where I can.

On Easter Sunday morning, the Owens family walked to Camp Ground church. The Godwin family went to Bethel church, but everybody in the Bethel Community relied on Camp Ground Church for social activities other than Sunday services, and the most enjoyable for the young men and the pretty young ladies were the basket dinners held on Saturday evenings about every other month or so, and each young lady came prepared to share her basket dinner with the highest bidder, and as a young man I learned early on to pay close attention to how Vesta decorated her basket dinner which hers was as the usual thing the best decorated and I'd be willing to bet on Vesta's fried chicken tasting better than any other. It came to be accepted that my first bid on Vesta's basket would receive one counter bid, just to bring in more money for the church, but all the young men knew that my second bid was to stand as the highest bid, and that handled that and before the sun went down, me and Vesta spread her quilt out on the ground out behind the church where the tall green grass was trampled down by visitors to the cemetery, and this was the way that Chester came to court my sister Nancy's girl Nora, and Jack came to court Cleo Kilgore, and when all the quilts were spread out on the ground for picnics they lined up with edges touching which made a cheerful, colorful display and pretty near covered up every bit of open ground and that is why the cars and wagons were parked out along the road in front of the church just to make room for all the spread out quilts.

On the walk home from Camp Ground's Easter Sunday morning service, Theda was walking between John and Sally. She was preoccupied with the flowers along the side of the road and she stopped to pick some of the little light blue violets and the bigger dark purple ones. She also picked some of the weed used to dye Easter eggs a soft yellow, even though all the Owens children were all too old for that foolishness.

"Papa, what day of the week is it?"

"Theda, this year Easter Sunday falls on Sunday. The only time that Easter Sunday actually falls on Monday is in odd numbered years following the even numbered years when Good Friday falls on Thursday? By my calculation, that won't happen again for several years."

Theda was dumbfounded with all this rig-a-ma-roll and John laughed out loud at the serious look on her face. That night was the start of revival at Pleasant Hill Church, and as you know during revival week, there's a church meeting every night for the purpose of reviving the faithful's trust in the Lord. These nightly meeting include preaching, individual testimonials, and singing a lot of favorite gospel hymns, followed by socializing outside in the church yard which for some of the county might be the biggest draw for it can get mighty lonely in the back woods of Alabama.

Vesta, Theda, Little Ruth, Sis, Beulah and Pauline, three Owens girls and three Godwin girls, as a usual course of action, walked the ten miles along the narrow wagon roads to the Pleasant Hill Revival, and on this Easter Sunday evening these six girls hushed their chatter as they approached the burnt grocery at the corner where the main Bethel road runs into the Jacksonville Road because they all knew this intersection to be the site where a small but busy country grocery store once stood, and they got a little scared just thinking about the eerie charred remains. They always quickened their step past where a man pitifully burned to death, and now with just enough light in the sky so as to see new growth of honeysuckle vines disguising the only reminder of a once thriving business reduced now to no more than a slight clearing in the trees covered knee high in honeysuckle vines, and the stone stacks set in place as the building's foundation rose above the green honeysuckle vines along the clearing's perimeter outlining the exact position of the grocery.

In revival meeting that night when it was Mrs. Reynolds's turn to give her testimonial, she stood up from her seat on the back pew and told the sad story as to how her whole family stayed sick all through the long winter and into the spring, they're still sick with her being the only one able to nurse them and carry out the chores of farming and cooking and cleaning, and when Mrs. Reynolds gathered together her cotton dress material and bunched her skirt in her hands to pull it tight across her back-end so as to sit down, she raised her head one last time from a half-standing-half-sitting position and declared in a high pitched and loud plea to the congregation, "So I just want you all to pray that they'll get well or do something."

Vesta, Theda, and Sis were sitting on the pew right in front of poor old Mrs. Reynolds, and the three girls politely continued their gaze toward the altar instead of looking straight up into Mrs. Reynolds face. In the crowded church, Little Ruth, Beulah and Pauline found a place to sit on the opposite side of the center aisle and two rows closer to the preacher. It was common courtesy for the worshipers to turn around in their seats to face the person giving a testimonial and that is what Little Ruth, Beulah and Pauline did merging their faces with everybody else in the church, but when Mrs. Reynolds delivered her unusual last request, Vesta, Theda and Sis in unison and ever so slightly shifted their gaze from the front of the church toward Little Ruth, Beulah and Pauline and naturally, the six girls needed only a quick glance to communicate their inner thoughts so it was a simple fake for Little Ruth, Beulah and Pauline to appear to be looking at Mrs. Reynolds when in reality they looked directly into Vesta's, Theda's and Sis's eyes, bringing the six to look at each other in the exact minute when Mrs. Reynolds made her high volume and unlikely prayer request, and not one of the six girls could hide her reaction and very quickly Little Ruth, Beulah, and Pauline realized their best tactic was to twist back around in the pew to face the preacher and they did, but it was no use for they could not stop their giggles and with heads bowed, their shame added to the ridiculous situation and the more they tried to stop laughing the more they had to let it out, and pretty soon they realized all attempts to stifle resulted in a humiliating jiggling of the pew, and one by one the others sitting on the same pew leaned forward to glare at the silly girls until in a last desperate struggle for decorum, they held their white handkerchiefs over their mouths and pretended to cough and this managed to hide their antics from most of the other worshipers. Here I should point out that no polite lady (young or old) considered herself properly dressed for any event outside the home until she stuffed a white handkerchief into her dress pocket, and proudly, all of these small white cotton squares were finely decorated with embroidery and less often with highly cherished, hard to come by, lace remnants, home tatted of course.

After the preacher's call for repentance and acceptance of Jesus, the congregation sang all verses of the favorite, 'Just As I Am, Without One Plea" and the girls sang in beautiful harmony without one missed note as several in the congregation answered each verses' call, "Oh Lamb of God, I come, I come!" To conclude the service, the preacher delivered the last prayer over the heads of those who answered Jesus's call by walking the aisle, and kneeling at the altar, and tonight's repentants accounted for more than half of the congregation, and with the last, "Amen," the preacher preceded everyone to the church door, and the six girls stood patiently in line to politely shake the preacher's hand before they scooted out the door and down the steps.

They hurried beyond the cemetery into the road, and when they were safely beyond the dim candlelight of the church and more importantly, beyond the ears of the believers, they were finally free to laugh until their sides hurt, and their rowdy antics continued throughout their passage along the moonlit narrow dirt road, but magically they were able to contain themselves and remember their decorum as a half a dozen wagons forced them off the road and into the weeds where each girl stood solemnly nodding, 'goodnight' because each girl understood the consequences if a neighboring believer conveyed to their families even a slight lapse of respectable behavior, which was all important in the social life of the county, and even though the Pleasant Hill settlement was somewhat removed from their own Bethel community, every single resident of Pleasant Hill knew each and every single member of the Owens and Godwin families.

When the final wagon passed, and the girls were back in parade down the center of the narrow dirt road, they soon approached the burnt grocery and settled down to walk in serious silence. No one made a peep of noise as they creped by the site practically on tiptoe, and this time as they passed the terrifying burnt grocery remains their foreboding was multiplied when the moon slipped behind a thick cloud, and they found themselves in total darkness, and their instant irrational rejoinder was to run with abandon through the pitch-black darkness. After running at top speed down the long straight stretch of road, their lungs collectively exhaled the life from their bodies when they heard the sound of a screech owl. They weren't actually handicapped by the darkness because even if they were blindfolded, they could easily follow any curve in the road for they knew every inch of this road and every other road and trail, for that matter, in the county or at the very least in this part of the county, and they knew the terrain like the back of their hand, but the screech owl dissolved their sense of security for it was always a fooler in that it sounded so much like a woman screaming, and the girls imagined that a tortured woman was following them home. As the eerie scream continued they ran at super human speed 'til they were out of breath, and when they slowed down to rest, once again the ghostly shrieking in the thick woods unwittingly started their feet to running again, and this time they didn't slow until they were totally exhausted and completely out of breath, and they stopped out of necessity, dropped their heads, placed their hands on their knees and gasped for air, but now in their self conscious silence, a profound collective revelation gave way to a quite literal life altering decision.

Each girl sheepishly looked to the other for confirmation of their shame, and they understood with clarity that they were running away from something they actually had very little of, that being 'fear,' and how could it be that tonight unexplainably and along this dark road which they'd walked in safety and security all their lives somehow they allowed their stupid fear to reduce them to scattered incoherence and idiocy when their actual goal was the exact opposite; they wanted to be and were strong, fearless and completely in control, and this sobering, inward look at themselves became a reckoning for all the girls as they straightened their rounded shoulders and pushed their heads up to face the sky. "What are we running from?"

The girls looked from one to the other as they grabbed hands and formed a tightly united, shoulder to shoulder line of attack, and they felt a power surge as their dependence on and support for each other literally forced them to grow taller, older, more mature and definitely harder to scare, and their clarity of purpose became a hand in hand pact to face fear head on, now and forever more. They vowed to walk instead of run right now, this minute, tonight and always, throughout life for why let fear rule? Running scared is no way to live your life, and now their show of bravery bolstered each one and by the evidence, that was all it took to convince the screech owl to move on and find someone else to frighten and the girls one by one, smiled up to the sky, and listened as the screeching gradually became fainter and fainter and now they deliberately walked at a slow, leisurely pace and the bright light of the full moon showed them the way, and as their sense of security returned their hearts stopped pounding, their lungs filled with air, and just now their senses were wrapped in the sweet honeysuckle aroma.

In the winter of 1929, after her fifteenth birthday in August, Sis moved out. Like Thomas, she packed her one change of clothes in a clean white sugar sack and she asked me to drive her into town, so I did. In town she wanted me to wait on her while she went into some of the stores to ask if she could get work, and when she came out of O.D. Lipham's, a lady followed her to my car.

"I heard you ask for work, aren't you a Godwin?" the lady asked.

"Yes, ma'am."

"What's your given name?"

"It's Sis, ma'am."

"Are you sure that's your given name?"

"Well, ma'am, Sis is what I've always gone by."

"Alright, Sis, my name is Mrs. Dalton Sewell, and I need someone to help me around the house. Do you want to follow me home, young man?"

I replied, "Yes 'um."

I drove Sis to the front of Dalton Sewell's house, let her out and drove off. I was glad to know where to find Sis, and every week or two, I went by to check on my little sister, and I could tell Sis was happy working for a very rich lady, the pay was good and her room and board was free. One time when Sis came out of the house and climbed into my car, she started telling me that share croppers worked Dalton Sewell's one thousand acres of farm land on the north side of town. One thousand acres, she's richer by a long shot than I guessed.

1932

All the years Sis worked for Dalton Sewell she got one weekend off a month and many times she spent her Saturday off at our sister Nancy's house. Nancy and her husband Jess Kilgore, had a big family like everybody else, and they owned a farm that bordered on the Tallapoosa River near Mc Bride's bridge. Before going to get Sis, first, I drove through the Bethel Cemetery to the Owens home place to pick up Vesta and she rode into town with me to get Sis, and then I hauled the two girls out to Nancy's which was a double back toward Bethel, but I liked the little bit of time alone with Vesta, and she was as pretty as a picture at age sixteen, and she had a laugh that would stop your heart. Her cream colored skin was smooth and radiant, and I noticed a few little freckles sprinkled across her small, slender nose. I stood right at six feet tall and Vesta was five feet four inches tall and slim like me. She had a healthy glow with just a little touch of pink on her high cheekbones. Her eyes were rich, golden brown about the color of sorghum syrup mixed up with a little butter, and her eyes complemented her glossy, naturally curly, auburn colored hair. Every time I looked at her, my heart skipped a beat for she was the prettiest girl in all of Alabama and Georgia. Both Sis and Vesta could drive real good, but today I drove while these silly girls laughed and had a high old time cutting up with some foolishness, and when I let them out and drove away from Nancy's house, I could hear the racket over the loud noise of the car engine when Nancy's girl Marie joined in their laughter.

Since it was a warm spring day, the girls walked across the field and down to the Tallapoosa River. To save their shoes they left them on the back porch and walked bare footed through the newly plowed fields, but their feet were still tender from wearing shoes all winter, so they danced and hopped in an effort to cushion the sharp gouging little rocks that dotted the field. Every jump and cry made them laugh even more, and when they finally waded into the cold river water they found some relief for their aching feet, and they watched mesmerized as tiny drops of blood rippled away and blended into the muddy water.

Their spring time topic of conversation centered around the dreaded dose of castor oil which all three girls along with everybody else in the county followed the annual "purge and renewal" ritual, and they allowed as how it was time to get it over and done with and the sooner the better, but believing in the benefits to their health did nothing to forestall the revolted shutter as each girl grimaced at the thought of swallowing the vile tasting elixir. They suffered the agonizing, barefooted walk back through the plowed field to the house, and before climbing up the back porch steps, each girl stepped into the bucket of well water sitting to the side of the steps for Nancy was just like Sis to keep things neat and clean and did not allow the girls to traipse into the house with muddy feet so with wet but clean feet, Marie tiptoed into the house, crossed the kitchen to the cupboard and returned to the back porch with the bottle of castor oil and the biggest spoon she could find.

The girls drew straws and Sis drew the shortest straw so that meant she had to go first, but before she poured the dose of castor oil into the spoon, she tried to work out the quickest and least painful way to get this foul tasting remedy into her system. She decided that it would be beneficial if she could immediately follow the castor oil with a drink of cool water so she filled the dipper from the well bucket and asked Marie to hold the dipper ready while she poured the smelly liquid into the big spoon. She instructed Marie to hand her the dipper as soon as she had the big dose of castor oil in her mouth, and at some point during her staging, there was a slight glance of conspiracy between Vesta and Marie. They realized this presented an unparalleled opportunity, and Sis suspected nothing and was unaware of Vesta's wink. As soon as Sis had the gorging dose of castor oil in her mouth, Marie splashed the entire contents of the dipper into Sis's face causing Sis to loose her breath as she swallowed the castor oil without tasting it, and then Sis swallowed again and again gasping for air. When she finally caught her breath, her eyes were as big around as saucers, her hair was dripping wet, her dress was soaked, and she could barely speak, but through her coughing and sputtering she said, "Ah shit Marie, that's not the way I meant for you to do it."

Marie and Vesta slid down to the porch floor to sit on their ankles, and in their wild laughing/crying hysteria, they collapsed further to the porch floor and began rolling side to side, back and forth clutching their stomachs as if they'd been the ones forced to swallow the castor oil, and their uncontrolled giggles drove Sis right off the porch, for she couldn't fathom how they could find such a dirty trick to be funny, and she stomped down the steps and into the back yard all the while wiping her face on her sleeve and squeezing the water from her drenched hair. She sulked and leaned against the big oak tree, arms folded at her waist, and the idée occurred to her to set out walking away from these mean girls and back to town, but her bad mood evaporated when Nancy called the girls into the kitchen for dinner and directed Marie to draw up the jar of buttermilk from the well, and Sis hoped this meant the table would be set with cornbread and the year's first tender turnip greens cooked with plenty of pot liquor and served with a cool (from the bottom of the well) glass of buttermilk.

For might near two years I worked at the Owens saw mill and one morning as I ran the last few steps to work, I wondered why the steam fired engine was not screaming, and the next thing I knew I was looking at the saddest site I'd every seen. John was standing where the sawyer's station had been and on the ground all around him was black soot where the sawmill used to be. The shed was burned to the ground, the metal boiler was blackened and twisted, the belts and pulleys were no where in site, and the wagon loaded with slabs yesterday was now reduced to the charred and distorted metal pieces of the tongue and singletree reinforcements, the tie-down hooks from each side of the bed, the long back iron rod bed stabilizer with the middle tightening wing nuts, and four metal outer wheel circles. This eerie ghost-like outline of the wagon lay on the black ashes next to the now mangled firebox defined only by the hideous and barely recognizable burned metal. My eyes scanned the site and confirmed that of course the firebox door was latched shut, but embers must have survived the dousing shovel of dirt. I guess the shock of it was too much for John for he was standing shaking his bowed head back and forth like he was telling a child, "No."

Chester and Jack were not much better off than their Papa and all three were reverently silent in the face of yet another devastating tragedy. I don't know how, but I controlled the sobs ripping through my gut, but not the tears rolling down my face and maybe it was good for me to let go of my torture but they could not find such release. I went over every detail in my head of the last minutes at the vibrant work place the day before, and I could see in my mind the usual precautions we always took to prevent a fire, and all I come up with was the wagon loaded with slabs left standing where we backed it up to the firebox and just one live floating ember escaping from the fire box smoke stack and settling on just the right spot of dry bark on just the perfectly positioned slab and the wind breathing just enough air into the flame and all the unlikely circumstances come together in unusual alignment to start a fire powerful enough to contort iron and pull the safe harbor of a man's lively hood right out from under him. You have to remember it was the middle of a depression that held our nation in suspended agony, and big John Owens had to let go of the one best means he had of feeding his family not to mention the countless unselfish acts of kindness that he'd come to be known for. We finally turned away from the pile of rubble, and it occurred to me as we trudged out to the road and down the hill to the house that the remains of the saw mill were cool enough for us to stand in the ashes and so that meant the fire must have occurred early last night, and I recalled that a quick shower of rain woke me laying on the ground at the still, so the best I could figure, that shower of rain came after midnight, so but for that little bit of rain, the saw mill fire could have spread into the woods and I said so and Chester and Jack were glad for the idée that it might have been a more devastating and crippling blaze, but John Owens showed no relief as he continued to look only at the ground and shake his head back and forth.

God Bless John Owens for he was always a stalwart of strength, a tower of kindness, and a harbor of peace and laughter for as long as any of us could remember, but now he crumbled before our eyes, his jokes were silent and his eyes were dull. He could find no reason to laugh and he described the world as gray and lifeless and ugly and because he could find no hope of starting over in the saw milling trade, Jack and Chester went out on their own and got jobs at other sawmills and for a while they both worked for Ab Whitley. And weeks after the fire the Owens family finally told Doc about John's condition, and Doc went with me to the Owens home place to see for himself.

John's diagnosis was a very serious mental shut down or nervous break down but Doc knew of a place in Tuscaloosa where John could get the help he needed so Doc wrote to the state hospital for the mentally ill and when Doc received back in the mail the description of the treatment at the state facility called Bryce State Mental Hospital, he was pleased to learn the methods used there were based on the philosophy of the first superintendent Peter Bryce who was considered a psychiatric pioneer. Doc carefully read every detail and was especially interested in the printed words that proclaimed all patients committed there were treated with courtesy, kindness and respect at all times and the use of shackles, straitjackets and other restraints were abandoned way back in 1882. The hospital has many work programs for the patients and Doc decided that John Owens could benefit from the farming program. All this took months of letter writing and when the day finally arrived for John to go off, I offered to drive John in my car for Chester and Jack couldn't spare the time away from work at Ab Whitley's saw mill. Sally would not let us go without her so she and Vesta sat in the back seat and made the long trip in silence, as did John and me.

To this point in my life, considering the difficult times I've been through, well I can honestly say the hardest thing I ever had to do was to drive away and leave John Owens, but there's comfort in the fact that the Bryce State Mental Hospital is a very nice big house three stories tall, with big white round columns also three stories tall along the wide front porch which creates a porch on the ground level, and the second and third levels too. Every member of the staff dresses in white cotton and not a single one was rude or mean-natured, and that made the whole thing a little easier, but Sally and Vesta both cried like babies all the way back home to Cleburne County, and I'd be lying if I tried to make you think I didn't.

I have to tell you that once Sally Owens faced and conquered the loneliness she found back at home, she proved to be stronger than anyone could have imagined and first of all, she did the one thing she could do for John and that was to write a letter to him every day and the only days she did not write to John were the days that Vesta or Theda or Little Ruth did write to their Papa, and these women made sure that John Owens got a letter in the mail every single day. The peddler, along with every body else in the county, knew that John was sent off for it was not a deep dark secret to be ashamed of and for the entire time that John was in Tuscaloosa, every day of the week but Sunday of course, the peddler made a special trip off the main road which was his usual route except for the two days a week he'd always left the main road to go by the Owen's home place, past the Roberds place to Campground Church before returning to the main road by way of St Michael's Church. The peddler did this just so he could pick up the daily letter to John Owens addressed to the Bryce State Mental Hospital, Tuscaloosa, Alabama. No one in the county looked down on or thought less of John Owens, but instead and as a matter of fact, it seemed like everybody now used this as a chance to repay John Owens for the countless times he has given his time and money to help others, and that included everybody in the Bethel Community, so now the tables are turned and acts of kindness come daily from the good folks who know the best way to help John Owens is to help his wife and family. Every one of Sally's letters to John tells of how somebody in the Bethel community brings garden vegetables, or comes by on wash day to help Sally and the girls with the heavy toting, or comes by before dawn and milks the cow not leaving a name or nothing but the full bucket of milk by the front door. These acts of kindness give Sally plenty to write about so as to fill up a whole page every day of writing to John and that's another thing that is given to Sally, the peddler gives Sally a pencil, paper, envelopes and stamps, and he doesn't take credit for it him self, but always tells Sally the names of the neighbors that each give a penny or two and the stamps alone cost a precious three cents a piece, but every time the peddler accumulates three cents in donations, he brings another stamp to give to Sally and just about every time he gives Sally a stamp or paper or envelope, he reminds Sally of a story for her to write of a neighbor's remembrance of John's kind acts in the community now retold to the peddler or in some cases it's a new funny story told to the peddler for the first time, cause everybody knows that John loves to laugh and laughing in his case will be good medicine.

John stayed in Tuscaloosa for just a few months, and when he came home it was a happy day and many neighbors stopped by to slap him on the back and tell him he was sorely missed and a few even hugged the big old bear of a feller, and John was glad for it, but after a while when all the excitement wore off, the time came for him to make some decisions, and he knew in his heart that saw milling was evil for it was doing the work of saw milling that fateful day hauling lumber to town when Jack was hurt and the thought of that desperate, helpless feeling he felt that day as he mindlessly carried his injured son will forever be linked in his mind with the hideous, brain numbing feeling he had when he buried not one but two babies, and no matter how big and strong a man is, lifting a shovel full of dirt and throwing it into a hole in the ground to cover up a baby well that's certain to break any strong man's back, and he will not recover no sir, even if he gives every effort to it, he will not recover if he lives to be a hundred years old, and now as John's mind wondered to that black morning when he stood in the middle of the burned out saw mill, another kind of mental torture took hold of him, and he submitted to it and understood this to be another demon that will torment him forever, and he believes the only sane means remaining to him by which to support his family and make a little money is to plow the fields in the spring, work the mules through the fields plowing up weeds in the summer, harvest the crops in the fall and scatter manure to fertilize the fields through the winter.

John the farmer

He knows that he can do the peaceful work of farming and feel good about it for it is a real connection to the renewal of life meaning farming is working at a satisfying pace that includes watching the crops grow, and it is a soothing work to tend the livestock and marvel as they drop their young which captures a warm place in his heart when the newborns stand for the first time on wobbly, spindly unsure legs and every time a hen's chicks hatch it brings a real good feeling when the little peepers scatter away from the hen only to scurry back under the protection of her wing. All aspects of farming are slower and more gratifying, and this is a side of life that appeals to John more than the hectic routine of running a sawmill and even though he enjoys the challenge of sawmilling he knows that he needs a calmer more relaxed way to get through the day-to-day business of living, and he now accepts that he simply is not suited to the constant hectic pace making thousands of split second decisions which sawmilling requires, and when he analyzed it with a clear head, he seemed to get a lucid view of his former self which painted an image of him butting his head into a rock wall over the last few years and for what? Now, looking back it became obvious that sawmilling separated him from the part of living that matters most to him, and making more money simply translates into buying more things and creating more problems and coping with more pressure. Just as a dog shakes itself free of water, John can shake himself free of worry and stress and move into a slower pace in life and sit on the porch more and talk to his wife more and visit with passing neighbors more and listen to his own heart more and slow down to look at the beauty all around him and take pleasure in the little things especially on the day's when the peddler comes by to share the gossip of the county.

Chester and Jack continued to work at Ab Whitley's saw mill and the work was regular enough to sustain a steady income so Chester married his sweetheart Nora Kilgore who is one of my sister Nancy's girls and by marrying my niece Chester became a part of my family and I was proud to claim him. And on June 5, 1933 Jack married Eb Kilgore's girl Cleo who was Nora's first cousin (Nora's daddy is Jess Kilgore). John and Sally were lonely for their boys, but at the same time they were glad to have them both married to fine young ladies, and Vesta, Theda and Little Ruth made the old house bright with the sounds of their constant racket which in the span of five minutes can include singing, laughing, crying and endless chatter, and John and Sally live in harmony with each other and with nature, and they treasure their fleeting and precious time together and John is back to his old tricks of teasing his wife and girls and everybody can see he places a premium on the things that really matter like walking down to the June apple tree to collect apples for a pie, and chuckling at the sheep as they bounded away kicking up their heels in delight to be rid of the wool he shears. These normally unnoticed things are more valuable than anything store bought and when you understand where true value lies well then, all parts of every day fall into place in a settled mind. And all the neighbors in the Bethel Community once again began asking as to Sally's well being just to hear John chuckle and give his ridiculous reply, "Oh all right I guess, mean as hell."

Also the neighbors passing by took pleasure in hearing John's deliberate effort to confuse the mule a pulling the plow, and above all John began to use his old and treasured reference, "If they put me to plowing when I get to heaven, well it'll just be a trip for nothing."

1934

The years of the Great Depression were difficult all across the United States, and certainly, in the backwoods of Alabama. All of his life, Doc struggled financially in his practice of medicine, I guess he never found financial success, but he certainly found professional success and sadly, at the young age of forty seven, Doc died on January 17th and that was a sad day, for everybody knew my oldest brother to be a brilliant man and a servant to the whole community all the desperate years through the depression and back as long as he'd been a doctor. He was respected and loved by all his patients in Cleburne County, and they would have paid him enough money to make him a rich man if they just weren't so God forsaken pore. It was common knowledge that because of his talents and intelligence, he could have moved to the big city and practiced medicine caring for rich people, but he didn't, he stayed in the country and cared for people free of charge, and he never turned away from anyone in need, and he treated every person with dignity.

Little Ruth was thirteen years old, Vesta was eighteen, and I turned twenty-three that summer. About once a month, all the young folks in the Bethel community got together for a barn dance. A favorite place was Eb and Lulu Kilgore's barn across the road from their house for it was big and new and it was the cleanest barn in the county. The center of the new barn was a big open room with only two small livestock stalls off to the west end. Once the manure was shoveled out and the dirt was swept with fresh-broke field broom straw, the hard packed earth was a good surface for dancing, and there was plenty of room for the music makers. There was never any kind of a shortage of music makers because it seemed that just about everybody could play either the fiddle or a juice harp or a tub drum and clackers. Jack and his bride Cleo lived in the little house on Eb and Lula's land so they were close by, but Chester and Nora lived on up the road a lot closer to town, but not so far as to keep them away from a dance. Once or twice, Sally & John Owens had a dance in their house for their barn was old and divided into stalls on both sides of the open hall leaving no space big enough for a barn dance, but to make room in the house they moved all the furniture, except for the pump organ, out of the big fireplace room, but even without the furniture, it was still way too crowded because all of the Bethel Community showed up. So the music makers moved outside onto the porch facing the road and everyone danced in the road on the hard packed dirt for it was the middle of summer and the night was warm, and if I needed any more convincing that I was in love with Vesta, that was the night that did the trick because outside dancing under the stars and among the lightning bugs there was a cool breeze blowing that pushed Vesta's beautiful curls into a soft frame around her creamy white face, and the moonlight sparkled in her eyes and holding her close to me made me feel like the most important man ever to take a breath. At first she was disappointed that she could not play the pump organ in unison with the music makers which the pump organ did blend real good with the fiddles, but it was lucky for me that the pump organ was too heavy to move outside, and she was freed up to dance with me, and we just floated around keeping time to the music through out that mysterious and powerful night, and I was so happy to have her in my arms that my feet didn't touch the ground all night.

When Vesta finished her schooling at Crossroads, she started going to high school in Heflin. It was too far to travel from the Owens home place to Heflin every day, so Vesta stayed school nights from late Sunday to Friday evening with her uncle, John's brother, Roy Owens and Roy's wife Eula. Their house was out on the main big road that runs all the way from Atlanta to Birmingham through Tallapoosa and Heflin, and staying with Roy and Eula was a lot closer to Heflin and the school bus which back then was just a little vehicle with one row of seats on each side of a center aisle and not much bigger than a car, and Roy's place was the end of the line for the school bus coming all the way out of town from Heflin. Every morning before sun up, Vesta had to be ready to go when the bus turned around in Roy's yard and usually it was just about dark when she got off the bus back at Roy's place at the end of the day. She endured all these long hours and concentrated on her books and many times she did homework while riding the bus if the sun was up, and she completed the first two years of high school, and the third year which was to be her last year because back then high school only went through the eleventh grade, Vesta started, but could not finish the last year because of the great depression which Heflin High School closed because of lack of funds and the state of Alabama had no money to pay any teachers.

Thomas wrote home on a regular basis. The adventures of travel gave him fodder for wordy, descriptive, newsy letters. Some letters were mailed from Cuba, and he painted a mighty pretty picture of that island. He wound up owning a bakery in Havana. He always had a gift for gab, and in my earliest years, I remember over the years Thomas telling me and Sis many made-up stories. Sis was especially enchanted with a swan story, and I liked it too. We kept Thomas's letters and read them over and over again for they were our special connection with Thomas and the outside world.

1935

Vesta was very disappointed when Heflin High School closed because of lack of funding. Nobody has a job, so nobody pays school taxes, so nobody can work as a teacher without pay, which then of course if there's no money to pay teachers then there's no money to pay to heat the school building and pay the power bill for the building. It's around and around no money no money so the power company has to close and the roads don't get fixed and it's a step back for our democracy, so I guess until somebody figures out how to turn the tide, we'll keep on going back from a thriving country on the move to better and better times, to a failing country who can't pay the bills. Vesta wanted very much to get her high school diploma for education was very important to her, but on a higher note to me, with her no longer in school, I saw this as an opportunity, and I talked the prettiest girl in all of Cleburne County into marrying me.

Vesta sewed a gray dress to wear on our wedding day, and her gray dress matched my best gray suit, and I remember she tied a white cotton string bow tie around her neck under her round collar. It looked real pretty hanging between the points of the collar, so we both wore gray with white at the neck for I had a gray and white striped necktie.

She recited the rhyme,

"Get married in blue,
And you'll always be true.
Get married in gray,
And you'll live far away."

We drove to the big city of Anniston, Alabama and found a justice of the peace and after we said 'I do' and signed the marriage book, we ate supper in a nice café. Then we walked around town looking in the store windows and through the picture window of a drug store we saw a nickel photograph booth so we went inside. We sat down inside the booth, I pulled the curtain shut and dropped a nickel in the slot, and we posed looking straight into a mirror which concealed a camera which automatically snapped two flash pictures of us on our wedding day. Then we went in the theater to see a moving picture show before we checked into a motel for one night, and all in all we thought it was a perfect day.

Back at home we stayed a few nights at the Owens home place until I found a house to rent in Steadman north of Tallapoosa. We were very happy in our little home, and I worked at my whiskey still through most nights, and slept a few hours in the cool of the morning before making my rounds delivering whiskey to my regular customers. Once in a while Vesta asked to go with me, but I flatly refused, I don't want any member of my family involved in any way with the whiskey making business so she stayed at home and kept busy sewing for us and others, but she didn't make any money at it because nobody had any money to pay her, but she sure could make nice dresses and things.

She did make a little money from her brood of chickens and mostly she sold eggs to the peddler each week, and sometimes the peddler bought live fryers from her and this happened usually on Friday so as the customers would have fried chicken for Sunday dinner. To manage the size of her brood, Vesta had a couple of setting hens. She packed the setting hen's nests and most times she had a dozen or more baby chicks from each setting hen. The young chicks became tender eating fryers within a couple of months and Vesta's customers relied on her to supply them with the tender young fryers and not the tough old laying hens.

After working for Dalton Sewell for six years, one day Sis told me she was about to get married. I knew she'd been seeing a feller, but I didn't know much about him except I had a suspicion that he was a bully. I didn't say so to Sis, and maybe I should a because sure enough, when she'd been married to him for just a little while, Sis walked away from the old town grist mill where they lived. The bully operated the grist mill which was located in the part of Tallapoosa called old town where Sis moved into his upstairs living space, but real quick it was plain to Sis that she'd made a mistake by marrying a cruel and hateful man so she left him one morning when he was too busy in the mill to notice and she just walked out the door and didn't look back. Sis walked over to Chester and Nora Owens's rented house in town. Chester and Nora were newly weds like Sis and me and Vesta. She stayed all day with Nora until Chester came in from working at the saw mill, and then Chester and Nora drove Sis out to our house in Steadman, and I drove into the yard about the same time they did and could see that Sis was sad and scared. She told me right off about leaving her husband and what she called 'her few little rags' that she figured would be lost forever. After Chester and Nora drove off down the road, I told Sis I was gona take her back to the grist mill and get her 'few little rags,' but when we got there, she was afraid to get out a the car, but I wasn't because I've never been afraid of anybody or anything and so I walked into the grist mill, and I called up the steps.

"Who-ooo anybody here? I've come to collect my sister's things."

In reply the rascal started a coming down the steps with a butcher knife in his hand.

I said, "I know you're the bully, but I've come now, and you might as well put the knife down right now cause I don't want any trouble, but I guess I got to warn you, I'm for damned sure not afraid of trouble from you or nobody else, so keep a coming at me with that knife and you'll wish you'd a made a different choice."

He came closer to me still holding the knife, and I let him get to the bottom step and then I hit him in the eye as hard as I could, and it all happened so fast that he dropped the knife as he doubled over in a pitiful ball down on the floor. I took the steps two at a time, and upstairs I grabbed Sis's clothes off the pegs in the corner of the room, and as I walked past the crumpled man still curled up on the bottom step, I said, "It's best that you stay away from Sis."

He did, and he never bothered Sis again for he knew I meant business.

Me and Vesta were happy that a baby was on the way and I was glad to have Sis a staying with us which calmed my jitters about Vesta being by herself through the night, but it came to a end when about two weeks later, Sis asked me to take her to Bremen to see about another job that Dalton

Sewell told her about, this time in the Hightower home. Sis got the job in Bremen, and we were glad for her, but we both wished she could a stayed with us longer, anyway it seemed like a good time for me and Vesta to move back in to the Owens home place because we knew time was drawing near when I'd have to go off to prison, and I sure wasn't about to leave Vesta to have my baby all alone. My court date came up about getting caught by the smartest revenuer I'd ever seen at least that's what I told Vesta because I didn't want her to worry that anybody could a been so low down dirty as to turn me in, anyway, she knew about me getting caught back before we got married and that's all she needed to know. What I didn't tell my sweet wife was that at the time I got caught, I was paying the law the usual amount, but the only explanation was that I couldn't be protected in this particular situation which I had a strong suspicion was the result of Bud Forley's mischief, and so the revenuer made his move and caught me red handed and now me and Vesta both knew my time to go off was at hand and so we moved back in with John, Sally, Theda and little Ruth and it was both happy and sad. Happy for us to be in the house with Vesta's always laughing and joking family and sad because our time together was dwindling away and we dreaded saying the last words to each other for it seemed like we'd both stop breathing if we were not together, but what has to be has to be, and we knew there was no way to avoid saying our goodbyes. Sally and John slept in the front bedroom, the girls slept by the fireplace in the big house, and the little back bedroom was ours, where we felt cozy and protected from the hurtful separation looming ahead. I couldn't stand the thoughts of leaving my beautiful wife so I didn't think about it, instead I thought about our baby and I decided this looked like a good arrangement because I could see how much Vesta loved being back home with her family, and I enjoyed their company just like I always had, and I knew I could go off feeling confident that Vesta and our new baby would be happy and safe and well cared for by her Papa and Mama and the girls. We had a real good Thanksgiving dinner that year with ten people crowded around the table in the Owens kitchen, John and Sally, the two girls, me and Vesta, Chester and Nora and their baby Norman, and Jack and Cleo which Cleo was pregnant too and as big if not a little bigger than Vesta and I don't know about Cleo, but we had it figured out that Vesta would deliver in January.

The next week, I went off with a heavy, lonely feeling in my heart knowing I had to serve a two year sentence, and on the ride to the Federal penitentiary, after my sentencing, I got a real weak feeling of worry and anxiety about Vesta, but it was some comfort to know she had my Model T and she wasn't the only one who could drive it, for everybody in the Owens family could drive even Little Ruth, except for Sally of course and even if the Model T was ten years old, it was still a good running car, but I still had a bad feeling about leaving my pregnant wife so far out in the sticks with the only the doctors in town now that Doc was gone.

I spent my prison time south of Talladega close to Sylacauga, Alabama. It was a miserable place and the stinking stench alone would make you sick to your stomach. The workdays when we'd leave the building and dig out-a-doors helped get me through. The work place was a quarry maybe ten miles away, and to get to the work site, we rode in the bed of five or six shackledee old wagons pulled by slow moving worn out old mules, I couldn't stand to creep along sitting in a crowded old wagon bed, so I mostly walked along side and I walked faster even carrying the damned old chains around my ankles and wrists. I liked walking instead of just sitting and waiting for time to pass. The guards were mostly good to me cause I kept my head down and didn't say nothing except when asked a direct question. After working a five or six hour morning we knew when it was about dinner time when we saw the give-away of the dinner wagon coming and that was the buzzards circling in the sky above the dinner wagon for the buzzards followed the stench of the stinking food. Some times there were maggots in the slop dished out for us to eat and I ate stuff that would turn my stomach inside out in just a few minutes, and as a result, I lost a lot of weight and I wasn't strong enough to do much digging, but I kept at it so as not to call attention to myself.

Vesta wrote me a letter at least once a week, and I read each one over and over and I kept them in a stack on the shelf in my cell and sometimes the poor old fellers who didn't get any mail wanted me to read out loud some of Vesta's letters. I didn't want to share her precious words with nobody, but I did because I felt so sorry for the lonely and hopeless. I didn't have no paper or pencil to write back to my wife except for once or twice when I knew by the panic in her words that I had to let her know I was still alive and so when she wrote frantic words a few times, I got my hands on a pencil and wrote between the lines of her sweet letter, folded it back shut, and crossed out my name on the outside of the folded sheet of paper and wrote her name and by the way, it was with a swelled chest full of pride that I wrote out Vesta Godwin, Bethel Church, Muscadine, Alabama for I knew I was the luckiest man alive to have Vesta as my wife.

Dear Shug,

You've been gone just a week, but I swear it feels like two years. I am keeping my fingers crossed my darling husband, that you will get a parole, because I can't stand to think that our baby might not get to see his own daddy until he is two years old. I know the parole board will see you for the good man you are and will let you come home to your loving family. Bert and Mose have come down just about every day to find out if I've heard from you. It will be good when I can read to them a letter from you, please write so I will know you are still alive.

> All my love forever,
> Vesta

When you read Vesta's letters you might notice that she writes using exact spelling and grammar. I did not learn spelling and grammar but Vesta has helped me to learn some and when I did finally write to her I studied how to say what I wanted to say by rereading her letters. I made the decision that I could make this prison sentence do me some good by making me learn and it made me feel a little less hopeless to turn at least one thing into a positive about this whole mess. So anyway, this new thinking got me off of feeling so useless and lost. We both knew that I could learn anything I set my mind to, but until now I never wanted to learn the foolish, but all that aside, Vesta's grammar perfect letters to me while I was in prison are written proof that my wife is the best part of my life.

Dear Shug,

I was thinking about names for our baby. If you have a special name, please let me know because I want you to know you're the most important person in my life and of course, our baby's life. I know you'll be the best daddy. My dearest, please try to put your mind in neutral, like we talked about, and maybe that way you will get through this bad time. I like 'Carroll' for a boy's name and 'Joan' if the baby is a girl. I don't talk about this to anyone but you because naming our baby is a job for us and no one else. I'll close for now, with longing in my heart for the best most decent man alive on God's beautiful earth.

My love forever,
Vesta

I was in the pen for two weeks, when Christmas rolled around and it was hard to face being hemmed in like a animal and sometimes I wondered how I could stand it, and one thing is for shore, I would a gone crazy as a bat but for the sweet letters I got from Vesta, and a few days before Christmas day I got a boxed package, and when I opened it, I looked at the golden brown crust of six fried dried apple pies and one was whole but the other five were broken into little pieces, so I ate the little pieces and had a real good feeling in my belly, so I saved the whole pie in Vesta's little box that looked like it was maybe a shoe box from Sears and Roebuck, but it was a small pair of shoes for a little person, maybe Little Ruth, and Vesta wrapped the pies individually in clean white cotton rags.

Dear Shug,

I'm sending you some dried, fried apple pies that I made this morning. I hope the guards will let the package go through to you. I can't stand to think about the awful food you have to eat. I miss you so much my insides ache. The only consolation is that our baby is moving around inside my belly to remind me that I have a big piece of you right here with me.

It's a warm December, and there's been no rain to speak of. Theda wanted me to go fishing down at the branch. We didn't have any fishhooks, so she used the pliers to bend a hatpin into the shape of a fish hook. We walked down to the branch, and I sat warming in the sun while she threw the string and hatpin into the water over and over again. She didn't even try to put a worm on the hatpin, and you know what? I caught just as many fish as she did. I told this joke to Papa and he laughed, but Theda did not laugh, in fact she got a little mad at me. When Mama heard Theda say a few angry words, she scolded Theda with one of her sayings, 'Remember Theda, the least said, the easiest mended.'

Theda snapped back into her usual cheerful self after that, and we were laughing and hugging when she made me promise that I'll go fishing with her again tomorrow.

I love you forever,
Vesta

This was a favorite letter to read to the other inmates for they laughed with me each time I read it to them.

Vesta had our baby on January twenty-fourth 1936, the warm December weather faded quickly away and was followed by extreme cold. In my prison cell far away from my wife, I knew something was bad wrong and I was sick to my stomach with worry. I was still saving my last uneaten fried apple pie, it sounds crazy, but somehow just looking at the whole pie helped me detach myself from the unmentionable conditions of that stinking hell on earth and every day I looked at the beautiful brown crust of that last apple pie and felt closer to home and when a letter in Sally's handwriting came, I couldn't rip it open fast enough. It was a long letter telling me of Carroll's birth which I read silently to myself for I wanted the sobering words to remain forever unspoken and when I had it memorized, I tore it into a million pieces and threw it in my piss bucket for it was all too personal and sacred to share.

Vesta went into labor in the early morning hours on January twenty first, after a bad backache all day the day before. Knowing the baby wasn't due to be born for another two weeks, Sally thought it was safe to give her daughter a dose of liver powders to ease the back ache, but it turned out that the liver powders might have been a factor in the early onset of labor pains, and after Vesta suffered for three days, screaming and crying in agony, Sally realized that her daughter's difficulty was exactly the same trouble she'd had with birthing her own babies, and Vesta's labor pains might go on forever because she wasn't dilating and just as Sally's sister Ollie had suffered and died, the same might be Vesta's fate for hard contractions pushed the baby futilely against a too small opening grossly inadequate for a baby to be born, so late in the evening on the third night, Sally called John into the back room to see for himself, and the site of Vesta's weak and sweat covered body caused a familiar catastrophic fear to wash over John Owens for he had seen his young wife in the same predicament and all the grief he'd felt so many years ago came flooding back, but he showed no signs of indecision but rather with rational purpose and solemn intent he strode from the room rolling up his shirt sleeves with each giant step and without delay he set about washing his hands with lye soap and boric acid, cutting his fingernails real close with his pocket knife and tying a clean white rag around his neck and again at his back so as to cover his belly for he wanted only the clean cloth to come in contact with the baby's head.

When he returned to the back bedroom, he told Sally to go wash up because he'd need her help and then he began comforting his daughter in a low soft voice, "Vesta, honey, first things first, I'm gona turn you sideways on the bed so your Mama can sit on the bed behind you and prop you up in a sitting position and Theda and Little Ruth can hold your ankles to give you something to push against, and I can help birth your baby because you're never gona have this baby unless I help you. I can see the top of the baby's head, so it's lined up right, but I have to force the opening to stretch, and it's gona hurt honey, but I have to do it because it's the only chance we've got for you and your baby to live through this. I won't let either of you die. I won't."

So with the frail and weak Sally on the bed supporting her daughter and Theda and Little Ruth holding Vesta's limp legs, big John Owens began to forcibly widen the space for the baby by pushing one finger at a time and slowly encircling the baby's tiny head, of course Sally's smaller hands would have been better at this but for the fact that her small hands were simply not strong enough, so John continued the process he had first performed so many years ago and the emotional pain he experienced blurred his vision but not his sense of purpose as he knelt at the bed's edge sharing his grief with his little wife as if they were one unit and not separate beings, and when he could feel the baby's soft little head, he caressed each tiny ear, and then with his fingers cupped around the baby's head as a shield of protection, he pushed his big hands apart and away and the slightly enlarged opening slowly widened with the warmth of slippery thick blood and Vesta screamed and writhed in pain and Sally managed to support and inspire her powerless daughter into one last effort to expel.

Theda and Little Ruth were silent with shock as they watched what their Papa could only feel, the red blood now gushing and pooling on the bed beneath Vesta. John Owens gently coaxed, "You're gona be all right, you're my little girl, and I won't let you die, or your baby, I know how to do this, I learned when I helped your Mama birthing all of you younguns."

Everyone in the room was imperceptibly emitting sobs and whimpers as John continued applying pressure to widen the opening for the baby and finally, the baby's little shoulders were visible and big John Owens mumbled that he was holding in his hands all that mattered in the world, and he was able to pull the baby by hitching a finger under each sweet arm and Sally and the girls understood that a lesser man would have tired and given up but not John Owens for he was stubborn and persistent and driven to heroics and sure enough the baby slipped out into the world, and Sally carefully laid her daughter's head down on the pillow, climbed down from the bed and pushed her weary husband from the room, and with a newfound strength, she gently picked up her little grandson and held him head down by his slippery feet all the while being very careful to make sure the bed was just below the precious baby in case her grip slipped and failed. Theda standing beside her Mama looked down without breathing and cupped the tiny head in her hands and when he started gurgling and crying, Sally raked blood from his mouth, lifted his head and slowly guided his body down onto the bed. Vesta asked to see her baby and Sally lifted him once more into her arms and gently placed this miracle of life on Vesta's chest, but then came the worst moment of all as they watched with horror when Vesta's arms failed to fold around her baby.

Vesta was the first to speak. "I can't move my arms," she screamed. "Don't let my baby fall, I can't hold him."

Sally scurried onto the bed again this time on her knees beside her daughter's prone body and as she held the baby tight to Vesta's chest, she cuddled the pair and used her own arms in place of Vesta's to hold the baby tight against her daughter's chest. Sally mumbled for Theda to hold Vesta's head up so she could look at her baby, as Little Ruth climbed on the bed and positioned herself behind Vesta and pushed her into a semi sitting position. With Ruth behind and Sally in front, they held Vesta's arms around the baby and Little Ruth pushed Vesta's head up with her own head, but as Vesta's head rolled forward and began to fall down onto her chest, Theda caught Vesta's forehead in the palm of her hand and supported the dead weight so that Vesta could murmur to her newborn the sounds of a loving mother. Sally whimpered like a lost puppy as Ruth freed one hand to catch Vesta's head as it rolled back away from Theda, and Little Ruth gently let her sister's head rest in the crook of her elbow, and sadly the reality settled in as they realized that Vesta had no control over her body. Theda was now on the bed too and somehow these two girls and Sally held Vesta in a sitting position with the baby snuggled at her breast. Sally opened Vesta's gown and no one dared move while the baby nuzzled in search of mother's milk and Vesta smiled and cooed at the site of her baby.

"He's just like Shug, the prettiest baby I've ever seen," Vesta wailed.

John was in the big room stoking a roaring fire and the light of the fire coming through the open doorway shed more light on the bed making it obvious to them all that Vesta was sitting in a huge puddle of blood, and she was still bleeding. She'd pass out if they didn't stop the bleeding. They could hear Papa sliding furniture around in the big room and Sally told the girls to stay on the bed with Vesta, and she went to the kitchen to get a pan of water to bath her daughter and grandson. She bathed the baby first and wrapped him in clean soft cotton, then she carried the baby into the big room to the bed now warmed, full on in front of the fireplace, and Sally directed John to go clean up and come back to tend the baby, and when John returned, Sally and the girls washed away the blood and revealed bleeding gashes. John's strength had torn the birth canal, but the blood helped the baby slide through, and now to stop the bleeding, Sally held cold compresses on the wounds. Theda drew fresh water from the well and constantly refilled the wash pan. Ruth brought a bucket of hot water and started bathing Vesta's face, neck, arms, and legs, and somehow they removed the bloody nightgown and dressed Vesta in a clean one, and John gathered his daughter's lifeless body into his arms and carried her into the big room where he placed her on the clean feed sack sheets beside her baby, and he rolled her onto her side and tucked a quilt at her back so she could happily look at the fire and her newborn.

She said, "Papa, will I be paralyzed for the rest of my life?"

John's reply was gruff, "No, you'll be rocking your baby tomorrow."

In my prison cell, I ate the last one of my Christmas fried apple pies the last week of January, 1936 because it was starting to smell soured, and I noticed the crust was just beginning to show a little green mold, but it tasted real good, so good that I ate every bite in one gulp. Nobody said anything to me, but I knew the inmates and the guards too were feeling sorry for me. I guess it was plain to see that I was going just a little bit crazy.

John was wrong; Vesta did not rock our baby the next day, and in fact she could not move her arms or legs for two weeks, and for those two long weeks John, Sally, Theda and Ruth worked long hours doing everything possible to prevent infection and further complications, and I'm grateful to them for writing me a line or two just about every day and I'm grateful to the peddler for coming by the Owens home place more than his regular once or twice a week. John kept a fire going night and day, and Sally fed her daughter broth and tiny bits of crumbled biscuit and held the baby to Vesta's breast to suckle, and every day, little Ruth and Theda washed a mountain of sheets and quilts, night gowns, and the baby's soiling rags, which was a tiresome job, but the girls knew they had no choice so they drew water from the well and filled a wash tub set on the kitchen table inside out in the bitter cold, and they scrubbed each blood stain with lye soap and they carried the heavy tub of clothes outside the house and down the hill to pour the dirty wash water away from the well, so the water would run into the field, and back inside they rinsed out the lye soap with more cold water which again they hauled outside to pour down the hill before picking up each wet piece to wring out the water which Theda started twisting at one end while Ruth twisted in the opposite direction at the other end, and they completed this process with each piece and trudged up the porch steps to sling each individual piece over a straight back chair on the back porch, only to start all over again wringing the water from another piece, and when they finally hauled the empty tub up the porch steps, they dropped all the clothes from the straight back chair into the empty tub and toted the heavy load into the house where the girls now shivering in their soaked coats and dresses hurried to spread the wet clothes on straight back chairs lined up in front of the fire. Almost instantly, steam started to rise as the clothes began to dry, and the girls stood first facing the fire and then backed up to the fire all the while holding their frozen hands and flapping their wet skirts over the flames. Their job seemed never ending, but the girls continued without complaining because their goal was noble and selfless and they knew in their hearts that their work might very well save Vesta's life and the life of her new born baby boy. In fact when either one of the girls came close to whining, the other recalled especially sweet memories of cutting fire wood, milking the cows, making Easter nests, fishing, cooking, reading, and laughing always laughing with their beloved sister. These young girls were fine and descent and noble, and they both deserve a lot of credit for being unselfish. The two showed maturity beyond their years and resolved with a solemn pack spoken in secret that they would do everything in their power to heel their sister and help her walk again.

The mother and baby needed constant care, and John and Sally realized that any chance of survival included frequent bathing of Vesta's wounds, changing her bloody gown, changing the baby's wet rags and changing the wet sheets and quilts. For two weeks someone was on the bed at Vesta's side every minute of every day and when the duty fell to John, he was just as gentle as the women. He'd hum a tune and hold the baby to his daughter's breast or he'd tie a dry rag on his grandson or spoon broth into Vesta's mouth, or change her wet clothes and sheets for dry ones. John realized that his daughter's severe paralysis made her unaware of her own body functions and this worried him more than anything. She reminded him of a helpless little bird, and he longed for the minute when she'd laugh again. It was a sorry thing to see her looking so frail. She was supposed to be the capable and happy oldest daughter. To brighten his own mood, John asked, "What are you gona name this fine young man?"

Vesta replied, "I like the name Carroll, but I'm waiting for an answer from Shug. I won't name this darling baby without Shug's approval. Do you like that name, Papa?"

John's smile widened into a chuckle to smother his tears of joy when he saw Vesta's arm curl around Carroll and slowly she lifted the precious bundle to her lips. It was the sweetest kiss big burly John Owens had ever witnessed, and from that minute, Vesta recovered quickly. She was back walking the next day and working the next week. She was too weak to do much, but she wanted to be useful, so she helped with the cooking while she watched the baby Carroll in a basket on the floor by the kitchen fireplace. The meals around the big kitchen table were loud again, and most of the sadness drifted away when the joking and foolishness returned. The baby grew stronger every day, and at the supper table one night, Vesta read aloud a letter from me.

February 24,1936
My dearest,

I am mighty proud to have a son named Carroll, and I want to tell you that even far away from you in this cold prison cell, I went through the birth with you. I had the cold sweats and a vomiting sickness for three days starting on January 21st and for those three days I couldn't shake the deep down feeling that something was bad wrong. When I got Sally's letter telling me of your paralysis, I was having black clouds of troubling thoughts that wouldn't leave me alone. Anyhow, I was glad to get your letter my darling, telling me that now you can walk again and hold our baby. When that letter came and I knew it was your handwriting, I didn't even really have to read it for it was proof you are no longer paralyzed, and my dark lonely idées were gone from my head, and in their place was the picture of my beautiful wife holding our baby. I am thankful for the news of you and Carroll well and waiting for me to come home.

Your loving husband,
Shug

March 24, 1936
Dear Shug,

Every time I look at Carroll, I have to say, "What pretty blue eyes." I learned in school that brown eyes are dominant over blue eyes; but that has to be wrong, because Carroll's eyes are just as blue as yours and not brown like mine. Mama keeps saying that Carroll's eyes will probably turn brown, but he is two months old now and his eyes are still blue. I'm glad that he has your blue eyes instead of my brown eyes.

Love always,
Vesta

April 2, 1936
Dear Shug,

I hope that you will get the early release so you can come home. I miss you with every breath I take. It is a boundless pleasure to watch Carroll grow, but the joy would be so much sweeter if you were here. He coos and smiles and studies his fist, he doesn't cry, but sometimes he whimpers to get our attention. He knows that he is the center of our world, we cherish him and somebody is holding him most of the time. Sis comes every Sunday all the way from Bremen. Bert, Mose, Joe, Beulah, and Polly come several times a week. It warms my heart to know your family and mine love Carroll just as much as we do my darling.

My Love Forever,
Vesta

April 27, 1936
Dear Shug,

Yesterday, Carroll rolled over from his stomach to his back, and today Sis tried to get him to crawl to her, she showed him how to lift himself up on his hands and knees, but he is still too wobbly to crawl. He smiled like he was proud, but then he settled back down to the pallet, and rolled over and over all the way to Sis. He wound up on his back right at Sis's knees and she was clapping and singing to him, and he laughed and cooed and kicked his legs in the air and acted like he was just about to carry on a conversation. I think he is very intelligent.

I love you,
Vesta

May 30, 1936

My dearest Shug,

Please don't ever worry that Carroll might not know you. I am certain that he understands when I read your letters to him. I read one of your letters to him every day and I talk to him about how happy we will be when you come home. I call you 'daddy' when I talk to Carroll, and he is so smart that he actually acts like he's about to talk back to me. I know he's only four months old, but I think he said, "Daddy" when I picked him up and showed him your new letter yesterday. He knows you are coming home to us as soon as you can, I am certain he knows. We love you,

Your wife and son

In June, 1936, I got parole. I jumped a train and headed north to Cleburne County Alabama, and as the train pulled into Heflin, while it was still rolling along, I jumped off because I knew I could run faster than that old slow train. I hitched a ride from Heflin all the way to the road at the old Jasper Hicks place, and I ran the distance to the Godwin home place in record time, and I started yelping out as loud as I could when I'd passed over the bridge in the holler, and sure enough Bert and Mose come running down the hill and I was completely out of breath so we slowed down just a little but kept on walking up to the yard, where Sis, who was a short, puny little woman took the steps in one giant leap and just about knocked me down when she slung her arms around my neck, then I held on tight to her narrow shoulders as we turned south and walked on down the road to the cemetery and the Owens home place where I'd hold my baby for the first time ever, and I'd hold my wife. It was a hot sunny day and I shore didn't need my suit coat which I had on when I went into prison and naturally wore when I walked out so I handed it to Mose who walked beside me and Sis, but Bert run ahead of us and by the time the three of us reached the top of the hill above the Owens home place, Bert was running back up the hill from the house to us with a precious bundle in the crook of his one arm, and when I saw what Bert was toting I took off running again lick-a-dee-split and left Mose still talking about the last letter from Thomas. Bert run as fast as he could back up the hill to me with his one arm holding my little boy tight to his chest and he was way ahead of Vesta who I saw running down the steps of the front porch, and I couldn't keep the tears wiped out of my eyes, but I tried to because I didn't want Mose and Bert to see me cry like a girl. I was squatted down sitting on one ankle the way I've always liked to rest and cuddling Carroll in the crook of my neck and I might have smothered him but I came too when I felt Vesta's soft warm tears splash on my arm, and she was kneeling like she was praying and she had a death grip on me and our baby boy and nothing else in the world mattered, it could a been raining or sleeting or it could a been the middle of the night for all I knew, I don't remember breathing or thinking or feeling nothing but the sweet touch of my family, and I give up that Bert and Mose would just have to look the other way if they didn't want to see me cry like a girl for finally after a lonely God forsaken six months in hell, I was holding Carroll and my wife was holding me, and my first thought was that Carroll knew me just like Vesta wrote he would, and my heart pushed out through my chest as he stretched up his little arms and put them around my neck and hugged me and life was never one bit sweeter than at that precious minute, and years later, Vesta told me through clinched teeth that she would never forgive Bert for running ahead of me to get Carroll because she wanted to be the one to show me our baby for the first time. I always tried to convince her that I didn't see Bert's face at all that day because the only thing I could see then or for that matter the only thing I'd ever see in my memory of that day was her pretty face, and as I stood up I lifted Carroll and squeezed him so tight that he started to wiggle and Vesta and me just about crushed the life out of each other and our little boy and I'm not ashamed to say I was crying big soaking tears onto her soft, shiny red curls and I guess we'd still be standing there locked in each other's arms except for Carroll, and he tolerated our sentiment just as long as he could and then he let out a holler that woke us both from a dream and I walked on down the hill holding Carroll in my left arm and my gorgeous wife under my right arm with both her arms around me and that sweet minute froze in my mind like a picture on the big screen of the Grand Theater in Tallapoosa and that's the first time for me to understand one of John Owens's favorite sayings of which there were plenty sayings, but just then I understood what he meant by, 'That's where my hat blew off' and I surely knew right then what he meant, for it felt like my hat blew off and I couldn't think or move or function except for in a distracted, forget-ever-thing-else-in-the-world-but-one-thing sort of way, and it sure wasn't chasing a hat in the wind, but that idée finally made sense to me, and when we reached the steps to the porch, Vesta hollered out, "Mama, Papa, Shug's here!"

And before the words really left her mouth, John and Sally came running out the door and across the porch and half way down the steps where Sally put her arms around me and Vesta for we were stuck together like fly paper, and then John hugged all of us, and then he started shaking my hand and pumping it up and down so hard I wondered if my arm might disconnect at the shoulder and Vesta ducked out of the way because it was dangerous to be in the line of John's pumping action. And all the time Carroll was gurgling and cooing in my left arm and a holding on to my neck like he knew me.

I said, "Honey, Carroll knows who I am!"

Vesta crooned, "Of course he does!"

"It's alright, honey, just let it go! I'm home now, and we won't look back, we'll just look ahead."

Sally said, "Supper'll be ready in a little while, you men wash up!"

It was obvious that Sally wanted the men out of the kitchen. The men went to the back porch to wash up, and inside Sally barked orders for Vesta to kill a chicken, Theda to bring in more green beans and tomatoes from the garden and Sis and Little Ruth to run down to the June apple tree and collect apples for a pie while she started water boiling to cook the apples and she stirred up the dough for a pan of biscuits and the pie crust, and in no time a tall, we all crowded around the table, me next to Vesta with Carroll sitting on my lap, John on one end of the table and Sally on the other end, Mose on our side by Vesta and on the other side on the bench against the wall was Bert, Theda, and Little Ruth. Sally asked us to bow our heads and she said, "Thank you Lord for bringing Shug home."

After super, we all sat around the fireplace in the big house and for some reason my eyes watered such that it was a hindrance to watch my wife as Carroll leaned back in her lap and they were so lovable and cute when Vesta whispered in his ear, and he slid down to the floor and crawled over to me and pulled himself up to stand in front of me holding one to my pants leg and when I put my hand on my knee he wrapped his little hand around my finger and he pulled me to the shore of the lake of loneliness where I'd been floundering, and I was no stranger to him and that idée caused my eyes to water up again.

At ten o'clock, Sis, Mose, and Bert stood to go home, but not before we had another round of hugging and it seemed like they'd hug me and turn around to line up to hug me again and I didn't mind.

Carroll was asleep in Vesta's lap, and she put him down in the middle of the bed by the fireplace and Theda and Little Ruth climbed in on each side of him, and me and Vesta went to bed in the back bedroom, and I couldn't get out of my mind the picture of what happened a half a year ago in this little back bedroom, and my stomach did a flip, and I felt light headed at the thought of my wife and son coming so close to death. I think that whole situation is what has made me get light headed when I see blood and sometimes when I just THINK about seeing blood, but it's a problem I have to deal with for now anyway.

It was obvious and gratifying that night to watch everybody look at Carroll with adoring eyes, and being handed around the room or crawling from one to another and climbing into laps and each and every single chosen lap belonged to a person completely and totally devoted to my son. Bert, Mose, and Sis were as yet unmarried as was Theda and of course Little Ruth and with Carroll being the only child in the room, they seemed to claim him as their own which they did with a tenderness that touched my heart and John and Sally demonstrated their rightful ownership with pride and wonder and winks of congratulations every time Carroll displayed his endless sweet personality and charmed ever body with his wit and intelligence.

We stayed at the Owens place for about a month and I had a chance to show John just how much I felt indebted to them for delivering Carroll and tending to Vesta and the baby through the long two weeks of Vesta's paralysis, and I had to wipe the tears out of my eyes when he put his big old arm around my shoulders, he couldn't say nothing either, and it was a real welcome feeling to know he didn't have no hard feelings toward me, and when we could speak, I learnt from him that a time or two when Vesta was in labor, he thought about loading her into the Model T and hauling her into town to a doctor, but it was too cold for Vesta to be jostled around in the Model T and she might very well a died on any ride to anywhere, and the other possibility was driving into town for a doctor to bring out to the house, but first of all John Owens didn't want to leave Sally alone to handle things while he was gone for it would take a long time to get to town, find a doctor, and bring him back to the Owens home place, and we both regretted the loss of my brother Doc who died just about two years to the day before Carroll was born, but when all was said and done, John Owens delivered Carroll and cared for Vesta as good as any doctor could a.

While we were living at the Owens home place, every single day some one of the ladies (Sally or Vesta or Theda or little Ruth) cooked a big celebration dinner for me because I was skin and bones, and actually more times than not, all the women worked in the kitchen together from early in the morning a laughing and having a high old time, which was food for my soul, and laughter cures a lot of ails, and they had dinner on the table right at noon, so after dinner, I could go off and do the work of getting my business up and running again, for we needed money to move out on our own and of course my business kept me away from the house all afternoon running around buying supplies and then I worked through supper and into the night til the early morning hours when I'd creep quietly into the house and crawl into bed beside my sweet wife. So the mornings were most times quiet in the house so I could sleep, they'd all find chores outside with Carroll right in the middle of milking, gathering eggs, toting firewood, and any of the many things to be done about a place, and most days about eleven o'clock an hour before dinner I woke to the sound of the women in the kitchen, and the dinner was fried chicken because Vesta used the feeble excuse that her brood needed some thinning, so just about every morning she caught a pullet, rung it's head off and pluck out the feathers. One morning she got mad at me when I walked out on the porch with Carroll in my arms and held him up so he could watch his mother kill the chicken for I wanted him to know that in order to have a good dinner of fried chicken somebody has to kill the chicken and that was the first of many arguments about how to raise our children. Vesta had never before let Carroll out side the house when she killed a chicken, and she was mad as a hornet at me for insisting that he watch for I believe that a kid has to see and understand all sides of life and you're never too young to face reality, and I think that life is sweeter when you know that along the way bad things are necessary to reach good things. Vesta argued that she wanted to protect him from the bad things, and she made a point that struck me as contradictory when she said, "I want him to love everybody and everything and live his life working to make things better for himself and all the people in his family."

Well I've worked all my life to make things easier for my family, but it don't stop there, I've never met a man I didn't like, even in prison, and if I have a gift to give on this God's earth, it is that I don't carry a grudge or talk mean about people or trample any human down into the mud for in my book that is wrong, because if you let anybody have a chance to show their worth, they will, and you'll be better off for it. I think I'm more like John Owens in that respect, for he has always set a standard of accepting people as basically good and because of it, there's many a men that John Owens counts as his friend but in reverse, there's some of his friends can call a mighty few besides John as their friend, and there's a few people who have no one to call friend except the one and only John Owens. So I studied on this while I was in prison, I'm still a young man, and starting there in prison, I tried my best not to judge but instead to give ever pore ole sorry bastard a chance to feel like somebody. John Owens still holds to his idee that if somebody is a trying to bully another, there's a flag a waving and that flag is really a plea for friendship, and that's why his advice is to stare the bully down and give him a chance to be a friend. He says it works ever time.

Now I saw a big chasm forming between me and my wife, and she knew it too, for I feel I can laugh with the pore ole sorry bastards of the world and hell, stand beside them shoulder to shoulder, but she wants to advance our family to a position where we can be respected for our education and work ethic and ambition and achievements, and in her way of thinking that is the way to reach a place where we can be benevolent toward the pore ole sorry bastards of the world, but back to the notion that she can protect Carroll from the ugly things, well I don't make any headway with her, and she for damned shore can't make any headway with me, but we agree on one thing, we love each other and our baby Carroll more than any slight disagreement can push us apart, and if these finer points define a problem for us it is a very insignificant problem except of course for the fact that we are both bull headed enough to teach our children the way we damned well please, and I'll continue to set Carroll a going down the path to make his own way, and Vesta will continue to set him a going under an umbrella of protection.

Vesta went inside holding the plucked, headless chicken by the feet. She washed the chicken and cut it into pieces and then dipped each piece in the flour in Sally's biscuit pan. Sally had hot bubbling lard waiting in the big iron skillet on the cook stove, and as Vesta dropped each piece of chicken into the hot grease it spattered and popped, and I held Carroll in my arms beside the hot stove as we continued our disagreement, and all at once our little boy screamed in pain when one pop of the hot grease landed on his leg. Of course this made Vesta mad again, and she tried to take Carroll from my arms, but I would not let go and to Vesta's shock, I started laughing, and we were both surprised when our brave little boy started laughing too. With this Vesta couldn't hide a little chuckle herself, and I turned to a room full of Owens's all joining in the laughter. It was an important minute in our relationship with each other and with our little boy. I guess that hot grease splatter on Carroll's leg helped me decide how I would approach the huge responsibility of raising him, and yes, it was a turning point for me. Vesta was still mad at me I could tell by the way she pretty much tried to break the dinner plates as she slammed them down on the table. The room was very warm, but the fire was beginning to burn down in the cook stove, and when we sat down at the big kitchen table, Sally found a place in a straight back chair to the right of John so she could 'jump and run' as she called it to get things anybody might need from the cabinet to John's left or from the stove when the second pan of biscuits was ready to come out of the oven. Sally usually sat at the opposite end of the table from John because that was the best seat from which to 'jump and run' but from that day on, ever time I ever ate at the table with John and Sally, Sally insisted that I sit in her place, she said it was a more fitting place for me. She always treated me with a high degree of respect that I found hard to accept let alone deserve. John too, always acted like

I was a very important person, and I appreciate it but again I don't really understand. Anyway, the Owens family took it upon themselves to fatten me up because I looked like a scarecrow when I got out of prison.

At the table, John told the story of going into Tallapoosa to O.D. Lipham's store and standing at the counter waiting to pay for his snuff when the poor old woman in front of him told the clerk she was buying a new pair of over hauls to bury her husband in. Her next question to the clerk was, "Are these over hauls still guaranteed?"

John laughed that distinctive whopping big contagious laugh of his, and of course, everyone at the table laughed with him, then Vesta asked if he remembered the poor old woman's name, and John answered, "No I don't remember, that's where my hat blew off."

I rented a house just up the road toward town, and we didn't have much, but we moved our few belongings into the old rambling house, and we were grateful every day to have each other and a brilliant little boy who made every minute of every day a miracle of discovery. Vesta wanted to protect him and watch him like a hawk, but I took great pleasure in watching him fall when he ran too fast chasing the chickens in the yard. She wanted to smother him with love, and I wanted him to learn for himself just what the world was all about. She wanted to show him a bird flying overhead, and I wanted him to notice and see the bird with his own eyes. She wanted to hold him up in the water at the swimming hole, and I wanted to let him go under and sputter and spit until he learned by himself how to float at the top and hold his breath if he went under water. We were as happy as any family could ever be. Vesta was still recovering from Carroll's extremely difficult birth, and when I saw the torn tissue, I realized that she absolutely needed more time to heal before we could consider having another baby so we slept together in a gentle embrace, unless Carroll slept between us, which he did most of the time, but sometimes he stayed in the little bed we set up for him in our bedroom. Vesta wanted him in the same room because she worried that Carroll might be afraid, I always answered that worry with a strong statement that my son was not afraid of anything, and Vesta started saying this to little Carroll every chance she got. She'd say, "We're not afraid of anything, are we darling?"

We talked about teaching him to be independent and self sufficient, and he was, and in fact the little rascal was head strong and willful, just the way we wanted him to be. He was spoiled too by my brothers and sisters, by John and Sally and Theda and little Ruth, and Doc's grown girls especially Beulah and Polly, for they all displayed a pride of ownership, and they came inside our house anytime they passed by and a lot of the time they made a special trip to see our amazing little boy, and nobody gave it a thought to feel jealous, instead they all wanted him to be a part of their lives and many was the time they took him along with them to town or back home, and he spent the night away from me and Vesta a lot, and actually more than we wanted him to, but we could not be selfish when they all loved him so much, and we talked about how both the Godwin and the Owens families were always close, but now we all grew closer, maybe because everybody knew the sad story of Vesta's paralysis after Carroll's birth, and my sickness in prison at the very same time, anyway something caused all members of both our families to love and cherish our little Carroll, and he was sweet with giving his love right back to everybody, and every time Vesta caught a chance to hold Carroll and believe you me the chances were few and far between, but anyway Vesta always kissed him and said, "What pretty blue eyes."

I had to agree with her, Carroll's eyes were as blue as the sky on a clear day, and one day that summer Vesta put her hands on each side of my face and said, "What pretty blue eyes," meaning my eyes, and I argued that Carroll's eyes were bluer than mine, but when Vesta went in the house and brought out a hand mirror to where I was sitting on the porch, I looked in the mirror and I knew for the first time that she was right, my eyes were as blue as the sky.

Again, I was making whiskey for a living, only this time I was more careful about getting caught. It was 1936, and the depression was supposed to be over, but you'd never know it in Cleburne County, Alabama, and me and Vesta worked all the time, I mean, we were never idol, there never seemed to be enough hours in the day, and in just a few months, I had most of my good whiskey customers back. Like I said, work took up most of our time, but our first and foremost occupation was caring for Carroll who was a handful; his daring spirit left us dumbfounded as he fearlessly backed his way down the steps and into the yard where he wrestled with the dogs. He even learned to call the cow into the barn, and somehow, he knew to position himself on the front porch each day just when it was time for the peddler to come. At this house being located on the main road that runs past Bethel Church, the peddler passed by every day except Sunday. We were within a half mile of the split in the road where the main road continues straight on to Bethel Church and Bethel School and the narrow side road runs down the hill off to the left to the Owens home place. At the split in the road the peddler turned off the main road on Monday, Wednesday, and Friday to go past the Owens home place and on Tuesday, Thursday, and Saturday he stayed straight on the main road to go past Bethel and within a few hundred yards of the Godwin home place, but at our location in this house, we appreciated the convenience of having the peddler come by every day, and we began to rely on our little boy as an alert system which gave us plenty of time to hurry out of the house to the edge of the yard and down the steep bank to the dirt road with Carroll in our arms bubbling over with excitement to meet the peddler.

We worked out a car share situation whereby Vesta could have mobility for grocery shopping which she did for our new little family and also for her Mama and Papa. She went to visit might near every day so anytime John and Sally had a list of needed staples Vesta made the trip into town and many times John or Sally or Theda or Ruth rode along with her which was a big help to Vesta. Of course, Sally and John and Theda and Ruth missed Carroll when even a single day went by without seeing the little feller, and Carroll surely had no need that wasn't filled, filled to overflowing and then some.

I blocked both Carroll's association with and Vesta's involvement in my whiskey making business, which meant I kept them distinctly apart and never allowed Vesta to buy supplies for me or so much as ride in the car or for that matter even look at the car when it was loaded with whiskey or whiskey making supplies. I was very strict about my wife and my son being totally removed from even the slightest connection to my illegal business. The closest they got to the whiskey trade was when Vesta drove the car and followed my directions and stopped the car when I told her to let me out. From this she knew the general vicinity of my still, and she probably guessed the approximate location for she knew the spot on the road that we called our meeting place, but every time as quick as she let me out of the car, I darted deep into the woods so as to be completely out of sight before I turned track toward the still. I made it simple and like always, she had certain knowledge of nothing more than the meetin' place, and from that meetin' place, she had no idea of the direction or even which side of the road.

In a few months in the fall of the year, I had enough money saved to buy a 1936 Ford, and it was a beauty and the first day I drove it home, I got Vesta and Carroll in the car with Vesta behind the wheel, and I was mighty proud of her skill at maneuvering through and around the muddy ruts in the road, and we went on over to the Owens home place, and when we pulled into the yard, John and Sally hurried out into the yard with Theda and Little Ruth right behind them. Vesta and Carroll stayed there with the women while me and John went for a ride with John driving, and real quick John got used to this fancy car and said he liked it more than the Model T cause he liked being inside out of the weather, and he just about ran into a ditch with excitement when I showed him all the improvements this car had over the Model T. I wanted Sally to learn to drive too, but she would have none of that business.

Me and Vesta worked together at building a chicken house with laying-hen nests all the way to the six-foot ceiling. We attached skinny pine pole horizontal perches along the front of each row of nests which the design was Vesta's idée, and it did make gathering the eggs easy and fast, and Vesta increased the size of her chicken brood to about fifty laying hens and fifty to eighty pullets, and she managed to fill the peddler's orders for both eggs and pullets even when he needed double the usual amount, and Vesta proved herself to be a good business woman for the peddler as her sales partner used his one day off a week to modify his wagon/store with chicken coops which he built under the wagon house a taking up some space of the wheel, but in the rare times when a wheel had to be changed, the chicken coop was easily removed first. The chicken coops each had a solid floor, spindles on all four sides for air, and a door facing out through which to pack the chickens and to retrieve them for a sale, and with one (5 to 7 chicken) coop in each wheel well up to 28 chickens could be transported out of the rain or hot sunlight and handy for catching as customers wanted to buy, and mostly the orders were placed a day or two ahead of the actual day needed giving the peddler notice as to how many of Vesta's pullets he'd need and of course the most were needed on Saturdays for Sunday dinners. And it was on rare holiday occasions that Vesta provided as many as twenty-eight pullets, which filled the peddlers coops to capacity.

Carroll loved to go with his mother into the big chicken coop, and he was pretty good at scattering the chicken feed from his mother's arms, and I agreed with Vesta on this one for a little tike like Carroll could a been pecked pretty seriously down on the ground on the same level as the roosters. This became another job which Carroll took charge just like he took charge of watching for the peddler. I worked my still through the night and delivered whiskey to my customers during the day, and in the morning Carroll never bothered me when I was sleeping; and in fact, just the opposite because I often wished that he would act just a little bit like he needed me for something, but then I guess I got what I deserved for teaching him to be independent, and Vesta too took a great deal of pride in Carroll's independence, and really that was the best if you thought about it, but once in a blue moon, Carroll hugged me and my heart melted into a puddle on the floor as I hugged him back, anyway the adventure of watching Carroll made our days fly by and on top of ever thing else, Vesta still sewed for all the neighbors which she'd drive back to the Owens home place so she could sew on the Singer treadle machine, but it wasn't long until I surprised her with a Singer sewing machine of her own. The new Singer sewing machine cabinet was simpler in design than the scrollwork wrought iron of the old one at the Owens home place, but the new one was a good sturdy sewing machine just like all Singers; but naturally, Vesta preferred the looks of the classic beauty of the old sewing machine.

Of course, like all the neighbors, we had no electricity so the new sewing machine was also a treadle type, and it was an amazing site to watch Vesta make any sewing machine hum along; and she made clothes for Carroll and just like always, she followed a picture in the Sears and Roebuck catalog as a guessing guide for how much material to buy from the peddler. As always she made sun-suits or shirts or shorts from start to finish without a pattern, and she got real creative in designing scenes of ducks and cattails, or fish and bubbles, or puppies and kittens, or a lamb looking up at a little boy, and she embroidered one little boyish scene on each sun suit and each shirt, and these creative and imaginative decorations captured many a stranger's eye in town on a Saturday afternoon. Once in a while if the embroidered scene was particularly intricate, Vesta sketched it out on the material with a pencil in order to get the details just right, but most times she didn't need any pencil. She was very artistic.

At Christmas, Vesta told me we'd have another baby by the end of summer, probably in August, 1937. Thankfully it was a mild winter, a far cry from the bitter cold of a year ago, and by his first birthday, Carroll was walking and a lot of the time Vesta drove the Model T over to the Owens home place and from there she and Carroll wondered through the familiar woods for she was very smart about taking care of herself, and she told me she practiced an exercise of holding in the birthing muscles as she walked because she felt somewhat uneasy and wondered how difficult it might be to carry another baby with the muscles scarred from Carroll's difficult birth, and she convinced me that by strengthening the birthing muscles, she would increase the likelihood of carrying the baby to full term. It made sense to me. On these walks through the woods, Vesta taught Carroll to listen to birdcalls and carefully observe the different trees. She recognized new leaves in the spring, full leaves in the summer, and the colors of the falling leaves in autumn, and when there were no leaves in the winter, she recognized the pattern and texture of the tree bark, and as they walked through the woods, she talked about all this and as a result, some of Carroll's first words were oak, maple, and sweet-gum, and that's not all, when he was one year old he could carry a tune real good and as they walked they sang hymns and the "Have You Watched The Fairies?" song.

Have you watched the fairies when the rain is done?
Spreading out their little wings to dry them in the sun?
I have, I have,
Oh! Isn't it fun?

Have you watched the fairies all along the line?
Singing out their little tunes in little fairy rhymes?
I have, I have,
Oh! Lots of times!

Have you watched the fairies dancing in the air?
Dashing off behind the stars to tidy up their hair?
I have, I have,
Oh! I've been there!

Me and Vesta agreed on most things about Carroll but when I noticed Vesta correcting Carroll's grammar, I accused her of wanting our little man to talk like a refined gentleman, and that's not all, for a while she made a point of correcting my English until one day I had it out with her, and she give in and apologized to me and promised to treat me with the respect she said I deserved, but she put her foot down and maintained the importance of correcting Carroll's English, so I backed off and let her do the English teaching, and it didn't hurt my feelings for I remember way back before we got married when she tried once or twice to correct my English, but it was just too late for me to change so I didn't, except some easy to remember ways, but I decided in that one respect, she could have her way with the children, and what I wondered was how she learned good English anyway, and she explained she learned from the teachers in school and from reading books, and from listening to the actors in the movies and the speakers on the radio which sounded reasonable to me but listening to a radio was not possible except in town, for electricity still was not available out in the country, and so our little boy learned to use correct English and once when he giggled and pointed at me when I said something like, 'I done it,' Vesta was quick to pop him on the knee and put her foot down in a very stern reprimand as she shook her finger in his face and said, "You will respect your daddy."

And that did it, for never again did Carroll laugh at me, but I do suspect that my wife repeated the same warning more than once as the other children came alone, but I have to say there was never another time that any one of my children even came close to showing me the least little bit of disrespect, and for that, my wife deserves the credit. Me and Vesta have a mutual respect for one another, it's easy and natural for I know she is smart and she knows I am smart, and we are very careful to appreciate and hold on tight to the good and let go of the bad and that's a pretty good way to be married and stay married.

The summer of 1937, I stayed at home as much as possible, and when I had to leave to buy supplies or work my still, I made a point of picking up John or Sally or Little Ruth, or many a time all three because we all worried about Vesta's trouble delivering. Anyway Little Ruth stayed with us most of the time and stayed all night every night so as not to leave Vesta alone. Little Ruth at age sixteen was still very small like her mama and sisters, and it was looking like she'd be called Little Ruth all her life, anyway John and Sally just about insisted on at least one of them staying with Vesta every single minute, and I didn't mind one bit. We were pretty sure the baby would come the last week of July, and one day about the middle of July I left Little Ruth with Vesta and Carroll and drove into town by way of Mc Brides Bridge. This trip into town, as I drove along approaching a house where a recently widowed woman lives with a whole house full of little children, and as I got closer and closer I thought I heard a woman's scream so I slowed down, but for the most part, the noise of the engine drowned out the screams, but off to the right just out of the corner of my eye, I saw someone jump off the porch with a baby in her arms, and she ran down the hill to the road a waving her one arm like somebody crazy, and I had to slam on my brakes to keep from hitting the woman and all the while the poor little baby was jostled and bounced around and just about come out of her tight grip, and there was no doubt that she was the one a screaming like a banshee, and a course I swerved off the road into the ditch and come to a standstill, and she ran around the front of my car still a screaming, "Shug, stop, please stop!"

She came right up to the window of my car, and holding the baby on her hip, she rested her other hand on the car window and leaned her pitiful head down on her hand and shuttered with sobs, and I didn't know what to do, but I said, "What in the world is wrong?"

When she could finally say something, she lifted her head up and wiped her nose on her arm and brushed the tears off her cheeks and said, "Shug, I know you to be a descent man. You've got to help me. I'm here with no ma or pa or sisters or brothers, just me and my five little children. The oldest is seven, and we're starving to death. My husband was killed three months ago and left me with another baby on the way. When I go around town asking for a job, everybody looks at my belly and they ask about my five children, and that's that. There's not a chance they'll give me a job."

She pulled on my shirtsleeve and dropped her head again this time in shame.

"Shug, you know I wouldn't ask for charity if there was no other way!"

Stone-faced, I looked at her while my mind worked on a remedy. The racket of my old jalopy gave me time to think, I had my hands on the wheel, and she was hugging her baby and swaying from one foot to the other in a desperate and helpless and mindless distraction.

"I'm on my way to town. I'll get some groceries for you. I'll be back by here in a few hours."

She backed away, and I drove off. By the time I got to Tallapoosa, I had the problem worked out. First, I paid a visit to four of my 'quart-a-week' customers and left each one with directions to a new drop off point. They'd never be the wiser and for them nothing else would change, all they'd know was they'd be still drinking my special recipe, but now each one of their new drop off points would be in walking distance of the widow's house.

On my way home, I pulled into the widow's yard. She came out on the porch and while the oldest little boy toted in the sacks of flour, sugar and coffee, the bucket of lard, and the slab of bacon, I explained that next Monday, I'd leave a gallon of whiskey and a few groceries on her porch, and besides that I'd leave four quart jars. "It'll be your job to fill four quart jars with whiskey and hide each quart of whiskey and when no one is passing by either early in the morning at sun up or after dark, you'll hide each quart in it's own hiding place."

Then I carefully told her the precise hiding place locations, two on this side of the road, each in opposite directions from the house, and the other two on the far side of the road and up closer to the river. "If you have to deliver any quart jars in the daytime, take the children with you and carry along a bucket to hide the jar of whiskey from passing cars, and pick some blackberries along the way or pick up a few apples in a neighbor's yard or walk into a field and pick a roast near or two, all of this will look natural as a reason for carrying a bucket if anybody happens by, but it'll be a good cover up of the real job of delivering the quart of whiskey, and at each drop off point, you'll find the pay for the whiskey in an empty quart jar and that's so's you don't have to make but one trip a week to each drop off point."

Next, I explained she'd find the gallon of whiskey next week at the downed pine tree out behind the house, "Oh yeah, I can't ever again leave the gallon a whiskey on your porch."

Next she assured me she owns a bucket for "picking blackberries."

Also I gave her a few bits of paper and a pencil for when she has to leave me or a customer a note, and I explained she needs to leave notes regarding new drop off locations all along maybe ever four or five weeks or quicker if any slight compromise occurs. I told her to leave the empty gallon jar at the downed pine tree right out behind her house on Sunday of next week and that way I can pick it up and leave a full gallon of whiskey in it's place on Monday. This is just another addition to a department of my business that I keep strictly to myself, and this new responsibility adds no hardship to my growing list of charity cases, but in fact it gives me more peace of mind, for if somebody needs help, I hope to high heaven they got to know all they need do is ask and if it can be done, I'll sure do it.

Now, fifteen years later, when I think back, I took on the job of caring for this pore old woman when our second baby was born, and that second baby is about grown herself now and I'm proud to say that our second baby has been good friends with that pore old woman's youngest baby who a course is in the same grade in school.

When Carroll was one and a half years old, on Tuesday, August 3, 1937, Vesta went into labor. Little Ruth was in the room a tending to Carroll and Vesta wanted me to go get John and Sally so they could stay with her while I went into town to get Doc Gilmore, a reminder here that Doc Godwin died in 1934, so that's why I made the trip into town real quick to get Doc Gilmore and he had an easy job that day for he was in with Vesta less than an hour when he opened the door and let us all in to see our beautiful, baby girl, Joan, who was born without much fuss and like Carroll this new baby had blond hair and blue eyes, but we were soon to discover her easy birth didn't help atall a keeping her contented. Vesta and baby Joan slept the rest of that day and on through the night, and Joan was as sweet as any angel for the first week of her life, but after that Joan made up for her uneventful birth by crying and fussing constantly for four months. Vesta's milk didn't agree with her so we tried cow's milk and I bought a bottle in town with a rubber nipple that stretched over the glass lip, but Joan cried like her stomach hurt no matter what we did. Sometimes we fed her Vesta's milk and sometimes we fed her cow's milk, and when she was four months old one morning at breakfast, Vesta was holding our beautiful, screaming little girl baby and eating her own breakfast of biscuits and gravy when suddenly it occurred to Vesta that Joan might be hungry, so she pinched off a tiny bite of biscuit and sopped it through the gravy and gently poked it into Joan's sweet little mouth, and that minute a miracle happened for she quit crying, and me and Vesta and Carroll looked at each other in shock and disbelief and Carroll smiled a timid little smile and after a minute or two of the sweet sound of silence, our little boy slowly dropped his hands from his ears down to the table and stared at Joan with his mouth hanging open, and then his smile turned into a cheer of victory, and he clapped his hands which captured Joan's attention and before she could start up the wailing again, Vesta poked a second bite of biscuit and gravy into her little mouth and Carroll climbed down from his chair, walked around the table, and kissed his little sister a big old sloppy kiss and Joan smiled at him like he was a angel, and Vesta couldn't poke food into her mouth fast enough, so we decided our pretty little blonde baby girl had been crying because she was hungry, and that gave us a guilty feeling that maybe we were bad parents, and that night Joan slept through the whole night and gave my poor wife a chance to rest up a little.

Vesta's health went down because of the sleepless four months partly because she was so physically exhausted and also partly because the delivery ripped the birth canal again, and this was very painful and also a drain of strength. When she got so she could barely walk, Vesta allowed as how the best thing to restore her own good health was movement, so little by little she got back to taking the children for walks through the woods. She wanted to walk near her home place in the woods she knew so well, and like before she packed the children into the car a holding the baby while Carroll stood up in the front seat, and off they went to the Owens home place to walk the woods with John and Sally for most of the time both of them went along on the walks for they could see how weak Vesta was and they too were concerned with her slow recovery, and both John and Sally worried when Vesta was alone. That year we had a very happy Christmas out on our own with our two brilliant and wonderful children, and I brought home from town a big sack full of oranges shipped in from Florida and another sack full of nuts shipped into our country from all over the world. It was a very special treat, which we gladly divided and delivered to the Owens and Godwin home places, and the pleasure the nuts and oranges brought is a sweet memory. Life was good.

As soon as Joan could crawl she followed Carroll around the house and watched his every move and these two cute as a button children stole the biggest part of my heart that up 'til then had never been used. My love for Vesta is matchless and has it's own special private place in my heart just where it's been from my earliest memories, and of course I love my brothers and sisters with a powerful love that I feel for no one else and a course my nieces and nephews (especially Doc's kids) are indistinguishable in my big family unit, but as important as they all are to me, and I got to emphasize they are mighty important, still my two children opened my eyes to a new and deep responsibility that makes me gasp for air, it's a more rigid responsibility sort of for they look to me and Vesta for meeting their vital requirements. When I come in at the end of the day and here Carroll and Joan come a running and crawling to me and screaming, "Daddy, Daddy, Daddy!" my knees double down and it feels like warm sorghum syrup has replaced my leg muscles and maybe my legs might not even hold me up, but sliding to the floor, I get a reward like nothing I've ever experienced with Carroll and Joan in my arms where I can breathe in their sweet aroma and hug my face into their silky soft golden blonde hair which sparkles and gleams in the sunlight just like my Pa described Ma's hair to me when I was seven years old a sitting on the old iron bed, and my heart still aches for Pa and Ma, but now I look at my children and I touch Vesta's soft auburn curls and I loose track of time. I am lucky beyond imagining, my children with Ma's golden hair have a steel lock around my helpless heart. The fuel of these potent feelings kindle my reason for living and that's something that's been part of me all my life back as far as I can remember to my earliest years when I was responsible for Sis and I accept it for the blessing it is which in my way a thinking is the only reason to put one foot in front of the other for nothing else carries any sense or reason, and many times in my mind, I relive the lesson my daddy taught me while we were sitting at the Ingram grave. His words were, "Don't make the mistake Liziebeth Ingram made, you got to take care of yourself first son, so you can be strong to take care of the ones you love."

So, back then, my new job of daddy put a glad and happy lilt in my step just as it does to this day. I don't remember being a kid, I've never been free from responsibilities and obligations, but I have no regrets; and I count myself lucky beyond belief and especially now when I can watch Carroll and Joan run and play and laugh and act like children, it is a reward worth a million dollars, but I do know that very soon, I'll start teaching them to accept their own responsibilities for that is the greatest thing I can pass on to my children, "Take care of yourself first so you can be strong and take care of the ones you love."

Just then I watched as Joan a holding onto a kitchen chair pulled herself up to a standing position and in a flash, without a word or sound, my grown-up little boy was standing behind her to catch her if she fell, and the best part was that Joan managed to turn to her brother and let loose of the chair and fall toward the haven of her brother Carroll's outstretched arms, and of course he caught her. So, now I know Carroll already accepts his responsibility for Joan and that is as it should be. I hold family far and above all other beings on this earth, but at the same time, I count a great many people as my family. No sir, blood line alone does not make a person my family, and I'm gona before God Almighty, do all I can to take care of those of my blood line and those not.

We were living in a different rented house when we celebrated Joan's second birthday on August 3, 1939. That house was built right along side of the railroad tracks south of Tallapoosa. After I paid the first month's rent, we again packed up our furniture on wagons and loaded the children into our 1936 Ford, and we drove in the lead with John coming along behind us in the first wagon and then followed Chester, Jack, Mose and Bert lined up in a parade of five wagons in all. Not too far along down the road, I had to pull off to the side and let the wagons pass while Vesta got out of the car and waded out into the tall grass a puking, and this continued two more times along the way, but we caught up to the wagons, and she acted like she was embarrassed which was her normal woman's reaction, but just the opposite for me, I felt no embarrassment, and to the contrary, it made me mighty proud to know we'd be having another baby in the spring. We lived in that little house by the railroad tracks for just a few months before we got out of there because like with both previous pregnancies, Vesta was puking sick, and every train that went flying by so close to the house that the dishes were practically rattled off the shelf caused a commotion that added to her worry and her trouble carrying the baby which this time was more painful than before because of the torn tissue from Carroll's and Joan's birth which was a pitiful site and gave me great concern, but even with the pain, Vesta was happy that another baby would brighten our lives, but this nervous time for Vesta of course meant she never let Carroll or Joan out of her sight even for a second for fear they'd get to the railroad track; so most days she gathered the children into the car and headed back to Alabama to her Papa's; and finally, with a desperate plea, she asked me to find another place for us to live as far away from the railroad tracks as possible, and she went on to say, "Find a place to buy, I don't want to rent anymore, I'm tired of moving, I want to move into a safe place that we'll call home for the rest of our lives."

So I made a deal with Otis Bennett and paid him $100 and my '36 Ford for a two story house and twenty-one acres of land three miles to the east of Tallapoosa, Georgia, and in January, we loaded up five wagons one more time (and for the last time) and moved into our own home place, and finally Vesta reached the point at which she could settle down a little and find some peace. She let four-year-old Carroll and two-and-a half-year old Joan play outside while she worked inside the house or if it was washday, she worked outside of course, and many a time, she repeated the phrase to me that she, "Kept one eye on her work and one eye on Carroll and Joan."

But at least she was able to work at something with a clear conscience that the children could not get into a really dangerous situation for this place was quiet and peaceful and already felt like our permanent home place, and here the dirt road runs right by the house and curves around the house making two ninety degree turns. Approaching from the south the first turn curves due west and at the southwest corner of our yard, the second ninety degree turn continues the road on to the north, and at that time the road was not regularly traveled by any car except my own and our closest neighbor, N. H. Arney who owned and farmed a good bit of land just to the north of us. He was very successful, and I'd known the man for years and I knew him to be honest and the sort who kept to himself. He never got into any sort of trouble and in those days, he had to keep his nose clean for he was a nigger, and I use that word here because back then that was a common way to refer to a man of color, but that word implies disrespect so to be fair, I won't use it again in telling you about N. H. Arney and his family, for as long as I can remember, they've been one of our closest neighbors, and we have more respect for them than we have for some of the high and mighty Ku Klux Klan members who go around stirring up trouble and preaching as how they're superior, which when you examine every one individually or the Klan as a whole, well they could use some of what the church stands for which is love and humility. Anyway, back then there were only three other houses along our road and those good neighbors went to town only about once a week and two of them made the trip in a wagon, but N. H. Arney drove a car, and as he passed by the first day after we moved in, he pulled into the yard real slow and hollered, 'Mr. Godwin, are you in there?'

Which he yelled from sitting in the driver's seat behind the wheel of his car, and that made me think on how a Negro has to conduct himself with caution until he understands how white folks are going to act, and I opened the front door to the house and jumped down past the stoop step and walked through the white gravel sandy yard right up to the side of the car, and when I stuck out my hand to shake his hand, well I could almost see the beads of sweat on his face, and he shook my hand after he turned off his engine. Then he stepped out of his car, and we stood in the white gravel sandy front yard and talked for a long time, and then I was mighty proud of Vesta when she brought out two glasses of well water, and N. H. Arney took off his hat and nodded his head with reverence as he gladly took the glass of cool water, and as N.H. Arney held the glass to his mouth he held onto his hat and tipped his head back and I noticed that he was an old man and his hair was might near all gray.

When Vesta went back inside the house, we talked on, and he told me he was living by himself since his wife died and his only young un named Thelma is married to Ulus Collins and lives in Bremen, and she and Ulus have a boy named Troy born a year before Carroll, and a girl named Georgia Anne born a year after Joan. This good man tipped his hat to me and vowed that he'd drive slow around our house, because naturally, there will be times when the children might be playing in the road. He thanked me for the well water, handed me the glass, and shook my hand again with the grip of a relieved man, then he backed out of the yard and drove off to the south.

On the rare occasions when a different car passed by, it necessarily slowed to make the two sharp turns, but Vesta was acutely sensitive to the sound of an approaching car and of course when she recognized N. H. Arney's car by sight or by sound, she knew the children were safe, but when it was a strange car, she was out of the house, across the grassy yard, down the bank and in the road waving her arms at the driver until he got the message and only when the car came to a complete stand still did she gather Carroll and Joan and scurry them up the bank and into the yard, but no driver minded the delay and besides that most times they stopped in to visit for a while, and that was always appreciated.

When we'd been in the house for about two months, on a Wednesday, March 20, 1940 before I left the house to go to work at my sawmill, Vesta told me I'd better drive into Tallapoosa and get Dr. Downey for our next baby was about to be born. When the doctor went into the one bedroom (not counting the upstairs big room) he came back out of the bedroom pretty quick with baby Marilyn in his arms which was a name me and Vesta both liked, and that little baby girl had John Owens red hair, which was laying in soft little curls matted down around her sweet face. I fumbled in my billfold to pay the doctor, and then I took Marilyn from his arms and held her to my cheek with a new fulfillment of blinding love and I walked into the bedroom where Joan and Carroll were already on the bed with their mother lying on clean sugar-sack sheets. Still in that room our neighbor Mrs. Brown finished placing and tucking in the clean sheets and then she made herself busy picking up the bloody sheets from the floor and gathering up all the bloody rags and Vesta's bloody night gown, and she took them outside to the wash pot where she drew water from the well, washed the clothes in cold well water so as not to set the blood stains and scattered the wet clothes out to dry on the hog wire fence. Then Mrs. Brown came back in the house and cooked a good dinner of biscuits and gravy. It was just about straight up noon when Mrs. Brown finished washing the dishes and offered to stay all day, but I told her she'd better go on home and tend to her own work because I planned to take the day off from the sawmill. So I drove Mrs. Brown home and went on to the houses of my sawmill hands and told them we'd not be working atall today which they'd all pretty much figured out for themselves, and when I told them about our little red headed baby girl, they were all mighty glad to hear the good news, and over the next week my sawmill hands' wives and the neighbor wives took turns coming to stay with Vesta and our three children, and they cooked for us and cleaned our house and visited with Vesta and our three little children for these people are good, kind and giving people, and now these people of this Pine Grove Community way over the line into Georgia and on past a good three miles east of Tallapoosa have become just as much like family as the good folks of the Bethel Community in Alabama.

Vesta's recovery was again very slow and painful; the doctor ordered, "Repair surgery and the sooner the better."

Vesta and I talked it over several times about when and how we'd go to the nearest hospital which was in Villa Rica, and finally in October 1941, when Marilyn was a year and a half old, on a Saturday, we made the trip to a Villa Rica doctor's office where the doctor examined Vesta and explained that her bladder was actually hanging free from her body, and so the doctor made a telephone call to the Villa Rica hospital, and he set the day for surgery in the middle of December, two months down the road. While Vesta was in the office with the doctor, I mostly waited with the children in the waiting room but when the doctor wanted to talk to both of us the three children were well cared for by the nurse. We left the doctor's office about mid-day, and instead of driving west to Tallapoosa, we decided to take a ride on east into Atlanta which was the first time Vesta returned to Atlanta since her Papa took her there after she broke her arm when she was nine years old and that was way back in 1927, and now in the fall of 1941, fourteen years later, we enjoyed a very nice visit to Atlanta, and I guess we'll always remember every detail of everything that happened along then for those days were the lead up to December 7, 1941, the day the Japs bombed Pearl Harbor, anyway, our growing family found Atlanta to be a big city where thousands of cars lined up and crawled around like ants. On the drive into town we passed by the Coca Cola plant and on up closer to Peachtree Street, we passed by the Varsity Drive-In eating place on North Avenue situated just east of the Georgia School of Technology, and we heard the roar of a crowd of people watching the Georgia Tech Yellow Jackets play a football game, and then I drove on another block or two and turned right to go south on Peachtree Street just to take a closer look at some of the tall buildings and with the evening sun lighting up the western sky, the buildings were exaggerated by long shadows, and I doubt that I'd have noticed the display if not for Vesta's effort to point out all these minute details to our children. At Five Points, we turned around and drove back north on Peachtree Street, back to North Avenue and the Varsity where I pulled in, and we ordered hot dogs from sitting in our car, and Vesta changed the baby's diaper while I took Carroll and Joan to a little public toilet room which both Carroll and Joan took turns flushing, and we washed our hands under a spigot of running water. The hot dogs, French fries, onion rings, and fried peach pies were delivered right to our car, and it was a feast like nothing we'd ever enjoyed before. But the daylight was fading and our uncommon day in the big city was over. So I reluctantly drove west past the Coca Cola plant and back across the Chattahoochee River heading straight into the setting sun; and from the Chattahoochee River Bridge, we rode on home to the west; and I was mighty glad to have a car with a good set of headlights. I kind a figured the children would fall asleep which Joan and Marilyn did, but Carroll was way too excited to sleep, and he blabbered about all the street lights in Douglasville, Villa Rica, and Bremen. Carroll was almost six years old and acted more like he was a grown man. Anyway, that day in the big city of Atlanta was a day to remember, but before we could return to the Villa Rica Hospital for Vesta's mid December surgery, our world turned up-side-down when on December 7, 1941, which was a Sunday, we passed through Tallapoosa a headin' west on our way to Alabama to have Sunday dinner with John and Sally at the Owens home place, but in Tallapoosa, we met a crazy, frantic, unbelievable site for that's got to be the only time in history the store owners' opened their stores on Sunday, but that day they did, and the commotion was something never seen before or since for might near every citizen was standing on Head Avenue a listening to radios broadcasting the horrible news.

We filled out our 1940 census papers a listing Tallapoosa as our permanent address and I imagine that's just how the Federal government managed to track me down and I worried a lot about what would happen to my family when the draft got to me, but in fact, when my draft notice came in the mail, it was a surprise deferment because I was a saw miller and since the country's war effort needed lumber and steel a plenty the draft deferment letter even went on to tell me if my saw milling came into a slack, I could find employment in the steel mill in Gadsden, Alabama.

By this time the saw milling actually did reach a slack because Lee Worthy bought the old vacant Lithia Hotel in Tallapoosa and right away signed a procurement contract with Uncle Sam, and Lee Worthy gave jobs to a good many saw millers as he started the work of tearing down the old hotel which was in it's hay day the largest wooden structure in the world. Thus in and around Tallapoosa during the first years of World War II saw millers had to find other jobs for the demolition work provided lumber a plenty for the war effort.

To understand positioning, let me tell you that Thomas (Kit) was still out traveling the world and in the late 1930's his letters were post marked "Cuba" for he moved there, bought a vacant building in Havana, outfitted the premises with mixing counters, baking ovens and cooling racks, and to deliver the baked goods he bought a half a dozen panel trucks, and although there was political unrest in Cuba, still Thomas increased the size of his bakery to fifty employees including bakers, sales clerks, and delivery drivers. He had three shifts working round the clock to keep up with demand, but of course there was only one shift of sales clerks working the normal business day hours selling breads and desserts over the counter. When the mafia took over and opened up casinos and racetracks everywhere Thomas sold his Cuban Bakery for he figured that Cuba was getting too dangerous. Thomas made out all right and actually made a little profit. Once again a free man and shed of his Cuban interests, about 1939, Thomas decided to move to Davenport, Iowa to work for the man who owned the Federal Bake Shops. Thomas met the man way back when the two of them went to Business College together and they'd kept close tabs on each other. So in moving to Davenport, Iowa Thomas swapped the dangerous and exciting life in Cuba for the safe and secure life of middle of America.

My one armed brother married Vesta's sister Theda, and a course Bert received a draft deferment and with his Business School Certificate in hand, he found a job a working for Mr. Decker who owned the Western Auto Store in Anniston, Alabama, and Theda with her Teacher's Certificate from Jacksonville State College in hand, found a teaching job in Fruithurst, Alabama. They rented a little house in Fruithurst, where Theda lived all by herself except on Sundays when Bert traveled the thirty miles home to Fruithurst from Anniston. All this detail is necessary to explain why Vesta wound up a living with her sister Theda in Fruithurst in 1942. When I had to get out of the saw milling business and find a job, just like my deferment letter said, I found work at Republic Steel in Gadsden, Alabama. So my first day working at Republic Steel in Gadsden, I found Eb Kilgore's son Leo Kilgore, and I know I've said it before, but I'll say it again, ever body from the Bethel Community seemed like kin, and Leo and his wife Polly were from the Bethel Community and in a round about way Leo and Polly really were family because Leo's sister Cleo married Jack Owens, and anyway, when I got the job at Republic Steel in Gadsden, of course I knew ahead of time that Leo worked there and naturally, Leo would have it no other way but for me to sleep on their couch in their little bitty apartment in Gadsden, but it helped them out a little too because I did pay them a little bit of cash money rent. So I worked in Gadsden which is 30 miles to the north of Anniston and Bert worked in Anniston at the Western Auto Store, and Theda worked in Fruithurst which is just a little over 30 miles to the east of Anniston, and Vesta didn't want just her and our three little children to live in our house 3 miles to the east of Tallapoosa, Georgia because maybe I'd never have enough time to come all that way on my one day off a week for our house east of Tallapoosa was a good seventy miles one way from Gadsden and aside from not having time off just buying rationed gas for a 140 mile trip was out of the realm of logical, instead what seemed logical was for Vesta and our three children to live with Theda in Fruithurst, Alabama.

You got to remember during World War II gas was rationed and nobody thought a thing about it because it's just the normal thing if your country is at war well you make sacrifices for the war effort, well the gas rationing was a main factor which prompted all our moving about, but once we were settled in with me in Gadsden, Burt in Anniston and Vesta, our children, and Theda in Fruithurst, the whole situation worked out just fine. Burt had Wednesday afternoons and all day Sundays off from the Western Auto in Anniston, and I had Sundays off from Republic Steel in Gadsden, so it worked out on Saturday nights I drove my car to Anniston, and from Anniston me and Bert took my car one week and Bert's car one week to drive to Fruithurst a getting in late after the children were asleep, but Vesta and Theda waited up and the four of us always had a good late supper, and we'd tip toe around and slip into bed around ten o'clock and Carroll, Joan and Marilyn slept on pallets on the floor in our bedroom, and it was heaven on earth just to sleep in the same bed a holding my beautiful wife in my arms, and sure as shooting, early Sunday mornings some one of our three children woke up the whole house a laughing and playing and nothing could a been any one bit better than that.

Carroll went to first grade in Fruithurst, and he loved to go to school, and he was reading by Christmas, and in the meantime, back in Tallapoosa, Chester and his wife Nora (who was my sister Nancy's daughter) were still a renting a place to live so instead of renting any longer, they moved into our house 3 miles east of Tallapoosa which was a good thing so they could keep up the place for we all understood an abandoned house just goes down the hill of disrepair. Our furniture was still in the house so now with their own furniture added into the mix, Chester and Nora had plenty of beds for their three little children Norman, Gene and Ellen, and Nora was pregnant with their fourth baby, and all this rigmarole is to set the stage to tell you that Nora's fourth baby was born in our house 3 miles east of Tallapoosa, and on April 13th Little Lynda was born and she was very little, just weighed one pound which was no bigger than a puppy, and the baby and Nora both about died, and Dr. Downey came back ever single day and some times twice a day and the neighbors especially Thelma Collins, were faithful to help out and Chester and Nora and their little brood were just as accepting of the coloreds as me and Vesta and our kids, and Thelma and Ulus Collins understood this sort of a situation immediate on entering a room, and of course if Chester and Nora had been high and mighty whites who consider coloreds as unequal well that too was immediate understood. It was a touch and go situation if the new baby would even live, and Nora was in a very bad way and needed the help of everyone willing, and Little Ruth and John and Sally on the Owens side and my sister Nancy and Jess Kilgore (Nora's parents), and Sis on the Godwin side, combined with the neighbors well anyway at least one person was there to nurse and care for Nora and Little Lynda every single minute of every day and night. It was a very close call but Nora and Little Lynda both pulled through, and when Little Lynda was just over a week old, on Sunday, Bert and Theda, me and Vesta and our 3 children loaded up, left Fruithurst and went back to visit to our house gladly occupied by Nora and Chester, and it was a pitiful sight to see Nora so weak. Vesta was first to hold Little Lynda, and a course, when the baby wet her diaper, Vesta knelt down beside the bed and opened up the baby's flannel wrap, and when she opened the wet diaper, from across the room, I heard Vesta's gasp, and I inched a little closer, and it was obvious to me why Vesta's hands were shaking for Little Lynda's legs and arms were too short for her normal torso, and Vesta all of a sudden was sobbing into her hands, so I grabbed a clean flannel wrapper and covered Little Lynda for I didn't want her to get cold. Next, our little Pretty (two year old Marilyn) leaned onto her mother's shoulder as Vesta, still kneeling, now sat on her feet in a crumpled curled up ball with her head bowed into her hands, and sweet Pretty Marilyn, not understanding her mother's sorrow, wound her arms around her mother's neck and whispered, "Mother, Mother, Mother" over and over and over until Vesta finally wiped her tears away, and in a frantic swoop, gathered our little red headed toddler into her arms. At this point, I could tell by looking at Nora and Chester that they were in a daze of disbelief, and it was plain to see the time was not right to talk about their sweet baby's too short legs and arms, and it went on for several months that Nora and Chester didn't talk about it to anybody, but all the family on the Owens side and the Godwin side slowly began to accept that Little Lynda was getting healthier and prettier by the day, but a sadness prevailed as we watched this sweet little doll baby girl learn to laugh, and crawl, and talk, and walk all on a normal timetable, and unconsciously, our sympathy for Little Lynda turned into adoration and admiration beyond any boundary, as she seemed determined to be normal whether we all believed it possible or not, and she amazed us all with her ability and intelligence and capacity, and she hit the ball right out of the park as she conquered every obstacle with a daredevil attitude you just had to admire and adore! To this day, I don't think the children realized or for that matter gave a flip that Little Lynda was short. All that stuff is immaterial and the only thing that does matter is that the children accept Little Lynda for the smart and beautiful person she is, and did I say she is as smart as a whip and as beautiful as any little fairy. Now once and again, I notice the grown-ups jump to accommodate when a barrier (or what they perceive as a barrier) pops up in Little Lynda's way, but Little Lynda has never once accepted as her due or disparaged as her right anything out of the ordinary in the way of help or accommodation or free pass consisting of unusual gratuity, no sir re, Little Lynda doesn't want any special privilege, that's obvious, and she pretty much dares everyone to raise their own limits as she figuratively, gains stature.

In June, two months after Little Lynda was born, the defense contract at Republic Steele in Gadsden run out; and consequently, my job ended after only one year; but with the year's worth of steady income, we managed to save a good bit of money, and when Chester moved his family into town, we gladly moved back into our house three miles east of Tallapoosa, and I looked around and did some timber cruising to buy a tract of land with enough ready to cut timber so as to keep me saw milling for several years.

The job prospects were still good in Haralson County for a good percentage of wives were working at good paying Defense jobs at the Camouflage right in the middle of Tallapoosa. Some men worked at the Camouflage but mostly it was women who worked at weaving huge nets used in the war effort to hide machinery like airplanes, tanks, jeeps, trucks and even boats which might become a target of German or Jap bombs if they were found by the spying eyes flying overhead. Now this job weaving these big camouflage nets was important and made all of Tallapoosa proud to be a part of the fight, and already a good Tallapoosa friend of mine named J.D. Thrower off fighting in Italy opened up a brand new camouflage net and discovered it was made right here in his home town, and when his letter to his family arrived telling of this amazing coincidence the whole town knew of it in a few hours and that's all we talked about.

Vesta had her own jalopy for now it was a necessity because the school bus didn't come along our road and every school day morning Vesta drove Carroll to second grade and Joan to first grade, Vesta sewed for three little children, and she had no choice but to do a little sewing every single day, and that was a time when all commodities were rationed, and it was patriotic to live according to the rationing for we had a War to pay for. As a consequence, Vesta made our children's clothing from any and all grocery sacks be it sugar sacks or coffee sacks or flour sacks, and she wasn't above using chicken feed sacks either (and she joked about using her spare time to tend to a small brood of chickens which provided eggs and on Sundays a fried chicken dinner. At this point, I don't have to repeat it, but I got to for any person a looking at our children's home made clothes well they naturally denied the outrageous idee that they were made from such low down material as chicken feed sacks and the children looked just as well dressed as the high flalootin' rich kids a wearing store bought dresses and shirts for Vesta has a design and sewing talent that seems next to impossible.

One Saturday night after a long day saw milling, when I pulled up to the house, I was glad to see Mose's car sitting in the yard, and I know he just pulled up a few minutes ahead a me for he shut off his head lights as I drove up, and next thing I knew he come a running over to me a waving a piece of paper and telling a story loud enough to wake up the Collins neighbors in the house way down the road, but it made no never mind for the news he had to tell was important, and he scurried me into the house so he could read Thomas's letter for it was pitch black dark outside. So once we were all in the house by the kerosene lamp, Mose held his twin brother Thomas's letter to the light like he was a reading it, but as he said the words, he was looking at us and not the paper, and so Mose quoted Kit's words to us from memory.

October 27, 1942
Davenport Iowa
My Dear Family,

I am doing well and hope this finds all of you doing well too. As you will recall, I've been working at Federal Bake Shops here in Davenport, Iowa since I moved here from Havana Cuba. I like this part of the country and I like working for my friend, but I have made a decision that I must share with my family.

Today I enlisted in the Navy. I have been thinking about this idea since the Japs bombed Pearl Harbor almost a year ago. It seems the right thing to do and my reasoning is that I should represent our family because I am not married as all my young brothers are married with children to care for except Bert and Theda, but in Bert's case of course having only one arm, he could not enlist and instead he is needed stateside. His job at the Western Auto is important to the war effort. Men working help to make our country strong.

I am 37 years old, single and healthy. I feel it is my duty to fight in this Great War. We all know Pa's brother Joel fought in the Civil War and was buried where he died in Richmond Virginia, and our own brother James fought in World War I, and now I feel lucky to be accepted to serve. The enlistment process started today and I should be called up soon. My recruitment officer will use my 18 years of experience as a baker, my high school diploma, and one year of business school as a basis for beginning my service with the rank of Steward First Class (Chief Commissary Steward). I will most likely serve on a ship in the Pacific Theater.

There's no need to worry, I consider it an honor to fight for my country, I will be safe, and I will see exotic places. You all know of my thirst to see the world.

My Love to All,
Thomas

This letter from Thomas marked a change in our family ritual, everyone continued to work their jobs and our older brother Joe Godwin (never married) continued to live at the old home place and some of the time he lived alone but through the War years it seemed that some family member was moving back home just about every month as circumstances dictated. You got to understand the War years were definitely a hardship of course, but a far sight better than the Depression years. Joe, born in 1901 (the 7th child of Hugh and Mattie Godwin) kept the home place producing a little bit of this and a little bit of that, and sometimes it might of been real hard to pay the taxes on that much land (at one time 640 acres) and sometimes Joe might notify us that a sale was about to take place on the court house steps, and that's how I came to own another 40 acres of the old home place, and remember I inherited the 40 acres up by Obie Laminack where to this day stand the two giant pine trees that my Pa never cut but instead left standing as seed trees.

Doc died way back in 1934 and Essie went on living at the Godwin home place up until the last of her six children were out on their own, at which time Essie moved into a little house down at The Junction, which is the settlement that built up when the main east west highway #78 was paved. The Junction is real close to the small village of Muscadine, which is right along the east-west railroad tracks and just a mile or two south of the Junction. The railroad tracks run parallel to Bankhead Highway and the tracks run right through Tallapoosa and Heflin. Through the war years especially, it seemed like different relatives moved in and out but Joe lived his entire life at the Godwin home place, he was born there and he died there and in between he spent every single day and every single night right there, and now with Thomas fighting in the War, of course his letters to "Godwin Family, Cleburne County Alabama, and from Thomas Godwin US Navy" in the return corner of the envelope, well naturally the letters are delivered to the old Godwin home place, and just as quick as Joe gets and reads a new letter, he takes off into Tallapoosa to share the letter with Mose, and then on down the line Mose takes the letter to Mary Lizzie or Nancy or Sis or Bert or me and that way every body hears from Thomas.

It was a time when all Americans pulled together and worked for a common cause which was to fight the enemy, the Japs in the Pacific and the German's in Europe, and nobody complained about drinking coffee without sugar or for that matter, drinking the coffee substitute called Postum when coffee was not to be found anywhere. There were many times when storeowners could not find a single sack of coffee atall anywhere but most times instead of coffee Postum sat on the shelf. The rationing didn't bother anybody and to the contrary rationing gave a sense of active participation in a valiant cause.

We had a German prisoner of war camp not far from Gadsden, and Gadsden's always had a large Jewish community, and everything seemed like a great big War effort with all the Tallapoosa women working together at the Camouflage. At first only about a hundred women worked there and of course they came from the Bethel Community and the Pine Grove Settlement and from all around Tallapoosa; but when that first contract for 800 camouflage nets was fulfilled, then bigger contracts allowed the Camouflage to expand and hire about 400 women who went to work with a noble purpose that influenced the preparedness of our troops in uniform for it was necessary to hide our military equipment from enemy spy planes and the Camouflage in Tallapoosa made the giant nets to spread out and prop up over airplanes or a fleet of jeeps or command tent centers housing the top brass right down to the fighting armed forces. From the start when the Camouflage opened, Little Ruth worked the second shift, and when the work force expanded to include Vesta, Little Ruth continued to work the second shift, but Vesta worked the first shift so as to be working in the daylight hours same as me cutting timber. Since Vesta's first shift started an hour and a half earlier than school, every week day morning Little Ruth came out to our house as Vesta was leaving, she waked up Carroll and Joan, and Marilyn, helped them get dressed, made them a little breakfast, and then drove Carroll and Joan to school but she kept Marilyn with her until the end of the school day when it was time to pick up Carroll and Joan, and then Ruth and our three kids met Vesta coming out of the Camouflage for school ended before Vesta'a shift ended and now with her shift of work behind her and Ruth's shift of work just beginning well Ruth went into the building to work the second shift and they swapped the children, and at about midnight when Ruth's shift ended, she left work and went home to get a short night's sleep before again coming to our house and tending to our kids, and in this mix, I left home first before daylight for I picked up my saw mill hands and we started our work day at the Rifle Range in the serene first light of a new day.

The Camouflage worked two shifts, six days a week, but I took Saturdays off from saw milling, and my saw mill hands who had children of their own were glad to be at home on Saturdays while their wives worked at the Camouflage because of course somebody had to be at home with the children. On many a Saturday, I took Carroll, Joan and Marilyn out to a ceremony or celebration like the one in June 1943 when the American Thread Company officially opened it's doors in the old cotton mill building. This was a big economic boost to Tallapoosa's prosperity, and while Vesta worked that Saturday, I had our three kids eating free barbeque. Many times military convoys drove right through town, and when we were lucky the convoys came through town on Saturday or Sunday when we could join the crowd standing and waving and cheering and whistling and hollering in support of our troops.

I remember one warm Saturday morning when I was at home with the kids and Vesta was already gone to work at the Camouflage, I called upstairs to wake the kids before I made them a little breakfast of warmed over biscuits and hot Postum. My three kids sat with me at the table and we talked about the work their mother was doing, and I could see that they understood more than I would have guessed, and as Carroll said something about Uncle Thomas fighting for our "way of life" I just listened and let him finish his thought, but the mood changed when my son decided it was time to hurry so he and Norman and Gene could "get over to Papa's" to help him with the heavy work, and I found it hard to hide my grin a thinking about Carroll's independence and how grateful I am for it. With orders to hurry, Carroll sent his sisters upstairs to get dressed as he went into the one bedroom downstairs to put on his work overalls and a short sleeve shirt made for him by his mother of course, and in the mean time I could hear the girls upstairs in the one big room helping each other get dressed in their matching green print batiste dresses which Vesta made out of a little bit of store bought cloth, and her description of the dresses was that each had a fitted, shirt waist, button up-the-back bodice, short puff sleeves, gathered skirt, wide waist sash to tie in a bow at the back, and for loving adornment in green thread she crocheted a row of briar stitching connecting the two piece rounded collar. When the girls came back downstairs, Joan combed Marilyn's hair and tied it back away from her face with a narrow-ribbon-strip of the matching material hemmed and turned (again Vesta's words) and next, it was Marilyn's turn to comb her older sister's hair, and when Marilyn tried to comb through a 'rat's nest' Joan screamed in pain, and little Marilyn handed me the comb, and I combed around the tangle (leaving it be) and hand scooped up Joan's fine, thin blonde hair and as best I could with big fumbling hands, I tied Joan's matching 'ribbon' in place. Now with an urgency to get on the road, we piled in the car and headed for town where we stopped by to pick up Chester's boys, Norman and Gene, and then we went on over to the Owens home place because Carroll and Norman and Gene were working for their Papa and many times the three boys stayed overnight on Saturday night, and sometimes when school was out for the summer, they stayed and worked for a whole week at a time, and John Owens paid them a little bit of money to drop corn, or slop the hogs, or hoe the weeds in the garden or pick up apples, or any number of chores. A course, John Owens made the chores fun, for he loved to laugh and his three young grandsons learned that work makes the living sweet, and a whole lot of the sweetness found in work is the attitude toward work and making the work a laughing matter is the best part. Carroll, Norman and Gene adored their Papa for the stories he could tell and for the love he could convey.

Back to that warm Saturday morning after I left Carroll, Norman and Gene at the Owens home place, me and Joan and Marilyn drove the dirt roads back to the paved Highway 78 which some call the Bankhead Highway, and heading east back to Tallapoosa, we reached the Tallapoosa River and slowed as the last military jeep as part of a very big convoy pulled off the pavement and onto the large white-graveled space on the east side of the river. I could not resist pulling off the road too, just as a courtesy to the soldiers that every citizen counted as family, and I just wanted to let the soldiers know. So as we got out of the car, officers and non-coms came over to shake my hand and to complement me on my pretty little girls, and if I do say so myself, Joan and Marilyn looked like angels in their green print dresses and white shoes and socks, and we walked around through the crowded jeeps, and when we got to the edge of the river, we looked down the steep, vine covered five foot cliff and watched as twenty or more soldiers played a game of tag in the river water. Where the water was the deepest it came up to the soldiers' chests, and these young boys sure did enjoy splashing in the cool refreshing water, and when the water antics settled down, and it looked like the soldiers wanted to climb out of the river, I took Joan and Marilyn by the hand and turned to walk back toward my car, so the soldiers could climb back up the riverbank to their clothes which were laying in piles on the white gravel. The piles of uniforms laying on the ground meant the soldiers would be a climbing the riverbank a wearing only their undershorts that is if they were wearing anything atall. So a course they waited until my little girls were a safe distance away.

As we sauntered along back through the dozens of army jeeps and trucks, we came to one soldier a sitting in the shade a leaning against a jeep, and he stood up and came right up to me and asked if he could take a picture of my pretty little girls, and I was proud to say "of course." So he positioned Joan and Marilyn a standing up on his jeep's front bumper, between the head lights, and with his elaborate camera he snapped just one picture which happened just as Marilyn slung out her right hand a trying to catch her balance, but it was no good and she had to jump two-footed off the jeep's bumper, and the photographer said a looking through the camera lens that it was a real good shot and "The little one's thrown out hand looked like she was a waving."

The photographer was so sure it would be a very good picture that he told me he'd present it to the military newspaper for printing in "The Stars and Stripes" and I'll go on ahead a few months and tell you that we got a copy of that sweet picture in the mail from that military photographer, and he was exactly right, in the picture it looks like Marilyn is waving. I never tire of looking at that sweet picture for it captures Joan and Marilyn at their sweetest and they look like the prettiest little girls in the whole country, and anyone can see by looking at that picture of my girls wearing matching hand made dresses, and by looking at the smiles on their faces and by the attention to details like the ribbons in their hair and the lace on their white socks proving that Joan and Marilyn are loved and cherished for the angels that they are, and in the picture printed across the jeep's bumper is: "2A-168-S * PHOTO 3"

Military Jeep Picture
Marilyn & Joan Godwin

It was good news from Sis for she and her husband Huitt Davis had a baby girl Beverly Gayle on June 8th and another letter came from Thomas.

That fall Carroll started fourth grade and Joan started third grade in the big brick, two-story grammar school building in Tallapoosa. Up until that summer (1945), Vesta worked at the Camouflage, but now Vesta didn't want to work for she wanted to start Marilyn in the private kindergarten at the Harris house on Kiker Street up town which we decided a half day for Marilyn. Vesta was vital as a driver, and she went into town two times a day, once to deliver all three children to school, and once at noon to pick up Marilyn for now there was a school bus route past our house to pick up the whites on our road, but the Collins children Troy and Georgia had no bus to pick them up, and since we never noticed Thelma Collins drive past our house on school mornings well that meant she drove straight out west from the forks of the road directly in front of the Collins house, straight past the giant oak tree right in the middle of the forks, and well she took the short cut uptown past the farm house of the older couple Mr. and Mrs. Brown, and not many white people took notice of the travesty occurring ever day which colored kids all around Tallapoosa got to school the best way they could and some walked miles to the Carver School on the south side a town, but I took notice, and it was a worrisome thing for me, but I kept it to myself so as not to worry my wife and kids, and even though I'm sure Vesta took notice, we didn't talk about it, and maybe that was wrong. I guess I should have stood up for what's right, and in this case, I guess I should a been an actual brave man instead of hem hawing and letting it slide and not saying what was obvious, "The colored school was separate, but by no means was it equal."

Back to the bus a picking up white kids, our school bus picked up the widow Ruby Brown's children, then our children, then the Nichols children and the Wright boy Neal, and the bus went all along the dirt road from Highway 78 to Highway 120. I understood the many and varied arguments against Vesta working at the Camouflage, she should be at home this last year before Marilyn starts first grade next year. It is definitely beneficial for Marilyn to go to this kindergarten and at the same time have afternoons at home with her mother.

Ruth and Sis kept on a working at the Camouflage, but Sis did take a few weeks off after Gayle's birth, and to make it possible for Sis to go back to work, Sis and Huitte hired a young colored girl to take care of the house work and more important to sit with their sweet baby Gayle and Louise Hammock was the colored's name, and she was a fine, upstanding brave young lady, and honestly the whole of the south was full a fine upstanding brave coloreds who lived in deep poverty, and I know the living in poverty part well, but the poverty of whites in the depression had not a single smidgen of likeness to the poverty of coloreds, and that should have caused our country to cry foul and make a turnaround in regards to colored people, but it didn't, and in 1945, there was no sign a any such speaking out in the name of coloreds. No sir, and the filthy coward bullies in the KKK continued on preaching hatred, and they enjoyed the power of control by fear, and one man's speaking out couldn't do much to change things, but me and Vesta raised our kids to value our good neighbors, and make no never mind the colored part, and in our minds, we went on living by the same code and in little ways here and there, I established a barricade separating me and mine from the filthy KKK and now and then I got the chance to stare down one of the bastards and say to his face, "I know you're the bully, but I've come now."

Like John Owens taught me they would, the cowards just about melted into a puddle at my show of strength and the starring-down business kept us safe, me and Vesta and our three kids, and I don't reckon a cross was ever burned in the Collins yard, and for damn sure no cross was burned in my yard, and word got out who would tolerate the dirty shenanigans of the KKK, and it was common public knowledge who simply would not stand for it, and I hope to yell it from the top a Tally Mountain in the case that maybe there's a KKK scaredy-cat that didn't get my message.

One day when Thelma walked up the road to visit Vesta well Thelma talked about her cousin Louise Hammock, and this was the first we knew that Sis's colored helper was related to Thelma Collins, and knowing this emphasized just how respectable Louise Hammock is!

1946

The need for Vesta's corrective surgery was a constant and looming frustration and urgency, and by the end of January, Vesta wrote to Villa Rica for an appointment with the doctor so's to assess a strategy for carrying our fourth baby to term, and when we met with Dr. Berry, he detailed the necessary precautions Vesta should strictly follow. She should avoid lifting anything over ten pounds, she should avoid emotional stress, she should not drive a car the clutch being the possible danger, she should not lift the children or climb the stairs, or lift heavy wet clothes, she should rest and sit down most of the time, so I spelled my wife as much as possible, but I was out of the house for a full work day five days a week.

Since Vesta could not drive it fell to me to take Marilyn into town to kindergarten, and again we fell back on Ruth for she was always there right behind us ready to help us in whatever way she could and now her job was to pick up Marilyn at noon and bring her home, and she was glad to do it and Ruth and Otto were as happy as any married couple could possibly be for Ruth was pregnant with their first baby due sometime in May, and it being their first baby, Ruth was a far site healthier than Vesta who'd struggled a birthing three babies already, and Ruth truly enjoyed the time with her sister and little niece and many times Ruth took our little Marilyn home with her to Alabama for Ruth and Otto lived with Otto's mother (my oldest sister) Mary Lizzie.

I had my eye on cutting timber off the vast acreage of a tract of land known as the Rifle Range in Waco, it was called the Rifle Range because during World War I, it was the site of shooting training, and since World War I, it stood vacant for thirty years, a plenty time for the growth of a nice stand of pine trees, and it was understood, the federal government would post the Rifle Range for sale sometime, but for now, I kept busy cutting smaller tracks of timber here in Georgia and across the state line in Alabama, and it was a constant thing managing the buying, the cutting and the moving of the equipment on to the next work sight.

In a small community word spreads at amazing speeds and women from all over heard about Vesta's predicament, and every day two or more ladies come by to help Vesta and one woman in particular was Arbelle Pruitt now married to Floyd Cobb and she too was pregnant with their first baby. You'll remember the story of baby Arbelle way back when her Ma and Pa brought her to the Godwin home place and Doc lanced the risen as big as a man's fist on the little baby Arbelle's neck, well that baby was now grown and expecting a baby of her own. At the end of 1945 and into 1946 pregnant women were everywhere, and in the Owens family alone there was Vesta and Ruth and Jack's wife Cleo, and on the Godwin side Sis and three of Doc's kids were all expecting, and we had no shortage of help for dozens of women volunteered because everyone understood the serious consequences if Vesta strained herself in any manner which meant she let her work go undone for the first time in her life, but our family and good friends from all over Haralson County, Georgia and Cleburne County, Alabama came and helped out, and we had close neighbors who lived right down the road like Thelma Collins who was just two years older than Vesta. Thelma Arney Collins (married to Ulus Collins) was Mr. N.

H. Arney's only kid, and she and her husband Ulus moved back in with Mr. N. H. Arney bringing their two children Troy and Georgia about the same age as Carroll and Joan, and our neighbor in the other direction was the widow Ruby Brown, and she had a boy also named Carroll, and Carroll Brown was our Carroll's age. Ruby and her four children lived on the dirt road towards town over close to Highway 78, and also the other direction there was another Mrs. Brown, an older lady who also helped out (we had two neighbors by the name of Brown) we bought our milk from the older Mr. and Mrs. Brown who owned the fields in cultivation that came right up to the dirt road by our house, and we can see that neighbor Brown's house looking north west across their cotton crop. Like I said, on most days two or more of these good women came to check on Vesta and help out with one thing or another, and I appreciated all the help, but as the new year 1946 marched on into May, Vesta was as big as a barn, and her situation was precarious at best for she had labor mimicking pains that scared us both and I warned everyone to keep quiet about Ruth's pitiful situation. I did not want Vesta to grieve herself into a premature birthing. Then's when Sis started coming by after her shift at work and bringing her baby Gayle and Sis didn't mind atall doing the heavy work which she did the washing more than once, and Sis loved our kids like they were her own, and that's sure a good feeling, and raising kids is made easier when there's a wide range of adults taking turns at doing the raising.

The third week of May, when Ruth went into labor, she lay in torture because she had the same problem delivering that her sister Vesta had and her mother Sally had and her aunt Ollie had and who knows how far back in the family this problem went, but Ruth was writhing in pain in her mother-in-law Mary Lizzie's house, and Otto and his mother didn't understand the situation and after two days Otto went to town and brought back the doctor and I won't mention his name because he did a bad job a delivering the baby and actually used a metal instrument to force pull the baby into the birthing canal and in the process he killed the baby, and the biggest regret was that Otto didn't go get Ruth's Papa, big John Owens, for John Owens was the one who delivered Carroll ten years before and now at age twenty-five Ruth was strong and healthy but when she fell unconscious she was unable to communicate to her husband even if she did know who could help her deliver (for she'd seen him deliver Carroll) and in a pitiful state and faced with a life and death situation, Otto and his mother (my oldest sister, Mary Lizzie) didn't know what to do, and a tragedy took place that could a been different but as it unfolded there wasn't nothing to be done to prevent it, and it was something that haunted Ruth and Otto and they never got over it, never.

After the doctor's rough treatment, Ruth remained unconscious for two more days and during that time, Otto buried their little baby girl they'd already named Shirley, and Ruth didn't know a thing about it, and Otto was scared to death that his wife might die too, but he saved her life by feeding her and bathing her with cool water to bring down her fever and finally the bleeding stopped, and she barely opened her eyes and asked to see her baby, but she was not conscious long enough to hear of the death, and that's when I had a spare minute and drove over to Mary Lizzie's house and found Otto himself in a semiconscious state and Mary Lizzie was pitiful telling me the sad story, but she told me to go home and, "Do what ever it takes to help your sweet wife."

Mary Lizzie always treated me more like her son than her little brother, but I guess that was understandable considering she was twenty four years older than me, anyway as soon as I could, I made arrangements to handle the complicated birth of our fourth baby and the first thing was carrying out Dr. Berry's strict orders relieving Vesta of heavy lifting and getting workers to help Vesta. Next, I made a full proof plan to transport Vesta the twenty-five miles to the Villa Rica hospital as soon as possible after her water broke, and this required some intricate coordinating. First, I talked it over with our widow neighbor Ruby Brown, and she played a very important part for she had a telephone and the plan was for Vesta to send Joan (almost nine) and Marilyn (now six) walking from our house to Ruby Brown's house the very minute her water broke. I rehearsed the plan with Joan and Marilyn, and more than one Sunday afternoon the three of us (me and my two little girls) walked over to the widow Brown's house just to practice, and one day I gave Ruby Brown the telephone number of the taxi service in Tallapoosa which was a one man/one car business, but he promised me he'd drop whatever he was doing when he got the call from Ruby Brown, and he'd come a flying, collect Joan and Marilyn on their return walk home, continue on to the house, pick up Vesta, and haul Vesta and my girls to the hospital twenty five miles away in Villa Rica, and by the time they arrived at the Villa Rica hospital, Dr. Berry would be a waiting because Ruby Brown's next call was a long distance call from Tallapoosa to Villa Rica, warning the hospital that Vesta was in a taxi on the way, and the final phase of the plan was for the taxi to bring Joan and Marilyn to me at that time cutting timber off the pretty good sized track of land known as the Rifle Range,

Sure enough on Tuesday, July 23,1946, all phases of the plan were set in motion and luckily the plan worked out just right. The taxi carrying Joan and Marilyn showed up and found me and Carroll in the woods cutting timber at the Rifle Range at about four-a-clock when the sun was high in the sky, and naturally, first thing I warned my girls to watch out for snakes and black widow spiders, and at the end of our work day, about an hour later, I packed my three kids into my pick-up truck, and one of my saw mill hands drove the log truck delivering all my hands to their homes, and I drove lick-a-de-split straight to the Villa Rica hospital where our fourth baby was already born, another sweet little girl, a tiny little baby girl, and we named her Janet Rose, and I held her for the first time in my dirty saw-miller's work clothes, and just like with Carroll, Joan, and Marilyn the first time I held Janet Rose in my arms I thought I'd pass out from the bushels of love weighing down on my heart so that I could barely breath. Vesta didn't wake up until it was about dark, and in the mean time, Carroll held the baby, and Joan held the baby, and Marilyn held the baby, and six year old Marilyn giggled and was mighty proud to hold a newborn baby for the first time ever in her life, but Joan claimed superiority because she'd held Marilyn as a baby and now baby Janet Rose was the second newborn baby she'd ever held in her arms, but then Carroll took the prize because Janet Rose was the third newborn baby he'd ever held even though he admitted he didn't remember anything atall about holding Joan.

Next, with my three kids out of the room, I got an earful from Dr. Berry that the surgical repair work went well and Vesta's bladder was attached again, and my wife would be more comfortable right away and completely pain free in a few weeks. He cautioned me to get help to come in and cook and clean and tend to the children so's Vesta could stay in bed and speed up her recovery for walking around might pull out some stitches and lifting any weight atall might cause internal damage.

When Vesta finally woke up, she was vomiting from the ether they used to put her to sleep; Dr. Berry assured me they did not put her to sleep until after the delivery for the ether might have interfered with the birthing. Now the new baby was sleeping in a bassinet right next to her mother, and we all took another turn holding the baby, and then the nurse brought in five bowls of soup and five pones of cornbread, and Vesta ate a good bit and said she felt lots better, and then Dr. Berry sent Carroll, Joan and Marilyn back to the waiting room so's he could check Vesta's stitches, and he decided she'd have to stay all night in the hospital, and then before Dr. Berry left the room for the night, I unloaded a worry that'd been haunting me all evening. I picked up our tiny little newborn Janet and laid her on the bed at Vesta's feet, then I carefully unwrapped the soft white cotton flannel blanket and the sight of the littlest baby I'd ever seen caused tears to gush, "Doctor Berry, is Janet deformed? She looks too little to be a healthy baby! Can't we do something, what can we do?"

My sweet wife answered me before the doctor had a chance to speak, "Shug, our baby's normal, don't worry, you remember when we first looked at Little Lynda her fingertips didn't reach the upper part of her thigh. Look Shug, compare Janet's arms and legs to her body and look down at your own arm's length at your side, your fingertips come halfway down your thigh, and now stretch Janet's little arm, go ahead you'll see it reaches half way down her thigh just like yours. Don't torture yourself, I see our baby's strong resemblance to Little Lynda and they're both beautiful look-a-likes, but Janet's body is well proportioned."

I made the measurements like Vesta said, and she was right. I felt satisfied that Janet was normal, "But why is she so little, will she grow and catch up or will she always be such a very small size? Will she even be as tall as Miss Sally?"

This time Dr. Berry answered me, "Your baby might be two or three weeks premature because of the difficult situation under which your wife carried her, but she will grow and catch up. Because she is so tiny, it is likely she'll always be small, but she's healthy, and she'll walk and talk right on schedule. Like your wife said, don't worry."

I thanked Dr. Berry, shook his hand, and he left the room. Vesta then told me the story of her Aunt Ollie, Miss Sally's only sister who died in childbirth out in Oklahoma, and then her husband, Mr. Hooper mailed her hope chest and clothes back to Miss Sally, and the clothes in the hope chest fit Miss Sally, but no one else in the family because no one else in the family is small enough to wear Aunt Ollie's clothes, but "Now maybe when Janet is grown, she'll be the right size to wear Aunt Ollie's clothes."

When I wiped away my tears, I hugged and kissed my wife and tiny baby, then I stuck my head out the door and called Carroll, and here he came a herding his sisters back into the room, and when I told the kids we'd go on home and come back tomorrow, Carroll, Joan and Marilyn made the rounds hugging and kissing before I took the three children home for the night, and as we walked out the door, we promised we'd be back tomorrow. At home, I heated water and one by one each of us bathed off, and the children, dressed in their clean homemade cotton pajamas, crawled under a quilt on the couch and waited for me to be the substitute reader which I particularly enjoyed reading a sweet story that this time was Carroll's turn to choose, and he surprised me when I read a poem at the end of the story, and he spoke the words aloud as I read:

> They are dressed in colors as bright and gay.
> They budded and blossomed for this May Day.
> The woods are alight with the birds that sing,
> Making so merry because it is spring!
> Come out, come out and skip with the breeze.
> We'll play hide-and-seek in the shade of the trees.
> Tra lalala, lala, tra lalala lala
> Come, come, come, come,
> Come out in the fields and play.

When I blew out the kerosene lamp at nine thirty, Carroll chose to sleep upstairs and Joan and Marilyn slept in the other bed in the room with me, and I didn't hear a peep out of anybody until late the next morning when the widow Ruby Brown came a knocking on the front door which no one ever knocks on the door, so the first tap caused me to shoot up in bed, and I jerked on my pants and invited Ruby and her children to come in, and while she cooked us a little breakfast, we told her about our perfect tiny, little Janet Rose, and quick as we could, we got dressed and headed back to Villa Rica in hopes of bringing Vesta and Janet Rose home. It was still a weekday so's by now the log truck was back in the work place at the little track of land near the Rifle Range and my saw mill hands were working cutting and snaking logs.

While me and my three kids went to the Villa Rica Hospital, the widow Ruby and her children worked a cleaning up the house, and it was a dirty mess because Vesta had been in bed most of the last six months trying her best to carry our baby to full term, and weeks later Vesta got a little mad at the good widow Ruby Brown when she heard tell from somebody how Ruby Brown tattled about how hard she and her children worked cleaning up the house and still only, "Scraped off the top layer of dirt."

Vesta came home knowing the dirt would have to stay in place for a few more weeks because she had to get 'bed rest' and let the surgical repairs have time to heal, and it was on Sunday, the 28th of July when Ruth and Otto came to see the baby, and that was a real sad day for Ruth and Otto, and all we could do was watch the pitiful sight as Ruth and Otto held Janet Rose, and they seemed to grow stronger in hopes of having another baby, and Ruth and Otto offered to take the baby with them and tend to her for a few days, and it would a been a good idea, but Vesta asked if Ruth's milk was dried up and it was so Vesta suggested instead that Ruth come to our place every day to help with baby Janet and that plan seemed to please everyone, and Ruth and Otto unloaded and set out on the table the supper they brought and at that point Ruth warned Vesta she'd get her bowls back the next day, but Vesta joined in the teasing with, "If I can get out of bed atall in the morning before you get here I'll hide your bowls and tell you the children broke every one."

Vesta and her sister carried on like this all the time, I guess it was a trait they inherited from their Papa, and the next day was a work day for me and my sawmill hands, but before I left the house, Ruth drove into the yard a bringing with her John and Sally so they could see their youngest grand baby, and they stayed about all day long and after Ruth and Sally did the washing the women stayed indoors tending to the newborn and Ruth openly grieved for her own loss but admitted her love for Janet helped her to stifle some of the pain, and at the same time she admitted the best thing for her and Otto was to have another baby as quick as possible. While the women carried on about babies and such, John took Carroll, Joan, and Marilyn walking through the woods beyond the barn and the pasture down into the blackberry valley and on past the old pear tree which now stands as the only evidence of a hundred year old home site, and this was a long walk and when they finally came back up to the house it was about five o'clock and I drove into the yard from cutting timber all day. Inside the house while I was washing up, I heard Carroll and Joan excitedly telling the story of a red devil they saw walking through the woods way off down beyond the old pear tree. They each gave explicit details about the red devil, "He was about half as tall as Papa, had bushy red clumps of hair all around his head and neck and chin, he walked a swaying side to side and he breathed fire and moaned when he stepped on a briar for he was barefooted."

Marilyn and her Papa did not see the red devil, but Carroll and Joan rattled on describing his thick wide shoulders and his long rope tail, and no one knew quite how to respond to this wild yarn and actually everyone tolerated it as a sign of Joan's and Carroll's very creative imagination. John kept quiet about the devil story, but Marilyn shivered and squealed with horror, and then is when Vesta from the bed (which we'd set up in the living room) chastised her oldest children, "Stop this silly mess, you both know we are not afraid of anything, there is no such thing as a walking around real devil, and I won't stand for your nonsensical tales that are designed to scare and confuse and simply put, the both of you better stop and think about what you're doing, and remember how good it feels to honestly say and mean it that you are not afraid of anything. That's what we are all about, we are not cowards, and no one can really frighten us about anything because we rely on our strength, and there's no greater force in the world than the force of our family united, standing up to bad things and mean things and unfair things."

With this tongue lashing, Joan and Carroll slinked out of the room and Carroll tiptoed back into the room just long enough to take Marilyn by the hand and lead her out on the front porch to sit in the swing between him and Joan, and it was quiet out there and all we could hear was the creaking of the swing.

Just about ever day after Janet was born when Vesta had to lay low a recovering, our good and kind neighbor Thelma Collins along with her two children, Troy and Georgia walked up the dirt road the short distance between the Collins house and the Godwin house.

When Janet was born, Troy was eleven years old and Carroll was ten, and it was easy for the two boys, our blonde, blue eyed Carroll and the very dark colored Troy to find plenty to do like for example, in a distance contest a throwing rocks into Mr. Brown's field of cotton from the road bank in our back yard, or racing up and down the dirt road in a running contest of speed and agility, or climbing trees just to see who could get closest to the blue sky, and the favorite pastime of these boys, when they had time to play instead a work, well it was flipping rocks from a flip to a specific target, and it was the pact of cooperation agreed on by these two boys that they ended each day's contests in a tie, no winner declared, and thereby they'd know exactly where to take up and continue the contest the next time, and with all the rock flipping outside usually in the back yard, it was the usual thing for Joan and Georgia (one year younger than Joan) and little Marilyn to play outside in the front yard, usually down by the big pine tree on the path to our garbage dump, and under the big pine tree, the girls raked the pine straw into lines and blanks delineating the walls and doorways of a make believe play house, and the "raking and building" was more fun than the pretend living in the pretend play house, of pretend cooking or sleeping or rocking the baby or reading the paper, and as a consequence the more fun "raking and building" never ended for more than a few minutes at a time because there was always a demand for another make believe room or porch or sidewalk, but these sweet girls, one colored and two white made good use of vivid imaginations and many times their make believe turned them into office workers, or telephone operators, or school teachers and there was no room in their play for hatred or inequality, no sir, the girls were equals in intellect and creativity and purity and honor just as they viewed the whole world and in their child's minds they were sure it could be no other way.

Just as the kids played together in harmony and peace in the summer time, come fall they went back to school separate, allowing the common reference of 'separate but equal,' but anyone who might have entered the white kids' fine brick school houses up town in Tallapoosa, well nobody with eyes can call the white school system equal to the colored school when the white kids have a ride on a school bus to and from their home no matter how far out a town, the white grammar school and the white high school have a full time janitor, Mr. Thurman, a hard working man who stays busy all day every day in winter for he stokes the coal burning heat system that sends hot water to radiators in every room, he cleans the black boards and sweeps the floors in every room every day, he oils down to a rich glow the wooden floor boards in both buildings, he cleans the boys' toilets and the girls' toilets, and in the grammar school there is a small library, and in the high school there is a fine large library, there is a lunch room with cooks working every school day cooking lunch, there is a playground with a swing set, a jungle gym, and a merry-go-round, there are two teachers and two rooms for every grade in grammar school, and in high school there's a science lab complete with gas feeds to each student station for firing Bunsen burners, there's a designated typing room with modern manual typewriters at every student station, and there's even electric typewriters at two student stations, there's a home economics room with a refrigerator and a stove for learning how to cook, and there are electric sewing machines for learning how to sew, and most importantly, all grades from first through twelfth, all students get new textbooks as the old textbooks start to show wear and tear. Public education for white children is fine and all these tools offer a good education to the white children who of course are greatly appreciative but this grandeur is not in any respect, not in any regard, and certainly not seen through the colored's eyes as equal opportunity for all. The colored school called Carver, is located on the south side of the railroad tracks, and the brutal truth is there's no school bus service, and the kids walk miles if their family has no car or truck, there's no janitor and the teachers build fires in pot belly warming stoves, there are no blackboards to clean and no floors to sweep and oil, there's no running water, and there are only outhouses, there is no science lab, there is no home economics room, there are no typewriters, on the playground there consists of rope swings hanging from tree limbs, there are as many as fifty children for each teacher, and worst of all, the colored students never, and I do mean never, get a new textbook, instead they learn from hand me down textbooks that have a dozen or more names of white children scribbled inside the front cover.

I have to blow off some steam and lower my head in shame every time I think about the hateful UNequality.

Time marched on and before long our kids were back in school, and it made no never mind that our kids had no inkling why they did not see Troy and Georgia on the playground or on the school bus or in the classroom, no sir, some questions never formed in the minds of our children, and to be fair, the colored children like Troy and Georgia maybe they actually got a better education for it was something they had to really want, they had to really work for, and not something just handed out for free. I can say with confidence that our children learned everything put before them and actually soaked up learning like gravy on a biscuit, and I got to give Vesta credit for inspiring our kids to be faithful and respectful and grateful for Vesta saw real early in her own life that education is an equalizer, and the best ladder atall to climb out of the depths of poverty.

Vesta's recovery was obvious, she was feeling stronger every day and of course the stronger she got the more she yearned to pack up and go visiting her Papa and Mama. So every Sunday she gathered all four children, now three girls and still only one boy (who, by the way) is every thing a man could ever want in a son, he is strong and caring and intelligent, and he doesn't shy away from work, but for that matter neither do the girls. Vesta is very strict with all the children, she has high standards and make no mistake, my wife is a strong person in her own right, and there is no way in hell one of her children is going to cut up or slack off or amount to nothing, and I approve of her preaching, and it is a daily thing for her to warn the kids about the dire consequences if they somehow fall out of her graces.

In the fall after Janet was born, Carroll was in 5th grade, Joan was in 4th grade, and Marilyn started 1st grade. We were all glad to be back in our own home, and for now I continued cutting timber off of small tracks anywhere within a few minutes drive and this went on pretty good keeping me earning a descent living. I bought timber for cutting without buying the land, but I still had my eyes on the tract of land called the Rifle Range just south of Waco, Georgia. The Rifle Range is close by and has enough timber to keep me and my saw mill hands busy working for several years, and the rumor is it will come on the market sometime in the next few years, but I can't wait around, and I have plenty of work cutting timber in Georgia and Alabama for after the War, people are building houses every where all across our great big country, and any timber I cut I sure have no problem selling at top prices.

I enjoyed the time visiting back at the Owens home place, but many Sundays instead of going with Vesta and the kids, I worked a cutting timber all by myself for I would have been counted as a heathen by the whole country if I'd a required my sawmill hands to work on the Sabbath

Black Widow

One Sunday, I was working alone and when I sat down on a log which I felled the day before, I reached under a big white rock at my feet in order to flip it over and get it out of my way, and when I reached under the edge of it, well I felt a stinging on my left wrist, and on the underbelly of the big white rock I was surprised to see a spider's nest made of thick layered perfectly round spun spider webbing so thick it looked more substantial than any fragile spider web and more like a wad of cotton picked right out of the field, and it's white color was perfectly matched and blended in to the white rock, and there were several pea sized white pods containing baby spiders, and I kind of shuttered in respect when the biggest Black Widow spider I'd ever seen in my life danced away from me in what seemed to be a slow motion effort, and too soon, she disappeared under the cover of another rock, and there was no doubt atall she was a Black Widow for her extended body behind her head and legs was as round as a marble and she mesmerized me with her long, stout, agile legs working in concert as she danced away, graceful and confident in a bewitching performance.

Black Widows are dangerous poisonous, and I had to think fast because I knew my time was running out and sure enough there were two fang marks right on the blood vein on the inside of my left wrist, so I started walking back to my truck holding my left hand down to my side so's maybe the poisoned blood might stay in the extremity tips and prove harder for my heart to pump the poison up my arm and through my body. I left my saws right where they lay, I didn't dare carry the weight, I intended to keep my heart beating slow and luckily the spider bite was on my left wrist which in the driver's seat I continued to hold down between the seat and the truck door. I closed the driver's door (on my left of course) with my right hand

and for just a second as I leaned out and reached for the door with my right hand, I rolled my left hand palm up so's to examine the bite area and the fang marks were now swollen by a good bit, and I cranked up the truck and backed out of the woods looking over my shoulder until I got back out to the public dirt road where I continued backing out of the logging road and into the public road where I dug out a ditch in the dirt road scratching off and speeding forward like it was a matter of life and death for it was, and when I reached the Bankhead Highway, I didn't slow down atall, instead I pealed off a good inch of rubber from my tires entering the paved highway and turning the ninety degree turn to the left heading due west toward Tallapoosa. I barreled along as fast as the eight cylinder motor would carry me to Dr. Downey which I didn't call him Dr. Downey, hell he's been my close friend all my life and I call him by his name which is Perrin, and flying up Dead Man's Curve I relived the Bowdon football game way back when me and Perrin played and won. When we played that football game together, Perrin's daddy was Tallapoosa's Doctor. Driving myself to Perrin that day, it seemed like I had all the time in the world to think of our young Doctor Downey's distinguished military record, which began after he finished Tulane Medical School in New Orleans and Intern Residency at St. Joseph Infirmary in Atlanta. He became a naval flight surgeon when he reported for active duty in 1941. He landed with the Marines on Guadalcanal and received the Presidential Citation and the Pacific-Asiatic Service Medal with three combat stars. On Guadalcanal, he started the program of air evacuation of the wounded. He was discharged after the war with the rank of Commander. Everybody in Tallapoosa kept close track of our military boys.

In town, I took the right turn onto Alewine Avenue with only two wheels toughing the ground, and two blocks north, I tore up the dirt a skidding right onto East Mill Street and immediately veered left into Perrin's yard a blowing the horn, and luckily the Methodist church across the street had let out, but it made no never mind if church was in or not, if they were a praying or not, I was, like I said, a running out of time, and Perrin came a flying out of his house as I blared out, "I been bit by a Black Widow!"

Perrin motioned for me to slide over and let him drive, he backed my truck into the dirt street carving more trenches as he slammed on the brakes, turned the wheel and blasted down the street to his office where he ordered me to stay put and don't move and like a flash he was in the building and back out again running toward me with a shot and a vial of antidote, which I knew all this from a conversation with him not long ago in which he told me that now since it is available he keeps the antidote on hand in his office, and in one fluid motion he filled the syringe, dove into the cab past the stirring wheel and jabbed the shot into my upper left arm, and the prick brought me out of unconsciousness and the world was a spinning like I'd never seen it do before, and my tongue was as thick as a Varsity hot dog and everybody in Georgia knows that measurement, and next thing Perrin was a slapping me hard, and I'd a slapped him back but the only thing I could move was my eyeballs, and I'd a cussed him out if I could a got the Varsity hot dog out of the way.

I passed out for a good little bit, and when I came to, I was still in my truck, but now the truck was parked in my front yard, and I could see Perrin's wife in their car sitting in my yard, and she was behind the stirring wheel holding their little toddler Charles, and Vesta and Perrin were running from the house to me and right behind them was Perrin's and Lila's first grader Carroll (same name as our Carroll), and when I fumbled around making inaccurate attempts at catching a hold of the door handle so's to open the truck door, Perrin commanded me, "Shug, I said stay put."

So I stayed put and I wondered why he thought it was ok to yell at me like I was a nobody, but I accepted that I had no choice for now my stomach was cramping real bad and when Perrin saw me begin to heave, he told his Carroll to get in the car with his mother and then he opened the truck door, and all I could do was lower my head to the edge of the seat and gravity did the work of it and before I could spit I was a vomiting out the door onto the white sandy front yard, and the waves of heaving and puking went on and on and on and on until I was as weak as a girl and sweating like a sissy, but after a while, Perrin cranked up the truck and repositioned it so's he could pull me out of the cab on the passenger side without stepping in the gallons of vomit on the white sand, and that thought brought on another convulsion, but this time nothing but bitter bile came up, so Perrin pulled me out of the truck and just about carried me into the house and plopped me down on the bed, and again I wondered why he thought he could get away with man handling me, but that silly thought was gone as quick as it occurred and from that point on, well, I didn't hear anything or think anything or say anything for hour after hour, after hour, no sir, I just looked at the ceiling and watched the shadows deepen into night.

Vesta was real sweet to me but she didn't get any kind of response out of me for I was back to concentrating on the ceiling and the mystical-eye-rolling feat that took every ounce of strength I had in the world. My stomach hurt, I MEAN MY STOMACH HURT. I never thought I'd die, I guess I truly believed the antidote would save me, but I did think a time or two that I was going to be old and gray without a tooth in my head when I finally got up out of this bed and walked like a living breathing human being.

I remember refusing food one time, but come to find out when I woke up for real Vesta told me I'd been in bed for forty-eight hours, and it was not Sunday any more, and it was not Monday, no, good-God-a-mighty, it was Tuesday, and the one meal I thought I refused was in actuality the fourth meal I refused, but Tuesday evening I gladly accepted the meal and I ate a good bit but then my stomach started cramping a little so's I took the signal and stopped eating and the next thing I knew it was Wednesday morning and I rolled over and threw my feet to the floor and stood up like I was somebody. Now that was all there was to it, I was alive, and I was hungry and I wanted to get back to work, but for damn sure I'd check for Black Widow spiders before I stuck my hand under a rock or anything atall from now on

1948

We were as happy as any family could be, Vesta was feeling good physically and she was very happy to mother our four children. Twelve year old Carroll was a fine sawmill hand, Joan and Marilyn helped their mother a washing dishes every day and washing clothes on Saturday, and little tot Janet was walking and talking, Vesta spent some little time every day designing and sewing remarkably beautiful dresses for our three girls, and you got to admit she is as talented as any big outfit in Hollywood at designing and sewing.

With good news rumbling everywhere, I whistled all the way to my sawmill hands' houses picking them up to go to work, and at the Rifle Range I spilled the beans with the very exciting news that power lines were going up to our house and on past our house which meant that our house and the eight houses on our dirt road and all the houses along the paved Highway 78 all the way past the Pine Grove Church east of Tallapoosa including the Dead Man's Curve settlement would be getting hooked up to power lines. With this positive turn of events, I bought a couple of acres at Dead Man's Curve right along the Highway 78 pavement and planned ahead to the time real soon when I can build two buildings, a country store and a grist mill and in the building process I plan to wire the two new buildings with electrical wire ahead of the actual electrical lines coming our way. The gristmill is something the farmers need and right there is a natural location for a country store and a gristmill. On either side of the paved Highway 78 residents travel dirt roads to intersect with the more traveled Highway 78 which with a new country store and a grist mill will save them lots of travel time and it is a convenient time for me to build because I am flush with money and still a making money ever day a cutting timber.

All our Saturday mornings were filled with the normal chores around the place, we had a cow and some chickens and a horse named Dan, and of course we always had a yard full of stray dogs, but the dogs, for the most part, took care of themselves, and by two or three in the afternoon, everyone bathed off a little with a dishpan of warm water, and we got dressed up in Sunday-go-to-meeting clothes all of which were designed and made by Vesta except for my clothes of course and Carroll's for she'd never made my clothes, no sir I want store bought clothes, and now that Carroll is about grown he too wears store bought clothes like me, and in the common ritual, we piled into the car and I drove to town and it was a sociable thing to find a parking place and go inside and sit down for a meal at the Smith's Southern Café on Highway 78 or at Hat's Café on Head Avenue, then as a usual thing, I took Carroll in the pool hall with me, and Vesta and the girls either sat in the car or walked around to other cars and visited with the crowd of people spending their Saturday in town.

Most Saturdays in town, we got the chance to visit with Sis and Huitt and their sweet little Gayle, and in Gayle's short life her mother has miscarried three times and the doctor describes her problem as being a miss match of hers and Huitt's blood types, and no matter how much they want of course to have more babies, it will never be possible and although Sis and Huitt are luckier than Ruth and Otto for Ruth still can not get pregnant, well Sis and Huitt have one healthy and beautiful baby girl and over and over again, Sis got pregnant and within a short two or three months each time she miscarried, which was in itself a misery like Ruth and Otto loosing their one baby Shirley, but of the two couples, Sis and Huitt are luckier to have one baby, whereas it is beginning to look like Ruth and Otto will never have even one baby, and their sadness about it is obvious.

Sometimes on Saturdays Joan or Marilyn knock on the pool hall door and ask to speak to me, and when my girls tell me they've found something they want to buy, I give them a little money, and they go running off leaving me to grin with fatherly pride in having such pretty and sweet girls, but of course the girls are never allowed inside the pool hall and for that matter they can not even look inside from the doorway, and even the adult women are strictly forbidden, but inside the pool hall all the men or just about all the men and boys are playing pool and smoking or chewing tobacco, and it is no place for a lady, and that suits the men just fine.

As a usual thing, I take my family into the Grand Theater for the matinee, which includes a cowboy movie, a weekly serial, a comedy short and previews of coming attractions, but some of the time, Vesta and the kids attend the matinee while I shoot pool. By the time the sun goes down, it's time to eat again and many times we drive up to the Smoke House Drive-In and eat in the car and many times it is nine o'clock or later when we finally get home and on closer to ten o'clock when the kids stop jabbering and go up stairs to bed.

One Friday, after putting in a full day cutting timber, about sundown I met with the man who is to start building the country store and grist mill for me, and by the light of the head lights, he showed me his pencil drawing and I checked the measurements and added an outside-entry toilet to the design for ultimately, I plan to dig a well on the property and for sure the electric lines will reach the site in the next weeks and I'll have the means to pump water for the toilet, anyway it was pitch black dark when I drove home, and it was a little unsettling when I walked up to a very dark front door for not a single kerosene lamp was burning inside the house, but when I opened the screen door and stepped into the house, all of a sudden Carroll in the kitchen, Joan in the living room and Marilyn in the bedroom flipped a switch and electricity lit up the house like it was daylight and everybody yelled, "Hey daddy!"

Of course Carroll, Joan and Marilyn planned every detail of this surprise before I got home, and it was lucky that I was late getting there which the pitch black moonless night outside made the electricity especially brilliant inside the house.

AND THAT'S WHEN EVERYTHING CHANGED or at least that was the beginning of the transformation! Electricity opened up a world we'd never even dreamed of. There were no limits to the advantages of electricity, and we spent our spare time dreaming about what electrical gadget we'd buy first, and as was the practice back as far as I can remember, we got our ideas from the Wish Book (the Sears and Roebuck Catalog) and Vesta decided on an electric wringer type washing machine, which we bought from the Hardware store in town and when it came in I hauled it home on the back of my pick-up truck, and the first time we used the wringer type washing machine, we set it up in our kitchen beside the wood burning cook stove. The concept of washing clothes inside the house was an amazing and novel symbol of progress, but we quickly discovered we needed more stuff like galvanized tubs to make the automatic washing machine work for us, but of course we could see the potential outcome of this great time and labor saver, but we missed the obvious which in a new situation often times becomes limited to specific knowledge of which we had none, and until the needed extras of the whole process are in place, well things can turn out to be more inconvenient than first imagined and for us the first complication was drawing up bucketful after bucketful of water from the well which of course is a normal process whether filling the new giant electric washing machine basin or filling the old iron wash pots sitting out in the yard, but now bringing the drawn buckets of water up the porch steps and into the house added a new dimension to the wash day work for we had to traipse back and forth out the back door and down the steps to the well, draw up the bucket of water, pour the water from the well bucket to the toting bucket, and back inside pour the toting bucket water into the new wringer type washer tub, and finally, with the clean pristine well water filling the wringer type washing machine to the brim, we felt real stupid when we could not poke the clothes in the washing machine without the well water overflowing the basin, so we had to remove bucketful after bucketful of water, and next we discovered the necessity of two new galvanized tubs to hold rinse water, and it was two tubs because Vesta always liked to rinse the clothes twice. We had three iron wash pots sitting on the ground outside by the hog wire fence, but they were useless for several reasons, first being they were too heavy to use for hauling water or wet clothes and besides they had no handles, and we could not touch anything to the black-soot-covered-cauldrons without smearing the fire's residual grime into the clothes and all these considerations eliminated the cauldrons as being useful in conjunction with the new wringer type washing machine.

Finally, we decided the first load of clothes had agitated long enough, but first let me back track and describe how the wonderful automatic agitation caused the washing machine to walk around the room and even once unplug itself from the wall electrical outlet for when that amount of weight is being vibrated, well naturally the amazing automatic wringer type washing machine extends itself to the limit of the electric cord, which in itself is no more than five or six feet long, and the constant movement/agitation made for a definite self repositioning for part of the fancy design included little metal rollers on each of the four legs which were a good idea to be practical when moving the machine, but were not such a good idea when the agitator motion naturally set the machine to rolling around on it's little rollers, and that not being the focus, we realized we'd made another miscalculation for we could not drain the dirty water from the washing machine basin through the very handy attached drain hose because we had no way a disposing of the dirty water beyond catching it in the toting bucket which we did, and slowly, we caught and poured outside, and caught and poured outside, what seemed like a hundred loads of dirty wash water until finally the wringer type washing machine tub was empty.

This process would have certainly been easier if we had a water plumbing and drainage system but a course we had neither, and this experiment rendered a long list of necessities 1) drainage pipe system 2) plumbing pipes delivering clean water 3) electric pump dedicated to pumping well water through the plumbing pipes 4) tubs for rinsing 5) tubs for toting wet clothes.

Although we had no tubs, we persevered and reached a point where if one of us fed the wet clothes into the automatic wringers and the other one stood right there to catch each piece well it might work. It was a Saturday and the kids were bathing and getting ready to "go to town" and youngest Janet was on the back porch with a wash pan dipping and re-dipping and re-dipping a rag into the water before squeezing out as much as a little squirt could squeeze before slapping her face with the wet rag and then slapping her legs and arms and all the while saying over and over again, "I'm ready to go to town."

This Janet scene was an exact repeat of the same performance we'd seen over the past several Saturdays, and of course it endeared our youngest, but nevertheless our modern day washday resolution was still a distant goal. We decided to put the clothes through the electric wringer, (this wringer is two 'rolling pin' cylinders rolling against each other one on top and the other on the bottom in a swing-arm housing, the swing-arm allowed the wringer to follow a circle around from washing basin to first rinse tub, to second rinse tub to third dry tub (for receiving the wrung out clothes and delivering them to the drying clothes line) and we perfected the art of fishing an article from the water, holding it in place on the intake side and feeding it between the rolling pins and on the outtake side catching each piece individually, which if we had the needed three tubs, we could pretty much let the wrung out soapy clothes fall as they might into rinse water tubs one and two, and ultimately let the final wringing drop the clothes into the last dry tub for transport to the clothes line. Instead our job was made unnecessarily difficult stacking the wet clothes on the table, and using our drinking dipper to completely empty the soapy water from the wringer type washing machine basin, returning the wet clothes to that same basin, refilling the basin with countless buckets of drawn rinse water, re-plugging in the washing machine to our new electrical socket, letting the agitator extract some of the soap, painstakingly repeating the wringing and stacking and emptying process and finally one load of wash yielded stacks and stacks of wet clothes covering the kitchen table, and I might add each stack of wet clothes was dripping water into rivers on the floor, which indicates of course that the mechanical "wringers" were somewhat less than efficient, but dutifully we hugged the wet clothes to our bodies, and lugged them out to the hog wire fence and spread them to dry where the two of us should have stripped down and hung out the sopping wet clothes we were wearing, and back inside the house, we faced the tedious task of mopping up all the water standing on the kitchen floor.

Considering all these missteps the one biggest glaring solution was to buy some galvanized tubs, and beyond that it became apparent we should begin our electric transformation with an electric well pump, plumbing pipes, a kitchen sink with a drain pipe, and then go from there, and realistically this life changing electric conversion shifted our attention to construction because with soon to be five children, we definitely needed more space and what better time to add on to the house than right now.

We were sitting pretty, and when the Rifle Range comes up for bidding and I'm lucky enough to win the bidding, there is enough timber standing on the Rifle Range to bring in a steady income for several more years, and Vesta soon will be managing a country store in the new building at Dead Man's Curve, and we talked it over and considered every angle, and it seemed like a good way to increase our income without taking Vesta away from the children. We understood Vesta's job a running a country store and raising a family would demand her attention on many different levels, but she liked the idea as long as everybody in our family and all her store customers understood that nothing was more important than our children's needs

While we were building our store, Chester was a building a new-car-showroom-building in Tallapoosa sitting right on the north side a Highway 78 between Robertson Avenue to the west and Spring Street to the east, and as soon as he opened the doors on his new Pontiac Dealership, I bought a brand spanking new 1949 Pontiac, Chieftain, and I paid him cash money, two thousand two hundred dollars. It was the real pretty modern style, two-tone, dark green top, light green from windows down, and Chester might of had it on the showroom floor for a few minutes when I stopped in to visit and saw the Chieftain, and I could not resist the wide shiny chrome front bumper and the Pontiac Indian Chief hood ornament, and boy howdy it was a mighty fine car with white side wall tires, a dash board radio, and six cylinder in-line engine.

A few weeks later, I drove to Carrollton in my old pickup truck, and drove back home in a brand new, 1949 Dodge two-tone green and yellow pickup truck and for good measure, loaded in the brand new Dodge pickup truck bed was a brand new Famous James motorcycle for Carroll.

So in one year's time, after getting wired for electricity, we bought a brand new Pontiac, a brand new Dodge pickup truck, a brand new Famous James motorcycle, we built the store and the grist mill, and enlarged our house by adding two bedrooms, a hallway and a real indoor bathroom with a sink, a bathtub, and a fine indoor commode. Besides that, we built a garage and a mate building we call the well shed, which as a logical solution followed our first experience of washing clothes in the electric wringer type washing machine which showed us we'd be better served with a wash house built over and around the well including an electric well pump pumping water through a direct line water hose from the well into the washing machine basin and rinse tubs. We designed the wash house with a rot-proof concrete floor slightly sloped to accommodate all spilled water and route every drop into a nine inch drain pipe cemented into the floor and dug through the ground with a gradual slop such as to deliver the dirty wash water underneath and beyond the well shed's west wall and of course deposited down-hill of the well so as not to contaminate the well water.

Just about as soon as the construction crew added each new board to the well shed, Joan and Carroll stood waiting with pencils in hand to write on the inside (unfinished walls) and the main words they wrote were, "Kilroy was here."

Which this phrase, had something to do with a ship yard riveter during the War, and in the years following the War, 'Kilroy was here' could be found written inside just about anything.

Over the next months, the construction crew enclosed the back porch and made the area into a kitchen with it's own sink and drainage system dug parallel to the wash house drainage pipe and both the kitchen and the wash house drainage pipes emptied into the grassy yard beyond the west wall of the well shed where Vesta transplanted a shrub from an abandoned old house-place way over yonder in Borden Springs, Alabama. Whenever Vesta and her cousin Geneva (Vesta calls her "G") passed by any flowers growing wild along the road, they made a mental note to come back together in the fall after the sap goes down and safely dig up and transplant the discovered treasures, and even though both these cousins are bothered with back aches, together they can take turns digging and consequently both their yards are full of Redbud trees, Dogwood trees,

Rose of Sharon bushes, Nandina bushes, Weigela bushes, Rose bushes, and many others, and as soon as the well shed was built, Vesta decided to make good use of the kitchen and wash house waste water by letting both empty into the grass and she planted a shrub to soak up the water and at the same time force the children to walk around the soggy, muddy spot thereby protecting her new linoleum rugs from muddy tracks. That fall Vesta and G planted a flowering Quince at the west end of the well shed, and the very next spring the scraggly multi-stems burst into red blooms and fresh little green leaves, and Vesta said, "If I had the time to stand there and watch the flowering Quince, I'm sure I could actually see the stems growing taller, and every time I do walk by, it's noticeably taller, and even if it's been only one day, I'm sure it's grown a good six inches. I reckon my flowering Quince thinks Valvo soap powder, Babbo scouring powder, and Purex bleach are guano."

Of course, I tore down the old outhouse and shoveled dirt to fill in the hole because we are living in modern times now, and our fancy indoor toilet has a running-water-spigot into the sink, and another running-water-spigot into the nice big stationary bathtub, and a sit-down-seat called a commode which flushes all body waste right down through drain pipes which empty into a new septic tank buried in the ground outside the bathroom window.

Ruth & Otto visited with us at least once a week, and as a usual thing they were at the Owens home place on Sundays, and they could not hide their envy when they see our little Janet for all this time, might near a year and a half, they have desperately hoped for another pregnancy and a baby of their own, but as a substitute they focus their attention on our little Janet, and they both dote on Janet, and every now and then for no apparent reason they bring a gift to Janet, and they take delight in watching her open up a package, and that spring of the year when Janet was not yet two years old, they brought a tiny little tea set which has a marble size tea pot and two itsy-bitsy little cups each about the size of a black-eyed pea, and it is mesmerizing to watch Janet pretending to drink from a pea sized tea cup.

As soon as Ruth and Otto left that day, Vesta gathered up the tea set and tied the tiny pieces in a handkerchief and put it high on the shelf out of Janet's reach, and when Janet asked for the tea set Vesta explained that she can play with the tea set only when Ruth and Otto are here to play with her, and that satisfied Janet until Ruth and Otto came back the next week at which time, Otto was Janet's choice of a playmate, and it was a sweet thing to watch a grown man holding a miniature tea cup in his giant bear paw of a hand, and the ritual of pouring and drinking imaginary tea seemed never to end and brought smiles all around until on this Saturday afternoon everyone including Ruth and Otto loaded up to go to town and Janet rode with Ruth and Otto, and we planned to meet for supper at the Southern Café where we enjoyed the special which was chili (served of course over a slice of loaf bread) and then we all ambled along toward Head Avenue with Ruth a toting Janet, and Vesta and Ruth bought tickets at the ticket window of the Grand Theater, and me and Otto decided to shoot pool instead and as me and Otto walked past the National Clothing Shop we met Beulah toting their baby Laurel (but everybody calls her "Dolly") and we mentioned to Beulah that Ruth and Vesta and our four kids were already in the theater, and likewise Beulah informed us that Morris was already a shooting pool, and late that night when the kids were finally asleep, Vesta put away the tiny tea set and noticed one cup was missing which caused no alarm for the pea sized pieces were bound to get lost, and we thought no more about it until the next day after the usual Sunday visit to the Owens home place, Vesta removed Janet's dirty diaper, bathed our little Sugar Pie in a wash pan of warm water, pulled a clean night gown over her head, and after reading to the children, Vesta handed the sound asleep Janet to me and I tucked her into bed. Then I found Vesta in the bathroom opening Janet's dirty diaper in order to dump the stool into the commode, but she stopped in her tracks and called me to come see, and there in Janet's diaper was the missing pea sized tea cup, and Vesta gently stuck a broom-straw (pulled from the store bought broom) through the tea cup handle and separated the lost tea cup from the stool (my kids called it shoe-shoe) and she then dumped the stool into the toilet and dropped the tea cup into the soapy bath water still sitting in the wash-pan.

Remarkably unnoticed by any of us, Janet swallowed the teacup the previous afternoon, and it took about twenty-eight hours to pass through her little body from her mouth to her diaper, and Vesta retrieved the tea cup from the wash-pan and transferred it into a cup containing enough

Purex bleach to soak and disinfect the tiny tea cup, and before we went to bed, she reunited the complete tea set and tied all the pieces in a handkerchief and hid it in the back of a top drawer well out of Janet's reach.

In the fall 1950, Carroll was in the eighth grade, and he was old enough to play football, and I'm tickled to have my son learning the game of football. I have been attending most of Tallapoosa High School's football games as far back as I can remember, well since my initial game in which I had to PLAY, and the man that got me into that predicament was Bant Bailey, and now me and Vesta buy just about all our furniture from Bant Bailey at his partnership store 'Bailey and Barnes Furniture' up town. Carroll learned real quick how to operate his Famous James motorcycle, and he needs it for getting to football practice, which is after school every Monday, Tuesday, Wednesday, and Thursday. The coach is a young man I like a lot, Ray Wood, and he is very good at explaining the rules of football, and sometimes Ray Wood has his two little daughters with him at practice, and they are as cute as buttons and very well behaved, and while their daddy is coaching the players, the little girls play make believe off the field, in the bottom level of the wooden stands which run eighteen feet off the ground at the highest bench, and I can tell Ray Wood's two girls are very careful climbing up and back down, but they know better than to climb too high, and after practice one day, I said something to Ray Wood about his little girls, and he told me their names, the oldest is Pat and the youngest is Jane and Pat is a sweet little mother hen taking care of Jane, and Jane is the same age as my Janet and it gives me encouragement that Ray Wood's Jane is just as little as my Janet which I still sometimes worry about Janet's size, but seeing how little Jane is too, well it puts that concern out a my head once and for all.

Part of the job of running a sawmill is making sure every worker has access to a supply of gas which there'd be no power saws cutting if there was no supply of gas, so of course it's a constant job driving into town and refilling the gas cans, and it's my idee to refill gas cans when about half of the cans are empty, and it's an easy thing to coordinate gas buying trips to town so's they occur during the hours after school when Carroll's at football practice, and this way, I'm learning all about the game, right along with Carroll, but I can't stand there all day and watch and listen to football practice, so that's why Carroll needs the Famous James motorcycle so's he can transport himself without bothering his mother who's mighty busy, and now in the mornings Carroll sends his books (if he brought any home to do homework) with Joan and Marilyn on the bus, and he cranks up the Famous James and rides the back way which is a dirt road all the way up town, and he parks the Famous James at Chester's house, and usually, he gets to the Grammar School building ahead a the bus, and when the bus pulls in, he gets his books from Joan or Marilyn and heads on to the High School building. Grades eight through twelve are in the High School Building, and Joan and Marilyn are still in the big two-story Grammar School Building. This year is Carroll's first year in High School, and he's a little bit scared to ride a motorcycle up to the school building and park it and go inside for everybody to see because it's common knowledge he's too young to have a driver's license, but age has never been a factor for kids a growing up in the country for necessity dictates if you live out in the country, well there's a need to learn how to drive as soon as you can reach the petals as far as common sense and family safety is concerned.

By October 1950, construction work was complete on the store building and the grist mill building, and a cabinet maker was maybe about half way done building display shelving for the store building which in itself was a big job because each of the buildings are a good fifteen hundred square feet (thirty feet wide along the highway and 50 feet deep back from the highway). This large size country store requires two rows of double-sided shelving down the middle and one row on each side of one-sided shelving along the west wall and along the east wall, and with the shelves put in place we'll have three aisles each ten feet wide running from the front door area (on the north end of the building) to the back of the store. I gave the cabinet builder instructions to build each stand alone display shelving piece eight foot long and to start the lowest shelf off the floor by eight inches, and separate the shelves by two and a half feet, and the bottom shelf will be two feet deep, the next shelf up will be twenty inches deep, the next shelf up sixteen inches deep and the top shelf twelve inches deep. The two sided shelves will be exactly twice as deep as the one sided units.

While the cabinet builder worked inside the store building, I planned the mechanical workings of the grist mill but of course this was a side line job to my main source of income which is cutting the vast stand of timber off the Rifle Range, and make no mistake, saw milling comes first and defines my very existence for I guess I'd be a saw-miller if in fact I had to pay out good cash money for the privilege, and I'll be thankful right up to my last breath for the sweet acid smell a pine sawdust, but I don't stand back when faced with a challenge, and now I realized there's a need for the farmers in the Pine Grove settlement. Definitely a need for the means by which to process their corn crops which corn is the money maker for much of the northwestern quarter of Georgia and the northeastern quarter of Alabama.

Here is where I want you to understand one basic characteristic of me as a human being, and that is I'm not a man that considers any other human being on this God's green earth to be inferior to me, no sir re, and as proof, the very first farmer I consulted was N. H. Arney right down the road from me not some white farmer, but my closest neighbor, who is a colored farmer, and I also consulted with his son-in-law Ulus Collins, knowing both these good men work the fields growing corn, and from the handshake agreement with my closest neighbors well I carried that along with me a talking to white and Negro farmers, and simply put, I have been explaining if they're white, well they'll use the services of my new electric grist mill with full understanding that they might wait in line behind farmers of color, for there'll be no preferential treatment, no sir, it'll be the one that gets there first that'll be grinding first, and by God, that's the fair thing, and not a single farmer so far, wants to change my reasoning on the subject. In this Dead Man's Curve settlement I know and it is common knowledge that for the most part the KKK has little if any presence but to be fair there is one respected family of grown boys and one out of the whole bunch is KKK. The rest of the settlement is full of good, kind, and fair anything but KKK.

1951

I brought in a little old bitty blue bicycle, which 5 year old Janet named Blue Label, and with no hesitation, she pushed Blue Label up the road to the big oak tree at the edge of our yard, and she stayed out there all day on Saturday a pushing the bicycle up the hill (not much of a hill) getting it situated leaning toward her so's she could swing her skinny leg over the seat, this she did from a stand still for running and mounting all in one fluid motion was not possible for Janet to accomplish for she was a good two inches too short to throw her leg over the saddle. And only by standing on one tip toe could she accomplish the mounting feat of straddling the little bike with her tip toes barely touching the ground on either side, and over and over again, she panicked and jerked her feet from the ground to the peddles and started off down the slope weaving back and forth, and if she fell once she fell a hundred times, and if anybody came out to the road to offer help, it just made her mad.

One of the times when she was a starting off down the 'hill' Carroll jumped up off the couch inside the house and ran for the front door a yelling loud enough to be heard all the way up town, "Janet, watch out here comes a car!"

At fifteen, Carroll was the self appointed monitor for the little one (aw hell he was the monitor for the whole family) but especially when he heard a car coming or a car cranking up in the yard, that's when he was up and running to make sure the little one was not in the car's path, and this time coming up the road was teenager Troy Collins, our next neighbor down the road, and he was slowly passing by as was the usual thing for all the neighbors were very careful of our children a playing in the road. Troy was driving his own car which was black and yellow two tone, and Carroll in no time atall was standing on the road bank at the walnut tree and looking down right at Troy's fine black and yellow two tone car and Troy came to a complete stop and held his breath as little old bitty Janet fought to stay upright on two wheels, and she was so intent on learning to ride the bicycle that she didn't even raise up her head until she was about to run right slap dab into the stopped, engine-off, yellow and black car or rather the car's radiator, well not the radiator but the protecting chrome bumper right in the middle of the radiator, well the chrome rounded into a circle about the size of a wheel. Troy was a coming out of the driver's door and Carroll was about to jump off the road bank, but all this took place in a silent second, and when Janet suddenly became aware of her predicament, she knew enough to jump off the bicycle and guide it to the road bank where she waved and smiled at Troy like she was somebody. When the one white teenager and the one colored teenager could finally breathe, Carroll and Troy nodded to each other and Carroll turned back toward the house, and Troy slipped behind the steering wheel, eased the car door shut and pulled away from Janet now at the curve by the exposed roots of the persimmon tree. The three and a half foot high bank was taller than little Janet. She pushed Blue Label back up the 'hill' to her launch spot.

That night, Vesta held Janet's forehead while she vomited into the toilet some of her frustration and shock. Our determined little girl told her mother about the yellow and black car, and Vesta sat on the side of the bath tub and gently helped a bruised and bleeding little girl wash off the red dusty grimy dirt, and for a few minutes the three of us were in the bathroom together when I came in to sit on the commode for a while, and when I stood up a pulling up my underwear. I quickly turned away from little Janet Rose as she cut her eyes up at my back side past her mother still sitting on the side of the bath tub, and said, "Daddy, you've got the funniest old tail."

The next day was Sunday and of course, Vesta took all four kids to the Owens home place, but she didn't drive for Carroll was fifteen years old, and he'd been driving since age eleven when he could barely reach the gas peddle, clutch and brakes, and Joan and Carroll usually got up a fuss about who's turn it was to drive, and they were both so bull headed that Vesta had to referee their fights, but it was a usual thing that Carroll drove one way and Joan drove the other way, and that Sunday morning when I was about to leave the house to work alone cutting timber at the Rifle Range, well Joan and Carroll were about to finish their coffee and biscuits when I heard Joan scream, "That's hot, you mean inconsiderate, ungrateful heathen."

I was about to go out the front door when I deciphered that Carroll must have flipped a spoonful of his hot coffee at Joan, and next thing I knew, Carroll was dashing out of the kitchen into the dining room and right behind him came a cloud of airborne white sugar for Joan picked up the sugar bowl and with a skilled over-hand pitch, she threw the sugar bowl and all at her brother, and it was a pretty good pitch too for it plowed through the doorway and slammed into the dining room wall just missing Carroll's head. Carroll didn't loose a beat but kept on running past me out the front door to the edge of the front porch where he jumped over the Nandena bushes and tore out running past the car and truck down towards the barn, but he had to keep his speed up until finally Joan stopped and hollered something which I hope never to know the exact words, but I figured it was best left unexplored.

Carroll wound up sitting in the back seat of the Pontiac on the trip over to the Owens home place that day for Joan won the right to drive when he flipped her with hot coffee, and then he did not wait for her to catch him and beat the living daylights out of him. I drove off in my truck as Vesta and our four children piled into the two-tone green and light green 1949 Pontiac.

We are all mighty proud of Chester and Jack for they are both running thriving businesses in Tallapoosa. Jack since 1945, when he bought some land at 22 Gordon Street and set up his sawmill, added a planer mill, and built a shed he calls the office. Jack bought the Parmley place just up on the main road from the Owens home place in the Bethel Community, just down the road from the house where Joan was born, and he built a very nice house for his family, and he cut the timber, cleared pasture land, planted fruit trees, and built a big old barn and a pig sty and mostly Cleo and the children tend to and milk the cow, slop and butcher two fine hogs each year and beyond that they plant vegetables in the garden and a little corn in the fields, and this is a lot of work, but the canned garden vegetables and preserved fruits and smoked bacon, pork chops and hams feed their family all winter. At present they have four children Mary Jo (is Carroll's age), Wanda and Golia (are about the same age as Joan and Marilyn) and their youngest is Lynwood (one year older than Janet).

Where as Jack built a big new house out in the country near John and Sally, Chester bought a fine big house in Tallapoosa right by the High School building, and he added on and about doubled the size of the house for he and Nora have four children Norman, Gene, Ellen, and Little Lynda, and to speak of Little Lynda, she is as cute as a button, and smart as a whip, and nobody has let on that her height might be abnormal and Little Lynda thinks of herself as normal and as good as anybody, and it's obvious she is capable of doing anything she sets her mind to, and the whole town pretty much claims her and protects her just like our neighbors do out of town on the dirt road, but in town Little Lynda plays on the dirt city streets just like she owns everything in sight and not one person complains for she is a sight to see walking around in her mother's high heel shoes and maybe one of her mother's hats on her curly head of hair and every now and then Nora gets a little put out with her daughter, but when she tries to make any kind of behavior change Nora is the one who ends up giving in to her little whipper snapper and waiting for Chester to come home and put Little Lynda on the straight and narrow, but that is doomed to failure because Little Lynda has her daddy wrapped around her little finger, and she knows just how far to carry her pouting and huffing and in no time atall she's got her daddy taking her and her pets, and Lord knows she's adopted all the cats and dogs in town, and with a sweet smile and a 'please' Chester is taking a car load of cats and dogs for a ride, and Little Lynda is standing up in his lap a 'driving the car' and it's usually a brand new Pontiac off the show room floor.

Little Lynda started the fourth grade that fall and her older brothers Norman and Gene are in high school, Norman in the eleventh grade and Gene in the ninth grade and as usual in the morning, when it is time to head out the door for school, either Norman or Gene swings Little Lynda onto his shoulders, holds her tight to his head, tucks his books under his arm and goes a loping across the front yard, cuts across the Strasberg yard, across Bowdon Street and hauls Little Lynda to the Grammar School building. Little Lynda, now in the fourth grade which means she is up stairs and naturally her brother totes her up the stairs and right into the fourth grade room thus saving Little Lynda the difficult climb, and the point of this daily ritual is so's Norman or Gene can protect their little sister from any and all cruelty, but for the most part, the brothers have already whooped all bullies who might even look at their sister the wrong way, and the remainder of the students carry the protective business to the next level, and thereby insure that any remarks directed at or about Little Lynda are charitable and amiable and goodhearted, and that's just what Norman and Gene make for damned sure is the case.

No single member of her huge family has ever told her that she is handicapped by being little, no sir re bob, she's operated like she's just as tall as anybody, she's approached ever challenge head-on a never hesitating, and I truly believe her spunk was inborn as a natural part of her being, and she just proves to everybody that if she is brave enough to simply ignore what some might consider a hindrance and go on and live her life, well she can fool the whole world.

Back to her "country home" she usually spends at least one night a week with us, and it makes no never mind if it's summer or winter, school in or school out, she is just as much at home with us as she is in her town home, and sometimes Chester gets kinda huffy and tells her to, "Why don't you just pack up your clothes and move in with the Godwin's?"

Then is when Little Lynda uses her powerful charm, stays at home for a few days and convinces Chester there is room for two families in her sweet heart and never for a minute could anybody take his place. She calls over what all he's done for her when he and the elder Doctor Downey took her all the way to Johns Hopkins University in Baltimore, Maryland where they actually wanted to do a series of operations on her legs a cutting them into, separating them by about a half a inch, and letting them grow back together forming new bone, and in theory, with each procedure she'd gain about a half an inch in height. Chester was sure glad to have Dr. Downey with him in Baltimore, Maryland, and they talked through all the side effects and the worst possibility was that Little Lynda might become dependent on pain killers for everyone agreed the bone cutting and separating would be extremely painful and a second major consideration being that Lynda would not walk atall while the bones were 'growing' back together, and what if somehow the new 'growth' turned out to be weaker than a bone needs to be, what if the weakened half inch of new bone left Little Lynda in a wheelchair. No, it was too risky and Chester finally declined that radical approach, but he did agree to let the doctors fit his daughter with braces to straighten her bowed legs, and the straightening alone would itself give her an inch or more of height. So the doctor and Chester flew back into the Atlanta airport with Little Lynda wearing braces on her legs, and she wore the braces all the time for the next two years, except for the few times when Little Lynda's tears got the best of her daddy and Chester got out a screw driver and dismantled the dogged old braces to give Little Lynda an hour's rest from the braces gouging into her flesh.

Thomas got a letter from our cousin, our half sister Martheny's daughter, which the letter had to do with timber cutting on land owned by our cousins in south Georgia, and in talking it over with both Vesta and Thomas, well I went ahead with plans to haul my saw mill down to south Georgia. Back here while I was off working in south Georgia, with Thomas's help, Vesta would be ready to move on bidding on the Rifle Range as soon as it was announced for sale by the government, and no sense waiting for the kettle to boil, I packed up and hauled my sawmill and timber cutting equipment five hours south of Tallapoosa. The job in south Georgia looked like it would take us maybe three or four months, and once I got there, I knew for sure that I needed one more hand working so's every power saw I owned could run cutting every day.

In south Georgia, as soon as we got the sawmill set up, my hands knew what to do, and I set about finding and hiring a local south Georgia man, and I took off into the next small town and sure enough just a rolling into town in my pick up truck and sitting on a bench around on the back side of the Main street store entrances, well right off, I talked to one older colored lady, and when she found out I was a looking for sawmill help, she asked me politely to wait until she walked back home for to tell her grown-man-son Posey Greer, for he was in need of a job, and she'd send him right back into town, "Mr. Godwin, he'll think his ship has finally come in for he's pined away many a year wishing he could do the job of timber cutting and saw milling."

"How far is your place from here, ma'am?"

"Not far, just a few miles."

"Well if you don't mind, I'll drive you out to your place, and I can talk to Posey quicker that way, if you will ma'am, crawl into the cab a my pickup truck."

"No sir, Mr. Godwin, that won't do. I'll be walking on out a town to the east, and you can drive that way, and when I'm good and out a sight a every house along the way, well then you can stop along side the road, and then I can climb in your pick-up truck ride with you and not be noticed, and I'll show you the way."

These indecent maneuvers in regard to the colored 'allowed and not allowed' always punched a hard solid blow to my sense of what's right and what's wrong, but there's nothing to be done here in south Georgia where if I stir up a ruckus, well when I leave the KKK might very well just make things a whole lot worse for Posey Greer and his family, so I did as Posey Greer's Ma told me, and pretty soon we drove into her yard, and it was a right nice house on a few acres a land that was every-inch plowed into vegetables gardens, and out by the main road, well we pulled off the road right by a little shack, where her husband was selling their vegetables to folks driving by.

Like his Ma said, Posey Greer acted like he'd just been handed the moon, and he was quick to climb into the back a my pickup truck, but I made no never mind and went on a talking to Posey's mother, and my question was if she'd cook one good meal a day for me and my whole saw milling crew, and vegetables and cornbread would be welcome, and the bargain we struck was a sweet deal for her and a sweet deal for me, and we decided I'd bring my crew to her front door ever evening just about dark, and we'd eat her cooking while it was hot, and she offered and I accepted that me and my crew a saw mill hands could camp in the barn out a the rain, and she'd give out hot coffee and a cold biscuit ever morning, which she said had already added in when I offered her more pay. That's how we worked it out and Posey Greer's family made this a real enjoyable work trip, and his Ma even took in our dirty clothes and returned to us clean clothes, and on Saturday evenings everybody took turns shaving and bathing in the barn, and I like to think we gave that family a boost up out of the dreary confines of following KKK forbidden guidelines.

As soon as my kids' school let out, Vesta packed them up and drove south, and I settled Vesta and the girls in town at a cousin's house, and Carroll was raring to get to work, and he worked a good day's work just like the others, and he and Posey passed the time of day, and we decided maybe Posey was born a few years before Carroll, maybe as early as 1930, and Carroll decided that Posey was as honest as the day is long and to be trusted without restriction.

In south Georgia, the week that Vesta and my three girls were in town, at the end of ever day, Carroll drove one lumber truck and I drove the other lumber truck and we delivered the saw mill crew to the Greer place, and then we went on into town, and my cousin was pleased to make supper for us every night, and her little house was real comfortable, situated on a white, sandy city lot, and she even had indoor plumbing which we took turns showering (and it's a mighty pleasant experience even if the water is cold) but actually in south Georgia in the summer time who in the world would want a hot shower? And sitting in clean clothes at the supper table, well it's hard to think there might actually be anything better, and Vesta and Joan and Marilyn rattled on about picking lemons off a tree to make the pie, and early in the morning when we pulled out, well Vesta, and the girls pulled out too, and they're driving over to the Okefenokee Swamp where they'll see alligators, and with the mention of that word, the youngest joined in and recited all she'd learned which amazed every one at the table. After supper each evening before the sun went down, we all sat outside on the front porch where Janet wanted to jump off the end of the porch into the sand and feel her bare feet burrow into the warm white sand, which I didn't make no never mind about her playing in the white sand barefooted, but that first night after supper when my cousin and Vesta finally finished cleaning up the kitchen and came out on the porch to join us, well my cousin, was strung out, nervous worrying if Janet would get ring worms playing in the sand barefooted. Vesta buckled white sandals back on Janet's little feet, but my cousin couldn't stop her fretting.

The next week, Vesta and the kids went back up to Tallapoosa, and Joan helped her mother drive some of the time on the back roads when it was miles between towns and miles between meeting any other cars, and back home the first night when Vesta poured hot water in the bathtub and Janet sat down in the warm water, Vesta got down on her knees to lather up some of the Ivory soap and scrub Janet's dirty little feet and ankles (which this time wasn't the caked on red clay we in north Georgia call "rust") but instead, Janet's south Georgia dirt was browner than "rust" and well, Janet is always the main one to walk around barefooted in the summer time, and that night when Vesta scrubbed away the dirt from around Janet's ankles, well it was obvious Janet did in fact pick up ring worms in south Georgia for the rings were right there in plain sight, and the next morning, Vesta gathered up Janet and took her into town, and when Dr. Downey heard the story and examined Janet, he decided there were than one ring worm obvious so he wrote out a prescription for two bottles of medicine (each about the size of a co-cola), and Janet said it didn't taste too bad, and she was real good about taking her medicine, but that's nothing new, because we always emphasized if you're sick, you take your medicine, and there's no exceptions to that simple rule.

By the end of the summer, I hauled my sawmill back up from south Georgia in time of course for Carroll to start tenth grade and football practice, and I thanked the Greer family for treating us kind and fair, and when I stopped by my cousin's she was real sweet and asked us to come back, and I made sure to invite her to come stay with us in Tallapoosa, and she thought she might like that.

Moving my sawmill back home right at that time was a lucky thing, and after delivering my hands to their homes, I got a surprise at my own home when Vesta handed me the opened notice that the Rifle Range land is to be auctioned off at the Federal Building over in Atlanta, and this was remarkable timing, and I might just as well leave all the sawmill equipment on the log trucks sitting in the yard while I go to the Federal Building, and my twin brothers Thomas and Mose want to go to the auction with me and in just a few days, early one morning, before daylight, the three of us set out for Atlanta in the Pontiac, and Vesta had my pickup truck if she needed to go anyplace, but Ruth thought it'd be good to spend the day with Vesta and Janet just in case if anything happened. Well at the end of that momentous day, I came in from the federal auction the proud owner of the Rifle Range, and my sawmill hands were just as happy as pie that we'd all get settled in to working close to home and looking forward to cutting timber off the Rifle Range for three or four years.

On a cool day in May just a couple of months before Janet's sixth birthday, the older kids were in school, and problem is it's unanimous for all four of our kids have the same problem, and to treat the sinus infections Dr. Downey instructed Vesta to have the children drink a dissolved aspirin and a smidgen of baking soda in a small amount of warm water, and besides giving them the aspirin/baking soda, he instructed to "wash"

the sinuses with warm salt water injected directly into the sinuses with a medicine dropper. The "recipe" being one teaspoon of table salt dissolved in one pint of boiled water, let it cool a bit, then using the sterilized (with boiling water) eye dropper squirt the warm salt water into the sinuses and the best position for accomplishing this is for the patient to hang her head up-side-down off the side of the bed or couch and squirt a couple of eye droppers full of the warm salt water into each nostril which the whole process is complicated but actually effective in controlling sinus infections, and pretty soon as the youngest learned this procedure well then it was something that all our kids knew how to do and when to do it, so while Vesta continued coaching with the eye dropper, I decided to spell Vesta (for she was about three months pregnant with baby number five and still suffering from morning sickness. I took Janet with me up town in the two-tone green Pontiac Chieftain for I needed an inner tube patch for a log truck tire so's my sawmill hands could get on with loading logs. The log truck was a sitting in place jacked up on the jack at the Rifle Range waiting to be loaded with logs.

I switched the log truck flat tire from my pickup truck bed to the trunk of the Pontiac and drove up town with Janet standing up in the front seat leaning against me like me and Vesta thought was the safest for the little children, for that way we could hold the child in place with our right arm and body in case we had to slam on the brakes.

When I parked in front of Lively's Service Station up town, I got out of the car and took the key with me, I opened the trunk and wrestled the big flat tire onto the ground and set out rolling it into the service station repair bay, and while I was talking to the repair man I felt a little bit uneasy about Janet being out of my sight so I waved the worker off and walked backwards out of the repair bay while telling him I'd be back in an hour or so to pick up the tire, and when I turned toward the two tone green Pontiac, Janet was leaning out the driver's rolled-down window. I looked down at the black grease on my hands and told Janet I'd just get a rag out of the trunk to wipe off the old black grime, and when I shut the trunk and got around to the driver's side of the car, I opened the back door (with it's window rolled up) and I tossed the dirty rag in the floor board behind the driver's seat. I stood there a minute or two still wiping my hands, and Janet leaned over the seat to look up at me and ask me if she could please have a co-cola out a the co-cola box and a bag a peanuts to pour in the co-cola, and of course she wanted to stick her little hand down inside the co-cola box and pull up the bottled co-cola from the cold standing water, and I said I reckoned so just as Janet pulled herself back to a standing position in the front seat right behind the stirring wheel. I could see she'd hooked one foot into the stirring wheel and still facing the back seat she was moving the stirring wheel back and forth with her little ankle doing a little dance and when it comes to dancing she turns every opportunity into a performance if she sees any way atall.

What happened next is a little unclear in my fuzzy brain, but I think I threw the rag onto the floorboard, stepped back and slammed the door and simultaneous with slamming the back driver's side car door I heard a mournful sound that will haunt me forever when little Janet screamed, "Daddy! Daddy, Daddy!"

All I saw were the sweet little fingertips of Janet's right-hand wrapped a little ways outside the window post between front and back door, and the miniature fingertips were kind a waving but staying right there in place on the window post, and then Janet stuck her head out the driver's rolled-down window, but this was out of balance for my little Sugar Pie because she could not move her right hand out of the way and off the window post, so she had to turn her little head sideways and poke her head through the opening between the upper edge of the window frame and her own skinny little arm, and with her head tilted out the window and a looking straight at me, I thought she'd never stop crying and calling, "Daddy! Daddy! Daddy!"

I thought to myself, "You stupid son of a bitch! Open the Dod Damn Door! Don't stand here forever and a day, OPEN THE DOD DAMN DOOR!"

Somehow the back door mysteriously opened with my hand a pulling on it, and as quick as a knee jerk, Janet's right thumb pulled back into the Pontiac away from the window post and into the front seat of the car, and all I could see was a bright red baby thumb retreating in a flash of liquid, right up to Janet's neck and as quick as a wink the bloody thumb was the center of a growing, bright red, dripping, oozing sickening, horrifying bloodspot, and some how my wobbly legs got me in position behind the stirring wheel, and my worthless arms opened and caught my little Sugar Pie, and my good-for-nothin' left arm held her sobbing spasms to my

chest, and her left hand squeezed her bloody right wrist to her little neck in an automatic protective position, and my left arm curled around her tiny shoulders, and my right hand pushed the key into the ignition and my own uninjured, clear of blood, vile, hateful right thumb pushed the starter button while my left foot pushed the clutch to the floor, and the car lurched forward while my right hand turned and twisted the stirring wheel around and around in what seemed like about a hundred revolutions, and I floored the gas peddle right through town flying east past the stand pipe, down the hill, up the hill, left off of 78, scattering gravel on the dirt road past the Gladden place, past Ruby Brown's place, past the Jaillet place, to the forks of the road which I took the ninety degree forks with my back wheels skidding to the right pushing the front wheels to the left and kicking up dust and dirt and rocks into a plume tagging along behind us, and the Pontiac's six inline engine took the hill like it was flat as a pancake, but now for some unknown reason we were stuck in thick sorghum syrup covering every inch of the last hundred yards to the curve at the old oak tree which went by slowly enough to give the hands of a watch plenty of time to move from mid-day, past midnight and into tomorrow, and all that long unending, eternity all I could think of was the co-cola and peanuts I'd promised my little girl, and I would have had time to leave my little girl a lying on the seat in the car while the car poked along slow as cold sorghrum syrup, and I could've opened the car door, got out and run back the three miles to town, got her promised co-cola and peanuts, returned to her and this old good for nothing two toned green Pontiac, creeping along and there I'd be back in place sitting behind the stirring wheel holding my little girl before she even missed my arm under her sweet head ....
but here I go again, there's got to be something bad wrong with a daddy who thinks of such nonsense at times like this, but finally my watch did in fact turn past midnight and into a new day, and finally, I turned at the old oak tree and finally, I actually slammed on the brakes and pushed the white sandy yard into two heaping piles solely for the purpose of stopping the wretched two toned Pontiac, and next thing I know somehow Vesta is waiting in the yard. How'd she do that? How'd she know? Can't she do something to fix this? Why is she sauntering along? Don't just float over to me this way! Why can't she fix this? Why can't she hurry! How'd I get covered with blood and where's my little Sugar Pie? Where's my wife?

When my lungs decided to keep me alive, I was out of the two tone light green and dark green Pontiac Chieftain, and inside the kitchen with no recollection of walking or crawling or nothing but somehow here I was in the kitchen. At the table I propped myself up with one knee in a chair and holding to the chair's ladder back, I stopped the dizzy swaying and watched as Vesta carefully examined Janet's quivering right thumb while Janet snuggled her face into her mother's neck and finally spelled me as she cried over and over, "Mother! Mother! Mother!"

Vesta decided we'd go on up town to see Dr. Downey at the Downey Clinic and a finer clinic cannot be found in these parts. I drove us up town with Vesta promising that everything would be alright, and we didn't miss a beat as we entered the Downey Clinic with Vesta toting Janet, and the nurse (Sara Walker) motioned us through the waiting room and back around to the operating room, and Perrin appeared like magic wearing a white jacket with a small white stand-up collar, and Vesta bent over Janet and told her it might hurt just for a few minutes and then my beautiful wife, smiled at me and started humming the "Have You Watched the Fairies" song, and Janet was as brave as any little girl could possibly be. I had a clear mind, and it came to me in a sudden realization that the only time I pass out is when I have no immediate responsibility, and as long as I am holding any one of our children, that is the signal to my crazy brain, that I can't be passing out, any fool with eyes can see how dangerous it'd be if I passed out and crashed to the floor, so that's all it takes to keep me from passing out,

I can watch Perrin stitching right through Janet's bloody skin and I'm no sissy about it, I'm not even a little bit light headed, but I bet you anything, if Perrin puts down the needle and walks out of the room, right there in front a me, then the next second, I'd faint like a girl knowing I'd involve no one but my own self. This having children is a very powerful thing! That's exactly the way I had it figured because I'm not the fainting sort of a man, hell, when I was sixteen years old, I carried my brother all the way from the bridge down in the valley to the home place while Bert's left arm dangled by a little thin slice of skin, and I could feel the severed arm hitting me in the shin with every single step, and that night I stood by my brother trying to keep him breathing while he was out cold and when he came to and relieved me of the immediate responsibility keeping him alive, hell I didn't faint then but I sure do faint a lot when it's something involving one of my children, so I'm holding one of Janet's feet, and it's both a comfort to me and a sock right in the jaw to me for it's her reliance on me that keeps me aware and awake.

Perrin stitched up Janet's right thumb as best he could, but because the thumbnail was completely sliced in two separate pieces, it was clear the thumbnail would never grow back together and since stitching through the thumbnail was impossible, Perrin cautioned that the wound must remain bandaged over the next several weeks as the thumbnail will require an extended amount of inactivity to avoid further injury, and he emphasized to our little Janet that she must not use the "bad" hand and that'll be unhandy because she's right handed, but she'll have to use her left hand for eating and drinking and such, and even though her right hand will be bandaged for a long time, she'll have to remind herself to hold the "bad" hand to her chest and cradle it inside her left hand to protect it, and Perrin didn't let up as he continued to train little Janet to take every precaution with the "bad" thumb.

Vesta told me later that she watched as the doctor could only minimally press the two-piece nail together, and he made every effort to reposition the thumbnail, and we all understood from the doctor's relentless cautions that any contact between the "bad" thumb and any solid material would bring excruciating pain, and on a parting note once again, Perrin's advise was to "Soak the wound in Epsom Salts water and apply clean bandages daily."

Back in the car, Janet Sugar Pie sat between me and her mother, and my first words were to ask Janet, "Sugar Pie, do you still want a co-cola and peanuts?"

I parked in front of the pool hall, my front right tire to the curb, on the west side of Head Avenue, and quick as I could I dashed into the Red Dot Grocery Store, I bought a whole case of co-colas and an unopened box of peanut packets, and it was a pitiful pay-out that was no where near re-payment for shutting the car door on my little girl's thumb. For a long time I was a sorry good-for-nothing moping around like a fool holding onto my wife's apron strings, and when I came out of it a little, well I tried to sort through what I've become, and I decided that I forgot and forsook my number one principle of being a good daddy for back when we just had Carroll and Joan, Vesta wanted to cradle and protect both our little children, but I wanted just the opposite, and we argued about it, but I wanted to stand back and let the children find their own way of protecting their own sweet hide like I'd always had it to do. I don't regret it, but the simple truth is I had no choice except to learn how to take care of myself (and Sis of course, I always took care of Sis) But now I feel like I am at a crossroads in raising my own four children, and sometime I changed and started acting like another Vesta, and one mother in this house is enough, but here and now, I protect my kids and shield them and forget to let them learn a few things on their own. Well it's not too late, and just as soon as Janet's thumb heals, well then I'm starting with Janet and just like Janet persisted in teaching herself to ride a bicycle for no other reason than her obsession to do it, well she was bound and determined she could, and that relentless attitude is the very place I'm getting back to in my own mind, just as soon as Janet's thumb heals, and I mean it too!

That summer 1952, Boot Goolsby bought a Streetcar, and he had it hauled right to Dead Man's Curve and he set in place along Highway 78 just east of our country store, and it took about all summer wiring it up to the electric lines and hooking it up to the well water and inside all the wooden Streetcar seats were unbolted from the floor, and a service counter (with bolted down stools) was built right down the middle, and a front door was cut on the north side facing the highway, and on either end of the food service counter some of the wooden seats were arranged around tables and bolted to the floor forming sit-down booths. Behind the service counter is where a gas cooking grill was hooked up, and a dish washing sink was fed clean well water, and the sink's drain was connected to a dug-in-septic-tank-sorta-barrel buried deep in the ground with punched holes draining the dishwater into the ground away from the well up the hill in the yard. Boot's wife Lavada sewed cafe curtains and hung them along the windows and the Streetcar Cafe was in business serving mostly hot dogs, chili, and co-colas. This was a welcome addition to the busy Dead Man's Curve settlement.

Through the summer, Carroll mostly ran the country store but of course he had his mother's help as she ran in and out, rushed off to William's Brothers, and on a weekly basis, tallied up the customers credit receipts, but Carroll ran the cash register, stocked the shelves, and swept the floors before arranging straight back chairs into a conversation circle inside the wide front doors where visitors bought a co-cola and a pack a peanuts and listened to one feller in particular, who was a good neighbor and a kind person in all regards, but he had a flaw and that being, he liked to hear his own voice talking nonstop whether anybody was listening or not, it didn't matter and he kept on a talking flapping his jaw just for the sensation of hinging it up and down. This man's nickname (to his back a course) was "Windbag"

and every time Vesta blew in, Janet blew in right with her, and sometimes Vesta left Janet with Carroll and I guess Janet was a listening to every word said, and understanding a whole lot more than anybody was ready to admit, but sure enough one day when Janet blew into the store ahead a her mother, she passed directly by Windbag's chair, and she threw up his hand in greeting and said, "Hello, Windbag!"

Nobody let on, but they all held their breath waiting for some sort of condemnation from Windbag, but Windbag must have decided to let it slide with no hard feelings, for he actually silenced his constant jaw flapping for a few days.

Fall, 1952

In the fall when Carroll started his junior year in high school, Janet started first grade. On weekends and week days after school, Carroll has always worked helping me, and now our prospects are clearly in the black cutting timber off the one and only Rifle Range not some pathetic timber-only tract, but cutting timber off my own land which will bring in steady money well into the future, and Carroll can make good money working for me all he wants to but of course except during football season for he enjoys that game just as much as I do. Many times after football practice, Carroll came on to the Rifle Range in time to work an hour maybe two, and Joan works the soda fountain at Robert's Drug Store after school every day except for Wednesday, and all day on Saturdays and for two hours on Sunday mornings, and twelve-year-old Marilyn helps her mother with the washing which now takes place in the well shed and is a site easier than it was before we got electricity, but it remains a whole lot of back breaking work, and in the winter when the weather is cold and rainy, it is mighty inconvenient since the well shed has no heating system, and the water from the well is painfully colder than body temperature, so instead of dipping her hands into the cold water, Vesta uses a good strong and sturdy stick, and she has devised a "dig and snag" method of retrieving clothes so as to pull them up and out of the cold water and send them through the wringer with a minimum of hand contact.

Even in the winter, the clothes dry pretty quick outside on the clothes line unless it is raining of course, and on rainy days, the wet clothes are strung out on collapsible, wooden, clothes-drying-racks inside the house, and it is a nuisance to maneuver through the maze of drying racks, and no matter where the clothes hang to dry outside or inside, the wrinkles have to be ironed out and Marilyn is Vesta's ironer in charge of ironing everybody's clothes to wear to school the next day, and so while Joan and Carroll work at their paying jobs, Marilyn works at home, and no ifs, ands, or buts about it, she works hard, but no harder than is the usual thing in any big family, and it is a natural thing in our family for everybody contributes, and the children work at home or they work at paying jobs and no body gets by without working, and Carroll and Joan bring home their payday and every member of the family benefits from it.

Vesta takes care of the cooking, every morning she makes fresh biscuits and a skillet of hot bubbling gravy and that, along with hot coffee, gives every one of us a good start, me for saw-milling and the kids for learning in school, and all along every time a teacher has a chance to talk to me or Vesta, we learn how much they enjoy and appreciate teaching our children, and that is a matter of great pride and frankly, hope for the future. Vesta has set high expectations, and I don't interfere in that area, because I'm not blind, I can see what's plain as day, our kids have great potential, they are blessed with good minds and simple ever day rituals are paying off. The books we have in our home are tattered from use and everybody knows the words by heart and from repetition comes reading.

Sewing for three girls takes up a lot of time, and Vesta is already teaching Joan and Marilyn how to sew, but in the afternoons while Marilyn stands at the ironing board which is set up in the dining room just outside the kitchen doorway, Vesta cooks supper, and Vesta and Marilyn talk and listen to the radio, and now we have a new radio made of white Bakelite with a big-as-your-fist round knob to dial in the radio station, and the main station we receive is WLS in Chicago which broadcasts mostly singing during the day, and at night Vesta and the kids listen to serials unless Vesta is upstairs quilting, she quilts in the evenings if the temperature upstairs drops enough to make it tolerable, but mostly her quilting upstairs takes place in the fall of the year and the spring of the year for it is too hot up stairs in the summer and too cold up there in the winter. While Janet's hand was bandaged, Vesta made sure Janet was upstairs with her while she quilted each evening after supper.

Every Saturday Joan worked at the Robert's Drug Store, and toward the end of the day, the whole family according to our tradition got all cleaned up and went into town, and most Saturdays, Vesta took Marilyn and Janet into the Grand Theater, and me and Carroll spent time meeting with Mr. James McDonald at his house up town, and we planned and wrote letters and filled out Federal Government paper work, and it was taking shape and the pieces of the puzzle were falling into place, and it now seemed a good possibility that sometime in the next several years, I'd buy timber cutting rights on National Forests to the west of a little town called Magdalena, two thousand miles from Tallapoosa out west in New Mexico.

Joan worked after school at Roberts Drug Store, and she walked from the high school up town to the Drug Store, but on school nights the Drug Store closed at seven. Joan got there from school in time to work about a four hour shift three to seven, and after school when it was not football season, Carroll as a usual thing rode the bus home and changed into his work clothes then drove the Famous James wearing a good winter coat up to the Rifle Range where he worked with us until dark, at which time I hauled my sawmill hands home in the pick-up truck, and Carroll drove the Famous James home and switched to the Pontiac and then drove up town to pick up Joan, and by the time we all got home, supper sure tasted good.

It's always been the case in Tallapoosa that stores and banks and everything closes on Wednesdays at noon, and so that one day a week, Joan didn't have a job at the drug store for it was closed, and she rode the bus home, and many a Wednesday, Little Lynda rode the bus too. This one Wednesday, when Carroll got off of the bus at the house, he noticed a flat tire on the Pontiac so before he came on to the Rifle Range first he changed the flat tire on the Pontiac, and then he drove the Pontiac up town in order to leave the flat tire at the service station, so about dark when we were a little late leaving the Rifle Range, I followed Carroll home, the Famous James had a good working headlight and taillight but it made me uneasy for him to be on the busy Highway 78 at night, and when we pulled into the yard, Carroll parked his Famous James in the garage and jumped in the pickup cab with me, then we delivered all my sawmill hands to their homes, and me and Carroll went on to meet with Mr. McDonald again, and Carroll told me he was embarrassed to show up at Mr. McDonald's front door in dirty work clothes, but I set him straight right quick, for dirty work clothes or nothing else to do with work is cause for embarrassment and in fact, it's just the opposite, grimy clothes, dirty fingernails, greasy hands, pine needles in your hair and every single bit a evidence of hard work is to be showed off as a badge of pride and honor, and when Mr. McDonald opened his front door, it was obvious by the look of respect on his face that he understood the exact same hard work code of conduct I was a talking about.

Vesta heard the commotion in the front yard when Carroll parked his motorcycle in the garage, and when she heard us drive off in the pickup, she put our supper plates inside the slightly warm oven and went upstairs to quilt. Upstairs with her mother, Janet played jacks on the wide-pine-board floor, and she liked the cozy play area under the hanging quilt. This was Vesta's idea to hang the quilting frame from screw eyes screwed into the attic's sloped ceiling, and on the floor under the anchor-less quilting frame, Janet chased the little rubber ball about the room and when the little rubber ball hit the cracks between the floor boards which sent it a bouncing away, but chasing the ball was as much fun as picking up the jacks, and Janet had a time learning to catch the little ball with her left hand in order to take care of her right thumb. By now, the whole family just trusted Janet to manage about holding back from using her right hand and she seemed glad for the responsibility.

At the same time downstairs in the kitchen, Joan and Marilyn and Little Lynda were washing up the supper dishes in an assembly line which began with Marilyn stacking the dirty dishes on the sink's left hand grooved white enamel drain board, next in line to the right was Joan washing in a dishpan full of hot soapy water, and next in line was Little

Lynda rinsing each piece through a dishpan of clean rinse water and finally, Marilyn took the wet dishes from Little Lynda and dried and stacked each dish on the table. Some times Marilyn's job got backed up and when that happened, Little Lynda placed the dripping wet dishes and pots and pans on towels spread out on the sink's grooved white enamel right drip side which both sides of grooved white enamel channeled water into the basin just fine, but the enamel was a slippery surface for laying down wet dishes and that's precisely why the girls placed a rag over the water channeling grooves which of course even though the non-skid dish towel was sopping wet, it still cushioned and protected and held in place the wet dishes while excess rinse water dripped away. (Little Lynda did everything standing up in a chair, and no one ever even noticed, it was just a matter of fact) At the end of the assembly line, Marilyn was racing around trying to keep up with her job of drying and putting away, and when Joan wiped off the table and picked up the last dirty item which was the empty gallon milk jar, well at this point Joan, Marilyn and Little Lynda conspired to avoid washing the last dirty item for they reasoned the dish washing water was getting too cold and greasy to do any good atall cleaning the big glass gallon milk jar, so naturally it seemed the only logical thing to these three girls was to pour just a tad bit of milk from the full gallon milk jar (in the refrigerator) into the empty gallon milk jar and then put both gallon milk jars back in the refrigerator.

As soon as Joan carried the dishpan out onto the back porch and gave it a sling tossing the dirty dish water out into the grass, Marilyn used her now wet drying rag to dry down the two dishpans before hiding them under the sink, and now free to follow their own devices, the three girls set out to make some fudge which they'd been trying different made-up recipes over and over again and not yet had they found a good combination of coco, sugar, flour (just a pinch) and butter, and they were pretty sure no other ingredient was needed so they turned the stove eye to high, stirred and mixed constantly as the butter melted, and of course they each took a turn stirring the concoction and tasting a little lick off the spoon, and this time they decided they might have the correct combination, and it was time to thin the fudge with a little water, so with the fudge a bubbling in the pan, and Lynda (standing in a chair) stirring it, Joan went to the white Bakelite radio on the floor under the ironing board, got down on her stomach and dialed in WLS in Chicago, and all three girls shuttered when the spooky music came on and the scariest voice in the world said, "Who knows what evil lurks in the hearts of men? (cynical laugh) The SHADOOW KNOOWS!"

Joan crawled back into the kitchen, stood up, and took the stirring spoon from Lynda, Marilyn ran some cold water into a glass, returned to the stove and held the glass as Joan scooped up just a tiny bit of the bubbling fudge and dropped a drop or two into the cold water. They all held their breath watching the two fudge drops dissolve in the cold water. In unison they all wailed, "It's not forming fudge balls like it's supposed to."

Always the optimist, Lynda said, "We've just got to boil it some more, turn up the heat and keep stirring!"

Joan turned up the heat and stood there stirring the fudge well out of direct line of vision of the front door, and when 'The Shadow Knows' radio show played more spooky music, and the evil voice tried to trick a young girl, Lynda squealed like a helpless little puppy, and she and Marilyn huddled together with Lynda's chair positioned so that both girls were looking through the dining room toward the front door and just at that minute when the scary music reached a crescendo, Lynda and Marilyn heard a tap, tap, taping and when they looked through the dark dining room, they could see the outline of a man's face looking through the glass panes of the front door, and the screen door squeaked farther opened and Lynda jumped off the chair and started the longest journey of her young life running through the dining room, into the living room, up the stairs to safety, and Joan and Marilyn were bringing up the rear as fast as their wobbly, wet noodle legs could possibly carry them.

Upstairs, Janet scurried under her mother's arms and stood there with her eyes as big as saucers hoping no one was actually dying, and Lynda was the first one up the stairs and a close second on her heels came Marilyn fighting off Joan's attempts to take second place, and Vesta stifled a grin as she awaited an audible explanation through the chicken squawking turmoil which the disclosure finally came in a whisper from Lynda, "There's a man's face at the front door."

Against the mighty forces of a gang of children trying to intervene, Vesta stood up from her quilting, straightened her shoulders, crossed the room, and descended the stairs, and when her left foot reached the bottom step, she looked up to see four faces peeping over and through the banister; and finally, she could hide her laughter not a minute longer, and her bravery bewildered the kids sure to their core they were catching a LAST glimpse of their beloved mother.

It was just before school let out in 1952, that I hauled in our brand new, first ever television set. It was a little old bitty thing, but when Carroll put up the antenna, we got a pretty good picture, and one of the first shows we watched was on Saturday night, and it was a singing show with Dorothy Collins, Gisele Mackenzie, and Snooky Lanson singing songs that our kids knew all the words by heart. The television is amazing, but I guess I like better the old days of listening to Vesta read a story to our kids and watching the creativity spelled out on their faces. I know television is the entertainment form of the future, but I'm not sure this can actually be called progress.

In the fall, Janet and Dolly were together in Mrs. Fitzgerald's first grade class, and Beulah and Morris were just as glad as we were to know our little girls were together, but a few weeks into the school year, Vesta worried that Janet might be watching the other children play and not joining in at recess because Janet's shoes and socks were as clean at the end of the day as at the beginning, and up town on Saturday, Vesta talked to Beulah only to find out that Dolly's shoes and socks were also too clean at the end of the day. As it turned out, the worry was for nothing, and Ruth handled the situation when she took Janet and Dolly into Robert's Drug Store and paid Joan for two small dishes of ice cream. When Ruth had the two first graders sitting at one of the small soda fountain tables, she recounted to them how as a young girl in school herself, she always liked to play jumprope or hop scotch way back when she was in first grade, and when Janet looked to be on the verge of tears, Ruth pulled her into her lap and asked, "What's wrong, Sugar Pie?"

Through her sniffles, Janet said, "Doctor Downey told me I had to hold my bad thumb and always remember to protect it, so I'll never get to play jump rope or hop scotch."

Amazingly, when Janet recalled Dr. Downey, Ruth saw him walk into the Drug Store through the back door that leads directly into the Pharmacy, and with a mission to accomplish, Ruth instructed Janet and Dolly to stay put at the little table while she went to the Pharmacy Counter. In a matter of minutes, Dr. Downey was sitting in the fourth chair and telling Janet he needed to examine her bad thumb. Janet dutifully put her spoon in the cut glass ice cream dish, slid down to the floor and stepped up to the doctor. Perrin examined her thumb and pronounced, "Janet, your thumb is completely healed, and you should never again protect it in any way. From this day on and forever, you have to forget that your thumb was ever hurt."

Then Perrin asked for a bite of Janet's ice cream which caused Janet and Dolly to giggle at the amazing spectacle of the doctor eating from a little girl's spoon, and the next Monday afternoon when the bus delivered the kids back home, as usual when Carroll stepped off the bus, he handed his books to Joan and turned to swing Janet from the bottom bus step and hoist her onto his shoulder. Janet giggled as usual when Carroll climbed the bank from the road to the back yard, and with some momentum he ran across the grass, and up the porch steps two at a time, and as smooth as dancing a waltz, he delivered Janet into the house and hugged his little sister.

Vesta greeted the children as usual with a kiss and the question, "How was school?"

In turn, starting with the oldest each rattled off the day's accomplishments, and finally when it was Janet's turn, she first looked down at her red-clay-powdered dirty socks then smiled her very own accomplished little smile before twisting and turning from one foot to the other and saying dauntlessly, "Dolly and I had a pretty good time today!"

This was to be a "home made ice cream" night, but me and Carroll had to miss the celebrating, and that night right after supper, I heated, on the electric cook stove, two big buckets of water. Next I hauled the hot water to the bathroom and settled down in the luxurious, modern bathtub. I scoured off the dirty and grimy evidence of a descent hard day's work and even went so far as to put a drop or two of liquid "shampoo" on my black hair. With a couple of rinsing splashes, I stepped out of the bathtub, dried off and dressed in a white shirt, dress pants, and a corduroy suit coat, which gave me a feeling of self esteem and confidence. On this particular Wednesday night, I put on my newest felt hat and the two of us (me and Carroll) went into town to meet with Mr. James McDonald who was excited and anxious to tell us the good news.

Earlier that afternoon when Carroll was still in school, I was still at the Rifle Range and it sort of shook me up to see this influential man dressed up like a banker, traipsing along our logging roads and waving his arms until I shut down my power saw. As I made my way toward him, my sawmill hands kept on working and paid no attention. That's when Mr. McDonald asked me to bring Carroll and come to his house to sign more papers, and then he shook my dirty hand, turned away from me, and found his way back to his car. We quit work a good bit before sundown, and at home we each took a bath and got all gussied up in Sunday go to meetin' clothes, and Carroll backed my pick-up truck out of the yard, and we headed into town, for at age sixteen, my son is a fine right hand man, and I for one want him with me making and signing any and all business deals.

In the mean time, Vesta, Marilyn, Little Lynda, Janet, and Joan were on the back porch watching the sun go down as everybody took turns cranking on the ice cream freezer. It's another worm fall and cold ice cream sure tastes good.

I carried Janet into the house and Vesta went ahead of me to make a place for her in our room. Janet sleeps in our room, Carroll has his own room and Joan and Marilyn share a bed in their room which has furniture Vesta calls the Blonde Waterfall Set, and Vesta has outfitted all three rooms with bedroom sets of matching furniture, they're very nice, but tonight unlike the other nights when Lynda spends the night, Joan and Marilyn are both sleeping upstairs where Janet and Lynda usually sleep, but tonight Lynda's sleeping-room-mate didn't go up the stairs but instead she crawled into bed with her mother, and both Janet and Vesta fell asleep without a bath. Before the girls went upstairs, Lynda polished Janet's shoes for school in the morning, and then the bath marathon began and Lynda went first just as soon as the three buckets of water came to a boil on the kitchen stove which we have an electric stove with four eyes, but one eye is burned out so we can heat only three buckets of water at a time, and while Lynda was in the bathtub, the next three buckets of water were getting hot on the stove and so on and so on. The butane gas space heater puts out good heat to warm the bathroom and bathtub, and that warmth helps us to slow down our inquisitive brains and gear into a sleep mode. These are mainly Carroll's words by the way, for I never in my life had a bit a trouble sleeping with or without a bath.

There are still three beds upstairs, and tonight all three beds will be occupied. The kids polished their shoes (Lynda polished Janet's) and lined them up along the wall behind the potbelly-warming stove so they'd be warm to put on in the morning. Marilyn already ironed everybody's school clothes, and Lynda had a starched and ironed dress or two upstairs for Nora came around every week when she was sure Lynda had no clean clothes at our house because it was a usual thing for Lynda to spend the night at least on Wednesday night and more than that if she could get by with it.

Early this morning, I drove around to my workers houses to tell them we'll not be working today, and about 10 o'clock me and Vesta did something we've never done before, we (just the two of us) went over to visit with John and Sally. They were both in good humor and pretty soon we understood why, the peddler stopped by with both of their Social Security Checks. The checks come every month, guaranteed and boy howdy what a game changer that is!!!!!!

By Halloween all the leaves were on the ground, and as usual I pulled into the yard ahead of Carroll who drove the log truck on uptown to pick up Joan, and as I drove into the yard, I noticed the leaves off the old oak tree were raked into a pile, and I got a little out a sorts a thinking that Vesta might a been out raking leaves today, and when I shut down the engine and opened the pickup door, I jumped like a scared sissy when I heard Janet's "Hey, Daddy!"

I got to admit I was scared! Ya damn right I was scared! Probably as scared as I'd ever been in my life! My youngest popped her head up from the pile of dead leaves that she'd raked up into a mound right under the old oak tree, right there, right exactly where I drive into the yard, hell right exactly where anybody drives into the yard! I threw down my coat hard against the ground and covered the space between me and Janet in steps longer than I am tall, and I was grittin' my teeth the whole way, and by the time she could see my face, she stopped calling out to me, and she stood still as the tree trunk, and without a peep she followed my directions said through clinched teeth, "Get into the house this very minute, and I mean it!"

I tried to calm my racing heart by pacing and blowing, and I had to push my hands down to the center of the earth inside my pockets to keep my feet on the ground, and I was still in the yard when Carroll and Joan pulled in taking the usual path right under the old oak tree, and distracted by me, Carroll drove right smack dab through the pile of leaves where Janet would still be in the pile of leaves, and Carroll would a killed her for sure. Carroll stopped and rolled down his window and said, "Daddy, what in the world are you doing? Are you raking up leaves?"

I blew off some more frustration and motioned them to go on in, and when I finally picked up my coat and went in the house, Vesta had Janet sitting on the couch, and she slipped out of the living room and let me have a private minute with my youngest, and then is when I had to sit down on the other side of the room because I was afraid I'd hit my little girl, and so help me God, that's the only time in my life I've ever been unsure of myself in that regard. I started with, "My first question is, have you ever before hidden in a pile of leaves?"

Janet replied, "I thought up hiding in the leaves just a little while ago."

I pushed out, "Janet, you have to take care of yourself because there might come a time when you don't have anybody else to take care of you."

"Yes, Daddy."

"By now you're old enough to know what's a good idee and what's a dangerous idee. Did you think hiding in the leaves was a safe place to hide?"

"Yes Daddy."

"When I passed by in the truck, could you see through the leaves?"

"Yes Daddy."

"Did you have an idee how close the pickup truck wheels came to you?"

"Yes Daddy"

You have to take care of yourself first and then you have to take care of others who might need you"

"Yes, Daddy."

"Did you think the pickup truck wheels might roll over you?

This time she had no answer.

"Now listen to me! Hiding in the leaves right where I pull into the yard could a killed you. It was a very, very dangerous thing to do. If the pickup truck wheels had rolled over you, I'd a killed my own little girl, and that is something a man cannot live with. Starting right now and for the rest of your life, you have to consider if you're putting yourself in danger of being killed."

With that, I left her alone, and I joined everybody else at the supper table, Carroll and Joan were eating, Vesta and Marilyn already ate. Not a word was spoken, but it was plain to see, they'd heard what I had to say to Janet. They heard Janet come in and sit down on the couch, but they could only guess what she was thinking.

Right then, I made a decision that Carroll's place for a while is at home with his mother except of course when he has football practice after school, but his mother needs him for she's overloaded with work and minding a little girl, and Carroll's not needed at the Rifle Range, and Vesta didn't argue for I think she felt a little bit responsible for the 'hiding in the leaves' episode, for she was in the house all the whole time that Janet was raking up leaves, and just one head stuck out a the door might have prevented the whole situation, but she's said many times, she "goes in a long lope from before sunup to after sundown."

I said nothing about Vesta's situation of course, but it was plain as the nose on your face Vesta went through a time of self blame, and we all proceeded with a new found determination to teach and preach and watch and protect, but over the next two weeks the whole idee was being distorted, and I could see a trap was being set by everybody 'cept me in which Janet would most certainly become more dependent and less independent on influences outside of her own self reliance, so in two weeks of the incident, I came in a little early from the Rifle Range, and at the table that night with all four kids present I said, "Janet, I'm gona give you a test for I want to understand just how much you've grown up since the mistake you made about hiding in the leaves.

Now, right this minute, I'm telling you what to do, and I won't take no for a answer, now listen to me, I want you to put down your fork, go outside on the back porch, go down the steps and across the grass to where the school bus stops. I want you to go down the bank and into the road, and I want you to stand there in the middle of the road until you see the headlights of a car coming. I want you to wait until the car's headlights are shining right on you, then I want you to start yelling and waving your arms up and down and make the car stop. I want you to stand there until the car stops, don't try to get out of the way, you have to stand there and make the car stop before it hits you. Now, I mean it, go on out there."

To her credit, she lifted her chin (but not her eyes) as she replied to the tabletop, "No sir."

I looked at her misery and asked, "Young lady, are you defying your daddy?"

This time she said, "Yes, sir."

I fired back, "Well alright then."

We ate the rest of our supper in silence, very serious silence, and I can tell you not a word was spoken against or in support of Janet, and it was the only way I could get the point across that we are not put here on this God's green earth to spend every minute of every day protecting and making decisions for our littlest kid, no sir, she has to know how to protect her own self, she has to make her own decisions without first looking to someone else to point the way, and after supper there was no hugging or celebrating or congratulating, no sir by God.

The next night, I came in early again for a another word or two at the supper table which everybody hesitated about exchanging normal conversation, and again I pointed my questions at Janet, "Do you remember what we've taught you about standing up to a bully?"

"I remember."

"Tell us?"

"Raise up my chin and look the bully right in the eye and stare him down."

"Does it matter how big the bully is?"

"No."

"Will the bully make you afraid."

"Yes."

"Was I the bully last night when I told you to go outside in the dark and wait for a car?"

"Yes."

"Were you afraid of me?"

"Yes."

"Well you did the right thing last night, you hid your fear, and I'm mighty proud of you, and I know you don't have a coward's bone in your body."

Then's when I wiped away the tears gushing down my cheeks, I took my handkerchief out a my back pocket and blew my nose, and when I looked at Janet, her tears were not gushing like mine, and I asked one last question, "Is it a sign of a sissy to cry?"

"No sir!"

On the 20th of November1952, my wife's water broke about ten o'clock in the morning while nobody was at home but Vesta. She threw some towels over the mess on the floor, and she took some more towels with her to sit on in the car, and she drove herself up town to the Downey Clinic.

Inside the waiting room, Sara Walker saw immediately that Vesta's skirt and shoes were wet, so she turned away and went around behind the desk into the hall where she met Vesta and quickly got her onto the table in the operating room, and Sara helped Vesta to find the metal bar at the top of the bed and Vesta asked Sara if she'd call the high school and get the message to Carroll.

Carroll got the message, folded his algebra book shut, went down the hall to his locker where he stashed his books and pulled his coat from a peg on the wall before rushing out the side door at the south end of the building. He ran the short block east on Taliaferro Street, turned onto Spring Street and took this short block south at breakneck speed, and there he was at the west end of the Downey Clinic where he let himself in through the back door, and at the front end of the wide hall, he turned left into the operating room and when Dr. Downey came into the room and lifted the sheet covering his mother, Carroll said, "I know Daddy wants to be here when the baby's born."

With that thought, Carroll took off past the front desk, through the waiting room, and out the front door on his quest to find Daddy! Carroll wadded the wet towels and threw them over the seat into the back floorboard, and when I saw the Pontiac on the logging road, well I knew why, and I caught Bud Goolsby's eye, and when he shut off his power saw, I darted toward him and yelled that he'd drive my pickup to take all the hands home, and I motioned for him to take my power saw too, and then I was off a running for the Pontiac.

Carroll drove back to Tallapoosa, and in town Carroll turned right on Alewine and two blocks north, he took a left on Mill Street and another left on Head Avenue where I jumped out before he parked, but I got to the operating room too late, for Vesta was a sleep, and Sara Walker was bathing a baby boy! Another Boy! Another Boy!!! When Carroll came in he was excited, but he waited for me to hold the new boy baby first,

They wheeled Vesta out of the operating room and into a patient's room, and she was groggy, but with our help she staggered from the gurney to the bed where she fell asleep right off. Sara Walker kept our baby boy in the operating room in a bassinet all covered and tied up in a flannel blanket, but the nurse's attention was split for she had to focus on our baby and another lady who like Vesta drove herself to the clinic, for her husband was at work at the thread mill, and this woman's baby girl was mighty quick a birthing, and I heard her say this baby was number fourteen. When school let out, Carroll was there to get Joan before she walked up to the Robert's Drug Store and Marilyn and Janet before they got on the bus, and when Carroll herded the whole family into Vesta's room, their mother was asking Sara Walker to bring her baby, "I want to see my baby!"

Just in a few minutes, Sara Walker came back into the room carrying our baby, and I took him from her and the same dogged old lump forced my eyes to water, and the kids set up a delivery line from me to Vesta, and I handed the baby to Janet then she passed the baby to Marilyn, and Marilyn passed the baby to Joan, and Joan passed the baby to Carroll and Joan turned back to Janet and picked her up so's everybody could watch as Carroll leaned over his mother's bed and settled the baby in her arms, and by that time I was on the other side of the bed sitting in a straight back chair for my legs felt a little wobbly, and when Vesta uncovered the baby and proved to herself that he had two arms and two legs and two hands and two feet, then she leaned to kiss him, and she said, "Hello, Darling, your name is Randall John Godwin, and this room is full of your family, and we love you."

Everybody thought it was best for Vesta to stay in the Downey Clinic overnight, so Carroll drove us home. After taking her books in the house, Joan drove herself back up town in the pickup truck and she got to work right on time, and at seven when the drug store closed, Joan stopped by the Downey Clinic, and Vesta was glad to see her and told what the lady who had her fourteenth baby today said hours later when Sara Walker finally asked if she wanted to see her newborn, the pore old lady said, "I just don't care a thing about it."

Joan wasn't old enough to have a driver's license, but back then when you lived in the country, well you learned to drive as soon as you could reach the petals, and nobody really cared a thing about holding you to the exact letter of the law. I got to admit I think about it all along and my explanation being the Great Depression sort of put a different light on what's acceptable and what's not, and the logical thing being if Joan's got a job, well then the money she's making is better spent if she drives herself home tonight for why work making a dollar or two if you have to spend a significant amount of your wages on burning gas.

The next Thursday was Thanksgiving, our baby was one week old and Ruth brought the whole Thanksgiving dinner and made giblet gravy and biscuits after she got to our house, and just before we sat down at our dining room table, in come Otto, and first thing before dinner Otto wanted to hold our new little Randall John, and about five o'clock, Ruth packed up her dishes, careful to collect ever single one of her purtty bowls, and on her way out the door, Vesta poked fun at her sister by trying to divert Ruth's attention while Carroll joined in the joke and eased loose the handle of the big basket from Ruth's hand, and as silent as possible, with the basket now in his hand, Carroll slipped back into the kitchen and out the back door before Ruth started her ranting about there wasn't no way her sister would get away with her dirty thieving again.

Vesta and I never had wedding rings, it always seemed like an unnecessary expense, but after the war, I became a member of the Masons, and when I bought and put the Mason's ring on my finger, Vesta and the kids and especially Carroll asked me questions about what the Mason's ring meant. I didn't say much for I committed to the Mason's code of secrecy, but I did tell my family I want to become a better man, and to my son's credit, in 1952, after Thanksgiving when Carroll's football practice was over for the year, and I wanted him to stay close to home instead of helping me at the Rifle Range, well my sixteen year old son took it upon himself to scrounge up old bicycle parts, and after school ever day, he worked in the garage straightening and sanding and painting and buying and fitting a new chain and spokes and tires on a bicycle which his purpose he kept secret and didn't boast about it, but on Wednesday, December 24, 1952, when the pile of scrap parts was finally transformed into a fine like-new bicycle, well when I came home from the Rifle Range that evening about dark, Carroll loaded the like-new bicycle in the back of my pickup truck and drove out of the yard, and to this day, we don't know who got that like-new bicycle, but it's my guess, the proud new owner never knew my Carroll's name.

My wife was always a good example and having so many children to get ready for a new school year made her sympathetic to the agony that poorer mothers faced when they could not buy clothes and shoes for their children, Every summer when all kids went barefooted most of the time, Vesta crammed a pile of our kids soles-wore-out shoes (the brown leather uppers never wore out) into a feed sack and hauled them uptown to Johnson's Shoe Shop which was in the basement under the Post Office and across the street from the Jitney Jungle. At the end of the summer, Vesta claimed empty boxes from the Jitney Jungle and with specific families in mind she made up boxes of kid's school clothes, clean, starched and ironed, and kid's shoes newly re-soled at Johnson's Shoe Shop, and with the clothes and shoe sizes carefully calculated for the specific children Vesta delivered the boxes to the recipient's front porch with no knock at the door and no embarrassment conveyed for my wife has eyes in her head to see the need, and her small helping hand was meant as just that and nothing more, and with her youngest girl and baby Randall in the car, she backed away from the donation before any 'thank you' was offered, for it was her idee that if she waited around to hear a 'thank you' well that would not be in the true spirit of giving, and not a word was said, and Janet saw no reason to ask what or who, but she did get the idee it's a good thing to offer a little help.

The first Wednesday in December, when the kids got off the school bus, Joan announced she was taking the Pontiac up toward Cedartown where everybody says she'll find a good shaped cedar Christmas tree, and it was about time we had a pretty shaped Christmas tree for most years we had ugly trees, but they looked alright when lights and icicles (two-foot long, thin strips a metallic paper) covered every limb, and this year Joan wanted to try a cedar tree. Carroll stayed home with his mother and the baby, and fifteen year old Joan drove out of the yard with a Pontiac full, Marilyn, Janet and Lynda of course, and when they got way up about Cedartown, Joan found the dirt road she was a looking for, and pretty soon there were cedar trees on both sides of the dirt road, and she pulled to the ditch and shut down the engine, and the four kids took off a wading through the tall broom-straw and the girls were wearing borrowed blue jeans. When they saw pretty shaped cedar trees in the distance, as they approached right up to the tree, it was a usual thing for the back side of the cedar tree to be blank of limbs or distorted in some other way, but finally after an hour of hiking through the tall broom-straw, they found the perfect tree, and Joan started cutting it down by leaning the tree over and stepping on the trunk, and she bent over and sawed with the handsaw which was an awkward angle, so she handed the handsaw to Marilyn and held the cedar bent over while Marilyn did the sawing, and more than one time the girls had to change jobs and pretty soon Joan was itching all over, and it was best if Marilyn held the tree down while Joan finished the sawing, but then getting back to the Pontiac, Joan and Marilyn took turns dragging the cedar tree by the freshly cut trunk which they could not avoid the cedar sap getting on their hands, and by the time they finally got to the Pontiac, well Joan was covered in welts, but Marilyn and the other kids were doing just fine, so Joan got in the back seat so's she could lie down and twelve-year-old Marilyn drove the Pontiac with Lynda and Janet up front with her, and Marilyn found the old Jacksonville dirt road and took the shortcut home missing town altogether.

When Vesta saw the hives all over Joan, she told Carroll to put three buckets of water on the stove so Joan could bathe in the bathtub. Vesta was bottle feeding the baby, which she made the decision four breast fed babies were all she needed, and as soon as the first batch of hot water was poured in the bathtub and Joan shut the bathroom door, Vesta told Carroll to fill the buckets again, and when the second three buckets of hot water were boiling, Carroll carried two and Marilyn carried one bucket to the bathroom door where Carroll yelled through the shut door for Joan to let out the cold bath water and step out of the bathtub so's Marilyn could come in and refill the bathtub with hot water, for Vesta figured Joan needed another soaking, and this time Vesta stepped into the bathroom and added a little splash of Epsom salts to the bath water as she instructed Joan to soak as long as the water was warm enough, and she quickly left and closed the bathroom door to hem up the heat.

When Joan came out of the bathroom, she still had a bad rash all over, but she seemed to be a little bit better so Vesta told her to read a story to the kids (knowing this would get her mind off the rash), and all the kids except Carroll snuggled under a quilt on the couch and Joan started reading, and it was the story about a little fellow killing seven flies with one blow which the whole story was new to Lynda and the others loved the chance to hear it again, and in the meantime, Vesta was cooking supper with the baby on a pallet of quilts spread out on the floor in front of the couch in the warm living room, and Lynda and the others watched the baby kicking and cooing while Joan read the story, and Carroll hauled the cedar tree down the road to the nearest neighbors, and Thelma Collins surely appreciated it, but Carroll warned her to hand it on down the road to the next neighbor if any in the house came down with a rash.

When Joan finished reading the others stayed put but Lynda slid down from the couch and went into the bathroom where she climbed up to reach the liquid shoe polish bottle on the bathroom shelf, and she brought the glass bottle into the living room, and at a safe distance from the baby on the quilts (for Vesta could have washed the shoe polish spatters off of the baby, but she never could have removed brown shoe polish from her cherished quilts), and while the others watched a little television 'Our Miss Brooks,' Lynda sat down on the warm linoleum floor right behind the wood burning pot belly area heater and went first polishing her shoes for of course she needed extra time in the bathtub so's to soak off the shoe polish that she somehow manages to get all over her hands and face and legs as a usual thing. The same shoe polish splatters happened first of all every single time Lynda had to wrestle and wiggle and push side to side the cork stopper which shut and sealed the glass bottle top and also held secure the polish dauber suspended in the brown liquid at the bottom end of the heavy wire connecting the cork at one end to the polish dauber at the other end which reached to the inside bottom of the glass bottle where it could soak up the last drops of brown shoe polish. Second of all, every single time Lynda jabbed the polish dauber back in the glass bottle so's to soak up more polish, well when she pulled the full polish dauber back out of the bottle without draining off a little of the excess liquid polish, well she never remembered to squeeze out the excess polish from the dauber which was a simple matter holding the dauber against the inside of the glass bottle above the liquid line. Lynda was the only one unpracticed in the skill of polishing shoes for in town at her other home, she has Viney to polish her shoes instead of getting practice polishing her own shoes which here in the country was the only place where she did her own shoe polishing, and in comparison Lynda fell behind our kids who got plenty of practice polishing their own shoes from practically as soon as they could hold the polish bottle and wiggle loose the cork, for we didn't have a colored helper like Viney, so Lynda slopped and plopped a full polish dauber as fast as she could from the mouth of the shoe polish bottle to her shoes and thereby drops of shoe polish went flying.

In order to explain the Viney situation, Chester took little Viney in when day after day in town, he noticed her sitting on the concrete sidewalks around town, and before Chester said a word to the young colored girl, he of course talked it over with Nora, and they came to the conclusion that Viney could live in the little out-building house right beside their big house. The little frame house (with it's own running water and electricity of course) was a slightly newer building than the original part of the big brick house, but the previous owner was the one responsible for building the little frame house and after moving in, Chester doubled the size of the big brick house with the addition of bedrooms plenty for his family.

Like I said, by this time I was attending regular Masons meetings, and Chester was too, only he managed to produce the necessities of becoming a Shriner. The Masons and the Shriners went to the same meetings and the wives like Nora and Lila Downey were Eastern Stars. Vesta continue with her own personal charities and left the Eastern Star meetings to the other wives, but back to Viney, Chester and Nora set her up with all she needed to get by in the little frame house, the pore thing had nothing to move, for she had nothing; no clothes, no furniture, nothing, and she was mighty grateful for the chance to sleep inside and help out with the children, and of course, she helped Nora with the house work and cooking and Viney polished all the shoes every night, and at Christmas when the Eastern Stars handed out wine soaked fruitcakes, well Viney helped Nora with all that, and she became part of the Chester Owens family, and Nora tried to get her to sit down at the table and join the family at mealtime; and for a year or so, Viney refused to even consider sitting down at the table for she acted like it would be disrespectful to the white folks, and she was more comfortable serving up her plate in the kitchen and taking it to eat out in her own little home. I guess Chester didn't really pay no never mind to the situation for a long time for he was rarely at home by suppertime, remember he was a running a new car dealership, but when he finally understood the exact scope of Viney's feeling of inferiority, well he corrected the situation right quick with a direct order to Viney which was said out loud in a quivering voice, "Viney, you are a human being with a good quick brain, you are every bit as good as me, and I won't have it no longer, from now on, you will sit at the table and eat with the rest of the family, and I won't hear to anymore of this foolishness."

Friday night, Janet talked me into cutting a Christmas tree off our own land, and we planned to get up early Saturday. It was pretty cold and a thin layer a frost outlined the bushes and grass and broom straw, and we headed out toward the barn. I got there first and let down the bottom one-by-eight, bent over at the waist, crawl-walked under, and my sweet little girl passed through and replaced the fence plank before following me through the barn center hall, down into and through the blackberry valley and up the hill into the woods along the narrow road separating my land from Cochran's land, and when I turned off from the narrow road and set out through the woods, Janet was keeping up with me and a coming too close behind me for she let her excitement keep her little legs a running along, and it took three or four steps for her to match one of mine, and she didn't tire out, but instead she kept up pretty good, and I saw she followed too close behind me for she wasn't paying attention to the release of limbs when I pushed into the woods, and the first time I let a big limb sling back into her face I planned it as a warning for it was safely above her head, and she was able to duck under the force, and I was proud of her agility, but I didn't let her off that easy for this was another perfect instance when she'd better be taking care of herself. Each time we walked down a slope naturally, we had a good view and could see across to the next uphill, and Janet caught on to look ahead and pick out a good shaped tree top easily seen from a distance, then she directed our path straight toward her targeted treetop, and now's when I let 'em sling, deliberate lower and lower limbs and the first one caught her silky soft hair and carved a straight part passing through, and she cut her eyes at me (like Kit says was our Ma's habit) but she knew better than to whine, and for that I was grateful. Slowly, she began to catch on to my method, and sure enough she made an obvious and deliberate decision to track me at a greater distance, and there was no need to mention a word about it, but my first grader became older and more self reliant that very day.

I cut down a twenty foot tall loblolly pine, and it hurt me to the core despite the sweet-acidic pine sap aroma soothing me, but the top six foot of that tall straight loblolly pine turned out to prove Janet had a pretty good eye picking out a Christmas tree, and back at the house while I set it up on cross boards in front of the double windows in the living room, Carroll pulled down the box a Christmas tree lights, and he surprised us all when he pulled out a new box of icicles. The light strings were separated, and this year the light strings were wadded into the biggest tangle we'd ever seen except of course if you took into account the giant tangled mess of light strings last year and the year before that. If the truth be known, well, ever single year the tree decorating began with this exact same tedious untangling chore caused by putting the light strings away in a hurry the previous year. While Carroll, Joan and Marilyn worked on untangling the wadded up lights, Vesta rushed off to the kitchen with the baby in her arms, grabbed the baby's bottle out a the boiler of warm water, wiped it dry and brought it back so as to feed the tiny baby a bottle of milk, and she took a little break for herself as she surveyed the room full of bliss, but too soon it was time for Joan to go to work, and suddenly the peace and quiet turned once again to the ordinary pandemonium of a house full of two parents and their five kids (six counting Lynda a course!

Joan bought her own Christmas presents on her half hour supper break, by that I mean she picked the presents she'd open on Christmas morning. When she knocked on the pool room door I gave her a few dollars to pay for a blue plaid wool, button up the front, unlined jacket which she was sure would go real good with a light blue short sleeve sweater decorated with four pearls sewed into the neck line. I handed her the cash money through the cracked door of the pool room and she went into the National Clothing Store right next to the pool room and bought the blue short sleeve sweater out of the window display, and next she rushed across Head Avenue and around the corner at Robert's Drug Store into Glad Hat's where she bought the blue plaid wool, unlined jacket, and at home she wrapped up her own two presents and put them under Janet's right pretty tree.

Friday, December 19th was the last day of school before Christmas, and it was Janet's first school Christmas party, and Vesta sent tea cakes (made by Sally's recipe) and Carroll carried Janet on his shoulders across the frosted grass, and Joan toted the two paper sacks of tea cakes one for her class party and one for Carroll's class party, and Marilyn toted the sacks of tea cakes for her class party and for Janet's class party, and no body carried any books because nobody had any homework that close to Christmas, but the whole school had a high old time with a Christmas party in every room, which included a Christmas tree in every room decorated by hand-made chains of colored paper rings glued together with flour paste, and Dolly and Janet declared their room party must have been the best in the whole school for every single first grader got a present which was a pencil and permission to take a reader home so's they could practice their reading at home through the Christmas holidays, and Vesta waited as long as she could stand it before she packed up the baby and went into town to attend Janet's party in Mrs. Fitzgerald's first grade room, and while Vesta was a swaying the baby to sleep, Mrs. Fitzgerald whispered two things she'd been wanting to tell us, and that being one of the little girls by the name a Joanne Parmley made the comment, "Janet doesn't need to come to school because she already knows everything."

And the second being a sweet comment made by little Jimmy Thrower who said, "Last week when we were playing chase on the playground, I caught Janet Godwin, and she was the first girl I ever caught, and I didn't know what to do with her."

Mrs. Fitzgerald went on to say, "Janet and Dolly play every game on the playground Red Rover, Red Rover, and Chase, and Tag, and they swing and pump themselves, they hang upside down on the Jungle Jim, and they hold on tight and love to spin as fast as the Merry Go Round can go."

Back then, the teachers bought gifts for all their students, and they made sure that every child received a gift and some of the more needy got more than a pencil when they opened their special Christmas package.

Come Christmas morning, Carroll's surprise will be two new tires for his Famous James motorcycle for he's ridden a million miles on the Famous James, and the tires are bald and unsafe, and Vesta knew just exactly what secret purchases to make at the Dime Store for each time that week when she needed to go to town and get some groceries at the Jitney Jungle or the Red Dot, or pick up some dry cleaning at the Sanitary Dry Cleaners, well she made it her business to take the time to walk through the Dime Store real slow letting Janet study every kind of toy and plaything, and it was a baby-doll-bed that Janet lighted the most and so on Saturday when Marilyn took Janet into the Grand Theater, well then Vesta with the baby in her arms, bought the Santa Claus secret toy at the Dime Store, and a real pretty sweater set for Marilyn at the National and over on the other side of the railroad tracks at Lipham's Dry Goods, Vesta bought enough little-print cotton material to make a matching gathered skirt for Marilyn which completes a new outfit. Vesta was always sewing so it made no never mind to Marilyn what her mother was sewing, and in just a little while, Vesta cut out and sewed up a full skirt, gathered onto a waistband, with a placard closing in the full gathers and a button and a hand made buttonhole sewed into the waistband.

On Christmas morning, it was a squawking happy crowd as Janet marveled at how Santa Claus must have slithered through the pot belly stove pipe without getting a smidgen of black soot on his red suit and white beard, and he placed a baby-doll-bed and Marilyn unwrapped her surprise outfit and Joan unwrapped her sweater and jacket, and Carroll didn't do any unwrapping but he was truly surprised to find two new motorcycle tires under the tree, and right in the middle of the havoc in came Sis and Huitte and their sweet little Gayle, and Huitte was carrying Gayle's Santa Claus surprise which was a baby doll bed just exactly like Janet's Santa Claus surprise, and it was as good as it gets to see the looks on their little sweet faces when Huitte toted both baby-doll-beds up the stairs, and Janet and Gayle followed along behind toting their baby dolls. Huitte stayed up stairs a long while. "It took a long time up there, but finally we got the two baby dolls to sleep while Janet and Gayle tidied up their brand new baby doll beds.

Huitte could not have been a better daddy to his own little Gayle, and sometimes every one of us takes a deep breath for the problem Sis and Huitte have which makes it impossible to have more babies, but then it's not a far reach to soberly realize the endless mourning that Ruth and Otto are going through.

That was the best Christmas we ever had, but I've been known to say that many times before, and I'll no doubt say it many more times in years to come, for we have a big family, and we have a good modern house, and all our kids go to work when they're old enough and that seems to be age fourteen, and nobody ever feels sorry for us, no sir re, we are envied and we know it, and this year we have a little one that believes in Santa Claus, and we have a new baby Randall, and there's no getting around it, I have to enjoy and boast about what a blessing we have right here in this crowded room.

On out a week or two into January, one Sunday after Vesta and the kids pulled away from the house, out of the clear blue when I was about ready to leave the house to work by myself at the Rifle Range, a tall colored man walked up and knocked on the front door. When I opened the door, I was mighty surprised and pleased to see Posey Greer, and when I opened the screen door and reached to shake his hand he said, "Mr. Godwin, I ain't had a payday since you left south Georgia, would you have any work for me, Sir?"

I asked him to come in and sit down, but he wasn't having none of that, and I thought to myself, 'Here's a fine man who happens to be colored, and he's beat down to the ground with no hope and no nothing' I stepped out on the front porch and sat down in a cane bottom rocker, and I motioned for him to sit down in the other cane bottom rocker, but he sat down on the porch steps instead which put him in an inferior position looking up at my face, but the years of beating him down has backed him into a corner, and he never looked at my face atall, he talked to my shoe laces. He started out like he'd rehearsed the lines a million times, "Mr. Godwin, I want to work, but I'm not making no slur against any white man, no sir, I'm not figuring to take a white man's job, I don't think for a minute that I deserve a job from you, and I didn't come all the way up here expecting a thing, that'd be wrong of me and that'd be me telling you what to do, and I ain't that kind, no sir, I'm not, but if you can find it possible to give me a chance at work, well, I'd work hard for you, sir, yes sir, I would!"

This speech of Posey's was meant to offer not a word of accusation, not a word of self defense, and most of all not a word of implied equality, and it's obvious to me the pore old feller spent hours planning out just what to say, and it touched my heart and strung a chord of justice deep down inside of me that this man has not been allowed a good education, not been allowed to learn a trade, and well bad things can come of a situation that pushes a feller to desperation, and I study about questions like this, and I guess I've been planning my own speech, which right now is time to deliver face to face to Posey Greer, except from Posey's side it's more like 'from face to shoelaces,' and well my course is clear ahead a me, I've got to be the one to make a difference in this colored man's life. I like him, he's smart, he's a good worker, and right then when I stood up and put my hands on my hips, well it scared the pore feller, and he just about slithered away like a ground bound snake, but quick as I could I said, "Can you start today?"

Straight to my shoelaces, he answered, "Yes sir!"

I be dogged if either one of us could say another word, my speech was left unsaid for the knot in my throat, so I pointed his way to my pickup truck, and turned my back on him as I drew open the front door so's he'd never see.

That Sunday me and Posey worked in silent harmony, and about noon, I pulled a sugar sack from the cab of my pickup truck, we sat down on a log and I rolled down the white cotton sugar sack exposing about six of Vesta's left over breakfast biscuits, I nodded to Posey to help himself, and he ate four biscuits and just about swallowed them whole. At the end of the work day that first Sunday evening when I loaded up to leave the Rifle Range, I told Posey I'd give him a ride anywhere he wanted to go, and I explained to him that I always drive around to their houses and pick up my saw mill hands in the morning, and then I take them back home at the end of the work day, but Posey said to me, "I ain't got no place to stay, Mr. Godwin, and if it's alright by you, I'll sleep here at the Rifle Range on the ground under one a the log trucks or if it starts raining or gets too cold, I'll crawl in the cab of one of your log trucks, that is if that's alright by you, Mr. Godwin, sir."

I drove off and left Posey Greer to sleep in the woods, with not a bite to eat, and I worried about the feller, and at home that night with my mind made up, I had Carroll help me move some things around upstairs for everybody in my family was agreeable to giving a helping hand and letting Posey Greer live upstairs in our house while he's working for me at the Rifle Range, and all the current toys like Janet's baby doll bed, well me and Carroll moved Janet's toys out of the upstairs and into the dining room.

That first day of working with Posey Greer was a pitiful thing, for the colored man never once looked me in the eye, and if I talked to him, he looked down at his feet and sort of trembled in his loose shoes which were way too big, and he had great big shoes laced up tight so's the worn leather flaps at the laces actually overlapped, but that pair of way-too-big shoes was no doubt the only shoes he had to his name, and I felt so low down rich and sorry that I wanted to set right down on the ground and take off my own shoes and give em up to Posey Greer, but in truth, I acknowledged, if I did such a thing, well Posey Greer would likely die of humiliation for in his mind he is a beat down miserable unworthy colored man, and in my mind, somebody on this God's green earth has to do something to help him and let him know he is valuable in some way or a tother.

I'm not a man looking for a fight, and I'm not a man looking for recognition, but the next morning, Monday, the second day of Posey Greer working at my saw-mill, I carried breakfast to him, four of Vesta's hot buttered biscuits 'cept they were just a little bit warm by the time he ate them down in one gulp, and at noon, there wasn't no way me and my saw mill hands would let him keep on working while we ate our dinner, and when we finally set him down right in our circle, I handed him a stack of crackers and a can of potted meat which I opened with my pocket knife, and he was fidgeting, uncomfortable, and didn't open his mouth to say a word, but dod damn, he set there like he was somebody, and as usual just before the sun went down my saw mill hands shut down their power saws, and I motioned for Posey to do the same, and with Bud Goolsby, and C.W. Goolsby, and Dink Daniel and Boomy Daniel, a standing right there, I said, "Well, Posey, you're gona ride home with me tonight and there'll be no ifs, ands, or buts about it for I've already made up a bed for you in the upstairs at my house, and every work day morning, you will get in my pickup truck and ride to work with me."

I actually thought pore old Posey might jump out of his skin or fall down dead, he was so mortified; and with his head in his two hands, he looked at my shoe laces and said, "Mr. Godwin, I can't let you do such a thang, why the clan 'ill be burning crosses in your yard, your little children won't be safe, and I for sure will be strung up to the nearest oak tree!"

"Now look a here, Posey, I know the sorry cowards wearing them white ghost getups, and believe you me, I know how to handle bullies, I been taught well, and I'm sure every Klan member there is around these parts is a hell of a lot more afraid a me than I am of them. Why they know I'll shoot their asses if they come in my yard, and they know I don't answer to nobody, and don't make no never mind about worrying about my kids, for there's not a bully alive who wears a ghost getup or not that would live a minute after doing harm to one a my kids, and all a the high and mighty Klan know what for."

So, with a hand up from Boomy, and a pat on the back from Dink and Bud and C.W., Posey climbed into the pickup truck bed, and he rode along quiet and humble, not looking up at nothing, just as usual looking down at his great big old wore out shoes.

I figured I'd bring Posey along a little at a time, and when we pulled into the yard, I said, "Posey, I'll show you to your bed upstairs, come with me."

Which he did go inside the house and up the stairs, but when I pivoted away from him and headed back downstairs, well he followed me back downstairs and darted outside and into the woods, and there is where he stayed through the night, and when Vesta put some supper on a plate for

Posey, I took it outside to the front porch, and called out, "Posey, come and get your supper before the dogs eat ever bite of it."

I saw a little movement at the edge of the yard out by the old plum tree, but I didn't dare wait to come face to shoelaces with the pore old scared to death feller, instead I put Posey's supper plate down on one of the cane bottom rockers.

The next morning Posey was in the front yard a sitting in the pickup truck bed, and I toted a cup a hot coffee and three biscuits out to him, and the pitiful feller drank his coffee and ate his biscuits, and quick as he could, he knocked on the front door and handed the cup to Vesta when she opened the door, "Thank ye ma'am!" he said without looking.

Vesta shut the door and wiped away her tears, and my little Janet holding onto her mother's skirt, asked, "What's wrong, mother?"

"I'm sad, sugar, because some white people are mean to Negros, and they ought to be ashamed."

Our angelic first grader replied, "Well, the Negros will just have to stare down the mean white folks. They'll have to raise up their chin and say, 'I know you're the bully, but I've come now."

"I hope that happens someday, honey!" Vesta said as she lifted little Janet into her arms.

Posey was a natural with a power saw, he didn't need telling twice on anything and every move he made was careful and deliberate and correct, and he slept in our house upstairs for more than a year, but he never ate a single meal at the table with us, even though Vesta never failed to fill up a plate and set it on the table in front of an empty chair, instead a sitting at the table, Posey sorta slipped into the room a ducking and weaving and picked up his full plate and darted out of the house or upstairs to eat it, but as soon as he was pretty sure we were finished eating, he returned the plate to the kitchen, "Thank ye, Ma'am!"

Every Sunday Posey took the sheets off his bed and walked down the road carrying a load a dirty clothes, and for months we didn't know exactly where he went, we had a pretty good idee, and we know he found some place to bath and wash the sheets (Vesta still made our sheets out a sugar sacks and flour sacks and feed sacks) and when he came back in the house toward the end of the day, he was dressed up and he brought with him his clean, folded clothes and the clean, folded sheets and pillow case, and it was after his first payday; one day a week, he wore good Sunday go to meeting clothes and new shoes (that fit) for he made good money working for me, and Lipham's Store uptown has a back entrance for the colored, and he was more proud of his new shoes than anything else, but he kept on a wearing the old shoes to work.

Every noonday at the Rifle Range, we shut down power saws and came together to eat our dinner in the peace and quiet, all the men joined in talking except for Posey, and the usual main topic of conversation is New Mexico even if the working trip is still more a year or two away, and it is an exciting thing to discuss the ins and outs. Most of the men seem anxious and happy to plan, but some have already declared they can't go, and Posey never opens his mouth one way or tother.

In January, Janet and Marilyn both brought mimeographed notes home from school regarding tap dancing lessons which Mrs. Barbee from Carrollton plans to offer to students in grades one through seven or in other words the lessons are available to the kids in grammar school, and the lessons will be held in the Tallapoosa High School auditorium and that is lucky for Marilyn because she is in seventh grade which is the last year of grammar school, and the mimeographed note tells of a tap dance show to be held the last week of school. So it worked out that Marilyn and Janet stayed at school for tap dance lessons and missed the school bus, but that was nothing to worry about for Vesta most days could not contain her enthusiasm for she loves to dance as much as any person alive, and she closed up the store early and packed up the baby Randall and went on to town so's she could watch Mrs. Barbee teaching the tap dancing steps, and pretty soon Vesta knew the steps as good as Marilyn and Janet, and Mrs. Barbee handed out sketched costume pictures so's the work could begin buying material and cutting out and sewing the costumes, and Vesta got right on it for she had four costumes to make, two for Marilyn and two for Janet.

To dance to the music of Tuxedo Junction, Marilyn's costume is all black and white, real formal looking with a short little black skirt exposing her legs and a short to-the-waist black jacket, and around the bottom of the short little black flouncy skirt is an edge of black and white striped shiny satin, and the lapels of the to-the-waist-jacket are made of the same black and white striped satin material, and the to-the-waist-jacket is designed sort of on the order of a man's tuxedo jacket, and to top it off, the same striped satin winds around above the brim of a top hat with a bow at the back made out of the same black netting as the short-skirt petticoat. In contrast to this black and white costume, Marilyn's other costume is very colorful with a below-the-knee heavy skirt made out of multicolored, wide striped, rough not sparkly material. Marilyn will dance with Judy, Lynn, and Pricilla.

Janet will dance in a chorus line to the music, "Diamonds Are a Girl's Best Friend" and this is a group of first grade girls, Connie, Jane, Laura Hill and Kristina, and besides the chorus line, Janet will dance another number in a cowgirl costume with Bill Carter and Larry Thompson (two fourth grade boys who'll wear cowboy costumes), and the three will dance to the song "Don't Fence Me In"

Little Lynda will dance with Joe Barnes, Ronnie Strasberg, Beth Pluff, and Sandra Saturday and they'll all wear red shiny satin made to sparkle with sequins and rhinestones around the girls' necklines and covering the boys' lapels, and the girls will have more sequins and rhinestones on little "Roaring Twenties" pulled-tight-hats, and for a few minutes Joe Barnes and Lynda will switch from the tap dancing and buggie doing the 'Charleston,' which was the favorite dance of the "Roaring Twenties."

On the night of the tap dance show, me and Vesta got to the Tallapoosa High School auditorium early delivering our two dancers, and right behind us in came Chester and Nora following behind the star of the show, and Lynda's fan club (every single person in the auditorium), whooped and hollered making Lynda and the rest of us just about cry. Me and Vesta planned we'd take turns with our youngest, and we got seats close to the front just four rows back and Chester and Nora slid into the center of our row, and me and Vesta and our little boy sat on the end of the row so's we could take Randall out of the crowded auditorium if need be for he didn't much like all the "sissy stuff" but as it turned out, he wanted to watch one sister dance when she danced looking like a cowboy. It was easy to pick out our girls on the stage, and I know we're partial, but anybody with eyes could of course see Marilyn, Lynda, and Janet belonged in the spotlight (if there'd a been a spotlight). I'm not ashamed to say, I had to wipe away a tear or two, which was a nuisance and did nothing but blur my vision

On the drive home in our packed full car, my vision blurred again, already dreading the time when I'll be working far away from my family, and I go through this on a regular basis and in my mind, I call it the cycle of ambition, I am eager to make good money and I am so sad to leave, but that night, Marilyn pulled me back from the sad end of the ambition cycle when she told us what Lynda said backstage about her grandmother Kilgore (my sister Nancy), "Mama Kilgore thinks this whole tap dancing show is a floozy, doozy disgrace."

After school let out for the summer, first thing Beulah and Dolly came a calling, and the two little girls would have it no other way than for Janet to go home with Dolly and spend the night. By this time, Beulah and Morris had moved out of the little house uptown in 'old town' on Broad Street, and they now live in a big old house with a wrap around porch, tall ceilings and several outbuildings besides the big barn, and this house is over in Alabama, close to Bethel Church, and Beulah and Morris plan to move Dolly to the Fruithurst grammar school come fall but so far, Dolly and Janet go right on thinking they'll be together again in 2ⁿᵈ grade at Tallapoosa.

That night, Beulah cooked a good supper and Janet and Dolly ate every bite and then dashed back outside to play as long as the sun was up, and they ran circles around the house playing horse racing which their 'horses' was a broom and a mop held up end down, trailing the stick-handle end in the red dust, and making the broom-straw of one and the mop strings of the other into the horse's mane, and these races around and around the house continued on til about 9:30 when Beulah had to enter the race and physically grab hold of the runaway horses which the sweet girls loved that idee, and inside the house, when the girls bathed off a little and got their pajamas on well Beulah read a story (or actually Beulah quoted it from memory) a swinging the girls in the wide front porch swing, and the little sleepy heads leaned into Beulah sliding down til their heads rested in Beulah's lap, and both nodded off into a deep and worn out semi-consciousness, and Morris toted Dolly and Beulah toted

Janet inside to bed, and Janet opened her eyes in time to admire the tall, white French Princess Headboard matching exactly to Dolly's headboard, and Janet snuggled into white whole sheets with not a single seam atall. The next day, Beulah hauled Janet back home and finally Dolly agreed to climb in the car and start back across the state line under the condition that her mother would stop in at the Junction (run by Beulah's sister Ruth and Olin Cunningham) and part of this sweet deal was that Dolly could of course have a Nutty Butty ice cream.

Most times at the store Janet stays inside with her mother and the baby Randall. Vesta likes for Janet to stay inside so it is a smart thing for her to bring the big tricycle from the house, and the big tricycle keeps Janet occupied for hours on end for tricycle riding on the smooth concrete floor is exciting and addictive and speedy. Living around the Dead Man's Curve settlement there's a whole lot of kids to play with, and Larry Goolsby and Ivy Newman are both close to Janet's age, and Wilma, Carroll, Francis, and Ivy Newman are the kids of Ross and Lou Newman who live directly on the other side of Highway 78, and Francis and Janet like to play under the tall loblolly pine trees, sweeping the pine needles into pretend playhouse walls, and before you know it, they have a playhouse that only grows bigger and more elaborate as their minds form princess castles on the one extreme and one-room log cabins on the other extreme.

When school is out Ivy and Larry can find a multitude of pursuits to while away the summer days. Lou, Lavada, Barbara, Virgie, and Locket all work together raising the settlement kids who have open access to pastureland, the creek and the creek's culvert running under the highway. The kids cross under the highway through the culvert if no grownup is handy for it is a rule, the little kids can not cross the busy highway unless a grownup is right there to help, and our oldest kids qualify as grownups as do the oldest Newman kids and the oldest of the Goolsby, Daniel, Key and Pope families help the little ones cross the busy highway many times a day, and the older kids organize baseball games in the pasture, using rocks for bases and sturdy tree limbs whittled into bats, and for a baseball they wad up a plug of red clay mud inside an old sock or two, and it works pretty good tied in a tight knot.

There's a city boy named Jimmy George whose uncle Ralph McBurnett is planning to rent the store building when I take my sawmill and sawmill hands out to New Mexico. Renting out the store building will give Vesta a little income and free her up to do double time parenting our kids. Anyway one day when Jimmy George spent the day playing with the Settlement kids, he spent the whole day saying how much he loves the game of football, and in the baseball game, he ran like a banshee around the bases explaining he needs lots a practice running if he wants to be a good football player, which he understands the requirement being an ability to run like the wind, and over and over he kept saying I want to 'run' fast, I have to 'run' real fast, and every time he said anything atall, he added his desire to 'run' fast emphasizing the word 'run' and well by the end of the baseball game, Wilma made the decision he must be talking about taking a dose of Epsom Salts because in Wilma's mind Epsom Salts provides a good means by which to 'run' fast, and Wilma reasoned the Epsom Salts 'runs' could be very helpful to a speedy football player, and in her mind it seemed a logical thing to help Jimmy George with the 'runs.'

Ever time the kids play baseball it's the reward for being the winning team to go first jumping in the creek, and after the baseball game losers also have a turn in the cool creek water, well all the kids head back to the Ross Newman house, and today once they were all sitting on the shady back porch, Wilma went inside and found the Epsom Salts and mixed up a dose in a glass and brought it out to Jimmy George, and it served as another prize for that day Jimmy George was the top scoring baseball player, and when Jimmy George swallowed down the dose of Epsom Salts, well he shook his head to be rid of the terrible taste, but in the same instant he asked for another dose for if one dose helps any slow runner, then in his case two doses are bound to increase his already impressive speed.

Now some time passed before the city boy came back to play again, and when he did finally came back, well he was a little sheepish telling (mainly Wilma) the experience he had with the 'runs,' which he decidedly argued had nothing to do with being a good football player for such a predicament would have kept the great Johnny Unitas off the football field indefinately.

The kids go barefooted all summer, and there are hard packed red clay trails through the woods and through the pastures, and when the kids cross under the highway through the dark, cool, culvert (tall and wide enough for a train to pass through), but the inch deep, constantly flowing creek water forms patches of moss on the concrete culvert floor which the moss can be easily picked out (even in the darkest center of the culvert which in the center looking either direction there's plenty brilliant daylight at the end) and the moss clumps are real pretty and a bright green color and the culvert is tall enough for any grown man to pass through without his head reaching a single high strung ceiling spider web, and the kids and grown ups alike use the moss patches as stepping stones, for the moss is not as slippery as the slime.

Vesta and all the mothers never fail to warn, 'Watch for snakes!' The girls especially watch with every step, but the boys slough it off knowing and actually hoping they'll see a snake inside the culvert in the very shallow water, and on each end where the path winds down the hill to the culvert floor, the path passes through tall weeds that's true, but the path itself is wide enough to expose any part of a snake slithering along the open trail. All this being said, the girls use the under passage culvert only when there's no other choice, and many times, if Janet wants to cross from the Newman side of 78, to the country store side, well it's a simple thing easier than going through the culvert, she goes inside the Newman house and asks Lou to help her cross the highway, and it never fails when Janet goes inside the house, Lou Newman immediately starts filling up a plate with pinto beans from the pot always found on Lou's wood burning cook stove, now here is where I need to emphasize, this happens ever single time Janet goes inside the house, and here's the reason why, everybody, everywhere, makes note of Janet's small size, and Lou Newman calls our little Janet by the name of Banty Hen (taken from the small breed a chickens), and these good neighbors are not rich folks by any means, but they operate by the code of honor of feeding the hungry and it's Janet's size that indicates to the kind hearted Lou Newman that she's got to be hungry.

On Saturday morning in the fall of the year (September 26, 1953) our party line telephone became a reality which everybody on the dirt road was on the same party line together, and it's no problem sharing one party line, and it is easy to call each other on the party line by dialing in the number and then pushing down on the hang-up button which causes our telephone to ring and their telephone to ring, and if they pick up, the ringing stops, and that's when you let up on the hang-up button and say 'Hello' and they say 'Hello.'

The new telephone is a convenience that makes us wonder how in the world we got by without it, but finally in 1953, we have a modern black table type telephone with a dial for dialing in the number, and if you pick up the handle and hear somebody on the party line a talking, you put down the handle and wait a spell before picking up the handle again.

I guess the party line telephone benefits Lynda more than anybody for now she feels free to climb on the school bus just about every day knowing she can call her Daddy from our house, for Chester is more likely than Nora, but Nora is coming in a close second to getting fire eating mad at Lynda for staying out at our house all the time, and the bus driver, Mr. Clackum is real good about making it his business to wait until all his kids are for sure on his bus before he pulls away from the school, and there are many times when Lynda is the last one to come out of the school building, and thankfully Mr. Clackum hasn't yet pulled away a single time and left Lynda behind, and in fact it's got to the point, that Mr. Clackum and Lynda have worked out a signal, so's if Lynda isn't getting on his bus, well to save her from rushing all the way down the stairs from the 5th grade classroom, instead while she's still upstairs, she crosses the hall from Mrs. Rambo's room on the back side of the building to Mrs. Eaves' room on the front side of the building, and Lynda leisurely goes over to the front windows facing out toward the street area, and if she holds up a piece of paper to the window, that means Mr. Clackum has to wait for her, and she gets down stairs and outside to the bus as quick as she can. Both the fifth grade teachers, Mrs. Rambo and her sister Mrs. Eaves, understand this situation, and sometimes if Lynda is running behind all the other students, well the sweet fifth grade teachers know the routine, and sometimes Mrs. Rambo will take it on herself to cross the hall to her sister's room and go to the windows herself and hold up a piece a paper signaling Mr. Clackum to wait for Lynda, and likewise a few times, if Mrs. Rambo is otherwise occupied, Mrs. Eaves has crossed the hall, found Lynda and asked if she's going home with the Godwin kids, and that's all Lynda has to do for then Mrs. Eaves is the one to hold up the signal for Mr. Clackum to wait, and there are actually some days when Lynda does not ride the school bus to our house, and when that happens, well pore old Mr. Clackum waits and waits as long as he can, but finally he pulls off with a sigh of regret at missing the sunshine that Little Lynda brings to his work day a driving the school bus.

We all planned just how we'd wire money home to our wives from New Mexico, and now that the telephone lines are finally out into the country east a Tallapoosa, all my saw mill hands set in to have a telephone installed which will bring peace of mind to a man working almost two thousand miles away from his wife and kids, but in the case of Bud Goolsby since he isn't married, Bud paid the price for a telephone installed in his Daddy, Preacher Goolsby's house. Most of my sawmill hands live around the general vicinity of the store and gristmill at Dead Man's Curve. Until I leave for New Mexico, Vesta is running the store full time, except for trips into town to deliver or pick up the kids, and she orders weekly bulk grocery deliveries from Williams Brothers Wholesale Groceries which operates right uptown in Tallapoosa. Vesta has decided to set up some beds in the back room of the store for she reasons that once I leave the state and before Ralph McBurnett rents the store building in 1956, well there'll be times when she and the kids might overnight at the store, not every night but a night or two a week maybe, especially in the winter for it will be a difficult thing to keep the store open and cook supper and keep the house warm at home, and with longer store hours, Vesta can make more sales to the neighbors if the store is actually open when they get home from work. While I'm way out in New Mexico, Vesta will have the income from the store (sales at first and then rent later on) and the money that I wire home.

The New Mexico plans, so far, have connected me to a man named Mr. Blivens in Grants, New Mexico, and he has already called me on my own house telephone for Mr. James McDonald gave him my telephone number since he has been in touch with Mr. Blivens a long time now getting all the paper work filled in so's I can buy timber cutting rights on National Forests, and Mr. Blivens will be my contact person when me and my saw mill hands drive across the country hauling my sawmill and timber cutting equipment, and we'll drive straight to Grants, New Mexico, and from Grants Mr. Blivens will lead us into the National Forest west of a small town called Magdalena, and he'll show us on a map and in real life exactly where to set up the sawmill, and he'll point out on the map and in real life, the exact timber stand to cut. On my home telephone when Mr. Blivens called, he explained he's working on building a log cabin mess hall/bunk house, and he'll deliver a big old wood burning cook stove and he'll set up a rain and snow catching water tower that'll feed water into a galvanized water tub inside the log cabin, and he suggests I bring a cook who'll be in charge of all the cooking, and by the time we get there, the man who works for him buying and delivering coffee, flour, buttermilk, eggs, bacon, ham and fresh vegetables (when available) to other saw milling operations in the National Forest and he'll deliver the same supplies to my saw milling operation on a once a week routine.

The New Mexico plans and paper work and telephone calling is falling into place but until the day we leave, well til that day comes I have a job for Posey Greer as we finish cutting the vast stand of trees at the Rifle Range.

Sis miscarried for the sixth time, and it brought on a deep depression, and Huitte wanted Sis to quit working and let Louise Hammock (the colored baby sitter) go and just stay home for a while with Gayle, who was eight years old, and so that's what Sis did and just about every day, Sis came to the house and if nobody was there then she went on down to the store. In the fall of the year, after the Godwin reunion, Carroll was at football practice every day after school getting ready for his senior year, his last year playing the game he loves to play just about as much as I love to watch.

One Friday, Sis and Gayle wanted Janet to come home with them, it was the usual thing on Fridays for Janet to spend the night with Ruth and Otto, but not this Friday, so it worked out for Janet to spend the night with Gayle. It was still early in the day, and Sis took Gayle and Janet on home, and the girls played down in the cool cellar to get out of the hot kitchen where Sis was putting up tomatoes which Huitte especially likes though the winter months mixed in vegetable soup together with put-up okra and corn and green beans, and Sis especially liked her home canned tomatoes through the winter months added to home made chili seasoned hot with chili powders and a chili brick bought at the Jitney Jungle.

Sis and Huitte own forty acres on Steadman Road, and down off the road way back at the back west end, the forty acres borders on the Tallapoosa River, and it is a wide stretch of the Tallapoosa River, and when they first bought the land, well they thought about building a house on a hill overlooking the Tallapoosa River, but finally they made the decision it would be might near impossible driving a car up all the way from the river to Steadman Road if the hills were wet and muddy, so Sis and Huitte built a nice two bedroom house with a modern kitchen and bathroom and Sis and Huitte's bedroom is on the north west corner of the house, and Gayle's bedroom is on the north east corner of the house, and after eating a good supper, Janet and Gayle took a bath, and then Sis took a bath, and then Huitte took a bath and after the sun went down about nine o'clock, Huitte turned off all the electric lights in the house, and Janet and Gayle crawled into Gayle's big bed and the girls talked and giggled for a while before Sis called out, "It's time to be quite, girls."

But Sis and Huitte heard one more sentence from their sweet little Gayle when she spoke to her (younger by one year) first cousin and said, "Now Honey, don't be afraid of the clicking and popping you'll hear coming from the kitchen, it's just the fruit jar lids sealing tight as mother's canned tomatoes cool down."

On the first Sunday in October, 1953, the Godwin family got together for our first family reunion at Bethel Church, and the permanent outside long table built on stilt high legs and anchored to three tree trunks was plum full of food from one end to the other, good homemade cooking, fried chicken, home cured ham, fried vegetables straight from the garden, biscuits and cornbread, and cakes and pies enough for an army, and not all fourteen kids of Hugh and Mattie Godwin were alive to attend, but the second born Mary Lizzie was there, and she was born way back on December 28, 1887, and at age sixty-six, Mary Lizzie Hart was the oldest Godwin at the very first Godwin Reunion. I was forty-two.

We took all five of our kids, from seventeen year old Carroll right down to the ten month old baby Randall. Carroll was a high school senior in the middle of playing his last football season which me and Morris or Thomas or Mose or some of us went to just about every Tallapoosa football game, and the most fun for us men was walking the sidelines up and down from one goal post to the other watching every play from as close as we could get, and we didn't let on to a single person, but instead we passed ourselves off as 'boosters' only we never had time to actually attend Boosters Club Meetings, and we couldn't imagine the meetings would be any fun atall, but we sure had plenty of fun at the football games placing bets on each and every play, and sometimes, by the end of game, I walked away with most of the money from the billfolds of a whole great big crowd of men just like me who came to the games to be on hand if our son's got hurt, but once there, well what could the harm be in placing a few bets.

At that very first Godwin Reunion at Bethel Church, Doc's girl Pauline Godwin Laminack was big as a barn pregnant, but she came on to the reunion anyway, and Huitte Davis was standing right beside her when her water broke right there, that day, standing outside the church, and Huitte Davis made no never mind about telling nobody nothing, instead he calmly walked Pauline a few steps to his truck holding his left arm around her shoulders, and his right hand holding her right hand, and when he got Pauline sitting down inside his truck, he shut Pauline's door and waved to his wife (Sis) and their little eight year old Gayle who happened to be at that minute tending to Pauline's little boy Tony, and Huitte scattered a few rocks as he slammed into first gear and took off to the Downey Clinic.

It was a surprise to all for Pauline was just seven months pregnant not due until the first week of December, but there was no denying the water and the labor pains, and Huitte told me later he talked a mile a minute all the way to the Downey Clinic for he was as nervous as a cat in a room full of rocking chairs, and sure enough a little boy baby was born that very day, Sunday, October 4, 1953, and on the ride to the Downey Clinic, Pauline listened to the nervous Huitte Davis talking a mile a minute, and somehow the half question slipped out a Huitte's mouth a wondering why in the world Pauline would come on to the reunion feeling as bad as she did and Pauline's exasperated exhale and frustrated eye roll was followed by, "Well I'd already bought a new dress for this historic beginning of the Godwin reunion! What in the world was I to do, I had to wear my new dress didn't I?"

Now Pauline's story that started that Sunday because she had to wear a new dress continues in an unbelievable turn of events. Dr. Downey delivered a small seven-month baby boy, Pauline and her husband named the baby Barry, Pauline stayed overnight at the Downey Clinic, and Howard took her home on Monday the fifth of October. Pauline felt real tired all day at home on Monday, and through the night that night, she didn't sleep much atall, and little Tony was real sweet holding the tiny new baby Barry and singing "Bye O Baby" to his new little baby brother wrapped up in a flannel blanket and actually the little baby was the perfect size to fit in little Tony's arms.

The next morning was Tuesday October 6th, and Howard had to stay home from work for Pauline was in distress experiencing what felt exactly like labor pains, and by mid morning, her water broke again, Howard loaded Tony into the car, and quickly followed with the loading of Pauline who laid down in the back seat and Howard spread a sheet over her for she could not straighten out her legs and besides that she couldn't bring her knees together thus exposing her bloody private parts which if little Tony saw all of that, well he'd get every thing all mixed up in his mind about what in the world was going on. Finally, Howard was about to crank up the car when from the back seat, Pauline gently reminded him he forgot the baby Barry, and then Howard dashed back in the house, came back out again and laid the tiny baby right beside his right leg on the front seat, and one handed he drove faster than he'd ever driven right back to the Clinic. He kept his mind on one thing, and that was keeping the baby pulled tight to his leg while Tony was standing up in the front seat, and what felt like a century later, he pulled the car up to the Downey clinic, and to his credit, Howard did in fact remember to snatch up the tiny flannel blanket bundle, and into his other arm Howard scooped up little Tony, and he assured his sweet wife he'd be right back, and Pauline screamed out at him right irritable which was unlike Pauline, "You'd better get the Doctor out here RIGHT NOW!"

Believe it or not, the door to the clinic opened with a crash of the screen door against the outside bricks, and out of the front door come running two people dressed in white, and it was the nurse Sara Walker and Doctor Downey who'd heard Pauline's screams and boy howdy did they come a running! And just as Sara Walker got close to the car, well Pauline still lying in the back seat, reached her hands up over the top of her head and felt around for the door handle and pulled it up and just about ripped the car door handle out of the upholstery and chattering all the while like the world was a coming to an end and she said something like, "Somebody better get ready to catch a baby, and I mean it!"

Well Sara Walker was first to decipher the situation, and without a second's hesitation, she pivoted and turned a perfect one hundred and eighty degrees, and in a flash of white, she practically walked through the screen door on her way back inside the Clinic, and in a split second, she was back out of the Clinic carrying a stretcher which was nothing but two poles running along both sides of a strip of leather, and Dr. Downey already had Pauline half way out of the back seat and her arms grabbed around his neck, and she turned her head toward Howard and snapped through grinding teeth, "Howard, take Tony and the baby for a walk up town!"

As quick as a wink, Pauline was on the stretcher legs wide open, and Sara Walker with her arms behind her, toted the stretcher at Pauline's business end, and Dr. Downey toted the stretcher at Pauline's head, and it appeared that Pauline was a giving him a lecture through her still clinched teeth. Well the second baby was born just about as soon as Sara Walker and Dr. Downey put the stretcher on top of the bed in the delivery room right under the big brilliant light. Thankfully, Howard stayed away with the baby Barry and little Tony while Sara Walker cleaned up Pauline, and when Howard came back in and rounded the nurse's desk, it sounded like he was muttering to himself, and it sounded something like, "I'd like to know what Pauline has thought up now."

Now no one wanted to hold it against the father of twins, so not a word was said, and Pauline sweet as can be, held out her hand and asked Howard to put the baby boy in her arms, and "Please honey, get little Tony up here with me on this big old high bed."

Then Howard's surprise of a lifetime occurred when the nurse, Sara Walker, gently placed another bundled-up baby in Pauline's other arm, and she said, "Mr. Laminack, you and your wife have to name another baby, and this one is a girl."

Howard turned as gray as ashes, and about as light headed as if his brains were actually transformed into ashes, and there was no question or comment or happy congratulations or smug fatherly pride, no sir re, there was nothing from Howard, but sweet Pauline asked little Tony to kiss the two babies, and she explained away to her little boy that now he had a brother AND a sister ...... twins! Still nothing from Howard, so next

Pauline said, "Tony, honey, we named your new little baby brother 'Barry,' do you think it'd be ok if we name your new little baby sister, 'Bonita'?

One day in late October, 1953, when Marilyn was thirteen years and seven months old and in the eighth grade, Marilyn didn't take the school bus home, but she did make sure Lynda was on the school bus to take care of little Janet (which Mr. Clackum already had the signal to wait for Lynda anyway) and Marilyn didn't go home to start her ironing job, no sir, she walked up town from the high school building, and she walked up town alone for as a cheerleader, Joan was getting things worked out for decorating the goal posts making sure there was enough red and white crepe paper for the home team goal post and enough blue and white crepe paper to decorate the visiting team's goal post for this Friday is Tallapoosa High School's Homecoming game, and when she got up town, Marilyn went into the Red Dot grocery store and asked for a job, and the owner (which I won't say his name for maybe he could get in trouble for hiring a thirteen year old, anyway the owner of the Red Dot Grocery store asked one question and that being, "You're Shug's girl, aren't you?"

When Marilyn said, "Yes sir, I am."

The owner showed Marilyn where to put her books in the back room, and he showed her the telephone in the back room and he said, "Call your mother and tell her you get off work at seven o'clock."

Next, the owner showed Marilyn how to operate the check-out cash register which there were two cash registers up by the front door, and just in a few minutes Marilyn could read the price, punch in the numbers, and pull the side lever on the check-out cash register as fast and as accurate as any body he'd ever known. Now to be fair to the owner, he never asked Marilyn how old she was, and she was maybe tall enough to be fifteen, maybe, but anyway the owner had a real good worker and that much he was sure of, and for all he knew she was maybe fifteen.

By the end of the week, Vesta worked out a schedule by which she'd have time to iron all the kid's clothes for school, Carroll being a senior and Janet being in second grade well that meant Vesta had to iron three dresses and a shirt for Carroll which just one year before when Carroll was a junior, every day Marilyn had to iron three dresses and a shirt for Carroll and also a pair of blue jeans for Carroll, but now Vesta doesn't iron any blue jeans for Carroll or any knock about pants for me because now she has ten pairs of a real time saving, remarkable invention called jeans stretchers which she ordered from the Sears & Roebuck catalog. The idea being, when you wash pants and wring out most of the water, well you slide these collapsed metal frames inside each wet leg, and you straighten the wet seams running right down the middle of the stretchers, and positioning the seams down the middle naturally forces a crisp crease along the front and back of each leg, and finally you pull apart the top and the bottom of the metal stretchers and lock it into place in the widest position possible, and hang the stretched out wet blue jeans to dry and like magic when the pants are dry all the wrinkles have been stretched out and the creases are straight up and down in front and in back!

That Friday in school the Tallapoosa High School students, in a secret ballot, voted for Joan to be Homecoming Queen, and first thing Marilyn (in the eighth grade) and Carroll (a senior) asked for permission, and they both left their classrooms and found their sister the Queen, and they couldn't say nothing (for this time the ambition cycle thing blurred their vision) but they sure could hug each other, and at the football game, in his muddy, back field offense, football uniform number 43, Carroll escorted his sister the Queen at half time, and Joan had time to change in the restroom from her cheerleader uniform into the formal dress she wore to the prom last year, and me and Vesta and our two younger kids were mighty proud to witness the majesty. Carroll is one of the best players, and way back when he was in the 9th grade, when he first went out for football, he wanted to be the quarterback, but he admitted he couldn't remember the plays so instead he's played halfback every year, and the main quarterback this year is Hubert Dodson, and some of the other players are Dooney Bates, Gary Bailey, Mack Cain, Bob Downey, Billy Higgins, Alton Lively, Gene Owens, Gordy Smith, Curtis Thompson, and Jim Walton.

Football season was about over, when one day I took a few hours off just so I could drive over to check on John and Sally. When I pulled into their yard, John was hitching up the horse to the wagon and being as it was a warm fall day, well he decided he'd drive the horse and wagon into town with the same excuse he always uses, being he needed some snuff which has always baffled me why in John's head it's ok to dip snuff, yet the only whipping he ever gave a kid was when he caught Chester smoking a cigarette? On the other hand, I been smoking since I was twelve years old, and right in front of John Owens, but never once has he ever let on, and for that I appreciate being counted able to make my own decisions.

Just when John came into the house to wash up after hitching the horse to the wagon, well the peddler stopped his fancy truck with a house built over the truck bed and folding steps which are easily folded down when a customer wants to go inside the 'store' and the peddler climbed the steps to the porch and called through the screen door to Sally, "Misses Owens, here's a letter from OK."

Sally's heart visibly jumped into her throat just as it always does each time she receives a letter from her nephew in Oklahoma, and she scurried over and opened the screen door in a dither, took the letter from the peddler, and short of breath like a young girl who just ran up the hill from the spring, Sally thanked the peddler, and well I followed her out on the porch and the peddler said his good byes and descended the steps to his fancy new truck and cranked up and drove off while Sally sat down in her porch rocking chair, and I sat down in my porch rocking chair, and Sally opened up the envelope and read the words from OK:

October 1953
Dear Aunt Sally,

My dearest and only Aunt, I thank you for the letter wishing me a happy birthday, I am now forty-seven years old. I do indeed hope to visit you in person some day! It won't be this year however, for my sons are marrying age, and it looks like three will speak their vows very soon. They have chosen fine young ladies each and every one, I'll be happy and honored by each of the three weddings. My sons and I are busy building three homes on our land and before long I'll have more and better help with all the work a putting up for the three brides to be are handy in the kitchen.

I am your loving nephew,
OK

Sally hugged to her chest the new crisp pages of this latest letter from OK, and unashamed, she let her husband see the tears welling in her eyes, and as she stood up from her porch rocking chair, John came out of the kitchen and crossed the distance between them in two long strides, and in a sweet embrace the husband and wife cried angry tears for the loss of Ollie and Hazel and Paul nearly half a century ago. Their love needs no words and each understands that their pain must be tolerated and allowed to surface momentarily, but as quickly as the darkness came, it receded and left behind a renewed strength.

Sally gently retrieved from her apron pocket the worn, fragile pages of OK's letter received four months ago, and with the new letter clutched together with the old letter in her right hand she held the two letters close to her heart and then she opened the screen door, and inside the house she made her way to the fine Sears & Roebuck, light golden oak dresser where she opened the right top drawer and gently added the four month old letter to safe keeping, and simultaneously she placed the fresh pages and the brilliant white envelope into her apron pocket as has been her method since her first letter came from OK some forty-two years ago when a five year old OK was learning to write.

In her apron pocket, Sally carries the dimes tied into the corner of a lace edged handkerchief always ready and on hand to give a visiting grandchild, and in the same pocket she keeps OK's newest letter always ready to be read aloud when anyone comes a calling, but this time she read silently except for the occasional word whispered to herself, and this time there were no tears atall, just a longing to hug OK and give dimes to his grandchildren.

Out in the yard, Big John Owens yelped, "Geed up!"

Leaving Sally at home to read and reread her new letter, in his mind, he figured he'd get to town just about the time of day when Marilyn (Merrily) was a starting her after school four hour shift checking out customers at the Red Dot Grocery Store. He intended to go into the Red Dot and gather up some groceries and a couple of cans of snuff and wait in line for Marilyn to check him out, and he'd be a proud Papa to make a money transaction on one side of the counter and Marilyn on the other side.

In town, he parked his horse and wagon in the open space along side of the railroad tracks which his horse and wagon as usual blocked a little bit of the access to Williams Brothers Wholesale Groceries, but no one and especially not the friendly and kind Williams Brothers (Junior and Morris) let on atall. It was John's usual thing to go inside Lipham's, but today Lipham's was put on hold, and instead he hurried across the railroad tracks leaving the horse reins loosely tied to the wagon seat, and as he walked past the Robert's Drug Store, he could not resist stepping inside and surprising Joan who came running around the end of the fountain counter, and she was so surprised and happy to see her beloved Papa that she jumped up into his arms, and he laughed out loud as he hugged his sweet granddaughter and through his chuckles he said, "Whoa, this must be what Carroll and Norman and Gene call a tackle in the game of football."

"Oh Papa, I don't know how to tackle, I just know how to hug. Why in the world are you in town so late?"

"Well, it's hours before the sun goes down, and your Mama needs some snuff, and you know how she gets when she's about to run out of snuff, before I can get back with it, she'll be scrounging through ever empty snuff can in the house shaking it and knocking two together to collect a smidgen that'll maybe get her by for a few minutes. I'll be going on down the street to the Red Dot, and young lady, you better get back to work."

"Mother and the little ones are in the Red Dot right now getting a can of date nut bread and a stick of cream cheese, they're all in for a nice surprise when you walk in!"

With that, the giant man in overhalls sauntered on down the street glad handing two or more neighbors on the way, and the exact same thing happened when he walked through the door of the Red Dot, by that I mean John Owens was tackled again and this time by Marilyn and with all the commotion at the front door, here came Janet running up the aisle between the canned goods and she hung on tight to her Papa's overhall pants legs, and the giant man walked along through the store toting a little granddaughter on one shoe, and it was a scene that brought emotions to the surface when the other customers witnessed the unabashed love and devotion and adoration bestowed on this chuckling giant with a red face, yellow hair and a yellow handlebar mustache.

John Owens gathered up the items on his wife's list including the snuff of course, and then he took his place in the check out line behind his oldest daughter and being that Vesta had only the two items, John stacked his purchases on the counter and slid and shuffled along proudly managing little Janet on one shoe as he reached for and cooed to the baby Randall while Vesta paid for her can of date nut bread and stick of cream cheese. Then John Owens quietly and intently watched every move as Marilyn punched in the numbers of each item and added the price by pulling the big handled lever on the right side of her giant cash register/adding machine, and Big John Owens managed to disguise his pride in what he saw, it's obvious to everyone that Marilyn is a gifted grocery checker for she doesn't search for a single number on the adding machine no sir, without looking at the numbers, thirteen year old Marilyn punches in the exact addition amounts, and then when the customer gives her a five dollar bill, she effortlessly and silently counts up from the amount owed while simultaneously pulling out bills and coins, and finally aloud she counts into the customer's hand the exact change back. Well, John Owens imagines the heights where she will soar!

Carroll is taking geometry this year and some times he has homework to do, and Janet makes herself available whenever her big brother sits down to the dining room table because, and I'm not sure when this got started, but it makes no never mind what the homework subject happens to be, Carroll teaches Janet his high school subjects, and she can read the history lesson and answer the homework questions, but more amazing, Carroll is teaching her to work out his geometry problems and listening to his explanations well I can picture the equations and answers myself, and I guess it's a testament to Carroll's genius for his little-est sister, the one who just a little while ago was afraid to play at recess and chance damaging her split thumbnail, well that was possibly a difficult social problem for her, but if Carroll is her teacher, well she simply has no academic problem.

This is shaping up to be my last Thanksgiving and Christmas at home for every day more details fall into place about cutting timber off the National Forests in New Mexico, and the latest correspondence from Mr. Blevins describes his plan to put a crew to work framing in a wide and long mess-hall-housing-lodge and roof it nine feet off the ground using the slabs cut into shingles then when me and my saw mill hands get there we will complete the walls and doorways and windows all be it the windows will be hinged shutter type doors covering the window opening, there will be no glass, and this mess-hall-housing-lodge will be big enough for cooking and eating tables and five bunk beds (which'll be five beds at the bottom level and five beds at the upper level) enough to sleep me and all my sawmill hands. Mr. Blevins will direct his workers to cover the roof with shingles made from the slabs cut off of the lodge pole pines. Once felled, each lodge pole pine will be chain-saw-shaved of its slabs (being the builders won't have the use of a saw mill), and the plan is to deliver a cast iron wood burning cook stove and stove pipe sections. He'll purchase and have on hand ten half-size mattresses and pillows and blankets. Once we get there, we'll build our own free standing bunk bed frames inside the lodge, and we'll use our own rough cut boards which we'll run through the sawmill saving the buying of expensive smooth cut boards and hauling the smooth cut boards many miles into the National Forest to our work sight. In our first week, we'll complete the lodge, and we'll build an outhouse downhill of the creek and lodge so's not to contaminate the creek water; which we'll catch in buckets for cooking and drinking, and any weekly bathing in the cold creek will also take place down stream. Mr. Blevins will see to it we're outfitted with buckets, pots, pans, tin plates, tin bowls, tin cups, forks, spoons, knives, coffee pots, kerosene and kerosene lamps for many will be the meals we eat before the sun comes up and after the sun goes down. When we arrive in Grants, Mr. Blevins will have some of his log trucks loaded with kitchen supplies, bedding, and food supplies, and first thing, we'll drive the supply (log) trucks to the work site, so's we can get on with the work of loading rough cut logs, and I fully expect we'll sleep on the ground for a least a week while we do double time loading the log trucks and building the bunk beds for when the replacement empty log trucks come out in a week or ten days, well we for sure want the first rough cut logs (slabs cut off) ready to haul into town, and to be ready for the replacement log trucks, my priority is to first thing load the log trucks which means we'll sleep on the ground a night or two and then once the log trucks are loaded, in strict order we'll build the bunk beds and enclose the lodge. Now the roadway into the wild National Forest land is mostly to be a dry creek bed which might be unusable during the spring run-off, but by then working through the summer and winter months, we will carve out a higher-land road, and Mr. Blevins says we'll be our own surveyors a marking the high road layout and possible future, bridge sites.

As we settle in; letter writing will be done by the light of the kerosene lamps and the written letters will be hauled to the nearest post office sixty miles away which thanks to Mr. Blevins, every family back here in Georgia already knows where to send our mail.

The cleared area and framed in lodge will be waiting for us right in the middle of approximately four thousand acres of National Forest, and me and my saw mill hands will cut and load the rough boards, we'll cut off the slabs at the sawmill so's to free space and increase the number of logs we can load on the trucks thereby hauling more on each load in the constant running back and forth, hauling the rough cut boards into Grants, New Mexico, and once the logs are off loaded in Grants, gas tanks are filled, supplies to us are loaded and all this accomplished in one overnight, round trip to us begins again and takes a full day's driving. Turning around the log trucks has to be quick and best it's of course, if the trip out of Grants starts early in the morning coming right back to us for another load, and the business of driving and maintaining the log trucks will fall to Mr. Blevins for he has a fleet of log trucks and a crew of drivers who double as mechanics.

I've already made the cash money payment of $2000 paid to the Federal Government, which amounts to fifty cents per acre paid in full for the right of cutting timber off of the four thousand acre tract. The hardships involved are the very reason why the price is only fifty cents per acre, but some of the trees will be inaccessible on the sides of steep mountains, and considering all the hazards, the profit margin is blurred but still, everything considered, it stands to reason profits will be substantial which is only fair considering the hardship cost to me.

By my way of figuring, we'll be a finishing the Rifle Range cutting by summer and now I've got a mighty fine idee a taking my oldest, Carroll with me to New Mexico. He'll be a graduating from Tallapoosa High School this spring, and he knows for sure he'll go to West Georgia Junior College in the fall, and what better time for him to learn the saw milling trade? He'll be my right hand man just like always, and his friend Bobby Key (a year younger than Carroll) wants to go with us too, and I know there's no better start in a young man's life than hard work! I mean hard work in unfamiliar situations and circumstances, and taking these two fine young boys along to New Mexico will be as good a start as they can possibly have in life!

I'm jumping the gun here just a little bit, we're all raring to go, but first things first, we have to complete the job of cutting the timber off the Rifle Range, then Mr. James McDonald will sell the Rifle Range as soon as he can, but me and my sawmill hands will be far gone out to New Mexico, and the selling price proceeds from the Rifle Range will go to Vesta, and she will wire money to me as I need it and right at first I'll need a good bit so's to meet my saw mill hands' payday and keep gas cans full and food rations a plenty for the cook; but for the most part, after Mr. James McDonald pays himself for his trouble, well then Vesta will manage the Rifle Range money, which unforeseen difficulties, both in Georgia and New Mexico, will be paid from this lump sum.

By my way of figuring, we'll be finishing the Rifle Range cutting by summer and now I've got a mighty fine idee of taking my oldest, Carroll with me to New Mexico. He'll be a graduating from Tallapoosa High School this spring, and he knows for sure he'll go to West Georgia Junior College in the fall, and what better time for him to learn the saw milling trade? He'll be my right hand man just like always, and his friend Bobby Key (a year younger than Carroll) wants to go with us too, and I know there's no better start in a young man's life than hard work! I mean hard work in unfamiliar situations and circumstances, and taking these two fine young boys along to New Mexico will be as good a start as they can possibly have in life!

Pore old Posey Greer is still sleeping upstairs, I've asked him to go to New Mexico with us, but he has mixed feelings about leaving Tallapoosa because it's as plain as day, he's in love, and the young lady is very lucky to have a fine, hard working man like Posey Greer. Since Posey's been sleeping upstairs, we've always tried to include him but he won't have it, and it's my suspicion he's mortally afraid of the Klu Klux Klan and there's not a way in the world I can transmit my fearless attitude toward the cowards in the Klan into the mind of a colored man, and that intimidation makes me mad as fire.

The sorry, low-down, good-for-nothing Klans-men (or maybe I should refer to them as Klans-heatherns) anyway, it's my way of thinking when a human lets hate take over well, you're on a slippery slide to hell, for if you don't have tolerance and love in your day to day life, you don't have respect for your own self, let alone, and for damn sure, you don't have respect from others, and when that happens, you're walking around here on earth with one foot in hell already, a hell you create that feeds itself right here in the flesh. But that being neither here nor there, the fact remains, from day one of sleeping upstairs, pore old Posey Greer has never answered a single invitation to share in our family life, no sir, he's always managed to be gone on Sundays and holidays, and for the longest time we didn't have any idee where he went, but the pieces of that puzzle fell into place when Huitte Davis told me that his good colored worker, Gene Hammock has a sister Louise whose been a babysitting their little Gayle since Gayle was born, and the colored, good worker Gene Hammock and his sister Louise are first cousins to our neighbor Thelma Collins, and well from the first week when Posey arrived from South Georgia, he's spent most of his free time at the Collins house just down the road, and it's not much of a coincidence that Posey Greer met and fell in love with Louise Hammock.

When Posey told me he won't be going to New Mexico, me and him figured he'll have to find some place else to sleep, especially now that Carroll won't be at home in the house, and I made the decision to build Posey his own shack down on my land at Dead Man's Curve, and this way he'll be right by the highway and can hitch-hike and get abouts, and we'll build his shack right by the spring's fresh cool water where he can dip up a bucket, and we'll build a shelf inside the shack like a dry sink for the water bucket and wash pan, and he'll have the store to buy his groceries, and we'll build a food storage shelf above the dry sink shelf, and there's still a pretty good supply of slabs left over from the short period of time when I had my sawmill set up on the property up hill of the store and grist mill, and Posey can burn up the pile of slabs cooking and heating his shack. We'll build him an outhouse down in the ditch downhill of the culvert, and he likes the idee of being completely independent and right next to a supply of slabs and a spring of fresh water, and most of all, a store where he's welcome to walk right though the front door, and all of the neighbors around the store will be good to Posey, and they'll treat him like he's somebody. Hard for him to imagine!

But for Huitte telling me, I'd a never known, that Posey's Louise Hammock, had a white man's baby last year, and she named the half white baby Posey Greer, but it's doubtful she'll be allowed to marry the man she loves, the grown Posey Greer. For sure, this young colored couple have a future which will involve an unbearable burden, an irrational situation which goes against the laws of nature simply put, the only right thing to be done is for my Posey Greer to marry Louise Hammock, but that won't be allowed by some distorted twist of fate by which a white man can lay claim to Louise, and the immorality doesn't even occur as a passing thought to the white sorry bastard. I hate to hear of such mean things!

But on the good side, the new colored school, Haralson Consolidated, is finally under construction up at the Round Top on Highway 78 west of Waco off the highway to the north, and the new colored school (Haralson Consolidated) and the new white school (West Haralson) both will open by the fall of 1956 and maybe sooner, and there will be indoor plumbing and a school bus for the colored children, and that's as it should be!

Share the burdens

On Wednesday, November 25, 1953, the last day of school before Thanksgiving, when Vesta went into town to pick up Joan and Marilyn after their shift of work, well her plan was to buy a turkey at the Red Dot for this year our normal supplier, Willie Hill, a fine colored man who provides turkeys for just about all the settlement around the store, well Vesta went over to Willy Hill's place on Wednesday afternoon, and I'll be dogged if Willie Hill hadn't sold every single turkey he had, and Vesta first thought we'd have one of his chickens instead, but then she changed her mind and figured she could probably get a turkey at the Red Dot or the Jitney Jungle. So that evening, when Vesta parked in front of the Red Dot, the lights were already turned off inside the store, and here come Marilyn out the door a carrying a turkey in a sack about as big as Marilyn, and Joan and Marilyn got in the car at the same time, Marilyn in the front seat and Joan in the back seat with Janet, and Marilyn proudly put the big old turkey on the floorboard at her feet so's she could hold Randall, and Vesta was a little confused but right quick Marilyn bubbled over the situation, "We sold a lot of turkeys today, and when there was only one turkey left, and we were closing and locking the front door, well I took my pay and turned back to my cash register and rung up the price for the last turkey and I paid for it!"

Vesta's surprise dropped her chin about to the floor, "Well I thought I'd get here in time to buy a turkey. Willie Hill sold out! I'll pay you back. How much was it?"

Marilyn, said, "No, Mother, you won't pay me back, I'm proud to be the one to buy the Thanksgiving Turkey! That's precisely what I'm thankful for! I'm better off as an eager benefactor."

When they told me, and Marilyn repeated her same lofty words well I didn't say thank you or boo, but I thought to myself, "That's precisely the point, and that's precisely what we all are about! We share the burdens with no feeling sorry about it. Don't make no never mind."

By December 1953, the 1954 model cars were in the showrooms, the Chevrolet style was barely changed from the 1953, and out of all the new cars I liked best the Chevrolet Bel Air, and it's time to replace the five year old two tone green Pontiac, and well I traded in the Pontiac for a brand new 1954 Chevrolet knowing full well, I can't move outa the state and leave Vesta driving an old car, and planning ahead as best I can, it is a relief to have the store and to know Vesta can keep supplies on the shelves and bring in some money all along, and the neighbors around the store seem just like family as do the neighbors around the house, and I can't pick up and move way out west without peace a mind, and a course there'll be times when in New Mexico maybe I won't be flush with money to send home, and my peace a mind rests on my family being independent and separate of the hardships of cutting timber off a National Forest seventeen hundred miles away.

Mitnick Chevrolet up town had on the show room floor, a 1954 Bel Air four door Sedan, two tone India Ivory and Horizon Blue with a similar to the 1953 but more modern looking grille and tail light lenses. Like the 1953, the 1954's trim along the side has the same script and Chevrolet crest.

I'm proud to say I traded in the 1949 Pontiac, paid the difference in cash money and drove the Bel Air home, and it's got power steering, powerglide, power brakes, the floorboards are carpeted, it has a good heater and defroster, turn signal lights (we call blinkers), a handy windup clock, and a push button Deluxe Radio.

I have bought and paid for this new 1954 Chevrolet Bel-Air for the total of $1700. This will be Vesta's reliable car, which after a year or so she and Joan and Marilyn will drive to New Mexico.

One warm sunny Saturday afternoon the first week of December, Vesta had some things to do in town, so she left me at the store with the kids and whizzed up town in the brand new Chevrolet Bel Air to get a few cases of canned goods at Williams Brothers Wholesale Groceries, pick up a frier chicken at the Red Dot, leave some shoes to be re-soled at Johnson's Shoe Shop and mail off a catalog order to Sears Roebuck. I stayed at the store with our two littlest kids, but actually I only had the baby inside the store with me, and it suddenly dawned on me that I didn't know Janet's whereabouts, so I took the baby out in front onto the slab of concrete and called out to the east, "Who-oo, Janet."

I called out a few more times, and then I heard a squeal coming from the direction back behind the grist mill where I had my sawmill set up for a while a few years ago, and instantly my heart jumped out of my chest, and I couldn't run fast for the gravel was a spinning under my shoes, and the baby took the jostling to be a game which his giggles blended with Janet's but I didn't see a thing to giggle about, and then I skidded my leather soles to a stop at the base bottom of the ten foot high pile of sawdust. The base of the sawdust hill is as big around as three cars pulled nose in together, and above the height of my head. At the very highest point of the sawdust hill there Janet stood getting ready to jump to a sitting position and slide down the sawdust slide, only she don't know because I never told her, sawdust rots just like wood only faster, and her weight can cause the sawdust to cave in filling the caverns below, and God A Mighty help me to stop her. I yelled louder than any sawmill blade, "STOP RIGHT THERE. STOP"

She was still at the top, and I cupped one hand (the other was holding Randall) and I yelled for Janet to run, run like a snakes after you and run right straight to me. Keep running no matter what!

When she was safely down off the sawdust pile, I ordered, "Come in the store. Right now!"

By the time we got inside the store, Janet was as white as a ghost, but she stood up to me, and I'll be dogged, when I sat down, she put her hands on her sides with her hands doubled up into fists, like she was getting ready for a fight, and she demanded, "Daddy, there's nothing about the sawdust pile that could be dangerous."

This time I chose my words carefully, "You're right, it appears that the sawdust pile is just a great big soft slide, but there is a very real danger that you can't see because way down deep inside the sawdust hill, there can be caves where the sawdust is rotten, and your weight as little as you are well, that much weight can easily begin a cave-in, and you'd be pulled under and you'd smother to death as the sawdust sealed itself around you blocking out air to breathe."

As soon as Vesta returned from town, I told Janet to stay inside the store, and Vesta went into the store carrying the baby. I told them to stay put inside while I drove my pickup truck to the sawdust pile, and with the windows closed tight, I drove circles around and around the edge of the sawdust pile pulling in closer and closer to the center and more than one sawdust slide piled up to the rolled up window on the passenger side but the powerful pickup truck engine managed to flatten most of the sawdust pile.

You're just like Sis

The week before Christmas, I took Janet walking though the woods again to cut down a Christmas tree, and Janet showed me for sure she'll never again forget to keep a good safe distance behind me so's the limbs I let fly on purpose don't hit her in the face. It is Janet's job to decorate the Christmas tree because the older girls and Vesta have no time to get it done, and again this year, the decorating started with the tedious untangling of the giant wad of tree lights carelessly put away last year.

Wednesday the twenty-third of December, I gave out ten-dollar bills to all my sawmill hands. They all had two days off work (Thursday, Christmas Eve, and Friday, Christmas Day). Posey was glad to eat Christmas Eve breakfast biscuits, but he carried them out doors and then he was no where to be found around our house, but by now we understood his connections with our good neighbors and with Sis and Huitte, or I should say with the baby sitter Louise Hammock. On Christmas Day, Sis and Huitte and little Gayle got to our house about ten in the morning so's Gayle could show Janet her Terri Lee Doll which is about as big as Gayle.

Saturday, the day after Christmas, we all got back to work, me and Carroll and Posey at the Rifle Range, Joan at Roberts Drug Store, and Marilyn at the Red Dot, leaving Janet at home to take down the Christmas tree for Vesta had her hands full as usual, and when I came home tired as fire, Janet showed me how she wound each string of lights around a folded up paper grocery sack eliminating the tangled mess come next year, and when I was telling my youngest daughter how she's ahead of me in the planning ahead department, well just about that time Vesta walked through the room and smiled the sweetest smile in the world at her youngest girl, and for the nine hundredth time she said to Janet in a kind of put-out, teasing voice, 'You're just like Sis!'

It didn't hurt Janet's feeling one bit, for Janet's love and admiration for Sis is plain to see and Vesta's point is well taken because Janet is 'just like Sis' in many ways such as cleaning up the house and organizing and sorting and these skills are especially helpful at Christmas and in late summer before school starts for these are the two times every year when Vesta makes deliveries to the front porches around the county, and now Vesta depends on Janet for it's become Janet's job to organize and box same sizes of girls clothes and shoes and same sizes of boy's clothes and shoes.

On Sunday the 27th of December me and Carroll and Posey tore down Posey's bed upstairs which poor old Posey argued wasn't right for him to take a perfectly good bed, but I told him me and Vesta have already figured out that as soon as me and Carroll leave out to New Mexico, well Vesta and the three girls and Randall will all want to sleep downstairs close together, and the downstairs has a gracious plenty beds for all, and it naturally follows there's no need of a bed upstairs. So Posey gave up arguing, and accepted what he called his 'windfall' his bed stead, mattress, springs, pillow, two feed sack sheets, and two blankets along with a table and two chairs which Vesta said was in the way of her putting another quilt in the frame. When we got it all loaded on the truck, then is when Vesta went out to the well shed and brought into the front yard a big box filled with a water bucket and dipper, a cooking pot, an iron skillet, an iron kettle, two tin plates, two tin forks and spoons, and two tin coffee cups. Vesta carried this box full of kitchen supplies in her arms, and it just about blocked out her face, and sticking out the top of the box was what pleased Posey the most, an empty tin can in which Vesta had arranged dried broom straw, and the broom straw arrangement is real purdy, and when she took it out of the box and handed it to Posey, he said out loud to his shoe laces, "Thank ye ma'am, It looks like a picture I once saw in a magazine."

For a minute there I saw a scared look on Posey's face like he'd just lay down and die if Vesta tried to hug him, and she just about hugged him anyway, but thankfully pore old Posey dodged that embarrassment, and instead, my sweet wife, told him truthfully as how he'd brought nothing but kindness to our home.

The first day of the New Year 1954, was a Friday and me and my sawmill hands worked a full day, but at home that evening after supper, the Goolsbys from around the store came a serenading all dressed up in gypsy costumes. The girls, Preacher Goolsby's Ruth, Louise, and Janice, and Boot Goolsby's, girls Lucille and Dorothy and their mama Lavada wore bandanas around their heads, full colorful long skirts, men's work shirts belted at the waist and long colorful strings of beads. The Goolsby men Boot, Junior, Bo, Fuzz, Bud, C.W. and Preacher Goolsby wore bandanas around their heads too and colorful vests over their work shirts and jeans. Their voices blended in harmony while Vesta played the tunes on the piano. It was a serenade of creative and happy hearts, and I for one hope we enjoy often repeated performances.

The kids went back to school on Monday, January fourth, and when I got home from the Rifle Range, Carroll had the table set like some highfalutin' rich folk's table, and Joan, Marilyn, and Janet were babbling about all the rules of etiquette Carroll was teaching. When we all sat down to the table, Carroll described that in school, the Home Economics teacher made an announcement that all Seniors who want to learn good table manners could come to the Home Ec. Room instead of going to study hall, and it turned out that not a single senior was left in study hall for everyone of the seniors wanted to learn good manners. It's too late for me to become highfalutin' but, I got to admit, it seems like a good idee for the kids, for I do believe that all our kids are smart … I mean real smart, and it's just about a sure thing they will all get a good college education, and they will all get good high paying jobs, and if that's how it turns out, then they better for sure know good manners, and it's plain to see, if our kids learn good manners now while they're young, well then the good manners will come natural, and this is taking what Vesta has always preached about learning to speak good English and taking it to the next level. Vesta deserves credit here, for Carroll, Joan, Marilyn & Janet have already reaped mostly all A's in English, and having that head start in school, well it just goes to show, a good helping of self confidence can translate across the board, and so far our kids have mostly A's in every other course taught to them. Not one of our kids has brought home a single report card with a single grade lower than a B. It's got a lot to do with our kids, it's got a lot to do with Vesta, and it's also got a lot to do with the quality of the teachers in the Tallapoosa schools.

Me and Kit (Thomas to everybody but me) bought some farmland up beyond Bremen. The whole thing is Kit's idee, and he don't have any plans to do any farming himself, but he knows the old couple who needed to sell so's they can move out and go live with their only son in the big city. I am in on the deal just as pure investment, and Kit means to sell the farmland right quick. Along about the same time, Kit bought a store building right in Bremen, it is the southern most store front in the strip of west facing stores along Highway 27 just south of the intersection of 27 and 78 along side the east west railroad tracks. Kit is in the process of furnishing the store building with ovens, sinks, work counters, electric giant mixing machines, cooling racks, and electrical outlets every three feet around the walls and two or more hanging from the ceiling directly above every work counter. There'll be two or three glass display cases by the west facing front door and a cash register for to sell bakery goods to walk-in traffic, but the bulk of Kit's Dixie Bakery business will be deliveries made to grocery stores in Bremen, Buchanan, Tallapoosa, Waco, Villa Rica, Bowdon Junction, Carrollton and all the country stores along the way. He has ordered three panel trucks for what he calls the "pie routes" which pies will be included in the fresh-out-of-the-oven baked goods, but by no means will the delivery goods be limited to pies.

Of course, we all attended Carroll's graduation, and as soon as school was out for the summer, Carroll and Bobby Key came to work at the Rifle Range every day, and finally, (although I wish it wasn't so) by the tenth of June all the timber cutting is done, and now we have ahead of us the giant job a loading the saw mills on the log trucks and loading all the power saws and gas cans and tool boxes. I sold the oldest log truck, and I have two fairly new log trucks and one almost new Dodge pickup truck which we'll drive across the country to Grants, New Mexico.

My saw mill hands are feeling mighty adventuresome, all-be-it might be beneficial if they curb their enthusiasm at home, for the wives (to be left behind) are getting moody and especially Dink Daniel's wife Ora, and a few times she's been downright depressed, and Dink tells us about what she says, like once she asked the equation if Dink's free to pick up and move across the country, well then she ought to be free to do the same, and she might just pick up and move too and maybe not even tell Dink and maybe never let him know her whereabouts, and she'd for sure have the kids with her, all-be-it's not her choice to tell Wayne and Shirley what's what for they're about grown, but the youngest, Kay will be for sure right beside Ora where ever Ora might decide to go.

This adventure is counting real big in many a man's life, and I'm the first to admit I'd change my mind in a minute and not go out west atall if I could find timber to cut right around here in Georgia which I mean I'm looking for a good many thousand acres to keep me working and paying my hands for at least five years. I get real sad if I start thinking about missing out on what my wife and kids are doing on a daily basis, I know this is the best opportunity I have to make good money, and I exercise inner discipline, but I can't say it any other way, bam I stop thinking the sad thoughts, bam I stop! Right on the edge of the cliff before I fall, bam, I stop thinking about it. That's the only way I know of dealing with the situation.

We're getting everything packed up, and there's one thing I got to do before I go, I got to, I'm taking my littlest girl on a camping trip, and I want to take the baby along too, he's close to two years old now. I got it all planned out, as the sun is going down, we'll build a fire and have a wienie roast then just after dark, Vesta will come get Randall, and me and Janet will sleep under the stars by the creek that runs through the farm me and Kit bought northeast of Bremen.

"Boy Howdy! Daddy! We're going camping?

Vesta helped us throw some quilts and pillows in the truck, and I loaded the food box and then turned to pick up Randall who was ready and raring to go! In the truck, bam, I stopped thinking about it!

First thing at the farm campsite when I shut down the engine Janet scrambled out of the pickup truck and set out on a mission looking up and down the creek bank. As usual, Janet was barefooted. I'd worked a full day, and it was getting on about sundown, so while Janet was hunting rattlesnakes, I built a campfire, and using my pocket knife, I cut off three low hanging, new growth, oak limbs, cut each to about three feet, stripped the bark, and Janet was the first to start roasting her wienie on a stick, but just in a minute I had Randall's and my wienie sticks stuck out over the flames, and I used the intensity of the minute to begin my purpose. "Janet, you're getting about grown, and I know you'll be ok, but I want to talk over what's coming."

Janet, with her head tilted like Ma, groaned to the sputtering fire, "You're leaving for New Mexico."

Bam, I could not stop the pain in my heart...

Janet continued, "I'll take care of every thing around the house, Daddy, don't worry, I'll take care of Randall,"

When I could speak without sobbing, I went on, "You are my precious Janet and I know you'll take care of everything. That's as it should be. Also there's a special job for you while I'm gone. You have to write to me, I'm depending on you. This is a good opportunity, and a man has to provide for his family, but I can't survive the separation, unless you write to me every week. I have to know what's going on. Being far away from my family will be next to impossible, so you will be my lifeline. Your mother and Joan and Marilyn are too busy to write. I know you are busy too, but now you have to make time, no matter what, you have to make time to write to me every week. Can you do that for me?"

She vowed, "Yes, Daddy, I promise you that I will write you a letter every week telling you what's going on back here at home."

Janet took her first bite, and I forced myself to eat and then with perfect timing, Vesta's headlights searched for us, and quick as a wink, she loaded

Randall into the Chevrolet and took off back home. Then to make our bed on the ground I spread out three quilts in a stack and placed two pillows under the top cover quilt. As soon as I spread the last quilt, barefooted Janet slowly moved into place at her pillow's edge and subconsciously held her breath in awe as she surveyed the magical surroundings in one last fantasy filled look at the field of a million lighting bugs.

I kicked out the campfire, finished my cigarette, squashed it into the dirt, and crawled under the top quilt on my side. My youngest little girl pushed her pillow away so as to use my arm instead, and under the clear brilliant stars in the heavens above, I recalled some history.

"When I was eight years old like you are now, my Pa died, and the wagon a carrying him in a pine box pulled away from the old home place with me and Sis walking along behind. Sis was just four years old, and we stayed in the cemetery til after dark because we felt close to Pa there, and that evening in the cemetery alone with Sis and Pa, at eight years old, I began my adult life. It wasn't what I wanted to do, but I did it, for I had no choice. Now on a smaller scale, Janet you must begin your adult life and keep me involved with my family. You have made a solemn promise that you will write to me."

On Father's Day afternoon, June 20, 1954, all my hands met me at the store, nine men plus Carroll and Bobby Key, and all the wives and families were there hugging and crying. During that last week, all twelve of us worked on my pickup truck and three log trucks changing oil, adding water and antifreeze, examining and replacing worn out tires, bolting down into place spare tires, tool boxes, power saws, and gas cans and finally loading and chaining in place the saw mill components. Bud Goolsby will start out driving the pickup truck, Mitchell Daniel and Bobby Key will spell him off. Carroll will start out driving one log truck and in the cab with Carroll is Dink Daniel and Boomy Daniel, Earl Hart is driving the second log truck with Cliff Deering and Tommy Ballew riding with him, and I'm driving the third log truck, it's got the heaviest load and I'm afraid it'll be the hardest to handle. I'll have two in the cab with me Fred Houston and his boy June Bug. For the most part, I intend to drive the heaviest load most of the way and especially through the nights, but I plan to ride and get some sleep in the daylight hours. The others will switch around every few hundred miles.

Every man stashed his nap sack and lunch box in the pickup bed, somebody slung the canvas over the load and tied it down, and then it was time to say goodbye and there were more hugs and tears all around, but mostly from the women, for the men were electrified with energy and excitement, and finally, I called out to load up, and I pulled onto Highway 78 heading west and Carroll pulled in behind me, and Earl Hart followed Carroll, and the pickup truck pulled in line to bring up the rear, and I can tell you the road ahead was blurred with uncertainty, but mostly the road leading west was blurred with my tears which I kept to myself as best I could.

Part Three Tell Your Mother To Stop Running The Red Light

June 21,1954
Dear Daddy,

You left yesterday and not much has happened but I want to write anyway so you'll have a letter waiting for you when you get to New Mexico. I am going to spend the night with Mary Ann this coming Friday night. Marilyn and Joan are at work, and mother is making jelly. Randall is playing in the sand. I'm watching Randall and writing to you both at the same time. I don't want to start crying again, but I want you to know we all miss you and Carroll very much.

Love,
Janet

Mother showed me how to fold the school paper so it fits exactly in the envelope. I wrote my return address and the address in New Mexico.

Miss Janet Godwin
Tallapoosa, Ga

　　　Mr. Shug Godwin
　　　Grants, N.M.

Before Daddy left, he wrote down the Grants, New Mexico so I know how to spell it, and now with my first letter ready to mail, Mother drove us to the post office, I went in with her, and inside, Mother put Randall on the high counter, he wrapped his little hand around one of the bars, and then she lifted me up on the high counter too. I could hold on to the bars (like in a jail) and turn around to look at Mr. Roy Howe who stood behind the high counter in a window cut out in the bars. Mr. Roy Howe is a short man, but he seems tall behind the high counter, I think the floor behind the bars is up a step higher than the floor for the customers on the front door side of the bars or maybe Mr. Roy Howe is standing on a footstool. I had my letter to Daddy in my hand, and Mr. Roy Howe, the Post Master, asked me if he could help me. I was surprised that he spoke directly to me instead of to Mother. I said, "I need to buy four stamps, please."

He carefully tore off four stamps and as he handed them to me he said, "That'll be twelve cents."

I'm glad Mother had twelve cents because I didn't have a penny to my name. Mother helped me get off the high counter and back down on the floor, and I separated one stamp and handed to Mother the remaining three stuck together stamps. I licked the one stamp and put it in the upper right corner of the envelope, and then I saw Mr. Roy Howe's hand reaching out to me from the high counter, he looked sort of like a belly plane flying on the high counter top, so I touched his hand with the envelope and he took it, and I said, "Thank you. Do you know when this letter will get to my Daddy?"

Mr. Roy Howe replied, "Well this letter will go parcel post and it should arrive in New Mexico within a week. When did your Daddy leave out?"

I said, "Yesterday."

Mr. Howe said, "Well I suspect your letter will be waiting for him when he pulls into (he looked at my envelope and read) Grants, New Mexico."

I smiled at Mr. Howe and turned to follow Mother through the screen door, she held it open for me to come out behind her, then she let it slam shut. I like Mr. Roy Howe, he looks like an elf with his suspenders holding his pants above his round stomach almost up to his armpits, and he has a twinkle in his eye like he might be up to some sort of mischief. He remembers my name, and he talks to me like I'm a grownup.

When we were in the car, I asked Mother if she came out with the three stamps, and she felt of her little leather coin purse inside the front of her dress, and when she touched the front of her dress for reassurance, she jerked her hand back and slung her fingers to ease the painful pin prick, no it was a needle prick. It was a needle stuck in the front of Mother's dress, and the needle has blue thread in it because mother is making a blue dress for me, and she brought the dress with us and threaded the needle with blue thread so she can finish the dress at the store, all she has to do is hem the blue dress. Mother said, "I put your stamps in my pocket book."

My Mother always has her little coin purse with her, and mostly she carries it inside her dress pocket, but a few of her dresses have no pockets, and then she carries her little pocket book inside the top of her dress. To put her little pocket book away, she pulls the neck of her dress straight out from her throat and with her other hand she pokes the little pocket book down inside, and usually the little pocket book falls way down to her waist inside her dress, and to retrieve it, Mother locates it through the fabric then pushes it up until she can reach it at the dress neckline. My Mother always has pins and needles stuck into the front of her dress, and many times she forgets about the needles and pins and pricks her finger, and sometimes when she hugs her children, she draws a drop of blood, but that is just fine, and it's entirely worth the short lived sacrifice because the tiny drop of blood is just another good reason for my sweet mother to kiss (and as she says) 'love on' the injured.

We spent the rest of the day at the store, but before Mother unlocked the store, she walked me to the edge of the Highway where we looked both ways, and it was clear so she said, "Ok run on across, and have fun!"

Ivey Newman and Larry Goolsby (most call him Red because of his red hair) played in the pasture and Francis Newman, Kay Daniel, and I played inside the shady, screened in, back porch. We played school and Francis was the teacher, and I was an unruly student and the three of us laughed so hard tears rolled down our faces, and before long Francis's mother (who seems like a mother to all the kids) called the boys in to dinner, and she made everybody wash up on the back porch where she drew up a bucket of cool water. She used the dipper to fill the tin wash-up pan, and then she poured cool well water from a second draw up bucket into the kitchen bucket and she carried the kitchen bucket inside and filled seven little glasses with the cool, refreshing well water, and while we were washing up, the boys started a water battle on the back porch, but the girls rushed inside and sat down around the big table and the pinto beans and cornbread combination made a delicious dinner, and Lou Newman made me eat a second helping of beans. She always makes me eat because she thinks I'm too skinny.

At home that evening, I found the West Georgia Bank calendar in the junk drawer, and I drew a circle around the 21st of June, that way I'll remember when I wrote to Daddy, and I'll write again on Monday the 28th of June, and I'll be sure to write to Daddy every Monday.

Almost every Friday, I spend the night with Ruth and Otto, but this week Mother drove me to Uncle Thomas's house in Bremen. Uncle Thomas married Evelyn late in life, and Mother says he is lucky to find such a nice lady, and their only child so far is Mary Ann who is about my age. After supper, Mary Ann and I played with our dolls in the back yard while Uncle Thomas and Evelyn sat under the Mimosa tree on the east side of the house. Mimosa trees are not very good shade trees, but as the sun set in the west, we had a very cool place to play in the solid shade of the house. Just as the sun went down, Evelyn went inside the house and found two fruit jars and lids so Mary Ann and I could catch lightening bugs. It always starts the same way, catch hundreds of lightening bugs, fill the fruit jars and make lights to read by, maybe. It's a good idea, but it never works, so as always we let the lightening bugs fly away out of the fruit jars, and I went inside with Evelyn, and she turned on the water in the bathtub. I brought my shortie pajamas into the bathroom, and this was the first time I ever knew that hot water could actually come out of a bathtub faucet, and another first for me, was my first time ever to take a bath in deep water.

After Mary Ann's bath, we were talking and giggling to high heaven in Mary Ann's very own bedroom, which is like Dolly's bedroom and has two half-size beds. Mary Ann and I could not seem to settle down even though the house was dark, and it was very late. The door to Mary Ann's room actually has a doorknob, and with the door shut tight, we kept talking and giggling because we had a feeling of privacy behind the closed door (another first for me, that's three). It must have been really late when Uncle Thomas knocked on the door and came into Mary Ann's bedroom. He said, "I know you girls are very excited to be together, but it's time to settle down, you're keeping me awake, and I need my sleep because my workday starts at five o'clock in the morning. Saturday at the Dixie Bakery is our busiest workday. You girls crawl in bed, and I'll tell you a story."

Mary Ann stretched out on one half bed, and I stretched out on the other, and Uncle Thomas sat at the foot of Mary Ann's bed, and he did not read a story, he told a story that he made up as he went along.

"Once upon a time, there was a beautiful and lonely white swan who lived on a small pond. The pond was out in the country far away from people, and the seclusion pleased the beautiful white swan very much. It was quite handy that the pond had lots of fish swimming around just close enough to the surface so that the beautiful white swan could reach under water with her long graceful neck and catch a fish and eat it for breakfast every morning, and she could easily catch a fish for dinner and for supper too. Her life was peaceful and serene, but when a storm blew up naturally she knew her world was also filled with wonder and danger. She watched the majestic and powerful lightening carve the dark evening sky, and sometimes she dared to imagine or dream about sharing her life, but she simply did not realize that there might be other creatures in the world like her who have white feathers and long graceful necks. She knew that she was more beautiful than any creature because when the winds calmed and the waves subsided, she could see her reflection in the still water. She was a very big bird, and her only bird companions were the countless little varieties of twittering, fluttering, hopping, pecking, flying birds, but she was fond of these small birds and grateful for their friendship. One day as she watched the little birds flying and swooping about, she had a new idea, an idea that made her heart skip a beat as the image of soaring though the air inspired this beautiful large stately white swan. She thought to herself, 'these little friends have feathers like me, and they have wings like me, and considering the similarities, it must follow that if they can fly, well then I should be able to fly also'.

So the next morning, after her breakfast fish when the sun rose in the eastern sky, the big beautiful white bird swam to the edge of the pond, climbed out of the water, and waddled up the hillside to a cliff that she had never noticed before and she thought it handy to have a cliff that jutted out over the pond. So from this ledge, the big beautiful white swan jumped out into the air, and when she spread her wings a wondrous thing happened. She was able to glide in downward spiraling circles, but that only whet her desire for more, so while still in flight, she learned quickly that she could also climb through the air back up to the height of the ledge and beyond! She spent day after day jumping into the air from the ledge until one day, she learned she could take off from the water's surface, and now she realized her power was boundless, and she climbed higher and higher into the air until she could see over the mountains that surrounded her little pond, and there beyond her wildest dreams was a world full of beautiful white swans, and these swans were calling her to come join them, and that's what she did."

I stayed awake to the very end of the story, but it was obvious that Mary Ann was sound asleep. Uncle Thomas kissed Mary Ann's forehead, and then he kissed my forehead, and I could not help but hug his neck because he looks so much like my Daddy. I miss my Daddy and it makes me cry when I think of him so far away, and before Uncle Thomas tiptoed out of the room I realized he had a tear welling up in his eye, but I stopped my tears by thinking about the beautiful swan, and the next thing I knew it was morning, and the sun was streaming in the window. Mary Ann yawned awake and we scrambled around to get dressed because we had to follow the aroma of eggs and bacon and grits. It was already almost nine o'clock, and after we straightened up Mary Ann's room, Evelyn gave us each some money in a little coin purse, and she walked us across their front yard to the edge of Highway 78, and she helped us cross the Highway to the cement sidewalk that goes all the way to up town Bremen. Evelyn told us we could walk to town and spend our money on anything we wanted. It was very shocking and at the same time very exciting to think I could look through all the stuff in the stores and buy anything I wanted, but after looking at all the toys and dolls and doll dresses and paper dolls with sheets of cut-out dresses, I decided that what I really wanted most of all was to surprise my Mother with something she might like. So I left Mary Ann in the toy department, and on the other side of the store, I found things like irons, and pots and pans, and then I found a very beautiful, flat, cut-glass dish with a cover a little bigger and the exact same shape as a stick of butter.

The minute I saw it, I knew Mother would like it, and so that's what I bought with my money. Mary Ann paid for a toy, and I paid for the butter dish, and we started the long walk back home, and as soon as we could see her house, of course we saw her mother standing in the front yard, and we were so excited that we started running and Evelyn met us on our side of the Highway and when it was clear, the three of us crossed back to the house. It was time to put my dirty clothes back in my book satchel, and I carefully protected the glass butter dish at the bottom. Mary Ann and I both sat in the front seat with her mother as Evelyn drove us west through Bremen to my home. I was so happy to see Mother, and she was happy to see me too, but when she bent over to give me a smack, sure enough I got stuck, and this time it was a little more dangerous because I got stuck right in the eyebrow while Mother kissed my hair (remember she's like that), but as usual, the injury floated away into nothingness when my Mother loved on me and drew me onto her lap as she sat down in the wing-back chair big enough for Mother, the baby and me. Evelyn and my Mother talked and talked and talked, and Mary Ann and I escaped upstairs to play, but it was really too hot up there, and besides it was time for Mary Ann to go.

As mother unpacked my pajamas and dirty dress, she had a confused look on her face, so I said, "Evelyn gave us money to buy anything we wanted, and I wanted to buy something for you!"

Mother loved the butter dish just as I knew she would.

Monday
June 28, 1954
Dear Daddy,

I spent Friday night with Mary Ann. Uncle Thomas made up a bedtime story about a beautiful white swan. On Saturday, Mother bought groceries at the Jitney Jungle. On Sunday morning, I went to Sunday School, Mother drove me to the Baptist Church and she drove Joan to work at Robert's Drug Store.

Love,
Janet

I licked a stamp for the letter to Daddy, and Mother told me to hurry on out to the mailbox because it's time for the mailman. Our mailman is Mr. Jaillet. He's Brenda's granddaddy, and I got to the mailbox in time for him to personally take Daddy's letter from me and hand me the mail to take back into the house. Every day except Sunday, we go to the store after Mother gets the housework done. We do not go to the store on Sunday because there's a law or something that makes it impossible to open any store on Sunday, and for that matter, no one works any sort of job on Sunday, except for cooking of course. We would probably have to go to jail if we cut the grass, did the wash, mopped the floor, or swept the yard. Our Sunday afternoons are filled up with my favorite thing in the whole wide world --- going to Mama's and Papa's. Every Sunday, to help out Mama and Papa, Mother takes a few cans of vegetables from the store, but she loads the cans in the trunk of the car when we are leaving the store on Saturday.

I brought the mail inside to Mother, and Mother stopped her sewing, stuck her needle into her dress, and opened the mail. It's been one whole week and one day since Daddy and Carroll left for New Mexico. I have mailed two letters, but there's still no letter back. Suddenly, I heard a huge and very loud engine, but then it sputtered and quit, and then I saw in Mr. Brown's cotton patch an airplane!

With no more explanation, Joan, Marilyn and I ran out the back door followed by Mother carrying Randall. We formed a steady stream down the back steps and across the grass to where an airplane was almost ready to land. It took just a minute to focus on the very large bird now getting ready to touch the ground in Mr. Brown's cotton field! Yep! Look! Just as I thought, the pilot is a regular man walking toward us!"

Joan, "I can see the man's face. He's looking straight at us."

Mother, "He's waving!"

We went down the bank and into the road drawn by an airplane? The pilot was tending to parking his airplane and the plane finally came to a complete stop when the wheels could no longer flatten the cotton bushes. I was first to climb the hog wire fence, twisting over the one line of barbed wire at the top, and dropping to the other side. Joan and Marilyn followed in quick succession, but Mother decided to stay put in the road holding the baby. The pilot climbed out of an open cockpit, and as his feet touched the ground, he ripped goggles from his face. The pilot walked past the three of us to the fence and said to Mother, "Howdy Ma'am!"

I'm not kidding, this man in a leather jacket, leather gloves, and leather hat with flaps buttoned under his chin, said, 'Howdy, Ma'am.'

I'll never forget the look on my Mother's face. She didn't say a thing, but the baby held out his arms to the pilot, and the pilot took the baby, over the fence. Mother was frozen like somebody had tagged her and said, 'Freeze tag!' The pilot held Randall like it was the most natural thing in the world, and then he said, "I ran out of gas, I'm sorry to destroy some of your cotton crop, but I had to put her down."

I thought to myself, 'This will be the best ever letter to Daddy and Carroll."

The pilot handed the baby back over the fence to Mother and asked, "Ma'am, I need to buy some gas, can you drive me to a filling station? I'll pay you for your trouble"

Mother found her tongue and said, "I can drive you, but I don't have a gas can, Shug took all the gas cans to New Mexico."

The pilot turned away from the fence and headed back to the airplane, "I have a gas can in the Stearman," he called over his shoulder.

Once we were inside the house, mother invited the pilot to have a seat in the kitchen and finish off the breakfast biscuits, and even though they were cold, the pilot ate every single one with generous portions of Mother's home canned pear preserves, and she heated over the perked coffee while we waited for Joan and Marilyn to get dressed for work which didn't take long, and it was certainly worth the few minutes wait because that way Mother could make only one trip to town. Call it stewardship or stinginess, Vesta Owens Godwin takes to heart, Papa's admonitions to conserve gasoline, water, food, cloth, soap, kerosene, electricity, long distance telephone time, and this list goes on and involves every aspect of life. The only bad thing about making one trip into town is that Joan and Marilyn will miss the Stearman's takeoff. When the pilot sat in the front seat of our new Chevrolet, he said, "Nice car!"

The baby crawled into the pilot's lap, and as soon as we were settled in the back seat, I thought I'd go on and be quick about it, and it took just a minute for everybody to catch on when I called 'A' and proudly proclaimed 'A" for airplane.' We usually only play the alphabet game on Sunday's when we are taking a longer trip than just to town, and usually I call the first letter, and then they have to find something outside the car that starts with an 'A,' 'A" for "Airplane' and according to the rules of the game, I had to say it before we lost sight of the airplane which of course happened when Mother backed away from the house.

July 5, 1954
Dear Daddy,

This week an airplane landed in Mr. Brown's cotton field. All we had to do was go outside and stand there and watch an airplane land. The pilot got out and said he ran out of gas. Then when Mother took Joan and Marilyn to work, the pilot rode to town and filled up his gas can. He poured the gas into his airplane and then waved goodbye and took off. I wish you and Carroll could have seen the pilot and his airplane.

Love,
Janet

The next day the mailman delivered the first letter from Daddy.

June 27, 1954
Dear Family,

The drive across the country was long and monotonous and we thought Texas would never end. It most certainly is the biggest state in the U.S. When we left Tallapoosa, we went straight to Birmingham and on to Tuscaloosa. We hit Columbus and Greenville Mississippi, and Texarkana Arkansas. In Texas we went through Paris, Wichita Falls, and Lubbock. In New Mexico we drove from Clovis to Vaughn and on to Grants. Last month before we got here, Mr. Blevins had his workers set up a campsite in the mountains next to a rushing creek in the National Forest. They built a roof on lodge pole pine logs set in the ground and the roof is 9 feet off the ground at the lowest point of the slope. We spent two days building tables and bunk beds and it wasn't much trouble to wall in the lodge with slabs, which we left two opening windows on each long side and one opening window on each end, and we've already added slab shutters mounted with hinges so's we can leave the windows open in summer and shut them tight in winter. We have a right nice place to live. It rained one day, but our lodge roof did not leak a drop. The lodge is situated such that the ground falls away on all four sides so there's no chance the dirt floor will flood. We have mattresses and pillows and blankets. There are two kerosene lamps on our long eating table and two lamps on the cook's table and beside each bunk bed we built a small boxy table to set lamps on. I'm writing by the light of my kerosene lamp. Right by my bed the wall has a crack in it because we used green slabs to build the walls and when green lumber dries out it shrinks. When it's dark and everybody blows out all the lamps, I can see five stars through the crack by my bed. I've named the five stars Carroll, Joan, Marilyn, Janet, and Randall. Up a little higher in the sky, there is a brighter star and that's your Mother. It makes me feel close to my family because you are probably looking at the same stars.

Love,
Your Daddy

Early one morning toward the end of the summer, I was in the back yard and Mr. Brown called my name and I went to the fence and he asked me if I'd like to help him pick cotton, I said yes, and went running in the house to tell Mother, and she said yes and I blasted out the door, down the steps, and over the fence!

Mr. Brown came to me with a brown paper grocery sack because he said they'd stand up on the ground if we rolled down the top a little bit all around the sack. Mr. Brown did the rolling down and handed me the paper sack, but he wore a very large cloth sack with the strap slung on his shoulders. We worked at a pretty good pace walking though the cotton rows heading north. Mr. Brown made it to the end of his row way ahead of me. At the end of his row, Mr. Brown turned to work back toward meeting me in my cotton row, but I kept on picking and pretty soon he motioned for me to come back south in the next row then Mr. Brown did some more high cotton stepping over the rows through my row into the next row over, and now the two of us each in a separate row picked back to where we started. I was just a little ahead of Mr. Brown so that first time, I poured my full grocery sack into Mr. Brown's shoulder strap sack. Then he shouted that I could stay put in the area with his cloth shoulder strap sack and keep empting my grocery sack into his cloth bag. Then Mr. Brown parked his full cloth shoulder strap sacks and picked up an empty cloth shoulder strap sack from the supply of extra cloth sacks left lying all along the north end of the field. I picked my grocery sack full only three or four more times because I was thirsty and tired, but Mr. Brown thanked me for helping and said I was a good worker, and then I climbed the fence and barely got one leg over the top getting myself in a half sitting position when a sharp barb tugged at me, but I was barefooted and wearing shorts and the barb gouged deep into the flesh of my inner thigh. I managed to swallow a scream as I looked over my shoulder and thankfully found Mr. Brown picking to the north away from me, and I had a modicum of dignity remaining as I climbed the steps to the back porch. I decided not to tell Mother about my barbed wire wound and inside the privacy of the bathroom, I washed the blood away and painted Mercurochrome over the gash.

July 12, 1954
Dear Daddy,

I helped Mr. Brown pick cotton. We worked for about three hours, you are right, working makes you sleep really good.

Mother is making school dresses for me and Joan and Marilyn, and she ordered jeans and shirts for Carroll. She ordered some from Spiegel and some from Sears Roebuck, and some from Montgomery Ward.

Love,
Janet

P.S. I think I am looking at the same five stars and the brighter one higher in the sky.

The rolling hills between our house south, southeast toward Highway 78 are in 'cultivation' (to quote my mother), and actually all the land between us and town (to the west) is also in cultivation, and because there are no woods between us and the highway, from our front yard, we have a view of the Drive-In-Theater screen, but from our distant vantage point, the Drive-In-Theater screen is so small that I can block it out completely with my hand, so in the miniature version of course it's impossible to watch and understand the picture show, and the only sound we hear is the occasional, intermittent background music. I have decided the picture show's background music is louder than the words spoken by the actors and actresses, but even so, the background music is very faint by the time it reaches our front yard. The picture show of course projects motion on the screen, and the colorful movement makes it fairly easy to find the Drive-In-Theater screen in the dark of night, but it is virtually impossible, to find the screen in daylight even when I search from standing in the exact night-time spot, my conclusion: it's easy to understand why a white motionless screen would not be discernible in sunlight.

On the other side of the house, when we sit on the back porch, we can't see any stores or houses in town day or night, but at night, we can see the halo of the city lights reaching miles high into the dark sky. There are many times when we see powerful searchlights dancing as giant flashlight wands stretching and searching far off to the earth's neighboring planets. Mother says these searchlights possibly mark the opening of another store, and it's certain when Chester's Pontiac Dealership opened, he had searchlights tempting customers to his showroom.

By five o'clock, we are usually home from the store, and that's when I like to sit on the back porch and listen to the huge loud speakers mounted on top of the Methodist Church up town. The speakers are connected to a record player, and the crystal clear notes of 'The Old Rugged Cross,' 'Come Home,' 'Blessed Assurance Jesus is Mine,' 'Go Tell It on the Mountain,' and my favorite, 'In the Garden'. This beautiful music floats all the way out to our house. Mother says if the land between here and town were covered with tall trees instead of plowed fields, well then the sound would be muffled and would not reach our porch. In that case, I'm very glad for the plowed fields. Recently however, Mother amended her reasoning when I told her that Charles Downey and Robert Allen told me at the pool, that the new Methodist minister Reverend Irwin has decided to blast some of our good Tallapoosa citizens off the bar stools at Bruno's by cranking the speaker volume to the loudest possible notch. The Minister Irwin chose five o'clock because that's when the manufacturing plants end their workday, and many of the workers go straight from work to Bruno's Beer Joint. Mother and I think it's a funny story, and we imagine the yellow bricks of the Methodist

Church chattering like false teeth with every boom of the base notes, but we are in the perfect position to really appreciate the music which is at music box volume by the time it travels three miles to us, but back up town, it's not a laughing matter inside the Downey home right there directly across the street from the Methodist Church. Charles says he thinks he's getting hard of hearing and maybe even deaf as a result, and his daddy, Dr. Downey gets all blustery with indignation every time five o'clock rolls around, and he says he's for sure not getting one tiny little bit more religious, but actually the opposite is the case, and that's where Charles said, "Janet, my mother said I'd better not be repeating a single word of what Daddy says."

Charles says his mother closes all the windows and doors and puts cotton in her ears just so she can cook supper, but it's easier for Charles and his brother Carrol to ride their bikes out to the ball park or anywhere, any direction just so long as it's away from home and the Methodist Church. Finally, after months of eardrum splitting chimes, Dr. Downey decided his only course of action was to survey the results inside Bruno's Beer Joint.

Inside the beer joint, the jukebox was playing at a nice modest volume, and a worker in a booth against the west wall stood up to shake his Doctor's hand, and another former patient asked the Doctor if he could buy him a beer, but the Doctor declined appreciating the offer just the same, then another worker told a very funny joke and everyone including Bruno had a good laugh. All this took place in a quiet, somewhat dark and smoky, very comfortable small room. Dr. Downey's inquisition definitively ruled out loud chimes as even the slightest imposition on the beer drinkers, and in fact, if these workers are inside Bruno's Beer Joint every day at five o'clock, it stands to reason that not a single worker has the slightest notion that outside the confines of Bruno's beer joint there are deafening chimes running the remainder of Tallapoosa's citizens completely out of their minds. With the scientific results presented above, Dr. Downey, made his way from Bruno's Beer Joint to the Methodist Church manse, where he knocked on the front door, and as Minister Irwin opened the door, Dr. Downey caught him pulling cotton from his own ears. The Minister asked the Doctor to come in and the Doctor presented his findings, and ended with the plea, "I beg of you, please turn down the volume!"

With that, the Minister ventured to assess the results and moaned, "If the loud chimes do not disturb the beer drinkers, and in fact, the loud chimes sent you INTO the beer joint, well then the score is beer joint plus one, and church minus one. I'm convinced the whole endeavor is an abysmal failure."

Three miles east of town, this precipitated a marked downgrade of my private-back-porch-chimes- entertainment which from that day forward literally became as fickle as the wind, no really the only time the chimes are audible on my back porch is in the event of a fairly steady west wind.

July 13, 1954
Dear Family,

Carroll and Bobby Key are the cooks, and they are getting pretty good at it. There's always a lot of joking and carrying on like Bud can't tell if they battered and fried up some deer droppings instead of potatoes just as a means a getting back at us for complaining about the food. But they are learning to cook biscuits just about as good as your mother's. They tell us it takes three days a boiling dry beans so's they're tender enough to eat. Carroll has decided it's the high altitude (we are in the mountains) and Carroll has come up with some confounding explanation that water boils at a lower temperature at higher altitudes. Or I might have that backwards. That's neither here nor there.

Love,
Your Daddy

July 21, 1954
Dear Daddy,

We went swimming two days this week. I am working toward being a good swimmer, I can swim laps back and forth from side to side in the shallow end, but I can't dive off the side because I still have to hold my nose, but I can swim one time from one side to the other side in the deep end.

Love,
Janet

July 19, 1954
Dear Family,

At night after supper I read your letters to everybody, and they read their letters out loud too. We get a kick out of hearing about what is happening in Georgia. Sometimes I get homesick, but it helps that Carroll is here with me. I dread when he has to go back home, but he's already paid the money to West Georgia Junior College, and he needs to get a good education. We work from sun up to sun down, and we eat our breakfast and our supper by the light of kerosene lamps. We saw a bear yesterday. He stayed out of our way and we stayed out of his. He acted a little afraid of the loud power saws and saw mill. We see lots of deer every day. They walk right up to us, but we scare them away.

Love,
Your Daddy

July 19,1954
Dear Daddy,

Mother wants a map of New Mexico, and please mark your location. I think that is a very good idea. If you can take some pictures with the brownie, send the undeveloped roll of film and Mother will send it off at Roberts Drug Store.

Love,
Janet

July 20,1954
Dear Family,

Carroll, Bobby Key and Dink Daniel are planning to leave about the middle of August to come home. It makes me sad to say goodbye, but at the same time I'm glad for Carroll to get started on his college education. Mr. Blevins says I might have to drive them to Socorro, New Mexico where they can get a bus north to Alamosa, Colorado, and from there they can connect to a bus heading east. They have earned some pretty good money for working long hours from sun up to sun down every day including Sunday plus Carroll and Bobby Key got a bonus for serving as our cooks all summer. Every time Mr. Blevins pays me, I turn right around and pay my hands.

Love,
Your Daddy

If the neighbors around the store need to buy a can of Campbell's soup or a box of Babbo detergent, or a tube of Ipana toothpaste, they understand that Mother is performing a great balancing act splitting her time four ways for her children while running the household and the country store, and the store saves gas for the entire settlement if they buy their incidentals right there rather than driving four miles into Tallapoosa. So when they need something, they first look out their window to see if the 1954 blue and white Chevrolet is parked in front of the store, and as a result, during the time that the 1954 Chevrolet is parked in front of the store just about all the neighbors are drawn to the village meeting place, which makes for a party atmosphere that takes place when the worker's eight hour shift is done and one by one they get out of their carpool car in front of the store. Mother plans her day around her customers, and she knows they come in very tired, but ready to have a little fun. In the country store unlike Bruno's Beer Joint, the refreshment is a Co-cola with peanuts poured into the bottle. And while the grow-ups are laughing and carrying on inside the store, the kids are playing outside never lacking purpose in the invention of the next great game.

I like to play outside with the kids, but some days I like to stay inside and listen to the grownups, and usually by the end of the day, I have a list of questions for Mother, like what does 'I swanny' mean? Mother thinks it's some mild form of 'I swear' because actually saying 'I swear' is impolite, and next I asked Mother what does it mean to get your 'hackles up'? Mother knows exactly what that one means, "Hackles are in fact, a rooster's neck feathers which buzz out and stand up when he's in a fight and hackles also refers to a cat's or dog's neck hair, and although people don't have feathers they do sometimes feel that the hair on their neck might be standing up"

I know what it means to walk along at a slow pace, but what does 'slow poke' mean? Mother can't help me with 'slow poke' and I answer my own question about why the last in line is called a 'cow's tail' that's because the cow's tail is at the back end of the cow.

August 3, 1954
Dear Family,

There is a closer post office to send letters, so from now on, send them to: Magdalena New Mexico. One of Mr. Blevins' drivers told us about Magdalena so last Saturday, we decided to take the day off, and we found the dirt roads that got us to Magdalena in about 55 minutes. That's a good bit closer than Grants. I stopped by the Post Office in Magdalena so they will expect letters from Tallapoosa, Georgia.

Love, Daddy
P.S. Happy Birthday, Dolly Dimples

On Saturday night, August 21st, the telephone rang, and I ran to answer, and Carroll said "Hello, Sugar!"

I screamed my big brother's name into the phone and probably broke his ear drum on the other end of the telephone line, and Mother came running to the telephone like she might be worried, but just in a second, Mother smiled that smile that can melt your heart into a worthless body organ hanging suspended in your chest. Carroll and Bobby Key and Dink Daniel arrived in Alamosa, Colorado on a bus from Socorro New Mexico. When they went inside the cafe that serves as the bus station, the man working behind the counter told them the bus heading out of town to the east might show up in three days, or at least that is the schedule, but that bus comes all the way from California and the mountain roads sometimes cause unheard of delays, but "You're welcome to take a room at the hotel across the street."

The three sat down on two hard benches in a corner of the bus station/ cafe and methodically they examined their alternatives. If they got a hotel room, maybe the bus would show up in three days, but by then they'd have to pay the hotel bill and then more than likely they would not have enough money to buy their bus tickets, and besides who wants to waste time sitting around in a hotel room? No, the hotel room is out! Ok then, maybe they could hitchhike back to Georgia, but they'd probably have to split up because how many drivers would have room for three hitchhikers? Not many, and they don't want to split up. No, hitchhiking is out! Ok then they could start walking but that was foolish because it would take a year to walk all the way back to Georgia. No, walking is definitely out! The only alternative is to buy a car and start driving across the country, and Bobby Key wants to buy a car anyway, and really the main reason he wanted to be a part of the crew on this amazing adventure was because he wanted to make enough money to buy a car, and he knew if he worked all summer pumping gas in Tallapoosa which is about the only job available to a teenage boy, well one summer working pumping gas won't pay enough to buy a bicycle let alone a car. So that settled it, Bobby Key bought a car in Alamosa Colorado. It is a pretty good car too, it's a 1948 Ford Coupe, and it has four new tires on it and a pretty good spare tire. That's when Carroll called home collect, and Mother in turn called Bobby Key's family and Ora Daniel with the news they're driving across the country in Bobby's Ford Coupe.

August 17,1954
Dear Family,

I drove Carroll and Bobby Key and Dink Daniel to catch the bus in Socorro New Mexico this morning, and I waited about a hour with them, but the bus is late, so I'm writing this so I can mail it to you before I leave Socorro, that way you'll have some idee when to expect their bus in Tallapoosa. I got a long drive back so's I can get back to work. I am going to tell you all right here and now how much I love my family, because I sure do. I wish Carroll could stay with me, but he and Bobby have to get back home in time for the start of school, Bobby will be a senior in Tallapoosa High School, and Carroll will start his first year at West Georgia Junior College. I'll drop this in the post office and be on my way back to the campsite. I'll be glad to get to work.

Love,
Your Daddy

The last Friday night before the start of school, Lou Newman and Mother took their little children (and that includes me and Francis, thank goodness) to the Drive-In-Theater. Mother and Lou packed supper, and we ate in the car while watching a Dean Martin - Jerry Lewis picture show. Mother made enough fried baloney sandwiches for everyone, and Lou made chocolate cake for dessert. Mother wrapped each individual sandwich in waxed paper, and Lou cut the flat cake into three-inch squares and wrapped each piece in waxed paper. The sandwiches and the cake were messy, but it was no problem because Mother planned ahead and brought a bucket full of clean wet bath-cloths enough for everyone. The picture show was funny, but not as funny as we made it out to be because each giggle in the car caused a ripple effect, and doubled and re-doubled in intensity and pretty soon it didn't matter what was happening on the big outdoor screen, our only reaction was laughter.

The next day, the last Saturday before school, the Thread Mill had a company picnic, a fish fry at Alec's Lake (the pool). The pool was closed to everyone except Thread Mill employees and their families. The cooks kept fish frying constantly because the huge crowd of people were invited to come back for seconds and even third helpings, but working with huge quantities of fish presented a dilemma for the cooks, and at one point a couple of the crates of fish were mistakenly left stacked in the panel trucks too long. All the ice cubes melted, but when the cooks opened the crates, the fish looked good and had no bad odor, so the two crates were dropped into the vats of boiling hot frying lard without a second thought. There might have been a little doubt as to the lard's freshness because one cook wondered out loud about the slightly rancid whiff coming from the giant vats, but as the wind picked up the odor was blown away and quickly forgotten. Every Thread Mill employee went from enjoying the fish dinner to jumping in for a refreshing swim in the pool, but pretty soon everything turned sour when a diver on the high dive, leaned over the side rail and vomited onto the grass below. The vile smell prompted another to throw up, and a chain reaction shuddered like a tidal wave through the crowd, and swimmers hurried to climb out of the pool or else contaminate the water. The food poisoning passed rapidly from one to the next, to the next, to then next, and no one seemed immune, but for the few still healthy, it became a matter of urgency to crank up and drive away hopefully to distance themselves and find safety in there own homes. It wasn't meant to be, and the food poisoning became an epidemic. The first and worst of the sick made their feeble way to the Downey Clinic. Sara Walker, alone in the clinic on a Saturday afternoon, called the Doctor and practically before she could hang up the phone, Dr. Downey rushed into the building, through the waiting room, around behind the nurse's desk and into the patient rooms. One by one, he examined the sick and administered drugs until his medicine supply was depleted, but still outside the front door the long line of the poisoned puking into their own buckets reached all the way to Bowman's store. Sara Walker called both local pharmacists, Ken Roberts and Charles Hilderbrand and they emptied their drug store shelves and delivered the supplies to the Downey Clinic.

At that time, we had another Doctor in Tallapoosa, Dr. Allen set up his offices in the building between the Downey Clinic and Bowman's store, but that particular weekend Dr. Allen and his family, were out of town on vacation.

Carroll's home! He won't be riding the school bus anymore, and that means I have to walk through the wet grass, but I'm selfish to think only about me. I have to think about somebody else besides me. Carroll has it arranged that his ride to West Georgia Junior College in Carrollton will come by our house, and Carroll and two more riders will pay a little to help buy gas. It's good to have Carroll home from New Mexico even though the only time he's actually in the house is when he's sleeping.

I love school, I love the teachers, I love to read and write and do arithmetic, I love making friends and this year Linda Sue Chandler, and Linda Dobbs, are in my class again. We've been together in first grade (Mrs. Fitzgerald) and second grade (Mrs. McClendon) and now in third grade (Mrs. Simanton). I love all my teachers, and I have a lot of friends who are not in my class like Kristina Walton and Laura Hill Merrill and Connie Gentry, and Janet Wood and I guess I made friends with Kristina and Laura Hill through Connie who was in my second grade class. I like the boys too. It's fun to ride the merry go round when Jack Nixon and Denver Morgan are pushing because they make it go really fast. I like to play red rover, red rover because Jimmy and Johnny Thrower, Rod Lipham, and Robert Allen always call to 'send Janet right over' because they know I can't begin to break even the weakest link, so they get to add me to their side, and of course they put me on the end, and of course the next person called to break through (to my new side no matter who it is) knows the best link to break is at my end of the human chain, and so when my weak link is broken the strategy is always the same and that is to take the strongest person back to the other side, and that person is usually Denver Morgan. Anyway, I get shuffled back and forth, but I like it.

Every Friday the teachers organize a race, a whole grammar school race, and it's a pretty long race too, the starting line is even with the swings and the finish line is all the way to the merry go round, and every one has to run in the race, and in the case of running fast, I think being light weight is to my advantage, because I win the race just about every Friday! I beat the whole grammar school! It's wonderful to win at something physical, and because I'm a fast runner, when we choose soft ball teams, I get called early and sometimes I'm the first one called, and to make it even better, I'm a good batter too. My specialties are running and batting, and I can sometimes hit a home run. I can't catch or pitch, but I can hit and run! Golly gee, winning is so exciting that sometimes I can barely breath.

Carroll has a Saturday job, he rides his Famous James motorcycle to the Dixie Bakery in Bremen because Uncle Thomas gave him a one-day-a-week job. Carroll calls this job his 'pie route,' and it sounds pretty good. Carroll gets up early and arrives at the Dixie Bakery about six o'clock, just as the fresh baked goods are coming out of the huge ovens. If there are any celebration cakes, they went into the ovens first, and they come out of the ovens first so they can cool a bit before Uncle Thomas writes special celebrations and names on the newly spread icing. As boxes are filled and labels are attached, Carroll loads up the panel truck according to a list of orders and then he drives from delivery to delivery in and around Bremen, Buchanan, and Tallapoosa and Waco. Once those deliveries are completed in about five hours, Carroll returns to the Dixie Bakery where the huge ovens are once again emptied and this time they are turned off as the bake day comes to an end, and this time the pies, cakes, cream horns, and breads are already packed in labeled boxes, and as the last chore of their work day, the other workers have loaded up another panel truck allowing Carroll to make a quick turnaround leaving the empty panel truck and pulling out in the loaded panel truck and this time he delivers to Temple, Bowdon Junction, Carrollton, and Bowdon. Uncle Thomas has two full time weekday panel truck drivers, both work eight-hour delivery shifts five days a week. On weekdays it takes a little extra time at each stop because the next day's orders must be discussed and the order forms filled out and collected. On Fridays, the full time delivery drivers collect orders for both Saturday and for Monday, thereby relieving Carroll of any connection to that chore. Carroll's Saturday workday already goes from about six a.m. to five p.m. with no time allowed for taking orders. While Carroll is making the morning deliveries, the Bakery is buzzing with workers mixing and baking to fill the afternoon deliveries allowing Carroll to work one eleven hour shift and deliver the same amount of goods as the two eight hour week day drivers. Carroll says it's good pay and good work because of course he likes to drive, and all three panel trucks are the latest model, and whenever the panel trucks are out on the road they are advertising for the Dixie Bakery since 'Dixie Bakery' is spelled out on both sides, and that leads to the second reason why Carroll likes the job, he gets to visit 1) with the store owners and 2) with other customers who like the products produced at the Dixie Bakery. Carroll says this pie route is the perfect way to spend his Saturdays and getting paid for it is a very nice added bonus.

On Saturday mornings, Mother scurries around the house getting the work done before she loads everyone in the Chevrolet, first she takes Joan and Marilyn into town to work, and while in town Mother buys sewing supplies at Lipham's and gets stamps at the post office and usually somebody's shoes need mending so she leaves a pair of shoes at the shoe shop, and she leaves and picks up dry cleaning because we wear a lot of wool clothing. Carroll has two sports coats and two pairs of dress pants, and Joan and Marilyn have a few wool suits, (which Mother made of course) and I have a wool sweater set, it's a dark green and the under sweater is sleeveless and has pearls sewn into the neck line and these pearls match the same design sewn into the long sleeve top sweater. Mother made me a matching dark green cotton print skirt gathered full at the waistband. The print design is rows of little white fish.

Almost every Friday night, I spend the night with Ruth and Otto. I have been spending Friday nights with Ruth and Otto just about as far back as I can remember, and I understand why it means so much to Ruth and Otto, because their only baby Shirley died at birth two months before I was born. Ruth and Otto are good to me, and now that Daddy is in New Mexico, both Ruth and Otto are especially kind and loving, and I try never to let them see me crying, which I do every night before I go to sleep. If I let anyone know that I cry every night it would just make them sad too (I'm not talking about my Mother not knowing because my Mother knows everything), so I keep my tears to myself, and it's when I repeat the memorized prayer, "Now I lay me down to sleep, I pray the Lord my soul to keep, If I should die before I wake, I pray the Lord my soul to take."

I can get though that part o k, but after saying that part, I start my list of 'God Blesses' and of course my first 'God Bless' is my Daddy, and that's when I visualize my Daddy looking through a crack in the wall at five stars and one of the stars is named Janet. There's something so sad about that, it's not fair that Daddy began his adult life when his Pa died when Daddy was my age, and it's not fair that Ruth and Otto lost their only baby two months before I was born healthy. When I spend the night with Ruth and Otto, the next morning sometimes I follow Otto through the fields, and it's a game I like to play that I step only in his footprints, and to make the game a little more fun, sometimes he lengthens his steps and in that case, I have to leap through the air, and then he shortens his steps and the smaller the steps get the more I have to giggle watching big old Otto taking sissy steps, anyway, Saturday mornings are busy with Ruth and Otto, and I know the fun we have helps them deal with their loneliness, but about noon we get cleaned up and since noon in their house in Alabama is eleven o'clock in my house in Georgia by the time we get cleaned up and drive into town it's time for dinner in Georgia at noon so they take me to dinner in town, mostly we eat at the Southern Cafe where I order chili (which is chili poured over a slice of loaf bread), but sometimes we eat at Hat's on Head Avenue where I order a hamburger, then after dinner, Ruth and Otto deliver me to the store, and by the end of the day, when it's time to close up the store, Mother loads us up in the Chevrolet and we take off up town to get Joan and Marilyn. At home after supper, Joan and Marilyn take their baths early and wash their hair, then Joan uses bobby pins to pin curl her hair, and I'm next in the bathtub, and mother washes my hair at the kitchen sink, and mother is teaching me how to pin curl my hair. She says the key is to pick up a section of hair and start a curl at the end of the hair then roll it up around and around keeping the hair tip ends in the middle of the curl until the curl is touching the scalp, then with one hand hold the curl flat to the scalp and open a bobby pin with the other hand and pin the curl to the scalp. Mother won't let us open the bobby pin with our teeth, she's like Papa always wanting us to take care of our teeth. By the way, Marilyn has naturally curly hair so she doesn't have to pin curl, but sometimes she sort of pin curls large sections of hair because she says it kind of straightens some of the tightest curls.

Next, on the Saturday night agenda is to watch television, Mother sits in the wing back chair, and as we watch intently, first the baby (he's almost two) crawls into Mother's lap, then pretty soon, I crawl into the wing back chair and lean against Mother, and she pats me and makes me feel like somebody, It's so cozy and I love it with both of us in Mother's lap, but we are careful not to bring Joan's attention to the situation because many times when Joan catches two of us in Mother's lap, she actually starts yelling at us to, "Get out of Mother's lap, you're both too big to be sitting in Mother's lap, you are big enough to understand that Mother needs a break."

Joan's like that, but I'll bet you one thing, when she was little like us, I'll bet a whole lot of money that she sat in Mother's lap too. Anyway, when she starts yelling, we get out of Mother's lap and lie down stomach down on the linoleum floor facing the television. Mother buys a new linoleum rug every spring during spring-cleaning which is when Joan and Marilyn dismantle the wood burning warming stove and chimney pipes and haul the heavy warming stove out to the garage for the summer. Joan and Marilyn and Mother get dressed up in ragged old work clothes most of which are Daddy's and Carroll's worn out jeans and shirts and they wear the rags to take down and move the pot belly stove because whatever they are wearing is ruined the minute they touch the black soot. When the big old warming stove is out of the way, Joan and Marilyn (mostly Marilyn) paint the walls, covering up the smoke stains, and sometimes they roll up the old linoleum rugs and carry them to the garbage pile down below the house, and other times they roll out the new linoleum rugs on top of the old ones, but this stack of linoleum rugs can't be too high or else everyone trips over the edge sticking up in the air. Every year at spring cleaning time, Mother gets Carroll and his friends to load two upholstered chairs or the couch into the back of the pickup truck only now our pickup truck is in New Mexico so Mother borrows one from Chester or Jack. We have four upholstered chairs and the upholstered couch, and once every year mother hauls two upholstered chairs or the couch to the Upholstery Shop, and for about a week, instead of the soft upholstered missing furniture, we sit on hard chairs brought in from the kitchen. Mother calls this her rotation procedure, which results in never having on display old worn out upholstered furniture.

Oh yes, I almost forgot, there is one other spring time ritual, every year Mother pays a visit to Thelma Collins and brings home a Wandering Jew plant. You see, our big old house is so drafty that inside in the winter time the temperature drops below freezing for at least one night, and one night below thirty two degrees is all it takes to kill the Wandering Jew plant, but Thelma's house is more air tight than ours, and so every fall, Thelma starts a new plant from a few cuttings off of her giant Wandering Jew plant, and by spring cleaning time, the new-start Wandering Jew plant is ready for Mother to pick it up, and it has become a tradition by now, and both Mother and Thelma rejoice in the friendly arrangement, and I've heard both these ladies laughing that it's just another fine excuse to visit.

Anyway, back to sitting in Mother's lap, we stay on the linoleum floor for a while lying on our stomachs, kicking our feet back and forth, and propping our chins in our hands, but it's not long until both of us are back in the wing back chair with Mother. It's just the coziest place in the world to be, and besides we're a little jittery on Saturday nights waiting for the telephone to ring, and usually about eight o'clock it rings, but somebody is usually standing right by the telephone and that somebody grabs up the receiver on the first ring (cut-short), and somebody else turns off the television, and we take turns talking to Daddy. There's a pay telephone booth in Magdalena. I miss my Daddy.

Joan works at Roberts Drug Store two hours on Sunday morning, and I ride with Joan to town and while she is working I go to Sunday school and church. Between Sunday school and church, all the Sunday school children walk up to the Drug Store, and we order a coke from Joan, and we sit at the little tables and drink our cokes, and then we hurry back to church, and I usually sit with Kristina and her mother. Connie, Jane, Kristina, and Laura Hill have been good friends of mine since first grade when we danced in the chorus line to "Diamonds Are a Girl's Best Friend." Kristina's mother wants me to call her Ona Faye, but that's hard for me to do. She is so nice and sweet, and she brings Kristina's little sister Teresa to the nursery, and sometimes when Kristina and I get fidgety in church, she hands us little note pads and pencils, and Kristina and I pass notes back and forth. I get serious and sing along during the hymns, I love to sing, and many times I feel compelled to walk down the isle during the repeated last verse of the last hymn, especially if it's 'Come Home' or 'Just As I Am.' I try to be a good Christian, and I like to go to church, and Mother makes lots of nice dresses for me, and I have white dress up shoes and white lace edged socks, and my Sunday school teacher tells me how lucky I am to have a Mother who can sew, and I know that.

Last Sunday, Kristina and her mother were not in church, but Brenda Cobb and her mother Arbelle were in church so I sat with them. Brenda's mother wants me to call her Arbelle and I do. It seems o k to call her Arbelle because the first time I met Brenda's mother she told me about when she was a baby herself and her parents took her to Dr. Godwin because she had a big, old, fist size pone on the side of her neck. Arbelle wanted me to know that my Daddy's brother was the Dr. Godwin in the story. Brenda is another really good friend of mine, even though so far we've had different teachers in school. That day in church, Brenda and I didn't get fidgety at all, and in fact, we both listened to every word preacher Skaggs said, and at the end when the preacher made his appeal to 'give your life to Jesus', I could do nothing else. The music director lead as we sang all the verses of 'Just As I Am', and then the preacher said a few more words to emphasize the invitation, and finally the music director lead as we sang the last verse one more time and that's when I gave in and answered the irresistible pull. It was a compelling, defining moment singing the last verse softly almost in a whisper and acappella for added mystic. I was very sober about walking down that isle, because I want to honor the teachings of Jesus. I truly believe that it's wrong to judge other people, and I truly believe that every human being is worthy of love and dignity, and I have some first hand experience about what happens when a person is judged to be less than worthy. I know my Daddy did a very brave thing when he took Posey Greer into our home, I have heard my Daddy talking to Posey Greer, and I figure somebody has been mean to Posey Greer, and I'm old enough to know that's a sin against Jesus.

At the door, I shook the preachers hand and walked out of the education building, and Joan pulled the Chevrolet up close to the sidewalk, and as soon as she stopped the car, Mother opened the back door and I climbed into the back seat with Mother and Randall. Marilyn was in the front seat and I was happy to tell my family that I just joined the church, and then I added, "Mother, the preacher will baptize me at the Bremen First Baptist Church on Tuesday after school, and I'll be the only person he baptizes that day so it won't take long."

Just as we passed Obey Laminack's house, Joan slowed down and veered to the left to drive down the hill along side Obey's pasture fence, Joan drove though the shallow little branch at the bottom of the first hill, and when she drove across the bridge at the big creek that's always my cue to climb over the seat and into the front. As usual, I rested my chin on the dash board, and held my breath until we rounded the hill top, and magically, before our very eyes appeared the most perfect place on earth, and yes, when I climbed the steps to the porch and skipped over to Papa, thankfully, my ears flopped just like they're supposed to. I want to live m life like Mama and Papa and Mother and Daddy, they're good to everybody, and everybody knows they are fair in all things.

My Daddy helps a lot of people all the time, we don't know who or when or how because Daddy never advertises, but somehow we found out that Daddy went all over the county taking up money to rebuild a house that burned and left the family without a home.

Our Christmas parties at school were on Friday, December 17, 1954, and school was out til Monday, January 3, 1955. I spent the night with Ruth and Otto, and on my way home we had dinner in town, this time at Hat's on Head Avenue, and then Otto went into the Pool Hall to shoot a game or two, and that made me miss Daddy because if he were in Georgia instead of way out in New Mexico, he'd for sure be shooting pool with Otto. Ruth and I first went into the National Clothing Store next to the Pool Hall and Ruth bought a new shirt for Otto, and to keep the secret, the lady working in the National put the shirt in a box and wrapped it in red and green Christmas paper. Next, we went into the Dime Store just on the other side of the Grand Theater, and Ruth held my hand and together we walked up and down each of the four wide aisles. It was an amazing way to look at toys because holding Ruth's hand meant I didn't have to look where I was going, instead I looked only at the toys, and on a very high shelf way above my head, I found a tea set that was the prettiest thing I've ever seen. We wandered through the Dime Store for a long time, and each doll was more beautiful than the last, and every play stove and ironing board seemed to glisten, and I saw another baby doll bed just like the one I have at home. There was a Dale Evans set that included guns, holsters, and a cowgirl hat all packed in a box with a clear cellophane cover. Every thing in the Dime Store was unattainable both physically because it was out of my reach, but also unattainable because of the huge prices. I certainly did not say a word about wanting anything, that's never been my style. The Dime Store has always been a place for me to look and not touch. I distinctly remember looking at the tea set many times that day. It was high on a shelf, completely beyond touch. It was packed in a green box, and each precious breakable cup and saucer, the teapot, the cream pitcher, and the sugar bowl fit perfectly into it's own specially cut out place, and I was spellbound by the tiny flowers painted on each piece. Too soon it was time to go. Otto met us at the car, and we drove to the store. After Ruth and Otto left, I told mother about all the toys in the Dime Store, but I didn't dare tell her about the tea set. It wouldn't have been right.

The next Monday Carroll had no classes, and he went with me to find and cut down a Christmas tree. It's always fun to be around Carroll, he talks about the future when we are grown up with a college education, and we are scientists or teachers or doctors or lawyers, and no dream is too big because we don't mind hard work, and the hard work of getting a good education will prepare us to do important things like discovering cures for horrible diseases. Carroll's lofty thinking is inspiring, and I love to dream along with him because I have a feeling down deep inside that he's right! I found the tree I wanted, and Carroll cut it down, dragged it back to the house, and nailed cross boards to the trunk, Carroll offered to help me decorate the tree, and when he discovered the orderly strings of lights that

I methodically put away last year, he said, "See, this is an excellent example of problem solving. Bravo, little sister!"

As soon as the sun went down, we plugged in the Christmas tree lights, and as usual the tree was misshapen and honestly ugly, but also as usual, no one complained because who in the world could begin to hope to find a loblolly pine tree in the shape of a Christmas Tree. That year the television was on the north wall side of the living room next to the up right piano, and before Mother finished her work and came into the living room, Randall and I were lying on the floor on our stomachs watching television and laughing to high heaven at Sid Caesar and Imogene Coca. Soon after Mother came to join us, Randall crawled into her lap, but I stayed on the floor as the three of us watched 'Babes In Toy Land' and during a commercial, I noticed a new present under the tree. I waited until again everyone was engrossed in the picture show then I slid the new present across the floor over in front of me, and I could read the faint pencil writing on the wrapping paper, 'To Janet, From Ruth & Otto."

Thinking that no one was watching me, I put my head down on the floor and tried to lift the paper away from the box, and if I held my head at just the right angle, I could barely see the top of the box inside the paper. My heart began to pound when I saw the color of the box! It was a green box! An involuntary tear dropped from my eye and splashed on the floor as I dared to hope for the unthinkable. Christmas wasn't until Saturday, how could I restrain myself until Saturday? Every night I went through the same ritual until one night I accidentally ripped the wrapping paper a little. Oh, why did I do such a thing? I was horrified to think someone might realize I'd torn the paper, no one said anything, but my guilt was a huge burden. On Christmas morning, I opened the tea set first, I planned it that way knowing as soon as the torn paper was ripped off in shreds, the evidence against me would finally and forever be destroyed, and I would be rid of the painful disgrace I carried on my rounded shoulders, and I promised myself never again will I ever get into a situation of such calamitous disadvantage.

Mother's wringer type washing machine broke right after New Year's Day 1955, and she figured we'd have to buy another one, unless Carroll can find the time to work on it, but that's doubtful because Carroll is taking a full load of courses at West Georgia, and working his 'pie route' all day every Saturday, but there is a handy alternative washing machine up town, a brand new coin operated Laundry Mat opened up, and after school one day, Mother loaded up all the huge pile of dirty clothes tied into sheets (opposite corners tied over the bundle), and we headed up town. The Laundry Mat occupies the middle unit of a brand new three unit building just down the hill off Highway 78 on Robertson Avenue. Inside the brand new coin operated Laundry Mat everything is clean and sparkling, the floor tiles are the new wear resistant kind, and the left side of the long room displays a line up of brand new washing machines from the front picture window to the back wall. There are a few brand new clothes-folding-tables scattered down the middle of the room, and two more new tables stand side by side along the back wall, the big new automatic clothes dryers back up to the other windowless wall opposite from the automatic washing machines, but the line up of automatic dryers extends only about midway from the front door to the back wall because one huge dryer can easily dry all the clothes washed in three or even four washing machines. Along the right wall where the dryers stop there is a long 'bench' made up of formed individual chairs. Mother told me to stay right with the baby every second and, "Keep him inside, while I sort the colored clothes from the whites."

Mother thinks of everything, and this time she brought a book for me to read to Randall, and I had the big old baby on my lap for a little while until he got too heavy and cut off the circulation to my feet, so then I put him down in his own formed chair seat, and I sat in the next chair seat and continued reading and leaning over to let Ran see the pictures. The long row of formed composite, extremely modern straight-back chairs were individually mounted and seemed suspended in air, but on closer scrutiny they are welded in place along three 15 foot long steel rods, one 15 foot rod runs along behind the chair backs, another 15 foot rod runs along under the seats exactly at the bend from seat to back, and the last 15 foot rod runs along the floor connecting all the center support posts of each chair bottom. This floor rod has balancing feet all along the floor to keep the whole thing from tilting back or forward. This long bench made up of connected colorful chairs serves as seating for ten people.

Randall tired of the book reading and I took him out front where we watched the rain coming down slightly on the cement side walk/front porch under the long brown metal awning, which handily channels the rain to down spouts at each end of the wide building. Mother was busy packing the last of the colored clothes into washing machine number five when I opened the front glass door and urgently slipped Randall through the opening all the while yelling, "Mother, Mother! Mother! Stop! You can't put the colored clothes in these machines. We'll have to take the colored clothes back home, you can't put colored clothes in these machines!"

Mother stopped loading the colored clothes and faced me and with her hands splayed on her sides, she asked, "What?"

I looked straight ahead at Mother and with my right hand I led to look at the front door, "Right there on the front door it says in big letters, WHITE ONLY! Right there on the front door."

I wondered what had just happened to make tears well up in my Mother's eyes. I was baffled, and I felt like I'd said something very mean, and my sweet Mother finally cupped her face into her hands and said, "Honey, it doesn't mean clothes. It doesn't mean 'white only' clothes."

At this, I felt indignant with incomprehension and I demanded quietly, "Well what in the world does it mean?"

Mother said, "Honey, it means white people only."

Then it was my turn, "You mean Thelma can't wash her clothes here?"

That minute is when like my Daddy at age eight, I became an adult, that minute I carried this knowledge a step farther, and that minute I realized that's why Posey Greer looks like somebody has been really mean and stomped him into the ground.

January 10, 1955
Dear Daddy,

I am sorry that I did not write you last week. I know I broke my promise to write you every week, and I don't have any excuse, but I am sorry.

I hope we never have to be apart at Christmas again. I think I should be ashamed of myself because all of us here in Georgia have each other to help us get through the lonely missing you, but you have nobody except your saw mill hands to help you get through the lonely missing us.

Carroll is taking another full load of classes this quarter, and he'll continue with his Saturday morning 'pie route.'

We're all fine except for missing you!

Love,
Janet

Last week when I should have written a letter to Daddy, I was preoccupied thinking up questions about what Thelma and her family can do and what Thelma and her family can't do besides use the brand new coin operated Laundry Mat. Mother settled most of my questions by driving me around town and asking me to read out loud WHITE ONLY signs on the front doors of most stores, then my question was, "Well where do colored people buy their groceries, and shoes and clothes and cloth and seeds?"

Mother revealed, "They can't go inside the stores except through the back door."

"Mother, where does Georgia go to school?"

To answer that question, Mother drove me right up to the colored school called Carver, and that old shackledy building might just fall right down on top of the colored children one day. Every day at the store, I look out the window toward Posey's shack, and there's never any smoke coming out, and about the fourth or fifth day, Mother and Vergie Newman and Lou Newman and Lavada Goolsby, and Barbara Goolsby all walked out to Posey's shack. The four white ladies knocked on the door and waited and waited and knocked some more, and finally Mother opened the door, and Posey is not there. Mother said, "Posey's Sunday go to meeting new clothes are hanging on a nail in the corner by his bed. His new shoes are visible under the foot of his bed which is made up as clean and neat as can be, and there's coffee in a cup sitting on the table beside a plate of cold turnip greens."

Mother and Vergie and Lou and Lavada and Barbara talk about Posey all the time now, and nobody can remember the last time they saw Posey, but it was way back before Christmas. I want to write Daddy and tell him about Posey, but Mother said, "You can't do that to your Daddy. He's way out in the mountains over a thousand miles from here, and there's nothing he can do about Posey, and if we tell him Posey is missing, he'll just grieve, but there's nothing he can do about it."

I know Mother is right, but it sure is hard to write to Daddy and keep a secret from him. At home that night, Mother went to the front door when somebody knocked, and it was Thelma and first thing, we all wondered why she knocked, she usually opens the door and makes the sing song 'Who ooo' sound, and then she comes on in, but not this time, this time she waited for Mother to open the door. In the living room, Thelma sat down in the wing back chair and didn't say anything for a long time, and finally Mother stood up and crossed the floor and Thelma stood up and they hugged each other, and Mother said through her tears, "Posey's missing."

"Yes um, Posey's been missing a long time, Louise told us last Sunday."

Mother said, "Sis tells me all you have to do is look at her sweet little boy to know who his white daddy is, but nobody is brave enough to mess with him. Can you tell me?"

"No'um, I can't tell you because we're all better off leaving that white man alone. He's mean as a rattlesnake."

I stayed in the room with Mother and Thelma because I was starting to think what my Daddy would do if he were here right now, and I almost decided to blurt it out to Thelma, but Mother quickly smoothed down my hair as a loving warning, so I didn't say what I wanted to say. But I'm sure when Daddy finds out about this, I am sure, as sure as I am that the sun will rise in the morning that my Daddy will have something to say to the white man who is as mean as a rattlesnake. Thelma stayed just a few more minutes, and the cold January night air that blew in when she opened the front door, made me shiver, but the shivers were not shivers of fear, no sir, 'I know you're the bully, but I've come now, you mean as a rattlesnake.'

I asked Mother if we could tell Papa about this situation, but Mother warned against it, "Let's just wait until your Daddy comes home. He'll know what is to be done."

I'm proud of Mother, she's brave, and if the Rattlesnake Man comes up to our front door, Mother will greet him with the shotgun loaded, and with one look at her resolute fearless face, the coward will turn tale and run. That's a sure thing.

No one went inside Posey's shack again, and I think everybody soothed their grief by thinking that one day he'd open the door and walk right out of there and come in the store to buy a coke and some peanuts. BUT he never came out of his shack, and one Sunday morning Mother picked up the ringing telephone and yelled into the hand set, "What?"

The next thing Mother hung up the telephone and called to everybody to, "Wake up, we have to go to the store! Wake up! Let's go!"

We were an uncombed, bedraggled, pajamas crew flying out of the yard, over the dirt road and down the highway, and the minute we entered the downhill Dead Man's Curve, all questions were answered by an ugly black blight where Posey's shack stood yesterday, today it is a smoldering pile of twisted iron bed frame and barely recognizable small wood burning stove. The stove pipes, the galvanized bucket, the tin coffee pot, and the tin cups appear to have been shoved in anger into lumps of debris in the otherwise smooth soot and ashes, and nothing else is even slightly discernible. The ugly black stain forces your eye to crawl up the hill where the dangerous sawdust pile is no more, now burned and completely eradicated, and to the east luckily the bald red clay gave no fuel to encourage the flames past that point and the store building and grist mill building are completely untouched.

Mother told me that she won't now and never will use the man's name, but she can tell me the story of a man whose house is in the outer limits of the store settlement, and he likes to dress up in the white KKK costume, and it's common knowledge because just about every week, he brags about burning another cross on Friday or Saturday night, and he does his bragging in church on Sunday morning, but the other church goers who actually try to follow the teachings of Jesus pray that he one day discovers the error of his bullying insanity. The good people are the majority, the KKK are the minority, the brainless few. In the past, Rattlesnake Man has come into the store a few times and each time the good people promptly left, and Mother picks up the baby, and herds me behind the cash register counter, and my Mother cuts him short with obvious disdain. I give my Mother credit, she is a strong woman, and it's amazing to watch as she skillfully maneuvers the bully into a box with no outlet no acceptance no vent for his little minded hate. In the days following the fire, Mother got word of his boasting buffoonery taking credit for running the colored man out of the community and burning his shack, but he must have realized he'd bragged to the wrong people because he never, not once over many years time has been brave enough to show his coward's face in my Mother's presence.

In the summer of 1955, Little Linda and I spent a whole day with Mama and Papa. Mother picked up Little Linda and drove on over to the most perfect place on earth, and as usual Linda and I were holding our breath as we rounded the hill top, and no words were spoken, why waste words trying to describe the most perfect place on earth? Mother breezed in and out all the while saying what sounded like instructions to her parents, and then she raced back to reality and the immediate job of opening the store.

Marilyn has a second job on Saturdays this summer, and she rides to work on the back of the Famous James motorcycle hanging on to Carroll. She wraps cakes and pies at the Dixie Bakery, and along down the middle of the metal work table runs a strip of electrified warming metal, and once the clear wrapping is in place around the pies and cakes, the workers, Marilyn included, slide the wrapping's loose edges over the warmer strip, and unbelievably, the wrapping is sealed shut and airtight.

The games Linda and I played that day at the most perfect place on earth were so much fun! Scattering corn for the chickens lent revelation and understanding when the roosters, hens and chicks fled from the shadow of a hawk, and Papa followed his granddaughters up the ladder to the barn loft, and once on sure footing, he produced two pitch forks whose name finally made sense as the girls learned to pitch the forked bundles of hay down to the stalls below through shoots designed precisely for the purpose. Between chores, the girls spent their earned break running down the hill to the spring, the winner of the race took the first drink of cool water from the jelly glass retrieved from the giant oak's steel rod keeper. Every detail of every matter, every accomplishment, every delight, every laugh inside the perfectness adds to the all encompassing feeling of safety and belonging and fairness and might-makes-right so much so that inside the insulation there is no possibility that mean people can ever invade. John Owens is mighty, literally, he is well over six feet tall and weighs over three hundred pounds, and his might enforces right. He is kind and loving and gladly carries out the assignment of banishing ill begotten acts and deeds, meanness is just not allowed.

Inside the kitchen, Mama leads with gentle composure, "You want to make teacakes? Well we better get busy. First, let's tie your aprons on, and both you girls pull up a chair to stand in, and next, we sift the flour because one bite into a lump of pure flour would certainly ruin the taste of a good teacake. All the flour lumps have to be sifted into powder. Now, that you see how to do the sifting, both of you girls have to sift enough flour to fill your mixing bowl half way to the top."

Linda's attention was drawn away as she continued turning the sifter crank, and guess what, she sifted the flour right onto the table, but I pushed the side of the sifter back into place directly over Linda's mixing bowl, and the force of my push, caught Linda off guard, and she stopped sifting. She dropped the sifter into her bowl, and swiped at the wasted flour on the table's oil cloth covering, and with the bottom edge of her long apron, Linda dusted the flour from the oil cloth into a cloud that threatened to choke us both. It was no laughing matter, but nearly choking made us both laugh all the more, and Linda looked like a scene from 'I Love Lucy' with flour even in her hair and on her face except for her eyeballs which the whites of her eyes took on a yellowish tint when compared to the absolute white of the flour. Thankfully, Mama was in the back room when the flour cloud pushed us to the brink of hysteria, but as soon as Linda rubbed up the last of the wasted flour and tossed the wet rag into the dishpan, Mama came back into the kitchen with the next of our instructions. It's pretty much a given that Mama noticed our ghost white powdered faces, but Mama knows nothing of chastising children, and concurrently she praised our sifting skills as she honed her own benevolence.

When our tea cakes came out of the oven, Mama picked up a plate full by her proven effective 'grab, slide and toss' method (with thumb and forefinger grab the edge then slide slightly to begin a perfect toss onto the plate) and the three ladies joined Papa on the front porch to watch the rain coming down in waves of hypnotizing power. The delicious teacakes chased the chill away as we rocked and watched and reached for another teacake. In short order the plate was empty, and Mama took it inside and returned to the porch with quilts for each, and even Papa spread one around his shoulders. Quilts are all important in our lives, and as we rocked and snuggled, Mama started the story telling that inevitably follows the spreading of a quilt, and her somber story took us to the far away state of Oklahoma, and Mama stood with each new chapter and made her rounds pointing out Aunt Ollie's scraps sewn into the quilts. My quilt has a scrap from Aunt Ollie's brown traveling suit, and with the retelling of that story, I asked, "Mama, do you have Aunt Ollie's brown traveling suit?"

"Yes, I do, come inside now girls, and let me show you Ollie's hope chest sent from Oklahoma all the way back here to me in Alabama more than fifty years ago."

After supper, Carroll pulled into the yard in the two tone blue and white Chevrolet. Carroll's almost as tall as Papa and certainly towers over Mama, and when Mama said, "Well Towey! You are a sight for sore eyes. I chased a yellow news bee from the kitchen just a few minutes ago, and I guess seeing you is just about the best news I could possibly hope for!"

Mama's greeting let a hint of concealed emotion escape through her sweet words, and her quivering lip brought tears to my eyes, and as quick as a wink, I climbed to stand in the nearest straight-back chair, and I wrapped my arms around Mama's narrow shoulders and as a result, Mama had to take her lace edged handkerchief from her apron pocket, but Carroll intercepted before she could blow and the sweetest thing happened, Carroll gave Mama a big old bear hug, and she handled the awkward display with her favorite dismissal, "Pshaw!"

The sound of a car approaching caused a marked change in Mama's attitude, enough of the emotional and on to the practical. Mama began her customary and flustered search for her glasses allowing as how, "Some of you children see if you can't see who that is."

Carroll delivered Linda to her town home, and at her country home three miles east of town, everyone had already taken their turn in the bathtub, and mother had water boiling on the stove, so I went first ahead of Carroll to wash off the hay stems still tickling my neck, and as soon as I came out of the bathroom, Carroll came toting two pots of boiling water which he put down on the sink and while my dirty bath water drained from the bathtub, he scurried back to the kitchen for the third pot, and when Carroll came out of the bathroom in his pajamas, he padded barefooted to the living room, and as the television show ended, he turned off the television set. Carroll is good about turning off the television, he says we need intelligent conversation more and television less, and tonight he ventured to get our opinion on the topic discussed today in his biology class. He's taking a full load of courses this summer at West Georgia, but this fall he will take one quarter of courses at Jacksonville State and then transfer to Georgia Tech. He has made up his mind to get a degree in engineering, and he is working within the requirements as listed in the Georgia Tech catalog, and this way he won't waste money taking unneeded courses, this summer quarter at West Georgia will be his last there because West Georgia offers no more of his required courses, this fall he will take Georgia Tech's required drafting courses at Jacksonville State just over the state line in Alabama, and by January, Carroll will enter Georgia Tech as a junior.

Carroll directed the pajama meeting in our living room to come to order, "At Tallapoosa High School all of you will take biology and you will learn about evolution, I'm taking biology at West Georgia this summer, and again today, we learned more of the intricacies of evolution. It is a very complicated scientific theory that traces connections of all life on earth and begins to reveal why scientific medical testing done on monkeys and mice can accurately predict the results when the same tests are administered to humans. It's an introduction to the grand scheme of God's creation from the universe scale to the amoeba scale. My professor talked about a shocking regression in our country by some ignorant fundamentalists who argue against the science of evolution without ever studying evolution, and sadly, irreverently and mistakenly, they try to fit God into a box the size of the human brain."

Marilyn spoke next, "I know God created the heaven and the earth, but I don't know how long it took, seven days in God's time could be seven million days in our time."

Joan spoke, "I think evolution glorifies God!"

I spoke, "I think it discredits God's power to dismiss evolution, and irreverence of God's power is blasphemy."

Mother had the last word in this discussion, "We believe in education, that's how we progress. God's power should not be restricted by the limitations of human understanding."

I am at the First Baptist church all day long every Sunday. I miss going to Mama's and Papa's but I want to attend Sunday School and Church, and Training Union and Church, and now there is another activity offered while school's out for the summer and that is Sunday afternoon Bible Drill practice and once a month, we host or travel to Bowdon, Bremen, Temple or Buchannan to compete in an actual Bible Drill. At Bible Drill practice, we have learned to open the Bible in the exact middle to quickly find Psalms, and half way between Genesis and Psalms to find Judges, and half way between Psalms and Revelation to find Matthew. Our Bible Drill team is small, but we are very fast, and we have won all but one Bible Drill so far. Brenda Cobb is at the Baptist Church all day on Sundays too, and in between morning Church and mid-afternoon Bible Drill practice Arbelle takes us to Crossroads Cafe, and during the free time between Bible Drill practice and Training Union, Brenda and I walk around town when it's not raining, and if it is raining Brenda's mother picks us up, and sometimes we go to visit Brenda's Uncle Clarence and Aunt Josie.

On the telephone with Laura Hill Merrill, we decided it's her turn to come out here to play, so on Mother's daily errand run into town, we stopped by Laura Hill's house, she and her brother Phillip live with their grandparents. Dr. Hill is Tallapoosa's only dentist. Laura Hill's sweet Mama came out to visit a minute with Mother, and then Laura Hill hugged her Mama and climbed into the back seat with me. Mother turned the car back toward town because she remembered one more thing she needs to get, so Laura Hill and I stayed in the car with my two brothers while Mother went into the Jitney Jungle. Randall can be so cute, he's about two and a half and right now he loves to play peak a boo, and he gets sort of silly hiding himself behind his own two little hands like he really thinks we can't see him because he can't see us.

At home, Laura Hill drew out a hopscotch game in the white sandy front yard, but she was distracted by the plum tree hanging full of not yet ripe plums. I said, "But the persimmons are ripe.

Laura Hill was smart enough not to fall for that old trick, I guess even city girls know a green persimmon draws the inside of your mouth into knots which just about curl your lips inside out, and with the negative image of green persimmons that's when I thought about the positive image of the blackberry patch down in the valley behind the barn, and for sure the blackberries are really and truly ripe, and that means they are sweet and juicy. We took a bucket with us to the blackberry patch in case there are enough delicious ripe blackberries to make a cobbler. At the barn, to get into the pasture, of course we had to let down the fence planks, and once inside the fence, we made a detour up the steps into the barn loft where we sat on the floor at the west haymow door and dangled our feet off the high ledge, and a cool breeze rustled through the tree tops and channeled through the loft, in through the west haymow door and out through the east haymow door.

Daddy built the barn before I was born, but the ten years have not diminished the powerful perfume of the never painted pine boards, and I love the sweet acidic pine aroma because I can close my eyes and imagine Daddy coming home from the Rifle Range. The barn loft is my lookout to the world and especially to New Mexico. I can pretend that Daddy is near by, but sometimes Randall is sitting in the haymow door beside me, and he usually talks about jumping to the ground hundreds of feet below, no maybe thousands of feet. I don't like to talk about it, I don't even like to think about it, but one day Ivey Newman jumped out of the barn loft and he said it was fun.

All that aside, the blackberries will be rotten on the ground by the time we get to blackberry patch, so we stopped our swinging legs, pulled them inside the loft, and carefully stood up holding on tight to the door frame, and pretty soon after a last look at the whole wide world, we went back down the barn steps to the ground. I noticed Laura Hill watched her feet and carefully placed each next step as we made our way through the dark, wide-open barn hall toward the blinding bright sun in the eastern sky. Laura Hill continued watching her feet down the hill to the blackberry patch, and I enjoyed it very much when she said, "I'm being careful to avoid stepping in horse manure."

Of course that is a reasonable thing for a city girl to do, but somehow, it seems too much effort assigned to what maybe should come naturally and maybe indicates that Laura Hill doesn't really connect with the country surroundings. I guess I should have given more warning, but she jumped like I'd said BOO when I said, "Laura Hill, do you want to pet old Dan?"

Laura Hill jerked her head up away from the intense avoidance of horse manure, and to her surprise Old Dan stood directly in her path, and she just about butted heads with our big old horse, but I have to give her credit, she acted normal and not one bit afraid when she rubbed Old Dan's face, and she had the great idea of picking a handful of blackberries and holding them in her outstretched hand for Old Dan, and our big old horse gently ate them right out of her hand, and Laura Hill watched spellbound as Old Dan's big old flapping lips carefully picked up the blackberries, and that made us both giggle to high heaven, and Old Dan snorted out his own merriment, and we expected him to laugh right out loud. Old Dan went back to grazing on his preferred grass, and Laura Hill and I ate the first one hundred or so blackberries right there in the blackberry patch, but then we remembered to get busy picking a bucket full so Mother can make a blackberry cobbler. As long as Laura Hill and I were close to the bucket, we picked the blackberries and dropped them in, but pretty soon, we were miles away from the bucket, so I picked until both my hands were full, and then I skipped back to the bucket. I guess I really didn't pay close enough attention to notice that Laura Hill was picking and putting the ripe juicy blackberries into the fold of her white blouse, and as I made my way with the bucket closer to the unpicked millions, I saw the disaster, but I tried not to alarm Laura Hill, and with deliberate calm, I said, "We have enough for a cobbler, we'd better head back to the house."

Mother put the bucket of blackberries on the kitchen cabinet and said, "Oh, Honey, you girls come with me."

In the bedroom, Mother found a tee shirt that fits, but it was too late because Laura Hill was transfixed on the mirror and the hideous black stain around her mouth revealing to her what I and Mother had up to that minute not disclosed, and as Mother sat down on the bed, she pulled my bewildered friend onto her lap, and Mother rocked back and forth as

Laura Hill's gushing tears prompted Mother's coo, "You have nothing to be embarrassed about, Honey, we've all been through the exact same thing, every single person who's ever eaten fresh blackberries learned exactly what you have just now learned. Don't you worry one little bit! The stains will come off of your beautiful face and I assure you, I know how to get the stains out of your white blouse."

Mother stood up and gently settled Laura Hill's feet to the floor, and we followed Mother into the bath room where she pulled a bath cloth and a towel from the cabinet, and said, "Laura, honey, we'll wait outside the door for you to take off your blouse and hand it out. Then, you wet the bath cloth and rub up a lather on the Ivory soap bar, and then scrub the blackberry stains from your face and stomach, and I'll put your white blouse to soaking."

Mother put Laura Hill's white blouse in a dish pan mixture of cold water, about a teaspoon of Purex, a sprinkling of Snowy, and a little Babbo detergent, and when Laura Hill came out of the bathroom, her silky smooth face was a little bit red but stain free, and in comparison, I checked my face in the blonde waterfall dresser in my sisters' room; and luckily, there are no blackberry stains on my face, but unluckily, in contrast to Laura Hill's creamy smooth complexion, my face is freckled and no where near as flawless as Laura Hill's, her's is the color of whipped cream, mine is freckled and red like Papa's especially if I am laughing. I have begun to secretly give each of my friends a superlative, and long before today, I gave to Laura Hill the 'prettiest.'

In the kitchen, Mother found a long wooden spoon and showed us how to push and pull Laura Hill's white blouse through the soaking water, and in the mean time with her hands now free, Mother made a batch of biscuits. Laura Hill and I took turns pushing and pulling until she became intent on watching every move of Mother's biscuit routine. First, burrowing a neat round hole in the middle of the almost full flour pan. Next, opening the refrigerator and digging out a handful of lard, then squeezing the lard into the flour, adding buttermilk a splash or two at a time until the batter became more and more pliable and finally, pinching off a round dough ball and tossing it back and forth from right hand to left hand until it is perfect in size and consistency. In quick succession and precision, Mother filled the biscuit pan with symmetrical rows of dough balls, and when the biscuit pan was full, she knuckle flattened each ball, opened the oven door, and slid the biscuit pan into the hot oven.

Mother called us in to dinner, and I found Randall in the living room lying on the couch as he emptied his bottle of chocolate milk. Mother regrets the day she filled the big old baby's bottle with chocolate milk because now that's all the spoiled rascal will accept when he demands, "Pix me body."

Mother replies that if Randall is big enough to ask for a bottle, well then it must follow that he's too big for a bottle, but her method of weaning is to continue to fill the one and only remaining glass bottle until it breaks, then that's it, a broken bottle won't hold liquid, plain and simple, and even a two and a half year old can grasp that result. The worse part is that everybody gives in to the big old baby, and boy howdy he is spoiled, but I guess it's what we all get for jumping to his beck and call.

I smiled looking at his sweet sleeping face and decided to leave in place the drop of chocolate milk oozing from the corner of his mouth. Also, I made the conscious decision to leave the empty bottle lying exactly where Randall tossed it to the floor because he has a super sense that wakes him the very minute anyone touches his bottle. Better to leave it, and if someone steps on it and breaks it well, he knows this last bottle cannot be replaced.

I think Laura Hill had a good time with us today, and I know she loved Mother's buttered biscuits and tomatoes, and by about five o'clock when Joan's ride stopped in the road to let her out, Mother took Laura Hill's white blouse out of the soaking water and rinsed it through two rinse waters, and then she rolled it up inside a towel and stepped on it to 'squeeze out as much water as humanly possible', and in just a few minutes Mother ironed it dry, completely dry! Laura Hill changed and left the tee shirt in the dirty clothes hamper inside the bathroom. Mother then chased down the baby, then Laura Hill and I climbed into the back seat of the Chevrolet, Mother backed out of the yard, and we returned Laura Hill to her home up town. I wish I could have spend-the-night parties, but that is not possible because we have too many people and too few beds.

August 29, 1955
Dear Daddy,

School starts next Tuesday, the day after Labor Day, and as a 'right of passage' Ivey Newman talked me into jumping out of the barn loft. Don't ask me what a 'right of passage' is because I don't know, but Ivey and Red both know exactly what it is, and they know how very important it is. The three of us were swinging our legs out the west haymow door, and next thing I know, they are teaching me how to jump and how to land. It's about seventy-five or a hundred feet or more to the ground, but they instructed me to push off from a sitting position, and that alone would save me ten feet or more, and they also advised me never to lock my knees straight, but instead to anticipate the minute of contact and imagine the ground to be mushy, and that's what I did, and sure enough just before I hit, I deliberately cannon balled my legs (not holding them, no sir) and it really did ease the shock, and I swany the ground actually did feel mushy. I feel a wonderful sense of relief being done with the right of passage.

Love,
Janet

September 5, 1955
Dear Daddy,

I'm in fourth grade this year, and Joan is in her first year at West Georgia Junior College. Carroll is taking drafting classes at Jacksonville State, and two nights a week he sleeps on the couch in Gary Bailey's apartment in Jacksonville, Alabama. He pays a little rent and saves a little gas. The two nights that Carroll is not at home, Marilyn sleeps in his room, I sleep in the bed with mother and Randall sleeps in the other bed. We like it that way and my dog Snippy sleeps under our bed.

Love,
Janet

September 12,1955
Dear Daddy,

On Thursdays, after work Marilyn walks back toward the High School to attend Mamboco at the Tallapoosa Presbyterian Church. The Presbyterian minister Pierre DuBose started up this teenagers' social club, and Marilyn enjoys the games they play and each week after game time, they have a wienie roast. The boys Wayne Duncan, Wade King, and Harvey Nixon get a fire started while the girls Marilyn, Judy Evans, Joyce Mann, and Lynn Littlefield set out the hot dog buns, potato chips, ketchup, mustard and co-colas.

Love,
Janet

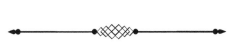

September 19, 1955
Dear Daddy,

It's sad, but this is Gayle's last year at Tallapoosa Grammar School. Next year she'll go to a brand new school right across the street from Sis and Huitte's house, it's called West Haralson, and it opens next fall 1956, and close to Waco, they are building a new colored school right across Highway 78 from the Round Top and that new school opens next year too, and next year, Gayle goes to West Haralson and Thelma's daughter Georgia, goes to Haralson Consolidated. It's a good thing that the old colored school, Carver, will be torn down because it's not safe and looks like it might fall down any day, and for the first time ever, the colored students will ride a bus to and from their new Haralson Consolidated School, and Mother said, "That's progress, and progress for colored people is long over due."

Love,
Janet

Daddy plants thought seeds, in fact he rarely tells us what's what, he speaks in outlines deliberately hushing before reaching a conclusion. Carroll learned Daddy's technique and now in Daddy's absence, it falls to Carroll to be the pretend arbitrator, and like Daddy, it's not always obvious when Carroll's cultivating our reasoning process, and I respect his skillful manipulations. Mother on the other hand, insists that we consider all opinions but there's no doubt as to her position, and also there's no doubt that she expects us to fall in line with her and her conclusions which of course leaves no room for independent counter intuition. That's where Mother differs from Daddy, they both have strong beliefs, but Daddy wants us to develop our own carefully considered conclusions, and Mother considers it her prerogative to dictate morality. In the final analysis neither will accept anything less than benevolence, they don't like bullies, they don't tolerate hate, and they won't acquiesce to anything less than the high road. In both our parents, there's an understanding that life's not worth living in malevolence. These are the rules. Malicious behavior is unacceptable, so you better be starring down bullies and changing lives for the better and don't wait about telling people you love them because tomorrow might be too late.

Sept. 26, 1955
Dear Family,

Things are going really good out here, the weather cooperates most of the time but when it's raining that's when we write our letters home which explains why I haven't written for a month or more, but it is raining today, and we are writing our letters and cleaning up to go into Magdalena.

It hurts to the very core of me, but this will be another Christmas away from my family, but I've been thinking, Vesta, I want you to put out the word we're ready to rent out the store building and grist mill, and that way getting the word out 7 or 8 months in advance of next summer, well that gets me to the good part! Since our work out here is going good, well as soon as school is out next summer, I want yall to come out here to Magdalena, and Carroll can come on out here in January. I've read and re-read the letter about how Carroll won't start at Georgia Tech until the fall of 1956. I know he's been thinking as to how he can make the most money, and it's plain to see he'll make the most money working out here. Today when we get to Magdalena, I plan to ask around if there might be a house we can rent for the summer, if not maybe we can get a good rate at the Grayson Hotel.

Love,
Your Daddy

Mother opens letters from Daddy as soon as the mail man drives away from the mail box, and usually everyone except the baby of course reads Daddy's letters as soon as they see a new one on the dining room table, but today Mother waited until Marilyn was home from work, Joan was home from West Georgia, and Carroll was home from Jacksonville, and then she drug Daddy's letter out of the front of her dress where she hid it to keep it secret, and then with all five of her children corralled in the living room, she read the letter and the house was just about jolted off it's foundation when everybody started jumping up and down and Carroll did a dozy-doe with Mother and Marilyn swung the baby around and around, and Joan and I danced a clover dance, and the strangest thing happened when the noise died down, it was like a giant looking in through the roof maybe pinched all of us or stuck us with a pin or something, but the laughing stopped and the crying started! I guess the crying is because of Christmas.

All Mother had to do about putting the word out was to say to Lavada Goolsby, "We're ready to rent out the store for a while."

Lavada turned on a dime, went back to her house, picked up her telephone, and called her cousin Ralph McBurnett, knowing he's been talking about running the store and gristmill ever since Shug Godwin built it. Mother and Ralph McBurnett decided he'd pay for the remaining stock so Mother made a meticulous price list, and to be fair, she asked Ralph to do the same, and each reached a total price within fifteen dollars of the other. So Ralph McBurnett borrowed a little money and bought out Mother's supply of canned goods, co-colas, and whatever else remained on the shelves, and from that day, Mother's life became a whole lot easier. During the times when Mother is at home alone with the baby, she spends a lot of time visiting with Thelma just down the road, and Thelma is at home during the day, but she is not at home any night of the week because she works as the cook at Club 78 up town. The early morning is a busy time for Mother and Thelma, but when that hubbub quiets down, they can have dinner and visit until early afternoon. Except for these visits, white women have little or no contact with colored women which makes Mother's and Thelma's friendship all the more precious. It's unlikely that Mother could know from any other source that Louise Hammock is now a cook at Smith's Cafe and has more than one child by the same white man, and she's making it pretty good, but her grief is endless, and still there's no word from Posey Greer.

October 3, 1955
Dear Family,

I know Ivey Newman and the other boys have a good time jumping out of the barn loft just like me and my brothers never could resist the fun of pushing the others into the old dried up well, but I need to say directly, I have back troubles to this day and the pain started back then when I was pushed into the deep dry well one time too many. Janet hid in the pile of leaves and I got so mad at Janet that I tried to make her put herself in a dangerous situation, but she stood up to me. Now listen to me, don't be jumping out of the barn loft not even one more time. I expect Ivey, Red and Janet to follow my directions and never jump out of the barn loft again. Janet, I want you to go to your Mother right this minute and tell her that you are making a solemn promise to me never to jump out of the barn loft again and never let anybody else jump either. I'm not mad at you Janet, but go on to your Mother right now and make the promise to your Daddy.

Love,
Your Daddy

This year my teacher is Mrs. Florence Barnes. Jane Wood, Brenda Jaillet, Kristina Walton, Brenda Cobb, and Sandra Payne are in my class upstairs in the front corner room, but Connie Gentry and Laura Hill are across the hall in Mrs. Helen Barnes's back corner room. I love fourth grade because we study geography every day, and I love learning about different places in the world like the high mountain meadows of Switzerland where the young boys heard the cattle and then live there all summer in a shelter or lean to. I want to see Switzerland's high mountain meadows someday! I love learning about the mosaic sidewalks in Rio de Janeiro, Brazil, and the Copacabana Beach and Ipanema Beach, and the giant statue of Jesus high above the city on Corcovado Mountain and the cable car up Sugarloaf Mountain. I want to see Rio de Janeiro someday! I love learning about the tsetse flies that transmit sleeping sickness in the jungles of middle Africa. I love to look at pictures of Africa's exotic animals. I want to see zebras and giraffes and elephants someday! I hope when I grow up, I can travel around the world and actually see a kangaroo in Australia, and the Great Wall of China, and the frozen tundra, and the Eiffel Tower and the Amazon River, and I hope I get to see a play on Broadway! My list includes many countries and cities and jungles and forests, and I can add to my list at home now because Mother bought a set of Encyclopedias! Now not just in fourth grade geography class but at home I can dream about traveling the world.

I am a Girl Scout! Brenda Jaillet's mother Delores is our leader, Brenda Cobb, Connie Gentry, Sandra Payne, Laura Hill, Kristina Walton, Jane Wood and I meet every other week mostly at Brenda Jaillet's house. We have already learned the Johnny Appleseed prayer/song :

> The Lord is good to me,
> And so I thank the Lord,
> For giving me the things I need,
> The sun the rain and the apple seed
> The Lord is good to me.

I have a lot of best friends. Sometimes I go home with Kristina after school, and behind her house we explore a huge forest that runs down the hill to a creek, there's a swimming hole but it's too cold to go swimming this time of year, we found a dirt road and crossed it to climb a pasture fence, and two horses galloped over to us as if they were asking for an apple or a sugar cube, we promised them we'll come back someday with treats. Kristina feels sad because her parents bought an old house in town on Cleveland Street, and as soon as it is remodeled, they are moving into town, she's worried about who will bring treats to the horses when she moves away. Kristina's little sister is Teresa, and the baby is Molly each have special scrapbooks, Kristina showed them to me, her mother is making the three scrapbooks, Kristina's Keepsakes, Teresa's Treasures, and Molly's Memories. I'm glad to know about the scrapbooks because now I want to keep important things like letters from Daddy because someday, I plan to have a scrapbook too.

Sometimes Jane comes to play at my house and sometimes Laura Hill comes to play, but they never come at the same time. Last Saturday, Mother took me to Connie's house. It's a big old two story with a huge front porch and a swing. There isn't much of a yard, and the front yard is even smaller than the back yard. There is a large stone house that actually is the next door house, but the stone house has a very large front yard which makes it an odd situation with the stone house facing the back of Connie's house. When Mother let me out at Connie's house, Jane, Laura Hill and Kristina were there too. Jane lives in the house on the same street (Boulevard Avenue) and like Connie's house, Jane's house has a small front and back yard but unlike Connie's house, Jane's house does not back up to the Stone house instead it backs up to a forest and consequently Jane's family has a lot more privacy than Connie's family. There is one more house well it's actually under construction at the corner of Boulevard Avenue and Head Avenue beyond Jane's house. Mr. & Mrs. Otis Bennett are Kristina's grandparents, and I know that name because Daddy has told us a million times that he bought our house and twenty-one acres of land from Otis Bennett, and the price was a hundred dollars and a 1936 Ford. I met Kristina's grandparents that day and Otis Bennett asked if I was related to Shug Godwin, and I said, "Yes Sir,"

Then Otis Bennett said, "I know your Daddy because I sold him the house where you live."

I said, "Yes Sir, I know."

Then Otis Bennett said, "I know your Daddy is doing well cutting timber off out in New Mexico. Your Daddy is as fine a man as you'd ever want to know."

I didn't say anything more, I was kind of choked up, and besides, by then everybody was running out the door and heading across the street to walk the foundation where the Lithia Hotel once stood. We found Rod, Denver, and Charles at the Lithia Hotel ruins. I've heard about the Lithia Hotel, built in the late 1800's, and I know it was the largest wooden structure in the country, and it was built because the Lithia Springs were thought to be healing waters. The hotel flourished for a while, but it closed in the Great Depression because no one had any money, and during World War II, Lee Worthy bought the building and tore it down because the United States needed lumber in the war effort.

Connie's Granny made dinner and we ate our sandwiches on the front porch. I sat on the steps with Laura Hill, the boys sat in the yard, and Connie, Jane and Kristina sat together on the swing, and the pimento cheese sandwiches were the best I've ever eaten. When we returned our plates and glasses to the kitchen, Connie asked Granny if we could walk to Kristina's house on Cleveland Street which is very close to Charles Downey's house and Granny thought it would be ok, but she said, "If the renovation crew is working on Saturday, don't go inside."

We agreed with Granny's instructions and then we walked down the hill through the valley and up the hill toward Charles's house, but we turned left and walked to the end of a single lane gravel road, and Kristina said, "At first I didn't like the idea, but now I think it'll be perfect to live close to my friends, but Laura Hill, you and Janet will have to promise me you'll come play at least every Saturday."

The following Friday, all four girls (Connie, Jane, Kristina and I) walked home with Laura Hill after school. Mama kissed her granddaughter, and then she did the sweetest thing in the world, she kissed Connie, she kissed Kristina, she kissed Jane and she kissed me. She told us we'd find a snack on the kitchen table, and there was a plate full of tiny little triangle shaped boloney sandwiches with the crust cut off. They were nothing but boloney and mayonnaise, but they were so delicious, and I think maybe the flavor was enhanced by their appealing size and shape.

Anyhow, when the plate was emptied, the five girls decided to run out to the ball park, and we cut through a narrow street I'd never even noticed before, and when we reached the ball park fence, the boys on the other side were running around playing tag I guess, but when Jack Nixon spotted us, he waved and bull horned his hands around his mouth and directed us to go north along the fence and then of course it became a race: boys (Jack Nixon, Denver Morgan, Jimmy Thrower, Johnny Thrower, and Bobby Bates) inside the fence versus girls outside the fence, and I'm proud to say, I beat everybody to the hole in the chain links, but I knew enough not to go through until somebody got there to hold the sharp barbs out of my way, and when we were safely through the break and inside the fence, I heard my sister Marilyn's voice, and we all took off running to the goalpost where Marilyn and the other cheerleaders and majorettes were holding a ladder against the horizontal part of the goal post, and Marilyn was the person way up high off the ground wrapping crepe paper around and around the goal post, and she was wrapping Bremen's colors : blue and white.

The Bremen Blue Devils will play our Tallapoosa Red Devils tonight, and Joan and Carroll will go to the game, but I don't really like to sit still on the bleachers and do nothing but watch a football game. If I could jump around with Marilyn and the other cheerleaders then I'd like to go, but of course I can't do that, so instead, the five of us girls are having a spend the night party at Laura Hill's house. It's my first spend the night party, I've heard about spend the night parties, but I've never been to one, and I can say for sure I can't wait! The best part is a secret, and it's been awful keeping the surprise from Jane, because her birthday was yesterday, and to make it a really good surprise, there was no celebration at Jane's house last night, but today while we were in school Jane's grandmother made a birthday cake and delivered it to Laura Hill's house, and after supper Mama will go to the kitchen for the cake and when she comes back into the dining room, we'll all sing Happy Birthday, Jane! After we have the cake, we'll bring out the presents. I'm sure it will be a really good surprise! Jane is such a good friend! I think she and Laura Hill are the prettiest girls in our whole entire school! I continue to give my own secret superlative to each of my friends, and actually, Jane's superlative is most glamorous. She really is as glamorous as a famous movie star! It's just the way she walks and talks with sweet flirtation sort of like a young Marilyn Monroe.

The boys walked us back to Laura Hill's house and we got there just at the same time as Laura Hill's grandfather Dr. Hill.

After the surprise cake and presents, Doc Hill and Mama turned out all the lights in the house and closed the door to their bedroom on the front or east end of the house which faces Bowdon Street, but in the back bedroom, the farthest west room, the five girls sat on the floor in the dark and planned a daring escape. Connie's always the daredevil, and when we were absolutely sure Doc and Mama were asleep, we slipped out of the house and ran as fast as we could all the way up town to the Grand Theater. We bought tickets and settled in the perfect seats (they were all open) and the movie had already begun, and our first glance at the screen brought an in-unison-scream as Dracula sucked the life's blood from a pretty girl's neck. I can't account for anybody else's reaction because I for one turned my eyes from the movie screen, and I fit my entire face in the space between my seat and Connie's seat, and except for occasional glimpses at the screen; I watched the floor behind our seats instead of the movie. At one point, I summoned the bravado to search for the doorway out of there not knowing how I could possibly escape on legs made of mush, and when I scanned the exit, it was blocked by the silhouette of a man, and I'm pretty sure it was Dracula himself. That movie scarred me for life, and years later, I still get the cold sweats just thinking about the horror. I certainly understand that the entire story of Dracula is science fiction and has no connection to reality, and I remind myself 'I'm not afraid of anything,' but a thousand or more times a day I verify that the silver cross is in place around my neck. After that Connie seemed to think and talk about Dracula more than any sane person should from my point of view, but her obsession has helped me find the perfect superlative for her, and for now Connie is the most unconventional.

Monday
December 19, 1955
Dear Daddy,

Yesterday, we went to Mama's and Papa's fiftieth anniversary celebration! I'm not sure if I have told you, but Ruth and Otto bought a house on Highway 100 about halfway between Tallapoosa and Cedartown. It's an old house but they have remodeled it, and now it's very modern, it has shiny hardwood floors, gas heating, and two very nice bathrooms with hot running water. Ruth has an automatic washing machine in the kitchen, which is very handy. It is on wheels so she can move it and hook the hose up to the sink water faucet to fill and also hook the discharge hose into the sink to drain, however she does not have a clothes dryer, instead she hangs the wet clothes on lines inside the large screened-in back porch. She never has to set foot outside the house to do the laundry beginning to end.

Of course Otto's mother, Aunt Mary Lizzie moved into the new house with them, and another son Grady and his wife Bonnie live just on the other side of the highway. There is a small country store on the property situated very close to the highway, and either Ruth or Otto is in the store from daylight to sundown everyday except Sunday of course, and they have customers stopping in all the time. Friday was the actual 50th Anniversary, but Ruth had the celebration on Sunday so as not to interfere with the customers. I spent the night in the new house on Friday night just like I always do, and then on Saturday morning I helped Aunt Mary Lizzie make cookies.

Love,
Janet

Carroll and I cut a Christmas tree again, I decorated it with little travail, I read "Twas the Night Before Christmas" to Randall. Mother bought a Christmas turkey from Willie Hill, and another wrapped gift to me appeared under the tree, but I have little or no interest. It's just not right; it just doesn't feel like Christmas without Daddy.

Monday
January 2, 1956
Dear Daddy,

I cannot wait to see you! This Christmas was ten times harder than last year. I hope we never ever spend another Christmas apart. I got a little Ginny Vogue Doll. She's seven and a half inches tall; she has blue eyes and long brown, wavy hair. She's a walker, and with each step, she turns her head from side to side. She's wearing a fancy red and white dress, a white petticoat and bloomers, white socks, red shoes, and a wide brimmed red and white sun hat. I can attach her red and white parasol to her hand. I showed Mother and Ruth the Ginny Doll in the Dime Store. She is a beautiful doll, and I understand how lucky I am to have her, but I'd trade her without regret for five minutes with my Daddy!

Love,
Janet

On Saturday, January 7, 1956, Carroll answered Daddy's telephone call that came right on time at eight p.m. Carroll asked Daddy to read off the telephone number of the pay telephone booth in Magdalena, but Daddy was a little short with Carroll for what he considered to be a distraction and finally said, "Yes Son, I can give you the telephone number of this telephone booth, but first let me speak to your Mother."

Mother almost cried out, "Hello."

During Mother's silence it was plain to see that Daddy was saying something very sentimental, and then Mother said into the telephone, "I love you too."

Then Carroll took the telephone again, listened for a minute and said, "Oh no, I forgot."

Carroll had a pencil in his hand, and he opened our telephone book to the back page and wrote down the number Daddy called out to him, and then unfairly Carroll hung up the telephone. Amidst groans and grumbles, Carroll dialed the 'O' for operator and asked for information please, and she gave him the long distance telephone numbers for all the airlines at the Atlanta Airport, and again Carroll wrote the numbers in the back of the telephone book. The very first airline he called gave him the name of the one specific airline that has regular scheduled flights from Atlanta to Kansas City and from Kansas City to Albuquerque. In his next call, Carroll quickly made his reservations, wrote down the flight numbers and departure times and arrival times, and agreed to bring cash to Atlanta on the day of his departure, and then he quickly hung up the phone so as not to waste time talking long distance because there's a charge per minute. It's exciting to think that he will fly in a few hours the same distance it took Daddy and his crew the better part of five days to drive. With his Albuquerque arrival day and time, Carroll dialed the number of the pay telephone booth in Magdalena, and Daddy answered ready with a pencil and paper.

Finally, Carroll handed off the telephone to the next in line, rushed to intercept Joan and whisper something in her ear, and slipped out of the house, cranked up the Chevrolet, and drove away. (It's important to note that as always the car keys were in the Chevrolet.) Once everyone had a few minutes on the telephone with Daddy, sadly time was up or else Mother won't have enough money to pay the telephone bill.

Every time after talking long distance to Daddy, the first few minutes are very still and quiet as if our collective hearts in our collective chests need silent time to recover, and tonight is no different except that maybe our hearts are more severely broken than ever before, but then again that's hard to imagine because every Saturday night when the hang up click reverberates, we begin once again the slow and painful march through a long and debilitating seven days, but inevitably as the week progresses, the dread regret turns once again to eager hope.

We went about a usual Saturday night and cast our votes for or against television, conversation, word games or books. Not a single hand went up for television, games or conversation, and I suppose my tightly clutched library book helped to rig the vote. One of the best parts of being in the fourth grade is that fourth graders get to go to the library every week, and because fourth graders are responsible, all fourth graders are allowed to bring a book home and keep it all through the Christmas vacation.

The Grammar School Library is in a dark windowless room about the size of our bathroom, but it is an enchanting place lined on three sides with floor-to-ceiling books. The library is on the front side of the building, upstairs between Mrs. Eaves fifth grade room and Mrs. Phillips sixth grade room. On library day, one row of students (usually six) go at the same time, and there's no room inside the library for another single person. This year on the last day of school before Christmas when it was my row's turn, I headed straight for the book that Linda Sue Chandler had last month. The title of the book is Mabel, and Linda Sue told me it's about a little girl who can talk to the animals in the forest, and she understands their language in reply. I think I'm the reason why everybody voted to read tonight because I've jabbered on and on about my attachment to this book. Everybody in my family knows how I feel connected to the crows that live in the woods around our house. I think the crows are very smart, I feel they are protective of me, and I'm sure they actively warn me of dangers when they caw-caw and sure enough I see a big snake slithering away, and when I'm sitting alone on the ledge of the west hay mow door, their warning caw is harsher, shriller than their soft comforting caw as I push through the tall rabbit tobacco and broom straw fields of winter. The crows are constant companions when I am outside the house alone, and especially when I go deep into the woods looking for future Christmas trees, I am quite convinced the crows talk to each other in relays from the first one ahead of me to the next ones in line over me and on to the last ones behind me. Tonight it's my turn to read aloud. I finished two chapters by the time Carroll came crushing through the front door singing:

Happy Birthday to you!

It was instantaneous and unanimous: everyone sang along except Mother of course:

Happy Birthday to you!
Happy Birthday, Dear Mother,
Happy Birthday to you!

To get Mother's birthday cake, Carroll drove ninety miles an hour to the Dixie Bakery in Bremen where he unlocked the front door, left a note and some one dollar bills in the cash register, and quickly pulled from the huge refrigerator a very pretty white iced cake with Happy Birthday written in red on top between two bunches of red roses! Mother couldn't stop her splashing tears. Joan and Marilyn dashed into the kitchen and came back with a knife and six plates and forks, and Mother said, "This is the first store bought birthday cake I've ever had."

On a warm Saturday in March, Jane came to play and first thing when her Grandmother Crabtree left, we ran up the stairs because in school yesterday, we planned that we'd play dress up! I told Jane about the beautiful clothes Mother makes for Joan and Marilyn, but it's not fair to say that Mother makes them all by herself because Joan and Marilyn do most of the cutting and sewing, and they are pretty good seamstresses in their own right. Mother encourages them to create their own designs, select the material, figure the yardage, cut out the pieces and sew them together. Inside a pattern envelope, there is a pattern-piece placement diagram and on the back of the envelope, there's a yardage chart, but Mother teaches to ignore the suggested piece placement because it wastes a lot of material, and consequently whatever the yardage chart calls for, it's safe to subtract about a yard and still have more than enough material. Both my sisters learn fast, but they do require frequent consultations with Mother. The next step beyond creative pattern piece placement and active fabric conservation goes far beyond the moment's goal of a new dress to wear to the next party, Mother's very core quality is frugality, and consequently all fabric scraps are saved no matter how small because each and every scrap can be used to piece together quilt tops. There's always a material scrap grocery sack and usually it's upstairs, and when there's several full scrap sacks Mother takes them to Dorothy Hicks who lives in a red brick house across the road from Dink Daniel's house down by the store. Mrs. Hicks cuts the material scraps into quilt top design pieces and finger-work-sews them all together into beautiful designs and when she's finished a quilt top, Mother pays her $2 and she begins the process again. Then Mother buys batting and a large piece of material for the lining and mounts the three layers into the quilting frame upstairs, and usually Mother completes the quilting of two or three quilts a year.

Next year in the spring, Joan will graduate from West Georgia Junior College, and with a business degree, she will have no trouble finding a good job in Atlanta. A whole bunch of Joan's clothes are upstairs for safekeeping until she needs them to wear to work. If she gets a really good job as a successful businessman's secretary, then she'll need a lot of nice clothes. These homemade clothes are 'original designs' based on the actual clothes worn in the movies by big stars like Audrey Hepburn and Janet Leigh. Mother says it's a waste of money to buy multiple patterns when it's so simple to cut pattern variations … meaning the exact same dress bodice can be slightly altered to button up the front or the back or zip up the side, and the sleeves can be lengthened or shortened and if you want a sleeveless dress, there's no problem cutting a facing to fit, and as for the neckline it can be easily faced as a scooped or squared or jewel neckline, and a collar can be large or small, stand up, or rolled, squared off or rounded. Each creation is unique in color, fabric and design, and the best part of all is that today, Jane and I can play dress up! With each change of costume, Jane and I swagger to and from the big mirror leaning against the chimney. I feel a little awkward in too-big high heel shoes, but Jane is as beautiful and graceful as any movie star! I try to copy the way she walks, but it's hard because she can point her toes like a ballerina, or she can drag her feet while dramatically shoving her hips side to side. She is very convincing. "Jane, I know when we grow up, you'll be famous for your glamor and charm. No kidding! I think you'll be Drum Majorette! Just wait and see!"

We were giggling to beat the band when we heard footsteps on the stairs, right away we saw Mother's head as she rounded the stairway curve, and we stood smiling as Mother came toward us with two plates; oh boy beef stew over loaf bread! Mother set the two plates on the little play table and carefully moved it directly in front of the window, Jane followed my lead and pulled up a small chair, and as we ate, Mother sat down in her quilting chair which brought her knees (tightly bound into her dark print cotton dress) to the height of our little table top. Jane warmed to my Mother and asked, "Did you make all these beautiful clothes?"

Mother's reply gave more credit to Joan and Marilyn than to herself, but I added my observation that Joan and Marilyn are 'learning' how to sew, and perhaps if their teacher were not readily accessible, they might never actually learn! Mother got my meaning and laughed with relish, and it was plain to see that Jane also understood the joke for Jane and Mother both cackled their shared boisterous laughs that echo and etch a treasured place in my heart, both my mother and my friend are free spirited and compelling, and their zest serves as a magnet for who can resist their draw? I've never known anyone to dislike my Mother, and the same is true of Jane.

We ate every morsel, and the three of us felt a comfortable oneness. My Mother has the power to 'sprinkle fairy dust' and spin a web of security, Mother protects; Daddy expects self-reliance. The soothing spell was broken when Mother reached to pick up our empty plates, and the final reality returned when Jane said, "Thank you, that was delicious."

At school on Monday it was a warm spring day and time for all first graders to get polio vaccination shots. Every year the downstairs grades (first, second, and third) are first to line up one by one and walk the short distance to the Downey Clinic where Nurse Sara Walker and Dr. Downey make quick work of immunizing the children. First graders get their arms scratched with a special hypodermic needle, which actually is more than one needle in a cluster. It really doesn't hurt at all because the needle cluster is designed simply to abrade the surface, which makes the word 'shot' a misnomer. This year the first three grades get a sugar cube polio booster, but fourth graders don't get a polio booster unless they did not have one last year, I guess two sugar cube polio boosters, one in second grade and one in third grade make me resistant to polio. When my fourth grade class reached the Downey Clinic, word spread down the line that we have to be ready to show our polio vaccination scar. Most everybody followed instructions to wear short sleeves, except for one or two, and Nurse Sara Walker found two names in her book who need the second polio booster sugar cube, and on the spot she asked them to open wide and stick out their tongues while she placed the sugar cubes. Next, she made a short announcement to everyone, "Remove long sleeves, before you go into the building."

I was near the front of the fourth grade line, and as the first dozen or so fourth graders passed through the screened front door, I watched as they rounded the nurse's station and continued down the hall to the last room on the left, which is the exact same procedure as previous years. I shuffled along reluctantly getting closer and closer to the screened door, but I stopped in my tracks when I heard a scream from inside the clinic, and it sounded like a boy screaming, and I kinda froze in place until Sandra Payne nudged me from behind, and I wanted to say something to her like 'did you hear that scream?' but my mouth dried up like the Sahara desert, and I couldn't say a word. Nervously, I looked around and realized nobody else heard the scream, so I passed off the notion that maybe I should be afraid, after all what chicken coward screams at getting a shot, and I decided somebody must have slipped on the shiny waxed floor! Once inside the Clinic, the line moved quickly around the nurse's desk and down the wide hallway toward the last room on the left, and when I stepped inside that room, I saw Dr. Downey rolling around on a wheeled, backless stool. He twisted toward a table full of shots, picked up one, and smiled at Dorothy Shealy who was right in front of me, then he pushed off the floor and creaked toward Dorothy. He caught her left wrist, held it steady and planted a long needle into her upper arm. He is very good at moving around on the rolling stool, and by the time I finished that thought, he was pushing a long needle into my upper left arm.

It happened so fast, I didn't have time to scream, but when I hurried to catch up to Dorothy, she was crying as she made her way through a connecting bath room into the actual farthest patient room on the left, and as we re-emerged into the wide hallway, I tried to lift my left arm to comfort Dorothy, but it hurt, a lot, and then I remembered the shot we got last year in third grade … typhoid … same as this year … the typhoid shot last year made my arm very very sore!

When Daddy was only four years old, his mother and brother died in the typhoid epidemic of 1915, and occasionally, Mother recalls sad stories of children paralyzed with polio way back then before there were vaccinations, these are sad stories but more often Mother approaches the topic from the positive angle and recounts how lucky we are to live in a country that is almost polio and typhoid free, when I get home today I have a question for Mother, "Who pays for the shots and vaccinations we get every year?"

Mother's answer, "In this great country, the government pays scientists to figure out how to make us immune to fatal diseases, and then the government pays to produce, ship and administer the vaccinations! We live in the greatest country on earth!" Mother is good at explaining.

I turned my attention to a pile of unfolded clean clothes on Mother's bed, and I found my favorite striped, long sleeve play tee shirt and blue jeans. I had a little trouble pulling the blue jeans up to my waist under my dress, so I carried my tee shirt into the kitchen to find Mother. First, she unbuttoned the back of my dress, then she pulled the short sleeves down over the blue jeans, and I stepped out of the dress. I gingerly poked my arms into the long sleeve tee shirt, and finally Mother helped me lift my 'typhoid shot' arm just as the telephone rang. Brenda Jaillet wanted me to come play. Mother thought it a good idea to get my mind off the still painful shot.

Brenda's mother (my Girl Scout leader) reminded us that we should exercise our typhoid-shot arms, so we decided to take two jelly jars down to the honeysuckle vines at the edge of the woods behind her house. We have been planning this endeavor for a long time. First we broke off long boughs of honeysuckle vines and dragged them into the open yard. We, like all the kids in the state of Georgia, know how to produce a drop of nectar from each aromatic white honeysuckle flower. So we began collecting nectar by gently pinching and breaking the stem while leaving intact the pollen tube, then we slowly pull the pollen tube through the long trumpet style, and in so doing we produce a drop of clear sweet nectar at the bottom of the flower. We sat there on the ground for hours methodically pinching, producing and depositing each nectar drop into the jelly jars, until we began to realize maybe this form of exercise might not actually be considered exercise at all because both our typhoid-shot arms were aching, boy howdy, and on inspection we decided her jelly jar and my jelly jar might actually contain a half of a teaspoon of sweet nectar, but when we tilted the jars to our lips well there was not enough nectar to roll along the inside of the glass jar and into our mouths. We growled the disappointment, snatched up the jelly jars and lids, and pounded up the hill into the house. Mrs. Jaillet does not drive, so I called mother to please come get me.

On the way home, we stopped in at the Drive-In-Theater, Mother had a recipe to give Maggi. The Jackson family operate the Drive-In-Theater and live on the premises in a very nice building that doubles as a snack bar for movie goers and a home for the Jackson family. That was Monday, and the very next day when Mother picked us up at school, we ran to the car through a downpour electrical storm. Of course it was hours before sundown but the dark angry clouds hid the sun and except for the lightning's brilliant illumination, the sky was as dark as midnight. At home someone called and asked to speak to Mother, and we heard Mother say, "I'm on my way!"

Mother hurried us back outside into the car, and she backed out of the yard and went flying out to the Drive-In-Theater where she pulled up close to the Jackson family home, and as she opened the car door she ordered us to 'stay put' in the car! Mother blasted into the Jackson family home leaving the door wide open revealing a total blackout inside the home. We could not imagine what in the world was going on, but we stayed silent and 'stayed put' until we saw Mother at the doorway motioning me to roll down the car window. "Mrs. Maggie was talking on the phone when the place was hit by lightening! She's here alone and she's a little stunned so I'm going to stay with her for a while, you two stay put in the car!"

In just a few minutes, the sun came out! The rain stopped and a glowing, ethereal rainbow wrapped up and over the Pine Grove Church lending an unworldly peace to what was until now an ordinary afternoon.

The two of us kids needed no entertainment and certainly playing a game of 'eye spy' or 'the alphabet game' would be sacrilegious. Through the still open doorway, we saw the lights inside come on, and directly, Mother came out of the Jackson home, and on the drive back to our house, Mother told us the person Mrs. Maggie Jackson was talking to on the phone is the person who called our house to ask Mother to go check on Mrs. Maggie, and when Mother first walked into the Jackson home, Mrs. Maggie was still lying on the concrete floor, but she was awake enough to ask Mother, "Well Vesta, come on in, would you like a cup of coffee?"

At the end of every school year, we have a class picnic. When I was in first grade the class picnic was in someone's yard (in town), and before leaving the Grammar School, all the first grade girls changed from dresses into swimming suits and to be proper the girls were required to cover their swimming suits with shorts, tee shirts, and for the walk, a towel. Finally, when the chaos inside the boys' bathroom subsided, most of the boys wore only a swimming suit with a towel hanging around their shoulders, and not a single girl complained about wearing three layers, no sir, for a complaint of that nature could only be characterized as improper behavior. So, finally, we set out walking, and at the destination house we threw our towels onto the front porch and the boys took the initiative because they could wait no longer, and quickly a boy opened the water spigot, and the boys shivered and turned bluer with each run through the sprinkler's very cold water spray, but as it turned out, the extra layer of clothing actually kept the girls a little bit warmer than the boys but still the girls were very bashful.

Both my class picnics at the end of second grade and third grade were at Alec's Lake, and both years, my Mother, and Randall of course, came over to the swimming pool because she insisted the life guard might need help watching so many children, another case of Mother's protective instincts, but actually there were plenty of mothers helping watch the kids and many more mothers down in the valley arranging the food on the weathered picnic tables.

At the end of fourth grade, my class picnic was at Tanner's Beach, and we rode in a school bus, and our instructions were to come to school wearing our swimming suits under our clothes for we might not have time to change before we board the bus, but for sure we had to bring a brown grocery sack with our name clearly written on the outside. We were told to pack a towel and dry clothes. This year, Mother had her camera with her and she took a picture of me and my friends.

The last day of school was on Tuesday and it was a tumultuous day for two reasons; first Joan came home finished with her quarter at West Georgia and Joan and Marilyn came with Mother to pick me up, and we did not head east to our home, instead we headed west, way out west but that day was also the last day ever for Gayle at Tallapoosa City School.

In a dizzying pace the wonders revealed to me in fourth grade geography, the variety of merit badges earned at Girl Scout meetings, the 'substitute-daughter' Friday nights with Ruth and Otto, the devout Sunday First Baptist Church classes both before and after the never changing Sunday visits to Mama and Papa all came to a screeching halt when school let out for the summer on Tuesday, May 29, 1956, the day before Memorial Day. At the end of that momentous day, the last ever school bus pulled away from the Tallapoosa City School because the city school is from here to fore just that: a school for walkers who live within the city limits, except in our case. Mother wants her children to continue at Tallapoosa City School, and of course that is allowed provided that we are transported to and from school by some means other than riding the school bus. Haralson County School buses from now on will deliver white students to and from the new West Haralson School and colored students to and from the new Haralson Consolidated School, and that is really something for the colored students, and I know how amazing and unbelievable it is because it's plain and simple, the coloreds have never had the privilege of riding on a school bus and I know all this because I listen when Mother and Thelma talk, and they talk all the time.

About two years ago, Mother and Thelma got all excited about a Supreme Court ruling that makes 'separate but equal' against the law because it is separate, but it's never equal, and Mother actually thought the state of Georgia would obey the new law and de-segregate the schools and the coloreds and the whites would go to the same school but of course, Mother was wrong and instead the state of Georgia started construction of new schools everywhere, and specifically in Haralson County, two new schools were built to be ready to open this fall 1956, and one new school is for the coloreds and the other is for the whites, but Mother keeps holding out, "Surely this time the two schools will be exactly separate but equal, after all it is 1956, for crying out loud."

When that last bell rang, a teary eyed Gayle came from her 5th grade room into my next door fourth grade room and she hugged me because she'll miss us when we are in Magdalena, New Mexico, and she is especially sad that she'll never again be a student in this big old, rambling, two story school house. It is logical that she should attend the new West Haralson School after all it is located a stone's throw from her home directly on the other side of Steadman Road. For the last time, Gayle and I walked arm in arm down the wide steps, around the landing, down the remaining wide steps and outside. It's a long and wide gravel walkway out to the street, and as we neared the one remaining bus, we made no effort to hide our gushing tears, and with one last hold-on-tight hug Gayle climbed on the bus, and I slapped the tears from my face and dashed beyond the bus to our 1954 Chevrolet nosed in to the curb behind the parallel-to-the-curb yellow bus. Randall was already in the back seat and Mother, Joan, and Marilyn filled the front seat. I climbed into the back, and in the floor board on one side of the hump was our metal thermos jug and six tin glasses each it's own color. We use these tin glasses all the time at home, mine is the pink one, and if by accident, someone drinks out of my pink tin glass, make no never mind, I'm not particular about drinking after anybody.

While we were in school that day, Mother and Joan and Marilyn loaded up the trunk of the car with stacks of folded clothes and ten or more grocery sacks some stuffed with shoes and some stuffed with underwear, and the bags saved space so's everybody could reach two cardboard boxes full of food. Mother planned ahead to take non-perishables like big jars of peanut butter and jelly, several cans of potted meat and sardines and a big box of soda crackers, but for the first day on the road she fried enough chicken and baked enough biscuits to fill two shoe boxes. When nothing more could possibly fit into the trunk, Mother and Joan loaded two pillows and a quilt in the back seat and three pillows and a quilt in the front seat.

At last Mother cranked up and turned the car around and drove south away from the school, and at Highway 78, she turned right and headed west following the signs to Birmingham. Marilyn took Daddy's letter out of the dash and read the list of all the cities we will drive through on our way across the country.

"First go through Birmingham, then Tuscaloosa Alabama, Columbus Mississippi, Greenville Mississippi, Texarkana Arkansas, Paris Texas, Wichita Falls Texas, Lubbock Texas, Clovis New Mexico, Vaughn New Mexico, Socorro New Mexico and finally, Magdalena New Mexico."

Then Marilyn read more from Daddy's letter, "The highways are paved, but there are many long desolate stretches with no sign of human life, and I won't rest unless you promise me you'll fill up each time the gas gauge gets down to half a tank."

Next, Mother read off the numbers and directed Marilyn to write the odometer mileage on Daddy's envelope, and that way when we get there, we can figure exactly how many miles Magdalena is from Tallapoosa.

Our 1954, two toned, blue and white Chevrolet has top quality, stain resistant, upholstered seats and the carpet on the floorboard is also stain resistant. Randall and I played 'I Spy' but that was short lived because we limited the things we 'Spied' to the inside of the car, and of course the colors inside the car consist of a very narrow field, but the 'Alphabet Game' could have gone on forever or at least as long as the hours and hours and hours it took to drive across the country, and the big old baby played the alphabet game pretty good for a three year old, but sometimes Marilyn or Joan helped him out and whispered something like 'u for under a car' or some other tricky letter and as we made our way west, Mother said, "You children are learning so fast, I think I can smell your hair burning."

Randall played the alphabet game from the ridiculous position of sitting on his pillow on the floorboard on the opposite side of the hump from the ice water thermos jug, and once he gets onto something, he can't find a quitting place, and it aggravates me a little because when he has a guess of something outside the car that starts with the letter of the alphabet in play, he first has to waste time standing up and actually looking out the window (that's how we play the game, for crying out loud), but he keeps on getting on my nerves getting hints from Joan, and sure enough if I say something, he makes one of his rolling eye faces at me, but it's comical and usually I'm the first one to laugh, and then there's no alternative but for everybody in the car to laugh with us!

If the big old baby happens to be asleep, no one speaks a word, and everyone welcomes the soothing silence. Usually, Randall conks out on the floorboard with his pillow against the hump, and I learned to place my pillow back to back with his for a little quiet time. After naptime, it's time for a change so I put my pillow in the middle of the seat and prop my legs on my door's armrest or the rolled down window, which is most comfortable for me because I love the wind against my feet. In this feet higher than head position, I watched a million power poles slide by, and up front, Mother, Joan and Marilyn took turns driving and unlike driving home from south Georgia, this time it's perfectly legal because Marilyn turned sixteen on March 20th and of course she has her actual driver's license.

Her sweet sixteen-birthday party was a wienie roast in the back yard, which is getting to be a very popular way to celebrate. I think everybody enjoys watching a fire send twisting sparks into the night air, and teenagers like to play 'spin the bottle' and when the bottle lands on a girl and the next spin lands on a boy, well then that boy and girl have to walk together all the way around the house in the dark, and then when they get back to the fire, they have to sit side by side on the ground, and of course there's always a lot of teasing about whether or not they kissed while they were alone in the dark. It's a funny thing to hear all the teasing, but it's sort of revolting when some boy inevitably asks, "Did you suck heads?"

We stopped at a filling station in Birmingham, Alabama, and when the attendant filled the gas tank and finished cleaning the windshield, mother paid the man with a twenty-dollar bill. He went inside to get Mother's change back, and Mother asked him if we could park at the edge of the gravel drive up area and have our supper, and then Mother said, "We are beginning a three or four day drive all the way from Tallapoosa, Georgia to Magdalena, New Mexico."

The attendant was truly impressed that a young mother and her four children would undertake to drive such a long distance, and he replied, "Yes'um, you're welcome to eat your supper here, but before you move to the edge of the gravel, first I'd like to check the oil in your engine, and the water in your radiator, and the air in your tires."

The man added a little oil from an already opened oil can, and Mother tried to pay him for it, but he wouldn't hear to it, "No'm, I can't charge you for leftover oil that's already been paid for, and let me just tell you this ma'am, right on down the road a piece, you'll cross over the creek bridge, and on the other side a mile or two, you'll come to a big d-up, and just keep it going slow till you're past the d-up."

Both before and after eating the greasy fried chicken picnic supper, we washed up in an indoor, very clean, hot-and-cold-running water restroom. I made note of the 'White Only' sign on the restroom door, makes me wonder why colored people would pay good money to buy gas at such a filling station unless of course they are about to run out of gas, in which case the shame should be on the mean white people. Mother was especially appreciative of the hot soapy water cleanups thereby eliminating the chance of grease spots on her beautiful quilts, and back on the road again, I stood up on the back seat and leaned over Joan's left shoulder and asked, "Mother, I heard that man warn you about a big d-up on the other side of the creek, what in the world is a d-up?"

Joan and Marilyn thought my question was pretty funny, and Mother choked back her own laughter as she explained, "Honey, the man was talking about a dip in the road a mile or two on the other side of a bridge. Here we are at the bridge, now we're going over the bridge, now I'll drive a mile or two, and now we've found the dip in the road. That man mispronounced the word 'dip.' He gave it two syllables, but there's only one syllable."

I wasn't done yet, and my next question was not in the least bit funny, "I noticed a 'white only' sign on the restroom door, where do colored people go to the bathroom?"

Mother again, "Honey, there's a lot of mean spirited white people in this world. My guess is colored people stop alongside the road and find privacy in the woods. It's a sad situation, and believe you me, I'd change it if I could."

With a heavy heart, I returned to the feet higher than head position, and Randall fell asleep on the floorboard, his pillow on the hump, and hours later, I felt someone reposition us from heads-together to feet-together thereby allowing the one quilt to cover both. We drove into the darkness, and many miles deeper into the black night, Mother quietly pulled off the road at another filling station. Despite Mother's best intentions Joan, Marilyn and I woke up but Randall did not; he only burrowed deeper into his individual pillow. We had no means of telling time, no watches and the electric clock on the Chevrolet Bel Air dashboard was a good idea that never worked, but luckily, this gas station also has a big, neon encircled, wall clock, and Joan asserted she's slept a good long nap and it's her turn to drive so Mother might have a chance to rest. Like the other filling station attendant, this one also washed the bugs off the windshield and checked the water and oil, but he took the short cut of only kicking the tires, and then mother gave him exact payment. Mother rounded the front of the car to the passenger side, Marilyn slid to the middle of the front seat while Mother plumped up two pillows and settled under the quilt with Marilyn.

Joan drove out her half a tank of gas and stopped again to fill up, and this time there was no clock inside the filling station, but the darkness was so profound that at the very least sunrise must be three or four hours away. Mother asked the attendant if we might use the restroom, but she went alone, and meanwhile Marilyn slid into the driver's seat as Joan paced back and forth from the front bumper to the rear getting a little exercise, and I rolled up my window against the very cool night air. Mother paid the gas bill, made her way around to the passenger's side and slid into the middle of the front seat. Joan crawled into the space in the front seat by the passenger door and tucked her big full cotton skirt around her legs as she pushed off the vent plunger just under the dash, and Marilyn started her first turn behind the wheel. The relative warmth without the opened vent lulled me quickly back to sleep, but by daylight the strong sun's rays through the back window warmed my feet and woke me up. I find it very comfortable to sleep with my feet above my head, just as I sometimes fall asleep at home in the wing back chair. I've always had a hot feet problem, just like my Daddy, and thinking about Daddy sent a jolt through my heart and brought me to my feet and my head surged upward slamming into the thankfully padded ceiling. "My feet are hot!"

Mother said, "You're just like your Daddy! And Sis. And Nora. They always have hot feet."

There's nothing she can say that pleases me more! I'm 'all Godwin' and I think Mama and Papa and Mother and Ruth are in that line up shoulder to shoulder with Daddy and Sis and Nora! I love my people, and I can't wait to see Daddy! But we're still in Mississippi! Boy howdy the United States of America is huge!

We were in another of the long straightaways of nothing ahead and nothing behind when Mother asked Marilyn to pull off the road while she went around to the trunk to find a specific sack in the food boxes, and with Mother back in the car we rolled on along, and Mother passed out biscuits wrapped in wax paper, and Randall followed her directive and pulled the thermos jug up onto the back seat, positioned himself on his knees in the floorboard, and one by one he retrieved tin glasses from the floorboard, held each precisely under the water spigot to exactly half full not wasting a single drop, and as we sipped our cool water and devoured our biscuits, Mother said out loud what everyone was thinking, "I wish we had a pot of hot coffee!"

For the next six or seven thousand hours, we saw only a few farm houses and a few farmers plowing their fields, and Mother made me switch places with Randall so he could stack up all the pillows except for one of course, and when the big old baby climbed high on the stack of four pillows, he screamed 'yipee' as he slid down on my head. I handed the thermos jug and tin glasses over the seat to Mother, and she helped me crawl over the seat and into her lap where I was glad to stay out of the line of fire as the rambunctious Randall slid down his pillow mountain again and again, and I have to admit, Randall is very creative, and we had a rip roaring good time laughing to high heaven!

That day when the sun was straight up in the sky, we pulled into Greenville, Mississippi, and Mother said, "Oh, there's a carnival in town. Find a parking place, Marilyn. I'll bet we can find some good home cooking, these people know how to celebrate Memorial Day!"

Randall clamored, "First, let's go ride the Ferris Wheel" and "I'm not one bit hungry!"

But he changed his tune when Mother pointed out a chili-over-hotdogs booth, and she bought five hot dog plates and five Co-colas, and the nice lady behind the makeshift pine-boards-on-saw-horses counter added the money to a cigar box and explained we're welcome to sit at the picnic tables set up under the big oak trees all along the dirt street leading to the Ferris Wheel at the far end. Those hot dogs didn't last long, and I almost blurted out, "This is better than a Varsity hotdog!"

But this time I'm the one who changed my tune and swallowed that silly comment because I'm not sure what my family would have done to me if I had uttered such profanity! Next, Randall rode the Ferris Wheel with a big sister, and Mother offered to ride with me, but I could tell she didn't really want to, so I saved her the misery by saying, "Ah, Mother, let's just watch."

Mother's anxiety vanished and privately, I relived the day last summer when Joan and Marilyn decided we'd go for a ride up to the top of Tally Mountain. Joan drove up, we examined the ranger's tower, and Marilyn drove down, Mother sat in the middle of the back seat, I had the big old baby in my lap on Mother's right side. Several times the road to the top switched back sharply on itself, and with each return Mother gave up her stranglehold on the now downhill armrest in favor of the current uphill armrest. I think she honestly pictured the car sliding sideways down the mountain against the grain, and her worst miscalculation was that somehow, everything would be ok if she shifted her anchor from one armrest to another with each switchback. My Mother is as strong willed and overpowering as anyone I know, and this revelation of her one silly weakness almost causes bile to back up into my throat.

Back to the case at hand, for dessert Mother bought an apple pie at another food booth, and another very nice lady placed the money in another cigar box, and Mother carried the pie as we sauntered back in the direction of our car. Once there Mother found a knife, the roll of wax paper, and five forks, Joan found a couple of clean bath cloths, and Marilyn stacked the tin glasses and pulled the thermos jug from the floorboard. At another shaded picnic table, Mother cut the pie and shoveled each piece onto a square of wax paper while Marilyn and Joan found an outside spigot to refill the thermos jug and wet the bath cloths. The carnival distraction relieved the tedium and with the apple pie's disappearance, Joan returned the pie pan to the pie booth, and the wet bath cloths cleaned the sticky from every face and hand, and now refreshed and full we crawled back into the Chevrolet.

For an entire day, we seemed to crawl through Arkansas, and I guess we're in one of those thousand mile segments of highway with no sign of human life. Did Daddy use the word 'desolate?' I'll never forget that word's meaning. There's nothing ahead into eternity almost as if nothingness is a constant realm all it's own, and the last ten thousand miles were just as much a void. Marilyn is the one who asks again and again, "What state are we in now?"

And the answer is always the same: TEXAS

In the back seat, Randall and I found time to think our own thoughts, thank goodness for that, and in the front seat, the rotation from passenger's side to center-hump-seat to driver's side continued with every half tank of gas, and I'm not exactly sure but I think we plugged along for forty days and forty nights and still we were in TEXAS.

In the blur of time immaterial, we ate peanut butter and jelly sandwiches for breakfast and sardines and crackers for dinner, and peanut butter and crackers for supper, and mostly all that eating took place when we pulled off the road in a 'dry sandy shade-less God forsaken back side of hell' (those are Mother's words), and I wish Marilyn would stop asking that question because I'm tired of hearing the answer: TEXAS!

Long past the point of delirium, and it's quite possible we've all screamed our lungs out, but believe it or not, like promised redemption Mother slammed on the brakes and stopped right in the middle of the highway, make no never mind, there's not the slightest possibility of a wreck on God's flat earth, no sir because there's no other traffic, and nothing to hit, not even a fence post! We followed Mother's example, vacated the Chevrolet, tracked at top speed her dusty trail back a few feet, finally to turn and adore a worn out, bent up, rusting metal sign on which the ancient, painted, pealing letters seemed to spell out 'Welco to New xico' There was no fanfare, no dancing girls, no flashing lights, zero ado, so we returned to walk west into the setting sun retracing our steps to the car left wide open, and I quickly preempted Marilyn, "What state are we in now?"

The five members of my family slugged along with no apparent resolve, but they were Johnny on the spot with a resounding reply probably heard in Magdalena hundreds of miles away. NEW MEXICO!

Mother decided this was as good a place as any for a quick redundant supper, but then back on the road new found energy kept us singing songs and telling stories until after a while I noticed Mother seemed unusually quiet. Mother's spontaneity creates a warm surround that when lost even for a few seconds, leaves a void deprivation that yearns for the return of her vivacious input. Now, silently, everyone came to understand something's wrong, and unwittingly our boisterous party mood became sullen and sober until finally Mother blew off her pent up worries and thanked the good Lord for lights up ahead, but just that second she declared, "Ugh oh. We're out of gas!"

She let the car's momentum move it off the road, then she directed every single one of us to, "Put your shoes on, we're all walking together to find help at that light in the distance."

As we walked along, the whole situation made everyone very nervous, in the dark Randall kept 'practicing walking backward' (his excuse to throw us off) when actually we cherish his protective instincts. No one said it out loud, but that's just what the man of the family should be doing at a time like this….walking backward in order to see headlights maybe a split second sooner than anyone else knowing full well a split second can be a life saved.

When the light in the distance ahead became a building, and a little closer to the building we made out a gas pump, and closer still we made out the tail end of a vehicle parked on the other side of the building, we relaxed our guard somewhat, but still the smell of danger kept us quiet and focused.

The nice old fellow at the gas station pumped gas into a two gallon galvanized bucket with a funnel tied to the handle, he carefully lifted the bucket up and into the bed of his truck, then he decided it'd be safer if, "All you children stay here, your Mother and I will go get your car, and we'll be back before you can say boo."

During that separation from Mother, I don't know about the other children, but I said boo about a thousand times! It's unlike me to be so anxious, and I made every effort to hide my fear, but ultimately, thankfully, my doubts were unfounded and I could not stop my feet from running to Mother when she parked the Chevrolet beside the gas pump, and before we piled into the car once more, the nice old fellow showed us to his well kept bathroom. When everyone else was again in place in the Chevrolet, I stalled and hem-hawed outside the back car door until I had a chance to signal the nice old fellow to stoop to my level and with strong conviction I hugged his very dark neck and said, "Thank you for being so nice to us."

The nice old colored fellow said he appreciated the business, it's not every day he sells a full tank of gas and to boot, Mother bought five candy bars as a sort of celebration. With all the hullabaloo behind us, Joan and Marilyn did some serious before-dawn driving through a somewhat hilly part of New Mexico, and when the rising sun jolted us awake, and Mother handed out the usual breakfast of peanut butter and jelly sandwiches, Marilyn found Daddy's last letter in the dash and with the brilliant sun behind us, she read aloud what I have memorized:

Dear Family,

We will be waiting in Magdalena; Socorro is the last town you'll go through. Drive on west through the desert, and you'll begin to see a few houses scattered along both sides of the highway and then suddenly you'll be in town. I have made a deal with the owner of a big house. He travels a lot, and won't be home very much over the summer months. He says about five years ago he rented the entire house to a Jones family who's youngest was five year old Bob.

He will reserve one room as his, leaving plenty of room in the rest of the big old house for us. His room has one doorway into a wide center hallway and another doorway that connects to the bathroom. The wide hallway leads all the way from the front door to the back door down the middle of the house, and the far end of the hallway serves as a spacious dining room. This gentleman explained the house was once back in the 1940's a maternity hospital, but it was sold when a newer multipurpose hospital was built in a neighboring town.

Back to your arrival, as soon as you drive into town, get ready to see us on the right side of the highway. My pickup truck will be parked right in front of the house.

Don't drive too fast across the country, for if you do, I'll worry myself into a state!

All our love,
Your Daddy & Carroll

Then the morning hours flew by at warp speed, and miraculously the meager earth bound Chevrolet folded her wheels up into the belly, and covered ground as if launched by a giant sling shot, and then: SOCORRO!!!!! We all know Socorro is to Magdalena what Temple is to Tallapoosa! One final gas station fill up and wash up, and Mother took the wheel for the last twenty-seven miles of what seemed just yesterday an endless journey. Let me verify, we left Tallapoosa not yesterday, not the day before yesterday, but Tuesday and today is Friday, the 1st of June, we have been in this 1954 Chevrolet for more than seventy-two hours, and now we're within walking distance of Magdalena! When the remaining miles could be no more than five, Marilyn once again retrieved Daddy's envelope with scribbled numbers from the dash, and quickly she subtracted the Tallapoosa odometer reading from the current odometer reading, and now cruising down the road, we are loudly and in unison cheering on the home team by counting the miles from Tallapoosa to Magdalena: "Seventeen hundred and thirteen, seventeen hundred and fourteen, seventeen hundred and fifteen, seventeen hundred and sixteen, ... There's Daddy! There's Carroll!"

Everything is right with the world!

Mother plowed the Chevrolet into the red dust behind Daddy's truck parked on the right side parallel to the paved highway, Daddy and Carroll are wildly waving their arms as if they think we don't see them, and from our viewpoint, Magdalena's landscape lacks detail, oh there are probably buildings other than the house we've read so much about, and there are probably cars and trucks other than Daddy's truck, and there are probably people other than Daddy and Carroll, but not as seen through our windshield!

I don't remember pulling the lever to open the car door, I don't remember my feet touching the red dust, I don't remember anything other than Daddy's dark tanned face, and Carroll's sunburned face smiling wide and happy. In deliberate, incremental jerks Daddy's arms wrapped around Mother when she apparently began floating downward, she must have tripped but Daddy caught her arresting contact with the ground, and in the center of five, Carroll and Daddy are covered with arms much like a morsel of food is covered with ants at a picnic. There is hooting and hollering and laughing! The army of ants unpacked the car, each carrying clothes and shoes and thermos jug and tin glasses, and pillows and quilts, and tales of the odyssey deserved knee slapping from Daddy and 'Really?' from Carroll.

Mother bathed the big old baby in the giant kitchen sink while he complained and resisted with, "Daddy likes me real dirty."

In quick succession, Randall, Marilyn, Mother, Joan and I took baths in the huge claw foot bathtub, and hot water came through the bathtub spigot! We were sweaty and grimy because this little town of Magdalena is situated in a desert and that means the temperature most summer days is well over ninety degrees, and there's no rain in sight, but how can this be? "Daddy, how can it be cool inside this house?"

Daddy and Carroll toured us around to all the windows and doors in order to explain the cool inside temperature, and the secret is the adobe (mud) walls are more than a foot thick and can capture the cool night air through opened windows and hold it inside behind daytime closed windows and shutters. In the tour, Daddy and Carroll saved for last a long cavernous bedroom on the front southwest corner of the house. There were four double sized beds, each made up in brilliant, store bought white sheets, turned down in invitation to the weary, and on cue with no words wasted, the beds became populated, Carroll in his own, Randall and Mother in another, Joan & Marilyn in one and I crawled over Daddy to claim my place next to the wall.

Against the brilliant sun, every window's inside shutters were drawn shut, and in the coolest, most peaceful place on earth, as motion ended everyone slept, everyone except Daddy and me. I could not go to sleep, but I thought it best to pretend, and secretly I had one eye slightly opened toward a very tanned Shug Godwin, and my heart just about exploded when Daddy's long slender fingers quietly wiped away his tears. The love in our family is palpable, and unwittingly, I composed a quick little poem in my head:

I'll climb the highest mountain;
I'll swim across the sea.
I'll move the sand from the desert,
If that's what you need of me.

And Daddy wiped another tear, but I did not cry because the moment was not about me, This is all about Mr. Shug Godwin. It's about his accomplishment, his organizational skills, his adventurous spirit, his adherence to honesty, his willing daredevil attitude, his devotion to family and friends, his mental capacity, his ambition, his not just survive but come out on top, his attention to detail, and last but certainly not least his inspirational aura. He is a hero now and forever.

That Friday began for Carroll and Daddy at the sawmill campsite, where they bathed in the bath tub situated in the corner of the bunkhouse next to the roaring hot cook stove and the back door, then each in order dumped the water from the bath tub and shaved and dressed in their knockabout clothes before driving sixty miles into town. In town, they kept themselves busy following the directions note left by the house owner. They found sheets and put them on the four beds in the one giant hospital ward, they stacked clean white towels in the bathroom, and they bought groceries at the town's well stocked mercantile, and with all preparation complete, Daddy planted himself under the big shade tree at the front door making sure of an open view to the east and Carroll hurried around the back of the stores to the Drug Store on the north end of town where he bought a double dip strawberry ice cream cone for Daddy and a double dip vanilla ice cream cone for himself. They are a mismatched pair, Daddy's complexion is dark as is his hair, Carroll's freckled face is sunburned red, his hair is John Owens yellow, but the two are both six feet tall, and they share eyes as blue as the sky.

As we came awake after a family afternoon nap, it's Friday night in Magdalena and the Godwin family (complete at last) filled the chairs at a large round supper table of fried chicken, fresh squash, coleslaw, snap peas and biscuits, and when Daddy could eat no more he declared, "I'm not asking for sympathy, but that's the best meal I've had since leaving home."

Carroll, Joan & Marilyn cleared the dirty dishes, and the assembly line made quick work of washing, rinsing (my job standing in a chair), drying and putting away the heavy each-it's-own-color dishes. Daddy, Mother, and Randall stepped out the side door from the room known as the hospital's sunroom. The narrow, west, side yard offered two chairs on either side of the door, and to the north behind the hospital house two parents watched from their front porch as their two little boys Pedro and Carlos played in the desert sand. Randall needed no introduction but Daddy shook the man's hand and Mother smiled and waved and told the story of driving non-stop from Georgia.

With the clean dishes back in place on the shelves, all seven Godwins retraced Carroll's earlier steps to the Drug Store where Mother said, "These ice cream cones take the place of a birthday cake."

And all around we wished "Happy Birthday Daddy."

With birthday cones in hand the family wandered up and down the main street busy with Friday evening customers. Then Daddy carried the big old baby as we strolled back home through the dusty red vacant lot common to the stores' back doors. Carroll walked beside us as Joan carried me and it felt so cozy and safe and happy and of course anyone would move all the desert sand for a reward such as this.

Carroll and Daddy took the next morning (Saturday) off and Daddy produced the key to a very small diner built along side the highway just a few steps to the east of our hospital house. This diner is completely stocked and ready for business, if Mother wants to run it for the summer. The rent, already paid, includes the use of the diner, and the owner made the point that he himself is usually the diner's best customer for he has no inclination to do any cooking what so ever. So we all followed our parents into the small diner noting the hours painted on the door, Monday – Saturday noon to six, and with the big old baby on his very own counter stool, Mother lifted the counter's east end, ducked under, and made her way along the narrow behind-the-counter workspace aisle, and midway she turned to face the seven-stool full house, and calculated that she could indeed 'run' the diner. In accordance with the hours of operation and the two posted menus one posted on the door the other posted over Mother's shoulder, Mother set out to cook up some Georgia chili and in the process, she located the other items on the menu, hotdogs in the refrigerator and potatoes in a bin for french fries. She vowed to have the menu items ready for noon customers, and while Mother worked behind the counter, Joan found some clean paper in my book satchel still in the trunk of the car, and skillfully she made new signs, one which she taped to the inside of the front plate glass window so that all outside can read,

"Tallapoosa Georgia = 1,716 miles"

and on the door inside the diner Joan taped new menus over the old:

Georgia chili-over-hotdogs
Georgia fried potatoes
Chili-less hotdogs

We were the buzz of Magdalena, (probable population - 1,000 people) and most days all seven stools and the four chairs at two small window-side tables were constantly full from noon to six, and as the diner customers gradually learned to enjoy the much too mild Georgia chili, they also gradually came to know our story. On Saturdays, a young twenty-year-old rodeo rider named K.O. came into the diner whenever Marilyn happened to be inside, and by another coincidence a young man named Sonny came in when Joan was present. K. O. wore tight blue jeans, and a tight button up cowboy shirt with a yoke front and back, and he always wore a cowboy hat, which he politely hung on the row of nails in the corner. Sonny on the other hand, wore blue jeans, a yoke-less button up shirt and no hat, cowboy or otherwise. Sonny came out from Mississippi to help his uncle for the summer, but as yet no one knew the details of 'helping' his uncle.

Meanwhile, every day Randall played with Pedro and Carlos, and I made friends with Shirley Grayson. Her parents own the Grayson Hotel just a block up hill from our house, Shirley is my age, and we play mostly in the Hotel attic, it's fun up there because there are lots of old time clothes and hats, there is one saddle and lots of furniture with mirrors. We make up pretend games, and sometimes we are so absorbed we forget to go downstairs for dinner. The hotel has thick walls but not quite as thick as our house, and it is Shirley's chore to open the windows and shutters at the end of the day and close the windows and shutters at the beginning of the day, and like our house the Hotel attic is amazingly cool during the hot summer days. Yesterday, Shirley's mother reminded us that she and Shirley are leaving town for a day or two, and with no one to play with I spent the morning hours alone in the sun room, I closed the three doors and privately worked up a dance routine to a song from 'My Fair Lady.' Barefooted as usual, I danced all over the sunroom mostly from mirror to mirror watching my feet and singing, 'On the Street Where You Live.' I finally tired of my solo performance and made my way to dinner in the diner where Mother greeted me with her usual 'hug and smack' (in layman's terms, she pulled me to her side and planted a kiss on the top of my head). Full of Mother's delicious fried potatoes, I found Randall and Pedro and Carlos under the pod-laden shade tree outside the big bedroom window. I stood in the shade with the three boys and listened as Pedro and Carlos described the really old headstones in the cemetery, and without letting me vote, it was a unanimous decision to hike out into the desert north of town. Just a few yards into the desert, I found a patch of beautiful cactus flowers, but evidently boys do not care even a tiny little bit about cactus flowers, and my cactus flower doting left me no choice but to run the remainder of the distance to the cemetery. One thing I've learned, the desert sand is hot, but the motion of walking or running dislodges the hot sand surface, exposing cooler sand and I like the warm massage to my bare feet. The very first week in New Mexico, Randall found a piece of wood which he whittled into a clunky, cumbersome shotgun, but the next Sunday when Daddy & Carroll showed up as usual in time for Sunday dinner, they took turns whittling on the wooden shotgun and now it looks almost real, and that day in the cemetery, I came to wish that the whittled shotgun contained ammunition more deadly than sawdust.

In the good sized cemetery, Randall and I hung back and slowly wandered from grave to grave along the south end (the end nearest town), and Randall kept examining and picking at the artificial flowers hanging from each head stone or wooden cross. He finds it hard to believe the flowers are fake and he wailed, "If they are made out of paper, why can't I rip them?"

My protective instinct kept me close to Randall, while Carlos and Pedro strayed farther and farther toward the northern side of the cemetery. Suddenly, Randall and I heard a voice yelling over and over again, "Rattlesnake, rattlesnake!"

The two bigger boys must have heard a whistle or a gun shot because in exact unison, they sprang into running mode like runners in an Olympic contest dashing toward us making sure to stay in the grave-less lanes so as not to show disrespect for the dead by walking on their graves which are meticulously laid out in precise rows with each grave's feet toward the east.

Daddy taught me the reasoning is that on judgment day, at the new day's beginning, the bodies will sit up facing the rising sun.

I have a personality disorder when faced with a dire situation, I have no alternative but to let my consciousness run through any number of unimportant, irrelevant side thoughts, and now in real time, when my mind finally again focused on the crisis at hand, the bigger boys came running lickady split past us (whoosh) back into and across the desert to town. I had to think fast, so I grabbed Randall's hand, held on tight because there's no option for me to carry him, it's not physically possible, despite the Boy's Town movie quote, "He ain't heavy, he's my brother."

I am totally devoted to my brother, and I'll come back later and kill snakes with my bear hands, but first I have to escort the big old baby out of the wilderness, so now I have to improvise and prioritize and thus I issued a directive, 'Run as fast as you can,' and the big old baby and I headed out across the desert, coming along in a distant Olympic third and forth but this race is not connected to any metal or ribbon, and there I go again, there's something wrong with a person who can't stay focused when lives are at stake, but somehow I had time to sort through my ramblings and realize another important positive, that being, it is possible to avoid hazards slightly lesser than a rattlesnake by being quick with decision making and implementation. All manner of growing vegetation in the desert presents a danger, seriously; I'm not sure which but I've learned some cactus needles burrow deeper and deeper into the body's tissue, and this time culling through pertinent information seemed essential to reality. Randall and I were both barefooted, as usual, and in order to cut by half the deadly possibilities, I screamed over my shoulder, "RUN IN MY TRACKS!"

With the imperative understood and demonstrated, I did not loosen my grip on my baby brother's hand, and in fact if attention to detail applies, my grip became multiplied and concentrated exponentially, and with peace of mind that Randall can run as fast as I can run, and not stumble or pull away, we covered a vast amount of territory, and very soon, I saw in the distance that the neighbor boys are standing on the neighbor's front porch, cheering us on as if we are winning the race for a million dollars, but I want nothing to do with any old dirty money in conjunction with possibly loosing my littlest brother! This is a time for serious action meant to protect and deliver, and if running through unforgiving obstacles doesn't qualify as serious proclivity, well then what on God's green earth can qualify?

I take all the credit for saving Randall's life that day, and I can tell you there's no mistaking the pounding in my chest today and any day if I dare to remember and relive the fear, and I can also tell you right this minute, this is a story which I myself will never repeat to my Daddy. No Sir Re! Because in this story, the line of responsibility is blurred up to a point, but when I followed the boys through the desert to the cemetery that day, I outlined and defined the line of obligation, and my action is something I regret! I should have used any leverage to keep three and a half year old Randall safely in town. He could have fallen into a man eating cactus, or stepped on a flower armed with flesh penetrating barbs! Of course I can still imagine the worst, but thankfully, the worst did not happen, but when I climbed into the bathtub that night, I saw and felt the actual innocent consequence of running a desert gauntlet in the blistering sun, that being the white precise outline on my body of my shorts and shirt against the brilliant red sunburn which is probably good reason for a visit to a real current day hospital, but I kept silent for to complain about my sunburn and receive treatment would be to admit my negligence. I did however, smear Jorgen's lotion on the accessible, and Camphor Ice soothed the splits in my lips.

With Shirley Grayson as my only friend in Magdalena, there are many days when I invent solitary pastimes, and I truly enjoy walking to the boundaries of town. One day I made my way from our house, to the opposite corner of town, and there I found a house at the edge of the desert that appears to be out of place. As you can imagine, every single sandy inch of the streets and yards are brown with no adornment, no trees but a few Pinion pines, scrub oaks and the occasional Hop tree like the one beside our house distinctive because of hanging pods. Of course, it seems a foregone conclusion that grass can never grow in the desert, but that notion is proven false with the one house at the southwest corner of town. It's a nice ranch type house made of brilliant white stucco, and in the front yard, there are several very tall shade trees that look nothing at all like the usual scrub oaks in this part of the country, but they seem to be giant oaks like the one in our front yard back in Georgia. Almost every day, I visit the house with the green grass and Georgia Oaks, and routinely, I find sprinklers soaking down the grass. I'm not sure how much water is sprinkled, but judging from the resulting green, it must be gallons enough to fill a boxcar every day. This white stucco is now my fantasy house filled with exotic excitement, and tales of riches, and I pretend there's a family who went all the way across the country to dig up the giant 'oak' trees and ship them 1,700 miles to Magdalena because there once was a sweet little girl who loved to play house under the giant oak trees, but when she died of a rattlesnake bite, her parents knew they could not live in Georgia ever again. I have a penchant for make believe ever since Uncle Thomas lulled us to sleep with a story of a beautiful white swan. His quickly made up specific details set an example for me which I'll never abandon, but which I'll use to encourage my own creativity venting dreams pent up and longing for release.

I have always gone barefooted in the summer time, I love to go barefooted, and it's especially comfortable in Magdalena because of the fine desert sand, however when I cross the paved highway, I have to skedaddle as fast as possible to avoid third degree burns to the bottom of my feet, but once I'm across the highway, there's no more pavement in town. Sometimes along the way to and from my green grass fantasy house, I pass by a pretty white wooden church with a tall steeple, and on Sunday morning, July 1st, I bolted out of bed, and as I polished my white Sunday shoes, I discovered a quarter size hole in each sole, but oh well, no one will ever see the holes in the bottom of my shoes. Sundays are very lazy especially for Carroll and Daddy, and today, Carroll interrupted my ironing with, "What are you getting all dressed up for Sugar?"

"I'm going to church. I've found a pretty white church with a tall steeple, the only bad part is the sign out front says they won't have Sunday School again until the fall, but maybe I'll meet some girls my age in the sanctuary, but even if I don't, living in town gives me the power to walk to church, I just gotta see how that feels."

I continued to sprinkle my cotton dress using the aluminum and cork sprinkler head made to fit inside the neck of a Co Cola bottle, and with the last ruffle ironed, I pulled the dress over my head and buttoned the top two and the bottom two buttons down the back. I sat on the bed and jerked white lace edged socks onto my feet, buckled the shoe straps, and quickly, found Mother in the kitchen. "Will you button my dress? I have proof that men are smarter than women!"

"Oh you do, do you?" Mother said through a smile.

I stood still so she could button, "Yes, Mother, men are definitely smarter than women because men never wear shirts that button up the back!"

I combed my hair and hurried out the door, and I reached the church just as the bell in the steeple tower rang out a joyous call to worship. I settled on a bench half way between the pulpit and the door, and a family with two very young children sat down on the same bench beside me, and on my other side a single old man sat down at the end of the pew between me and the opened window. I did not turn to look around, but I heard a lot of commotion as the church filled up, and when I did have a chance to look, I did not see a single person my age, but every person who caught my eye, smiled a warm welcome which was both calming and consoling, but my peace became hollow, and I began to fidget when I remembered the holes in my shoes, so I tucked my feet back under the bench reasoning that if I crossed my legs, the sole of my suspended shoe might be exposed all be it the bench was too high for crossing my short legs anyway. I decided to rest one foot and then the other over the opposite foot on a ballerina's tiptoe barely touching the floor under the pew. Midway into the sermon, a lady in front of me, stood to take her crying baby outside, and then her vacant spot revealed to me the feet of the people sitting in the next pew forward. With the forward feet and more importantly, one shoe sole completely visible, I became so embarrassed that I felt my face turn flaming red. Among a church full of strangers who knew nothing of me, I wanted to announce to the congregation that I am loved by a wonderful Mother and Daddy, and I have four loving brothers and sisters, but instead of proclaiming my status, my shoulders rounded under the awful weight of needed sympathy and pity offered to a very poor, family-less vagabond with holey soles for if I can see feet under the second pew ahead of me, then it has to follow that the people in the row behind the row behind me have had thus far a full view of the bottom of my shoes! Of course they have, and I've made the holes absolutely visible, unmistakably visible. When the preacher said the final 'Amen' I pretty much slithered out of there as fast as I could, but outside, several ladies hindered my escape and actually gave me reason to believe they are not the least bit interested in my shoe situation which serves as a much needed self esteem booster, and I now believe they know all about me and my loving family, and in fact, I'm convinced the citizens of Magdalena are proud of the Godwin story. At home when I took off my holey soles (I could not resist the pun), I thought I'd actually get away with throwing my white shoes in the trash, but the minute I tossed them in the can, of course my philanthropic Mother came into the room and retrieved the holey soles to hand down to another less fortunate little girl, and I whined, "Oh, Mother, it was so embarrassing. I'm sure the people sitting on the second row behind me had a good look at the holes in the soles."

But Mother made light of the sordid story with her own puns, "Don't fret, I'm satisfied the church was made more God like with two visiting holy souls."

Mother does that all the time, and her sense of humor has established an inner plum line for me, she brings me right back especially if I display a lack of inner strength, and for the most part, self pity doesn't enter into the equation, but contrarily, I know the worth of a smile and frankly, I'm not a whiner, I'm not a victim, I don't want any commiseration, I don't qualify for anyone's sympathy, and studying my mirror when I'm in a mock self pity mode the reflection is of a mundane, simple, nothing-special Janet looking back at me, but there is a physical transformation when I'm true to my inner effervescence. It's plain to see I'll fare better if I consecrate my being to a true bubbling selfless mode, and such an attitude is easy because I like people, and positive energy connects and lifts the spirit. Negative resentment clouds and alienates, and I will never fall into such a trap. I've learned from the best that laughter and down to earth sincerity alters. 'Putting on the dog' advances no one, and I should welcome my Magdalena 'holy souls' anchor.

At the end of that day, as the end of every Sunday, we said goodbye to Daddy and Carroll, that's the sad part, but the happy, I mean HAPPY part is we will see them again next Sunday, and this coming Sunday, Daddy is taking Mother, Randall and me on a dirt road trip. He knows all the dirt roads in these parts, and he thinks the scenery is best toward Truth or Consequences. He explained the small New Mexico town was renamed 'Truth or Consequences' because the citizens accepted the challenge of a radio show by that name and they won!

Usually Daddy and Carroll arrive Sunday mornings, and actually this works well because if they arrive on Saturday night, they face competition for the bathtub, but on the other hand, on Sunday morning there is no wait and each of the men in our family can soak leisurely in the tub. Carroll and Daddy regularly make comments about the luxury, and today, Carroll went first in the tub, and when he came out of the bathroom dressed in spanking clean, creased khaki pants and a white button up shirt, he found me again at the ironing board, but this week he knows of the plan, and he of course, understands that even if we don't see a single person on the dirt roads, it's polite to get dressed up for a family outing, and when I finished with the iron, Marilyn took over to iron Daddy's white shirt and khaki pants, and next Mother ironed her own dress and button up shirt for Randall, and I'm grateful that Mother pulled my holey white Sunday shoes from the trash last week.

We loaded up the car with a picnic dinner, four colorful metal glasses, and ice water in the thermos jug, and mysteriously, Daddy insisted that Mother pack towels and underwear for all, and on the way west out of town, Daddy stopped in at the Conoco station which is opened on Sundays because it is the last chance for fill up before travelers enter a vast unpopulated area west of Magdalena stretching all the way into Arizona, and our time in the store ended when the attendant came inside with the amount owed for the full tank of gas, and as we pulled onto the paved highway heading west out of town, I decided that I will come back to the Conoco station when I have a lot of time to look at the beautiful turquoise jewelry in the glass case!

We drove along dusty dirt roads kicking up a huge red plume of dust, and the scenery was 'breathtaking' to quote Mother, and the landscape is unique to us because back in Georgia never in a million years will we see dry canyons and thousand acre open range grazing lands separated by two-strand-barbed-wire fences and 'cattle crossings' which do the opposite and prohibit livestock 'crossing' but the tires of our car easily cross over. Daddy found his way to the first attraction, and when he slowed and parked the car under a lone shade tree like the ones growing in the green grass front yard of my fantasy house, I asked the name of the tree and Daddy's answer dictates the untruth of my made up story of grieving parents shipping huge shade oaks from Georgia to Magdalena. "It's a cottonwood, and that tells us this is a run off canyon in the rainy season because the cottonwood tree needs a supply of water."

We hiked a short distance to an open area littered with rocks as big as Daddy's hand, a nice change from endless sand. Randall was the first to pick up a rock, and then we all picked up rocks and their unusual shape prompted Daddy to say, "Look at the rocks in your hands, do they have similar characteristics?"

Yes, the rocks look like the rounded bark of a tree .... because they are trees turned to stone with the petrifying process over thousands of years, and now with this amazing information, we stood still to absorb and to marvel at the acres and acres of fallen petrified trees all around us for miles and miles! Lost in thought, Mother woke us and herded us out of the harsh desert sun back to the cottonwood shade tree where she spread out a quilt and produced the picnic dinner. As we ate our dinner, we watched a little chipmunk scurrying around picking up small seeds broken loose from a pod similar to a very small pinecone. The scampering little chipmunk is the first we've ever seen, and we talked of his ambitious search for food to store away for winter, and Randall said, "I'd help him if I had time."

There's a way of life expressed in the little boy's words, and yes we would help him if we had time. Back in the car, we left the petrified forest and the last shade tree and cruising along now over slightly rolling hills with no visual obstacles, it seems we can see for thousands of miles all around, and an hour into the desolation, Daddy stopped the car again, and this time he told us to strip down to our underwear, and then Daddy led the way about two car lengths off the road to a round livestock drinking tank bigger around than two 1954 Chevrolet cars parked side by side. Now that I recall the wonder of that livestock tank full of water, I realize not one of us had to ask because each of us surmised that the windmill water feed is situated over a deep well water source and with a breeze to fuel the windmill and the water pump the water level in the tank is a constant. Daddy climbed over the tank's edge into the warm, waist deep water. I followed Daddy's example and shinnied high enough up the side to throw one leg over and ease myself into the water, next Mother handed Randall over to Daddy where the big old baby did his treading water tadpole swim across to the other side, and there he held on while Daddy helped Mother climb in. We splashed and squealed and floated in our own private world, untethered to decorum or rules, and the soft blue incubator sky held us together in our game, and that private, secluded, wilderness swimming party will forever fuel memories of boundless love and devotion with an eternal life all it's own, never to be diminished, never to be lost, never to be erased.

The next week, as I promised myself, I walked down to the Conoco every single day, and boy howdy, I found a sterling silver and turquoise ring that is the prettiest ring in the whole world, and on Friday, the lady behind the counter, who remembers me from church, offered to let me try it on, and it fits perfectly! When Daddy and Carroll got home Sunday morning, everyone seemed to have forgotten that my birthday is tomorrow, but first things first, Carroll and Daddy got cleaned up and Mother cooked dinner, and then Daddy asked if anyone wants to ride down to the Conoco. As usual, he has to fill up the pickup and the gas cans enough to fill up the pickup bed and also as usual, I went with Daddy, and while the attendant filled up the pickup and all the cans, Daddy and I waited inside, and initially, I decided it's better not to mention the ring, but then contrary to my norm I couldn't help myself from blurting out, "Daddy, can I have this ring?"

As I said that, I pointed through the glass to the most beautiful ring in the world, and the same lady behind the counter stopped adding up Daddy's bill, and next thing Daddy asked the lady, "How much is the ring?"

She told him the exact amount without looking at the ring tag, I guess she remembers from Friday, and Daddy said, "Shugy Pie, (it's his nick name for me, and I'm very proud that it's a derivative of his own nick name) I have to pay for all of this gas first, but when the gas is added up, if it costs less than what I have in my pocket, and if paying for the ring does not take every bit of my cash then you can have it, but you have to understand I need a goodly amount of operating cash."

So I held my breath while Daddy handed her some money, and she gave him some money back, and still holding my breath, I waited while Daddy counted out the price of the ring and laid that much money on the counter top, and finally, he counted the cash money left in his bill fold, and I finally took a breath when he said, "That's enough to get me through the week."

Then he turned to the lady behind the counter and asked her to get the ring for me, and as she reached into the glass case, pulled out the ring and handed it over to me I held my breath so long that I thought I might pass out, but I simply could not force air into my lungs until Daddy actually paid for the ring, counted his money and verified he has fifty dollars left over, and when he did, finally I put the ring on my finger!

Pedro and Carlos and their parents showed up one evening with a very cute fat puppy, and the little fellow looks more like a bear cub than a canine. After playing all the next day with Husky, I had a great idea! "Let's go get Husky's last brother, Carlos says he's as black as night, and he has a cork screw tail, and he's as smart as Husky, and Carlos and Pedro wanted the black puppy but their mother has always said she won't have a black dog."

Carlos and Pedro agreed to go along and show Mother the way to the black puppy's house, and at the last minute their mother came along too because she wants to ride in our 1954 Chevrolet. The minute we saw Smokey, we agreed he was as black as soot, and soot is a byproduct of smoke and no other name fits. At home, we played with Smokey and Husky til well after dark, and then Mother's face disclosed her shock when Carlos and Pedro's mother jerked Huskey by the tail and dragged him whining between our houses to a rope anchored into the ground, and all through the night because the windows were wide open, we heard Husky begging to be set free. The next day, Mother asked Carlos and Pedro's mother if we could let Husky sleep with Smokey, and she actually thought it a good idea, as a sort of transition phase away from the mother dog, and so began the house training of two (not just one), but it seemed to come naturally for the two intelligent puppies, and after the first night, neither Smokey nor Husky had an accident.

The first Saturday night of every month, the Magdalena townspeople come together in the big sand lot behind the diner next to our house, and the town owns a movie projector, and somehow the town commissioners get their hands on full length movies. There is no big screen like the drive-in back in Tallapoosa, instead the movie is projected onto the long narrow white stucco building that is situated along the edge of the lot at the property line between us and Carlos and Pedro's house. We arrived from Georgia on Friday, June 1st, and the very next night Saturday June

2nd we watched an old 'Thin Man' movie. It's great! Once a month, the same thing happens, everybody brings quilts and pillows and the children run and play, and it doesn't matter if there's a lot of noise, because every house in town is dark and empty, nobody is trying to go to sleep, no sir, everybody crowds into the open sand lot behind the diner.

Almost every day, Mother me money for two ice cream cones, and the nice lady starts dipping up mine and Randall's favorite flavors when we walk through the Drugstore door. This is another bonus to living in town, back in Georgia, there's no place in the country to get an ice cream cone, and for sure we cannot walk all the way up town to the Drugstore. I love living in town, everybody in Magdalena is so nice, but our time is running out, Mother told us we have to leave this Friday, the 31st of August. Carroll left August 27th, he's hauling a load of logs across the country, and one sawmill hand is going with him. Carroll will sell the logs in Tallapoosa, and that money will pay his tuition and books at Georgia Tech. Classes at Georgia Tech and West Georgia Junior College and Tallapoosa city schools begin on the same day, the day after Labor Day, September 4th, and Daddy made sure to send Carroll home in the best log truck, and every night we go to the pay telephone booth at eight o'clock and usually the pay telephone rings at straight up eight o'clock, and it's Carroll checking in because Mother gets her way on stuff like that.

Daddy came into town to spend the last Thursday with us in Magdalena, and he took me and Randall to a lumber yard where Joan's boyfriend Sunny works, I'm not sure you'd call it a town, all I know is we went through some more barren countryside to get there, but it was worth it because Sunny took us for a ride on a Heister which is a really big piece of equipment that can lift thousands of pounds of lumber if it's stacked on a pallet. The pallet is a wooden platform that allows the Heister's lifting blades to come up under the heavy load, and once the pallet is in position on the lifting blades well then it's easy to drive around all over the place and put the heavy pallet down on a flatbed truck or back down on the ground in a different place. Daddy loves this heavy equipment stuff he'd have one of every Caterpillar made if he could afford it. He's still talking about someday building a dam to dam up the creek that runs across the east corner of the property back home in Georgia, he gets Carroll all excited when he talks about buying a Caterpillar bulldozer to move the dirt, but first he'll have to buy more land so the resulting forty acre lake will be on Godwin land only.

Our last night in Magdalena, Mother cooked fried chicken for supper because that's Daddy's favorite, and she made way too much so we can take some with us in the morning, and Daddy can take some with him too. It hurts so much way down deep inside that we look like ghosts walking around loading up the car, Mother can't stop crying and Daddy is as gray as ashes right through his dark tan, I want to sob and wail and beat my hands against the wall, but that would do no good, and probably might even do harm to my hands, and when that thought about harming my hands went through my head, I couldn't quiet the laughter rising to the surface, and the big old baby got kind a silly trying to make it even more funny, and his silly giggles were contagious, and pretty soon Mother, Daddy, Joan, and Marilyn came into the room, and that's what it took to stop Mother's tears, and when the laughter died down a little bit, Mother said again for the nine hundredth time, "At least we can laugh!"

We woke early, hours before sun up, and after breakfast, Daddy went on back to the sawmill, and all we had to do was bring our pillows with us because everything else was already loaded, and the big old baby fell asleep in the back seat before Smokey and I crawled in. Joan was at the stirring wheel with Marilyn in the middle in the front seat, and lickady split Mother turned off all the lights in the house and came running to the car with Husky in her arms! Since the beginning, when he wined all night tied to a stob, Husky has slept beside Smokey under a bed in our house, and Carlos and Pedro and their parents have enjoyed quiet nights, but in the process, 'possession is nine tenths of the law' and both puppies are now ours. Mother kidnapped Husky in the before dawn darkness, the lights in the house next door never came on, and with good reason because we said our 'goodbyes' yesterday, and yet Husky still slept last night next to Smokey, and the solitary noise of Joan's engine start up did not interrupt our neighbor's night's sleep, and not until we were safely half way to Socorro, did Mother lift Husky from her lap, up and over the front seat into the back seat. I don't recall thinking anything was out of the ordinary, and honestly, if our neighbors wanted Husky, they certainly would have said so yesterday.

Every tedious detail of the trip from Tallapoosa to Magdalena is etched in my mind forever, but the return trip remains a soft sweet memory at least after the initial stabbing pain of driving farther and farther away from Daddy, and I believe the puppies made all the difference at least they did in the back seat. These smart big old puppies probably weigh twenty pounds each, and they transformed the tedium into fun because they are still awkward in dealing with their rapid growth, which makes their movements clumsy and riotously funny. We did not have to play 'I spy' or any other silly game because the puppies kept us entertained even in their sleep when they look so angelic, but also in their waking devilish tug of war play-fullness. They are the ones who came up with games to play, and their imaginative frolics never ceased to amaze us. They changed the confines of the back seat into a boisterous giant playground, and we laughed ourselves from state to state on the one thousand, seven hundred and sixteen mile return.

Mother planned ahead for our Labor Day arrival back home and back to school the very next day, Tuesday, September 4th. She knows if we have time on our hands waiting for school to start, we'll naturally regret leaving Daddy too soon, and conversely, with no spare time to while away, we won't feel sorry for ourselves, and she's right as usual, and by Saturday evening, September 8th, we were fully back on track waiting for Daddy's call home at eight o'clock.

Carroll comes home from Tech every weekend, he sometimes gets a ride home but more frequently, he hitchhikes, which is an inconvenience because he brings bagged dirty clothes home. Mother spends all day Saturday and Sunday morning washing and ironing while Carroll works his pie routes, which Uncle Thomas re-scheduled to fit Carroll's time not the Bakery's, and Carroll is saving most of his pay to buy a car. He's making good grades in Mechanical Engineering, and he teaches me little snippets along the way, and he says teaching helps him to learn, and that's just fine with me, I'm glad to be a means to making good grades. Carroll has other responsibilities that take up most of his spare time, and the main one is locating and acquiring specific saw mill and log truck spare parts which is a good way to help Daddy, who is coming home for Christmas mainly to drive the log truck load of spare parts back to New Mexico because it simply is not possible for Daddy to locate and acquire spare parts in New Mexico. Besides the logistics barrier in New Mexico, in

Georgia, Carroll has the advantage of a working telephone and newspaper for-sale-ads, which actually make the locating and acquiring possible. Last summer in Magdalena when Mother let it be known that she's ready to put her foot down well the hope that Daddy will be home for Christmas became a reality. She won and Daddy will be coming home for Christmas from now on, and he will fly home and drive back in the vehicle driven home by Carroll, and at the end of spring quarter Carroll will fly out to Albuquerque, work with Daddy through the summer and again drive a load of logs home in the fall.

Our girl scout meetings are mostly at Brenda Jaillet's house, but on Saturday, December 22nd we met at Jane Wood's house on Boulevard Ave. Jane's mother showed us how to cut out paper-dolls from the Sears & Roebuck catalog and then glue (flour and water) the paper-doll to cardboard creased at the bottom so the paper-doll lady can stand up. By two o'clock, Jane's mother brought warm, fresh out of the oven cookies to the table where we were working, and she joked, "I'd better not put the cookie sheet down on this table or else it will be stuck there forever."

She is right and somehow, our flour and water glue got spread out all over the table, so she handed out the cookies in the living room and through the big picture window, there sat our two tone blue and white Chevrolet. The driver's door opened, and a man wearing a Dick Tracey felt hat got out and walked toward Jane's front door! I guess I dropped the warm cookie because the next thing I remember is grabbing a hold of the front door knob and just about tearing the door off it's hinges, slinging open the screen door and literally jumping through the air above all the steps into Daddy's arms, and it's a good thing Daddy is a strong man and I'm a small girl because just an ounce moved my way in that equation would have thrown Shug Godwin to the ground.

Daddy's home!

Mother tied the boxes shut with Christmas ribbon and Daddy placed six unwrapped cardboard boxes under the Christmas tree. Mine and Randall's are the biggest, and every night watching television, Daddy is right there guarding the boxes until Christmas morning! I don't feel the need to peak into my big box, instead, I want to stretch the time with Daddy, and my reasoning is if I look and learn the contents of my box, then the time will fly by, but it's my theory that suspense slows down time's passing and I'd like our time with Daddy to crawl by at a snail's pace, but it made no matter if I wanted time to slow down because Christmas morning came before I could count to ten, and we opened our big boxes from Daddy to find in each a western coat and western cowboy boots, and Santa Clause brought two bicycles, a blue girl's for me, and a red smaller one for Randall, and prevention was folly as the hours raced by and the very next morning Daddy and two new sawmill hands got on the road heading west, and by Saturday night at precisely eight o'clock, we got our first telephone call from Daddy, and it's a closer connection than before, and by that I mean there's a huge difference, a vast improvement because we can close our eyes and visualize exactly where Daddy is standing inside the one pay telephone booth in Magdalena, and finally, Daddy said to me, "Shugy Pie, your letter was waiting for me when I pulled into Magdalena."

December 26, 1956
Dear Daddy,

When you drove away this morning, I cried until my eyes were swollen shut and then Mother suggested that we try out our cowboy boots, and I can report, they work pretty good through wet broom straw, and they work real good through the woods, but when I decided to test them in the red clay mud on Mr. Jaillet's open land, well we got into trouble. We went straight to the biggest mud puddle just outside the south end of Mr. Brown's barbed wire fence, and the first one to wade into the mud was Randall, and I guess it's lucky that I can't run very fast in my boots, because by the time I got there my little brother was sinking past his knees and screaming hysterical warnings for me to stop and go get help, but on second thought he could have been sucked in over his head by the time I came back with help, so, I decided to tie one corner of my headscarf to Mr. Brown's hog wire fence, and when I stretched the headscarf out, Randall was able to reach the opposite corner, and the headscarf was a life line! He slowly pulled and elbowed his body into a position to lift one knee and then the other knee up and out of the mud and onto the hard shelf edge surrounding the sink hole, but in the process, his boots came off, and there was nothing we could do about it.

Love,
Janet

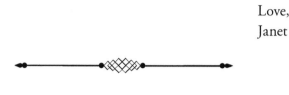

1957

The day before Valentine's Day every year at school is when we work all day decorating our own private mailbox with our name written in big letters, we cut out red hearts and glue them on, and sometimes we make crepe paper roses. This year Mrs. Eaves (my teacher) and her sister across the hall Mrs. Rambo have said already that we will not do any reading, writing or arithmetic today, no sir we will work on our mailboxes for a while, and then we'll listen as our teachers read aloud from the Laura Ingalls Wilder books. Mrs. Eaves and Mrs. Rambo started reading the series of books way back at the beginning of the year with "Little House in the Big Wood" and now they're reading aloud "On the Banks of Plum Creek" and they know we will finish the last book in the series, "Little Town on the Prairie" by the end of the school year because they do this every year and this year we are right on track. So all day today, we work on our mailboxes then we listen for a while, then we work on our mailboxes again, back and forth, and our Valentine mailboxes will dry overnight so they're ready first thing tomorrow on Valentine's Day when the students bring Valentine Cards and deliver the cards to the mailboxes. I delivered a little Valentine to Sandra Brooks, Bernice Langford, Jane Wood, Connie Gentry, Laura Hill Merrill, Brenda Jaillet, Jack Dryden, Jimmy Thrower, Jack Crocker, Denver Morgan, Linda Dobbs, Linda Sue Chandler, Nellie Moore, Sandra Payne, Charles Maxwell, Jack Nixon, Dorothy Shealey, George Kelly, and Kristina Walton and then I ran out of cards. Mother got the pack of little cards at the dime store, and she paid twenty cents for a pack that's supposed to have twenty cards but it only has nineteen. I've counted them a hundred times, there are only nineteen cards.

In the month of May the state of Georgia bursts into bloom and our yard, thanks to Mother and G is as pretty as any with azaleas, dogwoods and red buds. This past Christmas Brenda Jaillet and I both got new big girl's bicycles, and we decided to ride them all the way to town, of course we cannot ride our bicycles on Highway 78, but we can go the back way and avoid the highway altogether. Brenda's dad brought her to my house in his Georgia Power truck with her bicycle loaded in the back, but first things first, our mothers made each of us eat a good breakfast because it will take all day to ride to town and back. The weather this morning is cool enough to wear a lightweight jacket. Brenda borrowed blue jeans from her brothers because girls in Tallapoosa just don't own blue jeans mostly because you can't wear them to school. Elaine Bowman and I re-discovered the strict dress code again last week when we planned ahead to wear Bermuda shorts to school, and believe it or not we were sent home and couldn't come back to school that day, and lucky for me, my mother was at home when the principle called her, but Elaine had to wait in the principal's office. What I don't understand is why is it considered more ladylike to wear a dress to hang upside down on the jungle gym?

Anyway, Brenda and I set out for town on our bicycles, and first we rode down to Thelma's house where we turned left at the big oak tree in the middle of the forks-in-the-road, we rode past Mr. Brown's house, and when we rode down in the valley and past the new Williams' house, Marie called to us from an open window, and then we crossed the wooden bridge over the creek and started up the big hill that is parallel to the standpipe hill on Highway 78, and we both had to push our bikes up the hill, nobody could possibly ride up that hill, it's straight up! Finally, in the city limits, we rode all over town, up and down every street except of course for the busiest streets like Bowdon Street. We waved to a lot of people working in their yards or hanging out clothes, and a lot of cars tooted their horns at us and that made us feel good, but pretty soon, we wished we were back home, so we headed to the big hill, and boy howdy was that fun riding down that straight-up hill, but about mid way down, a big dog came running and barking at us, and Brenda was going a lot faster, and I saw her put her feet up on the handlebars! Never in a million years could I do that! I guess

Brenda can put her feet on the handlebars because her legs are a little bit longer than mine, but even if I had longer legs, I still could not keep my balance with my knees just about touching my chin. Marie Williams called out to us again, and we got off to push our bikes up the hill past Ola Ja Yates's house, then we passed Mr. Brown's house again and turned right at the big oak tree in the middle of the forks at Thelma's house, and it was after three o'clock when we got back to my house, and Brenda called her dad who was just leaving the Georgia Power office up town, and in just a few minutes he drove in the front yard and stashed Brenda's bicycle in the back and Brenda was gone! I can't believe we did it! Did I say, it's three miles each way? We really did it! In school the next week, we proudly told the story to anyone who listened.

1957

That Friday afternoon, Mother commented that Carroll is late getting home, usually on Fridays he's home by two thirty or three, but the times vary because he hitch-hikes home. It's a normal thing that Marilyn and Joan aren't home yet. I helped Mother in the kitchen until we decided to take a short break, and sitting on the couch, we heard the peaceful sounds of Randall playing in the back yard just outside the living room window, but right away we jumped up when we heard a car in the front yard. We both went to the front door, stepped out on the porch, and there was Gene Owens (as slow as sorghum syrup) getting out of his car, and the look on Gene's face scared the begeebers out of me, and Mother exhaled by way of a groan as a gray-faced Gene came up the porch steps. Mother backed into the house not daring to take her eyes off Gene, and when she sat down on a dining room chair, Gene squatted down in front of her and took her hands in his, and at first, he didn't speak because he couldn't catch his breath, and his appearance was totally changed from the Gene I know, and he gritted his teeth and seemed to physically jerk words through his vocal chords, and evidence of his struggle were the huge pulsing veins in his neck, "Carroll's been in a bad wreck. Daddy was coming home from Atlanta on Highway 78 at the Chattahoochee River Bridge, and traffic slowed to a stop in the westbound lane, and no eastbound traffic got through leaving the eastbound lane on the east side of the river completely free of traffic, and up ahead Daddy had full view of two demolished cars and victims' bodies laying around everywhere as if thrown out of a giant machine, and an unconscious lifeless young man lay on the grassy shoulder within a car's length and as Daddy opened the driver's door, he recognized the blonde hair and slight build, and his heart did a cartwheel in his chest as he dived for Carroll, and he shouted to heaven above, 'He's still breathing!' At that point, Daddy started yelling, "Help me! Somebody help me!"

A State Patrolman hurried over and Chester asked, "What happened?"

The State Patrolman said, "These boys are drunk, and they pulled right out in front of the old couple."

Chester looked around at the horrible sight and spit out his reply, "Well these other boys might be drunk I don't know, but I can tell you right now this one is my nephew Carroll Godwin, and by God, he is not drunk."

Chester frantically waved his arms toward the next car behind his Pontiac in the unmoving westbound lineup, and the driver got the message before Chester formed the words asking for help, and suddenly there were five people on each side of Carroll, and they gently picked Carroll up, every other one lifting only by clenching Carroll's clothes, and when they got him situated in Chester's back seat, a Patrolman pointed east toward his car and said, "Turn around and follow me. I'll escort you to Grady Hospital."

Like the parting of the Red Sea, the line up of westbound cars wedged themselves off the pavement giving Chester enough room to turn his Pontiac from westbound to eastbound, and another State Patrolman standing near by signaled and pointed the way as he yelled instructions to the ever growing number of people milling about, and Chester tore out of there with the State Patrolman's siren screaming out of control, and at the Grady Hospital Emergency Room the doctors and nurses were waiting outside with a gurney because the State Patrol escort car radioed the dispatcher to call ahead, and the doctors got right to work on setting a broken leg. When Carroll was returned to intensive care following the leg surgery, Chester found a pay telephone and called home with instructions to, "Go tell Vesta in person, do not call her with news like this."

About the time Gene finished the story, Joan and Marilyn got home, and calmly, Mother found a telephone number for Mr. Blevins in Grants,

New Mexico. When she hung up the phone she said, "Let's go, Joan, you drive, and Gene, you go back home and make sure somebody is by the phone every minute. It's crucial to answer every call, I'll be calling you every hour or so, and I gave Mr. Blevins your telephone number. You'll be our go between, Mr. Blevins is already on his way to get Shug."

Joan broke all speed records driving to Atlanta, and Mother murmured, "Don't worry, if we are stopped for speeding, we'll get an escort."

At the Chattahoochee River Bridge, debris still littered the entire area, and Mother put her hand over her mouth in an effort to force bile back into her stomach. When we reached Grady Hospital, Joan parked the car on the east side of the building in the long sunset shadow, and the five of us went up an elevator like the lady at the information desk said, and a nurse took us straight into intensive care where we found Chester sitting in a chair holding Carroll's hand, but he moved himself and the chair out of our way as Randall hurried to whisper something in Carroll's ear, Joan picked up the big old baby so he can see Carroll, I put my hand over Carroll's right hand, Marilyn took Carroll's left hand, and Mother stood at the head of the bed and bent down to croon loud and clear, "Honey, I'm right here!"

Carroll tried to open his eyes and a shutter rippled across his face, and the nurse said, "That's the first reaction we've seen."

Carroll's broken leg is immobilized in a cast, he's just come back from that surgery, they had to implant metal splints in his upper thigh, but he is able to move his good leg off the bed again and again as if he wants to get up and run out of here. Our vigil is accepted and not challenged, and Mother is resolute that we will stay by Carroll's side talking to him and gently touching him and taking turns sobbing and Carroll responds with more and more movement and agitation until ultimately a nurse wheeled in a transport gurney and said to Mother, "Everything is set up in x-ray. We'll introduce a dye, which reveals any organ damage. As soon as he comes back here, we'll come to the waiting room for you and your family."

It's probably dark out side, the clock on the wall says it is, but we don't know for sure because the family waiting room has no windows, Mother asks if anyone is hungry, we did not have supper yet, then she wonders if she turned off the stove, there is a pay telephone hanging on the wall in the family waiting room, and Mother has a pocket full of change so she calls Nora, Little Lynda will go check on the stove right now, but first

Mother reads off to Nora, this pay telephone number. Nora says that her brother Hershel who lives in Atlanta is on his way to Grady Hospital. In the waiting room while Carroll is in X-ray, I spend my time studying my dress fabric of course, Mother made this dress for me. A few months ago Mother ordered from the Spiegel catalog white lace collars which she calls 'ingenious' because they are attached to a base liner complete with button holes, and the collar is meant to be portable from one dress to another when buttons are sewn inside the dress's collarless neckline. As for me, I've never zeroed in on material before, in fact the design stamped on fabric is totally inconsequential, but at this minute, my dress material is the most important thing in the world, and I am thinking of exact words to describe it, because when I'm old and gray, I'm sure I'll recall every detail of this dress. The fabric background is a light tan and there are tiny black commas and larger pink commas lined up in every direction. Like Sally Owens, my folded hands mindlessly twiddle their thumbs, and this they do without cognitive recognition. No one speaks except for an occasional groan, and the groans come mostly from Mother. Hershel has come and gone, giving Mother a hug and promising to come back tomorrow. Herbie Jones and Buzzy Farmer are here, Mother answered the pay telephone, Daddy is on a plane, Hershel is back so it must be Saturday, I don't recall sleeping. We remain useless and senseless since they took Carroll away for an x-ray, we can't see Carroll yet because he's allergic to the dye they put in his blood, they need us to give blood but they won't take mine. WHY NOT? I can't eat enough to make me weigh a hundred and ten pounds, are they crazy? I don't need the blood; Carroll needs my blood! I hate 'em all! Ruth and Otto give blood and then take my little brother back home with them, it's lucky for everybody; they didn't try to take me back home! Finally, Carroll is back, but they've tied him down because of the allergic reaction. Herbie Jones and Buzzy Farmer can't stand to see him tied down so they took the belts off, and they're holding him down, and now Doony Bates, Hubert Dodson, Bob Downey, Billy Higgins, Ralph Lively, and Curtis Thompson are driving to Atlanta so they can take turns holding him down. Thankfully, it's my turn to sob into my hands, and I think I'll never stop crying! But I do because I have to when Mother comes into the waiting room again. Mother wants her sweater out of the Chevrolet. I know exactly how to find the car so Flora Moore McDonald and Martha

Marie Sheffield follow me. Finally, everybody goes home except Carroll's bodyguards, and I'm back in my chair in the waiting room.

Daddy is here! He walked right past my chair. I chose this chair because traffic from the hallway into intensive care comes through the family waiting room directly past this chair. Daddy has that same awful gray face as Gene, he hesitates slightly in front of me, but then goes on, I follow him into Carroll's room where the straightest path to Carroll opens up. Daddy sways and his head bobs as Joan pushes a chair under him. He kisses Carroll, and falls into the chair. I guess it's Daddy's turn to sob!

When he can speak, he tells Carroll a story, "Son, Friday night after supper, half the sawmill hands took their baths, and then it was my turn so I poured the two big pots of hot water into the tub, soaped up and rinsed off, but I settled down to soak a minute in the still warm water, when somebody yelled, 'Headlights are a coming!' It was Mr. Blevins, it took me just about two seconds to grab my clean knockabout clothes, and I put my socks, shoes, shirt and corduroy sport coat on as he drove licked-y split out of there, for we did not waste a single minute. As Mr. Blevins drove along, he told me the details about your wreck, and he took me to his house, and his wife already made my flight reservations to leave Albuquerque early this morning, I crawled into bed at his house, but I shouldn't a messed up the covers because I didn't sleep a wink, and before daylight, Mr. Blevins drove me to the airport. We landed in Kansas City, and I waited about an hour to get on the plane to Atlanta. On the Atlanta flight, I sat beside a very nice man, and when we landed here in Atlanta, he stood up in the aisle and got everybody's attention and he said, 'This man is Mr. Godwin, and he's trying to get to his son at Grady Hospital. His son had a bad wreck, will you all please stay seated and let him off the airplane first?' That's what they did, and when I stuck my head out of the airplane, Hershel yelled, 'Who oo! Shug, over here.' And here I am! Son, you gotta wake up, for I can't do all I have to do without you as my backup. It's just as simple as pie, I can't get along without you! But for now, Mr. Blevins will pay the sawmill hands and keep the operating cash so's to pay the weekly bills and wire money to me, and I'm counting on you to work again this summer!"

In Carroll's emergency care room, so he can hear every detail, Daddy and Mother plan to spell each other off, so Mother will take the daughters home in the morning (Sunday); and from home, on Monday, we'll deal with the last three days of school, because Memorial Day is Thursday the thirtieth and the last day of school is always the weekday before Memorial Day. Monday morning Mother will call the Tallapoosa School principal and Georgia Tech's Registrar, and Joan will call West Georgia Junior College. Then when the calling is done, Mother and the daughters will return to Grady so Daddy can go home. Little Randall will stay with Ruth and Otto, but they'll visit home anytime and especially when Daddy is there. My parents emphasize that we are not required to go to school or do anything if we feel uneasy, this is a tragedy, unusual and difficult, there's no way to minimize ramifications that are devastating and cannot be ignored, but at the same time, Mother and Daddy are reinforcing their belief that it's just a matter of time until Carroll is ready to come home, but until that happens, we're operating under altered rules that put Carroll at the top of the list! That's the main point; Carroll will have his family with him at all times! AT ALL TIMES!

When we finally got home Sunday morning, Mother was as white as a ghost, and I brought a pillow and a quilt from her bed to the couch just as she said, "I can't hold my head up!"

She doesn't need to hold her head up because the house is full of people cleaning up the kitchen and arranging the mountain of food brought by friends and neighbors, with each new dish, Little Lynda adds to a list of who brought what. Carroll's girlfriend Glenda McKibben and her parents came by, it's the first time we have met Glenda, she explained that she lives and works in Atlanta, and she came home yesterday but didn't learn of the wreck until Carroll was late for their date last night. That's when she called the house and asked to speak to Carroll, it was Norman Owens who answered the telephone, and he told her all about the wreck. Her ride back to Atlanta isn't until this afternoon, but when she gets back to Atlanta, she'll be able to take the bus straight from her apartment to Grady Hospital, and she can spell off Mr. Godwin, but the room echoed 'Shug' and she said, "I'll try to call him Shug."

Glenda picked up a broom and joined in the amazing work force of dozens of people sweeping and mopping the floors, washing the dishes, washing the dirty clothes, dusting the furniture, ironing school clothes, and the next dozen people to stop by had to move on to working outside the house, cutting the grass (even though it's Sunday), sweeping the porches, and hanging the wet clothes on the line until the Pine Grove Church Preacher stopped by on his way home from Sunday Service. He came inside and sat down next to Mother in a straight-back chair brought in from the dining room, and out of respect, everybody stopped working and came into the living room, and I sat in a wing back chair, and bowed my head as the Pine Grove Preacher began to pray, "Oh, Lord, in heaven, please take your son, Carroll into your loving arms

I heard not another single word the Preacher said, and I could not remain seated as I realized he must have later word than we have of Carroll's condition, and praying or not, my flight was irresistible, and with an, 'Oh no!' involuntarily escaping my lips, I ran from the living room into Mother's and Daddy's room, slamming the door behind me. I sat on the bed wishing I could climb out the window and disappear forever, but gently the door opened and in came Glenda, and the angel of mercy wrapped her arms around me and explained, "The Preacher didn't mean to say that, he doesn't know how Carroll is. You came from Carroll this morning, he didn't. He hasn't been to Grady Hospital to see Carroll. I agree with you that he began his prayer with an inappropriate request, but that's all it was, he doesn't know anything."

I cried a river while Glenda hugged me, and finally we heard everyone saying goodbye to the Preacher, and then Glenda went back to sweeping, and I left the house and ran across the road into the pine thicket in search of an open spot to say my own prayer in the sunbeams coming down directly from heaven, and as long as I stayed on my knees, my protection-squad of crows cawed me a sweet lullaby, and it helps if I repeat a stream of consecutive what Daddy said to Carroll, "We can't do without you, we can't do without you, we can't do without you."

At the hospital on Monday morning, to the non-responsive Carroll, Daddy starts, "Son, I know you've got a lot on your mind, but I need to tell you something, I'm staying in Georgia until you get out of the hospital, then I'll fly back to New Mexico, but you have to take time to recuperate, and when you're able, you'll come back to work along side a me!"

We watched for any sign of recognition, but if Carroll understands, he's not letting on, and for now, he doesn't move a muscle, or bat an eye, or say boo, and then Marilyn said, "Let's go home, Daddy, you're too tired to drive, but I'm not."

What seemed like an endless march back and forth, to and from Atlanta if examined from a distance, might have given us incremental hope, but seen up close and daily, Carroll's slow progress offered no promise, and as he continued to torture himself against tie down belts or loving hands holding him gently against the white sheets, sadly, our future became filled more with despair than hope, and I wondered more than once why our turn-around trips gave us no down time, either at home or at Grady, and when I mentioned my confusion, it turned out to be universal among my parents and sisters, every one of us seemed only to recall the in-transit car time.

Smokey and Husky have been uncanny at understanding our grief, and they want to stay close when we are actually at home, but sometime early in the week, we found Smokey in the house (he can let himself in and out) but there was no sign of Husky, and when we called to Husky, he didn't come, instead, a crying Little Lynda handed us a note from her brother, "Husky was hit by a car, I dug a new grave under the plum tree."

Our collective pain reached new depths and this time, no one waited in line to sob, and we were magnetically drawn to the Plum Tree Pet Cemetery where the newly turned dirt slashed and carved us to bits, and now we feel like the only remaining direction is up, away from all this sorrow, but how can we claim ascension with no means of lift?

Carroll stayed in intensive care at Grady Hospital for two and a half weeks, and somehow with smidgens of good news we began to rebound. Joan's degree from West Georgia Junior College came in the mail, and Tech will give Carroll credit for the courses he has completed because his grades are very good and in this particular situation, he is not required to take the final exams, and Marilyn will be a THS senior this fall and I'll be in the overflow sixth grade.

Last summer, while we were in New Mexico, the girls in my girl-scout troop earned the swimming merit badge, and now Mrs. Jaillet called our house and offered her daughter Brenda (the best swimmer on my list of superlatives) as my swimming merit badge counselor. Mother thanked her and offered, "It's worth a try, maybe it will change Janet's doldrums!"

At first, I refused because it seems ridiculous to splash around in some stupid pool when Carroll is waging a battle just to stay alive, but everyone ganged up on me and they won, and Daddy delivered me to meet Brenda at the pool. It was pretty early in the morning, and the water was colder than I'd ever known it to be, and Brenda's explanation is that, "the water cools overnight but the sun re-heats it quickly."

Brenda took charge of my Girl Scout Handbook and directed the accomplishment of each and every swimming requirement. Daddy took Randall with him. Brenda wanted me to go slow accomplishing each requirement, but I don't have and never have had a slow gear, so at dinner time Brenda had an on-the-go crackers and Co-Cola snack, as she continued to count repetitions and track time limits, and when I started the final requirement, I noticed Daddy was back and sitting on a bench half way up the hill toward the parking area, and Daddy's presence gave me new found stamina. So I finished the timed treading water and climbed out of the pool, and in order to keep my Handbook dry, Brenda took it to Mam-maw behind the concession counter leaving me standing alone at the water's edge. Someone touched my arm from behind and I saw nothing but the deep end. As I splashed water on impact, one thing reverberated, "I'm in the water again, I fumbled to orient myself and realized I did not have the strength to turn one hundred and eighty degrees toward the side, I could not reach and therefore push off the bottom, and I could not pull my weight through the water to the top. Suspended and helpless as a kitten, I watched the last bubbles of air escape from my lungs and rise to the surface, I simply could not save myself, and it didn't matter, I felt no panic, quite the contrary, I reached a place of serenity and peace, profound serenity and peace.

Then I woke up lying in the grass, someone forcing water from my mouth, and I regretted the rude interruption of my serenity and peace, and I vomited a fluid as bitter as green persimmons, and I found myself transported to the Chevrolet, my wet hair and bathing suit soaking the upholstery.

Our return home interrupted Mother's serenity and peace, Joan and Marilyn went to Grady Hospital alone today, and as Daddy told the story, I came to understand my close call:

Daddy's account, "I left Randall with Ruth and Otto, and returned to the pool about three o'clock, and I watched as Janet finished the swimming merit badge requirements. But when Brenda delivered Janet's handbook to her grandmother in the concession stand, well without warning Janet ended up right back in the water, and I watched her come to the surface only one time, and then her helpless body just hung there suspended under water, and knowing the lifeguard was cleaning the filters; I realized I'd better take off my shoes, and next I put my watch and my cigarettes in my hat, and I ran as fast as I've ever run in my life and jumped in over my head, and grabbed Janet's head and poked her face up and out of the water. I held her face out of the water while I swam pulling us both toward the rope, and finally when I could stand on the bottom, I picked her up and shoved her out of the pool, and others took over and not a minute too soon, somebody rolled her onto the grass and started pushing against her lungs, and when she revived, I carried her up the hill to the car.

The day that Carroll came home was happy and sad, sad because Daddy flew back to New Mexico, and happy because we know how close we came to losing our brother. Daddy got on the airplane wishing he could stay and knowing he couldn't, and when that happens, it's better to dwell on the good and forget the bad. We brought Carroll home to a roll away bed set up for him in the living room, this way he's closer to the dining room table, and he is 'famished' so he eats just about all day long, and that's a good thing because he is way too skinny, and he says it'll cushion the crutches under his arm if he can pad the area with some fat globules. I love it when he says things like that! And I've tried to catch him using made-up words, but sure enough if I look them up, he's right, 'globule' is a ball of fat! It's so good to have him back! Except for the no dancing part, he loves to dance as much as I do, mentally, he's back all the way and his mind is just as sharp as ever, but we can't jitterbug yet!

July, 1957
Dear Daddy,

As proof of Carroll's mental return, Joan has been sewing a dress and the electric sewing machine is right by Carroll's living room bed, and Joan's dress is made by a very difficult pattern, consequently, about every fifteen minutes she calls out, 'Mother, can you come help me!'

And of course Mother stops whatever she's doing and comes to help Joan, and all this time, Carroll is playing solitaire laying out the cards on his white bottom sheet, and I'm watching his dominate left hand shuffle and distribute, and my fascination keeps me close by as Joan calls repeatedly for Mother's help, and each time, I see Carroll roll his eyes, and shake his head, down deep I know he's enjoying every minute of Joan's agony. Some times, Carroll calls Joan 'Hon' which is short for 'Honey,' and it sounds like a joke and makes me laugh, but if I'm even smiling just a little bit, I have to turn away so Joan can't see because she might get a little ruffled if she knows she's the center of a joke. Joan has a very good sense of humor, but even so, if she is having difficulty and is not in a humorous mood, she can be a little bit aggressive (like the time she threw the sugar bowl at Carroll). I don't remember the sugar bowl incident, but Mother has emblazoned it into my mind forever. So back to the story, for the hundredth time Joan called Mother to come help and this time, Carroll calmly said, "Hon, why don't you just give up sewing?"

Even though Carroll is lying in a sick bed, I am certain if Joan could have found easy access to another sugar bowl, she would have again thrown the whole thing at her brother! The only difference is actually huge, this time unlike the first time when she desperately wanted to injure him, this time throwing anything at him would be for show because this time, she would not chance hitting him for anything in the world!

Love,
Janet

That evening Carroll answered the telephone, and he replied in short sentences, "No we don't." "I'm positive." "No chance of that."

When he hung up the phone, he asked for his one legged pants and pulled them on before quickly shaving and putting on a clean shirt. Then Gene came into the living room and passed the time of day until Carroll was ready, and they left in Gene's car because Carroll hasn't yet figured out how to drive. The two young men headed straight to the store where Gene handed Carroll the new set of store keys and the old removed store door lock, which Carroll laid down on the floorboard. Carroll told Gene to stay in his car and then positioned himself on the one step at the store's double doors. Within minutes, a half dozen pickup trucks pulled up and at least one man got out of each, and soon Carroll on his crutches, had an audience of overalls and straw hats before him as he said, "I don't want any trouble, I'm here to refund your rent money and ask you to return to me any and all keys you might have."

A shuffle of discontent made it's way from each pair of shoes to the next while Carroll conjured up the notion that he was speaking to empty shoes, unable to find or connect to a brain, and finally one defiant hollow voice asked, "Well just what do you intend to do if we hold you to the agreement?"

Carroll slowly and deliberately, pulled his crutches from under his arms and leaned them against the double doors. Then he opened his arms wide and said, "Well, it's like this, I am recovering from a car wreck, but if you don't take this refund and give me the keys, I'll fight each and every one of you in succession if one arm is tied behind your back, and think about this, I recognize all of you, and I know beyond a doubt that if you make me fight you, my Daddy will be on the next airplane from New Mexico, and without batting an eye, he will deal with the lot of you, and it won't be something you'll recover from in the next several years because you all know very well that my Daddy has a reputation, and he is honor bound to uphold every single detail that's ever been said about him."

Again, the brainless shoes did their shuffle, and for a minute Gene thought he might have to even up the odds a little, but then these cowards who conduct their business from behind white ghost costumes got a whiff of their own cowardice sweating from each armpit. The courage of a skinny kid on crutches melted their collective resolve, and the leader grabbed the money from Carroll's hand as they stomped back to their trucks throwing the keys on the ground. On the drive back home, Gene commented that their Papa John Owens knows of what he speaks because before their very eyes, the KKK bullies were beaten back not by physical blows but by inner strength that stopped just short of saying, "I know you're the bully, but I've come now."

With Husky's death leaving Smokey alone most of the time, he is unsettled and roams from house to house picking fights with the neighbor dogs, and I guess we never would have known about his wandering and fighting except for some extensive injuries which Carroll discovered. Smokey opened the screen door to let himself in, and instead of jumping onto Carroll's clean bed sheets, he placed one paw on the bed, and instantly Carroll understood why. Smokey was bleeding from huge gashes on his neck and side, of course Carroll called for help, and on closer examination, mother reckoned the wounds are not deep enough for stitches, and that's lucky because we've never used a veterinarian and actually we've never had that kind of money. Now realizing the danger involved, Mother changed her rules about Smokey in the car, and she began loading Smokey into the car each and every time she backs out of the yard, for she reasons that 'He's ill at ease at home alone, and that must be the reason he goes out searching for a fight.'

At first it worked like a charm keeping Smokey gash-free, but one fateful day, as Mother turned onto Head Avenue up town, Smokey became aware of the 'belongs-to-the-town' dog named Hobo, and without the slightest hesitation, Smokey jumped through the moving Chevrolet window onto the pavement leaving Mother helpless and alone in the car as the dogfight of the century ensued right there in front of the Grand Theater's Marquis advertising in huge letters this week's movie line up to be '*Wednesday, Thursday, Friday, August 21-22-23 King Kong vs. Godzilla, Saturday, August 24 double feature Gunfight at the O.K. Corral and Papa's Delicate Condition, and Sunday, Monday, Tuesday August 25-26-27 Gidget Goes to Rome.*'

Mother quickly parked the Chevrolet and true to her reputation, without even a twinge of fear, she managed to get close enough to the dogfight to grab one of Smokey's hind legs, and with a very powerful jerk, she proved her premise that Smokey will not bite her although she has her doubts about Hobo, but she was successful in defusing the fight, and Smokey quickly jumped back into the Chevrolet while Hobo retreated around the corner at the bank.

Brenda Cobb is at home alone after school until her mother comes in from work about suppertime, and while she waits, Brenda watches television, and she actually watched the very first American Bandstand show on Monday, August 5, 1957. She was glued to the television and at the end of that first show, she called me, and the next day, I watched American Bandstand too, and most of the time, Brenda and I are on the telephone watching the dancers and listening to the music together, and I like Kenny and Arlene best, and I dance the jitterbug holding on to a door knob as my partner.

I have a new little dog that I named 'Snippy' because of the way she makes Smokey leave her alone. She is a stray who just showed up one day, like most of our pets. Mother says the word is out that we take in strays so unwanted pets are 'dumped' on our dirt road close enough that they can find us, and consequently, we always have a yard full of dogs. Snippy is smaller than Smokey, she is a black and white long hair, shaggy dog; Smokey has black, short hair. Snippy knows somehow that she is mine, and every afternoon she sleeps in the wing back chair, and there's enough room for me to sit beside her to watch television. Smokey is calmer when Snippy is in the room, I guess he enjoys her company, but Mother still takes Smokey with her every time she cranks up the car because she knows if she tried to leave him behind he'd just chase her all the way to town. It's not unusual for Mother to 'run to town' taking Randall with her, and I'd rather stay home watching American Bandstand because I don't want to miss a single song and besides, there's nothing to be afraid of because everybody in the whole county knows everybody else, and except for the KKK there aren't any bad people. Marilyn works after school of course, just like always, and she is dating one of Carroll's classmates. Bob Downey went into the service right out of high school, and he was based in Germany, but he's back home now, and he takes Marilyn to a picture show almost every weekend, and during the week, he visits us at night, and it's always fun when he comes around because he likes to laugh as much as we do, and he kinda reminds me of Papa because he always has some kind of foolishness going on. It's different kinds of foolishness of course, but nevertheless it's still something silly and funny!

Carroll is working in New Mexico right through the fall quarter because he will never ever hitch hike again … never … under any circumstances, so with that as his guideline, he has to work and make enough money to buy a car. Then after Christmas, he'll go back to Tech. All this is good news! Daddy won't be so lonely, and I can breathe again, and without saying so, the other members of the family are just as relieved. Carroll's wreck rekindled a sad helplessness for Mama and Papa that goes way back to their two lost babies. Also, Carroll's close call has caused Ruth and Otto to noticeably revert to their loss, and it's possible they depend on me too much. I'm not complaining, no sir re, but it's not within my power to make them whole again. I certainly would if I could, but now that my life is expanding beyond the Friday night visits, well, they both realize I'm not a magician, and my name is Janet Godwin not Shirley Hart. Shirley is in a baby's grave and there's nothing to be done. In the meantime, as I slowly grow away from their 'Friday night family' I still spend the night at least once a month, and when I'm really lucky, Ruth and I spend all day Saturday helping Mama especially in the fall when there's canning to do. There's never a single misgiving as to how much I'm loved by Mama and Papa and Ruth and Otto, but the residue of sorrow sometimes brings Mama and Ruth to their proverbial knees, a position perfect for giving me a 'be careful' hug. Maybe sorrow is the razor that sharpens the edge of gratitude, and in this house, we appreciate our big family, and I can safely boast, I have never felt insecure! I offer up a prayer of thank you every night because I fully understand how truly blessed we are, and if anything, our gratitude has been sharpened by Carroll's near miss. I understand that the grief caused by the death of a baby never ends, never eases, but at some point doesn't that loss become less a sharp-knife open wound? I wonder if the pain is finally dulled enough to allow those left alone to begin to rebuild their lives with one tiny step over a vast period of time? I think of and hope for lofty goals delivering the parents from daily torture, but then I realize deep down that I am not equipped to judge, and it's not my place to presume, and shame on me for comparing Mama's and Papa's loss to Ruth's and Otto's, there's not a shred of connection, because Ruth and Otto have no other children and they will never have grandchildren, except through me as their sometime substitute daughter. They always give me a sweet gift at Christmas, this year it's a Five Year Diary, green leather bound, with a lock and key.

1957

We have a new gym with a full, hardwood basketball court, Marilyn went to a Sock Hop on that beautiful oak floor, and she said it's called a Sock Hop because everyone dances in their socks, shoes are not allowed. The hardwood floor and roll-away bleachers are on the street level and there are two double wide doors from the street right into the upper level, also, there's a basement that has no street side because that part of the basement is underground, but there is a walk out door on the back side of the building. On the basement level, there are two boys locker rooms and two girls locker rooms, one for the home team and one for the visiting team. When a visiting school comes for a game, the girls' basketball half-court game is played first. To clarify, on half of the huge court, the home team girls' offense and the visiting team's defense must stay within the half court boundary lines, and when the visiting team's defense gains control of the ball they dribble to the center line and pass the ball to the visiting team's offense playing on the other half of the full court. Besides the dressing rooms, there's a new lunchroom in the basement. The grammar school kids eat first, and we enter and leave the basement through the back door. When all the grammar school grades finish lunch, then there's an all Grammar school recess, and of course it's always a race to see who can eat the fastest and get out on the playground first. This is the best recess ever because there's enough time to play a baseball game, and enough kids to make up two teams, and selection of team members begins when one 'captain for the day' tosses a bat to the other captain, and the catch point is the start of back and forth hand over hand to the top, and the last captain might only get a half an inch of the bat, and if he can hold the bat to the count of ten, he gets to make the first team pick, but if he can't hold it to the count of ten, then he forfeits the first pick to the other captain. I love to play baseball, I'm a good hitter, I can run fast, and because I hit some home runs, sometimes I get picked first! Actually, it's rare that I'm picked first because I'm terrible at catching a ball and throwing a ball, but when I am the first pick, it makes me feel like a million dollars!

Brenda Cobb and I finished eating our hot dogs faster than anyone else, we dumped our scraps in the barrel, slammed our dirty trays in the stack, and in the excitement of being first on the playground, we tore out running through the wide empty hallway leading to the gym's back door. Mindless of the hazard, we raced to the back door, and Brenda actually won, but she miscalculated as she lead with her left hand placing it on a direct collision course with the glass, and the split second when her left hand pushed the unmovable, locked-in-place glass the inevitable catastrophe was set in motion. I reached the door in a close second behind Brenda as screams forced their way up from the abyss, and I watched and understood in slow motion that she was about to push the glass before releasing the lock, and my scream did nothing to dissuade her purpose, and horribly, her hand went through the glass, which would have been ok, if she'd followed her hand, body and soul through the glass, if she had continued the momentum with an impossible maneuver of letting her body follow her hand, well then the tragedy could have been avoided because breaking the glass doesn't do the harm, and this slow motion example proved that point and when I'm old and gray, I will still know how that rule plays out. In the reality of this scientific experiment, the sharp shards of broken glass cut through her recoiling flesh with merciless devouring greed leaving her entire arm instantly transformed into a blood-squirting appendage, and with the recoil finally complete, the little finger's only connection to the hand appeared to be a thin 'hinge' of skin allowing the finger to swing back and forth in a sickening display sending blood squirting everywhere on the door, the floor, Brenda's dress, my dress, Brenda's hair, my hair, Brenda's shoes, my shoes, all encompassing and debilitating.

"BRENDA, LISTEN TO ME, DON'T FAINT ON ME I CAN'T CARRY YOU. I'M RIGHT HERE! LEAN ON ME! WE HAVE TO SEE MR. COBB. WALK, BRENDA, DON'T STOP. WE HAVE TO GO AROUND THE CORNER OF THE GYM, NOW UP THE STEPS, AROUND TO THE FRONT OF THE HIGH SCHOOL BUILDING. I'VE GOT THE DOOR! *MR. COBB HELP, HELP, HELP, HELP!*"

Mr. Cobb dashed out of his office with his car keys in his hand, he ushered us back through the front door, down the steps, and into the back seat, mindlessly he handed me his clean handkerchief, painstakingly, I wrapped it around the still swinging finger and I held on tight transforming my hand into a splint, physically aligning and connecting the finger to it's stub, but when Mr. Cobb changed gears, I felt the little finger slide through the lubricant, and believe it or not, I felt through the dripping red handkerchief exactly when the skin hinge stretched to it's limit, and as a means to an end, I countered and relaxed the tension as a person with a one and only life long aspiration. In the short distance to the Downey Clinic, I had sufficient time to relive the accident again and again, and at the same time, I kept an accurate count of the car's excessive movements meant to do bodily harm to my friend, the jerks, stops, sways and violent centrifugal force as we rounded the two corners in route, and each excess required an adjustment, and with every corrective finger slide through the blood soaked handkerchief I dared not allow the slightest variance from stoicism. Brenda cannot see, no sir re, she's not strong enough, I accepted responsibility complete and utter, I accepted the quest for the holy grail, I accepted her need too great, I accepted the conquest unattainable. In semi-consciousness, I forced my libido into inconceivable and uncommon calm, and it seemed to be the recipe for reassuring Brenda, and when we finally traveled the short two blocks to the Clinic (by way of a detour through Texas), I managed to hold on literally and allegorically, and finally at the Clinic, as my feet hit the ground I locked my knees in the standing position and did not dare weaken as I escorted Brenda into the Downey Clinic up the hall and into the room with the giant light. Nurse Sarah Walker placed a chair next to the tall bed, and I climbed up still holding the red handkerchief in position precisely as Dr. Downey completed his role and gently lifted Brenda in his arms and positioned her on the high bed. I consider the maneuver a feat greater than hitting a home run, as Dr. Downey pried my fingers loose and Nurse Sara pushed my hand back toward me as if it were mine, but it's not mine, my hand is Brenda's she needs it, and I have no volition. Nurse Sarah soothed Brenda with cooing and stroking, and cooing and stroking, "You're fine, honey. This will hurt just for a quick second; then the pain will ease. You're fine honey!"

I was mesmerized by Nurse Sarah's calm stroking and purposeful pushing Brenda's hair from her face and soaking up thick flowing blood in a clean white cloth and another clean white cloth, again and again; and when I glanced at the trash can filled to the brim with red cloth, I surmised that Brenda has no more blood to bleed, no giant elephant could possibly have more blood after painting red every inch of our path to the office, every inch up the front steps, every inch of the hallway, every inch of Mr. Cobb's office and his car's back seat, every inch of the Clinic hallway, every inch of this high bed, and of course every inch of Brenda, every inch of me, every inch of Nurse Sarah, and every inch of Dr. Downey. I can give Brenda some of my blood; and in this case they will have to take it, not like when they would not take it for my brother, but this time Brenda is out of blood. She is out of blood!!!! This time they have to take it now! This time they will split my blood half and half, I don't need all of it.

Back to the task at hand, but first, I watch as fog rolls in, obscuring definition, wait just a minute, it's not right that I should faint, I deserve no attention, I will not be selfish when my needs are so pathetic, I will not faint, instead, I lean my head onto Brenda's pillow and easily conceal my short-lived escape. Nurse Sarah hovers until the Doctor tells her to call Arbelle at work, and when she comes back, she says, "Arbelle can't get here until her ride leaves work. They both need the pay, so she asked me to call Vesta, and Vesta's on her way. She'll take Brenda home with her and keep her until Arbelle gets home."

The minute that Mother walked through the door, that minute is the exact minute when I accepted the fact that I could no longer hold on. Unlike the short reprieve of an hour ago, this escape came as a black sheet spread over my head blocking all the light and all the sound, I visited a serene and blood free world, and when I returned, Mother was in charge and I floated about untethered as Mother took on my load. Mother is always there to sprinkle fairy dust when I need some magic, and she's the same Mother who holds me when I cry in the night, and then I realized that Nurse Sarah was mopping blood from my face. I was sort of on the bed, but mostly, I was in two sets of loving arms, one arm belonging to Mother and two arms belonging to Nurse Sarah, and Brenda had half of my Mother as of course she deserved the support and Dr. Downey's two arms made up her safe enclosure. There's no doubt in my mind, that I can do anything, I can fight and survive a vast travesty when there's no one around to take over, and concurrently, there's no doubt that Dr. Downey and Nurse Sarah can sew up the worst imaginable injuries, but the most *facilitating assurance* is that my Mother can be Brenda's Mother and Brenda's Mother can be mine.

Little Lynda has her driver's license, and one Saturday she blew into our yard driving a brand spanking new Pontiac, which she claimed, from her daddy's showroom. Before the dust settled, she asked from the whirlwind, "Aunt Vesta, Daddy told me to take Papa Owens to his dental appointment in Bowdon. I want Janet to go with me, where is she?"

Mother pointed upstairs, and that's where she found me, and luckily, I was already dressed in nice enough clothes to go inside a Dentist's office, but I did take time to comb my hair and brush my teeth (in the middle of the day?). Somehow it seems appropriate that the one person with the winning number of cavities this year, sixteen, well I should be brushing my teeth in the middle of every day with such a sorry record as that, and definitely, I cannot be so brazen as to go inside a Dentist's office with dirty teeth!

We high tailed it back uptown and sure enough, Chester wheeled into his Pontiac Dealership parking lot with Papa in the passenger's seat, and as quick as a wink, Papa made the switch into Lynda's passenger's seat as I climbed over the seat and positioned myself in the middle of the back seat so I can hang over the front seat and join in the, bound to be hilarious, conversation! Papa pushed his walking stick between his seat and the closed car door. He's dressed as usual in his newest and best overalls (he calls them over-halls} and matching denim jacket (he calls it a jumper), and no matter what he calls his clothing, he's a fine looking gentleman, big and strong and brave! Chester leaned down to look in through Lynda's window and chastised, "Now don't get into any trouble!"

Jokingly to myself, I thought Chester must have learned his ill temper from Mama, and then I smiled at the antonyms 'ill temper' and 'Mama' in the same thought! As my mind roamed on off point, I recalled Papa's often-stated critique when asked as to Sally's condition, "Ahh she's alright I guess, mean as hell!"

With a grin widening to the maximum that still fits my face, off we went south out of town, and first thing, Papa said, "Now, don't you go crying like a baby because your Daddy is always so mean to you!"

It was an exaggerated statement having no foundation whatsoever, and Lynda caught on real fast and replied, "Well the tears are blurring my vision, so I guess I'll have to pull off the road and let you or Janet drive!"

That started it, Papa quipped right back, and "Yeah pull over. With my eyes shut, I'm a better driver than you are! Here's my handkerchief, Janet can tie it over my eyes and I'll show you!"

I added, "My vision is blurred too, but it's not tears of sadness or fear, it's tears of frustration, because in fact I am the best driver, and yet I won't have a chance to make my case! So I dare you to pull over and let me drive or at least pull over and let us draw straws which is the fairest way to decide who should be driving this brand new car!"

Lynda pointed out that, "Age disqualifies you both, Papa because you have too much age and Janet because you have too little. I'm the duly elected driver all the way down there, and all the way back because my age is just right! Oh, and there is one other valid point to make, I am the only licensed driver in this car! And I'll tell you one thing, listening to your outlandish notions could be considered a distraction, and if you keep it up, and we have a wreck, well it's not my fault!"

"If you want to drive and you take the responsibility of driving, well then that automatically unloads on your shoulders the blame if we have a wreck! Everybody knows that." Papa's equation left Lynda trying to scratch her head, but it was a symbolic scratch for she did not dare take a hand off the stirring wheel.

Lynda, "Ahh, Papa, that's not the way to reason yourself through a problem, you're backing yourself into a corner without a paddle."

I piped up, "You're mixing your metaphors!"

Papa added, "You gotta stop thinking so hard, I don't like the smell of burning hair, and another thing, I'd hate for you to go around bald."

Without effort, Lynda maneuvered the new Pontiac right up to the Dental office's front door, and when she turned off the engine, Papa gave one last warning, "If you girls cut up in there like you've been cutting up all the way from Tallapoosa, I'm gona make them fit you both with false teeth!"

September 23, 1957
Dear Daddy,

We miss you and Carroll, but it's easier to imagine the two of you together, and company for each other, it's still sad, but not debilitating like what we've been through! I'm thankful every minute of every day that Carroll is alive!

Joan has found a job at AB Dick in Atlanta, and she shares an apartment with three other girls and two of them have boy's names like Joan's first name 'Billie'. Their names are 'Johnnie, and Freddie.'

Love Always,
Janet

Come spring the senior class will take their traditional class trip to Washington D.C. But first, between now and then, the class of 1958, will wash a lot of cars, sell a lot of magazines, and present a play in the early spring! Mrs. Williams, the English teacher, is the one who chooses the play, orders copies, and casts the characters, and she will spend many hours with the seniors rehearsing for the big presentation. Everybody in town gets dressed up to attend the annual senior class play.

When Bob Downey came over tonight, Marilyn told what she and the other seniors did today in Mrs. Williams' English class. In fact the seniors planned ahead so everybody whether they actually wear glasses or not brought to school either clear glasses or sunglasses, and it worked out just right because Mrs. Williams was a little bit late getting to class, and when she walked in the room, her eyes scanned the entire class and every single senior had a pair of glasses resting upside down on their face, and Mrs. Williams, as always, was very cool under pressure, and as she sat down at her desk at the front of the class, she removed her own glasses, switched them around and replaced them on her face upside down. For about half of the class time, no one made a comment, but finally when one person let a giggle escape, well then it spread immediately into a giant, feel good, deep hearty laugh!

The day finally came when all the seniors met up town at the train depot, everybody in Sunday go to meeting clothes and heavy over coats because of the extraordinarily cold weather so unlike spring time in Georgia. The chaperones joked with the seniors about lining up, boys in one line and girls in another, and 'behave like the good little girls and boys I know you to be and keep it quiet and don't mess up your clean clothes!'

I recall the same jokes when Joan's class left on their class trip. It's so exciting to watch the nervous pretend to be calm, and I envy these lucky people getting on a train, something I've longed for as far back as I can remember. When I hear a train whistle, the most romantic sound in the world, I plan my life of travel to the 'Far Away Places' like the song describes, and always that leads to dreaming about what I'll do when I grow up! Finally, the train pulled up to the Tallapoosa Depot, and it took no time to load the bags and people, and then they were gone, and as we were picking up the flattened pennies, the parents watched toward the east even as the train was clearly out of sight.

At home, Mother shared her concern about the weather, "It's supposed to get down below freezing tonight, and the butane gas gave out last week. It's been an expensive spring, I guess we can sponge bathe in the kitchen next to the stove with the eyes and oven turned on high."

Before Mother really completed that thought, I saw a truck pull up to the now empty coal pile outside Carroll's bedroom window, "Mother, Bob Downey is throwing something off of a pick up truck."

We grabbed our coats, and ran outside just as Bob pushed off a mountain of slabs cut into short pieces, "Why Bob, where'd you get the slabs? How much did you pay for them?"

Bob said, "I got them at Jack's plainer mill. He didn't charge a thing, and he even let his sawyer cut 'em up for me. He thanked me for doing this for his sister."

Georgia Collins graduated from the new Haralson Consolated (blacks only), and quick as a wink, she too boarded a train going north toward Washington DC, but Georgia stayed on the train and went on all the way past DC to New York City, and now Thelma visits Mother a lot especially when there's a new letter from Georgia and that's about once a week. Usually Thelma holds the week's letter until Sunday evening because Thelma's one day off is Sunday, and Sunday evenings Mother actually has a little free time because Randall likes to watch Sunday evening television, and of course, I have 'foreign ministries' that demand my attention. I can't say those words without smiling at Ruth's joke about my attending to 'foreign ministries' for what else could possibly keep me in church all day on Sunday. Ruth has spread this exaggeration far and wide!

It's serious business however that caused Georgia to move all the way up north to New York City, and even though I'm never home to hear Thelma read Georgia's letters, Mother relays every word to me, and we are very proud of Georgia because she has found a good job in New York. She is a cashier working regular hours and making good money at a super market called Daitchwell, and to boot, she's met Phillip Jennings who works in the dry cleaners in the same strip mall just a few doors from the super market.

On a sober note, Georgia's absence has caused a deep sadness in her mother and that gloom is passed along from Thelma to my Mother prompting her to take me on another tour of racial inequality in my hometown. Sometimes this horrid and unacceptable atmosphere causes a stagnation that seems to block the intake of air into my lungs.

Marilyn's Tallapoosa High School graduation was Thursday, June 5, 1958, and that afternoon after the ceremony and before dark, with the help of Bob Downey, Marilyn packed up all her clothes and shoes and shampoo, and moved to Atlanta to live in Joan's apartment because Joan offered her sister's name to the boss at A B Dick, and Marilyn's first day of work turned out to be Friday, June 6, 1958. So now in Atlanta, Bob Downey and Marilyn Godwin are dating.

September 1, 1958
Dear Daddy,

Good news, Marilyn and Bob are getting married on Christmas day! Marilyn bought a whole lot of white lace, and Lily is making the wedding dress. Mother and Marilyn will make the bridesmaid's dresses. Marilyn picked green wool for the bridesmaids' dresses and Janice Roberts and I are the two bridesmaids, and Joan will be the maid of honor. Most important of all, Daddy, this means you have to come home for Christmas because you have to give Marilyn away!

Love,
Janet

Thelma spends a lot of time with Mother, and Mother is glad for the company. Thelma still works as a cook at Club 78, but the cook works at night, and during the daylight hours she works as 'help' in Mr. Turner's home. Mr. Turner is the "T" in "T & W" Clothing Factory in Waco, and he's offered again and again that he'll be glad to have Thelma as the first colored working for him in his plant, but Thelma is slow to accept his offer, and now that Georgia is out of the immediate picture, she is seriously considering taking the T & W job. Thelma is ready to take her place in Haralson County history as the first colored to work in manufacturing. When she puts all the challenges aside, the reality for Thelma is she's lonely since Georgia graduated and moved to New York City, but time marches on, and well she is brave enough to run the gauntlet, especially with the fair minded Mr. Turner on her side.

We have reason to be very proud of Georgia, Thelma positively does not brag, just as all coloreds will tell you if she uttered a word of bragging, well then who's to know the form of bad luck that would change all the good news into horrible news, but a little at a time Mother has learned of Georgia's High School accomplishments. She was a part of Carver's Choral Group which traveled all over performing Negro Spirituals, and they performed just about every year on the stage right here in town at THS which is within walking distance of Carver. I don't know a whole lot about music, but I know it's easy to harmonize with Mother when she plays the piano, and I certainly understand how difficult it is for anyone to sing A cappella and stay in tune and not miss a beat, but that's how the Carver teenagers performed because they do not have a piano. Sometimes Georgia had a solo part, and she belted it out with her strong vibrant voice! At Carver they never had a school bus, but Georgia's Carver Drama Classes also traveled regularly to cities up north like Calhoun and Dalton and down south like Valdosta and Columbus. For the distant performances, the parents loaded up the teenagers in a convoy of cars traveling together in a safety caravan, and if there's one car driven by one of the teenagers well that car is kept in a central position with adult driven cars ahead and behind, because there are mean spirited white folks who do not hesitate to harass a colored person traveling alone, and particularly, when a young colored person travels alone, but the mean spirited whites ordinarily don't bother a group of older colored people traveling together.

As Thelma and Mother have become closer over the years, Thelma has opened up a little about the constant, ever-present danger a colored person faces in a white man's world, and sometimes, I am allowed to listen in, but Thelma prefers to keep quiet when I'm in the room, even though Mother wants me to hear what she has to say, but it's hard to change Thelma's hesitance because she carries grave concerns that I might hear too much and repeat too much and inadvertently bring danger to myself and my family and of course to Thelma and her family.

This very real hazard is a direct contradiction to what I have been taught in church ... we are supposed to love our neighbors as we love ourselves, and from my perspective, the colored people are better at that than the white people, too many whites truly believe that they are supposed to be acknowledged as superior, and they cannot distinguish the evil in that line of thought, and I don't dare verbalize, but often I wonder how these whites plan to explain themselves on judgment day.

In New Mexico, Daddy became accustomed to Carroll's working through the summer and last year and now this year too, Carroll stayed until Christmas. A few days before Christmas they loaded logs on the best log truck and headed across the country, but this time this year, it's to stand up in a wedding, I guess that's why Marilyn and Bob decided to get married on Christmas Day as a sure fire way of having Shug Godwin walk the bride down the isle and Carroll Godwin serve as Bob's best man.

Daddy jokes that once the logs are loaded, and they pull away from the saw mill camp, well the log truck takes over and the driver need only mash the clutch, the gas peddle and the brakes at the appropriate time because the log truck knows the way across the country. This time though, once they crossed over the state line into Mississippi, a State Patrolman pulled them over because they have an expired Georgia tag. As soon as they all came to a stop along side of the highway, Carroll and Daddy got out and walked back to the Mississippi State Patrol Car, only to return to the log truck cab in search of tag papers, and as Daddy leaned over to the dash from the driver's side, he held onto the stirring wheel to keep his balance, and the Patrolman standing at the opened driver's door, saw in plain sight, Daddy's Mason's ring on his left hand, and on December 22, 1958, the Patrolman made an exception in this case, "Mr. Godwin, forget about finding the papers, how long have you been a Mason?"

This question opened up a conversation in which Daddy and the Patrolman discovered they plainly share more than membership in the same secret society, these two men share the same *Fierce Loyalty* to the common good, and they both understand that no one on earth is better than the next man, especially and absolutely if he wrongly thinks he is superior because humility is a virtue and highfalutin la-di-da self pride is a sin against Jesus. These two good men, each a mirror of the other, carry on their own mini war against segregation. After hearing details of the Godwin story, the Mississippi State Patrolman said, "I have a Mississippi tag in the trunk of my car, most of us State Patrolmen have one on hand for situations like this."

He produced the Mississippi tag and a screwdriver, and proceeded to mount the tag on the log trunk, and then he said, "This tag will get you home to Georgia and back to New Mexico, and you can use it back and forth until it expires in 1963, and right now I'll escort you a ways down the road."

Shug Godwin shook the Patrolman's hand and turned away so as to conceal his emotion.

On Friday, December 26, 1958, the day after the wedding, Daddy spent most of the morning in town without a single word of explanation, and about noon, when he came in the house, he called to Mother, Randall and me, "Who-oo, come on outside!"

Sitting in the front yard was a brand new 1959, Ford Galaxie; two tone white and coral red! It's more luxurious than any car we've ever had! Daddy paid two thousand, five hundred, and eighty dollars, but the 1954 Chevrolet trade in brought down the actual amount of cash. It's a four-door sedan, V8, 2-speed automatic, with power steering, power brakes, tri-color hubcaps, radio, padded dash, and safety anchored front seat. The roofline is a larger version of the Ford Thunderbird. Daddy is right on schedule buying a new car every five years. He bought the 1949, Pontiac from Chester's dealership, the 1954, Chevrolet from Mitnick Chevrolet, and now with buying this new car in Tallapoosa, he has given equal patronage to the three car dealerships. We were speechless (a nice change of pace), but Mother spoke up, "Let's go for a ride."

We ended up in Alabama of course, and we gave Mama and Papa a ride to town and back, Papa needed snuff and Mama needed a sack of flour.

Sunday,
December 28, 1958
Dear Daddy,

My head is spinning, you were here and gone before I could count to ten. You were very handsome in your suit and tie, and Marilyn was as pretty as any bride in the world, and Bob is a good match for Marilyn, he's a good looking young man who can cut up and joke when it's appropriate, but he was very serious when he said his wedding vows.

Carroll bought a car today; it's a black two door 1953, Chevrolet. He says it's got a good motor, and the inside is as clean as a new car. The motor is more important of course, and the cleanest car in the world isn't worth a flip with a no good engine, but in my mind, it's sure a nice bonus to find a clean car!

I'm writing this letter so it'll be waiting for you when you and your two new sawmill hands get to Magdalena, so I'd better close and get this in the mailbox.

Love Always,
Janet

1959

I sort a hung around in limbo after Marilyn and Bob's wedding, I do all the same old things and still my most important responsibility is writing Daddy every week. I sleep better now in my cozy upstairs room and the credit goes to Marilyn for two reasons first she fixed up the space, and second she gave each of her bridesmaids a silver cross, and that's the very thing that wards off Dracula so when I go to bed, I make sure my silver cross is in position on my chest, and then the next thing I know, it's morning. Oh, I still have Dracula nightmares, and Mother still comes running up the stairs no matter what, but at least now I can go to sleep and there's no need for another wide eyed vigil watching over the window, and let him come on in if he wants to for now I'm confident he won't be sucking any blood out of my neck!

When I got in the car one day, Mother pulled me closer to her and put her arm around me, and she was crying and of course if Mother is crying there's no chance that I won't cry, and she said, "Honey, Snippy got hit by a car. Carroll's burying her right now."

All I could think was, 'I don't even want to watch American Bandstand without Snippy!'

So, I haven't watched American Bandstand at all, and I seem to be moving in slow motion most of the time, it sounds silly, but my chest feels funny and sometimes it's sore, and it looks swollen, and my old swimming suit doesn't fit, nothing fits, and I don't want to go anywhere not even to church, and I've always wanted to go to church all the time. Church is where I see my friends when school is out, and my Sunday-School teacher Charlene; and my Training Union teacher, and my Girl's Auxiliary teacher and the choir leader are caring people who make Church fun and never hateful or demeaning. Now for a little while, I'm not going to Church, and I can't explain any of these feelings, all I know is I cry a lot, and I try to figure any way possible to blame my quandary on somebody else or anybody else besides me, and I'm ashamed of that. I'm not the same as I used to be, but I don't know what's changed. It's a silly contradiction I know that, but I run up stairs like an idiot, no like a moron, just so I can be alone, but I don't want to be alone. I can't figure out why I feel so alone. I'm not alone! I miss my dog, and I worry that she's wet and cold in the ground, I wonder if maybe she wasn't really dead, and Carroll buried her alive, and at least once a week, I wake up crying and screaming, and Mother comes to me and sits on my bed, and draws me into her arms, and she rocks me back and forth and croons reassurances that Snippy is in heaven with all our other pets, and she's with Ruth and Otto's baby, and they are happy together. Eternity time is very different from Earth time, and for Snippy in eternity, it's been just a few seconds since she was here sitting in my chair as I watched American Bandstand, and she doesn't even miss me because she's warm and cozy and happy, and she knows pretty soon we will be reunited, and if I live to be a hundred, in eternity a hundred years is just about an hour. Even if it pours down rain and her body gets wet, she doesn't know it because her spirit is not in the ground. Mother explains that she is confident that eternity time is different from earth time because in Genesis God created the earth and the heavens in seven days, but it's obvious those seven God days are maybe as much as seven million years in earth time. It's not for us to figure out, and it's not for us to limit God's power by restricting Him to human timetables or human calendars, or human wisdom, or human anything, and if we do put God in a box the size of our brain, well that's blasphemy. Yes sir re, because we have to understand that God deserves credit for being far advanced and completely outside the realm of our feeble thought process!

Finally, school starts, my seventh grade year, and it is very exciting and I am jump-started out of my stagnation, I'm a cheerleader! The cheerleaders are in grades seven and eight. (footnote)

Mother made a circular navy blue corduroy skirt for my cheerleader uniform; it's called a circular skirt because if you spread it out with the waist in the middle, the skirt forms a perfect circle. All the circular skirts are hemmed just below the knee, and they are lined with yellow material and Glad Hats ordered yellow V-neck uniform sweaters. We had to pay for the sweaters, but the football players did not have to buy anything for their uniforms because the sponsors in each town donated lots of money (footnote)

After a couple of Midget games, Brenda Cobb and I decided we'd make felt navy blue 'T's' for the cheerleaders to attach to the front of the yellow V-neck sweaters. So one day after school, I walked home with Brenda, we left our books at her house then walked up town to buy navy blue felt material, and we discovered there is no such thing in Tallapoosa so we bought white felt and navy blue Rit dye. Before boiling the Rit dye, we cut out enough T's to make each finished 'T' two layers thick, then when each two layer 'T' was absolutely perfectly sewn together, we put the Rit dye and water in a big pot on the stove and when the solution was boiling, we turned off the eye and dropped all the T's into the hot dye, then we walked away from the stove. Mother came to town to pick me up, and Brenda turned on her television. The next week, we surprised the

Midget Football Cheerleaders, and we are very proud of the blue T's on our uniforms!

At the first seventh grade Girl Scout meeting, Mrs. Jaillet gave each of us a booklet to read at home in private, she most certainly did not make reference to the booklet's contents, and as a matter of fact, she said only one sentence, "Brenda will give you a booklet as you leave today, read it at home in private."

I'm apprehensive about the booklet, 'Just Between Us." And secretly I imaged horror stories that could be referenced in the simple title, and the dot, dot, dots lead me to wonder also what personal and embarrassing information might be included, and I blush just thinking about the mystery, and finally at home, I raced upstairs to hide my booklet, but what I really want to do is be rid of it, maybe I could take it to the garbage dump and hide it under the pile of wet trash, it's still raining and in no time it would probably dissolve into the earth, and then I could simply refuse to learn something that is obviously too private to talk about. All this uncertainty makes me dizzy, and my first problem is finding private time! No kidding, how in the world can I find time to read such a booklet? Mrs. Jaillet said only that we should read it in private, but the problem is simple, I never ever have any private time. So with all this confusion swirling about me, I conceded the long term battle for a short term fix and shoved the booklet into my top, right dresser drawer under my panties, but there in my panty drawer I noticed another complication, on top of my panties glaring up at me is a bran spanking new white bra right there in my underwear drawer! Did I say it's in MY underwear drawer? I felt the blush, I turned and looked in the vanity mirror hanging from a nail in the chimney, and sure enough, my face is as red as a beet! I knew it! I certainly do appreciate that Marilyn fixed up this room for me even though I know full well, my brother can barge in any time, but it is very handy that my nosey brother first has to come up the stairs, and the noise on the steps gives me a few minutes to hide my booklet. It's a remarkable coincidence that Marilyn and Bob came home from Atlanta and spent all day Saturday, hauling clothes and toys and everything else out of the big upstairs room and storing it for safe keeping in the barn loft, and then Marilyn painted the walls light blue, after dark when the paint was dry, she and Bob set up the two three quarter beds brought upstairs from Mother's and Daddy's room downstairs, both bed steads, springs, and mattresses were already upstairs leaning against the walls and Marilyn had to move them around as she painted. Not long ago Mother replaced the two three quarter beds with one double sized bed, and as a finishing touch, Marilyn hung the blue gingham checked cafe curtains and vanity skirt.

I had a brilliant idea to send my little brother to the muscadine vine down in the pasture north of the barn, I helped him find a bucket to carry the muscadine grapes, and Mother encouraged him by saying, 'I'll bet the muscadines are sweet and ripe!' And as soon as Randall was out of sight, I ran back upstairs to start reading.

Just Between Us

"Sometime between the ages of 11 and 17, we all graduate from girlhood to womanhood. We do this not only mentally, but physically. We find ourselves looking, acting, and feeling "grown-up." The physical process that tells us we have graduated to womanhood is call menstruation. It is a natural and repetitive process that runs through a definite cycle. This cycle may vary from 20 to 35 days, but generally, menstruation reappears about every 28 days. Naturally, when you first start to menstruate, you have loads of questions to ask. And perhaps shyness makes the asking difficult. That's why we, at Beltx, have prepared this little booklet … to give you a better understanding of the menstrual cycle by answering those questions … and to tell you things you should know about personal daintiness and grooming … what to do about sports … in other words, how to be your usual active, attractive self during "those days.""

O. K. that's as clear as mud! The only thing that fits me is the age, I'm twelve and twelve is certainly between eleven and seventeen. What about sports? Every 28 days what? Be my usual attractive self, dainty and groomed? I heard my brother in the yard, back home from the muscadine vine, as I quickly glanced at the next page. When I can read again in private, I'll be reading about 'old wives' tales' that are put to an end; Menstruation's not an enemy … it's a friend?

I quickly looked out the window and decided I have a few more minutes, so I flipped ahead and zeroed in on the dot, dot, dots in practically every sentence, the last page to read is page sixteen, then there's a Beltx dial calendar, and finally on the very last page there are items for sale and a clue of sorts is for sale, a pair of panties with a patented, built-in sanitary belt, also for sale are personal belts (no panties) with exclusive safeti-grip napkin clasps.

So far, I've read not a single word that might help me fill in the dot dot dots except for the one word 'panty.' If there's some need for napkins in my panties, well no wonder nobody will talk about this. I hear Randall on the steps and shove the booklet under my panties and bra ... I guess I'll have to wear the bra.

In the spring when Mother's yard full of blooming trees and flowers shockingly, were not the least bit helpful in lifting my spirits, I woke one morning with a wet sensation in my panties, and as I sat down on the commode, I was shocked into a coma at the sight of fresh blood stains, and a huge gushing blood clot plopped into the water.

The entire seventh grade year, one by one all my friends reported their 'start of their period,' and with each new announcement, I reread the booklet, but nothing conclusive evolved from my pitifully ill informed conjectures, and consequently, I simply was not prepared for the bloody shock that fateful morning. Still sitting on the commode, I wondered if I should yell for Mother after all this is right up there with the worst possible nightmare, but then I reasoned that if I called Mother to come to me, well then my nosey brother will certainly be included, and the thought of his prying eyes stopped me in my tracks and led me to the path of least resistance. I removed my panties, pulled up my pajama bottoms flushed the commode, opened the bathroom door, and tiptoed to the kitchen where thankfully, Mother was sitting alone at the table. With enormous relief that stung immediate tears, I stood very close to Mother and opened up my right hand revealing the hateful bloody panties. She put down her coffee cup, wadded my bloody panties into a ball, wrapped her other arm around me releasing her fairy dust once again, "There's nothing to be afraid of, honey. Come with me."

She took my hand and melted my fear and anxiety, and in the bathroom behind the closed door she taught me how to attach a Kotex pad to the brand new Beltx, "This is yours. Now wash yourself with a spit bath or get in the bathtub, if you'll be more comfortable."

With Mother's sweet response to my bloody panties, she accomplished all she intended in the way of explanation or commiseration or instruction or even simple clarity. I certainly understand and respect her position which is as best as I can decipher, simply that these things are not mentioned not even between a Mother and her confused daughter because verbal reference might break some taboo and lead the daughter to believe conversation about such things is acceptable, but it is UNacceptable at every level, and with painful isolation came the sobering expectation that I would never learn about menstruation from anyone, and there's probably no instruction books NONE to be found anywhere in the world!

My first menstrual period was certainly attention getting, at bedtime I saddled up with a new Kotex pad, and still I messed up my panties and the bottom sheet, and every day I had to take a replacement Kotex with me to school, and because I was absolutely horrified that someone might see what I carried hidden in my book satchel, as a matter of utmost secrecy, I found a good sized scrap of black material, and I devised and sewed a hide-away black bag, and then at school when Mr. Gladden let everyone go wash up before going to the lunch room, that's when I discretely retrieved the black hide-away bag from my book satchel. In the girls' room, in the individual private stall I made the switch from blood soaked pad to fresh pad, and in the commotion, no one saw me toss the old pad into the trash can or at least no one let on.

Almost every Friday, a friend comes home with me after school, mostly it's Kristina, Laura, or Jane. Connie is expected to walk home to Granny's fresh daily cookies, and Brenda Cobb's mother wants her at home inside their house safely behind locked doors. I think the accident (hand through the glass gym door) affected Arbelle in a transformational way. It stands to reason, Arbelle took a turn toward more control. It's understandably very difficult for Arbelle to be an absentee working mother.

On Friday, Jane was to be my 'friend over' for the afternoon, (no one can spend the night because I always spend Friday night with Ruth and Otto), and Jane and I came out of the grammar school building pushing and teasing and giggling like the little girls we used to be, but as we reached the car, Mother did the unexpected and called Jane to come to her side of the car, and then she whispered something in Jane's ear, and I heard Jane say, "Oh, that's terrible. No ma'am, I'll walk home, no ma'am, Mother likes me to walk home as long as I stay out of the woods and walk on the sidewalk all the way."

Then with my heart pounding out of my chest, I climbed into the front seat, and as a trumpet blew holes in my eardrums, I read Mother's lips. Oh, no, Smokey's dead. Oh no. Then Mother told us the story, "I took Smokey with me down to the store where I parked the car and walked with Virgie Newman to her house across Highway 78, and just as I was about to dig up an azalea, I was obligated to look up as a sixteen wheeler transfer truck laid down on his horn, and immediately, I took the entire scene in and reckoned I'd left the window down just a tiny bit too much, and Smokey was just barely able to escape from the car, and obviously, he was coming in search of me, and of course he had no inkling as to how to cross a busy highway, and I watched as the transfer truck tried to veer off target, but it was no use, and thankfully he died an instantaneous death never knowing what hit him He did not suffer"

We found no solace as Mother swiped the blurring tears away and drove us home to an empty house, and I have no hope of ever getting over this, my heart is broken, how many times can we hear the word 'dead'?

On Friday, May 29, 1959, we were promoted from Grammar School to High School (seventh grade to eighth grade), and the two weeks of preparation drilled into our heads the ultimate and undeniable importance of this transition from childhood, and as we practiced, we learned to appreciate the ceremony's significance. This grand and serious scheme is not to be taken lightly, no sir re, and together with my classmates who are better described as family, we will survive this transition and grow closer not because of some rule of independence, but because rightly, now and forever, we will lean into the empowering DEPENDENT circle, and again rightly, we will feel the envy of those outside our circle. Of course as we love, this is the way we are and the way we will continue to be!

Some of the logistics of transition are beyond our control, but through past ceremonies comes the regiment proven to attract and define, and as time has proven the benefit of tradition, the fifth grade teachers Mrs. Eaves and Mrs. Rambo exchanged places with the seventh grade teachers and informed us that the girls wear white dresses, the boys wear white shirts, dark sport coats and dark ties, and there is a large collection of freshly dry-cleaned ties and sport coats and just washed and ironed white shirts, and white dresses in every size from small to large. For tonight our assignment is to find out if we will borrow clothes so that Mrs. Eaves and Mrs. Rambo can bring the correct sizes to school. These two teachers are sisters who never had children of their own, and they enjoy being caretakers of the promotion clothes because they have seen miracles before, and they truly believe the white clothes actually inspire and convey dignity to the humblest, and it's fun to be the catalysts of transformation through apparel! The boys will wear their own blue jeans, and the emphasis is there's no disgrace in wearing borrowed clothes, and in fact, every single student sitting on the Tallapoosa High School auditorium stage is now and always will be treated with the highest degree of respect because it is no small accomplishment to pass grades one through seven!

During the two weeks leading up to the 'graduation' we practiced the ceremony every day, but nothing prepared us for the real thing because none of us expected that every seat in the large auditorium would be filled, and none of us imagined the stage would be so luxuriously decorated with magnolia leaves and huge pots of fresh flowers. When the day finally arrived, of course no one dared wear white on the playground, and the two seventh grade rooms were transformed into makeshift dressing rooms, the boys will change in the seventh grade room on the back side of the Grammar School building and the girls will use the seventh grade room on the front side of the building. As each seventh grader emerged from the 'dressing rooms,' the girls received red rose corsages, and the boys received white carnation boutonnieres.

This transitional milestone filled with traditional pomp and circumstance dictates the ceremony must begin precisely at two o'clock. First of all, Mrs. B.R. Stringer Jr. spoke a few words of welcome to a hushed standing-room-only audience, and then to my complete surprise, Mrs. Stringer called me by name and asked me to stand as she awarded a Certificate of Accomplishment for making all A's every year in grades one through seven, and I accepted the 'Certificate of Accomplishment' passed to me over the heads of my classmates, and thankfully, I did not have to say a word, but I am very proud and glad that Carroll took my picture with the Brownie. When Mrs. Stringer finally nodded that I should sit down, my face felt burning hot, and although I had no mirror, I'm quite certain it was brilliant red.

JULY, 1959

Graduation from Grammar School to High School
Certificate of Accomplishment
Janet is standing because she had all A's in grades 1-7.

I had a great 13th birthday party at Crossroads Cafe, Mother and I got there early and arranged little glove shaped place cards at the big round table in the back room. Mother ordered a hamburger, french fries, and a coke for each person, and the icing on top of the store bought cake outlined a pair of gloves. All my superlative friends were there, I got a lot of presents and coincidentally, Dennis Williams gave me a pair of white gloves. As soon as we finished our hamburgers, mother put quarters in the juke box, and I chose a few jitterbug songs and a few two step slow dance songs, and everybody danced every song, and my secret superlative list named Larry Jackson the best jitterbug dancer.

1959

The next Sunday, in Sunday School, Brenda Cobb and I decided to go to Baptist Youth Camp at Shorter College in Rome, so we put our names on the sign in sheet and brought our money back to Training Union. As it turned out Brenda and I were the only two attending Baptist Youth Camp from Tallapoosa. Mother drove us to Rome the last Monday before school started, and we shared our dorm suite (two bedrooms connected by a narrow hallway leading to our own bathroom) with two girls from Cedartown. Luckily, we both brought a lot of change because we skipped dinner and supper in the cafeteria every single day in order to buy a honey bun and a co-cola out of a machine! The caffeine in the co-colas kept us wide awake until two or three in the morning, but that was fun too because we've only been up that late at spend the night parties. Friday night, the last night of Camp, we were supposed to attend a church service, and we went into the auditorium and sat down, but boy howdy, we could not sit there very long because we both had to find a restroom and quick! And when we returned to the auditorium, we had to jump up and run right back to the restroom! We made it just in the nick of time, but then we consciously, solemnly decided that we'd better high tail it back to our room, and next thing we were running through the dark campus, and the week's worth of two co-colas a day worked a dirty trick on our bodies, and at one point, Brenda fell behind, and I heard her muttering to herself and for some unknown reason, I thought the whole situation was hilarious, and at the next street light, Brenda said, "I'm so embarrassed, I'm gona cry!"

When I asked why, she said, "I peed in my pants!"

At first, I was horrified, and I looked around, all around, 360 degrees around us, and when I was absolutely sure no one heard what she said, the absurdity of the situation sank in and even though I grabbed my crotch, I could not stop peeing in my pants too! I would have been humiliated beyond repair if I'd done such a thing under any other circumstances, but in the very last sane minute for us both, we realized we'd had far too many co-colas and at that point we were no longer in control of our own destiny, and we decided our momentary isolation was a gift from above, although possibly, this whole episode was beneath the jurisdiction of our Savior unless of course He was instrumental in orchestrating so as to teach us a simple lesson. But soberly we figured, this last week before entering High School, was the last chance for us to be little girls, 'little girls' not babies in diapers!

We stayed in our room for the remainder of the evening even though we missed the farewell party, and we reconciled by figuring they were probably serving honey buns and co-colas, and of course that brought on another wild laughing fit. In the dark room that night, Brenda asked if Mother was going to let me date now that we are in High School, and truthfully, I replied, "I don't know. I haven't thought that far ahead."

Brenda said, "Kristina has been dating Forrest Williams all summer."

The next morning, Saturday, Arbelle picked us up because that was the agreement since Brenda's mother doesn't work on Saturdays, and on the drive home, Arbelle asked if we had a good time, and we did, and she asked if we met any cute boys, and we did, and when she asked if anything special happened, we shook our heads no, and now in the daylight, last night wasn't one bit funny, so when Arbelle turned off of Highway 78 to take me home, Brenda turned to face me in the back seat, and she held out her little finger so we could finger pull our solemn promise never to tell another living soul about last night!

Aunt Mary Lizzie died a year ago, and I understand that Ruth and Otto have a longer and more painful affiliation with death than I, and every Friday night when I am free to do so, I spend the night with them because they are more alone now than ever. Ruth jokes that I have "Foreign Missions" that take up most of my time, but really, as far as Ruth and Otto are concerned, nothing has changed because I've always been active in church, it's just that now for me church has a greater lure, and my church life just took on a whole new social perspective, I've been promoted from the Junior Department to the Intermediate Department in Sunday School and Training Union, and now I can join the Youth Choir. I'm a teenager interacting with other teenagers, the THS freshmen, sophomores, juniors and seniors. Grades eight through twelve are in the High School building, but the eighth grade has no actual designation, informally, eighth graders are called sub-freshman, which leaves a bad taste in my mouth. I wonder if somewhere there's a sub-freshman pen (like a pig sty) where eighth graders are separated and must keep to themselves as the slime is cordoned off at the bottom of a pond? The sub-freshman term rankles, but doesn't inflict actual harm.

In just a few days, I'll be going to High School! I have said it a thousand times, I love school, I love to learn, and I love to interact with my teachers and my classmates, Mother made a new dress for my first day of High School, I picked out a soft aqua material, and I showed Mother a pattern in the pattern book, and without buying that pattern, she made the exact same dress as the pattern book picture, which is an amazing talent, but when I offer praise, Mother just kind of shakes her head and declares, "When you get to be my age, you'll know how to do all this stuff too."

That's sweet, but crazy, I'll never be able to do all the stuff that Mother can do, but I guess I'll just let it go because she's more emphatic than I'll ever be about anything. Back to my new dress for my first day of High School, it's a straight dress with no cut line (no seam) at the waist, but of course there are darts at the waist to give the dress some shape other than being just a straight old sack. It's a tight, straight skirt, sleeveless dress with a long zipper up the back, and to be worn over the dress, there is a very short 'jacket', which comes just below my bra line, and the short-sleeve 'jacket' buttons up the back. I have a pair of new black 'flats' (shoes with no heels - that resemble a ballerina's slippers), and I have my first ever tube of lipstick, it's almost white because Mother says I'm too young to wear any a bright color lipstick. I have white fingernail polish. I'm considering every angle. Did I mention it's my first day of High School?

Back the middle of August, Mother gave me a Tony regular home permanent, and of course a new permanent is always sort of frizzy for a week or two I've been washing my hair in the bathtub every night, and I push it up like Mother tells me, but then just before crawling in bed, I pin curl big sections of hair and every morning the permanent seems to be a little less frizzy, but I'm worried that I'll look like a clown with frizzy hair sticking out all over my head. I'm a nervous wreck getting ready for the most important day of my life.

I love school, I always love school! I love reading, writing, arithmetic, and coincidentally, I love socializing and on all counts boy howdy, High School is one hundred percent better than Grammar School! We change classrooms for each subject, we have a (complete with Bunsen Burners) science lab and Mr. Shell teaches the simple and powerful use of a slide rule and faster still than a slide rule he teaches the ease of mental estimates, and we have a (complete with stoves and sewing machines) Home Economics room, we have a typing room with a manual type writer at each desk and besides the manuals there are two electric type writers. On the other end of the hall from the typing room and the science lab, Mrs. Williams is a very good English teacher! She commands respect of course, but she actually laughs and cuts up with us! Mrs. Brewer is a Math teacher unparalleled in the universe! She makes Algebra fun! Imagine that! And the same goes for Mrs. Stringer who came from the Grammar School staff and is our French teacher, and the first day in French class, she said, "I don't know anything about French, but we are going to learn together. As a result, we are learning French at an amazing speed, and that's because of Mrs. Stringer's exceptional skills as a teacher!"

There are two High School boys who seem to want to talk to me, and I like to flirt with them, and we have time between classes for just that purpose! Wayne Newman is a real freshman (ninth grade). Remember I'm a sub-freshman (8th grade) and Frank Ellis is a senior.

I rely on my classmates, and that's a simple but profound statement, and Denver Morgan has a self proclaimed protector roll, which I appreciate, he is the most handsome in our class, but passing the time of day with my classmates isn't flirting, because like Denver said, "That'd be like flirting with your own sister."

Mother has said I can't date yet which is a good thing because nobody has asked me for a date, and if somebody does ask, well it will be an easy out, and besides I'm happy to go on flirting. All this time through the first six weeks of High School, I was very self conscious about the braces on my teeth, and Kristina's September birthday party in the early afternoon just after school on Friday was the last party I attended with braces because the welcome day finally arrived when Dr. Payne dismantled the cumbersome metal apparatus and freed my mouth to normalcy again.

It's important to give my sister Joan credit because I stood up and walked out of Dr. Payne's office knowing my sister who attends to detail paid the bill in full. Joan is a night student at Georgia State University while all day, every day she works a full day at Gulf.

Dennis Williams has a brother named Forrest who is in the ninth grade, he was in our overflow 6th & 7th grade class, but I really don't know him, on the contrary, I do know Dennis's sister Mira Jo. She is a Varsity cheerleader with Little Lynda and the two girls are in the middle of a hullabaloo about 'pulling down a stop sign' and dragging it to the High School building in the middle of the night, and it is positioned effectively blocking the door to the boy's restroom. The sign blocked the boy's restroom door from Friday night through Saturday and Sunday and now Monday morning honestly, Little Lynda and Mira are still comfortable boasting about their handy work, but that attitude quickly changed this morning when our principal called all the varsity football players and cheerleaders and all the high school Midget football players and cheerleaders into the auditorium. At first, while waiting for Mr. Cobb everybody was actually congratulating Little Lynda and Mira Jo for their ingenuity and bravery, but all the praise ended abruptly when Mr. Cobb stomped down the auditorium aisle, jerked his hands free from his pockets and clapped a thunderous bolt demanding attention. His opening line became a barbed wire fence clutching and confining the two girls to their now awakened sense of shame and fear, "You will go to jail!"

Past this volley, no one uttered a word, no one cracked a smile, and Little Lynda and Mira sat transfixed, knowing that any of the many students could pick up the challenge and offer them to their reckoning because their self-praise left no one wondering who, and up until this very minute, they proudly accepted sole ownership. After a stern lecture regarding proper decorum and civic responsibility, Mr. Cobb selected two Varsity football players, two Midget football players, two Varsity cheerleaders (not by coincidence he chose Little Lynda and Mira) and two Midget cheerleaders. His specific instructions, "The eight of you have twenty-five minutes to get the post hole diggers from my office, drag the stop sign back to his rightful place and dig a new hole. I will be in my office waiting for your return. Now get going, and as for the rest of you, give them five minutes clear passage through the halls, then get yourselves back to class."

I feel a power like none other if Frank or Wayne respond to my teasing. On any given day, Wayne will ask me to sit in the auditorium with him and I'm becoming more and more comfortable in one on one conversations, and the resulting ease is slowly diminishing the uncomfortable, red hot, blushing face, and I'm finding that it's out of the ordinary to disclose that I have a wide eyed understanding of the archaic divide of Negros from whites in 1959 United States of America, I don't mind saying that there's a change coming. Also, I find it rewarding to disclose that I have ambitions and far reaching life plans, and talking things over with a guy is beneficial but never have I yet found an acceptance that is true acceptance.

Since Sputnik last year, I day dream a lot about flying in an airplane and I fully intend to work somehow in the aviation or satellite industries, boy howdy, imagine all the jobs out there! Maybe I'm way off base, but I've noticed that Wayne's and Frank's respective eyes seem to glass over when I get started thinking and planning out loud. I guess I understand why the boys keep away from the gossip circle under the big tree outside. They are positively out of touch with the changing times, and they remain centered around male leaders and the important female figures throughout the ages are few and far between, but right now at this minute in time, I'm learning that practice makes perfect and serious talk gives me credence and reveals a level of maturity which makes me attractive, although I sense I am still bound by 'protocol' meaning, I must remain in the group that waits for someone else to do the asking, but no matter, I like the outcome of the brief minutes of one on one discussion, and I'm rapidly becoming more self reliant and self confident, but there is a disconcerting factor that comes into play which brings the fire hot redness to my face again: Wayne has told me that he loves me, and I'm not sure how to handle the declaration, he is an outward joker but actually, he is deep down more serious than I am ……... I love Wayne back, and who wouldn't? He is kind and thoughtful, and when I'm slow dancing in his arms, I like the way he seems protective and possessive, but is that love? By the same token, I love to dance with Frank I feel less pressured with him, maybe it's because he isn't in love with me, which gives me more latitude. It's difficult to live up to Wayne's lofty positioning, and surely he can see my shortcomings, but there I am at the top of somebody's list, and I'm not sure I can meet the requirements.

On the other hand, I have room to be myself and fall short of expectations which is in itself a source of freedom. Somehow, I can't put Frank into Wayne's category. I go back and forth in my mind because these guys are amazing in so many ways, Wayne has a rare trait that few people have but many people envy, he is able to flatter and convey a boost, and he makes it look easy, he makes me feel special, and I admire him beyond words. This description brings me once again to Denver while he fills in as Protector General.

After a Varsity game there is always a Friday night dance in the gym, and oh how I love to dance! Also, during football season, after the Friday night dance there's always a spend the night party, and this week the party is at Karen Smith's house which is conveniently next door to Charles Perrin's house. So by midnight, as soon as Mr. & Mrs. Smith were safely asleep, we slipped out. Charles had a kind of a sleepover, masculine style, which meant the boys were waiting for the girls on the Methodist Church steps, with the distinguishing masculine feature of a bottle of coke in each boy's hand, and as we inched closer and closer to the Methodist Church steps, we heard Denver insist that every boy, "Put out your cigarettes!"

It's a good thing they put out their cigarettes before we arrived because if word somehow got out that the boys were smoking in front of the girls, well they'd be next in line to go to Mr. Cobb's proverbial jail. There are certain rules of decorum that can't be diminished!

On the bus trip to a game, I like to sit with Denver because he tells me about Boy Scout Troop 128. The Faith Tabernacle preacher's son Billy Joe Brooks is the Scout Master, and Billy Joe's dad, the Reverend Howard Brooks helps in organizing camp outs, and trips to Atlanta to usher at all home Tech games, and I have to be very careful about saying anything that could be construed as negative about Georgia Tech because ushering has given Denver an all encompassing loyalty to Tech and only Tech. Next year, Troop 128 plans to usher at the Gator Bowl in Jacksonville, Florida, and of course the Scouts are hoping Georgia Tech will play in the Gator Bowl. Each time I listen to Denver's analysis I have a feeling that Denver is headed for a place of respect in the big scheme of things. He is as smart as anyone I know.

Another favorite bus seatmate to a game is Jimmy Thrower because he is a comedian, and seriously, he's never serious! He makes up comedy like the rest of us make up a simple plan to get through the day charged with the immediate hazards each teenager has to face and conquer. I usually sit with Charles Perrin on the ride home after a game because he is very good at explaining the decisions made by the players.

I sometimes have a fleeting vision that my class might be just like every other high school class, if that's the case, well all high school kids have it pretty good, but actually, I suspect that my class is exponentially special, and homeroom is our time to relax together, and what could possibly be more peaceful and reassuring than listening to Jimmy Thrower's jokes? I use the word 'relax' because we don't have to impress anyone, or play a role, or pretend we're something we're not, and our friendship within our class is reliable and strong and definitive, but we just never date each other.

Homeroom is first thing in the morning, and our homeroom is the library, and happily for the rest of the day the few minutes between classes is devoted as it should be to flirting and with the lines clearly delineated well I figure maybe I better warn Wayne and Frank to watch out, I'm here to flirt.

I feel bad that Connie and Kristina never come to parties, they have both sort of removed themselves from the social circuit, however it is a consolation that Connie actually has a lot of parties at her house, and Jerry Mathis from Bremen is always there, and Connie's parties are a lot of fun because there's no one with a better sense of humor than Connie, unless you count her mother Alison, but I'm a little concerned about Kristina, she doesn't come to Church or Sunday School or Training Union any more. Connie sings in the choir at the Methodist Church, which is lucky for the Methodist Church because Connie has a crystal clear singing voice, and that explains why we don't see Connie at the Baptist church. When I told Connie that I'm beginning to worry about Kristina, Connie was very blunt as usual, "Janet, let it go, Kristina is dating Forrest Williams, and she's rearranging her priorities, and we have to let her work it out for herself."

Somewhere, sometime, somehow, Kristina faded into the periphery, as did Forrest Williams, but the usual Tuesday night's activity of attending Midget League football games took on an added dimension having to do with a mischievous rascal from Forrest's family by the name of Dennis Williams. The Tallapoosa Midget team is considered to be the best team in the league, even better than Carrollton, but Carrollton has a huge advantage in the number of players, which gives them the unfair magnitude of having a perpetually rested team, but even with this asset, we almost beat them. So far this year we tied our first game against Buchanan, and we beat Bremen 13 to 0, we beat Mt. Zion 28 to 0, we beat Bowdon 41 to 14. Frank helped us decorate the goalposts for the home game against Carrollton which we tied 0 to 0.

At recess we no longer get to play on the Grammar School playground, instead now that we are in High School, we do have a break between second and third period, and it is called recess but it's just ten minutes (10:20 to 10:30). There are no jungle jims, no swings, no slides, and no merry go rounds, so we simple go outside and stand in a huge circle underneath the shade tree at the south west corner of the building. The big circle is made up of girls only, and the big circle pastime is nothing more than talk …..... (of course some might call it gossip). I don't know why, but the High School boys never stand in the big circle, my guess is that the High School boys think standing in a huge circle is silly.

Dennis is in seventh grade still in the two story Grammar School Building, so I don't see him at all during the school day, and he is lucky because he still gets to play on the Grammar School playground. I miss him and the Grammar School playground, but I'm glad to be a Midget Cheerleader because Dennis plays Midget Football and as a cheerleader I get to ride with the players on the bus to and from the games. Last week, as the players and cheerleaders waited for the bus in front of the High School Building, out of the blue, Dennis hugged me, and immediately after that hug, Jack Nixon tapped me on the shoulder and said, "I have something for you, Janet."

I turned to Jack and before I knew what was happening, he kissed me right on the lips, and of course, I blushed and fumbled, and the only thing I could think of was, 'Denver's right that was just like kissing my own brother.'

At that point, an alarm should have gone off, but no sir re, I didn't suspect a thing, and next, here comes Charles Perrin, and he said, "My turn!"

I did not see it coming, but Charles Perrin dipped me as if we were dancing the two step slow dance, and when he had me in the lowest dip ever, you got it, he kissed me, and when he finally stood me upright, it was Denver's turn, and my knees started wobbling, then Gary Gray, then Jimmy Thrower, then Wes Littlefield! Enough is enough! I put on my mean face and held up my hands straight out from my bruised lips which stopped Richard Allen in his tracks, and then as they all laughed to high heaven, the giggling gremlin Dennis who started the whole thing and for that matter Dennis stood right there his shoulder to my shoulder through the whole practical joke, except for the dip of course, and at that point with my mean face on and as red as a beet, well sweet little mischievous Dennis twisted me around so's my back was to him, and I felt it when the freckled face gnome pulled off a little white sign scotch taped to the back of my yellow sweater, it said, 'Kiss me please.' Well, that minute in my mind, we were back on the Grammar School playground where I could outrun every single boy, and I caught Dennis Williams just as he tried to hide from me behind the Nandena bushes, and with the pouting pixie in tow, I pulled him out into the open, and Pat, Patricia, Brenda, Brenda, and Karen helped hold him down while we smeared my pink lipstick all over his face each smear in the shape of outlandishly huge lips.

So now that my braces are off, I have a secret to keep because I really enjoyed the 'Kiss Me' trick, but it's mandatory that I never reveal to anyone and especially not to my mother because honestly, my Mother would swoon, and that is why I share it with no one, but I think often that now without braces I can dare Dennis Williams to put all manner of 'Kiss me' notes on my back, and they won't bother me because never again will I feel awkward when a boy's lips touch mine.

On the bus ride back home after the Bowdon game, Charles told me the inside story, "In the second quarter, we had the ball somewhere around the fifty yard line, when the quarterback called the thirty-six power play around the right end, and as he handed the football off to me, no one touched me as I made an easy forty-five to fifty yard touchdown. Bowdon was totally unprepared for the game, which made it an easy win for us. The final score was thirty-six to zero, and I believe Coach Harris held the score back because we could actually, score at will. The most special minute did not come during the game but after the game, when the final horn sounded, and the cheerleaders ran onto the field greeting the players like we had won a big championship game, and when you and I, Janet, walked off the field with our arms around each other's waist, well I couldn't help but think, 'What more could a football player ask for?' ...... Than walking off the field with his favorite cheerleader after a big win? That's a great moment I'll remember when I'm old and gray!"

See what I'm talking about? Do you understand now? I get choked up because I'm just a sentimental lightweight when it comes to stuff like this, and stuff like this is precisely why Charles is my friend, but of course, there is a wrinkle that presented itself and wouldn't you know it, the freckled scoundrel just happened to be sitting behind me and Charles, and that sweet 'walking off the field with your favorite cheerleader' line well it cranked Dennis's tickle box, and of course the entire bus then enjoyed my embarrassment as Dennis recited the part about the favorite cheerleader, and I tell you what, I'd teach that little imp a lesson if Coach Harris would look the other way!

It sounds like I'm a starched old fuddie-duddie, so let me say this: I love the attention, but a huge part of the reason I'm showered with this sort of attention is my blushing uneasiness which is completely authentic, but it translates to boys as an endearing and helpless quality, so I accept their perception totally, and I do not want that to change! I blush easily just like Papa, but also like Papa my fluster has nothing to do with my capability. Anyone can look at Papa and instantly believe he's a power to contend with and bullies better just watch out because he can crush you like a roach if he deems it necessary. My appearance is diametrically opposite to Papa's, where he is strong I am weak, but guess what, I learned well what he taught, and I suspect I am his best pupil, because blushing or not, weak appearance or not, I am not afraid of anybody or anything! Like I said, I enjoy the attention, and again, I don't want to change the slightest particle of how my friends perceive me, and if they are intrigued by a country girl's blushes well then I consider that a huge positive. I appear to be vulnerable, but in reality, there's no doubt in my mind that I am brave enough to stand up against evil and be counted as a force for good! Just like Papa and my Daddy, I will never stand aside and let an injustice go unchallenged, but my friends know this about me, and honestly, I am ready to stand up and be counted, and never in a million years could I be heartless in the face of hurt and discrimination, and if I'm given a chance, I can easily display inner strength, I'm not the swooning type, and I am positive that Dennis knows he owns a special place in my heart, and if he's busting open to have some fun, well he might as well just get on with it and get it over with, because sooner or later, he's gona figure out some way to make me chase him down and smear lipstick all over his cherub face, and furthermore, I'd have it no other way!

Friday night Bremen beat the THS Varsity 26 to 0. I sat with the Midget Cheerleaders, and during halftime when the THS band was on the field, the Varsity Cheerleaders were sitting in the bleachers with the Midget Cheerleaders. Dennis came to me and said, "Mike Murphy wants to meet you!"

"Who is Mike Murphy?"

"Aw, he plays on the Bremen Midget team, come on!"

I had no choice as Dennis pulled me up and off the bleachers and dragged me along side the field's white line. That's another long story I'll get to later, but for now, Dennis pulled and positioned me to come face to face with a guy standing practically under the blue and white Bremen Blue Devil's decorated goal post and next thing I know, this stranger is hugging me, and all I can think of is how good it's gona feel to put Dennis's face in a bucket of cold water. For real my face was burning hot, and I turned away and ran faster than any football player back to the bleachers and my still warm seat with the Cheerleaders. Brenda Cobb looked at me with a great big question mark on her face, and asked, "Who was that guy hugging you?"

"That's Mike Murphy."

"Who's Mike Murphy?"

"The guy hugging me."

We sounded like Abbot and Costello, and Brenda let it go when two Varsity cheerleaders, Little Lynda and Dennis's sister, Mira Jo turned to witness as Dennis grabbed my ankle from beneath the bleachers! I was quicker than Dennis by a long shot, and before he could react, I pulled his slender body right through the wooden boards and in another second, I would have had him in a death grip, but instead, with no fuss atall, Mira

Jo grabbed ahold of her little brother's ear and that simple wrestler's aid rendered Dennis still as a board and he finally sat down and nodded to his big sister when she demanded, "You will sit quietly, beside me."

Now with Dennis facing the performing Bremen Band, Brenda and I moved up a couple of boards so Dennis would be unable to hear our laughter at a rarely witnessed scene, Dennis the imp sitting as still and quiet as any angel in heaven. This is a comparison my subconscious has used many times because of the halo that glows in advance of Dennis Williams! I love that little imp!

When the band returned to the bleachers and Little Lynda and Mira Jo went back to the sideline with the other Varsity cheerleaders, I took advantage of the demure Dennis, which is a wondrous use of an adjective! In this most unfamiliar of circumstances, actually and politely conversing with Dennis Williams, I learned that Dennis and Mike Murphy have become true friends who happen to play on opposite football teams. They are so close that believe it or not, they talk on the telephone almost every day, and actually do their Civics homework together on the telephone. How about that!

At the after-game sock-hop in the gym back in Tallapoosa, I danced every dance, and I was in heaven! It's clear, I am an inordinately social fanatic, certainly, I enjoy solitude walking through the woods, dancing with the door knob, and writing my thoughts, but if I had to choose between time alone and time dancing (with a person partner), well there's no doubt, I choose dancing, I choose classroom discussions about a myriad of subjects but mostly about Sputnik, and I choose singing in the choir! Eighth graders are too young to have driver's licenses, all be it, I can drive a car (straight shift or automatic) because Mother and Daddy know it's a matter of safety and an actual necessity for country families (who only recently have had telephone lines in their reach) because emergencies of a wide range of possibilities can occur and consequently, I learned to drive as soon as I could reach the pedals. I'm pretty sure that city folks don't teach their children to drive, and so eighth, ninth, and tenth graders rely heavily on eleventh graders and seniors, and Frank's parents are generous with their 1957 black Ford Sedan, and it is a beautiful car! At Brenda's we put on a stack of 45's and danced some more. Close to midnight, Frank drove all the boys back to town but first he swung by my house because I have to get up early in the morning to catch the six o'clock bus to Atlanta and Dr. Payne's office for one of several required after-braces check ups, this one will be dedicated to fabricating a retainer.

Early next morning, Mother waited in the car while I went in to purchase my round trip tickets, and when I finally boarded the late bus, the driver let Mother go east on Highway 78 ahead of him, and this gave me time to make my way to the back of the bus while the bus was standing still. There were four white people and one Negro and I sat behind the Negro lady. From the back of the bus, I could see the driver's face in the driver's mirror, and I'm positive he watched me and approved.

When I heard on television that the Supreme Court is considering whether or not it is constitutional to force Negros to sit in the back of buses, well that's all it took for me to decide I'll do my part to express what I think.

On the afternoon bus, I had the bonus of riding with Denny Cole, I saw him first, and then he saw me leaning into the aisle, and he made his way to the back of the bus to sit beside me. I firmly believe if more good God fearing white people made the same decision, well then the colored riders would have no alternative but to sit in front of the whites and that would be good, and as far as I can see, the normal people in the world would welcome the Coloreds to have equality in every way. Mother and Daddy know of my strategy about this, and my parents agree because they ultimately put a lot of credence to this subtle sort of change that might just start with a ninety-seven pound white teenage girl! Oh I'm ready for the possibility of a confrontation if some mean KKK guy gets on my bus, but like I said before, I'm not afraid of anything or anybody and especially a grown man who hides his face in a white ghost costume. My Daddy stands as a giant among men, and any KKK riding a bus between Tallapoosa and Atlanta no doubt will recognize the name Shug Godwin because he is the man who laid down the gauntlet many years ago when he put out the word that he'd personally handle the situation if any cross is ever burned in our yard or the yard of any of our neighbors and that goes double for our closest neighbors the Collins Family! So I feel perfectly safe, and several drivers recognize me and smile in the mirror when they see me work my way to the back of the bus.

On Sunday morning I was promoted from the junior department to the intermediate department and my Promotion Certificate is signed by

Gay-El's dad, Morris Williams. Definitively, the best thing about being an intermediate is singing in the Youth Choir up a notch from the poorly populated Junior Choir.

I am currently active in the Girl's Auxiliary at the First Baptist Church, and the GA's have planned a hayride party, and it might be called a joint venture with the Youth Choir, except that the GA's are furnishing hot chocolate and cookies back at the Church Recreation Hall. I'm pretty sure that I am the most serious teenager in the world, but I truly enjoy the frivolity of flirting with Wayne and Frank. Last week during lunch break, Wayne pulled me into the auditorium to show me what he has carved into a seat-back, 'W. N. "84" + J. G.' This inscription containing his football jersey number ranks right up there with the Declaration of Independence (not to be irreverent but you get the general impact to such a jersey number carving). I love Wayne back but it's not a big love story. I recognize there's a difference between what I feel for him and what he feels for me, but not for a minute will I ever be the instrument of pain for Wayne. Secretly, I am convinced that Wayne, the proverbial knight in shinning armor has taken an oath of chivalry for he is the consummate gentleman, and that will be how the world always and forever credits him.

One afternoon a week, the Midget Cheerleaders stay after school for practice, and this being the last practice of this year, we have an audience although the number of by-standers correlates directly to the number of guys who have the afternoon off from work. As an example, Frank Ellis works at the Post Office where he does general cleaning, sweeping, moping, and dusting. Ralph Key, the Post Master and Lloyd Smith are usually working the afternoon shift when Frank is there, but this week Frank's day off coincides with our last cheerleader practice. The general atmosphere at practice is always whooping good fun egged on by the sneaky Dennis Williams who is at the base of every practical joke and today is no different! The freckle-faced bandit first announced that Frank is now available to be snatched up by some lucky girl because Frank just broke up with the 'other school' girlfriend (I think the other girlfriend is Ann Laminack who is a good friend of my cousin Golia. I like Ann a lot). Next, Dennis acts as town crier trumpeting the upcoming GA hay ride, but I wonder how he got that brand new bit of news? Next during a water break, I made my calculated advancement toward the water fountain and lucky for me it was a very warm day, but unlucky for me my curly new permanent was still in the initial stage of frizzes, I happened to approach the water fountain just inside the building and another of our audience, Little Lynda was at my side walking with me to the water fountain until at the last minute, she must have signaled to Dennis the exact second of my highest degree of venerability. Anyway, I had no time to prepare a counter offensive when out of the corner of my eye I detected the rascal Dennis running from outside into the hall, approaching the flowing water side of the fountain, and in an obviously practiced maneuver, he first covered my hand on the water-on handle with more than enough force to keep the handle in the wide open position, and then with his right hand he cupped the flowing water creating a shower directed precisely at my new frizzy permanent and before I could even begin to fight, I lost the battle, but with one perfectly landed kick to his shin, Dennis took off running away from me screaming like a banshee (what ever that is), out the double doors, down the steps, and into the grass, where I caught the little gnome by the shirt and pull-pushed him to the grass screaming, "Eat some grass if you ever want to walk again!"

The growing audience collectively held their breath, and I even heard a few sympathetic chastisements urging me to go easy on Dennis (EASY? ON DENNIS? WHAT ABOUT ME? WHAT ABOUT MY NEW TONY PERMANENT?) I was about to loose my composure, oh who am I kidding, what composure? Without looking in a mirror, I knew beyond a doubt that I looked like a drenched animal ready to scratch and bite anything within reach ...... When next the freckled faced imp picked a blade of grass, threw it in his mouth, and when he finished the slow and exaggerated mimic of a cow chewing her cud, he jumped up and swept me to the Nandena bushes along the building, and quickly he shoved me behind the line of bushes and discretely whispered, "Janet, just stay behind the bushes till your Mother comes to get you, it's the safest way to go unnoticed!"

"Dennis Williams, you make about as much sense as a fish out of water! GET OUT OF MY WAY!"

I said that part through clenched teeth, and when the spellbound crowd realized that I had to turn away from Dennis or else have him witness my withering anger turned into giggles thusly proving he's won me over again, yet again! The truth is I can't stay mad at him even if my permanent is frizzing up all over my head, it is simply not possible to stay mad at Dennis especially when Denver Morgan is counting him out. "Nine, ten, you are out Dennis."

The Thursday night Midget game was called off due to rain, and Friday night North Cobb beat the Varsity eighteen to seven. As usual after the game, there was a sock hop in the gym, then, the spend-the-night party was at Brenda Redding's. We played 'this, that, and the other' which involves taking walks around the building, holding hands with the game's selected partner. When my partner was Frank Ellis, he stopped in the dark shadows and kissed me right on the lips! I was speechless to say the least, but it was not just a fluke, because he kissed me again, and then he asked me to walk with him to the street corner (at Arbacoochee Road and Broad Street) on his walk home, and at the street corner, he kissed me again, but this time I pulled away from him and ran like I was in a race in grammar school. Then back at Brenda Redding's, everyone changed into pajamas, turned out the lights, placed a pillow in their assigned sleeping space on the floor, settled in, spread individual blankets, and finally the gossiping began, after all gossiping is the whole point of a spend the night party, right? As usual the gossip was inconsequential up until analysis turned to Frank Ellis, at which time Brenda Redding started with the disclosure, "Frank kissed me seven times right on the lips on our walk around the building."

At this point, I decided it best to refrain from contributing to the gossip by disclosing the small number of kisses coming my way. I acknowledged to myself there's a sharp stinging sensation attached to betrayal, but actually, it's good to know he's just a playboy, and this reality check is invaluable armor for my unprotected heart!

Appropriately, that very Sunday night, after singing the choir director's increased tempo version of "Blessed Assurance," in the closet room where we store our white choir robes, Frank dallied as I straightened and stored my white robe and when Frank and I were the only ones in the closet room, well he struck up a conversation and asked, "Do you want a ride to Crossroads?"

When everyone went inside at Crossroads Café, Frank sat down beside me as we ordered cokes and one order of French fries, and I noticed he was acting very silly, funny but silly, until he finally owned up to acting silly because tomorrow October 26th is his birthday and starting tomorrow at age seventeen, he will have to act more grown up. Those were his words, we'll see about that. The following Thursday, October 29th was our school Halloween Carnival & Sock Hop. I made it a point to flirt with everybody except Frank Ellis.

Going into the Midget Bowl, first we played and beat Villa Rica, and then in our next Bowl game against Buchanan we suffered a 'bad break' and it's an unknown if our team can win another single game in the tournament after Denver Morgan's accident! On Tuesday night November 3, 1959, in the Midget Bowl game against Buchanan, Denver broke his arm. Denver is a very good football player, but he'll be sidelined possibly forever because his arm is so badly mangled, and it'll be slow healing because it's such a 'bad break,' and there's a definite possibility the distorted arm might never again be strong enough to play football. Jimmy George was first to use the 'bad break' pun.

As a cheerleader in uniform, I wanted to run out on the field, concurrently as my circular skirt and sweater certainly transformed into a nurse's white, but unable to will the morph, I stood in regret as though somehow I was neglecting my duty to Denver, and I surmised of course that if I tried to play the roll of a nurse in cheerleader's garb, well that would be more obstructive than helpful for everybody (except me) so I decided to stand still on the sideline, and Jimmy Thrower happened to be the one Coach called to go in for Denver, and just at that minute, the players on the field opened up a safe passage corridor for Denver, and Jimmy Thrower and I froze suspended in disbelief not daring to breathe, and I physically forced my feet to dig in and stay put, and Denver's Mother appeared at the sideline's shortest position to her son, and I thought it odd how the sideline white chalk on the grass is as impenetrable as a ten foot tall prison yard fence, and from outside the players' boundary, ours was an orchestrated cry sent the short distance to Denver's ears as he struggled and slowly made his way from the bottom of the pile-on, and no one expected the hideous site of his once healthy arm transformed into a giant paperclip folding back on itself at more than one bloody point. Then in unison, the players retreated toward the opposite sideline as a car pulled onto the field straight along our sideline. Denver, his mother, and nurse Allison Gentry (Connie's Mother) climbed into the back seat, and the driver did a wide one-eighty leaving gashes in the green, conspicuous and shameful, but my thoughts placed the true and legitimate shame on the entire football tournament's culture as Jimmy Thrower made his required but frightened advance to the scrimmage line, I wanted to yell not a cheer, but a serious question, "Why bother, who cares? It's just a game! Let them win! We have to go with Denver! Doesn't anyone understand that? Denver needs us!"

Believe it or not, Denver showed up in school the next morning, and in homeroom, he told the story, "I was Left Tackle, Charles Perrin was Line Backer behind me, Jack Nixon was Left Half Back, Tim Cole was Left End, and Wes Littlefield was Left Guard. While in pursuit of the ball carrier, I jumped a Buchanan player lying on the ground, and in mid-air, I was hit on the side and behind by resolute Buchanan players. I reacted by stretching my hand out toward the ground and locking my elbow to 'break my fall,' and the arm snapped like a twig when the pile-on hit the ground, and my last memory of the normal is permanently etched, and I will always see Janet doing her cheerleader swing, hand in hand with cheerleaders passing thru each other in a weave type routine perfectly in rhythm with the Tallapoosa High School Band playing the 'Washington and Lee Swing.'

It was my uncle Jesse Newman who drove onto the field, loaded me, Mother and Allison Gentry into the back seat and carried me straight from the field to the Bremen Hospital where Dr. Allen of Bremen set the bones. Allison rode in the back seat and held my arm all the way. This was the only game my mother ever saw me play, as she feared her little boy would get hurt. In the back seat with nurse Allison and me on that unending trip, my Mother was in much worse shape than her son. The mistake I made was my conscious decision to 'break my fall,' and of course, I failed to consider the added weight, and very quickly, and possibly on the way down, I came to understand 'breaking my fall' was exactly the wrong thing to do."

In homeroom, Jimmy Thrower took his turn to explain, "I was on the sideline, not in the game, and when Denver came out of the pile-on, it was a nasty break and tough to look at. I broke my arm a few years before, and I back then thought my arm was a crooked mess until I saw Denver's. I remember Denver's mother coming to the sideline and asking Assistant Coach Harold McWhorter about Denver. I'll never forget what he told her, 'He'll be all right. He just warped his arm a little bit.' I had to go in and play the rest of the game (up until then I was safe on the bench) and I remember going to the huddle with my arms crossed on my chest and being asked by the quarterback if I was sick. I wasn't sick, I was scared."

In homeroom I was next with my account: "When Denver came out of the pile-on, right in front of me and Jimmy, we were witness to Denver's courage and spirit. Jimmy murmured, 'I don't know how Denver can walk off the field, he needs a stretcher!' As Denver neared the sideline, I wanted to hug him, but of course that would be a ridiculous thing to do. I'm not sure Denver could hear me, but I moaned his name as if his physical pain were actually my physical pain and not just a passing condolence, and if it is completely heartfelt, I think that specific sympathetic response is called 'empathy.' Denver's strength makes me proud, but on his face we saw his agony, of course, but his valor certainly transcends the ordinary and touts his courage."

After each game in the tournament, electricity arched from player to player on each bus ride home, and more than once, everyone yielded the floor to Denver by granting him the solemn right to joke and lessen the tension or if the minute required serious consideration well Denver was the judge, but for the most part, Denver's decree was light hearted, and in that case Dennis and Jimmy played again their usual crucial roles of stress eliminators with their new litany of jokes. Looking back, I can remember only one joke. Dennis asked, "When is a door not a door?"

"When it's ajar."

Before the game that night on Carrollton's football field, I remember the stark realization that there were Carrollton players covering their half of the field each within arm's length of the next as they engaged in their warm-up exercises, but the shock was that Carrollton players were still coming out of their dressing room. I remember Coach Harris saying, 'We counted 70 players on their team.' Denver, with his arm in a substantial cast sat on the end of the bench nearest the cheerleaders, and from that vantage point, he gained remarkable insight.

On the bus ride home the Tallapoosa players relived the game play by play in an accurate-to-every detail account of both team's performance.

Charles went first, "Coach Harris really motivated us. We were all up for the game. We wanted to beat Carrollton so bad we could taste it. In fact, yesterday afternoon Jimmy George, told me to play the game as though it would be my last, and literally, that's just what I did, and now I have to tell you all, this game tonight was in fact my last football game, because next fall I'm going to Berry Academy, and they don't have a football team. Anyway, tonight we were the underdogs, and Carrollton outnumbered us about seven to one. The huge number of players on the sideline (on the bench) was in itself totally intimidating. They have offensive and defensive squads so they are always rested and that is a huge factor, and I think the odds were fundamentally unfair, but no matter, true to form, our players take pride in playing both sides of the ball, and tonight, we played the best we ever played before. We played as a true team. In the fourth quarter, the score was Carrollton 7 and Tallapoosa 6, and we had one more opportunity to win the game as the clock showed about 3 minutes left to play. It was 4th down. We had the ball somewhere around their 5-yard line. In order to make a 1st down we had to score. In the huddle before we ran the play, we all motivated each other knowing that it was now or never if we were going to win. The quarterback called the 36, power play around the right end. This play meant that I would be running with the ball. We lined up, the quarterback called for the snap and then he turned and handed the ball to me. After receiving it, I could not believe what I saw. The field was wide open. I decided to go to the goal line via the shortest route so I made a sharp turn left and headed straight for the goal line. As I was running past the scrimmage line, a Carrollton player who was on the ground with one of our players on top of him grabbed my left ankle with his left hand. I went down like a lead balloon. It was by one left hand and one left ankle that we missed the greatest opportunity of a lifetime in beating Carrollton, ultimately, my last football season, our only loss was to Carrollton, but we lost to Carrollton twice. We were all sad after the game, but we knew that we had played the best we could play. In Tallapoosa, Coach Harris stood at the door outside of the bus, and as we got off, he slapped each of us on the shoulder pads and told us what a great job we did. I love Coach Harris. I think if Denver had been able to play, we would have won easily. One more thing, last year Jimmy George kicked the first extra point in our Midget Football League. I was the holder. The extra point was made against Buchanan at Buchanan."

Quite possibly, I've said this before, but again, I love school, I love reading, writing and arithmetic, which is a general statement, but quite specifically, I love grammar and diagramming sentences which could not be easier after all these years of Mother's correcting not only my English, but everybody's English! She has claimed the right and the moral obligation of correcting my friends' English! To prove that point, last week, on a warm fall day, Frank Ellis hauled home four girls and two boys, and my house was first stop, and the party came in the front door just as Mother came in the back door carrying a giant load of dry clothes from the clothes line, and even though she could barely see around the huge loosely stacked bundle of clothes, my sweet Mother dumped the clothes on the couch and herded everyone into the kitchen where she began by retrieving seven plates and a loaf of bread from the cabinet and without asking if anyone might be hungry, she placed a slice of bread on the first plate and ladled hot chili from the pot simmering on the stove, and one by one we took our plates, turned back into the dining room and pulled chairs up to the table as Mother returned to the living room couch and the task of folding clean clothes. Of course Mother could hear every word, and when Wayne said, "This chili is the best I've ever tasted, I wonder if I could have seconds."

Mother from the living room, "Please have seconds, all of you!"

Wayne from the kitchen, "I don't need no more loaf bread."

Mother from the living room, "You don't need ANY more loaf bread."

Wayne from the kitchen, "Yes'um, that's what I meant to say!"

This exchange is typical for my Mother because long ago she appointed herself as the "correct grammar patrolman."

Back to my love of school, Mother has guaranteed that English Grammar is easy, ridiculously easy for me, and Carroll has guaranteed that

Math and specifically, Geometry is easy for me ...... again 'ridiculously' easy. Carroll is a senior at Tech this year, his course load demands all his attention so he doesn't come home every weekend, as a consequence he doesn't have the time for his pie route, and therefore he's short on cash, but Joan is working and only takes one night course, and when I'm in Atlanta for a Dr. Payne appointment, more than once, I've seen Joan give Carroll a $20 bill, and they both have explained to me at least, that Carroll makes the twenty dollars last all week, plus he saves enough each week to make his rent on time, but he is losing weight.

When a student's subjects are ridiculously easy well of course that student can relax in class and feel free to ask questions, and of course between classes that student can enjoy interaction with other students, and the very next day after the impromptu chili party, in the hall between classes, I think Frank was actually trying to flirt with me but his method was all backward, I say that because when I walked past him, he stuck out his foot to sort of trip me up, and that's exactly what happened, I was sent stumbling down the hall trying to regain my balance, and as a consequence I glared at Frank as though he were a little boy, maybe in first grade, and with a cool head held high, I entered my next class, found my desk, stored my books, except for my History book, and deliberately, looked out the window at brooding dark clouds until the last bell rang, and Frank had to make good time getting to his own class.

Here I want to interject that so far in this my first year in high school, I have been a student of observation, and observing the girls specifically, I have come to realize that a junior seems to be the most popular girl, her name is Sara Will Saxon, and it's my opinion that her wide smile puts every one at ease, and her eagerness to interact gives her the opportunity to make friends, and frankly, she appears to be truly good friends with scores of girls and boys both, and I think I can make this a learning experience for me, because like Sara Will, I like to lead with a wide smile, I make friends easily, and my friends are girls and boys.

Wayne calls me several times a week, he's very sweet, and Mother has made it clear that Wayne is her favorite, in fact, if I don't begin telling stories the minute I get into the car, Mother asks, "What did Wayne do today?"

Mother knows that question will get me going because Wayne's antics of course, are the product of a super talented guy thinking up and executing funny and interesting plots and sub-plots. I sometimes wonder how he keeps it all juggled to come together just according to his plans. Now that I'm still mad at Frank for tripping me, he has been avoiding me, and that's just fine with me, but in town after school on Friday, Mother stopped at the Bakery, and when I got out of the car to go into the Bakery, Frank called out, "Hey Godwin, get me a Creamed Horn!"

When Mother and I came out of the Bakery, Frank was still doing his job of sweeping in front of the Post Office, and I did at least wave to him, but he needs to stop the kid stuff! I guess he doesn't get that message, because at Youth Choir practice on Sunday afternoon, Frank and Wayne sat behind me and now they are both acting like first graders tying paper scraps into my hair which actually hurts to high heaven when it's time to untie and get rid of them. In fact, Mother had to help eliminate the last couple of paper scraps, and I double dog dare either of the first graders to call me or look sideways at me because now I'm really mad!

It was a huge and happy shock after school on the day before Thanksgiving! Daddy is home! Not just for Thanksgiving, but for good! All this sounds wonderful and I can't stop giggling, but there's more to the story! Daddy's saw mill burned, and in fact, after supper, before anyone turned on the television, Daddy asked us to sit down in the living room so he could tell us the whole story which is sad, but at the same time, Mother's point of view and state of mind is directly the opposite of sad because the loss of income is serious of course, but having "your Daddy home is worth more than all the gold in Fort Knox,"

And I think I'm more on Mother's side! Daddy says we don't have to worry about money for a while and in the meantime he has two plans, 1) to buy up land mostly from neighbor Olly Goolsby so Daddy and Carroll can start building the dam just like Daddy has always dreamed! 2) Daddy will run for Haralson County Road Commissioner against Lee Worthy who is a 'good feller' but maybe it's time somebody else made some decisions around here! All that being said, Thanksgiving, the next day, was perfectly timed to be the greatest Thanksgiving ever! Thank you, Dear Lord for bringing my Daddy home safe!

On Friday December 4th, we got our school pictures back, and I exchanged pictures with my classmates, Frank, and Wayne, and on Tuesday December 15th we had our last Choir practice before the special Christmas program, and on Thursday we had our Christmas parties at school, I sat in the auditorium with Wayne, he is the perfect gentleman, and incidentally, Frank regressed to the first grade again when he loaded and fired a water gun repeatedly and mostly at me! After the big Youth Choir Christmas program, everybody went to Crossroads of course, and Frank sat beside me and held my hand under the table, and he whispered in my ear, "Try to get your Mother to change her mind about letting you date."

Instead of going home, everybody went back to the Baptist church where the GA's sponsored caroling 'walk around' was to begin, and most of the time walking around town on a cold Christmas caroling night, Frank walked with me and held my hand, and the week before Christmas turned into a time when Frank finally stopped the silly stuff, starting on the 23rd when Mother was in the Post Office: he came out to our car and asked me to go with him that night to the Methodist Cantata, and when he asked Mother face to face, she thought the Christmas Cantata was very appropriate for a first date.

The next night on Christmas Eve night, Charles called to say, 'Merry Christmas,' which would have been perfect except I know I acted very strange, and I'm sure he was confused by my repeated silences, and I can't stand to recall how un-caring I must have sounded, but for some reason, I thought it imperative that I hide my tears. It's odd how things work out, my first date was with Frank because he is old enough to have a driver's license, and this year is Charles Perrin's last ever year at Tallapoosa High School, and I'm such an idiot, I mean I'm not worth a flip! How can I be so insensitive?

I continue to flirt and I'm loving every minute.

On Monday, December 28, 1959 Pat Wade and I rode the bus to Atlanta, we sat in the front half of the bus because I don't plan to involve anyone in my crusade, it's a very personal and powerful thing that I've decided on my own, and I can't expect anyone else to make such a commitment. Joan had to work that day, but she borrowed her roommate Jonny's car to pick us up at the bus station. She always uses Carroll's car to pick me up, but Carroll is at home in Tallapoosa because of course, Tech is closed for the holidays.

Pat holds the 'most perfect everything' spot on my personal list of superlatives, her hair is always perfect, her clothes are always perfect, her sense of humor is perfect, she is the most perfectly kind person ever, and when I sit beside her in church, her crossed legs are perfect. I will explain: I am always fidgeting. Dr. Berry in Villa Rica said it's because I have poor circulation, and maybe that's why I have to shift sides and re-cross my legs about every five minutes, but Pat Wade sits perfectly still with the same leg crossed over the other, and it's my guess she could stay perfectly still until kingdom come.

When we found my sister at the Atlanta bus station, Joan took us to Dr. Payne's office for another of my after braces sessions, and this time he had the retainer ready for me and luckily it is a perfect fit, I'm supposed to sleep with it in place and come back again in about a year.

In the afternoon while Joan was at work, Pat and I rode a city bus to downtown Five Points and went shopping at Davison's first, then we walked to Rich's, and next we crossed the street to McCory's and shopped our way through McCory's to the other entrance on Whitehall Street, where we went in and out of dozens of little dress shops, and I think we both liked Three Sister's best, but we went back through McCory's to the Rich's close-out-basement because that's where we found the absolute lowest prices, and now I understand why Joan says, 'I can wear anything from a size 4 to a size 14 in Rich's basement. The prices are so low, heck, you might as well buy something and if you don't actually wear it, use it as a dust rag, it's cheaper than buying a scrap of material for a dust rag. That's probably a little skewed, but I like the idea! I bought two Bobby Brooks matching outfits, one in baby blue and the other in soft pink, each sweater and wool straight skirt is perfectly matched and each blouse is a matching print with a peter pan collar. Finally, Pat and I rode the city bus back to Joan's work, and Joan drove Jonny's car to her apartment, and we spent the night with Joan. It was very cozy, Joan already had a pallet made for us, and Joan made sandwiches for our supper. We were not very hungry because we had a great big Varsity dinner before shopping. Joan is so good to me, she's paid for my braces and Tuesday morning before work she drove us (in Jonny's car again) back to the Greyhound bus station. This time Joan went into the bus station and gave us a lecture on how to use the public toilets. Joan is very knowledgeable, and never in a hundred years would I question her advice. "First hang your purse on the corner of the door, then close and lock the door, next pull enough toilet paper to place a cover on the seat, next try very hard not to sit down at all, but if you loose your balance and have to sit down, then the paper seat liner will be better than sitting on the germ ridden toilet seat."

I am thirteen and Pat is fourteen, and we are completely at ease riding the Greyhound bus to Atlanta, it's about a two hour ride each way, and I'm sure we will take these shopping trips many more times, but I have to get a job first before we go again. This time, I had a twenty dollar bill that Daddy gave me for Christmas, and twenty dollars paid for my two Bobby Brooks outfits (found in Rich's basement), my dinner at the Varsity, my city bus rides in Atlanta, and my Greyhound bus tickets. The public transportation buses in Atlanta are clean and safe, and no one ever bothers us. Only occasionally, are there freedom riders on the Greyhound bus, and they are just as nice and polite as can be. I would like to talk to them, but I'm afraid they might get in trouble with the other white riders if I did. That's not fair but it's true. So it's my business and my business alone if I want to sit in the back of the bus. If somebody is blamed, then the blame is mine, but white folks for the most part just ignore me, but if someday some KKK idiot asks questions, then he better be asking me right to my face, and nobody else!

At home, Larry Thompson, this is the boy I tap danced with in the Tap Dance Recital when I was in first grade. Bill Carter made three of us who danced in cowboy costumes to 'Don't Fence Me In' Anyway, Larry called and asked if I could go to a movie with him tomorrow night, and the sweetest thing happened, when he picked me up, of course he came in to visit with Mother and Daddy, oh that reminds me, I have to tell Daddy's story first, then I'll tell the sweet thing that Larry did. So to back track, Daddy gets a kick out of teasing me, and that Tuesday night when Larry sat down in our living room, Larry and Mother kept a good conversation going while Daddy was preoccupied with the task of taking off his shoes. Yeah I know it sounds like a sensible thing to do in the privacy of a man's own home, but there's another factor to consider, and that is how bad my Daddy's feet stink! He could wash his feet every hour and still they would stink, and I mean STINK, if you are down at the barn when Daddy takes off his shoes and if there's a west wind, the odor travels easily and is not in the least bit diminished. With that being said, Daddy took off his shoes with the mild mannered Larry Thompson sitting right there on the opposite end of the couch, I had to bow my head in a futile effort to ignore the obvious, and as it turned out, something had to be done to stop my convulsions because I was laughing out of control, so with my head still bowed, I said, "Larry, I think we'd better get on to Bremen, the movie starts in twenty minutes.

Before Larry started the ignition, he reached over the seat and produced a gift wrapped with a big pretty bow. When he handed me the gift, I moaned, "Oh how sweet, I didn't get anything for you."

But he smiled sheepishly while I ripped the beautiful shiny paper, and then my breathing stopped when I saw such a lovely delicate chain with an unusual pendant, and on closer examination under the dashboard light I shrieked, "It's sputnik!"

With my mouth hanging open I looked back and forth from sputnik to Larry and back again to sputnik, and finally I said through my tears, "I thought no one was listening to me, I've been babbling about sputnik and the unimaginable idea of leaving the pull of gravity, going into space! This is the most thoughtful gift I've ever gotten! Thank you, Larry! I'm bowled over! Imagine that you were actually listening to me!"

When the movie ended, it was after 9:30 so Larry rushed me home because everybody knows of the strict curfew imposed by my Mother, and sure enough when I walked into the living room, Mother and Randall were watching television, but Daddy was already in bed asleep, and this gave Mother the opportunity to relive the story of Daddy's stinking feet which cut short any visiting that might have been done, and Mother's version ended the same as many stories she tells about Daddy, "Aggavatin thang!"

Her assessment of Daddy is not a secret, and when she calls him an "aggavatin thang" every single person in ear shot mimics her huge smile, and it's common knowledge that this descriptive language is not a slur, no sir re bob.

My brother Carroll (of course) is solely responsible for my inordinate fascination with sputnik! He has always encouraged me to be more than a country bumpkin, although I'm mighty proud of my origin just as Carroll is proud, and I'll gladly join in a knock down drag out fight if any snob ever makes fun of me or any member of my remarkable family or my remarkable friends! Carroll hopes to get a job in the space program when he gets his Degree in Engineering this spring, and he's thinking specifically of a job at Redstone Arsenal in Huntsville, Alabama, and there's no doubt in my mind that if that's where Carroll wants to work, well then that's where Carroll will work!

Back to the sweet gift from Larry Thompson, in the next week, I went about telling everybody, and along about then is when Larry Thompson acquired the nick name of 'Sweet pea' Thompson and I've always wondered if I used the word 'sweet' one time too many when telling the sweet story.

At Youth Choir practice on January 31, 1960, Frank Ellis asked me to be his date at the Athletic Banquet coming up two days before Valentine's Day on Friday, February 12th. I accepted his invitation to be his date, but a lot of my friends don't have a date because it's not required that a Midget Cheerleader bring a date, I could go to the Banquet without a date because the Midget football players, Midget Cheerleaders, the entire THS Band, the boys basketball team, the girls basketball team, the baseball team, the Varsity football players, and the Varsity Cheerleaders are included in the Athletic Banquet. Because Mother knew I'd go to the banquet with or without a date, she was already making my dress, and when Frank called specifically to get the color of my dress, I told him it is beige and white. He told me later that his Mother ordered the corsage in pink because she knows pink will complement the dress, and she was right. When Frank picked me up for the Athletic Banquet, he handed the pink corsage to Mother to pin on my dress. Frank picked me up early so we had time to stop by his house because his Mother wanted to see my dress. When I walked into their house, Mrs. Ellis made me feel like a million dollars when she said, "I think your Mother is a very talented seamstress, and if she weren't so busy sewing for her family, I think she could be as famous as Edith Head who designs and makes costumes for the stars to wear in the movies."

I responded with enthusiasm, "I always watch the movie credits and when I see Edith Head's name, I'm positive I will love the costumes. Thank you, I'll be sure to tell Mother about your complement!"

The first thing when Frank and I walked through the lunchroom door, the pesky Dennis Williams came running up to me and in a nervous song and dance, he said, "Janet, Denver's real sick, come here with me!"

What else was I to do but follow the imp into the gym's hallway, and although the light was minimal, I could see and smell a semi-liquid on the floor, "Oh! That's the worst odor I've ever encountered!"

Dennis volunteered, "My Mother says the worse it smells the sicker you are!"

"Where's Denver?"

"Come on, he's just inside the boy's locker room."

When we reached the door to the boy's locker room I said, "I can't go in there!"

Dennis insisted, "You have to! He's real sick!"

By that time Dennis was shoving me through the door into the boy's locker room and sure enough Denver was lying on the floor with his eyes closed! As Dennis held the door wide open, I reached for Denver's chest and thank heavens he was alive! But before I could process any of this bazaar scene, Denver yelled, 'Boo!' And about ten boys jumped out of the so-called private dressing areas and simultaneous with their yelling 'boo' they ran toward me insisting they were sick too! I was unable to verbalize at first, but I can tell you some very un-ladylike words were forming just beneath the surface, and finally my lips formed a profanity that never before has crossed my mind let alone has actually formed into the spoken word. In one more second, I would have unleashed the forbidden word, but alas Coach Harris saved me from disgrace as he passed through the wide-open hallway door carrying in his hand the "vomit." Actually, the vomit was swinging from his grasp between index finger and thumb, and my first thought was, 'How can that puke hold together?'

Couch Harris seemed unusually on the verge of smiling, but his inner core's serious foundation held together his solemn decorum, and he practically horse whipped Dennis with his stare as he threw the rubber puke against the rapscallion's chest, all the while pushing me back through the hall and into the cafeteria. I found Frank and took my seat beside him, and without ado I fumbled with the handmade menu/program booklet at my place. On the front of the booklet were the typed words,

Tallapoosa Athletic
and
Band Banquet
February 12, 1960
7:30 P.M.

Inside the booklet was a Program:

Invocation.......................................…...……….Mr. Eston Cobb
Introduction of Guests................…Mr. Charles Hilderbrand
(President Boosters Club)
Introduction of Band & Awards ......Mr. Henry J. Cavendar
Introduction of Football Players & Awards ...Coach Harris
President of "T" Club...........................…..............Charles Barnes
Superintendent....................…........................Mr. Eston Cobb
Dance

On the opposite page:

Menu
Fried Chicken
English Peas
Potatoes
Tossed Salad
Cherry Pie & Ice Cream
Iced Tea – Coffee

The lunchroom staff worked straight through from early morning, cooking two full meals the normal one in the middle of the school day, and then the one for the banquet that night and after serving the banquet food, they cleaned up, washed the dishes and put everything back into it's place for the beginning of the school week on Monday. These ladies are amazing, and I'm willing to bet they didn't get home by ten o'clock.

After the delicious banquet everyone went upstairs and while dancing with Frank I told him that I love his Mother because she is so thoughtful, and Frank responded with "She loves you too."

We had time to dance only three songs because of course I had to be home before ten o'clock. On the drive home, Frank stopped the car on our dirt road and turned off the engine and the headlights. We were just off the highway, and then in the dark, he kissed me and whispered, "I love you. I want you to go steady with me."

I didn't have time to say a single word because the headlights of another car coming off the highway almost blinded us. Frank started the engine and turned on the headlights, and the car behind us kept right on our tail, and when we turned into my yard, the other car turned into my yard too, it was Daddy, I'm doomed for sure. My guess is he's been to a Mason's meeting. We were caught red handed, and I pictured being tied to a hitching post and whipped with a hickory switch as soon as I entered the house, but actually, I was able to slip upstairs in a dark, quiet house, but early the next morning Mother woke me (very unusual on a Saturday morning), and sitting on my bed upstairs she gave me a tongue lashing like I've never heard before. The final judgment was a simple decree, "No more out until ten o'clock on weekends. From now on you will be home by nine, and every date must be a double date."

I did not see Frank on Saturday, but of course I saw him at Youth Choir practice Sunday afternoon, and Sunday night he drove me home after the choir's very moving rendition of 'How Great Thou Art.' I think our Youth Choir could be a huge success on tour, but how could that ever be possible, where would we get that kind of money. We do have a big performance coming up in September when Tallapoosa celebrates the Centennial! Our town was founded in September 1860, and the Youth Choir will wear period outfits and sing 1860's songs like Amazing Grace. I'm very excited for two reasons 1) I will wear Aunt Ollie's brown traveling suit, and 2) Mama told us that OK is coming from Oklahoma that very week. This will be his first ever visit with his only aunt, my Mama. Mama cries a lot when we talk about it, partly because it will be so poignant for OK to be here when I'm wearing his mother's brown traveling suit! Of course he knows all about the brown traveling suit because he's been getting and sending letters to Mama since he was five years old.

That Sunday was Valentine's Day, and after morning church service, it was the plan for Frank to pick me up at the Baptist Church. He and his parents go to the Presbyterian Church on Sunday mornings, but his parents come to the Baptist Church to hear the Youth Choir on Sunday nights. So after morning church, Frank picked me up, his parents in the back seat of their beautiful black 1957 Ford; and we all went to Crossroads Café for dinner. I was a little uneasy about my table manners, but everything went well except for an embarrassment when we were ordering. I was uncertain if I should order something really cheap in case I have to pay for my food, and if that is the case, well then maybe I should order French Fries and a glass of water, but when I heard what Frank's Mother ordered, it sounded so good that when it came time for me to order I blurted out like a poor heathen country girl, "I'll have what she's having."

Immediately, after practically pointing to Mrs. Ellis and referring to her as 'she' my face turned as red as a beet, and I squirmed uncomfortably in its hot burn. I was absolutely mortified that I would say something so impersonal, so impertinent and so brash. I wanted to cry, crawl under the table, and not come out until spring, but I was hemmed in and I had no choice except to sit there like a lump on a log and take the punishment, but believe it or not, for some reason, the benevolent Mrs. Ellis dissolved the awful embarrassment when she smiled the sweetest smile right at me sitting directly across the table. It was a signal of acceptance and forgiveness and understanding, and the understanding part made tears well up in my eyes, so again I had to hide behind my napkin, what a stupid fool I can be.

After dinner, Frank's parents walked home, their house is just a block away from Crossroads Café, and on the drive to my house, Frank asked about Friday night. When I explained Mother's curfew change, he quickly laid out a plan that includes my cousin, Ann Cunningham and he shouldered my mother's wrath with, "I don't blame your Mother one bit, I should have known better. I will make absolutely certain that you are home by nine, and we will double date probably with Ann and Rodney."

Just a few months ago, I was wary of Frank's immaturity or so it seemed, but now all that silliness has vanished and made visible a grown-up young man. We rode in silence until Frank turned off the highway, then he said, "Janet, do everything just as your Mother says, and I have to know if you will go steady with me?"

"I don't think Mother will allow it."

"I've thought it through, I want us to go steady, but I think it should be our secret commitment to each other."

I ventured, "OK we'll see if it works."

Next Frank said, "I'd like to come in and apologize to your parents."

Frank came in with me, but Daddy was not home and Mother was out back at the clothesline bringing in a huge load of dry clothes. As he held the screen door open, Frank winked at me and attempted to tease Mother with, "Mrs. Godwin I know you have a large family, but every time I'm in your home you are bringing in a mountain of dry clean clothes."

Frank pulled me out the back door and down the steps, and he made inroads with Mother when he helped me collect the remaining dry clothes. Inside, he offered to help fold the clothes, and Mother quickly instructed him to fold the towels, and Frank stood at one wing back chair, as Mother began throwing towels his way. I'm sure Frank thought nothing of his assignment, but Mother and I both fumbled through our embarrassment and the subsequent relief we shared as we quietly and methodically stashed all the female underwear just out of sight in the corner of the couch behind the huge active pile. When Frank had a chance, he again made points with Mother, "Mrs. Godwin, I want to apologize for Friday night. I want you to know that I respect Janet more than any girl I've ever known, and I would never do anything to make her or you feel compromised."

That's all it took, from that minute on Mother's sour expression dissolved, and her warm sweet smile returned. Daddy actually didn't meet Frank for some time even though Frank picked me up every Friday and Saturday night, and most times just to prove the point, Rodney and Ann came in to visit, but they visited with only Mother because Daddy was simply not around the house very much because he spends many long hours campaigning for the office of Haralson County Commissioner.

Monday, the day after Valentine's Day, was the beginning of Twirp Week at school. It was great fun following the list of rules for this turned-around-backwards kind of a departure from protocol. Everyone received a printed list of rules. There are eleven rules for Boys:

1. You shall not spend a cent on any female.
2. You shall eat lightly and watch your delicate figure.
3. You shall be angry if she does not call you.
4. You shall not call any girl at any time.

5. You shall keep yourself neat and feminine at all times.
6. You shall not leave on a date without at least 35c "mad money."
7. You shall not become ill on candy she gives you.
8. You shall look pretty and wear a perfume that makes you irresistible.
9. You shall have a manicure so that your nails will be in condition to use as weapons if needed.
10. You shall furnish transportation if the girl cannot.
11. You shall have a good time all week.

There are eleven rules for girls.
1. You shall ask for at least two dates during Twirp Week.
2. You shall be the one to make the telephone calls.
3. You shall defray all expenses on the date.
4. You shall buy him whatever his heart desires.
5. You shall open doors for him and let him go through first at all times, also you shall be expected to carry his books.
6. You shall walk him to the door after the date.
7. You shall not accept any gift from any male.
8. You shall be a perfect "gentleman" at all times.
9. You shall walk on the outside when walking down the street.
10. You shall furnish transportation if possible.
11. You shall be present at the Twirp Twirl.

Leap Year Twirp Twirl

Place - Tallapoosa Cafeteria   Admission- 50c couple, 25c stag.

Time- Saturday Night, Feb 20, 1960 8-11pm

Dress- School Clothes

Only girls may come stag. Twirp license admits couple or girl stag.

Girls only may lead.

The thing about 'secretly going steady with Frank' lasted about a week. As always, Mother made an effort to be in the room listening to my telephone conversations, and when I turned down a date with Wayne, Jimmy, Larry (Sweet Pea) and Brantley Thompson, well Mother lassoed me and jerked me to attention with her finger wagging in my face. Her query was, "Don't think for a minute I will allow you to go steady with Frank or anybody. This dating thing is a chance for you to have fun and get to know several boys, but it will not become a way for you to be monopolized by one boy. You are too young!"

Mother was right, and I made an oath to myself, 'I don't want to go out on a date every weekend because I miss my Friday nights with Ruth and Otto, and my Sunday afternoons with Mama and Papa.'

I suddenly got very sick, too sick to sing in the choir the last Sunday of February, and Monday morning the 29th of February (Leap Year) I could barely get down the steps and my coffee had no taste what so ever. I missed school Monday and Tuesday, but then beginning Wednesday March 2nd school was closed because of freezing rain, and as it turned out school was cancelled the remainder of that week and throughout the following week because everything stayed iced over for two full weeks, all the power lines, the streets and roads, the window panes, the cars, everything! This will be remembered as the "1960 Two Week Ice Storm."

My Mother always had the reputation of being the only person who can drive in and out on the muddy slick dirt roads after a soaking rain, but during the Two Week Ice Storm, even my Mother could not get out to buy groceries, but our salvation was Bob. Bob now drives a Volkswagen beetle, and the novelty car with the engine in the rear over the driving wheels works miracles, and Bob Downey brings groceries and other supplies twice every day. Marilyn and Bob have moved back from Atlanta and are living close by on our dirt road in the upstairs garage apartment.

Most of the two weeks duration of the ice storm, I was sick on the couch, and if I'd had the strength, I would have found a nesting place somewhere else, anywhere else, as long as I could get away from my littlest brother! Every morning, Randall starts the same ritual, and it's my guess he simply cannot justify in his mind that we are in fact icebound ………… this is something we have never experienced and Randall has no choice except to test the truth, and he does it endlessly, time after time every day, starting around eight in the morning and continuing throughout the day, almost on an hourly schedule. I can't really blame him, it is a remarkable sight outside, but the rest of us are content to look at the ice kingdom through the frosted window panes but not Randall, so to be able to venture outside into the frigid cold, he begins by layering his shirts. Starting with his regular white undershirt next to his skin, then comes his school wear plaid cotton button up shirt, then he covers the plaid with a larger shirt, borrowed from Daddy's drawer, a short sleeved t-shirt, then comes a sweat shirt probably Carroll's, because it reaches to Randall's thighs, and finally on the upper body he stuffs his puffy arms into one of Daddy's work jackets, and now with five upper body layers, he begins work on his lower body beginning with a pair of pajama bottoms that can easily pass for long under ware, then comes a pair of school jeans, next comes kid size camouflage army pants probably hand me downs which might have fit Randall last year, but it's fairly obvious that Randall wants to force the too short military type pants into to being his outer wear, and when you think of it, of course, the military look is the best look for an expedition into the polar region, but the camouflage requires a fight, and this same battle occurs over and over again. The battle being: when the camouflage pants are in place and finally zipped to the waist, my too tall, all legs, little brother pulls on a half a dozen pairs of socks, and a pair of hand me down high top brown leather boots. The boots reach his mid calf, and after tightening the laces and tying a very respectable (for a second grader) shoelace bow, he begins poking and stuffing the camouflage pants into the boots, AND THEN HE STANDS UP, AND THE TOO SHORT CAMOUFLAGE PANTS COME OUT OF THE BOOTS! Here is where I have to turn away to protect my little remaining sanity for he sits down and stuffs and pokes again, stands up and the camouflage comes out again, so he sits down and stuffs and pokes and stands up again and there comes a time when he noticeably stands up without stretching to his full height, and for long enough to get out of my sight, the camouflage stays poked into the high top boots, and he leaves me biting my fingernails and he finally disappears out the door. The worrisome behavior occurs at the top of each hour repeated with the same madness just so he can spend another five minutes outside!

The last three weeks of March were a whirlwind for Daddy, he was winding up his campaign, he finalized the deal to buy the Baker place, which includes a small two-bedroom house, and he put together a deal to buy more land along the creek. Back when the ice storm held everybody captive, it seemed that he didn't even slow down instead he found and bought a caterpillar and a pan, and after losing the election, men continued to stop by just to spend time with Shug Godwin because that name is more widely known now, and he seems to have become the go-to-man because he has cornered the market on the land along the creek and the Baker place, and it's coming to pass just like he's always talked about, Shug Godwin is actually going to build a dam that will contain 40 acres of water and at the dam's midpoint the water will be approximately 40 feet deep, and that is exciting enough to make Shug Godwin a very popular man!

So back to my dating, in the month of March, I had only one date and that was on Friday night the eighteenth, with Frank to the Senior Class Play. Here I want to mention again that Mrs. Williams picks the play and the actors and in a small rural/town, the residents are anxious to attend an annual play right here in our own high school auditorium. And this year's play 'The Perfect Idiot' was a success with Jackie Wood playing the part of Margaret Tennyson and Frank playing the part of Jackie Tennyson, Of course the heavy lift belongs to the Director, Mrs.Williams. It was fun at the senior class party after the play because when we walked in, everybody clapped for Frank and he deserved it, every member of the cast was applauded deservedly so.

After school on Tuesday the 22nd of March, 1960, the Tallapoosa First Baptist Youth Choir met at the church and filled up four cars for the ride to the Radio Station in Bremen. We recorded 'How Great Thou Art' and six other hymns, and we can expect to get the records back in about a month.

Papa is in town just about every time we are, and it's the best feeling in the world to see his horse and wagon parked along side Lipham's and Williams Brothers. One Saturday morning Little Lynda and I were going through the Dime Store killing time while Mother was in the Jitney Jungle, and when we figured Mother was probably about ready to go home, we walked from the Dime Store toward Hilderbrand's, and as we were about to cross Head Ave at the traffic light, we saw Papa's wagon, and just looking at Papa's wagon stirred up an excitement that just about bubbled over when we finally found Mother in the Jitney Jungle! "Mother, Mother Papa's in town can we ride home with him? Please!"

"Yeah, that's a good idea because I want to go over there in a little bit to pick up their dirty clothes so I can wash for them today and return the clean clothes tomorrow. I'll tell Chester."

Little Lynda and I ran out of the Jitney Jungle Denver was working that day, bagging groceries and hauling them to the buyer's car. I stopped for just a minute to say hello to Denver then Lynda and I hightailed it out of there and ran all around town like chickens with our heads cut off until we finally found Papa buying snuff in the back of Lipham's. We could not stop giggling as we informed Papa that we are, 'A going home with you!' He got that sneaky grin on his face when he finally understood what we were saying. "Well I do need some help shoveling manure so yeah come on home with me and you'll have a really good time getting some exercise and before you're done, it's my guess you'll learn to appreciate the ripe smell! It's about time the two of you ladies did an honest day's work!"

Little Lynda asked, "Where do we put the manure? On your bed?"

I said, "Ah Papa, everybody in the store heard you, and now there's no way to hide!"

Obviously everybody in the store heard all of it because everybody was laughing and slapping Papa on the back as we made our way out the front door. That wagon ride was more fun than anything else in the whole world because of Papa, and he helped us with the manure shoveling and somehow, the odor was pleasant, and working and laughing with Big John Owens has to be the next thing to being in heaven whether you're shoveling manure or not! Unfortunately, the time came when the barn stalls were rid of manure, and we had to put away our shovels. Little Lynda and I moped all the way to the house, but at the screen door the delicious aroma of fresh baked Tea Cakes changed us from slugging along to practically running through the screen. Inside the house, Papa caught Mama in a quick squeeze, and Mama said, "Pshaw, John. Let me go! Put me down!"

Little Lynda and I were hoping that Mother would forget about us and we'd get to spend the night, but about three o'clock Mother drove the 1959 Ford Galaxie over the hilltop, and we had no choice.

On Sunday, March 13th again Frank picked me up at the Baptist Church this time after Sunday School, and I sat with him and his parents in the small but beautiful old Presbyterian Church.

After school on Friday, April Fools Day, I stayed in town to attend a Tri-Hi-Y meeting, and when I finally came out the THS south door, Dennis was waiting for me. He knows full well my after school routine when I'm ready to go home, and many times he's walked with me on my way to Bowman's store and the pay telephone booth, but this time, when we reached the approximate mid-point he asked me to sit down on the Presbyterian Church steps.

Dennis started with, "Janet, I've got some bad news. You've been under surveillance driving the 1959 Ford Galaxie, and you don't have a driver's license. It's no use weather or not your Mother is in the car with you, it's still a Federal offense to drive over the state line into Alabama without a license, and you will be required to report to the Federal Court House. You'll receive the subpoena on Monday, and when you stand before the Federal Judge, he'll ask you five questions and the answers are: 'Yes, yes, yes, no, and yes.' Now, if you can't afford a lawyer, you will be represented by a public defender, but to be honest, it's not looking good."

At some point, I felt the blood drain from my brain, and it's a good thing I was sitting on the hard concrete church steps, but when my sanity returned well the debilitating fear was erased, and replaced with some pretty important questions like how in the world did the Federal Department of Justice get all this information to a kid named Dennis Williams, and then a sane but somewhat odd coincidence occurred when practically the entire Midget Football Team (including Denver of course) came slinking from behind the white church. I felt my heart flutter as I scanned the team because right down to the very last one they wore faces of misery and sympathy and support for a criminal caught red handed, but wait just a dog gone minute, there's no way! "HOLD YOUR HORSES! ARE YOU CRAZY? YOU GUYS ARE CRAZY!"

I aimed for the closest guy and it happened to be Richard, close enough for me to kick him in the shin, and then the team's collective laughter increased in volume as Richard danced around holding onto his probably bloody shin. As I hurried away toward the pay telephone booth, without looking back I heard the team's unison, "April Fool!"

I'm quite certain the team perceived my shaking body as evidence of crying, and as far as I'm concerned, they'll never know the truth, and another thing, I plan to use their own feelings of guilt against them, each and every one!

In the month of April, I did have a date with someone other than Frank, I went with Brantley to the Band Concert and when he took me home, he kissed me at the door, and I was very nervous that someone might be watching inside the front door's glass panes.

On Wednesday, April 13th all the Seniors left school at noon, and as soon as the last bell sounded, Brenda and I practically ran all the way up town to the train depot to see the Class of 1960 off on their train trip to Washington, D.C. The scene became very sentimental when Little Lynda's fan club stood protectively around her. Frank stood in the giant circle with his arm around me, and when the train finally pulled into town, Frank actually kissed my cheek before boarding. I was a little embarrassed with Frank's arm around my shoulders and the kiss, but I don't think it was enough public display to shock anybody, but I sure hope Mother never finds out about it.

When the train pulled away, I had a very curious feeling of loss, which I could not defend and certainly could not ignore. Brenda and I lollygagged back through town, and we stopped under the second level porch while I dialed my home number in the pay telephone booth, and when Mother answered, she understood it was her cue to come get me. Brenda waited with me, and Mother smiled at Brenda and said, "Get in sweetie, I'll drive you home."

On the train, between Tallapoosa and Greensboro NC, Frank scribbled the following:

Date: April 13,1960
Time: 10:21 p.m.
Place: On the "Southerner"
Somewhere between Greenville and Spartanburg South Carolina

Hi Jan,

I'm sitting in the Rest Room on the train with my suitcase in my lap, eating a tuna fish sandwich, smoking a Winston, talking to Denny and writing to Janet (That's you!) As you may have noticed, this train shakes around one heck of a lot. Gotta go for now. Poker players are running me out!

11:33 p.m.

Cavender caught the poker players so they left & I returned. Just me and Denny again. I lost my pen somewhere. This is Hilderbrand's. I was just sitting looking out the windooooow (Hit a bump!) at this "Carolina" moon. You know, it looks just like the one we have in Georgia. Remmmmminds (Hit another bump!) me of a little girl back in Tallapoosa.

I'm sleepy and tired but have no intentions of going to sleep. I guess I'm crazy but this is a once in a lifetime trip!

Here is a word from Denny --------- Sugar, please call Patsy and tell her I said, "Go by the Western or Economy Auto Store and get me a baseball bat. Just in case you're wondering that is in code. <u>Please</u>

Frank again   P.S. "I love ya."   Bye, Bye, That's to Patsy, not to you!

See ya later!

1:31 a.m.
Somewhere in N.C.

I found my pen. The train is getting rougher the further we go. I'm still in the Rest Room. All the chairs are taken so I'm sitting in the only place left. I'll let you guess where it is. I've also tried to sleep a little in here, but have just about given up!

I just put over 2 shrewd business deals. I sold Ronnie Brooks a 4c stamp, 2 sheets of paper, and an envelope for 50c. Mrs. Williams gave me the stamp. I sold Bosco the birthday card I bought to send to Smittie (at the post office) for 50c. It cost me 15c. He must be in love! (2 minutes later) Bosco just gave me 25c for a 4c stamp that I found on the Post Office floor. I'm going to give Rockefeller a rough time before long.

I sneaked off the train ~~twice~~ 3 times already. Once in Atlanta. That was legitimate (spelling?) I got off in Charlotte, ~~S.C.~~ N.C. and Spartanburg S.C. think I'll get to mail this at Greensville N.C. if I have time and can find a stamp. I'll probably have to pay dearly for one.

We're somewhere maybe it's Greensville. If so, I'll write you again later.

Lots of Love,
Frank

It wasn't Greensville
I sold 1 envelope, 1 stamp, & 1 piece of paper. The stamp cost me 4c.
I sold it for 25c
I think we are here.
Look under the stamp.

Frank

The postmark is 6 am, April 14, 1960, Greensboro NC, and Frank wrote 'Hi LS' on the envelope That's Lloyd Smith at the Tallapoosa Post Office. The minute I finished reading Frank's letter, I found Mother and read it to her, she loved it and later in the day, Mother insisted that I read the letter again to Joan, Marilyn and Carroll! They loved it too. It really is very funny! The last three words are totally indecipherable, but Joan took the letter and instantly read the last four words, "Look under the stamp."

Joan found the envelope, easily pealed away the stamp, and read aloud, "I Love You."

I blushed a brilliant red, and Joan decided, "You better hold onto to Frank!"

April 17 is Easter and for some reason, Ruth called the week before to make sure we'd be at Papa's in time for dinner, Ruth and Otto plan to get there early so Ruth can cook chicken and dressin' and all the trimmings. Also, she warned Mother to forget about the Easter Bunny this year because she has dyed three-dozen eggs, and Otto is anxious and raring to be the 'Easter Egg Hider and Chief.' As it turned out, that was the best Easter ever, I'm old enough to date, but not too old to hunt Easter eggs!

I don't care how that sounds, that wonderful Easter with Ruth and Otto and Mama and Papa will be a joy to remember lasting all my born days. I'm sure when I'm old and gray, I'll remember that warm cocoon of love.

As soon as Frank returned from the Class Trip, (they were gone for Easter) he called and asked me to go with him to the Prom. Mother immediately ordered my dress from Spiegal. It arrived on Monday April 25 four days before the prom. It's a beautiful sheer brilliant blue print fabric over a light blue satin under dress! I love it and it's a perfect fit. I weigh 97 pounds, which reminds me that Mother brought Aunt Ollie's brown traveling suit home from Mama's, I tried it on already, it's a very snug fit, and all I can think is, "No wonder Aunt Ollie died in child birth, I'll bet she weighed only 93 or 94 pounds."

May 19th was class picnic day, most classes went to Alec's Lake, but I didn't see any seniors. I danced with the best dancers in town, Larry Jackson and Ronald Gilbert, but Mother picked me up early. The following Sunday I went to the Graduates Baccalaureate Program in the First Baptist Sanctuary, and again Mother picked me up early, and this time I'm glad she did because we spent the whole afternoon with Mama and Papa! This was a quiet time, mostly sitting on the porch listening to Papa's yarns, he went down the list starting way back before his daughter married Shug Godwin and he said himself, "If it had been my job to pick husbands for my girls, I never could have found better men than they did."

Frank and I went to Kristina's amazing party on May 29th in their remodeled in-town house. It's impossible to count the number of 45's that Richard Allen put on the record player. He kept a huge stack actually on the spindle, but he arranged other stacks to use in their turn. Boy howdy, Kristina has all the latest and the most popular records! Kristina and her mother are the best ever hostesses! We danced in the den where they rolled up the rug, and in the kitchen, they had potato chips and co-colas enough to feed an army.

Frank has to pack up and leave for Auburn on June 8th his classes start the next day. He took me to the Bremen picture show the night before, he held my hand all the way through the movie, and in the car in my yard, and he held me as we said a prayer together, 'May the Lord watch between me and thee while we're absent one from the other.'

Frank was very good about writing letters, and by the end of June I had five letters, and I tried to answer every one, but I'm afraid I fell short. There never seems to be a shortage of necessary endeavors (which is a Godwin family characteristic) but the first distraction came in the form of Carroll's Tech Graduation on the following Saturday June 11th. We had to be in Atlanta at the Fox Theater at 8:45 am, but getting up before dawn on a Saturday morning was a small price to pay in order to share in Carroll's remarkable achievement. My brother was one of 978 Bachelors' Degrees awarded, with only 67 receiving a Bachelor's of Mechanical Engineering. I am so proud of Carroll, but one thing keeps nagging at me, during the ceremony I studied the 77th Georgia Tech Commencement Program cover to cover, and I watched very carefully for an actual female in a skirt to walk across the stage, and finally I found only one female name and Evelyn earned a Bachelor's of Aeronautical Engineering, but I missed seeing her skirt, so I'm wondering if 'Evelyn' is actually just another man. The absence of female graduates makes me feel diminished somehow, what can my future hold? What do I want to be? Am I confined to being a teacher? I acknowledge all my teachers are certainly worthy of admiration and praise, and I would do well indeed to be as strong and faithful and successful as any one of them, but why am I downhearted? Why do I feel less of a person today than I did yesterday?

Finally, June 24th, I took a bus to Atlanta for the absolutely positively last appointment with my orthodontist, and in Carroll's car with Joan, I had her full attention as I whined about the reason for my doldrums, and Joan actually snapped me into shape ready and willing to 'fight another day' when she said, "We will be the leaders, just operate with that in mind."

It's not unusual, but Thelma Collins avoids coming around on weekends. I can't explain this except that possibly she feels that a visit from her might diminish Daddy's privacy, but clearly in our house Daddy has very little privacy anyway. One weekday, Thelma came in to visit, and she was actually bubbling like a school girl, the reason being that her in-laws Elizabeth and John Collins (Ulus's parents) are celebrating 83 years of marriage, and the city of Tallapoosa is going to honor them with 'Collins Day' despite the Ku Klux Klan's cross-burning, phoned threats and other bullying techniques. To Mother's dismay she asked, "Did you say 83 years of marriage, how old in God's world are they?"

"John Collins is 100 years old, and his wife Elizabeth is 108. They got married when Elizabeth was 25 and John was 17. They had 16 children, Ulus is one of the eight that are still alive. Tallapoosa will furnish a car for their motorcade, and the minister Dr. Charles Pope, will conduct a short program concerning their history as slaves and their exemplary lives since being freed. Friends and neighbors have collected enough money to buy them both new outfits, and after the program everyone will have a chance to talk to them personally, and shake their hands. Then there will be another celebration at the Negro Mount Sinai Baptist Church. The police Captain, Chief Brown simply ignores the KKK's continuous threats."

Mother and Thelma giggled and hugged each other. It is really something to be excited about, and I too could not contain my giggles!

That Sunday, the day before the 4th, in the land of enchantment, Mama and Papa and Otto went with 'the children' down the hill to the spring, while Mother and Ruth washed the dishes and collected dirty clothes for Ruth's turn at doing the laundry. After a drink of the clear cool spring water, we walked along the branch and in the deep shade before breaking out into the pasture's brilliant sun, Papa made for sure that we admired the dancing water 'creasy' greens. The children and Otto ran ahead and scattered a sheep's gathering as Mama held onto Papa's arm in order to saunter slowly along toward the deeper branch water where a lifetime ago, Mama and her beloved sister Ollie slid through the bank's muddy collapse ruining their cotton dresses and aprons. All of their stories are emblazoned in my head forever, and before my eyes, this seen-from-a-distance image of Mama and Papa erased their wrinkles and transported them to their youth, and suddenly it became crystal clear to me just exactly why this hallowed place gives solace to our wounds, and dispels all manner of insecurity, and that being the lady and her husband can actually and absolutely sprinkle fairy dust.

On my birthday, Saturday July 23rd, I got cards from each of my sisters, Carroll and Glenda and one from Ruth & Otto, but the four envelopes were left unopened when Mother answered a mid morning call from Cleo. Oh! No! Say it's not so! Oh! Nooo! Jack and Lynwood found Papa on the floor this morning, Mama could do nothing but coo reassurances throughout the night while he pushed himself in an endless circle. His one unaffected leg proved itself to be in perpetual motion wanting to raise himself up to a normal standing position, but instead, his numb left side acted as an anchor preventing even speech. Mama COULD DO NOTHING to clean the urine and bowel excretions burning his fair skin. Jack and Lynwood toted him to the car, and placed his head in Mama's lap for the sound barrier breaking trip to the Downey Clinic. By the time we reached the Clinic, Papa was getting a wash basin bath, and in just a matter of minutes, John Owens's room was filled to capacity and overflowing into the hall, but I held onto my place standing by his head, remember I weigh only 97 pounds, I won't take up much space, and even if I weighed a hundred and 97, and took up way too much space, moving my feet away from Papa's side would be completely outside the boundaries of human capability. Ohhh! Noooo! Papa! Papa!

It's night outside? When did that happen? Someone is shooing the others out of the room, "Go home, get some sleep and come back tomorrow. Lynwood, Little Lynda and Janet are staying the night."

Lynwood and Little Lynda took their turn first in the waiting room, curling up in the chrome-armed vinyl two person chairs, and now alone with Papa, my dry throat and swollen tongue allowed me to talk, I kissed and held onto his big hand, "Papa, I need you to see if my ears flop. Papa, you've got some plowing to do here on earth, don't go! Please don't go .... when you get to heaven, they'll put you to plowing and you've always said, 'It'll just be a trip for nothing if they put you to plowing,' so just stay here with me, please, stay here!"

I lost count trying to sleep my turn on the vinyl torture chairs, and as dawn's light revealed a normal July Sunday morning, I wondered how the trees outside Papa's window had the strength to hold onto their leaves, surely all the trees in the world are sick with loss!

Again today, the crowd had to let me stand in my place next to Papa because frankly they had no choice, and then as the crowded room looked on, Joan rushed in, "Papa! Papa! That old chicken buzzed up her feathers and gritted her teeth at me!"

Everyone present witnessed Papa's slight smile, but then it was gone. About two or three o'clock, Mother took me home, and I slept in the back seat of the car until about five. After a bath and chili over loaf bread, Mother drove back to the clinic. No change, and again after dark that same administrator shooed every one out and away, and I stood next to Papa as Lynwood and Little Lynda (standing in a chair) went on and on about the sheep and the corn fields, and the three of us, "We are your favorites, right Papa? Well then of course you won't leave us, you can't leave us because what in the world will we do without you? You've spoiled us rotten, if you are not there who will protect us?"

Monday was a repeat of Sunday, the world remained in shock and disbelief. The only difference occurred early when Marilyn stopped by on her way to work at Dixie Steel, she had with her an apple and a pocket knife, and as she sat on the edge of Papa's bed she said, "Papa, while I'm at work will you peal this apple for me, I want to see the perfectly shaped empty apple pealing. You are the only person in the world who can eliminate the apple from inside leaving a hollow pealing. I really need to see it Papa!"

Like on Sunday, Mother took me home, I slept a couple of hours in the back seat, I took a bath and Mother made me eat. I think it might have been rutabagas, I really like rutabagas, but honestly I don't know what it was. Back at the clinic, this time was a little different, Lynwood, Little Lynda and I stayed in Papa's room through the night until dawn. The three of us stayed at the clinic all night every night, and Monday night we tried a different strategy thinking laughter might rouse Papa, because everybody knows John Owens loves to laugh, but each time, our pitiful attempt at laughing ultimately turned into wailing. We did not sleep, and at some point, we stopped talking and laughing and wailing just so we could hear Papa's breathing. Oh Dear Lord, don't take him from us.

Tuesday came and went following the exact pattern! Wednesday was another replica, and by Thursday, Oh Lord, Papa's breathing is more valuable than all the gold at Fort Knox. Friday, I hate all Fridays, just after dawn Papa stopped breathing, this time Mama, Chester, Jack, Mother and Ruth were in the room with us (me, Lynwood, and Little Lynda). When

Papa stopped inhaling, Daddy, Otto, Nora, and Cleo took up vigilance in Papa's room until someone from Miller's Funeral Home came to collect the body. Ruth and Otto took Mama home with them, while Daddy and Chester went with Papa to the Funeral Home. Everyone verbalized who is to call who, but as mistakes will happen, no one called Marilyn. As was her routine, she stopped by to see Papa on her way to work, but his room was empty, the bed was made, and Marilyn was alone!

Somebody planned Papa's funeral for tomorrow and as is the custom, Papa's casket will be open for viewing both tomorrow at the funeral and tonight in the log cabin part of his home. Ruth helped Mama get dressed up in her black Sunday go to meeting dress which she will wear again tomorrow. Mother worked on finishing her own blue dress for the funeral, it's very stylish with a rolled collar and three quarter sleeves, but tonight she is wearing a black print cotton dress. Every member of Papa's family arrived at the old house before dark, and at sunset when the hearse arrived with Papa's casket, I hightailed it out the back door, I can't stay inside the old house for it has been transformed into a lonely, miserable, loathsome, ugly, rundown old bat cave. Outside, I pretty much hid behind the smoke house, and I stood there like a statue with my feet in buckets of cement and I lost track of time, literally, I lost at least an hour because suddenly I realized the house was full of people, there were cars parked everywhere lining both sides of the dirt road and the fields on this side of the road are full of cars, and the front yard is full of cars, and the space between the corn crib and the barn is full of cars, and between the log cabin and the sweet gum tree there are about a hundred cars. All the electric lights are on in the house, I'm thankful they at least had electricity, but it's a mind blowing regret they never had running water, no indoor toilet, and tragically they never had a telephone. I can hear people laughing, and whooping it up, and I'm shocked at their stupid spectacle. The very idea! Who are these idiots? Don't they know my Papa is dead? There is a pain inside of me that burns and digs into my flesh, my muscle mass. I'm fourteen now, Papa had a stroke on my fourteenth birthday, and I think that I just won't recognize my birthday ever again. I've been a member of the First Baptist Church for as long as I can remember, I know beyond any doubt that Papa is in heaven, but there's no consoling and no reconciling, and the deep wound is dragging me into the depths.

Finally the intruders began to crank up their cars and figure a path out of the world's biggest traffic jam! I had no patience with their exit's snail's pace and I found the exodus rankled me as much as their laughter, and still it just kept on and on and on. Get out from here! Get on out from here. As the last set of headlights rounded the hill and left me in darkness, I made my way up onto the back porch, and inside the kitchen, Daddy was voicing an hourly crew to sit up with Papa, and for some reason, I had to run back down the porch steps and puke, and the bitter bile brought up more and more of itself until I continued to heave with no actual results, and before I could make it to the steps again, Mother was there, holding my forehead as the racking spasms contorted and dominated. When I finally could stand upright, Mother and I vented our anguish by standing in a tight embrace and crying enough tears to wash us both down the cultivated hill.

Every day, all day and all night we cried, occasionally we recalled another of Papa's finer observations, which gave us a minute of joy, but for the most part we cried. When the handkerchief drawer was empty, Mother sent somebody to town to buy more handkerchiefs and a lot of them because 'we're gona need them to get through this.' Saturday afternoon, when we walked into the Popular Springs Church, the front several rows were empty and reserved for us. Mother and I stood beside the open casket whose contents jolted us into the painful recognition that the powdered white remains will never again walk the earth or laugh out loud or see if a child's ears flop. I admired Mother's beautiful, also powdered white face with a constant stream of tears, and at the same time, I knew without a mirror that my face was contorted and brilliant red, but ask me if I care because I don't and there's not the slightest chance that I can be like my serenely beautiful Mother. I don't know who spoke or what was said, I think I remember some people standing up and singing Sacred Harp, but I could have imagined that, and actually after viewing the lifeless remains, everything else is a blur, except for Ann Laminack's sweet reach toward me as we followed the casket out the door and around the church to the gaping six foot deep hole waiting to imprison my white faced Papa forever.

Back home we went through the motions of eating because the mountain of pot luck food in hundreds of dishes not at all like Mother's dishes (or Ruth's pretty bowls) should be eaten for the sustenance and the dishes emptied and washed to make ready for return to the donor, besides it will surely go to waste if we don't eat, and everyone knows Papa could not stand to waste food.

Somewhere in the hollow core of carrying on after a devastating loss, I finally opened the four birthday cards that came in the mail a week ago, and although not right off, I finally at least counted the unopened letters from Frank, and including the opened letters preceding my birthday, in all in the month of July, I received eleven letters from Frank post marked on July 6, 8, 9, 11, 13, 15, 18, 19, 25, 27, and 29. For some reason I read the stamped July 25th letter first and oddly coincidentally, it contained glowing praise of Frank's x-girlfriend, Ann Laminack, and his funneling advice that I should count her as a very dear friend, and that is precisely how I will always feel toward her because of her outreach to my tortured face leaving Papa's funeral. Although I'm not sure, I probably wrote Frank several times in the first three weeks of July, but the last week of July, I could not write about Papa, not in narrative or description, because why? Don't ask me. I probably should have vented my grief, but nothing about this is probable, and for the time being the abnormal works for me.

On Tuesday, August 2nd, however, I pulled on a smiley facemask and attended Dennis' birthday party at the pool, and if anybody there knew about Papa's death, they mercifully kept quiet. For the sake of endearment, Dennis was in rare form, but luckily his antics were not directed at me, and in fact I do believe that he must have given a 'warning to be sensitive' lecture before I arrived because of course he knew about Little Lynda's Papa through her connection with his sister Mira Jo (Little Lynda's best friend) and of course he made the connection between me and Little Lynda.

The day after Dennis's party, I called the Tasty Treat and asked to speak to Norman, "Hey Norman, it's Janet, I'm wondering if I could get a job working for you."

"Yeah, of course, can you start tomorrow?"

"Yeah what time?"

"I'll meet you here at four o'clock."

I thought tomorrow would never come, but finally, Mother delivered me to the Tasty Treat, I let myself in through the side door by the juke box on the open air veranda where three picnic tables serve as the only sit-down accommodation, and inside the working hamburger joint, Norman's voice said, "Come on in."

When I rounded the milk machine/ice machine and came face to face with Norman, that's all it took, and we both let the tears flow. "I sure do miss Papa!"

We were useless for several minutes, then Norman took out his handkerchief, blew his nose, wiped his eyes, and handed me a paper napkin. We both seemed transfixed with the concrete floor knowing we'd start up crying again if our eyes met. Norman told the floor, "Well, Little Miss, there's just one rule around here, you eat anything you want, any time you want, and as much as you want!"

Just a couple of years ago, Norman bought two identical little cracker box houses right on Highway 78. He updated one as a home for his family, wife Jimmie Carol and their three little boys, Kevin, Kemp and Kraig. Inside the other little house, he removed all existing walls and replaced them with one wall through the middle dividing the work/storage area in back from the grill/customer area in front. He installed two 'walk-up' order windows, and paved both the parking area and the area between the two houses. As the finishing touch, he installed a corrugated metal awning connecting the two buildings and extending twenty feet from the order windows into the paved parking lot. Norman has a keen sense of conducting and establishing business. The set up allows him to open the Tasty Treat at 10am and close it at 10pm, and he's right there on sight and ready to intervene if a worker is late or a no show. He has perfected the 'Varsity style' chili added to every hamburger and every hot dog. He has divided the twelve hour work day into two 6-hour shifts, I will work the 4 to 10 shift five nights a week giving me a thirty hour work week making fifty cents an hour, that's $15 a week doing something I love to do, which is smiling and being friendly, never mind the physical work, I for sure don't mind mixing up the recipes and flipping the hamburgers, or even mopping the floors, and I feel right at home working for my cousin. Norman stayed with me for an hour or so that first day explaining every aspect of this line of work from greeting the customers, to filling their orders and taking their money, but he emphasized the most important detail of insuring that the customer will come back again and again, a worker's sincere smile. About five or five-thirty, Norman left me alone to handle the relatively light Thursday evening business, but on his way out the door, he offered a complement, "Just keep on smiling your sweet smile, Little Miss, and everything else will fall into place!"

Now alone in the Tasty Treat, I occupied myself with stacking and organizing the loose junk on top of the giant chest type freezer and in keeping with my 'just like Sis' personality, I tapped my fairy wand here there and everywhere making a place for everything and putting everything in it's place, after all, I am very proud to be 'just like Sis!' I quickly returned the dishrag to the hot soapy water in the deep sink when I heard someone knocking on the order window, and as I stepped from behind the partition, there in full sight stood Dennis! Standing there he looked so innocent, and there appeared to be nothing of the mischievous devil whose always teasing me and carrying on this that or the other, but sure enough there stood my very first customer and as soon as he recognized me, he put both hands down hard on the ordering ledge, and lifted himself into a sort of hand stand, and I wanted to reach out and pinch his freckled cheeks bunched into the biggest old smile ever, but instead, I calmly opened up the window and picked up the pencil ready to write down his order, but he stopped me with, "Aw, don't waste a piece of paper, all I want is a vanilla milkshake!"

I made the milkshake and handed it out to him as he slid his money toward me, then he informed me the milkshake is just right not too thin and not to thick. I wondered aloud how far he walked to get here. He answered, "I live real close down on Arbacooche Road, I can cut through the woods and walk the pipe across the gully and be here is five minutes!"

As he pulled vanilla milk shake through the straw, he impressed me with his sober, somber conversation, I was struck with his serious side! He is really very mature when there's no audience cheering him on, and when I told him so, his smile and nod opened up my heart like never before. I'm not saying he's never shown me the thoughtful Dennis, he certainly has many times, but especially now I cherish him to be the tender sweet guy who can hold his own in any competition and come out smelling like a rose because he is truly empathetic and as far as that goes, I've always known how important it is to feel what the other person is feeling, and I've been pretty successful with that, and now I know that Dennis Williams is as good at it as I am, and the two of us practice a lot at seeing things through the other's eyes! Long after he finished his milkshake, he stayed and talked to me, and for some unexplainable reason, not one other person came to order food or drink, Dennis and I had at least an hour to sort out the reason and make sense of the fact that we have always been such good friends, but at this point, just for good measure, he interjected, "BC means 'before Christ' right? Well how did the people who lived a hundred years before Christ, know they were living a hundred years before Christ?"

When I shook my head in disbelief, he smiled and for a second I thought he was joking, but no he was serious? He walked away toward the setting sun; I went back to my organizing task, and after dark, I did have a few more customers, and I helped them with an ever-widening smile!

Just to be true to my boss, I ate everything and anything that night and the other four nights that week and then sometime in the second week, it hit me with a wave of nausea, I do not want anything else to eat, and some months later, Norman made note with his triumphant observation, "So far, every single one of my workers eats to high heaven the first two weeks, and then becomes disgusted by even the thought of eating Tasty Treat food, it has worked every time! I'd say it is a complete success!"

Thelma Collins paid her respects when she was convinced it would not give the appearance to diminish our vast and all encompassing grief, she took on a pained expression and admitted that her long time boss at her day job cleaning his house in Bremen has actually co-conspired with her to make her the first Negro in all of Haralson County to be hired to work a forty hour job shift a making good money at his T & W plant in Waco. The down side happens to be the threatening telephone calls that started last week when somehow the KKK got word. Mother was duly proud of Thelma's courage, and that night Mother related the story to Daddy, and it was in fact a bit of really good news and a long time coming, and my Daddy slapped his hand on his elevated knee as his way of conveying his good wishes, "Well, I'll be dog gone!"

Toward the end of August, Thelma came to visit again, this time with a rolling account of the KKK's dirty tricks, now just beginning to ease up and give up. Thelma has out lasted the evil-no-counts and their harassments, and she is accepted and revered by the other workers at Waco's T & W because it's about time.

Also, interestingly, Thelma had in her hand a copy of the national Negro publication 'Jet Magazine' and inside is the complete story of Ulus's parents, Elizabeth and John Collins, and their day of honor in celebrating 83 years of marriage in the small Georgia town of Tallapoosa.

From Jet Magazine: 1960
Proud Georgians: Wed 83 years, Mr. and Mrs. John Collins
(100 and 108 respectively), ex-slaves of Tallapoosa, greeted
by, Mrs. Lewis Bell, one of hundreds who honored the
centenarians when the tiny Georgia town turned out to celebrate
"John and Elizabeth Collins Day."
KKK THREATS FAIL TO STOP GA. WHITES
IN TRIBUTE TO NEGROES
Despite a cross-burning and phoned threats by the Ku Klux Klan,
Nearly all of the 4,000 Negro and white citizens of Tallapoosa, in
northwest Georgia, turned out for a program honoring 100-year-old
John Collins and his wife Elizabeth, 108, in their 83rd years of marriage.
Remarked one citizen, summing up local feeling:
"Anyone married that long deserves the honor."
Parents of 16 children, of which eight survive, the Collins Couple led a
motorcade to the town square (wearing new clothing supplied by their
friends and neighbors), where city officials led a special ceremony.
Citizens shook hands and chatted with the couple, who were born
in slavery, Elizabeth was 12 years old when the Civil War ended,
after which they were honored at the Negro Mount Sinai Church.
Quipped Chief of Police E R. Brown, after the Klan actions:
"All the city did was furnish a car. What's the harm in that?"

Caption under picture of Police Captain:
Chief Brown ignores continuous threats from Klan

The first weekend of September, Tallapoosa is celebrating 100 years since founding, and on a very personal note, Aunt Ollie's sixty year old baby, OK is here, not just another letter in Mama's apron pocket, OK is really here! He is a tall, slim man with a head full of wavy salt and pepper hair, mostly pepper like his Aunt Sally. He arrived on Thursday, September

1st, by bus all the way from Oklahoma, and he described more than one leg of his bus trip as having Freedom Riders on board. Mother sympathizes every time she meets a Greyhound bus with it's head lights on, "There go some more poor old Freedom Riders."

The day after Papa's funeral, Ruth & Otto moved Mama's things out of the old house and into their remodeled house on Cedartown Highway. The first few days in Mama's new home were full of wonder because she now has to learn about running water, an indoor toilet, and how to actually use a telephone. Now she can keep in touch on a daily basis with her children and grandchildren at least the ones within the free calling area because no one anywhere can afford long distance charges to pile up every day. She came to recognize the telephone's 'busy signal' as 'it's still a blowing.' Ruth and Otto settled OK into their spacious third bedroom, and Mama relished every minute with her sister's only child, all be it, he is at least 59 years old. His Aunt Sally left all the talking to him, because her countenance is deeply rooted in an escape from verbal expression. He can understand her quiet sadness with certainty because he knows of her experiences with death, starting with the loss of her only sister, then in quick succession her baby Hazel, and next baby Paul, and now only a month ago she buried her husband. Mama took great pride in showing OK her treasure trove of his letters; she has every single one back to his first childish scrawl at age five. OK was duly impressed with the stack of tattered envelopes, worn thin by Sally's keeping the newest in her apron pocket handy for rereading and sharing until another letter arrives which in some cases is as many as six or seven months. OK became accustomed to the sight of his mournful little aunt sitting head slightly down watching her fidgeting fingers. Now in her late seventies, her hair is salt and pepper with more pepper than salt. Her face is smooth yet, only a few wrinkles, and although it is very seldom, when she smiles an enchanting sparkle creeps into her eyes.

Friday night September 2nd, Frank made it home from Auburn in time to take me to the ballpark Centennial Celebration. Reverend Skaggs read his own compiled history over the loudspeaker and next an adult choir sang several period hymns. The next night, again Frank picked me up, and tonight he found me dressed in 1860's style. Mother designed and made my dress of course, a blue plaid taffeta, long hoop-stand-out skirt and three quarter sleeves ruffled at the edge like the neck. To give credit where it is due, it was Marilyn's idea to make our hoop skirt petticoats with a hula-hoop sewn in along the hemline. Marilyn made her own dress which is more elaborate than mine, and Mother praised her delicate attention to detail, but shrugged off her own lack of intricacy with, "When I was young, I could do all that stuff, but not now."

At the Centennial Ball, Carroll and Glenda were also dressed in period clothes, although Carroll's was a simple black string necktie and black suspenders against a white long sleeve dress shirt. Frank and I love to dance, and he is at the top of my 'best dancers list,' but I have to give the absolute best dancer title to my brother Carroll, and that night only a few couples danced when a waltz was playing, and Carroll asked me if I can waltz, and I answered, "I've never waltzed, but I've seen waltzing on television."

Then a once in a lifetime thing happened as I softly counted the waltz rhythm .... Carroll followed exactly! Exactly, without a single miss-step **One**, two, three **One**, two, three **One**, two, three. We were gliding around the gymnasium floor like we'd been waltzing all our lives, and Carroll was masterfully leading me, and I was completely following him, and my hula hoop petticoat swayed back and forth, emphasizing and exaggerating the beat, and unbelievably, every other couple stopped dancing and let us have the entire floor.

Mother made my hula-hoop petticoat out of sugar sacks with the sugar advertisements still in tact. I wondered if the advertisements were possibly visible, at a distance of course, but visible as were my legs when the petticoat was at the highest sway point. When this possibility first occurred to me, I felt a twinge of embarrassment, but then my pride took over and made me hope, yes hope that everybody in that gym had a good long look at the sugar sack advertisements which were a testament to my mother's sewing creativity and ability, to my brother's and my dancing ability regardless of our station in life, and most assuredly, to life in a small Georgia town where very few if anyone looks at another's shortcomings, but instead everyone almost without exception appreciates the talents of each individual, and admires the gumption to pull yourself up to another rung.

For the Sunday night Youth Choir presentation at the First Baptist Church with every member of the choir wearing period costume, I was thrilled to wear Aunt Ollie's brown travel suit, and this of course brought Ruth, Mama, and OK to our house to witness. They decided to forgo attending the actual church service, and instead in the early afternoon, when they were settled in our living room, Mother called me to come let them see Aunt Ollie's travel suit. I was a little frazzled after finally getting my arms through the leg-a-mutton sleeves and barely matching the buttons with the button holes, and everyone groaned at the sight of this beautiful traveling suit stretched to the point of splitting at the seams, my words were, "Aunt Ollie definitely weighed less than 97 pounds!"

Ruth was first to consider, "No wonder she had such difficulty in child birth."

Luckily, I had a suitable white button-up-the-back lace blouse to wear as a substitute for the brown jacket. However, there was no fix for the skirt's too tiny waist band, but Mother was able to sort of safety pin it shut, and on my 5 feet, 1 and a half inches tall, the skirt length reached just below my ankles, indicating that Aunt Ollie must have been no taller than 4 feet, 10 inches, and I never would have guessed ahead of time that I'd be considered as over weight and too tall when compared with Aunt Ollie. OK summed it all up, "Now when I picture my Mother, the vision will forever be drastically altered, and I'll always wonder about how she managed to reach the top shelf in the kitchen. Did she climb onto a chair? "

As part of our singularly special production, Mr. Raiford Long, the youth choir director specifically changed the tempo of the hymn 'This Is My Story' which we practiced regularly throughout the summer, and if I dare say because I hate to brag, the presentation was very well received! The next day, Labor Day, Queen Betty Jo Bentley rode in the Centennial Parade. Then with the added bonus of another afternoon off, all the teenagers headed for the traditional season's last day at Alec's Lake and the party centered around the still new dance pavilion's juke box, this time my superlatives list of best dancers includes Frank Ellis, Ronald Gilbert and Larry Jackson, and I would not be surprised if the Patsy Cline 45's were worn out, wiped clean from over use! At the end of this perfect day, Frank got a ride back to Auburn with Mary Ann

Williams from Buchanan, her parents are driving her back and they have plenty of room for one more. I was at Frank's house to say goodbye, and I'm glad to meet the beautiful Mary Ann. Then waiting for Mother on her way to pick me up, at first I was a little uncomfortable, but when Mother arrived, Mrs. Ellis insisted that Mother stay and visit just for a while, and boy howdy, these two great ladies laughed to high heaven, and while I too laughed, the best entertainment for me was just watching!

At home, I took a bath and pin curled my still wet hair while everybody else watched television. I am at loose ends knowing three good friends are gone, 1) Frank is gone, 2) Charles left today for Mount Berry School for Boys the other side of Rome, Georgia, and 3) Richard Allen also left today for Baylor Military School in Chattanooga, Tennessee, they all traveled on Labor Day in order to meet roommates and be in position for Tuesday morning classes! I miss them all, I'm sad because it seems like I'm saying 'Goodbye' all the time. Richard doesn't dance, he says Music doesn't speak to him, but he is an excellent conversationalist, and sitting there in the moonlight he lamented his departure, and said out loud to the stars, "Leaving town is not my choice!"

I hope Charles and Richard are as good about writing as Frank is, and in regards to what feels like saying 'goodbye all the time' I think we have said a figurative 'goodbye' to Kristina, (the sweetest). She is simply never available, I haven't seen her since the party at her house, she is still dating Forrest Williams, and he totally monopolizes her time in school and out of school.

Frank came home for the weekend on Friday, November 4th, and on Sunday morning November 6th he and I sat with his parents in the Presbyterian Church. On Tuesday, November 8th Mother and Daddy voted for John F Kennedy, and that night at home, Mother and I watched the election results on television, and we were both far too excited to turn off the television and go to bed, so while the rest of the house slept soundly, Mother and I stayed glued to the television until Kennedy was pronounced the winner after 2:00 am!!!!!!!

On November 17th, I got a letter from Frank:

Monday 5 pm
Hi Babe,

I'm tired! Worked 4 hours instead of three today. So I went straight through from 8-4. No break. Last night I was up till 12:30 typing for Buddy. Up again at 6 typing again. I've got loads to do this week. But you know, I feel pretty good about everything. I have an Algebra quiz Wed. History quiz Fri. Have to hand in my note cards on my Research Paper in English Monday & a quiz on a book I haven't started (452 pages) Tuesday. My Research Theme is due after Thanksgiving.

So, if I don't write much (if at all) don't get peeved at me. I imagine I'll find time to write sometime though. I'd better go eat & study. I guess you're mighty glad to have your dad home for good. Be sweet.

I love you so much,
Frank
P.S. I know I'll have time to read your letters, so keep them coming, often. (Please of course.)

Coach Harris organized a THS bus trip to Auburn on Saturday, November 19th, the F.S.U. game at Cliff Hare Stadium. We stood ready to board the new red and white school bus as Coach Harris made his rules speech, "All right, there are twenty-seven of you and I certainly can count that high, but just as an extra measure to keep track of all of you, when you get on the bus, sit wherever you want to sit and sit with anybody, but remember where you sit and remember your seat partner because on the way back you are required to sit in the same place."

As usual Dennis was first to come up with, "Coach, twenty-seven is an odd number, who is gona be left sitting alone all sad and lonely?"

Coach got it, "You Mr. Williams are required to sit alone and just to make sure we do not forget about you, you have to stand at the door and hug everybody who gets on this bus and that is the rule not only here, but in Auburn, in other words, you have 26 people not just one seat mate who will be looking out for you, and the hugging will remind us to bring you back home."

Dennis was ready with, "Coach, I'm happy to hug the girls, but I don't want to hug Jimmy George!"

I was first to hug Dennis, first on the bus, and first to get my seat choice close to the front, then Connie sat down beside me and Denver sat just behind us and when Dennis was the last person NOT on the bus, he hurried up the steps and grabbed a hold of the seat back poles and swung himself into position and sat down in front of Connie and me! Already, I'm loving this! There's no one better to keep Dennis tethered to reality than Connie Gentry, but I was a little bit worried when Connie, knuckled Dennis's hard head and exclaimed, "Dennis, you need to loosen up, it's not healthy to be so hard headed!"

We were fully aware of the intended pun. Here we go, Dennis got it too and replied, "You are correct, that's what I've been thinking all along, I just have to try to relax, if I stay too tightly strung, why I might have a heart attack or something!"

All I could say was, "What have I done?"

But secretly, I love the banter between these two! Connie is the perfect counter balance to Dennis both physically (because of her thirty-to-forty pound too heavy weight) and figuratively because of her dry wit. Now as the bus lurched into motion, Dennis began wailing, Connie began eye-rolling and I began my delight of pinching both of Dennis's chipmunk cheeks, but his silent reaction was short lived, and he screamed over the engine's roar, "So Janet, is your sweetheart Frank going to sit with us at the game?"

I tried whispering, "No, he has to work."

Dennis shrieked, "What'd you say?"

It was no use, and as I shouted a repeat, my face turned as red as a beet and I gave in to the urge to pull his hair which of course made him bellow, "That hurts!"

We sat in a comfortable silence for a good fifteen minutes (possibly a record for Dennis) until he twisted onto his knees, leaned his back against the empty seat in the row forward, and as mischief washed over him, he asked the question, "If the sun warms the earth, why is it always cold at the top of Mount Everest? Isn't the top of a mountain closer to the sun?"

Connie blew her displeasure and moaned, "Shut up!"

But I took him on, "You are correct in that higher elevations are closer to the sun, but by an infinitesimal, teeny tiny amount which in a practical analysis is too minuscule to deserve calculation. The Earth is warmed by the sun and some say by a smoldering fire at it's center."

Connie ended my monologue with, "Shut up!"

She is a bully, but in a comedic manner, and I continued, "Dennis, I now have a superlative for you, I have my very own superlative list, and now you are the 'Most Existential!"

"Existential? Nobody is ever going to know what that is! Why can't I be the most debonair?"

I countered with, "Because you are not debonair!"

Dennis asked, "Well how do you know?"

Again I reasoned, "Well for one thing you have too many freckles!"

Dennis, "What's that got to do with it?"

I tried again, "Freckles make you cherub-like, and you can't be cherub-like and debonair at the same time!"

Dennis, "Cherub-like? Nobody knows what that is either!"

Connie weighed in, "Coach, is it too late for me to move to another seat?"

No response but from my angle, I could see the smile on Coach's face.

As the bus pulled into the huge Cliff Hare bus parking lot, there stood Frank, he's very handsome with his black hair and wide black eyebrows, but it's his dazzling white teeth that make me catch my breath, and right now his smile and slight pacing back and forth made me begin to worry that he might hug me, and heaven forbid, he might kiss me in front of everybody. Thankfully, he did nothing more than a sort of one armed hug around my shoulders, and to his credit he blushed as much as I did! Frank saw Judy and Kathy Kilgo and quickly said, "Be sure to tell your Dad I owe him a debt of gratitude because his friend got me this job at the cafeteria, but the only bad part is that I have to get back to work, wish I could stay with you but I have to get back."

Auburn won the game, and when the thousands of pedestrians finally got out of our way, the school bus nosed into a line up of at least a thousand buses trying to exit the bus parking lot! I wondered if we'd get home by midnight. At one point the driver shut down the engine, and the now famous as the most-existential, took this to mean he had no choice but to entertain.

He started his stand up routine with, "Janet has voluntarily put herself in the risky position of needing a best friend."

"I'll be her best friend." Rang out several times.

Dennis dug himself in deeper, "Well, you can't be her best friend because I'm her best friend! She might not admit it but I am, I'd resign from the job if she had anybody to take my place, but no, I'm stuck."

Again from the crowd, "How do you know all this? Do you have a mole in the FBI?"

Dennis blurted out, "My mole is a kid from Bremen. Anyone know Mike Murphy? His Dad is Tom Murphy who has just been elected to the State House of Representatives, and through his Dad, he gets a hold of a lot of information, but seriously, if you use his name they'll put me on the FBI hit list."

Again from the weary crowd, "Sit down and shut up!"

Dennis, "OK, so raise your hand if you think I'm debonair. OK, so raise your hand if you think I'm existential. Well OK, raise your hand if you want to thank me. You are a very tough crowd, but I get it, you secretly think I'm debonair and you'll thank me later in a more personal one-on-one right?"

The only thing anybody could be thankful for was when finally the bus's loud engine drowned out the entertainment and Dennis sat down.

Waiting for me at home was a letter from Charles:

November 16, 1960
Dear Janet,

May I express my sincere appreciation to you for kindness shown by you at school, while I was home. I am sure I am going to enjoy dreaming about you.

I count it a privilege to be acquainted with such a fine lady.

I don't know if I got your address right, but I tried. If I didn't I wish you would write me and tell me. My address is Charles Downey, Mount Berry School for Boys, Mt. Berry GA.

Love,
Charles

Norman closed the Tasty Tree on Thanksgiving, but I worked my 6-hour shift on Wednesday and Friday. Dennis was waiting at one of the picnic tables when I got there on Friday at 4pm, and of course he ordered a vanilla milk shake. When it's slow, I can count on Dennis to keep me company, and the day after Thanksgiving was very, very slow, maybe three customers besides Dennis, but it also was very, very cold, and finally Dennis went home to get a warmer coat, and sure enough he came back, this time in a big winter, heavy weight, coat and a boggan (that's what we in the south call a knit stocking cap). Dennis was subdued comparatively speaking, but he remains true to his superlative no matter if he's in a 'mood' and his existential question this time was, "Why doesn't the Bible say anything about the ice age or dinosaurs?"

All I could recommend was, "I think the 'firmament' part of God's creation includes a lot, God created the dinosaurs and they lived during a warm climate, and he created the wooly mammoths that lived during a cold climate like the Ice Age, and He created Adam and Eve. The thing I don't like is when people say the Bible writers meant the Earth was actually created in exactly seven days. As far as I'm concerned, that's blasphemy limiting God to what a human's mind can imagine, that's blasphemy of the worst kind! It doesn't matter if the word 'day' meant 24 hours or 24 years or 24 million years, God is great, far greater than any person who wrote down the books of the Bible."

Frank took me to the show in Bremen on Saturday night. He's leaving early on Sunday because he has so much homework to do. When I have to work after school, Mother comes to town and drives me the few blocks to the Tasty Treat. I could walk of course, and of course I appreciate the ride, and also I appreciate that Mother brings my mail. Frank writes me several letters every week, and I can read them and write one back to him in between customers, but today, the last day of November, the letter Mother brought to me is not from Frank, it's from Richard Allen postmarked Chattanooga Tenn.:

Sunday Aft.
November 27, 1960
Dear Rose, (I mean Janet)

I was glad I got to see you Thursday night. I guess things seem about the same to you at Tally High but a lot of things seemed different to me. It sure was a short vacation for me! I guess you don't get to see Frank much lately. It is a hard school at Baylor and they really make you study. On the weekends we have fun though, sometimes there is a party or a dance. Brenda J. called me about 5 times Friday night and asked me if I didn't call her. I don't know where she got that idea. I imagine it was just wishful thinking. (Hah) Tell her I really didn't mind her calling though. I guess you saw Charles on Sunday. I understand that he had to leave for Berry in time to finish plowing. Well, I hear my millionaire friend calling me so I'll stop for now. Write me a line or two when you can.

Richard Allen

On Thursday, December 1st, the mail mother brought to town was a letter from Charles postmarked Mount Berry GA I read this letter while working at the Tasty Treat.:

Nov. 29, 1960
Dear Janet,

I guess you know I was home the last weekend. I'm sorry I didn't see you! There's not much to tell about Berry. The main subject of the boys here is (GIRLS).

Out of 50 boys 49 use vulgar or profane language I guess you find that everywhere now days. The teachers are cutting down on using vulgar language, slowly but surely. The school itself is very fine.

I have a roommate some boys have a room to themselves. My roommate is OK but there are some better. I'm going to try to room with Bill Worthy, Lee Worthy's son. I guess you don't much like Lee Worthy since he beat your Dad in the county election.

The studies are not too hard. I'm making better grades than I did at home.

I'm taking English I, Algebra I, General Shop, Chapel, Bible II, General Science and P.E. The grading scale is: A - 92 to 100, B - 83 to 91, C - 74 to 82, D - 65 to 73, E - 60 to 64, and F below 60. All my grades are in the 80's.

The school is about the same as THS except for one thing. That is NO GIRLS. I just sit in my room and think about all the girls in Tallapoosa.

Yes blue and white are our school colors. I agree, red and white are better, but I'm liking blue and white more and more.

May I ask you a personal question in my next letter, and one thing else, what is your phone number?

Yours Affectionately,
Charles

It's a good thing I read the letter from Charles when I first entered the Tasty Treat because fifteen minutes later, Dennis knocked on the order window with the existential question, "Why is the basement cooler in the summer time and warmer in the winter?"

"The underground temperature of the earth is constant at about 66 degrees, and 66 degrees is actually warmer than winter temperatures, and cooler than summer temperatures."

Dennis, "What are you a walking encyclopedia? How do you know all this stuff?"

I gave Carroll credit, "My oldest brother knows everything, and when he tells me something, he makes it easy to remember. He's the reason school is so easy for me, and you can go on asking me questions forever, and we won't even come close to exhausting Carroll's knowledge."

Two letters from Frank, both postmarked December 12, the first at 8am, the second at 2pm.

Saturday 2am
Dec. 11, 1960
Hi Hon,

Just got in from the late show. Saw "Midnight Lace." That is honestly the scariest movie I've ever seen. OOOOOO!

Worked tonight. Work again tomorrow night. Had my History quiz today, Have no idea how I did. Don't feel too good about it though.

I'm coming home Tuesday! About 8:00 pm. Hey, you can't go to the show Tuesday night. You're still in school. Aren't you? You decide when we'll do what & it'll suit me fine. (Just so long as we are together lots!)

It hurts to think about not taking you to that dance, but it'll look better if you go with Sweet Pea. Go and have a good time! That's an order. Soldier.

I've got to go to bed. I guess this will be the last 'till I get home. I love you so much Jan. (Even at 2 o'clock in the morning) Please try to love me too.

Love Always,
Frank

Second letter postmarked Dec 12, 1960, 2pm

Sunday, 9:30 p.m.
Hi Jan-doe,

How are you?

You'll probably get this Tuesday morning, and I'm coming home Tuesday night, but I just wanted to talk to you.

I miss you. I love you.

Nights like tonight I really miss you. I went to church with Danny McDowell, the boy from Florence that you met at the ball game. When I go to church at night I want to sit next to YOU!

I will probably get home about 8:00 Tuesday night. (Georgia time). Like you said, we won't get to go anywhere during the week. If you don't already have something planned, how 'bout Friday night? Show date!

I may come to see you a minute Tuesday night. OK? I'll call when I get home and we'll see.

I've about gone crazy this week-end with nothing to do but sit and wait for Tuesday. It'll be worth waiting for though.

It sure is cold tonight. The wind is blowing like mad. Sure will make for good sleeping. I don't have to be up 'till 3:40 tomorrow afternoon.

Sure hate to think about you getting up early and going to school. (I'd give anything if I were in Tallapoosa getting up to go to Tally High in the morning.)

I'd better study math awhile or I might really be back there.

See you Tuesday.

I love you so much!

Frank

(2 more days!)

At work on Tuesday, December 13th, at about 8pm, I heard someone knock on an order window, but when I looked around from behind the partition, I saw no one at either window, but parked in plane site was Frank's parents' black Ford, and when I reached the west order window, I caught a glimpse of Frank hiding beneath the ledge at the east order window, and actually, when I opened the west order window, I surprised him and caused him to jump not me! Mother answered his call and told him where to find me. Everyone knows Norman's rule about never letting anyone inside the Tasty Treat and of course, never going outside the Tasty Treat, both of which make sense! Since there were no other customers, Frank did reach for my hand through the order window! On Wednesday, December 14th, Frank came to THS at lunch. We sat outside on the steps between the gym and the high school building. Of course, when the sub freshmen finished lunch, Dennis teased, "Well fancy seeing you two together!"

On Friday the 16th, we had Christmas parties at school and Frank showed up again, but we planned last night that I'd meet him on the front door steps, Mr. Cobb might have given him a pass but we both thought it better not to ask so we just sat outside for a few minutes. On Saturday night December 17th, Larry Thompson took me to the Christmas Ball, I wore Golia's pink, semi-formal dress and Larry gave me a beautiful orchid wrist corsage.

On Sunday, December 18th, I went with Frank and his parents to the Presbyterian morning service, and he took me to the First Baptist evening service. Then we went to Crossroads, we sat with Sara & Eddie, Frank held my hand under the table. On Monday, December 19th I went in to work at 4pm as usual, Dennis kept me company again as usual, and when Frank showed up too, the three of us talked until after dark when a few actual customers ordered hamburgers and french fries for supper.

I wish I could go back and erase all of Tuesday, December 20, 1960! Thankfully, I did not go in to work. If I'd been at work, what could I have done, what would I have seen, could I have changed what happened? The wreck that killed Dennis happened just a block west of the Tasty Treat! Frank called me from the Bowman Store pay telephone. He had a nickel. When the siren went off he was visiting with his Mother who works at the Clinic, we heard the siren at home 3 miles east of town; the siren blasted the short transport of Dennis Williams from the wreck to the Clinic. Dennis's brother Forrest was driving up the steep hill from the Hollywood Cemetery, up the steep hill onto Highway 78 and evidently, Forrest did not see the eastbound transfer truck, which involuntarily, plowed into Dennis sitting on the passenger side! I wish .... I don't know what I wish .... I know that instantly, everyone knew of the wreck, and instantly, a stunned crowd gathered at the Clinic, and instantly, the Williams family gave up the fight and surrendered to a changed world, and within minutes the Williams Christmas Tree appeared on its side tossed into their yard still bearing the icicles and garlands, but forever banished from inside their home. Someone pulled it away out of the yard and out of sight and hopefully it's in a gully underneath garbage, stinking garbage, a decorated tree forever bereft and useless and hateful. That night, I did not call my friends, my friends did not call me, it's impossible to imagine voicing this level of despair to a real live person, and for sure these things cannot be said into a cold black telephone, but the next day in the harsh sunlight, I decided to call all of this year's and last year's Midget Cheerleaders, and every single one agreed we should send flowers, so Mother drove me around to every house to collect the money, and she drove me to the flower shop where they will make a blanket (that's what they called it) of yellow roses that will exactly fit the teen/child size casket. Then Norman called that night, Mother answered and all she said was, "Thank you for that."

Norman told Mother that I won't work again until the day after Christmas, we wore our Midget Cheerleader uniforms to the funeral on Thursday, December 22nd, and from the pew directly behind the family, the Midget Cheerleaders turned to witness the entire Midget Football

Team carrying the small casket, most of the boys were also in uniform except for a few of the biggest boys who no longer can fit, and the biggest boys, eight of them were actually carrying the casket (not on rollers) up the aisle. The still ugly box (no matter that it was dolled up with the blanket of yellow roses) led the pitiful procession of blue and yellow football uniforms. I stiffened my resolve to hold down a wave of nausea! How can this be happening? If Dennis is in that ugly box, HE'LL SMOTHER! Pat Wade was squeezing my left hand, and Patricia Beam was squeezing my other hand, and with the sun through the window precisely focused on my space, I watched as huge tear drops splashed up from the hymnal in my lap right back up into my face, and pretty soon, I could visually transform the splash moment of impact into the center of a large flower (a water drop flower), and the tear-splash bouquet became large enough to fill the entire area between me and the pew to the front. I hate flowers especially tear-splash flowers, if I could I'd stop my mind from going on and on about stupid tear-splash flowers, I would if I could, but Mother says I get it from Daddy, "Your Daddy never has been able to stay focused in a tragedy, he wanders from one vision, one stimulus, to another and another, and sometimes he speaks out loud the stream of consciousness, and he finds courage in the inconsequential, it's nothing but a padding to ease the blow of the horrible. It's not running from the source of pain, but it is a little step back that pushes the unbearable onto a shelf for just a second, and that second of time is enough to validate acceptance and turn from denial to face the impossible and deal with it just like your Daddy has always come back from misfortune with extraordinary strength."

From the giant water bouquet's maniacal roving, I slipped into coherence and hateful acceptance of the moments ago unacceptable, and I seemed to understand what Mother called 'extraordinary strength.'

I don't recall going to the cemetery, I do recall getting into a strange car that stopped in front of the Presbyterian Church. Someone took me home, I don't know who, I hope I said, 'Thank you.'

I moped around for days, a living discount and completely contrary to my last couple of years of going around convincing everyone of my radiant beauty by disguising my so-so face in a bubbly personality, my simple strategy has been to smile away anyone's doubt and catch everyone up into the rouse of the beautiful Janet, my smile is the only claim to gorgeous, but it is remarkably effective.

This Christmas Eve, when Randall begged, I refused to read "Twas the Night Before Christmas." I refused to wrap the present Randall wanted to give to Mother, but on Christmas Day I took down our Christmas tree (Mother always wants it undecorated and dragged to the garbage dump on Christmas day), and this year I shared her urgency, and generally, I acted like a shrew, and the day after Christmas when I showed up at the Tasty Treat, I wondered if I'd ever get past this and instead of finding courage, I found it soothing to wallow in, "Why me? I'll never get over this, and forever I'll add into the loss of Papa, the Dennis sorrow."

But therein lay the route up out of this pain and sadness, and it's very fitting that the two biggest jokers, the two silliest darlings, the two most deserved angels are sitting right here with me wherever I look, there they are on the milk machine, there they are on the grill, there they are on the order window and the hood of the car outside, and now thinking about Papa and Dennis gives me reason to smile just a little crack of a smile for now, but nonetheless, a crack of a smile is better than the wicked witch's snarl. I've been viewed as beautiful because of my effervescent smile, and I will return to that personality, but not just now, not just yet because I'm too busy winnowing the chaff from the wheat. I have a lot of work ahead before I can actually smile again, but for sure I can and will find the "beautiful smile" and already my inner core is brimming over with Extraordinary Strength.

Five nights a week at 10pm, I close the Tasty Treat, and Norman has arranged with the Tallapoosa policemen to watch over me because there might be some mean person who would try to take the money drawer, although I can't imagine that any one could possibly be that unprincipled, but none the less, I have come to rely on the police. From the first, Norman has prompted me again and again, "Give the police anything they want and don't dare charge them. If they want hamburgers and french fries, fire up the grill and deep fryer and cook hamburgers and french fries. If they want ice cream or milk shakes or a bag of potato chips, give it to them, give them anything they want, and one night as I handed Jimmy Lambert a large co-cola, he said, "Janet, you're going to have to tell your Mother to stop running the red light."

There it was handed to me as an imperative, but the lighter than air smile changed into Extraordinary Strength and turned my gloom into a tangible wand of transformational smiling beauty.

All the outside lights and most of the indoor lights were already turned off, or else the two policemen could see my response to the notion that I could say such a thing to MY Mother! But to give Jimmy Lambert credit, I know exactly what he's talking about, and I could explain it, but he'd either take it as a complement to his policing skills or he might take it as a direct challenge, but either way, I'm not brave enough to tell my Mother that she should sit at the red light and in her very words, "Waste a gallon of gas waiting for non-existent traffic. Why we don't have any traffic in Tallapoosa! The police are there at the red light, they're always sitting right there in the police car, and they know that I can't pay 25 cents a gallon to sit there until a red light turns green. It makes no sense, besides if there is another car coming along; I wait for it to go by. I'm not irresponsible!"

If all the indoor lights were on, well I'd have to explain my facial expression, but they could not see my face, and I did get a little inkling that Jimmy Lambert might be just as afraid of my Mother as I am (and rightly so)! Into the uncertain, I rode high on the return Extraordinary Strength.

On Friday, January 6, 1961, I received in the mail a card with a sketched stained glass window surrounded with flowers. It is addressed to Janet Godwin & Cheerleaders, Tallapoosa Ga. The card makers message, "Thank you sincerely for your kind expression of sympathy. This tribute of respect will always be remembered." The small three by four card is signed, "Roselle Williams & family."

God bless the Roselle Williams family. I took the card to school on Monday, January 9th, and I made sure every single (last year's and this year's) Midget Cheerleader read the card. Every one of them donated money and every one of them read the 'Thank You' card. There are milestones in every life, and I am convinced that this is a pivotal point in my life, I've adjusted my trajectory; I've matured. Over the last few days, I've resisted the urge to throw the card in the trash, and now I've made the decision to keep this morbid little card, and it's now in place in my memories box along with my ticket to the Auburn FSU football game

Nov 19, 1960. We sat in the West Stand, we entered Cliff Hare through Gate 12, we sat in Row 5 and I sat in seat 12. My ticket is personalized on the back where Wayne Newman wrote the score. **Auburn - 52 - FSU - 6**

Back in school, there was no lock hanging on Kristina's locker, and the entire student body quickly learned that her locker is totally cleaned out, and within a matter of a few minutes, gossip enlightened everyone that she will never return to THS, she will marry Forrest Williams. She is pregnant at age thirteen and will have the baby at age 13.

Kristina (the sweetest)!

That first week after quitting school, Kristina mailed invitations to a Kitchen Bridal Shower. I found a hamburger press and a Deviled Egg plate and paid $5, 1/3 of my week's salary ($15).
Mother seemed to spin a protective cocoon around me. She set about re-tightening the leash
1) Only double dates.
2) Home by 9pm.
3) She introduced me to her finger shaking in my face.

I began to realize a phenomenon taking shape. My classmates starting with Denver, Jack, and Jimmy began to tighten our circle, and there seemed to be a conscious effort to block outside intrusion. The boys in our class made provision for the building of a security wall, and in quick succession the "strong together" wall was widened to include another and another until all in our class threatened with balled fists any possible infiltration and "strong together" became our unspoken motto. The pain caused by Dennis's death and Kristina's pregnancy could not be shirked off not yet, not now, and not for a while.

Of course I went to Kristina's Shower, and she was the sweetest bride ever, and we played adult shower games, and understood the significance. The general temperament was palpable and summed up with 'it just so happens that this new bride is young. So What?'
But for that attitude to spread to the boys in our class well that may take a while; then Kristina's Thank You note arrived in the mail, and I

took it to school and purposefully handed it to Denver first, then Jack, then Jimmy:

> February 13, 1961
> Dear Janet,
> Thanks so much for the Deviled Egg plate
> and the hamburger press. I'm getting hungry just
> writing. I guess you know how I love hamburgers.
> Love Always,
> Kristina

For my mother to ever say "so what? / no big deal" in dismissal of Kristina's indiscretion, well understand, by all that's holy, THAT WILL NEVER HAPPEN, and for that reason, I might as well withdraw from the fray, because I have to accept that my Mother's very core has been squashed.

Frank invited me to Auburn's ROTC Military Ball on Saturday night February 25, 1961. I found the perfect white chiffon dress in the Montgomery Ward Catalog, Mother agreed to let me get a store-bought dress because she just doesn't have time to make a Simi formal dress right now. Carroll and Glenda will drive me to Auburn and they will also attend the Ball, and we three will stay that Saturday night in a Motel and the next morning we will go to church with Frank and then we'll drive back home.

As it turned out, the Military Ball was wonderful. Everyone was in dress uniform. Carroll no longer has his Tech ROTC uniform, but somehow, my brother was able to borrow a perfectly fitting one. After that bad wreck, he will never again be qualified for acceptance in the Military because of the metal splints in his leg.

The ballroom was decorated with hundreds of US Flags and beautifully pleated Red White and Blue crepe paper swags. The military band played a lot of Jitterbug songs, and Frank Ellis and Carroll Godwin have to share the prize for being the best Jitterbug dancers!

The next morning Frank joined us for breakfast in the motel coffee shop, and we attended worship at the First Presbyterian Church. The minister to students Mr. Thomas Murphy preached the sermon.

All too soon it was time to go. Carroll and Frank shook hands, Frank hugged Glenda and then he hugged me too, and I'm certain my face was as red as a US Flag. Where did the time go? The remarkable weekend was over and done with, and I was still floating on cloud 9.

About once a week, I stay after school for a club meeting. There's Tri-Hi-Y, and Beta Club, and cheerleader practice in the fall and in the spring. Week by week I work my club meeting schedule around working at the Tasty Treat. Week by week there's no pattern of when I walk to the pay telephone. This leads me to wonder how I can invariably encounter Mr. Roy Howe as I walk alone from the High School to the pay telephone booth at Bowman's store.

Mr. Roy Howe is a short man with a round belly, red face and white hair. His sparkling eyes are an indication that he considers life to be just a great big game. He was the postmaster in Tallapoosa when I was in grammar school. Back then the post office was in the building that faces Highway 78, across Alewine Ave. from the Jitney Jungle. Johnson's Shoe Shop is in the basement of that building, and Gladhat's Clothing is next door to the west. I remember sitting on the counter at the post office holding onto the iron bars and watching Mr. Howe's mischievous expression as he counted out stamps for my mother. But now in these later years he is retired, and he walks every day around the town, for exercise and for company. He loves to stop and talk to the people he meets. I think he considers himself to be my guardian.

My monthly meetings, recur on the same day of the month, and I don't go to work on that day of the month. I walk alone from the school to the pay telephone, and for years now I've continued that pattern, and again for years, on every walk to the telephone booth, I meet Mr. Roy Howe, and I think he is waiting in ambush. That's a silly thing for me to say, but I guess Mr. Roy Howe's demeanor makes me silly. But that aside, I truly think Mr. Roy Howe has taken on the responsibility of protecting me, and that's the sweetest thing to think about. I'm not the least bit worried, and neither is

Mother, but the indications are that Mr. Roy Howe must be supervising just to make sure no one tries to scare me or hurt me.

He doesn't stop to talk to me every time, but when he has something to say, he stops and waits for me, and I continue walking toward him and I stop next to him so I can hear what nonsense he's going to say this time. I think he considers me to be a good listener, and I enjoy his funny stories, and he always seems to have another one.

One day for example he said, "You know my wife pays old bills. She pays light bills and gas bills, and grocery bills, and not a drop of liquor in the house."

I love to laugh, and this man is bubbling over to make me laugh.

Another time he said, "I've decided that every man needs a wife, there's a lot of things you can't blame on the government."

One day he had his city property tax bill in his hand, and he said, "There's just no explaining these taxes. No two people pay the same amount. I've decided that those tax assessors sit up there in city hall and wait for a train to come rolling along. They watch out the window and when the train slows down enough so they can read the numbers on the cars, well then they copy down the car numbers onto our tax notices."

Once he said, "You know the older I get, the stronger I get. When I was young, I could not carry twenty dollars worth of groceries out of the store. Now I'm old, and I can carry twenty dollars worth of groceries with one arm."

His sense of humor and his attitude that life is to be enjoyed and mocked made a lasting impression on me. I still can visualize the way he hitched his belt up above his potbelly almost reaching his armpits. He pursed his lips and sniffed his nose when he was about to say something jovial. One warm summer Sunday evening about twenty of us teenagers were standing in front of the First Baptist Church. We had been to BTU (Baptist Training Union) and youth choir practice was about to begin. I remember we were all laughing about something. Mr. Howe was walking past the church on his way home. (His house is just at the end of the block across from the old Christian Church at Lyon St. & Spring St.) He stopped and waited for all of us to give him our full attention. He puckered his lips, snorted, and with that twinkle in his eyes, he said, "Damn wild kids!"

Then he turned and continued on his way. We weren't offended. That was his greeting. We smiled after him. We knew we had his approval.

On Saturday morning October 21st 1961, Otto drove south into Tallapoosa to get some groceries. On the drive home, he crossed the Tallapoosa River Bridge, and blasted up the long hill heading north. He always drove too fast, and just as he rounded the top of the hill, a car pulled out in front of him. That's a very dangerous drive way and it's very possible that neither of the two drivers saw the other car. Otto's face was sliced off of his head. Someone in one of the houses called the funeral home and their emergency vehicle arrived on the scene in record time, they loaded Otto into the hearse because he was still breathing, they could see blood bubblies from a distance as he exhaled where his lips used to be. They broke the speed of light getting him and his separate face to Anniston because they know that Anniston has the best hospital. Someone called Ruth's neighbor, and that neighbor wasted no time getting Ruth into his car and he knows a back way shortcut to get to Anniston. Someone called us, and mother stopped washing the white clothes and still wearing a wet dress, Mother drove our car to Anniston. In the waiting room Ruth was moaning over and over, "First my baby and now my baby's daddy."

I pulled her to me and before she could resist, I had her in a hammerlock, and I made her listen to me, "I'm your little girl Ruth!"

When I had said that a thousand times, she finally said, "No you're not, honey, you're the next best thing, but NO you are not."

Ruth could not attend his funeral, she was obviously in an unmanageable state of shock. After a week and a couple of days she finally stopped moaning but the silence was more deafening. Mama was with her every minute for weeks and months and years. They were a solemn pair, each grieving for lost babies and lost husbands. Into the second year, Ruth put on a determined face and actually opened the country store, and it seemed that neighbors up and down Highway 100 from Tallapoosa to Cedartown, were on a rotating schedule to spend time with Ruth never leaving her alone.

All through the years in the face of tragedy, a favorite family slogan has been, "Another little chicken died."

I for one am ready for the end of dying little chickens.

1963

As soon as Connie got her driver's license, her parents bought her a car. It was a beautiful 1951 Ford Coupe. Most of us called it the Coupe. Her Daddy promised to keep gas in the Coupe if she followed a few simple rules. The only rule I ever knew about was the one that restricted Connie from driving outside of the Tallapoosa city limits except of course when she had to pick up at my house three miles east of town. For a long time, Connie was very strict in following this rule and on Friday nights we burned up a lot of Arthur Gentry's gas riding around Tallapoosa from the standpipe to the smoke house, turn around at the smoke house and go back to the standpipe, turn around at the standpipe, and go back to the smoke house, each time passing the Police sitting in the only police car at the red light at Head Ave.

Sometimes to relieve the monotony Connie turned at the red light (there was only one) and rode out to Crossroads Café and on out to the ball park where we turned around and drove back past Crossroads back to highway 78 and again started the dizzying back and forth standpipe to Smoke House loop.

On rare occasions we had enough money to buy a co-cola at the Smoke House or the Tasty Treat, and once in a blue moon when we were really loaded with cash, we went inside Crossroads Café and bought one order of French fries and 4 co-colas.

Referring to the "creative element" once again, one Friday night, Connie wanted to buy a gallon of gas so her daddy would not catch on. Remember he kept pretty close tabs on the gas situation. So that Friday night when we first broke the rule, Connie pulled in at the service station directly across from the Baptist Church. The gas station with the beautiful gas pumps that were colorful rounded top bake-o-lite domes. I recall them as ethereal rainbow works of art.

That night Connie pulled up to the beautiful gas pumps across from the Baptist church, asked the attendant for one gallon of gas, and then Connie collected our coins and when the attendant finished cleaning the windshield, she paid the man the dime, nickels and pennies. And that gallon of gas forever kept secret from Arthur Gentry, gave us a new found freedom as we headed out of town to Carrollton, and the campus of West Georgia College!

We rode around West Georgia pretending to be college students, and we went back the next Friday night and the next, and somewhere in there, Connie came up with the idea (creative element again) that we'd be more convincing if we were smoking cigarettes while we rode around the college campus.

So the next Friday night (I know these excursions were on Friday nights because I worked Saturday nights at the Tasty Treat) anyway, the next Friday night when Connie collected our money she took every last cent we had and while the man pumped the gallon of gas, she went inside the tiny little service station building and picked up a pack of cigarettes and this time when the man cleaned the windshield she paid him for both the gas and the pack of cigarettes.

When we got to West Georgia, we were all smoking, I mean we were puffing away because Connie figured we had to smoke all the cigarettes because she had no safe place to hide them, and if her daddy found them he might even take away the Coupe. The only course of action was to smoke all 20 cigarettes and that meant each of the four of us had to smoke 5 cigarettes.

Jane was in her usual place in the front seat, I was in my usual place behind Jane, and Gwen was sitting as usual behind Connie. At West Georgia, we had a favorite place to turn around right where a bunch of cute college boys stood watching the cars turning around, and we smoked as fast as we could as Connie entered the riding around traffic which took us to the bunch of cute boys watching us turn around.

We had to go real slow because there was a good bit of riding around traffic, and as we approached the cute boys on our 4th or 5th turn around, I noticed the Coupe was full of cigarette smoke, and Jane sitting in front of me had her window rolled down, there was no roll down window in the back seat, and Jane was trying to blow her smoke out the window but most times it didn't make it out the window but instead rolled over the seat and into my face, and the slow creeping along traffic caused Connie to constantly push the brakes, the clutch, and then the gas peddle alternately in a sickening rhythm, and by the time we finally reached the cute boys on our 4th or 5th turnaround, I had to get out of the car and I told Connie so. She stopped right by the cute boys, I shook Jane's seat, Jane opened her door, I scrambled out and just made it out of the Coupe in time to puke right in front of the cute boys.

That did it for our pretending to be college girls, it was entirely too much trouble and way too expensive. From then on, we went riding around INSIDE the city limits of Tallapoosa. Pretty soon our friends who COULD drive around OUTSIDE the city limits were telling us great and exciting tales of stealing watermelons from Gay El's daddy's watermelon patch, and we were very envious knowing we could not venture out into the country and sadly we'd never know the exhilaration.

But one night everything changed and just like it was meant to be, as we passed the police car at the red light, Connie glanced across to the other side of the railroad tracks and spotted a bunch of big ripe watermelons sitting in the dark front door alcove at Swint's Grocery Store. Clearly, it was a sign! There they were, picked watermelons sitting on the pavement OUTSIDE the store! Connie was right those watermelons were put there as a direct challenge.

We sheepishly continued to ride around TO THROW OFF THE COPS and Connie planned our great watermelon heist. Her first idea was that she'd stay in the Coupe behind the stirring wheel and Gwen and I would stay put in the back seat out of the way, and when she slowed to a stop right in front of Swint's Grocery Store, Jane would quickly open her car door, jump out of the car, grab up a watermelon and jump back in the Coupe all in one fluid motion, but Jane was having none of it. The outraged Jane screamed at Connie, "If you want a stolen watermelon, you'll have to do the stealing yourself." Jane was the only one brave enough to stand up to Connie.

So the plans were adjusted to accommodate Jane, and the ringleader, Connie came up with a workable plan. I can't emphasize enough that this whole rig-a-ma-role was Connie's idea, and the three of us were victims of a mischievous mind.

This time Connie planned to turn off highway 78 at the red light where we'd act nonchalant and wave and smile at the police, she'd drive right past Swint's Grocery Store, and turn right to go south on highway

100 all the while convincing the police we were innocent of any wrong doing, and as soon as the Coupe was out of site around the corner of the building, she planned to pull to the side of highway 100 at which time, Jane would open the door and get out and Gwen and I would get out too.

It looked like a fairly simple case of petty theft, so after one practice run, pretty soon Connie turned off of Hwy 78 and we all waved and smiled again at the police, and this time when Connie pulled to the side of the dark highway 100 just around the corner of the building in the cover of darkness Jane opened her door and jumped out, but she didn't make a move until Gwen and I were both out of the Coupe, and then the three of us tiptoed around the corner of the building and I remember Jane whispered, "I'll pick out a good one."

I thought she was surely crazy! We were in plain view! The police were right there! If they looked over their shoulder they would see every detail, but Jane took her own sweet time picking out a "good one" whatever that means! In the dark!

As soon as Jane decided on the GOOD one and bent over to pick it up, Gwen took off running for the get away car, with me coming along right behind her, but I took the time to glance back over my shoulder at Jane and I could barely stifle my giggles because Jane was running along taking tiny little steps and trying to manage a giant good one that she could lift no higher than her knees because she weighed about a 100 pounds and the watermelon had to have weighed at least 50 pounds.

We all wore skirts or dresses all the time, that was a rule, and Jane was just about tripping on her full gathered skirt hem because she could not straighten up and carry the weight of her precious good one.

I made it to the Coupe and into the back seat, right behind Gwen, and Jane heaved herself and the giant good one into the front seat and managed to slam the car door before Connie pealed off heading south out of town, and I fully expected to hear the siren and see the flashing red lights coming after us, but believe it or not we made a clean get away.

On Halloween night 1963, Jane begged and pleaded until her mother allowed her to take the car, but with one catch – it had to be returned in pristine condition. Connie, Gwen, Jane and I headed out for our usual "standpipe to Smokehouse" cruising – with a few detours through residential streets to see who was out & what they were up to. We saw lots of trick-or-treaters – playing more tricks than getting treats. –And among others we saw a carload of boys from our class – We smiled and waved – they smiled and waved. We kept seeing them around town and every time we saw them we smiled and waved – they smiled and waved.

We were at the corner of Robertson Ave & Boulevard in front of Otis Bennett's house when we met them again, so this time we stopped, and still smiling we rolled down the windows.

The car was full of our glass-mates, remember the classmates we were so close to that they seemed like our brothers, SAMMY – BOBBY – DENVER - & JIMMY, but our pride in our brothers was clipped at the root, and that was where and when the gauntlet was thrown. Those sweet classmates of ours, the ones we considered to be like our brothers, now took on an adversarial relation and, believe it or not, they bombarded us through the open windows with eggs. There was an egg explosion inside Jane's Mother's car – and Connie, riding in the front passenger seat got the brunt of it. Wiping the shells from her hair and with egg yolks running down her face, she looked at Jane and yelled through gritted teeth "Get Em!!!"

Now I was considered to be the intellectual of the group as I explained that we needed eggs for retaliation and at this point I directed Jane to go to my house because there will be plenty of eggs in our fridge. I'm fairly certain that Mother never knew what happened to all those eggs from her fridge!

Battle lines had been drawn and weapons accumulated in the back seat between Gwen and me. We cruised all over town looking for those low down, dirty varmints. Oh, there were skirmishes all right, with pumpkins and eggs flying between cars! We were so anxious to catch them and pay them back we actually came around the curve at the high school on two wheels. We braced for the rollover we all knew was coming, but the center of gravity of that old Nash was so low we finally settled back on all four tires.

I looked around to see if everyone was ok and Connie was leaning back at an odd angle. Seems her seat bracket had broken and she was partly in the front seat and partly in the back. Now this was pretty doggone funny to us, and we went into fits of hysterical giggling like only high school girls and old ladies can. But the most amazing part of all was that Connie had been able to do what no human is supposed to be able to do – She crushed raw eggs with her bare hands.

I would like to say we gave as good as we got that night – but sadly, no. We limped into Robinson's service station, and we washed the outside of the car using a spigot with a trickle of water, and our bare hands – by the way – the smell of raw eggs and pumpkin never came out of that Rambler.

November 22,1963

It was 6th period and I was in the typing room when over the loud speaker, Mr. Cobb's voice announced, "Our President has been shot." No one typed another word, and no one said anything except for one senior who said, "My Daddy will be happy."

Politics should never include "My Daddy will be happy" when a President has been shot."

Beginning in January 1964, I met several times with Coach Welch in his auditorium office behind the stage (he has converted one of the two small changing rooms each used only once a year at Senior Play) He has typed a personal data sheet listing me as single, 5'2" 101 pounds from Tallapoosa. My employer history lists Mr. N. K. Owens from December 1960 to June 1964. My extracurricular activities are Tri-Hi-Y President, Beta Club Treasurer, Cheerleader 5 years Co-Captain, T-Club, Senior Play. My references are Mr. E.R, Cobb, Principal, Tallapoosa High School, Mr. Bobby Welch 33 Spring Ave, Tallapoosa Georgia, Rev. S.T. Skaggs, Pastor, Tallapoosa First Baptist Monroe St Tallapoosa, Georgia and Mr. N.K. Owens Kiker St Tallapoosa Georgia. My grade point average is 94. My I Q score is high (without listing an exact number) I scored **very high** on A.F. Qualifying. My typing speed is 50 wpm (words per minute). And I know all letterforms. On my behalf, Coach Welch is corresponding with Universities and Scholarship programs. He obtained in my name a National Merit Scholarship Program 1964-65 'Handbook for Merit Program Participants' listing me as a participant and I qualify for a full ride scholarship to schools all around Georgia, South Carolina and Tennessee, but I want to go to the University of Georgia, and my paperwork for financial assistance to the University of Georgia arrived too late, but not giving up, Coach Welch found another scholarship program feeding only Universities within the state of Georgia and this program produces newly qualified teachers to fill the gap of retiring teachers. I am honored to accept this as my Scholarship!

An acceptance envelope from the "Office of the Registrar and Director of Admissions, University of Georgia Athens Georgia" post marked 10 cents ATHENS GEORGIA FEB 26,1964. The envelope itself is worthy of framing, because of a one inch wide red diagonal stripe labeled "Official Acceptance University of Georgia"

Tallapoosa High School Senior Class Educational Tour
To Charlottesville, Williamsburg, Jamestown,
Richmond and Washington
April 10-15, 1964

Friday, April 10th We left Tallapoosa at 6:19 PM aboard our special coach THE SOUTHERNER.

Saturday, April 11th: At 7:05 we arrived in Charlottesville VA. Our bus took us through the campus of the University of Virginia. We saw several buildings designed by Thomas Jefferson and we saw the famous Serpentine Wall. Thomas Jefferson figured out that a brick wall requires more than one layer of bricks to remain strong unless you use the serpentine method of laying only one layer of bricks. Next we had a guided tour of MONTICELLO the home of Thomas Jefferson,

Our bus took us through the historic countryside to Richmond, Va. with a stop at the famous St. John's Church where Patrick Henry made his famous 'GIVE ME LIBERTY, OR GIVE ME DEATH' Speech to the American colonists. As we traveled on to Williamsburg, (the Capital of Virginia in 1699) we learned that Williamsburg was recently restored to be as it was in the early founding of our country and the renovation bill was paid by a private citizen. Mr. Rockefeller paid the $60,000,000.00 cost.

SUNDAY APRIL 12ᵀᴴ: We took a trip to Annapolis Md. 'The Third Oldest City' in our country and home of the UNITED STATES NAVAL ACADEMY,

In Washington, we visited the Lincoln Memorial and the Marine Memorial of Iwo Jima, and we witnessed the changing of the guard at the tomb of the Unknown Soldier in Arlington National Cemetery. We also saw the Eternal Flame at the tomb or our late President, John F. Kennedy.

From Arlington we went to Mount Vernon, to visit the home of George and Martha Washington.

That night we went on a 'MOONLIGHT CRUISE' down the Potomac River to visit Marshall Hall Amusement Park. This 3000-passenger boat has a big dance floor and a great orchestra.

MONDAY APRIL 13ᵀᴴ: This morning we walked two blocks to the Archives of the United States to see the original CONSTITUTION OF THE UNITED STATES and THE BILL OF RIGHTS. We saw the Federal Bureau of Investigation. After the F.B.I. tour we walked one block up the 'Mall' to the Museum of Natural History to see exhibits that range from a stuffed elephant to the 'Hope Diamond'.

Next we visited Capitol Hill. We had a guided tour of both Houses of Congress: we went into the Supreme Court Building and toured through the Library of Congress. Then we went out Embassy Row, from there we went on to the Washington National Cathedral.

Our nighttime entertainment was to the nightclub 'Casino Royal', where we had a delicious dinner and saw the floor show featuring Chubby Checker.

Tuesday, April 14ᵗʰ: Toured the Bureau of Printing and Engraving, where our paper money, bonds, and stamps, are printed. At the Washington Monument we went all the way to the top, then we walked to the White House and toured inside the now home of President Lyndon Baines Johnson and his family.

We stopped in the Treasury Building to see the exhibit of the Secret Service. We saw counterfeit money compared with genuine currency, how coins are made and law-breakers caught.

We walked over to the Smithsonian Institute and the Jefferson Memorial.

Then our luggage was loaded aboard our bus and at Washington Union Station we boarded our special coach, 'The Southerner' for our trip home.

Wednesday, April 15th Arrived back home.

I love learning and this extended learning trip will always remain in my mind as the best (ever) learning experience!! I will someday travel the world!!!!! This trip opened new avenues for me. My vision will forever recall my first traveled trip, and Monticello will be for me the bedrock, the beginning (in my real time) of my understanding great intelligence. I wonder if other countries have such homes of great intelligence on display? I WILL FIND OUT AND I WILL SEE THOSE DISPLAYS!!!

Monday, April 20th 1964

As usual on Mondays at the Tasty Treat, Sandra Stewart and Mr. Lovvorn were already at work when I got there at 4pm. Five days a week, I work from 4 to 10pm, and from 8 to 10, I work alone. It was a very quiet day. Sandra was having a hamburger, and I made a chocolate milkshake for myself. Mr. Lovvorn was first to mention the howling wind that sounded like a train off the tracks heading straight toward us. I walked to the east plate glass window, to better see the trees being blown side to side with such power, I expected each one to snap at the folding point. Over my shoulder I heard Mr. Lovvorn speculate that the wind was crashing the jukebox into the side of the building, and next I was shocked to hear Sandra say, "I'm going out there to hold down the juke box."

This was such a ludicrous statement that I spun around yelling "NO!"

But it was already too late, Sandra was standing in the open door way, and immediately as the vacuum broke, I heard the 5 foot wide by five foot tall plate glass behind me as it started to crack, and I was able to take only one step away before the deadly shards caught me and carved my head, back and one leg. I looked down at the sight of my blue flowered dress being blown between my ankles, so that meant the skirt fabric had been cut away from the bodice fabric. As was the style, Mother sewed a form-fitting bodice, and attached a gathered skirt at the waist. I knew I'd have to hold the already sopping wet cotton skirt up off the floor or else trip and fall. I slipped and slide past the grill, and found Sandra on the floor behind the milk machine. I had no choice but to fall onto Sandra thus protecting her from the lethal breaking-glass shower of the front three huge windows. The milk machine was blown from atop the ice machine, and I dared to look up to see the milk machine dancing in the air just above me but being held in tow as it was unable to unplug itself. My cheerleader's voice could be heard for miles, "Get Up and RUN"

When the milk machine was slung out into the area that used to be the back cinderblock wall, I made myself heard over the deafening rain drops the size of chicken eggs, and only then did I dare stand up and follow Mr. Lovvorn's lead, and I screamed to Sandra, "Jump over the remaining wall!"

Now on a normal day none of us could have jumped up and over a 3 foot concrete wall and I did not see the competition, but I took flight up and over and down again with Olympic style and grace, and the egg sized rain pelted me when I knew there should be a metal ceiling above me, but there was no sign of the huge metal canopy. My second discovery was that the parking area was filled with cars, and every car door seemed to be open and screaming at me to get in! But my mother still warns against getting into a car with strangers. So I continued running through a maze of frantic helplessness. What can I do? What can I do? My question was not heard or answered, but there was a stranger who boomed, "GET IN THIS CAR! NOW! I SAID GET IN THIS CAR!"

Once in his car, I felt my blood spewing up from my head to stain the fabric ceiling. I felt my left leg bleeding a puddle on this stranger's floorboard. I tried to lean forward to stop my blood from ruining the passenger seatback, but when we both realized a power pole was falling and probably would sever the passenger door a determined hand pulled me toward him to safety, but I growled at the hand holding me back, and against all odds, I found the door's armrest and pulled the door shut just as the hand was doing a 180 and getting the hell out of there! The other cars were moving out of his way. I'm sure the hand belonged to a local person because he knew where to find Dr. Downey. This stranger was out of the car and knocking on Dr. Downey's side door only to run back, slide his arms around my bloody and tattered blue dress and carry me into the doctor's office. I think he was still standing there when Dr. Downey said, "Little miss 'Clean Socks' you have forty-eight stitches in your head, back and one leg."

Then I realized that Mother and Randall were in the office, and some one picked me up and carried me through two lines of people defining a path to the car, then Randall positioned himself in the front seat by the door and he pulled my feet into his lap as Mother guided my bloody head into her lap.

As the daylight turned to night, and the Dixie Steel Mill's shift let Daddy off work, finally Shug Godwin trotted into the living room, knelt beside the couch and folded me into his arms as Mother relived 'the day from hell' that guided Daddy by way of my words from "holding down the jukebox, to a stranger forcing me into his car, and finally Dr. Downey's forty-eight stitches."

For 7 days, I stayed put on the couch, too weak to walk alone or stand alone, "too weak for company" is what I heard Mother say into the telephone again and again, and when I finally assessed my condition in the bathroom mirror, my reflection showed my blonde hair as black, evidently blood turns hair black and disables a brush or comb, but the telephone rang on April 27th with an offer to wash my hair for free, so Mother drove me to the 'Beauty Shop' next to Bowman's store where Freda Gail would not take the one-dollar bill that Mother tried to force on her, and at home, Mother secured a few pin curls and left me to nap. The next morning, Tuesday, April 28th, Mother sat with me as I bathed, and she carefully helped me lift my clothes up and over my head, and she delicately combed my curls and placed new pristine white bandages, and from the car she parked outside Mr. Cobb's office, she walked me into the high school building straight to a chair in the library and in a few seconds my classmates appeared and as Brenda scribbled they finished a list of hourly assistance responsibility for the upcoming week They wouldn't even let me go to the girls' room alone. Every time I think about it, the tears start up again.

Into the Graduation ceremony, I was asked to stand, and then came the announcement:

Janet Godwin is awarded the Science Metal and the Math Metal, and she is awarded a scholarship to the University of Georgia.

Janet Godwin
Class of 1964
Valedictorian
Graduation Speech

There is a popular song that plays on the radio, some of the lyrics are: "People who need people are the luckiest people in the world."

Indeed we have needed our parents. There is a book in our THS library that contains several high school graduation speeches. In that book there's more than one speech that contains exact counts of the huge number of peanut butter and jelly sandwiches parents made over the course of twelve years. I figured the number 118,260 to be the correct number of sandwiches for our small class of 27, but I decided to list the solution as chili over loaf bread instead of PB & J. That's neither here nor there, but the point is to all of you dear parents, in this graduation ceremony there is not enough time to thank you. It's a debt each of us can never repay, but there's another possibility. Since it's obvious that we can't REPAY, maybe over the next years, our parents as grandparents can feel gratified each time we as parents make another chili over loaf bread.

We have needed our teachers who nurtured and challenged us, and also, in one case, the teacher learned the subject WITH us. At this point let me highlight the best French teacher ever. On the first day, Mrs. Stringer said, and I quote, "I know nothing about French, but we are going to learn together" and boy howdy we did!!!!! And we will always have a French vocabulary, not necessarily a social vocabulary because some of us will forever remember French profanity. We do love to laugh.

Although Mrs. Brewer is retired, she is here today, and without question, we needed Mrs. Brewer's amazing talent to teach us Math. Many times she made us stand back from the chalkboard and appreciate algebra's solutions as beautiful works of art. Geometry as taught by Mrs. Brewer is as easy as walking. Last week, my sister Marilyn came into the room where I was practicing this speech. Marilyn was in Mrs. Brewer's Geometry class six years ago, but as if it were yesterday, instantly when I mentioned Mrs. Brewer, Marilyn said, "The Pythagoras Theorem: In a right triangle, the square of the hypotenuse is equal to the sum of the squares of the other two sides."

I have nothing to add because that is a tribute to Mrs. Brewer beyond any I could recite.

Mr. Shell created whiz kids with his explanations of Biology, Chemistry, and Physics, and with time to spare he taught us how to estimate the answer to complicated formulas.

Mrs. Williams skillfully maneuvered our inaccurate grammar by teaching us easy to remember correction crutches, and she inspired all of us (especially me) to write modern day stories.

Now, let me say, emphatically, we the class of 1964 have needed each other! I can't emphasize enough the bond of shared happiness and shared sorrow. We have come to be more than classmates we are family, and one reason for our specific closeness is the common pain we have lived through together.

First of all, we discarded the notion that we were invincible when Brenda Cobb's hand and arm were sliced into shreds by the breaking glass in the door leading from the gym to the playground. Until that day, we were warm and cozy with the notion we were safe, from that day forward, not one of us will ever open a door by pushing against glass.

Once again, we stood helpless, on the Midget Football field and watched as Denver Morgan's arm was mangled and re-invented into a giant paper clip. The next morning in homeroom as Denver relived the horror, outside the door, those others in the hallway were separate from us, and our figurative circle welded together to be far stronger than any other group of 27 from the beginning of time and on until judgment day. Our willing responsibility for each other dates to these two tragedies.

Also, we recall the debilitating pain when we lost Dennis Williams, and when his antics were forever quieted we yearned for another laugh, just one more, please. But maturely and solemnly we accept that he's gone, and we draw strength from each other almost to the point of standing shoulder-to-shoulder ready for battle.

Our constant and reliable reason for being is to help each other, if one of us stagers from the heavy load, another one of us will step up to catch and bear the weight. If Sammy wobbles, Jack will be there. If Jane hesitates, Connie's arms will open wide, and whether we are aware of it or not, there are 25 of us patrolling Brenda's and Denver's back, and that will continue for an infinite and uncounted period of time. This support and responsibility for each other has become a solid that won't melt with time. Oh no, this solid is concrete. As we look ahead and go forward to find ourselves scattered around the world, no one in this class will ever walk the treacherous path alone. We truly respect and love each other.

These wise guys are serious when they need to be serious, and when there's no pressure, they are hilarious (Jimmy Thrower's name must be inserted here). So let us laugh, and let time go by, and ask us again in a decade or so if any one of us needs help, and if the answer is yes, then responses will resound from other towns or other states asking the questions, 'Where are you?' 'What do you need?' And the declaration will be, "I'll be right there."

But there might come a time when the world beyond our borders needs us and so be it! Our obligations are fathomless. If there's a need we will help. Why else are we on this God's Green Earth, but to help and love one another?

I love these guys!!!!!

Tallapoosa High School
Class of 1953
Elizabeth Adams, Archie Allen, Dorothy Allred, Macajah
Bagwell, Jacqueline Bennett, Joyce Bowman, Billy Jo Brooks,
Jimmie Carole Gable, Larry Nobles, Joy Owens,
Nelda Ruth Owens, Norman Owens, Janice
Pope, Juanita Virginia Powell,
Howard Priest, Jo Ann Richards, Betty Faye
Garner, Charles Hart, Martha Johnson,
Joyce Liner, Edna Mann, Avis Mize, Barbara
Newman, David Roberts, Maude Robinson,
Edward Robinson, Betty Joyce Walker, Byron Ward, Kenneth Williams,
Ruby Faye Williams, Roger Wood, Bruce Woody, Jr.

THS
Class of 1954
Billy Adams, Agnes Fay Alewine, Jacqueline
Bailey, DeLuna Bates, Mildred Bell,
Willene Byrd, Mary Martha Chandler, Jo
Ann Cobb, James Edward Deering,
Hubert Dodson, Robert Downey, Carroll Godwin,
Billy Higgins, James L. Hughes,
David Johnson, Clara Janice Little, Ralph A.
Lively, Flora M. McDonald, Doyle Mauk,
Gladys L. Nall, Betty Ann Nichols, Pat Nobles,
Clarence Robinson, Carol Sue Scott,
Martha Marie Sheffield, Edmund Smith, Ina
June Spearman, Curtis Thompson,
Jack Thompson, Barbara White, Marilyn
White, Jack Williams, Nora Wood

THS
Class of 1955
Carolyn Adams, Gary Bailey, William Bell,
Jane Cole, Ann Craven, Nan Craven,

Shelby Gable, Patsy Garner, James Roy Gilbert,
Terry Gladden, Joan Godwin,
Jimmy Harrell, William Hutcheson, Bobby
Key Helen Kittle Mack Lively,
Leon Mann, Barbara Morgan, Gene Owens,
Juanita Price, Marie Ray, Frances Saxon,
Charlene Smith, Jo Ann Smith, Mattie Smith,
Earl Tolleson, Sue Nell Tyra,
Geraldine Tucker, Nanelle Warner, Norma
Weathers, Clara Nell Williams,
Doyce Williams, Marie Williams

THS
Class of 1958

Audrey Arnold, Carolyn Austin, Juanita Bell,
Joyce Cheatwood, Lucille Cheatwood,
Priscilla Cumby, Lemoyne Dobbs, William B.
Emerson, Jr. Carolyn Little, Jack Lively,
Thelma Morris, Paul Nall, Billy Nichols, Harvey
Nixon, Willard Price, Charles Ray,
Judy Evans, Marilyn Godwin, Marie Hamrick,
Joyce Kittle, Janice Roberts, Paul Roberts,
Joan Swafford, David Warner, Wanda Willis

THS
Class of 1960

Dorothy L. Abercrombie, Jimmy Calvin Allen,
Charles Barnes, Ronald Keith Brooks,
Samuel MacArthur Cates, Ralph Walton
Cates, James Lowell Hildebrand,
Rebecca Howland, Linda Jane Jones, Martha
Jane King, Faye Marie Moore,
William J. Gordon Neal, William David
Crabtree, Dennis Benjamin Cole,
Jean Bowman Cole, Virginia Mae Croley, Frank
Daves Ellis, Margaret Linda Ellis,

Clarence Junior Gilbert, Linda Joyce Owens, Thomas Eugene Raiford Jr.
Linda Ward Robinson, Lon Evan Saxon, Sandra
Faye Turner, Brenda Joan Waits,
Mira Jo Williams, Jackie Wood

THS
Class of 1961
Patsy Baily, Marlon Beam, Claude Bedford, Bernda
Bell, Louise Burgess, Joann Brooks,
Phil Campbell, Bill Carter, Wadell Chaffin,
Carolyn Gilbert, Nesbert Godwin,
Stephen Hughes, James Lanier, Jimmy Lanier,
Jimmy Frank Meunier, Rodney Newman,
Beverly Ray, Joyce Roberts, Neal Saxon, Sara
Will Saxon, Mike Shackelford,
Jeanette Shealy, Margaret Ann Thrower, Brantley
Thompson, Larry Thompson,
Dru Walker, Gerry Gail Ward, Sandra Ward, Pat Wood

THS
Class of 1962
Gloria Beam, Cherrie Bentley, Diana Coggins,
Rebecca Crowe, Sue Easterwood,
Nancy Evans, Ronald Gilbert, Thomas Lee Harbison,
Donna Holder, Mary Beth Hughes,
Judy Kilgo, Gail Littlefield, Beverly McLeroy,
Wendell Morgan, Loretta Payne,
James Smith, Raiford Roberts, Shelby Jean Williams, Sandra Wilson

THS
Class of 1963
Richard Allen, Patricia Beam, Sandra Burgess,
Gary Cobb, Larry Dobbs, Larry Dodson,
Wendell Fielder, Jimmy George, Tony Gray,
Harry Greene, Michael Heaton,

Kathy Hildebrand, Marisa Jones, J. L. Little,
Wesley Littlefield, Margaret McLemore,
Diane Meunier, Wayne Newman, Virginia
Powell, Karen Smith, Nancy Smith,
James Thompson, Patricia Wade, Paul Waits, Jane Woody, Jean Woody

THS
Class of 1964
Robert Allen, Bobby Bates, Elaine Bowman,
Johnny Bowman, Gwen Brown,
Colleen Campbell, Cynthia Cauthen, Linda Sue Chandler,
Brenda Cobb, Eddie Dean, Louis Edgar, Bobby Farmer,
Constance Gentry, Janet Godwin, Brenda Jaillet,
George Kelly, Charles Maxwell, Denver Morgan,
Jack Nixon, Tommy Patterson,
Cynthia Pope, Sammy Self, Dorothy Shealy,
Linda Smith, Jimmy Thrower,
Johnny Thrower, Jane Wood

THS
Class of 1965
Naomi Dobbs Bentley, Bobby Lee Brown, Shirley Brown, David Brooks,
Barbara Ann Causey, Barbara Ann Chandler,
Thomas Cole, Virginia Coggins,
Diane Downey, Larry Dryden, Rebecca Feltrinelli,
Cathy Ferguson, Cary Fielder,
Judy Gentry, Larry Jackson, Kathy Kilgo, Larry King, Bobby
Lanier, Brenda Lanier, Glenda Lyle, Alton McWhorter,
Thomas Meunier, Donette Mullins, Alfred Rutherford,
Linda Ann Sheffield, Linda Smith, Marcia
Smith, Sandra Stewart, Jerry Gilbert,
Gary Gray, Peggy Hill, Ralph Hughes Robbie
Thompson, Phyllis Waldrop,
Gayner Elizabeth Williams, Ernest Olin Wilson, Jr. Danny Kay Wood

THS

Class of 1966

Michael Albright, Barbara Allen, Althea Almon, Peggy Barnes, Sammy Beasley, Francine Bowman, Kathlerine Broom, Max Burgess, Diane Clayton, Gloria Cook, Glenda Crocker, Sayre Beth Skaggs, Delaine, Cumby, Ronald Dodson, Gerry Eidson, Connie Elliott, Patricia Freeman, Janice Gaines, Dwight Gilley, Sandra Hamrick, Phil Hutcheson, Joseph Johnson, Billy W. Kilgore, Charles Lockhart, Floyd Mann, Kathryn McAdams, Sharon New, Cynthia Norton, Eugenia Phillips, Diane Pope, Judy Price, Nell Raiford, Ronnie Smith, Ted Straton, Dennis Treadaway, Danny Waldrop, Bobby Walker, Clinton White, Lynn Williams, Brenda Windom, Regina Wise

Epilogue

My deepest gratitude goes to Barbara Petty and Barbara Newman Goolsby

Godwin Lake can be found on any map of the Tallapoosa, Georgia area.

Posey Greer was born in 1920 and in 1952 when he would have been 32 years old, the second Posey Greer was born to Louise. That baby was fathered by the same raping, violent KKK scum.

Over the years, several people said to Vesta Godwin, "The Posey Greer who slept in your attic, was killed by the KKK in 1956, when you and your family were in New Mexico. Some months after his death, the KKK burned Posey's shack!"

Many people understood all this and everyone talked about it all the time, but no one had proof beyond a reasonable doubt and hearsay alone is insufficient to prosecute the filthy scum hiding in a ghost costume.

The second Posey Greer was the first young black student to integrate West Haralson School. Like his namesake, he was a good and brave young man.

(Footnote) The Midget Football Association included Bowdon, Bremen, Buchanan, Carrollton, Tallapoosa, and Villa Rica. The other Tallapoosa Midget Cheerleaders are Patricia Beam (Capt.), Karen Smith (Co Capt.), Brenda Cobb, Pat Wade, Brenda Jaillet, and Brenda Redding. The usual starting players on the Midget Football team rotate between Richard Allen, Timmy Cole, Charles Downey (Capt.), Jerry Gilbert, Gary Gray, Ralph Hughes, Bruce King, Wes Littlefield (Alt. Capt.), Bobby McElroy, Denver Morgan, Jack Nixon, Jimmy Thrower, and Dennis Williams.

(Footnote) Tallapoosa's Midget Football Sponsors were Bailey & Barnes Furniture, K & W Milling Co., Builders Supply, Dr. Downey, Sheffield Hardware, Roberts Pharmacy, Hildebrand Drug Co., the city of Tallapoosa, Mitnick Chevrolet, Johnson & Mitnick Frigidaire, American Hard Rubber, Wright Supply, Williams Brothers Wholesale Groceries, The Red Dot, West Georgia Bank, Jitney Jungle, Cook's Jewelry, Tallapoosa Truck & Tractor Co., Dr. Allen, Commercial Bank, Hick's Garage, Carter, Jaillet, & Hitchcock, Virgie Smith Jewelry, Pat's Fashion Shop, Glad Hat Clothing Shop, and Western Auto.

CPSIA information can be obtained
at www.ICGtesting.com
Printed in the USA
FFHW022113110419
51618304-57048FF